Oliver Burkeman

The Antidote

Oliver Burkeman is a feature writer for *The Guardian*. He is a winner of the Foreign Press Association's Young Journalist of the Year award, and has been short-listed for the Orwell Prize. He writes a popular weekly column on psychology, "This Column Will Change Your Life," and has reported from New York, Washington, and London. He lives in New York City.

Also by Oliver Burkeman

Help!

The Antidote

The Antidote

Happiness for People Who
Can't Stand Positive Thinking

Oliver Burkeman

Farrar, Straus and Giroux
New York

Farrar, Straus and Giroux
18 West 18th Street, New York 10011

Copyright © 2012 by Oliver Burkeman
All rights reserved
Printed in the United States of America
Originally published in 2012 by Canongate Books, Great Britain
Published in the United States in 2012 by Faber and Faber, Inc.
First American paperback edition, 2013

The Library of Congress has cataloged the hardcover edition as follows:
Burkeman, Oliver.
    The antidote : happiness for people who can't stand positive
thinking / Oliver Burkeman.
        p. cm.
    Includes bibliographical references and index.
    ISBN 978-0-86547-941-8 (hbk. : alk. paper)
    1. Happiness.   2. Positive psychology.   3. Negativism.   I. Title.

BF575.H27 B86 2012
158—dc23

                                                                    2012022880

Paperback ISBN: 978-0-86547-801-5

Our books may be purchased in bulk for promotional, educational,
or business use. Please contact your local bookseller or the
Macmillan Corporate and Premium Sales Department
at 1-800-221-7945, extension 5442, or by e-mail at
MacmillanSpecialMarkets@macmillan.com.

www.fsgbooks.com
www.twitter.com/fsgbooks • www.facebook.com/fsgbooks

10   9   8

To my parents

I have always been fascinated by the law of reversed effort. Sometimes I call it 'the backwards law'. When you try to stay on the surface of the water, you sink; but when you try to sink, you float . . . Insecurity is the result of trying to be secure . . . contrariwise, salvation and sanity consist in the most radical recognition that we have no way of saving ourselves.   – Alan Watts, *The Wisdom of Insecurity*

I was going to buy a copy of *The Power of Positive Thinking*, and then I thought, 'What the hell good would that do?'
                                                    – Ronnie Shakes

Contents

The Antidote

1

On Trying Too Hard to Be Happy

Try to pose for yourself this task: not to think of a polar bear, and you will see that the cursed thing will come to mind every minute.

– Fyodor Dostoevsky,
Winter Notes on Summer Impressions

THE MAN WHO CLAIMS that he is about to tell me the secret of human happiness is eighty-three years old, with an alarming orange tan that does nothing to enhance his credibility. It is just after eight o'clock on a December morning, in a darkened basketball stadium on the outskirts of San Antonio in Texas, and – according to the orange man – I am about to learn 'the one thing that will change your life forever'. I'm sceptical, but not as much as I might normally be, because I am only one of more than fifteen thousand people at Get Motivated!, America's 'most popular business motivational seminar', and the enthusiasm of my fellow audience members is starting to become infectious.

'So you wanna know?', asks the octogenarian, who is Dr Robert H. Schuller, veteran self-help guru, author of more than thirty-five books on the power of positive thinking, and, in his other job, the founding pastor of the largest church in the United States constructed entirely out of glass. The crowd roars its assent. Easily embarrassed British people like me do not, generally speaking, roar our assent at motivational seminars in Texas basketball stadiums, but the atmosphere partially overpowers my reticence. I roar quietly.

'Here it is, then,' Dr Schuller declares, stiffly pacing the stage, which is decorated with two enormous banners reading 'MOTIVATE!' and 'SUCCEED!', seventeen American flags, and a large number of potted plants. 'Here's the thing that will change your life forever.' Then he barks a single syllable – 'Cut!' – and leaves a dramatic pause before completing his sentence: '. . . the word "impossible" out of your life! Cut it out! Cut it out forever!'

The audience combusts. I can't help feeling underwhelmed, but then I probably shouldn't have expected anything different from Get Motivated!, an event at which the sheer power of positivity counts for everything. 'You are the master of your destiny!' Schuller goes on. 'Think big, and dream bigger! Resurrect your abandoned hope! . . . Positive thinking works in *every area of life!*'

The logic of Schuller's philosophy, which is the doctrine of positive thinking at its most distilled, isn't exactly complex: decide to think happy and successful thoughts – banish the spectres of sadness and failure – and happiness and success will follow. It could be argued that not every speaker listed in the glossy brochure for today's seminar provides uncontroversial evidence in support of this outlook: the keynote speech is to be delivered, in a few hours' time, by George W. Bush, a president far from universally viewed as successful. But if you voiced this objection to Dr Schuller, he would probably dismiss it as 'negativity thinking'. To criticise the power of positivity is to demonstrate that you haven't really grasped it at all. If you had, you would stop grumbling about such things, and indeed about anything else.

The organisers of Get Motivated! describe it as a motivational seminar, but that phrase – with its suggestion of minor-league life coaches giving speeches in dingy hotel ballrooms – hardly captures the scale and grandiosity of the thing. Staged roughly once a month, in cities across North America, it sits at the summit of the global industry of positive thinking, and boasts an impressive roster of celebrity speakers: Mikhail Gorbachev and Rudy Giuliani are among the regulars, as are General Colin Powell and, somewhat incongruously, William Shatner. Should it ever occur to you that a formerly prominent figure in world politics (or William Shatner) has been keeping an inexplicably low profile in recent months, there's a good chance you'll find him or her at Get Motivated!, preaching the gospel of optimism.

As befits such celebrity, there's nothing dingy about the staging, either, which features banks of swooping spotlights, sound systems pumping out rock anthems, and expensive pyrotechnics; each speaker is welcomed to the stage amid showers of sparks and puffs of smoke. These special effects help propel the audience to ever higher altitudes of excitement, though it also doesn't hurt that for many of them, a trip to Get Motivated! means an extra day off work: many employers classify it as job training. Even the United States military, where 'training' usually means something more rigorous, endorses this view; in San Antonio, scores of the stadium's seats are occupied by uniformed soldiers from the local Army base.

Technically, I am here undercover. Tamara Lowe, the self-described 'world's number one female motivational speaker', who along with her husband runs the company behind Get Motivated!, has been accused of denying access to reporters, a tribe notoriously prone to negativity thinking. Lowe denies the charge, but out of caution, I've been describing myself as a 'self-employed

businessman' – a tactic, I'm realising too late, that only makes
me sound shifty. I needn't have bothered with subterfuge anyway,
it turns out, since I'm much too far away from the stage for the
security staff to be able to see me scribbling in my notebook. My
seat is described on my ticket as 'premier seating', but this turns
out to be another case of positivity run amok: at Get Motivated!,
there is only 'premier seating', 'executive seating', and 'VIP seating'.
In reality, mine is up in the nosebleed section; it is a hard plastic
perch, painful on the buttocks. But I am grateful for it, because
it means that by chance I'm seated next to a man who, as far as
I can make out, is one of the few cynics in the arena – an amiable,
large-limbed park ranger named Jim, who sporadically leaps to
his feet to shout 'I'm *so* motivated!' in tones laden with sarcasm.
He explains that he was required to attend by his employer, the
United States National Park Service, though when I ask why that
organisation might wish its rangers to use paid work time in this
fashion, he cheerily concedes that he has 'no fucking clue'.

Dr Schuller's sermon, meanwhile, is gathering pace. 'When I
was a child, it was impossible for a man ever to walk on the moon,
impossible to cut out a human heart and put it in another man's
chest . . . the word "impossible" has proven to be a very stupid
word!' He does not spend much time marshalling further evidence
for his assertion that failure is optional: it's clear that Schuller,
the author of *Move Ahead with Possibility Thinking* and *Tough
Times Never Last, but Tough People Do!*, vastly prefers inspiration
to argument. But in any case, he is really only a warm-up man
for the day's main speakers, and within fifteen minutes he is
striding away, to adulation and fireworks, fists clenched victoriously up at the audience, the picture of positive-thinking success.

It is only months later, back at my home in New York, reading
the headlines over morning coffee, that I learn the news that the

largest church in the United States constructed entirely from glass has filed for bankruptcy, a word Dr Schuller had apparently neglected to eliminate from his vocabulary.

For a civilisation so fixated on achieving happiness, we seem remarkably incompetent at the task. One of the best-known general findings of the 'science of happiness' has been the discovery that the countless advantages of modern life have done so little to lift our collective mood. The awkward truth seems to be that increased economic growth does not necessarily make for happier societies, just as increased personal income, above a certain basic level, doesn't make for happier people. Nor does better education, at least according to some studies. Nor does an increased choice of consumer products. Nor do bigger and fancier homes, which instead seem mainly to provide the privilege of more space in which to feel gloomy.

Perhaps you don't need telling that self-help books, the modern-day apotheosis of the quest for happiness, are among the things that fail to make us happy. But, for the record, research strongly suggests that they rarely much help. This is why, among themselves, some self-help publishers refer to the 'eighteen-month rule', which states that the person most likely to purchase any given self-help book is someone who, within the previous eighteen months, purchased a self-help book – one that evidently didn't solve all their problems. When you look at the self-help shelves with a coldly impartial eye, this isn't especially surprising. That we yearn for neat, book-sized solutions to the problem of being human is understandable, but strip away the packaging, and you'll find that the messages of such works are frequently banal. *The Seven Habits of Highly Effective People* essentially tells you to decide what matters most to you in life, and then do it; *How to Win Friends and Influence People* advises its readers to be pleasant rather than obnoxious, and to use people's first names a lot. One of the most successful management manuals of the last few years, *Fish!*, which is intended to help foster happiness and productivity in the workplace, suggests handing out small toy fish to your hardest-working employees.

As we'll see, when the messages get more specific than that, self-help gurus tend to make claims that simply aren't supported by more reputable research. The evidence suggests, for example, that venting your anger doesn't get rid of it, while visualising your goals doesn't seem to make you more likely to achieve them. And whatever you make of the country-by-country surveys of national happiness that are now published with some regularity, it's striking that the 'happiest' countries are never those where self-help books sell the most, nor indeed where professional psychotherapists are most widely consulted. The existence of a thriving 'happiness industry' clearly isn't sufficient to engender national happiness, and it's not unreasonable to suspect that it might make matters worse.

Yet the ineffectiveness of modern strategies for happiness is really just a small part of the problem. There are good reasons to believe that the whole notion of 'seeking happiness' is flawed to begin with. For one thing, who says happiness is a valid goal in the first place? Religions have never placed much explicit emphasis on it, at least as far as this world is concerned; philosophers have certainly not been unanimous in endorsing it, either. And any evolutionary psychologist will tell you that evolution has little interest in your being happy, beyond trying to make sure that you're not so listless or miserable that you lose the will to reproduce.

Even assuming happiness to be a worthy target, though, a worse pitfall awaits, which is that aiming for it seems to reduce your chances of ever attaining it. 'Ask yourself whether you are happy,' observed the philosopher John Stuart Mill, 'and you cease to be so.' At best, it would appear, happiness can only be glimpsed out of the corner of an eye, not stared at directly. (We tend to remember having been happy in the past much more frequently than we are conscious of being happy in the present.) Making matters worse still, what happiness actually *is* feels impossible to define in words; even supposing you could do so, you'd presumably end up with as many different definitions as there are people on the planet. All of which means it's tempting to conclude that 'How can we be happy?' is simply the wrong question – that we might as well resign ourselves to never finding the answer, and get on with something more productive instead.

But could there be a third possibility, besides the futile effort to pursue solutions that never seem to work, on the one hand, and just giving up, on the other? After several years reporting on the field of psychology as a journalist, I finally realised that there might be. I began to think that something united all those psychologists and philosophers – and even the occasional self-help guru – whose ideas seemed actually to hold water. The startling conclusion at which they had all arrived, in different ways, was this: that the effort to try to feel happy is often precisely the thing that makes us miserable. And that it is our constant efforts to eliminate the negative – insecurity, uncertainty, failure, or sadness – that is what causes us to feel so insecure, anxious, uncertain, or unhappy. They didn't see this conclusion as depressing, though. Instead, they argued that it pointed to an alternative approach, a 'negative path' to happiness, that entailed taking a radically different stance towards those things that most of us spend our lives trying hard to avoid. It involved learning to enjoy uncertainty, embracing insecurity, stopping trying to think positively, becoming familiar with failure, even learning to value death. In short, all these people seemed to agree that in order to be truly happy, we might actually need to be willing to experience more negative emotions – or, at the very least, to learn to stop running quite so hard from them. Which is a bewildering thought, and one that calls into question not just our methods for achieving happiness, but also our assumptions about what 'happiness' really means.

These days, this notion certainly gets less press than the admonition to remain positive at all times. But it is a viewpoint with a surprisingly long and respectable history. You'll find it in the works of the Stoic philosophers of ancient Greece and Rome, who emphasised the benefits of always contemplating how badly things might go. It lies deep near the core of Buddhism, which counsels that true security lies in the unrestrained embrace of insecurity – in the recognition that we never really stand on solid ground, and never can. It underpins the medieval tradition of *memento mori*, which celebrated the life-giving benefits of never forgetting about death. And it is what connects New Age writers, such as the bestselling spiritual teacher Eckhart Tolle, with more mainstream recent work in cognitive psychology on the self-defeating nature of positive thinking. This same 'negative' approach to happiness also helps explain why so many people find mindfulness meditation so beneficial; why a new generation of business thinkers are advising companies to drop their obsession with goalsetting and embrace uncertainty instead; and why, in recent years, some psychologists have reached the conclusion that pessimism may often be as healthy and productive as optimism.

At the bottom of all this lies the principle that the countercultural philosopher of the 1950s and '60s, Alan Watts, echoing Aldous Huxley, labelled 'the law of reversed effort', or the 'backwards law':

the notion that in all sorts of contexts, from our personal lives to politics, all this *trying to make everything right* is a big part of what's wrong. Or, to quote Watts, that 'when you try to stay on the surface of the water, you sink; but when you try to sink, you float' and that 'insecurity is the result of trying to be secure'. In many cases, wrote Huxley, 'the harder we try with the conscious will to do something, the less we shall succeed'.

The negative path to happiness is not an argument for bloody-minded contrarianism at all costs: you won't do yourself any favours by walking into the path of oncoming buses, say, rather than trying to avoid them. Nor should it be taken as implying that there's necessarily anything wrong with optimism. A more useful way to think of it is as a much-needed counterweight to a culture fixated on the notion that optimism and positivity are the only possible paths to happiness. Of course, many of us are already healthily sceptical when it comes to positive thinking. But it is worth noting that even most people who disdain the 'cult of optimism', as the philosopher Peter Vernezze calls it, end up subtly endorsing it. They assume that since they cannot or will not subscribe to its ideology, their only alternative is to resign themselves to gloom, or a sort of ironic curmudgeonhood, instead. The 'negative path' is about rejecting this dichotomy, and seeking instead the happiness that arises *through* negativity, rather than trying to drown negativity out with relentless good cheer. If a fixation on positivity is the disease, this approach is the antidote.

This 'negative path', it should be emphasised, isn't one single, comprehensive, neatly packaged philosophy; the antidote is not a panacea. Part of the problem with positive thinking, and many related approaches to happiness, is exactly this desire to reduce big questions to one-size-fits-all self-help tricks or ten-point plans. By contrast, the negative path offers no such single solution. Some of its proponents stress embracing negative feelings and thoughts, while others might better be described as advocating indifference towards them. Some focus on radically unconventional techniques for pursuing happiness, while others point towards a different definition of happiness, or to abandoning the pursuit of it altogether. The word 'negative' often has a double meaning here, too. It can refer to unpleasant experiences and emotions; but some philosophies of happiness are best described as 'negative' because they involve developing skills of 'not doing' – of learning not to chase positive feelings so aggressively. There are many paradoxes here, and they only get deeper the more you probe. For example, is a feeling or a situation truly 'negative' if it leads ultimately to happiness? If 'being positive' doesn't make you happy, is it right to call it 'being positive' at all? If you redefine happiness to accommodate negativity, is it still happiness? And so on. None of these questions can be tidily resolved. This is partly because the proponents of the negative path share only a general way of seeing life, rather than a single strict set of beliefs. But it is also because one crucial foundation of their approach is precisely that happiness involves paradoxes; that there is no way to tie up all the loose ends, however desperately we might want to.

This book is the record of a journey through the world of the 'backwards law', and of the people, living and dead, who have followed the negative path to happiness. My travels took me to the remote woodlands of Massachusetts, where I spent a week on a silent meditation retreat; to Mexico, where death is not shunned but celebrated; and to the desperately impoverished slums outside Nairobi, where insecurity is the unignorable reality of everyday life. I met modern-day Stoics, specialists in the art of failure, professional pessimists, and other advocates of the power of negative thinking, many of whom proved surprisingly jolly. But I began in San Antonio because I wanted to experience the cult of optimism at its most extreme. If it was true, as I had come to believe, that Dr Robert Schuller's flavour of positive thinking was really only an exaggerated version of the one-sided beliefs we all tend to hold about happiness, then it made sense, first of all, to witness the problem at its purest.

Which is how I came to find myself rising reluctantly to my feet, up in a dark extremity of that basketball stadium, because Get Motivated!'s excitable mistress of ceremonies had announced a 'dance competition', in which everyone present was obliged to participate. Giant beach balls appeared as if from nowhere, bumping across the heads of the crowd, who jiggled awkwardly as Wham! blared from the sound system. The first prize of a free trip to Disney World, we were informed, awaited not the best dancer but the *most motivated* one, though the distinction made little difference to me: I found the whole thing too excruciating to do more than sway very slightly. The prize was eventually awarded to a soldier. This was a decision that I suspected had been taken to pander to local patriotic pride, rather than strictly in recognition of highly motivated dancing.

After the competition, during a break in proceedings prior to George Bush's arrival, I left the main stadium to buy an overpriced hot dog, and found myself in conversation with a fellow attendee, an elegantly dressed retired schoolteacher from San Antonio who introduced herself as Helen. Money was tight, she explained when I asked why she was attending. She had reluctantly concluded that she needed to come out of retirement and get back to work, and she'd been hoping that Get Motivated! might motivate her.

'The thing is, though,' she said, as we chatted about the speakers we'd seen, 'it's kinda hard to think these good thoughts all the time like they tell you, isn't it?' For a moment, she looked stricken.

Then she recovered, wagging a teacherly finger as if to tell herself off. 'But you're not supposed to think like that!'

One of the foremost investigators of the problems with positive thinking was a professor of psychology named Daniel Wegner, who ran the Mental Control Laboratory at Harvard University. This is not, whatever its name might suggest, a CIA-funded establishment dedicated to the science of brainwashing. Wegner's intellectual territory was what has come to be known as 'ironic process theory', which explores the ways in which our efforts to suppress certain thoughts or behaviours result, ironically, in their becoming more prevalent. I got off to a bad start with Professor Wegner when I accidentally typed his surname, in a newspaper column, as 'Wenger'. He sent me a crabby email ('Get the name right!'), and didn't seem likely to be receptive to the argument that my slip-up was an interesting example of exactly the kinds of errors he studied. The rest of our communications proved a little strained.

The problems to which Wegner dedicated much of his career all have their origins in a simple and intensely irritating parlour game, which dates back at least to the days of Fyodor Dostoevsky, who reputedly used it to torment his brother. It takes the form of a challenge: can you – the victim is asked – succeed in *not* thinking about a white bear for one whole minute? You can guess the answer, of course, but it's nonetheless instructive to make the attempt. Why not try it now? Look at your watch, or find a clock with a second hand, and aim for a mere ten seconds of entirely non-white-bear-related thoughts, starting . . . now.

My commiserations on your failure.

Wegner's earliest investigations of ironic process theory

involved little more than issuing this challenge to American university students, then asking them to speak their inner monologues aloud while they made the attempt. This is a rather crude way of accessing someone's thought processes, but an excerpt from one typical transcript nonetheless vividly demonstrates the futility of the struggle:

> Of course, now the only thing I'm going to think about is a white bear . . . Don't think about a white bear. Ummm, what was I thinking about before? See, I think about flowers a lot . . . Okay, so my fingernails are really bad . . . Every time I really want, like . . . ummm . . . to talk, think, to not think about the white bear, then it makes me think about the white bear more . . .

At this juncture, you might be beginning to wonder why it is that some social psychologists seem to be allowed to spend other people's money proving the obvious. Of *course* the white bear challenge is virtually impossible to win. But Wegner was just getting started. The more he explored the field, the more he came to suspect that the internal mechanism responsible for sabotaging our efforts at suppressing white bear thoughts might govern an entire territory of mental activity and outward behaviour. The white bear challenge, after all, seems like a metaphor for much of what goes wrong in life: all too often, the outcome we're seeking to avoid is exactly the one to which we seem magnetically lured. Wegner labelled this effect 'the precisely counterintuitive error', which, he explained in one paper, 'is when we manage to do the worst possible thing, the blunder so outrageous that we think about it in advance and resolve not to let that happen. We see a rut coming up in the road ahead, and proceed to steer our bike right into it. We make a mental note not to mention a sore point in conversation, and then cringe in horror as we blurt out exactly that thing. We carefully cradle the glass across the room, all the while thinking "Don't spill", and then juggle it onto the carpet under the gaze of our host.'

Far from representing an occasional divergence from our otherwise flawless self-control, the capacity for ironic error seems to lurk deep in the soul, close to the core of our characters. Edgar Allan Poe, in his short story of the same name, calls it 'the imp of the perverse': that nameless but distinct urge one sometimes experiences, when walking along a precipitous cliff edge, or climbing to the observation deck of a tall building, to throw oneself off – not from any suicidal motivation, but precisely because it would be so calamitous to do so. The imp of the perverse plagues social interactions, too, as anyone who has ever laughed in recognition at an episode of *Curb Your Enthusiasm* will know all too well.

What is going on here, Wegner argues, is a malfunctioning of the uniquely human capacity for metacognition, or thinking about thinking. 'Metacognition', Wegner explains, 'occurs when thought takes itself as an object.' Mainly, it's an extremely useful skill: it is what enables us to recognise when we are being unreasonable, or sliding into depression, or being afflicted by anxiety, and then to do something about it. But when we use metacognitive thoughts directly to try to control our other, everyday, 'object-level' thoughts – by suppressing images of white bears, say, or replacing gloomy thoughts with happy ones – we run into trouble. 'Metathoughts are instructions we give ourselves about our object-level thinking,' as Wegner puts it, 'and sometimes we just can't follow our own instructions.'

When you try not to think of a white bear, you may experience some success in forcing alternative thoughts into your mind. At the same time, though, a metacognitive monitoring process will crank into action, to scan your mind for evidence of whether you are succeeding or failing at the task. And this is where things get perilous, because if you try too hard – or, Wegner's studies suggest, if you are tired, stressed, depressed, attempting to multi-task, or otherwise suffering from 'mental load' – metacognition will frequently go wrong. The monitoring process will start to occupy more than its fair share of limelight on the cognitive stage. It will jump to the forefront of consciousness – and suddenly, all you will be able to think about is white bears, and how badly you're doing at not thinking about them.

Could it be that ironic process theory also sheds light on what is wrong with our efforts to achieve happiness, and on the way that our efforts to feel positive seem so frequently to bring about the opposite result? In the years since Wegner's earliest white bear experiments, his research, and that of others, has turned up more and more evidence to support that notion. One example: when experimental subjects are told of an unhappy event, but then instructed to try *not* to feel sad about it, they end up feeling worse than people who are informed of the event, but given no instructions about how to feel. In another study, when patients who were suffering from panic disorders listened to relaxation tapes, their hearts beat faster than patients who listened to audiobooks with no explicitly 'relaxing' content. Bereaved people who make the most effort to avoid feeling grief, research suggests, take the longest to recover from their loss. Our efforts at mental suppression fail in the sexual arena, too: people instructed not to think about sex exhibit greater arousal, as measured by the electrical conductivity of their skin, than those not instructed to suppress such thoughts.

Seen from this perspective, swathes of the self-help industry's favourite techniques for achieving happiness and success – from positive thinking to visualising your goals to 'getting motivated' – stand revealed to be suffering from one enormous flaw. A person who has resolved to 'think positive' must constantly scan his or her mind for negative thoughts – there's no other way that the mind could ever gauge its success at the operation – yet that scanning will draw attention to the presence of negative thoughts. (Worse, if the negative thoughts start to predominate, a vicious spiral may kick in, since the failure to think positively may become the trigger for a new stream of self-berating thoughts, about not thinking positively enough.) Suppose you decide to follow Dr Schuller's suggestion and try to eliminate the word 'impossible' from your vocabulary, or more generally try to focus exclusively on successful outcomes, and stop thinking about things not working out. As we'll see, there are all sorts of problems with this approach. But the most basic one is that you may well fail, as a result of the very act of monitoring your success.

This problem of self-sabotage through self-monitoring is not the only hazard of positive thinking. An additional twist was revealed in 2009, when a psychologist based in Canada named Joanne Wood set out to test the effectiveness of 'affirmations', those peppy self-congratulatory phrases designed to lift the user's mood through repetition. Affirmations have their origins in the work of the nineteenth-century French pharmacist Émile Coué, a forerunner of the contemporary positive thinkers, who coined the one that remains the most famous: 'Every day, in every way, I am getting better and better.'

Most affirmations sound pretty cheesy, and one might suspect that they would have little effect. Surely, though, they're harmless? Wood wasn't so sure about that. Her reasoning, though compat-ible with Wegner's, drew on a different psychological tradition known as 'self-comparison theory'. Much as we like to hear positive messages about ourselves, this theory suggests, we crave even more strongly the sense of being a coherent, consistent self in the first place. Messages that conflict with that existing sense of self, therefore, are unsettling, and so we often reject them – even if they happen to be positive, and even if the source of the message is ourselves. Wood's hunch was that people who seek out affirmations would be, by definition, those with low self-esteem – but that, for that very same reason, they would end up reacting against the messages in the affirmations, because they conflicted with their self-images. Messages such as 'Every day, in every way, I am getting better and better' would clash with their poor opinion of themselves, and thus be rejected, so as not to threaten the coherence of their sense of self. The result might even be a worsening of their low self-esteem as people struggled to reassert their existing self-images against the incoming messages.

Which is exactly what happened in Wood's research. In one set of experiments, people were divided into subgroups of those with low and high self-esteem, then asked to undertake a journal-writing exercise; every time a bell rang, they were to repeat to themselves the phrase 'I am a lovable person.' According to a variety of ingenious mood measures, those who began the process with low self-esteem became appreciably less happy as a result of telling themselves that they were lovable. They didn't feel particularly lovable to begin with – and trying to convince themselves otherwise merely solidified their negativity. 'Positive thinking' had made them feel worse.

The arrival of George Bush onstage in San Antonio was heralded by the sudden appearance of his Secret Service detail. These were men who would probably have stood out anywhere, in their dark suits and earpieces, but who stood out twice as prominently at Get Motivated! thanks to their rigid frowns. The job of protecting former presidents from potential assassins, it appeared, wasn't one that rewarded looking on the bright side and assuming that nothing could go wrong.

Bush himself, by contrast, bounded onstage grinning. 'You know, retirement ain't so bad, especially when you get to retire to Texas!' he began, before launching into a speech he had evidently delivered several times before. First, he told a folksy anecdote about spending his post-presidency cleaning up after his dog ('I was picking up that which I had been dodging for eight years!'). Then, for a strange moment or two, it seemed as if the main topic of his speech would be how he once had to choose a rug for the Oval Office ('I thought to myself, the presidency is going to be a decision-making experience!'). But his real subject, it soon emerged, was optimism. 'I don't believe you can lead a family, or a school, or a city, or a state, or a country, unless you're optimistic that the future is going to be better,' he said. 'And I want you to know that, even in the darkest days of my presidency, I was optimistic that the future was going to be better than the past for our citizens and the world.'

You need not hold any specific political opinion about the forty-third president of the United States to see how his words illustrate a fundamental strangeness of the 'cult of optimism'. Bush was not ignoring the numerous controversies of his administration – the strategy one might have imagined he would adopt at a motivational seminar, before a sympathetic audience and facing no risk of hostile questions. Instead, he had chosen to redefine them as evidence in support of his optimistic attitude. The way Bush saw it, the happy and successful periods of his presidency proved the benefits of an optimistic outlook, of course – but so did the unhappy and unsuccessful ones. When things are going badly, after all, you need optimism all the more. Or to put it another way: once you have resolved to embrace the ideology of positive thinking, you will find a way to interpret virtually any eventuality as a justification for thinking positively. You need never spend time considering how your actions might go wrong.

Could this curiously unfalsifiable ideology of positivity at all costs – positivity regardless of the results – be actively dangerous? Opponents of the Bush administration's foreign policies might have reason to think so. This is also one part of the case made by the social critic Barbara Ehrenreich, in her 2009 book *Bright-Sided: How Positive Thinking Is Undermining America*. One underappreciated cause of the global financial crisis of the late 2000s, she argues, was an American business culture in which even thinking about the possibility of failure – let alone speaking up about it at meetings – had come to be considered an embarrassing *faux pas*. Bankers, their narcissism stoked by a culture that awarded grand ambition above all, lost the capacity to distinguish between their ego-fuelled dreams and concrete results. Meanwhile, homebuyers assumed that whatever they wanted could be theirs if they wanted it badly enough (how many of them had read books such as *The Secret*, which makes exactly that claim?) and accordingly sought mortgages they were unable to repay. Irrational optimism suffused the financial sector, and the professional purveyors of optimism – the speakers and self-help gurus and seminar organisers – were only too happy to encourage it. 'To the extent that positive thinking had become a business in itself,' writes Ehrenreich, 'business was its principal client, eagerly consuming the good news that all things are possible through an effort of mind. This was a useful message for employees, who by the turn of the twenty-first century were being required to work longer hours for fewer benefits and diminishing job security. But it was also a liberating ideology for top-level executives. What was the point in agonising over balance sheets and tedious analyses of risks – and why bother worrying about dizzying levels of debt and exposure to potential defaults – when all good things come to those who are optimistic enough to expect them?'

Ehrenreich traces the origins of this philosophy to nineteenth-century America, and specifically to the quasi-religious movement known as New Thought. New Thought arose in rebellion against the dominant, gloomy message of American Calvinism, which was that relentless hard work was the duty of every Christian – with the additional sting that, thanks to the doctrine of predestination, you might in any case already be marked to spend eternity in Hell. New Thought, by contrast, proposed that one could achieve happiness and worldly success through the power of the mind. This mind-power could even cure physical ailments, according to the newly minted religion of Christian Science, which grew directly from the same roots. Yet, as Ehrenreich makes clear, New Thought imposed its own kind of harsh judgmentalism, replacing Calvinism's obligatory hard work with obligatory positive thinking. Negative thoughts were fiercely denounced – a message that echoed 'the old religion's condemnation of sin' and added 'an insistence on the constant interior labour of self-examination'. Quoting the sociologist Micki McGee, Ehrenreich shows how, under this new orthodoxy of optimism, 'continuous and never-ending work on the self [was] offered not only as a road to success, but also to a kind of secular salvation'.

George Bush, then, was standing in a venerable tradition when he proclaimed the importance of optimism in all circumstances. But his speech at Get Motivated! was over almost as soon as it had started. A dash of religion, a singularly unilluminating anecdote about the terrorist attacks of 11 September 2001, some words of praise for the military, and he was waving goodbye – 'Thank you, Texas, it's good to be home!' – as his bodyguards closed in around him. Beneath the din of cheering, I heard Jim, the park ranger in the next seat, emit a sigh of relief. 'OK, I'm motivated now,' he muttered, to nobody in particular. 'Is it time for some beer?'

'There are lots of ways of being miserable,' says a character in a short story by Edith Wharton, 'but there's only one way of being comfortable, and that is to stop running around after happiness.' This observation pungently expresses the problem with the 'cult of optimism' – the ironic, self-defeating struggle that sabotages positivity when we try too hard. But it also hints at the possibility of a more hopeful alternative, an approach to happiness that might take a radically different form. The first step is to learn how to stop chasing positivity so intently. But many of the proponents of the 'negative path' to happiness take things further still, arguing – paradoxically, but persuasively – that deliberately plunging more deeply into what we think of as negative may be a precondition of true happiness.

Perhaps the most vivid metaphor for this whole strange philosophy is a small children's toy known as the 'Chinese finger trap', though the evidence suggests it is probably not Chinese in origin at all. In his office at the University of Nevada, the psychologist Steven Hayes, an outspoken critic of counterproductive positive thinking, keeps a box of them on his desk; he uses them to illustrate his arguments. The 'trap' is a tube, made of thin strips of woven bamboo, with the opening at each end being roughly the size of a human finger. The unwitting victim is asked to insert his index fingers into the tube, then finds himself trapped: in reaction to his efforts to pull his fingers out again, the openings at each end of the tube constrict, gripping his fingers ever more tightly. The harder he pulls, the more decisively he is trapped. It is only by relaxing his efforts at escape, and by pushing his fingers further in, that he can widen the ends of the tube, whereupon it falls away, and he is free.

In the case of the Chinese finger trap, Hayes observes, 'doing the presumably sensible thing is counterproductive'.

Following the negative path to happiness is about doing the other thing – the presumably illogical thing – instead.

2

What Would Seneca Do?

The Stoic Art of Confronting the Worst-Case Scenario

Pessimism, when you get used to it, is just as agreeable as optimism.
　　　　　　– Arnold Bennett, *Things That Have Interested Me*

IT IS AN ORDINARY spring morning on the Central Line of the London Underground, which is to say that there are the usual 'minor delays' to the service, and a major sense of despair emanating from the closely packed commuters. The only extraordinary thing is that I am a few moments from undergoing, entirely voluntarily, what I expect to be one of the most terrifying experiences of my life. As we approach Chancery Lane station – but before the automated voice on the public-address system announces this fact – I plan to break the silence and proclaim, loudly, the words 'Chancery Lane'. As the train continues to Holborn, Tottenham Court Road, Oxford Circus and beyond, it is my intention to keep this up, announcing the name of each station as we go.

I am aware that this is not the most frightening exploit imaginable. Readers with experience of having been taken hostage by pirates, or buried alive – or even just having endured a particularly turbulent aeroplane journey, for that matter – could be forgiven for finding this all rather self-dramatising. Yet the fact remains that my palms are sweating and my heartbeat is accelerating. I've never handled embarrassment well, and now I'm berating myself for ever having thought that deliberately courting it might be a clever idea.

I am conducting this ritual of deliberate self-humiliation on the instructions of a modern-day psychologist, Albert Ellis, who died in 2007. But he designed it to provide a vivid demonstration of an ancient philosophy, that of the Stoics, who were among the first to suggest that the path to happiness might depend on negativity. Ellis recommended the 'subway-station exercise', originally prescribed to his therapy patients in New York, as a way of demonstrating how irrationally we approach even mildly unpleasant experiences – and how we might find unforeseen benefits lurking within them, if only we could bring ourselves to look.

Stoicism, which was born in Greece and matured in Rome, should not be confused with 'stoicism' as the word is commonly used today – a weary, uncomplaining resignation that better describes the attitude of my fellow passengers on the Underground. Real Stoicism is far more tough-minded, and involves developing a kind of muscular calm in the face of trying circumstances. This is also the purpose of Ellis's excruciating exercise, which is intended to bring me face to face with all my unspoken beliefs about embarrassment, self-consciousness, and what other people might think about me. It will force me to experience the unpleasantness that I am fearing, and thereby to realise something about the situation that is psychologically intriguing: that my beliefs about how staggeringly awful it's going to be, when they're brought out into the open and examined, just don't seem to match the facts.

Unless you are an unusually unembarrassable person, you can

probably empathise with the apprehension I am feeling – yet when you think about it, there's something bizarre about having any negative feelings whatsoever in this situation. After all, I know nobody in the carriage personally, so I have nothing to lose from them thinking that I'm crazy. Moreover, I know from past experience on the Underground that when other people start talking out loud to themselves, I ignore them, as does everyone else; this is almost certainly the worst that's going to happen to me. And those other people speaking out loud are often talking gibberish, whereas I am going to be announcing the names of the stations. You could almost argue that I'm performing a public service. Certainly, it will be much less irritating than all the leaking iPod headphones in my vicinity.

And so why – as the train begins to slow, almost indetectibly at first, for the approach to Chancery Lane – do I feel as if I want to vomit?

Behind many of the most popular approaches to happiness is the simple philosophy of *focusing on things going right*. In the world of self-help, the most overt expression of this outlook is the technique known as 'positive visualisation': if you mentally picture things turning out well, the reasoning goes, they are far more likely to do so. The fashionable New Age concept of the 'law of attraction' takes things a step further, suggesting that visualisation may be the *only* thing you need in order to attain riches, great relationships, and good health. 'There is a deep tendency in human nature to become precisely what you visualise yourself as being,' said Norman Vincent Peale, the author of *The Power of Positive Thinking*, in a speech he gave to executives of the investment bank Merrill Lynch in the mid-1980s. 'If you see yourself as tense and nervous and frustrated . . . that, assuredly, is what you will be. If you see yourself as inferior in any way, and you hold that image in your conscious mind, it will presently, by the process of intellectual osmosis, sink into the unconscious, and you will be what you visualise. If, on the contrary, you see yourself as organised, controlled, studious, a thinker, a worker, believing in your talent and ability and yourself, that is what you will become.' Merrill Lynch collapsed in the financial meltdown of 2008 and had to be rescued by Bank of America; readers are invited to draw their own conclusions.

Even most people who scoff at Peale's homilies, however, might find it hard to argue with the underlying outlook: that being optimistic about the future, when you can manage it, is generally for the best. And focusing on how you hope things will turn out, rather than how you hope they won't, seems like a sensible way of motivating yourself and of maximising your chances of success. Walking into a job interview, you're surely better off to err on the side of assuming you can triumph. As you prepare to ask someone on a date, it's surely advisable to operate on the basis that she or he might actually say yes. Indeed, a tendency to look on the bright side may be so intertwined with human survival that evolution has skewed us that way. In her 2011 book *The Optimism Bias*, the neuroscientist Tali Sharot compiles growing evidence that a well-functioning mind may be built so as to perceive the odds of things going well as greater than they really are. Healthy and happy people, research suggests, generally have a *less* accurate, overly optimistic grasp of their true ability to influence events than do those who are suffering from depression.

Yet there are problems with this outlook, aside from just feeling disappointed when things don't turn out well. These are particularly acute in the case of positive visualisation. Over the last few years, the German-born psychologist Gabriele Oettingen and her colleagues have constructed a series of experiments designed to unearth the truth about 'positive fantasies about the future'. The results are striking: spending time and energy thinking about how well things could go, it has emerged, actually reduces most people's motivation to achieve them. Experimental subjects who were encouraged to think about how they were going to have a particularly high-achieving week at work, for example, ended up achieving less than those who were invited to reflect on the coming week, but given no further guidelines on how to do so.

In one ingenious experiment, Oettingen had some of the participants rendered mildly dehydrated. They were then taken through an exercise that involved visualising drinking a refreshing, icy glass of water, while others took part in a different exercise. The dehydrated water-visualisers – contrary to the self-help doctrine of motivation through visualisation – experienced a significant *reduction* in their energy levels, as measured by blood pressure. Far from becoming more motivated to hydrate themselves, their bodies relaxed, as if their thirst were already quenched. In experiment after experiment, people responded to positive visualisation by relaxing. They seemed, subconsciously, to have confused visualising success with having already achieved it.

It doesn't necessarily follow, of course, that it would be a better idea to switch to *negative* visualisation instead, and to start focusing on all the ways in which things could go wrong. Yet that is precisely one of the conclusions that emerges from Stoicism, a school of philosophy that originated in Athens, a few years after the death of Aristotle, and that came to dominate Western thinking about happiness for nearly five centuries.

The first Stoic, so far as we know, was Zeno of Citium, born in what is now Larnaca, on the southern shores of Cyprus, sometime around 334 BC. 'He had his head naturally bent on one side,' writes the third-century Greek historian Diogenes Laertius, in his *Lives and Opinions of Eminent Philosophers*, which is the primary source of evidence for the early Stoics. 'He was thin, very tall, of a dark complexion, [with] flabby, weak legs . . . and he was very fond, as it is said, of figs, both fresh and dried in the sun.' According to legend, Zeno was a merchant who came to Athens aged around thirty, possibly after the traumatising experience of being shipwrecked. There, he began to study under the Cynic philosopher Crates; Laertius relates one of Zeno's early experiences at the hands of Crates, which may help explain Stoicism's focus on irrational beliefs as the source of emotional distress. According to the story, Crates gave Zeno a bowl of 'lentil porridge' and demanded that he carry it through the streets of Athens, but then Crates smashed the bowl with his stick, causing the contents to splatter all over Zeno's body. 'The porridge ran all down his legs,' Laertius tells us, whereupon Zeno ran away in embarrassment. 'Why do you run away [when] you have done no harm?', Crates called after him teasingly, mocking Zeno's belief that he had grounds for feeling ashamed. When Zeno began to teach philosophy himself, he did so under the *stoa poikile*, the 'painted porch' on the north side of the ancient agora of Athens – hence the label 'Stoic'. The school's influence subsequently spread to Rome, and it is these later Roman Stoics – above all Epictetus, Seneca the Younger, and Marcus Aurelius – whose works have survived.

From their earliest days, Stoic teachings emphasised the fundamental importance of reason. Nature had bestowed uniquely upon humans, the Stoics argued, the capacity to reason, and therefore a 'virtuous' life – meaning a life proper and fitting to a human – entailed living in accordance with reason. The

Roman Stoics added a psychological twist: living virtuously in accordance with reason, they argued, would lead to inner tranquility – 'a state of mind', writes the scholar of Stoicism William Irvine, 'marked by the absence of negative emotions, such as grief, anger, and anxiety, and the presence of positive emotions, such as joy.' And here lies the essential difference between Stoicism and the modern-day 'cult of optimism'. For the Stoics, the ideal state of mind was tranquility, not the excitable cheer that positive thinkers usually seem to mean when they use the word 'happiness'. And tranquility was to be achieved not by strenuously chasing after enjoyable experiences, but by cultivating a kind of calm indifference towards one's circumstances. One way to do this, the Stoics argued, was by turning towards negative emotions and experiences; not shunning them, but examining them closely instead.

If this focus on negativity seems perverse, it may help to consider the life circumstances of the Stoics themselves. Epictetus was born into slavery in what is now Turkey; though later freed, he died crippled as a result of his masters' brutal treatment. Seneca, by contrast, was the son of a nobleman, and enjoyed a stellar career as a personal tutor to the Roman Emperor. But that ended abruptly when his employer – who, unfortunately, was the deranged Nero – suspected Seneca of plotting against him, and ordered him to commit suicide. There seems to have been little evidence for Nero's suspicions, but by that point he had already murdered his mother and step-brother, and gained a reputation for burning Christians in his gardens after dark to provide a source of light, so he can hardly be accused of acting out of character. Seneca, the story goes, tried to do as he was told, by cutting open his veins to bleed himself to death. But he failed to die, and so asked to be fed poison; this, too, failed to kill him. It was only when he took a suffocatingly

steamy bath that he finally expired. Perhaps it is unsurprising that
a philosophy emerging from such circumstances as Epictetus's – or
in a context where a fate such as Seneca's awaited even those of
noble birth, if their luck ran out – would not incline towards
positive thinking. Where was the merit in trying to convince yourself that things would turn out for the best, when there was so
much evidence that they might not?

   Yet it is a curious truth that the Stoics' approach to happiness
through negativity begins with exactly the kind of insight that
Norman Vincent Peale might endorse: that when it comes to feeling
upbeat or despondent, it's our *beliefs* that really matter. Most of
us, the Stoics point out, go through life under the delusion that
it is certain people, situations, or events that make us sad, anxious,
or angry. When you're irritated by a colleague at the next desk
who won't stop talking, you naturally assume that the colleague
is the source of the irritation; when you hear that a beloved
relative is ill and feel pained for them, it makes sense to think of
the illness as the source of the pain. Look closely at your experience, though, say the Stoics, and you will eventually be forced to
conclude that neither of these external events is 'negative' in itself.
Indeed, nothing outside your own mind can properly be described
as negative or positive at all. What actually causes suffering are
the beliefs you hold about those things. The colleague is not irritating per se, but because of your belief that getting your work
finished without interruption is an important goal. Even a relative's
illness is bad only in view of your belief that it's a good thing for
your relatives not to be ill. (Millions of people, after all, get ill
every day; we have no beliefs whatsoever about most of them, and
consequently don't feel distressed.) 'Things do not touch the soul,'
is how Marcus Aurelius, the Stoic philosopher–emperor, expresses
the notion, adding: 'Our perturbations come only from the opinion

which is within.' We think of distress as a one-step procedure: something in the outside world causes distress in your interior world. In fact, it's a two-step procedure: between the outside event and the inside emotion is a belief. If you didn't judge a relative's illness to be bad, would you be distressed by it? Obviously not. 'There is nothing either good or bad, but thinking makes it so,' Shakespeare has Hamlet say, very Stoically indeed.

The suggestion here is not that negative emotions don't really exist, or that they don't matter, or that they can easily be brushed aside through sheer force of will. The Stoics aren't making any such claims; they are merely specifying the mechanism through which all distress arises. And they do mean all. Even losing your home or your job or a loved one, from this perspective, is not a negative event in itself; in itself, it's merely an event. To which you might respond: But what if it really *is* bad? Lacking a home and an income, you might perish from starvation or exposure. Surely that would be bad? But the same relentless logic applies. What makes the prospect of starvation or exposure distressing in the first place? The beliefs that you hold about the disadvantages of death. This view of how emotions work, as the leading Stoic scholar A. A. Long points out, is the underlying insight behind contemporary cognitive behavioural therapy, too. 'It's all there [in the work of the Stoics],' he told me. 'Particularly this idea that judgments are in our power, that our emotions are determined by our judgments, and that we can always step back and ask: "Is it other people that bother me? Or the judgment I make about other people?"' It was a method of thinking he regularly employed himself, Long explained, to deal with everyday distresses, such as road rage. Were other drivers really behaving 'badly'? Or was it more accurate to say that the cause of his anger was his belief that they ought to behave differently?

The distinction is crucial. The idea that it is ultimately our beliefs that cause our distress, as we've seen, is a perspective shared by Stoics and positive thinkers alike. Beyond this, though, the two traditions diverge utterly – and the divergence becomes most baldly apparent when it comes to beliefs about the future. The evangelists of optimism argue that you should cultivate as many positive expectations about the future as you can. But this is not the good idea that it may at first appear to be. For a start, as Gabriele Oettingen's experiments demonstrate, focusing on the outcome you desire may actually sabotage your efforts to achieve it. More generally, a Stoic would point out, it just isn't a particularly good technique for feeling happier. Ceaseless optimism about the future only makes for a greater shock when things go wrong; by fighting to maintain only positive beliefs about the future, the positive thinker ends up being *less* prepared, and *more* acutely distressed, when things eventually happen that he can't persuade himself to believe are good. (And such things will happen.) This is a problem underlying all approaches to happiness that set too great a store by optimism. Trying to see things in an exclusively positive light is an attitude that requires constant, effortful replenishment. Should your efforts falter or prove insufficient when confronted by some unexpected shock, you'll sink back down into – possibly deeper – gloom.

Applying their stringent rationality to the situation, the Stoics propose a more elegant, sustainable and calming way to deal with the possibility of things going wrong: rather than struggling to avoid all thought of these worst-case scenarios, they counsel actively dwelling on them, staring them in the face. Which brings us to an important milestone on the negative path to happiness – a psychological tactic that William Irvine argues is 'the single most valuable technique in the Stoics' toolkit'. He calls it 'negative visualisation'. The Stoics themselves, rather more pungently, called it 'the premeditation of evils'.

The first benefit of dwelling on how bad things might get is a straightforward one. Psychologists have long agreed that one of the greatest enemies of human happiness is 'hedonic adaptation' – the predictable and frustrating way in which any new source of pleasure we obtain, whether it's as minor as a new piece of electronic gadgetry or as major as a marriage, swiftly gets relegated to the backdrop of our lives. We grow accustomed to it, and so it ceases to deliver so much joy. It follows, then, that regularly reminding yourself that you might lose any of the things you currently enjoy – indeed, that you will definitely lose them all, in the end, when death catches up with you – would reverse the adaptation effect. Thinking about the possibility of losing something you value shifts it from the backdrop of your life back to centre stage, where it can deliver pleasure once more. 'Whenever you grow attached to something,' writes Epictetus, 'do not act as though it were one of those things that cannot be taken away, but as though it were something like a jar or a crystal goblet . . . if you kiss your child, your brother, your friend . . remind yourself that you love a mortal, something not your own; it has been given to you for the present, not inseparably nor forever, but like a fig, or a bunch of grapes, at a fixed season of the year.' Each time you kiss your child goodnight, he contends, you should specifically consider the possibility that she might die tomorrow. This is jarring advice that might strike any parent as horrifying, but Epictetus is adamant: the practice will make you love her all the more, while simultaneously reducing the shock should that awful eventuality ever come to pass.

The second, subtler, and arguably even more powerful benefit of the premeditation of evils is as an antidote to anxiety. Consider how we normally seek to assuage worries about the future: we seek reassurance, looking to persuade ourselves that everything will be all right. But reassurance is a double-edged sword. In the short term, it can be wonderful, but like all forms of optimism, it requires constant maintenance: if you offer reassurance to a friend who is in the grip of anxiety, you'll often find that a few days later, he'll be back for more. Worse, reassurance can actually exacerbate anxiety: when you reassure your friend that the worst-case scenario he fears probably won't occur, you inadvertently reinforce his belief that it would be catastrophic if it did. You are tightening the coil of his anxiety, not loosening it. All too often, the Stoics point out, things will not turn out for the best.

But it is also true that, when they do go wrong, they'll almost certainly go *less* wrong than you were fearing. Losing your job won't condemn you to starvation and death; losing a boyfriend or girl-friend won't condemn you to a life of unrelenting misery. Those fears are based on irrational judgments about the future, usually because you haven't thought the matter through in sufficient detail. You heard the rumour about cutbacks at the company, and instantly jumped to a mental image of being utterly destitute; a lover behaved coldly and you leapt to imagining lifelong loneliness. The premed-itation of evils is the way to replace these irrational notions with more rational judgments: spend time vividly imagining exactly how wrong things could go *in reality*, and you will usually find that your fears were exaggerated. If you lost your job, there are specific steps you could take to find a new one; if you lost your relation-ship, you would probably manage to find some happiness in life despite being single. Confronting the worst-case scenario saps it of much of its anxiety-inducing power. Happiness reached via positive thinking can be fleeting and brittle; negative visualisation generates a vastly more dependable calm.

Seneca pushes this way of thinking to its logical conclusion. If visualising the worst can be a source of tranquility, what about deliberately trying to experience a taste of the worst? In one of his letters, he proposes an exercise that was the direct predecessor of my adventures in embarrassment on the London Underground, though admittedly more extreme. If what you fear the most is losing your material wealth, he advises, don't try to persuade yourself that it could never happen. (That would be the Dr Robert H. Schuller approach: refusing to countenance the possibility of failure.) Instead, try acting as if you had already lost it. 'Set aside a certain number of days, during which you shall be content with the scantiest and cheapest fare, with coarse and rough dress,' he suggests, 'saying to yourself the while: "Is this the condition that I feared?".' You may not have much fun. But the exercise will force a collision between your wildest anxieties about how bad such an eventuality might be, on the one hand, and on the other, the reality – which may be unpleasant, but also much less catastrophic. It will help you grasp that the worst-case scenario is something with which you would be able to cope.

This all made intellectual sense to me, but I wanted to know if anyone really lived according to these principles today. I had heard rumours of a contemporary community of self-described Stoics, scattered around the globe, and my research brought me swiftly to something called the International Stoic Forum, an internet message-board with more than eight hundred members. Further investigation led to the story of a police officer in Chicago, who claimed to use the principles of Stoicism to keep calm while confronting violent gang members. At another website, a school-teacher from Florida reported back from the inaugural meeting of the International Stoic Society, held in Cyprus in 1998. Throughout all this, one name kept cropping up – as a moderator of the International Stoic Forum, as the tutor to the Chicago cop, and as the author of numerous web postings on the benefits of living Stoically. My intention had been to track down a Seneca for the modern era. I imagined that this person might have chosen to shun society, as Seneca did in his later years; that he might live, for example, in a simple rustic dwelling in the foothills of some Mediterranean volcano, spending his days in philosophical contemplation and his evenings drinking retsina. But the person to whom my enquiries led, in the event, was none of these things. His name was Keith, and he lived a short train ride to the north-west of central London, in the town of Watford.

Despite living in Watford, Dr Keith Seddon did fulfill certain criteria of otherworldliness. This became clear as soon as I saw his house. Set back from its better-kept neighbours by a tall hedgerow, in which I eventually located a very small gate, it resembled a wizard's cottage as conceived by Tolkien, had *The Lord of the Rings* been set in the London commuter belt. It was early afternoon, and raining hard. The front room, I gathered by peering through the large bay window, was empty of people, but crammed with teetering piles of books, along with an extensive collection of panama hats. It took several rings of the doorbell before Seddon answered. But when he did, he looked the part: a long grey beard, twinkling eyes, and a leather waistcoat, the whole thing topped off by one of his panamas. 'Come in,' he said, three times in a row, then led me out of the rain, through the hallway, and into a small side room containing a gas fire, a sofa, and two high-backed armchairs. In one of them sat his wife, Jocelyn. Much of the remaining space was taken up by still more books, squeezed into insufficient bookcases. Works of classical philosophy jostled against more esoteric titles: *The Book of Egyptian Ritual*, *An Introduction to Elvish*, and *Fountain Pens of the World*. Seddon ushered me to the sofa and went to fetch me a Diet Coke.

It was immediately evident that fate had not been especially kind to the couple. Jocelyn suffered from severe early-onset rheumatoid arthritis, which had left her badly debilitated. Though she was only in her early fifties, she now had great difficulty even raising a glass to her lips, a manoeuvre that required the use of both hands and clearly caused her pain. Keith was her full-time carer, and suffered himself from myalgic encephalomyelitis, or chronic fatigue syndrome. Both had PhDs and had planned on academic careers, but then Jocelyn's illness had got in the way. Now Keith's work as a tutor of correspondence courses in Stoicism, teaching students at private American universities, was drying up, too, and money was seriously tight.

Yet the atmosphere in the overheated little room was far from despondent. Jocelyn, it emerged, didn't describe herself as a Stoic like her husband, but shared a similar cast of mind: she said her illness had proven to be a 'dark gift', and that once she'd learned to ignore the people telling her to 'fight' it or to 'think positive', she had come to understand her dependence on others as a kind of blessing. She seemed serene; Keith, meanwhile, was practically bubbly. 'Being a Stoic is really a very uncomfortable position to be in!', he declared merrily. 'People throughout history have made this big mistake about happiness, and here we are, the Stoics, standing out on the fringe – beyond the fringe, really! – and shouting from over the horizon: "You've got it all wrong! You've got it all wrong!"'

Keith traced his beginnings as a Stoic to a bizarre incident that had happened to him at around the age of twenty, while he was walking through a wooded park not far from his home outside London. He described it as a shift in perspective – the kind of

jolting insight that often gets described as a 'spiritual experience'.
'It was quite a short thing,' he recalled. 'Just a minute or two. But
suddenly, for that minute or two, I was . . . ' He paused, hunting
for the right words. 'I was *directly aware of how everything was
connected together in space and time*,' he said at last. 'It was like
travelling out into space, perceiving the universe as a whole, and
seeing everything connected together in exactly the way it was
meant to be. As something finished and complete.'

I took a sip of Diet Coke, and waited.

'It was like an Airfix model,' he said, with an exasperated shake
of the head, which I took to mean that it hadn't really been like
an Airfix model at all. 'I had the sense that it was all done *on
purpose*, by some kind of agency. Not a God outside the universe,
pulling the strings, you understand. But as if *the whole thing itself*
were God.' He paused again. 'You know, the funny thing is, it
didn't really strike me as particularly significant at the time.'
Having briefly entered a mystic realm of cosmic consciousness,
the twenty-year-old Seddon forgot about it, went home, and got
on with his degree.

But after a while, the memory of those two minutes began to
gnaw at him. He read the *Tao Te Ching*, looking for clues
in Taoism. He explored Buddhism. But ultimately it was Stoicism
that spoke to him. 'It just seemed so much more solid and down-
to-earth,' he said. 'I thought: "There's nothing here that I can
argue with!"' His vision in the park, it turned out, mirrored the
Stoics' own idiosyncratic form of religious belief. They too held
that the universe was God – that there was a grand plan, and that
everything was happening for a reason. The Stoic goal of acting
according to reason meant acting in accordance with this universal
plan. 'Constantly regard the universe as one living being, having
one substance and one soul,' says Marcus Aurelius. 'Whatever

happens at all, happens as it should.' To modern secularist minds, this is certainly the part of Stoicism that is hardest to swallow. Calling the universe 'God' might be just about acceptable; that's arguably only a matter of language. But to suggest that it's all heading somewhere, in accordance with a plan, is far more problematic. Indeed, Keith explained with a sigh, he was always having to quell fractious arguments between atheist Stoics and theist Stoics on the International Stoic Forum – though as a good Stoic, naturally he didn't let it upset him all that much.

You don't necessarily need to accept the Stoic notion of a 'grand plan', however, in order to embrace its flip side, which is much more important to Stoicism in everyday life: that whether or not there is some agency bigger than ourselves, controlling the way things unfold, each one of us clearly has very little *individual* control over the universe. Keith and Jocelyn had learned this the hard way. They would have preferred to live without Jocelyn's arthritis, without Keith's constant fatigue, and with more money. But without their ever requesting it, circumstances had taught them Stoicism's central insight about control, and about the wisdom of understanding the limits of your own.

As Seneca frequently observes, we habitually act as if our control over the world were much greater than it really is. Even such personal matters as our health, our finances, and our reputations are ultimately beyond our control; we can try to influence them, of course, but frequently things won't go our way. And the behaviour of other people is even further beyond our control. For most conventional notions of happiness – which consist in making things the way you want them to be – this poses a big problem. In better times, it's easy to forget how little we control: we can usually manage to convince ourselves that we attained the promotion at work, or the new relationship, or the Nobel Prize, thanks solely to our own brilliance and effort. But unhappy times bring home the truth of the matter. Jobs are lost; plans go wrong; people die. If your strategy for happiness depends on bending circumstances to your will, this is terrible news: the best you can do is to pray that not all that much will go wrong and try to distract yourself when it does. For the Stoics, however, tranquility entails confronting the reality of your limited control. 'Never have I trusted Fortune,' writes Seneca, 'even when she seemed to be at peace. All her generous bounties – money, office, influence – I deposited where she could ask for them back without disturbing me.' Those things lie beyond the individual's control; if you invest your happiness in them, you're setting yourself up for a rude shock. The only things we can truly control, the Stoics argue, are our *judgments* – what we believe – about our circumstances. But this isn't bad news. From the Stoic perspective, as we've already seen, our judgments are what cause our distress – and so they're all that we need to be able to control in order to substitute serenity for suffering.

'Suppose somebody insults you – insults you *really* obnoxiously,' Keith said, leaning forward in his armchair as he warmed to his theme. 'The Stoic, if he's a good enough Stoic, isn't going to get annoyed or angry or upset or disconcerted, because he'll see that, ultimately, nothing bad has happened. To get annoyed, he would first have to have judged that the other person had harmed him. The trouble is that you're conditioned into making that kind of judgment all your life.'

This is a relatively small example: it's easy enough to see that a verbal insult need entail no personal harm. It would be vastly harder to make the same argument about, say, the death of a friend. This is why the notion of a 'grand plan' is ultimately so crucial to a thoroughgoing embrace of Stoicism: it's only by seeing death as part of such a plan that one could one ever hope to feel serene about it. 'Do not despise death, but be well content with it, since this too is one of those things which nature wills,' says Marcus. But this is a tall order. The best that Stoicism could do for an atheist, in this situation, would probably be to help her see that she retained *some* control over her judgments. She might be able to remind herself that it was possible to choose to be seriously but reasonably upset, instead of spiralling into utter despair.

Yet this hardly invalidates the usefulness of a Stoic approach when it comes to more minor, everyday forms of distress, which is where Seddon advised his correspondence-course students to begin. Try thinking Stoically, he told them, for the duration of a single trip to the supermarket. Is something out of stock? Are the queues too long? The Stoic isn't necessarily obliged to tolerate the situation; he might decide to switch to another store instead. But to become upset would be, in Stoic terms, an error of judgment. You cannot control the situation, so reacting with fury against that reality is irrational. Your irritation, moreover, is almost certainly out of all proportion to the actual harm – if any – that has been done to you by the inconvenience; there are no grounds for taking it personally. Maybe it's an opportunity to engage in the 'premeditation of evils': what's the absolute worst that could happen as a result of this? Almost always, asking this question will reveal your judgments about the situation to have been exaggerated, and cutting them down to size will vastly increase your chances of replacing distress or annoyance with calm.

It is essential to grasp a distinction here between acceptance and resignation: using your powers of reason to stop being disturbed by a situation doesn't mean you shouldn't try to change it. To take one very obvious example, a Stoic who finds herself in an abusive relationship would not be expected to put up with it, and would almost certainly be best advised to take action to leave it. Her Stoicism would oblige her only to confront the truth of her situation – to see it for what it was – and then to take whatever actions were within her power, instead of railing against her circumstances as if they ought not exist. 'The cucumber is bitter? Put it down,' Marcus advises. 'There are brambles in the path? Step to one side. That is enough, without also asking: "How did these things come into the world at all?"'

Or take somebody who had been wrongly convicted and imprisoned, said Keith. 'Now, that person, as a Stoic, is going to say that having been unjustly imprisoned, in one sense, *doesn't actually matter*. What matters is how I engage with the situation. Now that I'm here, rather than anywhere else, here in this time and this place – what can I do? Maybe I need to read up on the law and appeal my case and fight for my freedom. That's certainly not resignation. But, rationally, I'm accepting the reality of the situation. And then I don't need to feel distressed by a judgment that it ought not to be happening. Because it *is* happening.' For Keith and Jocelyn, this struck close to home. 'Without Stoicism,' he said quietly, gesturing at his wife and himself, 'I really don't see how we'd have been able to keep going through this.'

Later, as I headed back out into the Watford dusk, I had the sense of having absorbed some of Keith's rigorously rational tranquility, as if by osmosis. Back in London, buying food to make dinner for the friends with whom I was staying, I did indeed find myself at the wrong end of a long supermarket queue, attended by one overworked member of staff and a row of malfunctioning self-service machines. I felt a flash of irritation, before I managed to call the Stoics to mind. The situation was what it was. I could leave if I chose to. And the worst-case scenario here – a few minutes' delay before my friends and I could eat – was so trifling as to be laughable. My irrational judgments were the problem, not the supermarket queue. I felt disproportionately pleased with myself for recognising this. True, in the long history of Stoicism, it was a pretty minor triumph. It didn't really compare, for example, to staying tranquil while being forced to commit suicide by bleeding oneself to death, like Seneca. Still, I told myself – Stoically – you had to start somewhere.

For the Stoics, then, our judgments about the world are all that we can control, but also all that we need to control in order to be happy; tranquility results from replacing our irrational judgments with rational ones. And dwelling on the worst-case scenario, the 'premeditation of evils', is often the best way to achieve this – even to the point, Seneca suggests, of deliberately experiencing those 'evils', so as to grasp that they might not be as bad as you'd irrationally feared.

It was this last technique that was to prove especially inspiring, centuries later, to a maverick psychotherapist named Albert Ellis, who did more than anyone else to restore Stoicism to the forefront of modern psychology. In 2006, in the final months of Ellis's life, I went to visit him, in a cramped top-floor apartment above the establishment that he had named – with characteristic disregard for modesty – the Albert Ellis Institute, in uptown Manhattan. He was ninety-three and did not get out of bed for the interview; to accommodate his severe deafness, he wore a chunky pair of headphones, and demanded that I speak into a microphone.

'As the Buddha said two and a half thousand years ago,' he said, soon after we'd started talking, and jabbing a finger in my direction, 'we're all out of our fucking minds! That's just the way we are.' To be honest, I would have felt short-changed if he hadn't used such language early in our conversation, such was his notoriety for swearing. But I knew he had more going for him than entertainment value. A couple of decades previously, America's psychologists had voted him the second most influential psychotherapist of the twentieth century, behind the founder of humanistic psychology, Carl Rogers, but – amazingly – ahead of Sigmund Freud. This was especially generous of them in view of Ellis's opinion of much of the world of conventional psychology, which was that it was 'horseshit'.

In the 1950s, when Ellis first began to promote his Stoic-flavoured view of psychology, it was deeply controversial, at odds both with self-help's focus on positive thinking and with the Freudianism that dominated the profession. On several occasions, at psychology conferences, he'd been jeered. But now, with more than fifty books to his name – one typical bestseller was entitled *How to Stubbornly Refuse to Make Yourself Miserable About Anything, Yes, Anything!* – he exuded the satisfaction of intellectual victory.

A few days before, I had witnessed Ellis deliver one of his famous 'Friday night workshops', in which he hauled volunteers on stage in order to berate them, for their own benefit, in front of an audience of trainee therapists and interested members of the public. The first participant I watched had been beset by anxiety: she couldn't decide whether to give up her job and move across the country to join her long-term boyfriend. She wanted to marry him, and she didn't much like her job, but what if he wasn't the one for her? 'So maybe he turns out to be a jerk, and you get divorced!' Ellis shouted – because he was deaf, but also, I suspected, because he enjoyed shouting. 'That would be highly disagreeable! You might feel sad! But it doesn't have to be *awful*. It doesn't have to be *completely terrible*.'

This distinction – between outcomes that are completely terrible, versus those that are merely bad – might sound glib, or like a trivial quibble over vocabulary. To understand why it is neither, and why it goes to the heart of Ellis's outlook on the virtues of negative thinking, it is necessary to return to his youth, in Pittsburgh, in the first decades of the twentieth century. From an early age, thinking like a Stoic proved an urgent personal necessity for Ellis. His mother, as he remembered her, was self-absorbed and melodramatic; his father, a travelling salesman, was rarely around. At the age of five, Ellis developed severe kidney problems, condemning him to long stays in hospital throughout his childhood, during which his parents almost never visited. Alone with his thoughts, he drifted into philosophical speculations on the nature of existence and eventually read Seneca's *Letters from a Stoic*. The Stoics' focus on the importance of one's judgments about one's circumstances struck a chord; his unhappy existence, he came to see, might prove a surprisingly useful crucible in which to develop Stoic wisdom. And so, by 1932, when he was a gangly eighteen-year-old with a crippling fear of speaking to women, he knew enough philosophy and psychology to try addressing his shyness problem by means of a practical Stoic experiment. One day that summer – the summer that Amelia Earhart flew the Atlantic and that Walt Disney released the first Technicolor cartoon movie – Ellis arrived at the Bronx Botanical Garden, near his home in New York City, to put his plan into practice.

Every day for a month, Ellis had decided, he would follow an unbreakable rule. He would take up a position on a park bench, and, if a woman sat down near him, he would attempt to strike up an innocuous conversation. That was all. He ended up sharing benches, and attempting conversation, with a hundred and thirty women. 'Whereupon thirty got up and walked away,' he recalled, years later. 'But that left me with a sample of a hundred, which was good enough for research purposes. I spoke to the whole hundred – for the first time in my life.' Only in one case did the conversation progress far enough for Ellis and his benchmate to make a plan to meet again – 'and she didn't show up'. To an uninformed observer, the experiment might have looked like an utter failure. But Ellis would probably have rejected any such verdict as 'horseshit'; for him, it had been a triumphant success.

What Ellis had grasped about his unstated beliefs concerning conversation with women – an insight he would later extend to the beliefs that lie behind all instances of worry or anxiety – is that they were absolutist. To put it another way, it wasn't just that he *wanted* to be less shy, and that he *wanted* to be able to talk to women. Rather, he had been operating under the absolutist conviction that he *needed* their approval. Later, he would coin a name for this habit of mind: 'musturbation'. We elevate those things we want, those things we would prefer to have, into things we believe we *must* have; we feel we *must* perform well in certain circumstances or that other people *must* treat us well. Because we think these things must occur, it follows that it would be an absolute catastrophe if they did not. No wonder we get so anxious: we've decided that if we failed to meet our goal it wouldn't merely be bad, but completely bad – absolutely terrible.

Ellis's encounters in the Bronx Botanical Garden had shown him that the worst-case scenario – rejection – was far from the absolute disaster he had been fearing. 'Nobody took out a stiletto and cut my balls off,' he remembered. 'Nobody vomited and ran away. Nobody called the cops.' It was actually a good thing, Stoically speaking, that none of his conversations had ended in thrilling dates; if he had achieved such a spectacular result, it might subtly have reinforced his irrational beliefs about the awfulness of *not* achieving them. This 'shame-attacking exercise', as he later came to refer to these kinds of undertakings, was the 'premeditation of evils' rendered real and immediate. The worst thing about any event, Ellis liked to say, 'is usually your exaggerated belief in its horror'. The way to defuse that belief was to confront the reality – and in reality, getting rejected by women turned out to be merely undesirable, not horrifying or terrible. Later, as a working psychotherapist, Ellis devised other shame-attacking exercises; in one, he sent his clients onto the streets of Manhattan with instructions to approach strangers and to say to them: 'Excuse me, I just got out of the lunatic asylum – can you tell me what year it is?' It showed the clients that being thought of as crazy wouldn't kill them. In another, he instructed people to take rides on the New York City subway, calling out loud the names of the stations. When he told me about this, I replied that I thought I'd find such an exercise paralysingly embarrassing. Ellis said that was exactly why I should try it.

Explaining the difference between a *terrible* outcome and a merely *undesirable* one became a governing mission of Ellis's career. He went so far as to insist that nothing at all could ever be absolutely terrible – 'because', he wrote, 'when you insist that an undesirable event is awful or terrible, you are implying, if you're honest with yourself, that it is as bad as it could be.' Yet nothing could be 100 per cent bad, he argued, because it could always conceivably be worse. Even if one were murdered, 'that is very bad, but not one hundred per cent bad,' because several of your loved ones could meet the same fate, 'and that would be worse. If you are tortured to death slowly, you could always be tortured to death slower.' He did grudgingly concede that there was one event that might legitimately be viewed as 100 per cent bad: the complete destruction of absolutely everything on the planet. But that, he pointed out, 'hardly seems likely in the near future'.

This might seem like a bizarrely cold-hearted attitude to take towards such things as torture or murder; it seems tasteless to try to construct elaborate hypothetical scenarios merely to find something that could be worse than them. But it is precisely in the context of such extremely undesirable scenarios, Ellis insisted, that the strategy of focusing on the worst-case scenario – and distinguishing between *very bad* and *completely terrible* events – really comes into its own. It turns infinite fears into finite ones. One of his clients, he recalled, found herself unable to pursue a romantic life because of an extreme fear that she might contract AIDS from kissing, or even from shaking hands. If a friend suffered from such an anxiety, your first response might be reassurance: pointing out, in other words, how extremely unlikely it was that this scenario would ever occur. That was Ellis's first response, too. But, as we've seen, reassurance carries a sting: reassuring the woman that her fears were unlikely to come true did nothing to dislodge her belief that it would be unimaginably bad if they did. And so Ellis switched to negative visualisation instead. Suppose you did get AIDS, he said. That would be pretty bad. But absolutely horrific, or 100 per cent terrible? Obviously not: one could imagine worse scenarios. One always can. And one could imagine still finding sources of happiness in life, despite having contracted AIDS. The distinction between judging something to be 'very bad' and judging it to be 'absolutely horrific' makes all the difference in the world. It is only to the absolutely horrific that we respond with blind terror; all other fears are finite, and thus susceptible to being coped with. Grasping this at last, Ellis's client was able to stop fearing an inconceivably terrible calamity, and instead begin taking normal precautions to avoid a highly undesirable, though also highly unlikely, worst-case scenario. Moreover, she had internalised the

Stoic understanding that it was not within her control to eliminate all possibility of the fate that she feared. 'If you accept that the universe is uncontrollable,' Ellis told me, 'you're going to be a lot less anxious.'

Such Stoic insights served Ellis especially well in the months after I met him. His final days were afflicted not only by intestinal problems and pneumonia, but by a dispute with the other directors of the Institute. They fired him from the board, cancelled his Friday night workshops, and stopped paying for his accommodation, forcing him to move out. He sued, a judge ruled in his favour, and by the time of his death he was back in his apartment. True to his principles, he insisted that the contretemps had never made him upset. It was all highly undesirable, of course, but not horrific, and there was no point insisting that the entire universe fall in line with his wishes. The other members of the board, he told one reporter, were 'fucked-up, fallible human beings – just like everyone else'.

'Chancery Lane.'

I speak the words out loud, but in such a nervous croak that I'm not sure anybody hears them. Glancing up and down the carriage, I can't see any evidence of anyone having noticed. Then the middle-aged man sitting opposite me glances up from his newspaper, with an expression I can only describe as one of mild interest. I meet his eye for a moment, then look away. Nothing else happens. The train stops. Some people get off. Suddenly, it occurs to me that I have subconsciously been expecting something calamitous to happen – an explosion of ridicule, at least. Now that it hasn't, I feel disoriented.

As we approach Holborn, I say 'Holborn' – louder this time,

and less tremulously. The same man looks up. A baby two seats away stares at me, open-mouthed, but would probably have done so anyway.

It is at Tottenham Court Road that I cross some kind of psychic boundary. The adrenaline subsides, the panic dissipates, and I find myself confronting the very truth that Albert Ellis's Stoical shame-attacking experiment had been designed to beat into my brain: that none of this is anywhere near as bad as I'd been anticipating. I have been left with no option but to see that my fear of embarrassment was based on profoundly irrational ideas about how terrible it would be if people thought badly of me. The truth is that they aren't being outwardly mocking or hostile at all – mainly, no doubt, because they're much too busy thinking about themselves. At Tottenham Court Road, a few more people look my way when I speak. But I don't care anymore. I feel invincible.

Three stations further on, at Marble Arch, I get up and leave the train, beaming to myself, suffused with Stoic serenity. Nobody in the carriage seems particularly interested in that, either.

3

The Storm Before the Calm

A Buddhist Guide to Not Thinking Positively

You want it to be one way. But it's the other way.
— Marlo Stanfield in *The Wire*

IN THE EARLY 1960S, Robert Aitken, an American Zen Buddhist living in Hawaii, began to notice something inexplicable and alarming. Aitken was one of the pioneers in bringing Buddhism to the spiritually hungry West, and at their home in Honolulu, he and his wife Anne had opened a *zendo*, or meditation centre, catering mainly to the island's growing population of hippies. But something about a number of the new meditation students didn't seem right. They would arrive and sit down on their cushions at the appointed time, where they would remain still as stones, apparently meditating; but then, when the bell rang to signal the end of a meditation period, they would rise to their feet – and immediately collapse onto the ground. It took Aitken several weeks of tactful enquiries to establish what was going on. Word had got around, among the hippies of Honolulu, that attempting Zen meditation while under the influence of LSD was the ultimate trip, an express train to mind-blowing ecstasy.

As the craze for Buddhist meditation spread further through America and Europe, the notion that it was a shortcut to ecstasy proved a popular one. Back in the 1950s, that had certainly been what had appealed to Jack Kerouac, who embraced it with an enthusiasm he otherwise reserved for whisky and magic mushrooms. Blood circulation problems meant that it caused him agony to sit cross-legged for more than a few minutes at a time, but he battled on anyway, determined to penetrate new realms of bliss. Sometimes, it even seemed to work. 'Fall, hands a-clasped, into instantaneous ecstasy like a shot of heroin or morphine,' he wrote to his friend Allen Ginsberg, describing his early efforts. 'The glands inside my brain discharging the good glad fluid (Holy Fluid) . . . healing all my sickness . . . erasing all . . . ' More often, though, his knees simply hurt too much, and after a short time he would be forced, as one Kerouac biographer notes, 'to scramble to his feet and rub his legs to restore circulation'.

These days, the more prevalent stereotype about meditation is that it is a path not to ecstasy but to trance-like calm. It sometimes seems impossible to open a magazine, or a newspaper features section, without being preached to about the relaxation-inducing benefits of mindfulness meditation. The stock photograph most commonly used to illustrate such articles is of a woman in a leotard, on a beach; her legs are crossed and her eyes closed, and an insipid smile is playing on her lips. (If the topic of the article is 'using meditation in everyday life', it's sometimes a man or woman in a business suit, instead – same cross-legged posture, same smile.) The Australian meditation teacher Paul Wilson, the bestselling self-styled 'guru of calm', has done much to reinforce this stereotype: his books on meditation include *The Calm Technique*, *Instant Calm*, *The Little Book of Calm*, *The Big*

Book of Calm, *Calm at Work*, *Calm Mother*, *Calm Child*, *The Complete Book of Calm* and *Calm for Life*.

The idea of meditation as a path to calmness is somewhat more realistic, since calmness – unlike unbroken ecstasy – can indeed be one of its side effects. Yet all these associations have contributed to a modern image of meditation as a sophisticated form of positive thinking, which is almost the opposite of the truth. In fact, meditation has little to do with achieving any specific desired state of mind, no matter whether blissful or calm. At Buddhism's core, instead, is an often misunderstood notion that is starkly opposed to most contemporary assumptions about how to be happy, and that places it squarely on the 'negative path' to happiness: non-attachment.

At the root of all suffering, says the second of the four 'noble truths' that define Buddhism, is attachment. The fact that we desire some things, and dislike or hate others, is what motivates virtually every human activity. Rather than merely enjoying pleasurable things during the moments in which they occur, and experiencing the unpleasantness of painful things, we develop the habits of clinging and aversion: we grasp at what we like, trying to hold on to it forever, and push away what we don't like, trying to avoid it at all costs. Both constitute attachment. Pain is inevitable, from this perspective, but *suffering* is an optional extra, resulting from our attachments, which represent our attempt to try to deny the unavoidable truth that everything is impermanent. Develop a strong attachment to your good looks – as opposed to merely enjoying them while they last – and you will suffer when they fade, as they inevitably will; develop a strong attachment to your luxurious lifestyle, and your life may become an unhappy, fearful struggle to keep things that way. Attach too strongly to life, and death will seem all the more frightening. (The parallels here

Stoicism, and with Albert Ellis's distinction between what we prefer and what we feel we must have, aren't coincidental; the traditions overlap in countless ways.) Non-attachment need not mean withdrawing from life, or suppressing natural impulses, or engaging in punishing self-denial. It simply means approaching the whole of life – inner thoughts and emotions, outer events and circumstances – without clinging or aversion. To live non-attachedly is to feel impulses, think thoughts, and experience life without becoming hooked by mental narratives about how things 'should' be, or should never be, or should remain forever. The perfectly non-attached Buddhist would be simply, calmly present, and non-judgmentally aware.

Which, let's be frank, isn't going to happen for most of us any time soon. The idea of living without wanting things to be one way rather than another way strikes most people as a strange sort of goal. How could you not be attached to having good friends, to enjoying fulfilling relationships, or to doing well for yourself materially? And how could you be happy if you weren't thus attached? Meditation might indeed be the path to non-attachment, as the Buddhists claim – but it is by no means clear, to anyone accustomed to the standard approaches to happiness, why that's a destination that one might ever wish to reach.

What first led me to question this commonsense position was the title of a slim book by another American Zen Buddhist and trained psychiatrist. It was called *Ending the Pursuit of Happiness*, and its author, a man named Barry Magid, argued that the idea of using meditation to make your life 'better' or 'happier', in any conventional sense, was a misunderstanding. The point, instead, was to learn how to stop trying to fix things, to stop being so preoccupied with trying to control one's experience of the world, to *give up* trying to replace unpleasant thoughts and emotions

with more pleasant ones, and to see that, through dropping the
'pursuit of happiness', a more profound peace might result. Or,
rather, that wasn't the 'point', exactly, because Magid objected to
the notion that meditation had a point. If it did, he seemed to
imply, that would make it just another happiness technique, a
way of satisfying our desire to cling to certain states and eliminate
others. This was all deeply confusing. What would be the point,
I wondered, of doing something pointless? Why would anyone
try to end the pursuit of happiness, if not to become happy – in
which case, wouldn't they still be pursuing happiness, only by
more cunning means?

Barry Magid practised psychiatry in a large, sparsely furnished
room on the ground floor of an apartment block near Central Park,
on the Upper West Side of Manhattan. It was unlit save for a desk
lamp, and its two leather chairs were placed unusually far from each
other, against opposite walls, so that Magid's head seemed to loom
out at me from the dark. He was a tall, owlish man in his early
sixties, with wire-rimmed glasses, and when I asked him a rambling
question about Buddhism and non-attachment, he looked at me
with mild amusement. Then he started talking about something
else entirely.

What I really needed to understand, he told me, was the myth
of Oedipus. In Magid's view, the famous tale of the ancient Greek
king – who kills his father and marries his mother, bringing
disaster to his family and his city, and prompting him to gouge
out his eyes – was the perfect metaphor for what was wrong with
pursuing happiness. This had little to do with the 'Oedipus
complex', Freud's theory about boys secretly wanting to have sex
with their mothers. The real message of the myth, Magid
explained, was that struggling to escape your demons was what
gave them their power. It was the 'backwards law' in mythological

form: clinging to a particular version of a happy life, while fighting
to eliminate all possibility of an unhappy one, was the cause of the
problem, not its solution.

You may be familiar with the story. When Oedipus is born to
the King and Queen of Thebes, his horrible fate – that he will
kill one parent and marry the other – has already been foretold
by an oracle. His mother and father, desperate to ensure that this
never comes to pass, persuade a local shepherd to take the
newborn, with instructions to abandon him to the elements. But
the shepherd can't bring himself to let Oedipus die; the child
lives, and subsequently becomes the adoptive son of the King and
Queen of Corinth. But when Oedipus confronts them, some time
later, with the rumour that he is adopted, they deny it – so when
he hears about the oracle's terrible prophecy, he assumes that they
are the parents to whom it refers. Resolving to escape the curse
by putting as much distance as possible between himself and the
couple he takes to be his parents, Oedipus travels far away.
Unfortunately, the faraway place at which he arrives is Thebes.
Thereafter, fate drags him to his inevitable end: first, he becomes
involved in an unlikely dispute over a chariot, and kills its occupant, who turns out to have been his father. Then he falls in love
with his mother.

One obvious reading of this myth is that you can never escape
your fate, no matter how hard you try. But Magid preferred another.
'The quintessential point,' he told me, 'is that if you flee it, it'll
come back to bite you. The very thing from which you're in flight
– well, it's the fleeing that brings on the problem. For Freud, our
whole psychology is organised around this avoidance. The unconscious is the repository of everything that we're avoiding.'

The founding myth of Buddhism is practically a mirror-image
of all this. The Buddha becomes psychologically free – enlightened

– by confronting negativity, suffering and impermanence, rather than struggling to avoid them. According to legend, the historical Buddha was born Siddharta Gautama, the son of a king, in a palace in the foothills of the Himalayas. As was the case with Oedipus, his destiny had been foretold: it was prophesied that he would become either a powerful king or a holy man. In common with parents throughout history, Siddharta's preferred the job description that came with good pay and security, and so they dedicated themselves to making sure their son would grow to love privilege. They made his life a luxurious prison, pampering him with fine foods and armies of servants; he even managed to marry and have a son without once leaving his bubble of entitle-ment. It was only at the age of twenty-nine that he managed to venture outside the compound. There, he saw what have become enshrined in Buddhist lore as the 'Four Sights': an old man, a sick man, a corpse, and a wandering ascetic monk. The first three symbolised the inevitability of impermanence, and the three fates awaiting us all. Siddharta was shocked into abandoning his comfortable life, and his family, to become an itinerant monk. It was in India, some years later, that he is supposed to have achieved enlightenment after spending the night sitting beneath a fig tree, thereby becoming the Buddha, 'the one who woke up'. But it was those initial sights, according to the myth, that first awoke his understanding of impermanence. Buddhism's path to serenity began with a confrontation with the negative.

From Barry Magid's Buddhist–Freudian point of view, then, most people who thought they were 'seeking happiness' were really running away from things of which they were barely aware. Meditation, the way he described it, was a way to stop running. You sat still, and watched your thoughts and emotions and desires and aversions come and go, and you resisted the urge to try to flee from them, to fix them, or to cling to them. You practised non-attachment, in other words. Whatever came up, negative or positive, you stayed present and observed it. It wasn't about escaping into ecstasy – or even into calmness, as the word is normally understood; and it certainly wasn't about positive thinking. It was about the significantly greater challenge of declining to do any of that.

It was shortly after meeting Magid that I took the rash decision to spend almost a week with forty strangers, meditating for about nine hours a day, in the middle of a forest, in the depths of winter, many miles from the nearest town, in almost unbroken silence.

Which proved interesting.

'The basic meditation instruction is really incredibly simple,' said Howard, one of the two teachers charged with running the retreat at the Insight Meditation Society, a converted turn-of-the-century mansion in the remote pine forests of central Massachusetts. It was early evening, and all forty of us were seated on cushions filled with buckwheat hulls in the building's austere main hall, listening to a man with a voice so calming it was impossible to imagine an instruction he might give that you wouldn't be lulled into following. 'Sit comfortably, gently close your eyes, and notice the breath as it flows in and out. You can focus on this sensation at the nostrils, or at the abdomen. Just follow one breath in, and one breath out. And then do it again.' There were nervous chuckles; surely it wasn't going to be that simple, or that boring? 'Other things will come up,' Howard continued. 'Physical sensations, feelings and thoughts will carry us away into distraction. In meditation, when we notice that happening, we don't judge. We just return to the breath.' It really was that simple, apparently. What he failed to point out – though we were to discover it soon enough – was that 'simple' didn't mean 'easy'.

I had arrived at the Insight Meditation Society earlier that afternoon, sharing a taxi from the nearest major railway station, about twenty-five miles away, with an Israeli student I'll call Adina. As we bounced along uneven backwoods roads, she explained that she was attending the retreat because she felt lost. 'It's like I have no roots anywhere . . . nothing to hold on to, no structure in my life,' she said. I couldn't help wincing inwardly at her candour: we'd only just met, and as far as I was concerned this was over-sharing. But what she said next made sense. She was hoping that meditation might be a way not to stop feeling lost, but to come to see the lostness differently – to embrace it, even. The American Buddhist nun Pema Chödrön calls this 'relaxing into the ground-lessness of our situation', and it harmonises well with the idea of non-attachment. Chödrön suggests that 'groundlessness' is actually everyone's situation, all the time, whether they like it or not. It's just that most of us can't relax in the presence of that truth; instead, we frantically scramble to deny it.

Our taxi driver seemed lost in a more literal sense, plunging down rutted tracks through the forest, then reversing back up them again, cursing his satellite navigation system. The meditation centre proved seriously hard to find, which wasn't surprising; isolation was the point. When we finally arrived, I was shown to my room – a narrow, monkish cell, looking out over miles of uninterrupted forest. It contained a single bed, a sink, a small wardrobe, a shelf, and nothing else. I stowed my suitcase under my bed and hurried to the main hall, where a staff member outlined the week's ground rules. We would be expected to spend one hour a day helping to clean the building, or prepare food, or do the dishes, she explained. In a few moments' time, she would ring the small brass gong on the building's central staircase, and we would be expected to fall silent – with only a handful of exceptions, including emergencies and question-and-answer sessions with the teachers – for the rest of the retreat. Since we wouldn't be speaking, she added, it would be best if we kept our eyes downcast, too, so as to avoid the temptation to spend the week communicating via smiling, scowling, and winking. There would be no alcohol, no sex, no use of telephones or the internet, no listening to music, and also no reading or writing – since these, she said, could rupture one's interior quiet as surely as audible conversation. Then again, as the daily schedule we found pinned to the noticeboard made clear, there would be no time for any of that, anyway:

5.30 a.m. – Waking bell
6.00 a.m. – Sitting meditation
6.30 a.m. – Breakfast
7.15 a.m. – Work period (kitchen cleaning, food preparation, etc.)
8.15 a.m. – Sitting meditation
9.15 a.m. – Walking meditation
10.00 a.m. – Sitting meditation
10.45 a.m. – Walking meditation
11.30 a.m. – Sitting meditation
12.00 noon – Lunch, followed by rest
1.45 p.m. – Walking meditation
2.15 p.m. – Sitting meditation
3.00 p.m. – Walking meditation
3.45 p.m. – Sitting meditation
4.30 p.m. – Walking meditation
5.00 p.m. – Light meal
6.15 p.m. – Sitting meditation

7.00 p.m. – Walking meditation
7.30 p.m. – Dharma talk
8.30 p.m. – Walking meditation
9.00 p.m. – Sitting meditation
9.30 p.m. – Sleep or further meditation

'Well, that'll be the structure you were looking for,' I said to Adina, who was standing nearby. The moment I'd said this, it struck me as an annoying, smart-aleck kind of remark. What made it worse, somehow, was that it was the last thing I said. A few seconds later, we heard the deep ring of the gong, and silence descended.

It didn't take very long on the meditation cushion, how-ever, to discover that outer silence did not automatically confer inner silence. For the first several hours after receiving the basic instructions – the rest of the first evening, and most of the following morning – my mind was occupied almost exclusively by song lyrics, looping loudly on repeat. Inexplicably, and appal-lingly, they were mostly the lyrics to the 1997 song 'Barbie Girl', by the Danish-Norwegian kitsch-pop group Aqua, a track I had always despised. The music was interrupted only by occasional anxious thoughts about how I was going to make it through the week, plus stray entries from my to-do list that I'd forgotten to deal with prior to my departure.

In my defence, this – the mental chatter in general, not 'Barbie Girl' – is almost everybody's first experience of silent meditation. When you eliminate the distractions of external noise, and turn your attention inwards, what strikes you first is this: it's almost constantly noisy in there. It's not that the inner chatter is somehow generated by the attempt to meditate. It's simply that outer noise, the rest of the time, drowns out the inner noise; in the silence of the forest and the meditation hall, it all became suddenly audible. 'One realises', as the spiritual teacher Jiddu Krishnamurti once put it, 'that one's brain is constantly chattering, constantly planning, designing: what it will do, what it has done, the past impinging itself on the present. It is everlasting chattering, chattering, chattering.'

An understandable response to such chatter, when you're attempting to meditate, is to try to quieten it – to dampen it down, or perhaps even to try to stop thinking altogether. But one central principle of *vipassana* meditation, the variety taught at the Insight Meditation Society, is the opposite: to let the clamour be. As the Buddhist teacher Steve Hagen says in his pithy guidebook *Meditation: Now or Never*, 'we do not try to forcefully detach ourselves from the feelings, thoughts and expectations that arise in our mind. We don't try to force anything into or out of the mind. Rather, we let things rise and fall, come and go, and simply be . . . there will be times in meditation when we're relaxed, and times when our minds are agitated. We do not seek to attain a relaxed state, or to drive out our agitated and distracted mind. That is just more agitation.' This is the first big step towards nonattachment: learning to view passing thoughts and feelings as if one were a spectator, not a participant. Consider it too closely, and this idea becomes dizzying, given that watching your own thought processes is itself a thought process; it can be easy to feel caught in some kind of infinite loop.

Fortunately, it isn't necessary to resolve this conundrum in order to practise meditation. The technique, as Howard had explained, is simply to return – every time you realise you've been carried away by a narrative or by an emotion – to the breath. The following evening, during the teachers' daily talk, he quoted the Catholic mystic St Francis de Sales, a practitioner of Christian meditation: 'Bring yourself back to the point quite gently. And even if you do nothing during the whole of your hour but bring your heart back a thousand times, though it went away every time you brought it back, your hour would be very well employed.' There is more to non-attachment than this – and much more, it's worth emphasising, to Buddhism than non-attachment. But it is where it all begins.

It becomes easier to make sense of this when you realise that Buddhism, though we think of it today as a religion, was originally just as much an approach to the study of psychology. The central Buddhist psychological text, the *Abhidhamma*, is a ferociously complex tome of lists and sub-clauses and technical argument. But one of its more straightforward insights is the notion that the mind can be viewed, in many respects, as one of the senses – like seeing, hearing, smell, touch, and taste. Just as we receive smells through the 'sense-door' of the nose, and tastes through the sense-door of the tongue, it's possible to see the mind as a kind of sense-door, too, or as a screen on which thoughts are projected, like images in a cinema. This isn't how we usually think about thinking. Sounds and smells and tastes, after all, are just sounds and smells and tastes, but thoughts, we tend to assume, are something much more important. Because they come from within us, they feel more essential, and expressive of our deepest selves. But is that true, really? When you start meditating, it soon becomes apparent that thoughts – and emotions – bubble up in much the same uncontrollable, unbidden fashion in which noises reach the ears, smells reach the nose, and so on. I could no more choose for thoughts not to occur than I could choose not to feel chilly when I was woken by the ringing of the morning bell at five-thirty each day – or, for that matter, than I could choose not to hear the bell.

Seeing thoughts as similar to the other five senses makes

non-attachment seem much more approachable as a goal. In the analogy most commonly used by contemporary Buddhists, mental activity begins to seem more like weather – like clouds and sunny spells, rainstorms and blizzards, arising and passing away. The mind, in this analogy, is the sky, and the sky doesn't cling to specific weather conditions, nor try to get rid of the 'bad' ones. The sky just is. In this the Buddhists go further than the Stoics, who can sometimes seem rather attached to certain mind-states, especially that of tranquility. The perfect Stoic adapts his or her thinking so as to remain undisturbed by undesirable circum-stances; the perfect Buddhist sees thinking itself as just another set of circumstances, to be non-judgmentally observed.

Even more challenging than practising non-attachment to passing thoughts and feelings is practising it in the presence of physical pain; to be non-judgmental about being in agony seems preposterous. But it is here that some of the most powerful scientific evidence for cultivating non-attachment has been accumulating in recent years. Some Buddhists, such as Barry Magid, might object to the implication that the benefits of meditation need to be scientifically 'proven'. But the science is intriguing nonetheless – especially in the case of a series of experiments conducted in 2009, at the University of North Carolina, by a young psychologist named Fadel Zeidan.

Zeidan wanted to test the effects of meditation on people's ability to endure physical pain, and so, with refreshing straight-forwardness, he decided to hurt them. His research employed mild electric shocks – jolts that weren't sufficient to be harmful, but that were powerful enough to make limbs twitch – and partici-pants were asked to rank their subjective experience of the pain. Some then received three twenty-minute lessons in mindfulness meditation over the course of the next few days, showing them how to develop non-judgmental awareness of their thoughts, emotions, and sensations. When further electric shocks were administered, those who used the meditation techniques reported significantly reduced pain. (In a related experiment by Zeidan's team, using brain scans and pain created by a hot plate, meditation appeared to lead to less pain for every participant, with the reductions ranging from 11 to 93 per cent.) A critic might counter that the meditation was merely providing a distraction, giving the participants something else to focus on – so Zeidan had another group perform a mathematics task while being shocked. Distraction did have some effect, but it was nowhere near as large as that of meditation. And the meditation lessons, unlike distraction, lowered pain levels even when participants didn't actively meditate during the shocks.

'It was kind of freaky for me,' Zeidan said. 'I was ramping at four to five hundred milliamps, and their arms would be jolting back and forth, because the current was stimulating a motor nerve.' Yet still their pain assessments remained low. Meditation, Zeidan believes, 'had taught them that distractions, feelings and emotions are momentary, [and] don't require a label or judgment, because the moment is already over. With the meditation training, they would acknowledge the pain, they realise what it is, but they let it go. They learn to bring their attention back to the present.' If you've ever gripped the arms of a dentist's chair, in expectation of imminent agony that never actually arrives, you'll know that a big part of the problem is attachment to thoughts about pain, the fear of its arrival, and the internal struggle to avoid it. In Zeidan's laboratory, focusing non-attachedly on the experience of pain itself rendered the experience much less distressing.

As the hours turned into days at the Insight Meditation Society, however, my attachments seemed only to grow more intractable. By the second day, the song lyrics had faded, but in their place came darker irritations. Gradually, I started to become aware of a young man sitting just behind me and to the left. I had noticed him when he first entered the meditation hall, and had felt a flash of annoyance at the time: something about him, especially his beard, had struck me as too calculatedly dishevelled, as if he were trying to make a statement. Now his audible breathing was starting to irritate me, too. It seemed studied, unnatural, somehow theatrical. My irritation slowly intensified – a reaction that struck me as entirely reasonable and proportionate at the time. It was all beginning to feel like a personal attack. How much contempt must the bearded meditator have for me, I seethed silently, deliberately to decide to ruin the serenity of my meditation by behaving so obnoxiously?

Experienced retreat-goers, it turns out, have a term for this phenomenon. They call it a 'vipassana vendetta'. In the stillness, tiny irritations become magnified into full-blown hate campaigns; the mind is so conditioned to attaching to storylines that it seizes upon whatever's available. Being on retreat had temporarily separated me from all the real causes of distress in my life, and so, apparently, I was inventing new ones. As I shuffled to my narrow bed that evening, I was still smarting about the loud-breathing man. I did let go of the vendetta eventually – but only because I'd fallen into an exhausted and dreamless sleep.

One of the most obvious objections to non-attachment as a way of life is that it seems so passive. Granted, it might be a way of becoming more chilled out, but wouldn't it mean never getting anything done? The Buddhist monk spending decades in meditation might be at one with the universe, but it's not clear that the rest of us should want to emulate him. Attachment, this argument runs, is the only thing that motivates anyone to accomplish anything worthwhile in the first place. If you weren't attached to things being a certain way, rather than another way – and to feeling certain emotions, rather than others – why would you ever attempt to thrive professionally, to better your material circumstances, to raise children, or to change the world? There's a persuasive retort to this, though. Just as the Stoic notion of acceptance need not entail resignation, Buddhist non-attachment can be a rigorously practical way of accomplishing worthwhile activities. To understand why, consider the most ubiquitous and frustrating barrier to getting things done: the near-universal curse of procrastination.

You are probably already much too familiar with the truth that most anti-procrastination advice just doesn't work, or at least not for very long. Motivational books, tapes and seminars might leave you feeling briefly excited, but that feeling soon fades. Ambitious lists of goals and systems of rewards seem like a great idea when you construct them, but feel stale the next morning; inspiring mottos on posters and coffee mugs swiftly lose their ability to inspire. Procrastination sets in again, sometimes deeper than before. Which is, a cynic might suggest, how motivational speakers and self-help authors guarantee themselves a reliable income: if their products delivered lasting change, they would have much less repeat custom.

The problem with all these motivational tips and tricks is that they aren't really about 'how to get things done' at all. They're about how to feel in the mood for getting things done. 'If we get the right emotion, we can get ourselves to do *anything*!' says Tony Robbins, author of *Awaken the Giant Within*, whose books and speeches

fixate on this theme. (At Robbins's motivational seminars, participants are invited to pump themselves up by walking barefoot across
hot coals.) As we've seen, though, the ideas that self-help gurus
express so hyperbolically are often only extreme versions of how
the rest of us think. The most common response to procrastination
is indeed to try to 'get the right emotion': to try to motivate yourself to feel like getting on with the job.

The problem is that *feeling like* acting and *actually* acting are
two different things. A person mired deep in procrastination
might claim he is unable to work, but what he really means is
that he is unable to make himself feel like working. The author
Julie Fast, who writes about the psychology of depression, points
out that even when a person is so depressed that she is unable
to get out of bed in the morning – something Fast has experienced
for herself – it's more accurate to say that she's unable to *feel like*
getting out of bed. This isn't meant to imply that procrastinators,
or the severely depressed, should simply pull their socks up and
get over it. Rather, it highlights the way that we tend to confuse
acting with feeling like acting, and how most motivational techniques are really designed to change how you *feel*. They're built,
in other words, on a form of attachment – on strengthening your
investment in a specific kind of emotion.

Sometimes that can help. But sometimes you simply can't
make yourself feel like acting. And in those situations, motivational advice risks making things worse, by surreptitiously
strengthening your belief that you need to feel motivated before
you can act. By encouraging an attachment to a particular
emotional state, it actually inserts an additional hurdle between
you and your goal. The subtext is that if you can't make yourself
feel excited and pleased about getting down to work, then you
can't get down to work.

Taking a non-attached stance towards procrastination, by contrast, starts from a different question: Who says you need to wait until you 'feel like' doing something in order to start doing it? The problem, from this perspective, isn't that you don't feel motivated; it's that you imagine you need to feel motivated. If you can regard your thoughts and emotions about whatever you're procrastinating on as passing weather, you'll realise that your reluctance about working isn't something that needs to be eradicated or transformed into positivity. You can coexist with it. You can note the procrastinatory feelings and act anyway.

It is illuminating to note, here, how the daily rituals and working routines of prolific authors and artists – people who really do get a lot done – very rarely include techniques for 'getting motivated' or 'feeling inspired'. Quite the opposite: they tend to emphasise the mechanics of the working process, focusing not on generating the right mood, but on accomplishing certain physical actions, regardless of mood. Anthony Trollope wrote for three hours each morning before leaving to go to his job as an executive at the post office; if he finished a novel within a three-hour period, he simply moved on to the next. (He wrote forty-seven novels over the course of his life.) The routines of almost all famous writers, from Charles Darwin to John Grisham, similarly emphasise specific starting times, or number of hours worked, or words written. Such rituals provide a structure to work in, whether or not the feeling of motivation or inspiration happens to be present. They let people work alongside negative or positive emotions, instead of getting distracted by the effort of cultivating only positive ones. 'Inspiration is for amateurs,' the artist Chuck Close once memorably observed. 'The rest of us just show up and get to work.'

No approach to psychology better expresses the pragmatic

benefits of non-attachment than Morita Therapy, the school founded by the early twentieth-century Japanese psychologist Shoma Morita. The head of psychiatry at Jikei University School of Medicine in Tokyo, Morita was heavily influenced by Buddhism, and especially its perspective on thoughts and emotions as mental weather – as things that happen to us, and with which we can coexist in peace. 'People . . . think that they should always like what they do, and that their lives should be trouble-free,' Morita wrote. 'Consequently, their mental energy is wasted by their impossible attempts to avoid feelings of displeasure or boredom.'

One contemporary practitioner of Morita Therapy, James Hill, expresses this distinctive approach as follows: 'Many western therapeutic methods focus on trying to successfully manage or modify our feeling-states. The underlying assumption is that if our feelings can be altered [or] reduced, we will be more able to live meaningful and effective lives; that it is our feelings that hold us back . . . [But] is it accurate to assume that we must "overcome" fear to jump off the high dive at the pool, or increase our confidence before we ask someone out on a date? If it was, most of us would still be waiting to do these things. Our life experience teaches that it is not necessary to change our feelings in order to take action . . . Once we learn to accept our feelings, we find that we can take action without changing our feeling-states.' We can feel the fear and do it anyway.

By the end of the fourth day at the Insight Meditation Society, things were much improved. The bearded man's breathing had ceased to annoy. All of us seemed to have settled into the timetable that governed our waking, sleeping, meditating and eating; where before it had felt rigid and militaristic, now it cradled us through the day. I was actually starting to enjoy meditating – even the walking meditation, which involved moving at a glacial pace across the meditation hall, trying to divide the sensations of each foot-step into the component parts of 'lifting', 'moving' and 'placing', and which I had initially concluded was a waste of time. When, during occasional breaks, I managed to sneak out onto the forest paths behind the meditation centre, I found I had become hyper-attuned to my environment; every crackle of every twig underfoot registered like a splintering diamond. Meanwhile, the vegetarian food we were served in the dining room – nondescript lentil stews, peanut butter on rye crackers, that sort of thing – had started to taste extraordinary. I discovered subtle sub-flavours in peanut butter I'd never have imagined might be hiding there. The Massachusetts winter sunset, viewed from the building's main porch, was often so beautiful as to be almost painful. At night, I was sleeping more deeply than I could remember.

And then it all went wrong. Without my noticing the precise moment of transition, the silence of the meditation hall became a combination of courtroom and torture chamber. For hours, I was attacked by barrages of negative thoughts and their associated emotions – anxious ones, guilty ones, worried ones, hostile, bored, impatient and even terrified ones – as if they had all been gathering, just out of sight, for years, waiting for this moment to pounce. Above all, they were self-critical. I was suddenly aware – and somehow all at once – of countless occasions in my life on which I had behaved badly towards other people: my parents, my sister, friends, girlfriends, or colleagues. Many of these infractions were relatively small in the scheme of things – harsh words spoken, relationships insufficiently nurtured – but they filled me with sorrow. Months afterwards, I would encounter Buddhist writings suggesting that this was a well-recognised early step on the 'progress of insight', the stages through which a meditator is traditionally held to pass: it was called 'knowledge of cause and effect', and had to do with perceiving afresh how one's actions always had consequences. The sorrow that accompanied these realisations, from a Buddhist point of view, is a good thing; it is the fertile soil in which compassion can take root.

After about a day of this, though, I began to notice something. The situation in my mind was far from quiet or relaxed. And yet my constant efforts to return to focusing on my breath – to avoid becoming attached to thoughts or emotions – seemed to be having an effect. My vantage point on my mental activity had altered subtly, as if I'd climbed two rungs up a stepladder in order to observe it from above. I was less enmeshed in it all. As Shoma Morita might have put it, I was beginning to see it all as mere mental events, to be non-judgmentally noticed. Much of my thinking concerned the past or the future, but I was no longer being yanked off into daydreams or unpleasant memories; I was absolutely present, there on the cushion, watching the performance with something less like panic and more like interest. In some monasteries in the Zen tradition, a monk is charged with creeping up behind his fellow monks and hitting them with a thin wooden stick, or *keisaku*, in order to snap them into exactly this kind of utter presence. They didn't hit people with sticks at the Insight Meditation Society, but I felt like someone had. I was watching my own mind with total alertness.

The strangest part, though, and the part that is hardest to put into words, was the question of where I was watching all this *from*. If I'd stepped away from being enmeshed in my thoughts, where was this point of observation? Nowhere? Everywhere? I felt as if I had stepped into a void. I recalled my conversation with Adina in the taxi, and Pema Chödrön's advice about 'relaxing into the groundlessness of our situation'. It was suddenly apparent to me that I spent my regular life in a state of desperate clinging to thinking, to trying to avoid falling into the void that lay behind thoughts. Except now I was in the void, and it wasn't terrifying at all. By the time the retreat drew to a close, I found to my surprise that I didn't want it to end; I could easily have stayed another week. Moreover, I felt as if I were among friends. Even though I had never exchanged words with most of the other retreatants – and wouldn't have recognised them in the street, given that we'd been keeping our eyes downcast – a tangible sense of community had arisen in the meditation hall. When the gong rang to indicate that we could speak again, small talk felt scratchy and awkward; it seemed to interfere with the companionship.

'Well, that was . . . ' said Adina, trailing into silence when I encountered her on the porch as we made our preparations to leave. Encapsulating the week in a few words seemed futile.

'I know what you mean,' I replied.

By the time I made it onto the train back to New York, I had a throbbing headache: the normal noises of the non-meditating world were too much for my silence-adapted mind. Discovering the number of emails waiting in my inbox didn't help. But the stressed-out thoughts did slide away more swiftly than before. It seemed I could live with a little bad weather.

All this is only one small part of Buddhism's radical perspective on psychology. But the point is central to any 'negative' approach to happiness: it is rarely wise to struggle to change the weather. 'Clear mind is like the full moon in the sky,' Seung Sahn, a Korean Zen master of the old school, who carried a hitting stick, told one audience in America in the 1970s. 'Sometimes clouds come and cover it, but the moon is always behind them. Clouds go away, then the moon shines brightly. So don't worry about clear mind; it is always there. When thinking comes, behind it is clear   mind. When thinking goes, there is only clear mind. Thinking comes and goes, comes and goes. You must not be attached to the coming and going.' And if that wasn't sufficient to jolt his listeners into the realisation that they did not need to be attached to their mental storylines, that they could choose to observe their thoughts and feelings non-judgmentally, and thus find peace behind the pandemonium? 'Then,' Seung Sahn was fond of saying, 'I hit you thirty times with my stick!'

4

Goal Crazy

When Trying to Control the Future Doesn't Work

Future, *n*. That period of time in which our affairs prosper, our friends are true and our happiness is assured.
    – Ambrose Bierce, *The Devil's Dictionary*

IN 1996, A TWENTY-EIGHT-YEAR-OLD from Indiana named Christopher Kayes signed up with an adventure travel company to go trekking in the Himalayas. His intention, though it would prove ironic in hindsight, was to take a relaxing break. A punishing career as a stockbroker, and then as a corporate consultant, had left him burned out. Kayes had always been interested in the psychology of the business world, and so he had decided to pursue a doctorate in organisational behaviour instead. But first he needed time off, and when he saw an advertisement in a travel magazine for a group hiking expedition to Nepal, it seemed like the perfect answer. As the plane descended into Kathmandu, he recalled later, he was looking forward to 'a refreshing immersion in Nepalese culture', surrounded by the beauty of the Himalayas. But what Kayes encountered in the mountains was a troubling psychological puzzle that was to dominate his life for years to come.

While Kayes and his fellow hikers were exploring the foothills of Mount Everest, camping at night in tents, a disaster of historical proportions was unfolding near the mountain's peak. Fifteen climbers died on Everest during that year's climbing season, eight of them during a single twenty-four-hour period that has since entered mountaineering lore, thanks largely to the bestselling book *Into Thin Air*, by the climber and journalist Jon Krakauer, who was among those on the mountain at the time. Kayes himself encountered some of the climbers and rescue workers who had been involved – exhausted men, emerging dazed into the foothills, struggling to make sense of what had happened.

Even in the modern era of commercial Everest expeditions, when anyone with sufficient money and some climbing skills can pay to be escorted to the summit, it's still not that unusual for people to die in the attempt. What made the 1996 disaster so chilling – apart from the sheer number of dead – was the fact that it seemed uniquely inexplicable. The weather on the peak was not more perilous than usual. There were no sudden avalanches during the period when most of the climbers perished. The paying customers were all sufficiently skilled for the undertaking. *Into Thin Air*, controversially, attributed the tragedy in part to the stubbornness and arrogance of Anatoli Boukreev, a Kazakhstani climbing guide. There is some evidence for this, but it is ultimately dissatisfying as an explanation, too. Mountaineers, as a group, tend towards stubbornness and arrogance. Yet disasters on the scale of Everest in 1996 are mercifully rare.

In the end, what happened that year looked more like an outbreak of mass irrationality – an episode that reached its apogee around noon on 10 May at the Hillary Step, a wall of rock just 720 feet from the summit, in an event that has since become known as 'the traffic jam'. Teams from New Zealand, the United

States and Taiwan – thirty-four climbers in total – were all attempting the final stage of the ascent that day, from Camp Four, at 26,000 feet, to the summit, at 29,000 feet. The Americans and New Zealanders had co-ordinated their efforts, so as to ensure a smooth progression up and down the mountain. But the Taiwanese climbers were reneging on an agreement not to climb the same day, and an advance team of guides had failed to secure safety ropes at the Hillary Step according to plan, with the result that the smooth progression soon turned into a bottleneck.

Timing is one of the most important variables in any assault on Everest, and so climbers generally observe strict 'turnaround times'. Leaving Camp Four at midnight, a climber can hope to reach the summit by midday, or soon after. But if he or she fails to make it there by the pre-arranged turnaround time – which might be anywhere from noon until two in the afternoon, depending on weather conditions, and the team leader's attitude to risk – it becomes essential to call off the attempt and turn back. Failure to do so means the climber risks running out of bottled oxygen and facing Everest's most dangerous weather in the dark. Yet confronted with the traffic jam at the Hillary Step, the teams pushed on, disregarding their turnaround times. Back at Camp Four, the American mountaineer Ed Viesturs watched the climbers' slow progress through a telescope, and found it hard to believe what he was seeing. 'They've already been climbing for hours, and they still aren't on the summit,' he remembered thinking to himself, with rising alarm. 'Why haven't they turned around?'

Members of all three teams continued arriving at the summit for two hours after two o'clock, the latest safe turnaround time. Doug Hansen, a postal service worker from Washington state who was a paying client of the New Zealand group, was the last to do so, at the astonishingly late time of just after four o'clock. He had ascended Everest the year before, but had been forced to turn back a few hundred feet from the top. This time, he never made it back down. Like seven others, he was caught in intense blizzards as darkness fell, which made navigation of the mountain impossible, and sent temperatures plunging to −40°F. They lay dying, unreached by the frantic rescue attempts that saved several other climbers' lives. Years after climbing Everest had become a feasible project for amateurs as well as professionals, 1996 saw the highest recorded death toll in the mountain's history. And even today, nobody clearly understands why.

Except, just possibly, Chris Kayes. A former stockbroker turned expert on organisational behaviour might seem to have little to contribute to the post-mortem of a mountaineering disaster. But the more Kayes learned of what had happened, and as he continued to follow the case after returning home, the more it reminded him of a phenomenon he had witnessed all too frequently among businesspeople. The Everest climbers, Kayes suspected, had been 'lured into destruction by their passion for goals'. His hypothesis was that the more they fixated on the endpoint – a successful summiting of the mountain – the more that goal became not just an external target but a part of their own identities, of their senses of themselves as accomplished guides or high-achieving amateurs. If his hunch about the climbers was right, it would have become progressively more difficult for them to sacrifice their goal, despite accumulating evidence that it was becoming a suicidal one. Indeed, that accumulating evidence, Kayes was convinced, would have *hardened* the climbers' determination not to turn back. The climb would have become a struggle not merely to reach the summit, but to preserve their sense of identity. In theology, the term 'theodicy' refers to the effort to maintain belief in a benevolent god, despite the prevalence of evil in the world; the phrase is occasionally used to describe the effort to maintain any belief in the face of contradictory evidence. Borrowing that language, Chris Kayes termed the syndrome he had identified 'goalodicy'.

During his years in the corporate world, Kayes had been troubled to watch goalsetting achieve the status of religious dogma among his colleagues. The situation hasn't changed much today. The hallmark of a visionary leader, it is widely held, is the willingness to set big, audacious goals for his or her organisation, and then to focus every resource on achieving them. Individual employees, meanwhile, are encouraged, and sometimes obliged, to define their own personal work objectives, frequently in the form of 'SMART' goals. (The acronym stands for 'specific, measurable, attainable, realistic, and time-bounded'.) Numerous self-help books advocate ambitious and highly specific goals as the master key to a successful and satisfying life: 'By this time next year, I will be married to the woman of my dreams/sitting on the balcony of my beach house/earning £10,000 per month!' One of the practice's most passionate evangelists, Brian Tracy, in his book *Goals! How to Get Everything You Want – Faster Than You Ever Thought Possible*, insists that 'Living without clear goals is like driving in a thick fog . . . Clear goals enable you to step on the accelerator of your own life, and race ahead rapidly.'

Yet Kayes couldn't help but notice that it frequently didn't work out that way. A business goal would be set, announced, and generally greeted with enthusiasm. But then evidence would begin to emerge that it had been an unwise one – and goalodicy would kick in as a response. The negative evidence would be reinterpreted as a reason to invest *more* effort and resources in pursuit of the goal. And so things would, not surprisingly, go even more wrong. Kayes believed that a similar thing had happened on Everest in 1996.

Chris Kayes is now a professor of management science at George Washington University in Washington, DC, and as he has travelled the lecture circuit in recent years, using Everest as a metaphor for all that is wrong with our obsession with goals, he has frequently found himself giving offence. 'A businessperson should not study topics filled with such great tragedy and emotion,' one Russian student lectured him curtly by email. 'Questions of tragedy and the dilemmas of human existence should be left to the poet, the novelist, and the playwright. These topics have nothing to do with why we study leadership in organisations.' But Kayes couldn't let it drop. 'It would be accurate to say that I think about the Everest disaster probably every day,' he told me. 'Almost like it was a death in my own family. "Haunted" would definitely be the right word.' And there is persuasive evidence for Kayes's hypothesis about what happened on the mountain, hidden away in a largely forgotten psychology study that was conducted in 1963. The study's participants were professional mountaineers, undertaking an expedition to Everest.

That year, seventeen climbers were attempting to become the first Americans to reach the summit, and a psychologist named James Lester realised that the expedition presented an ideal opportunity to investigate what drove people to attempt such ambitious and dangerous feats. With funding provided by the United States Navy, Lester and a handful of colleagues gathered the mountaineers in Berkeley, California, where they administered a series of personality tests. Then – demonstrating an unusual degree of commitment to his research – Lester left sunny California for Mount Everest, accompanying the climbers as far as Camp Two, at 21,000 feet. There, he administered further tests on the climbers and their Sherpa guides. In his book *Destructive Goal Pursuit: The Mount Everest Disaster*, Chris Kayes relates Lester's basic finding about the typical Everest climber: he was someone who demonstrated 'considerable restlessness, dislike for routine, desire for autonomy, tendency to be dominant in personal relations, and a lack of interest in social interaction for its own sake. Their felt need for achievement and independence was very high.' No surprises there: Lester had confirmed the truism that climbers tend to be domineering loners with little regard for social convention. But more intriguing findings were to emerge from the daily diaries that Lester asked the climbers to keep for the duration of the three-month period they spent preparing for, then carrying out, their trek to the mountain's summit.

En route to base camp, the American team had split into two dissenting groups, each with a very different idea of how best to reach the top. The larger group favoured the well-established route via the South Col, a mountain pass ravaged by high winds, leaving it relatively free of snow. But a smaller group wanted to approach via the remote and never previously attempted West Ridge. (Even today, in a morbid statistical oddity, the fatality rate for the West Ridge is higher than 100 per cent, meaning that more people have died there than have reached the summit that way.) Noting the difference of opinion among the climbers, Lester made sure that their diaries included regular updates on how optimistic or pessimistic they were feeling about their chosen route.

Subsequent analysis of the diaries revealed an unexpected pattern. As the day of the summit attempt neared, the West Ridge group's optimism began to fade rapidly, replaced by a gnawing sense of uncertainty. That was only to be expected, given that their route was untried. But as the climbers' uncertainty and pessimism about the West Ridge option increased, the diaries revealed, so did their commitment to it. 'The more uncertain climbers felt about their possible success in reaching the summit,' as Kayes puts it, 'the more likely they were to invest in their particular strategy.' A bizarre and self-reinforcing loop took hold: team members would actively seek out negative information about their goal – looking for evidence of weather patterns, for example, that might render the West Ridge approach even more risky than usual – which would increase their feelings of uncertainty. But then, in an effort to extinguish that uncertainty, the climbers would increase their emotional investment in their decision. The goal, it seemed, had become a part of their identity, and so their uncertainty about the goal no longer merely threatened the plan; it threatened them as individuals. They were so eager to eliminate these feelings of uncertainty that they clung ever harder to a clear, firm and specific plan that provided them with a sense of certainty about the future – even though that plan was looking increasingly reckless. They were firmly in the grip of goalodicy.

The happy conclusion of the 1963 expedition – much as it spoils the neatness of Kayes's argument – is that the West Ridge climbers went ahead with their dangerous plan, and survived. Too many of the relevant participants in the 1996 drama perished, meanwhile, for us ever to know with confidence exactly how far the same thought processes were to blame. But Beck Weathers, a paying client that year who was twice left for dead on the mountain – he lost his nose and several fingers to frostbite, having dragged himself back to camp – testified to the plausibility of the notion. 'You can overpursue goals,' he reflected afterwards. 'You can become obsessed with goals.'

Mountaineers, of course, do not speak in the corporate language of targets and goalsetting. But when they refer to 'summit fever' – that strange, sometimes fatal magnetism that certain peaks seem to exert upon the minds of climbers – they are intuitively identifying something similar: a commitment to a goal that, like sirens luring sailors onto the rocks, destroys those who struggle too hard to achieve it. Ed Viesturs, who watched the 1996 tragedy through his telescope, spoke of this lure in vivid terms. 'When you're up there, you've spent years of training, months of preparation, and weeks of climbing, and you're within view of the summit, and you know, you have – in the back of your mind, you're telling yourself "We should turn around, 'cause we're late, we're gonna run out of oxygen . . . " But you see the summit, and it draws you there. And a lot of people – it's so magnetic that they tend to break their rules, and they go to the summit. And on a good day, you can get away with it. And on a bad day, you'll die.'

If you've ever read a popular book about the importance of planning for the future, you will almost certainly have encountered a reference – and quite possibly several – to the Yale Study of Goals. This is a now-legendary finding about the importance of creating detailed plans for your life: it is cited in the aforementioned *Goals!*, by Brian Tracy, but also in scores of other works, from the supposedly scholarly (books with titles such as *Psychological Foundations of Success*) to the more streetwise (the management manual *Train Your People and Whack the Competition*). The essentials of the study are as follows: in 1953, students graduating from Yale University were asked by researchers whether or not they had formulated specific, written-down goals for the rest of their lives. Only 3 per cent of them said they had. Two decades later, the researchers tracked down the class of '53, to see how their lives had turned out. The results were unequivocal: the 3 per cent of graduates with written goals had amassed greater financial wealth than the other 97 per cent combined. It is a jaw-dropping finding, and a powerful lesson to any young person thinking of just drifting through life. It isn't surprising, then, that it achieved the status of legend in the world of self-help, and in many corners of corporate life. The only problem is that it is indeed a legend: the Yale Study of Goals never took place.

Some years ago, a journalist from the technology magazine *Fast Company* set out to trace the source of the alleged study. No academic journal reference was ever cited when it was mentioned, so he began by asking the motivational gurus who liked to quote it. Disconcertingly, when asked for their sources, they pointed at each other. Tony Robbins suggested asking Brian Tracy, who in turn suggested Zig Ziglar, a veteran of the motivational-speaker circuit, and a regular fixture at Get Motivated! seminars. Completing the circle, Zig Ziglar recommended asking Tony Robbins.

Taking matters into my own hands, I called a senior Yale University archivist, Beverly Waters. She seemed friendly and eager to help, but when I mentioned the goals study, a note of frustration entered her voice. 'I did a systematic check, years ago, when this first arose, and there was nothing,' she said. 'Then the secretary of the graduating class of 1953 did another systematic check, and nobody he spoke to had ever been asked to fill out such a questionnaire, or anything like that.' She added that it was highly unlikely that it had happened in some other year, and been wrongly described as taking place in 1953, because the Association of Yale Alumni would have been involved – and nobody there could trace anyone who remembered it. Waters sighed. 'It's just too good not to be true, I guess,' she said.

Of course, the non-existence of one study about the benefits of setting goals does not disprove the suggestion that setting goals has benefits; there is plenty of very real research testifying to the fact that the practice can be useful. What the story indicates, instead, is how far the fascination with goals has gone. You might never have written down any 'life goals' yourself, and you might well disagree with the imaginary Yale study's implication that material wealth is the ticket to happiness. But the basic urge beneath all this is nearly universal. At some point in your life, and perhaps at many points, you likely have decided upon some goal – to find a spouse, to get a specific kind of job, to live in a particular town – and then devised a plan to attain it. Interpreted sufficiently broadly, setting goals and carrying out plans to achieve them is how many of us spend most of our waking hours. Whether or not we use the word 'goals', we're forever making plans based upon desired outcomes. 'Consider any individual at any period of his life,' wrote the great French political philosopher Alexis de Tocqueville, 'and you will always find him preoccupied with fresh plans to increase his comfort.' Tocqueville's use of the word 'comfort' should not distract us here; we are, of course, capable of setting far grander and more selfless goals than that. But the deeper truth remains: many of us are perpetually preoccupied with plans.

It is precisely this preoccupation that the followers of the 'negative path' to happiness call into question – because it turns out that setting and then chasing after goals can often backfire in horrible ways. There is a good case to be made that many of us, and many of the organisations for which we work, would do better to spend less time on goalsetting, and, more generally, to focus with less intensity on planning for how we would like the future to turn out.

At the core of this outlook is the insight that Chris Kayes and James Lester both reached in their studies of Everest mountaineers: that what motivates our investment in goals and planning for the future, much of the time, isn't any sober recognition of the virtues of preparation and looking ahead. Rather, it's something much more emotional: how deeply uncomfortable we are made by feelings of uncertainty. Faced with the anxiety of not knowing what the future holds, we invest ever more fiercely in our preferred vision of that future – not because it will help us achieve it, but because it helps rid us of feelings of uncertainty in the present. 'Uncertainty prompts us to idealise the future,' Kayes told me. 'We tell ourselves that everything will be OK, just as long as I can reach this projection of the future.' Obviously, climbing Mount Everest requires plenty of planning and implies a specific goal – reaching the summit. But to Kayes, the evidence suggested that in 1996, an aversion to feelings of uncertainty might have tipped the balance in favour of a fatal overinvestment in goals.

We fear the feeling of uncertainty to an extraordinary degree – the psychologist Dorothy Rowe argues that we fear it more than death itself – and we will go to extraordinary lengths, even fatal ones, to get rid of it. As we will see later in this chapter, though, there is a powerful alternative possibility: we could learn to become more comfortable with uncertainty, and to exploit the potential hidden within it, both to feel better in the present and to achieve more success in the future.

It is alarming to consider how many major life decisions we take primarily in order to minimise present-moment emotional discomfort. Try the following potentially mortifying exercise in self-examination. Consider any significant decision you've ever taken that you subsequently came to regret: a relationship you entered despite being dimly aware that it wasn't for you, or a job you accepted even though, looking back, it's clear that it was mismatched to your interests or abilities. If it felt like a difficult decision at the time, then it's likely that, prior to taking it, you felt the gut-knotting ache of uncertainty; afterwards, having made a decision, did those feelings subside? If so, this points to the troubling possibility that your primary motivation in taking the decision wasn't any rational consideration of its rightness for you, but simply the urgent need to get rid of your feelings of uncertainty. Here are the words of one blogger on psychology, David Cain, reflecting on how an intolerance for uncertainty once dominated his own choices: 'It's quite disturbing to take a mental inventory of where [the intolerance for uncertainty] has steered my life,' he writes. 'It's the reason I spent three years and ten thousand dollars learning computer programming, when I didn't really want to do it for a living. It's the reason behind every single day I've spent working on careers that don't inspire me. [Uncertainty] feels like you're sinking, and [that] it is positively imperative to scramble to the next patch of firm ground, whatever direction it may be in. Once you get there, you can let yourself breathe.' Clinging too tightly to goals is one of the principal ways in which we express the obsession with reaching that next patch of ground.

To understand one of the many reasons why goals can backfire, consider the experience of trying to hail a taxi in a major city during a rainstorm. If you've ever had to do this, you'll be familiar with the despair it can induce – and you probably think you understand why it's so difficult, since it seems like the kind of economics problem even a five-year-old could solve. When it rains, more people want cabs, and so demand outstrips supply, making it harder to find an empty vehicle. That's obvious, surely? So when the economist Colin Camerer and three of his colleagues set out to investigate the problem of the rainy-day taxi shortage – taking New York City as their field of study – you can imagine the kind of looks they might have received from their colleagues.

Except, as their research revealed, the reason for the problem isn't as obvious as it appears. Demand for taxis does surge when it rains. But something much stranger happens at the same time: the supply of taxis shrinks. This contradicts the standard economic assumption that when people stand to earn more money, they work more. You might have expected cab drivers, who have some discretion over the hours they work, to work the most when demand was highest. Instead, they clocked off *earlier* when it rained.

Further investigation revealed that the culprit was goals. New York taxi drivers rent their vehicles in twelve-hour shifts, and commonly set themselves the daily goal of taking in double the amount of money that it costs to rent the cab. When it rains, they meet their goal more rapidly and head home sooner. New Yorkers are thus deprived of taxis during exactly the weather conditions in which they need them most, while drivers are deprived of additional income at exactly the time when it would be easiest to earn.

The point is not that it's wrong for a taxi driver to choose more leisure time over more income, of course – that's an entirely defensible choice – but that it makes no sense to take that time off when it's raining. Far from behaving like stereotypically rational economic actors, the drivers appeared to act more like the pigeons in experiments conducted by the behaviourist psychologist B. F. Skinner. Having learned to obtain a food pellet by pecking on a mechanism in its cage, Skinner observed, a pigeon would indulge in a 'post-pellet pause', relaxing after having attained a predetermined goal.

A taxi driver's daily income goal is a very different matter to the goal of climbing Everest, and the researchers did not investigate the drivers' emotional motivations. But it is possible to see the taxi-shortage problem as another, more minor example of how uncomfortable we're made by uncertainty. The drivers, it would appear, preferred the regularity and reliability of a predictable daily income to the uncertainty of remaining open to the possibility of earning more. They had invested in their goals beyond the point that doing so served their best interests.

New York cab drivers were much on the mind of a university professor named Lisa Ordóñez when, in 2009, she and three of her colleagues embarked upon the heretical project of questioning goalsetting. In their academic field, management studies, the wisdom of goalsetting was rarely questioned, thanks largely to the work of two North American management theorists, Gary Latham and Edwin Locke. Over the course of the previous four decades, Latham and Locke had established themselves as the godfathers of goalsetting, publishing more than twenty books between them. Their credo was one of the very first things taught to incoming students at business schools: to be a success as an entrepreneur, what you needed first was a business plan, focused on specific goals. Anything less was unacceptable. 'When people are asked to do their best, they don't,' Edwin Locke told one interviewer. 'It's too vague.'

Ordóñez and her colleagues mounted the case for the opposition in a 2009 paper with a heavy-handed pun for its title – 'Goals Gone Wild' – in the usually rather dry pages of the journal *Academy of Management Perspectives*. The goalsetting that worked so well in Latham and Locke's studies, they pointed out, had various nasty side effects in their own experiments. For example: clearly defined goals seemed to motivate people to cheat. In one such study, participants were given the task of making words from a set of random letters, as in Scrabble; the experiment gave them opportunities to report their progress anonymously. Those given a target to reach lied far more frequently than did those instructed merely to 'do your best'. More important, though, Ordóñez and her fellow heretics argued, goalsetting worked vastly less well outside the psychology lab settings in which such studies took place. In real life, an obsession with goals seemed far more often to land people and organisations in trouble.

One illuminating example of the problem concerns the American automobile behemoth General Motors. The turn of the millennium found GM in a serious predicament, losing customers and profits to more nimble, primarily Japanese, competitors. Following Latham and Locke's philosophy to the letter, executives at GM's headquarters in Detroit came up with a goal, crystallised in a number: twenty-nine. Twenty-nine, the company announced amid much media fanfare, was the percentage of the American car market that it would recapture, reasserting its old dominance. Twenty-nine was also the number displayed upon small gold lapel pins, worn by senior figures at GM to demonstrate their commitment to the plan. At corporate gatherings, and in internal GM documents, twenty-nine was the target drummed into everyone from salespeople to engineers to public-relations officers.

Yet the plan not only failed to work – it made things worse. Obsessed with winning back market share, GM spent its dwindling finances on money-off schemes and clever advertising, trying to lure drivers into purchasing its unpopular cars, rather than investing in the more speculative and open-ended – and thus more uncertain – research that might have resulted in more innovative and more popular vehicles. There were certainly many other reasons for GM's ongoing decline. But twenty-nine became a fetish, distorting the organisation in damaging ways, fuelling short-termism and blinkered vision, all so that the numbers in the business news headlines might match those on the vice-presidents' lapels. But that never happened. GM continued spiralling towards failure, and went bankrupt in 2009; it ended up taking a bailout from Washington. At the Detroit Auto Show of 2010, the firm's newly installed president for North America, keen to show how much GM had changed, used the twenty-nine campaign as an example of what it would no longer be doing. 'We're not printing [lapel] pins,' he told a radio reporter. 'We're not doing any of that stuff.'

It is safe to say that Edwin Locke and Gary Latham's response to 'Goals Gone Wild' was among the more furious outbursts ever to have been published in *Academy of Management Perspectives*. Ordóñez and her colleagues were accused of being extremists, of using 'scare tactics', of abandoning good scholarship by stringing together anecdotes, of 'spreading falsehoods and insults', and of 'making unverified assertions'. 'Oh, my God!', Ordóñez exclaimed, when I asked her about the dispute. 'My face was hot for a week. It was just so completely personal. But put yourself in their shoes. They had spent forty years doing research into how wonderful goals can be, and here we were, coming and pointing out the pitfalls. It was nothing but a temper tantrum.'

The reason all this academic infighting matters to anyone else is that the two sides represent two fundamentally different ways of thinking about planning for the future. It was unfair, as it happened, for Locke and Latham to imply that Ordóñez and her colleagues had ignored experimental data altogether in favour of anecdotes. But the real lesson of 'Goals Gone Wild' is that the simplified conditions of the laboratory almost never apply in real life. In most artificial studies of goalsetting, participants are faced with a single task or simple set of tasks, such as the word game mentioned earlier; some of them are then encouraged to approach the task with a goal firmly in mind, while others are not. But as the case of GM suggests, outside the laboratory – whether in business, or in life in general – no situation is ever anywhere close to being this simple. In singling out one goal, or set of goals, and striving to meet it, you will invariably exert an effect on other, interlinked aspects of the thing you're trying to change. In an automobile manufacturing company, that might mean starving your research division of funding in an effort to meet a prede-termined market share. Applied to the personal realm, it might mean attaining your goals at the expense of ruining your life. During one course he taught, Chris Kayes recalled, 'an executive came up to me at the end of a session and told me his goal had been to become a millionaire by the age of forty. That's something you hear all the time in business schools. And he'd done it – he was forty-two, so he was right on target. But he was also divorced and had health problems. And his kids didn't talk to him anymore.' Another student had been furiously training for a marathon when he first met her. She succeeded in her goal – but at the cost of severe injuries and several weeks spent housebound.

This problem goes deeper than one might think. The standard answer to it, from the proponents of goalsetting, is that these are examples of people setting the *wrong* goals – overly ambitious or overly narrow ones. Of course, it's true that some goals are wiser than others. But the more profound hazard here affects virtually any form of future planning. Formulating a vision of the future requires, by definition, that you isolate some aspect or aspects of your life, or your organisation, or your society, and focus on those at the expense of others. But problems arise thanks to the law of unintended consequences, sometimes expressed using the phrase 'you can never change only one thing'. In any even slightly complex system, it's extremely hard to predict how altering one variable will affect the others. 'When we try to pick out any thing by itself,' the naturalist and philosopher John Muir observed, 'we find it hitched to everything else in the universe.'

The thinker who probably pursued this notion further than anyone else was the anthropologist Gregory Bateson, who spent a significant part of his early career studying everyday life in the villages of Bali. These villages, he concluded, owed their social cohesion and effective functioning to customs and rituals that he described as 'non-maximizing'. He meant that these traditions had the effect of discouraging villagers from focusing on any one goal at the risk of a detrimental effect on others. A Balinese ethos of frugality, for example, was balanced with a custom of occasional ritual displays of conspicuous spending, thereby preventing the quest for wealth from damaging other social goals, and holding competitiveness and inequality among villagers in check. The obvious contrast was with Western industrialised societies, where maximising economic growth had become the goal to which all else was sacrificed. If life in America or Great Britain was best compared to climbing a ladder, life in rural Bali was more like an endless but graceful tightrope walk, resulting in a 'steady state' of social thriving geared to no particular set of goals. 'The continued existence of complex interactive systems', Bateson argued, 'depends upon preventing the maximization of any variable.' This need not be taken as an argument for abandoning all future planning whatsoever, but it serves as a warning not to strive too ardently for any single vision of the future. As Chris Kayes pointed out, the mountaineers who died climbing Everest in 1996 did success-fully reach their goal: they ascended to the summit. The tragic unintended consequence was that they didn't make it back down alive.

What might it mean to *turn towards* uncertainty – to learn to develop a tolerance for it, or even to embrace it? To try to answer this question, I first sought out a recovering goal addict who I'd heard had some radical ideas on the matter.

I met Steve Shapiro in a poorly lit bar in New York's West Village, where he was drinking a pint of Samuel Adams lager, working his way through a cheeseburger, and keeping half an eye on the baseball game on the corner television. There was nothing about his appearance, in other words, to suggest that he was anything but a quintessentially all-American forty-five-year-old. His job description might have given the same impression: he was a consultant who travelled the country running workshops with businesspeople. His life unfolded in conference suites, airport lounges, and hotel bars; PowerPoint was sometimes involved. Yet behind his quick smile and open features, the real Shapiro was a kind of enemy agent, because the message he delivered ran counter to some of the most deeply cherished ideologies of American corporate life. He argued in favour of giving up goals, and embracing uncertainty instead.

Shapiro did, in fact, start out as an all-American achiever, committed to his goal of becoming a highly paid management consultant. His punishing hours destroyed his marriage. 'I'm not sure if my goals drove me to work the crazy hours I did,' he later wondered, 'or if I used my goals as an excuse to avoid issues in my personal life.' He tried to dig himself out of such crises by means of even more goals (at one point, he recalled, he had a five-year plan to become 'a leader in the innovation space'). But none of these plans changed his life. What made the difference, in the end, was a conversation with a friend who told him he spent too much energy thinking about his future. He should think of himself more 'like a frog', she said. Shapiro was wondering whether to feel insulted when she explained: 'You should sun yourself on a lily-pad until you get bored; then, when the time is right, you should jump to a new lily-pad and hang out there for a while. Continue this over and over, moving in whatever direction feels right.' The imagery of sunbathing on lily-pads should not be taken to imply laziness. Shapiro's friend's point was entirely compatible with his hard-charging, achievement-hungry personality; it simply promised to channel it more healthily. In fact, it promised to help him achieve *more*, by permitting him to enjoy his work in the present, rather than postponing his happiness to a point five years in the future – whereupon, in any case, he would surely just replace his current five-year plan with another. The idea triggered a shift of perspective for Shapiro that would eventually lead to his reinvention as an advocate for abolishing goals.

Unsurprisingly, perhaps, the companies that pay Steve Shapiro for his advice have sometimes proved resistant to this idea. ('People looked at me pretty funny sometimes,' he said.) Chris Kayes has encountered similar opposition: 'At any company I visit,' he told me, 'there's always some manager who says, "You know, that stuff they did on Everest – taking huge risks, ignoring the consequences, ploughing on regardless – that's what I *want* people to be doing round here!"' Shapiro's counterargument to his sceptical clients begins with what he calls 'the happiness and self-worth side of things': goal-free living simply makes for happier humans. In survey research he commissioned, drawing on samples of American adults, 41 per cent of people agreed that achieving their goals had failed to make them any happier or had left them disillusioned, while 18 per cent said their goals had destroyed a friendship, a marriage, or another significant relationship. Moreover, 36 per cent said that the more goals they set for themselves, the more stressed they felt – even though 52 per cent said that one of their goals was to reduce the amount of stress in their lives.

Bosses are more frequently persuaded, though, by Shapiro's other argument: that getting rid of goals, or focusing on them less fixedly, is often also the best way to extract results from employees. He seduces them with anecdotes about the effectiveness of operating goallessly, such as the tale of the Formula One pit crew with which he worked, whose members were told that they would no longer be assessed on the basis of speed targets; they would be rated on style instead. Instructed to focus on acting 'smoothly', rather than on beating their current record time, they wound up performing faster. Then there was the story of the sales team that went from missing its targets to exceeding them – as soon as it became company policy to keep those targets a secret from the salespeople. 'You can have a broad sense of direction without a specific goal or a precise vision of the future,' Shapiro told me. 'I think of it like jazz, like improvisation. It's all about meandering with purpose.'

More recently, the benefits of a goal-free approach to business have started to be substantiated by more than mere anecdote. A few years ago, the researcher Saras Sarasvathy recruited forty-five entrepreneurs who met a predetermined definition of 'successful': they each had at least fifteen years' experience in starting businesses and had taken at least one company public. She presented them with a detailed hypothetical scenario about a potentially lucrative new software product. (Confusingly, it was software to help entrepreneurs launch businesses.) Sarasvathy then conducted two-hour-long interviews with each participant, probing how they might take this promising but vague idea and make real money from it. She generated hundreds of pages of interview transcripts – and then hundreds more when, for the purposes of comparison, she conducted a parallel exercise among executives at older, larger corporations.

We tend to imagine that the special skill of an entrepreneur lies in having a powerfully original idea and then fighting to turn that vision into reality. But the outlook of Sarasvathy's interviewees rarely bore this out. Their precise endpoint was often mysterious to them, and their means of proceeding reflected this. Overwhelmingly, they scoffed at the goals-first doctrine of Locke and Latham. Almost none of them suggested creating a detailed business plan or doing comprehensive market research to hone the details of the product they were aiming to release. ('I don't believe in market research,' one anonymous participant told Sarasvathy. 'Somebody once told me the only thing you need is a customer. Instead of asking all the questions, I'd try to make some sales.') The entrepreneurs didn't think like high-end chefs, concocting a vision of a dish and then hunting for the perfect ingredients. They behaved more like ordinary, time-pressed home cooks, checking what was in the fridge and the cupboards, then figuring out, on the fly, what they could make and how. 'I always live by the motto of "Ready, fire, aim",' said one. 'I think that if you spend too much time doing "Ready, aim, aim, aim", you're never going to see all the good things that would happen if you actually started doing it. I think business plans are interesting, but they have no real meaning, because you can't put in all the positive things that will occur.' The most valuable skill of a successful entrepreneur, Chris Kayes is convinced, isn't 'vision' or 'passion' or a steadfast insistence on destroying every barrier between yourself and some prize you're obsessed with. Rather, it's the ability to adopt an unconventional approach to learning: an improvisational flexibility not merely about which route to take towards some predetermined objective, but also a willingness to change the destination itself. This is a flexibility that might be squelched by rigid focus on any one goal.

Saras Sarasvathy has distilled her anti-goal approach into a set of principles she calls 'effectuation'. It is an outlook with implications far beyond the world of entrepreneurialism; it might serve as a worthy philosophy for life. 'Causally minded' people, to use Sarasvathy's terminology, are those who select or are given a specific goal, and then choose from whatever means are available to make a plan for achieving it. Effectually minded people, on the other hand, examine what means and materials are at their disposal, then imagine what possible ends or provisional next directions those means might make possible. The effectualists include the cook who scours the fridge for leftover ingredients; the chemist who figured out that the insufficiently sticky glue he had developed could be used to create the Post-it note; or the unhappy lawyer who realises that her spare-time photography hobby, for which she already possesses the skills and the equipment, could be turned into a job. One foundation of effectuation is the 'bird in hand' principle: 'Start with your means. Don't wait for the perfect opportunity. Start taking action, based on what you have readily available: what you are, what you know and who you know.' A second is the 'principle of affordable loss': Don't be guided by thoughts of how wonderful the rewards might be if you were spectacularly successful at any given next step. Instead – and there are distinct echoes, here, of the Stoic focus on the worst-case scenario – ask how big the loss would be if you failed. So long as it would be tolerable, that's all you need to know. Take that next step, and see what happens.

'See what happens', indeed, might be the motto of this entire approach to working and living, and it is a hard-headed message, not a woolly one. 'The quest for certainty blocks the search for meaning,' argued the social psychologist Erich Fromm. 'Uncertainty is the very condition to impel man to unfold his powers.' Uncertainty is where things happen. It is where the opportunities – for success, for happiness, for really living – are waiting.

'To be a good human,' concludes the American philosopher Martha Nussbaum, applying this perspective to her own field of ethics, 'is to have a kind of openness to the world, an ability to trust uncertain things beyond your own control, that can lead you to be shattered in very extreme circumstances for which you were not to blame. That says something very important about the ethical life: that it is based on a trust in the uncertainty, and on a willingness to be exposed. It's based on being more like a plant than a jewel: something rather fragile, but whose very particular beauty is inseparable from that fragility.'

5

Who's There?

How to Get Over Your Self

Why are you unhappy? Because 99.9 per cent of everything you think, and of everything you do, is for yourself – and there isn't one.

— Wei Wu Wei, *Ask the Awakened*

IF YOU HAD SPENT any time in the park that dominates Russell Square, in central London, in the late 1970s, it is possible that you might have noticed a skinny man aged around thirty, with delicate, almost elfin features, sitting alone on a park bench and doing absolutely nothing. For almost two years, if his own account is to be believed, Ulrich Tolle sat on park benches all day, unless it was raining or snowing hard; then he sought shelter in nearby public libraries. He spent his nights on the sofas of tolerant friends – or occasionally, when their tolerance expired, sleeping rough amid the bushes of Hampstead Heath. All things considered, though, it is unlikely that you'd have noticed him. Tolle was a nobody. And he would not have considered this label an insult, either, since from his perspective there was a sense in which it was literally true.

A few months prior to the beginning of his park-bench period, Tolle had been living alone in a bedsit in Belsize Park, in north-west London. He had recently completed a graduate degree at the University of London, and he was depressed to the point of regularly contemplating suicide. Then, the way he tells it, one night when he was filled with even more despair than usual, something snapped. Lying nearly paralysed on his bed in the dark, he underwent a terrifying, cataclysmic spiritual experience that, he claimed, erased his old identity completely. It was 'a slow movement at first', he wrote, many years later. 'I was gripped by an intense fear, and my body started to shake . . . I could feel myself being sucked into a void. It felt as if the void was inside myself, rather than outside. Suddenly, there was no more fear, and I let myself fall into that void. I have no recollection of what happened after that.' He lost consciousness.

When he awoke the next day, he knew instinctively that he was no longer the person he had been before. But what had happened seemed even more wrenching and elemental than that: somehow, in a way he couldn't properly put into words, it no longer felt as though he had a clearly bounded personal identity at all. His 'me' was missing in action. In its place, he felt only a sense of 'uninter-rupted deep peace and bliss', which faded a little after a while, but never went away. 'I walked around the city in utter amazement at the miracle of life on earth, as if I had just been born,' he wrote. After a while, he gave up the bedsit. With no personal agenda, no to-do list, no mental narrative telling him that he had to become someone or get anywhere other than what and who he was, he found that the idea of spending his days on the park benches of Russell Square didn't strike him as strange behaviour. There was no reason not to. And so, in a state of peaceful content-ment, he did.

Some time after his bedsit crisis, Ulrich Tolle changed his name to Eckhart Tolle, and began to speak and write about his experiences. Several years after that, another cataclysmic force – Oprah Winfrey – helped propel him to the position he enjoys today, as the world's bestselling living 'spiritual' author, with the arguable exception of the Dalai Lama. These facts do not enhance his credibility in everyone's eyes, and some sceptics have questioned his account of his transformation. Tolle says he doesn't mind the doubters, although you might argue that he doesn't have much choice: when you've told the world that you dwell in a realm of infinite equanimity, you can't start getting all snippy when people don't take you at your word.

You might also reasonably suspect that a figure such as Tolle would have little to contribute to the 'negative path' to happiness. The books that clutter the mind/body/spirit shelves, where his reside, often embody the very worst of the 'cult of optimism'. And Oprah's endorsement is no less troubling, given that it has also been bestowed upon the likes of *The Secret*, that epitome of magical positive thinking, as well as upon a number of questionable self-help gurus. Tolle's own first bestseller, *The Power of Now*, was once photographed under the arm of the socialite Paris Hilton as she prepared to serve a forty-five-day jail sentence in 2007. None of this bodes well. But regardless of exactly what happened to him that night in Belsize Park, his insights are worth considering because of his perspective on a topic that most of us, most of the time, take entirely for granted: the idea of the self.

In this book so far, we have explored the many ways in which conventional approaches to happiness and success seem to backfire, for the same essential reason: that there is something about trying to *make ourselves* happy and successful that is precisely what sabotages the attempt. But there is an even more unsettling possibility. What if the problem is not just one of technique?

What if we are mistaken not only about how to change ourselves but also about the nature of the selves we're trying to change? Calling into question our assumptions about what it means to talk about the self might prompt an entirely different approach to the psychology of happiness. And *The Power of Now* – which is, in fact, mercifully low on references to 'energy fields', 'vibrational frequencies', and the like – calls these assumptions into question with the title of its very first chapter: 'You Are Not Your Mind'. Think about that, if you dare.

The notion that our commonplace assumptions about selfhood might need re-examining certainly didn't originate with Eckhart Tolle. It is an ancient thought, central to Buddhism and to numerous other philosophical and religious traditions – a theme recurring so frequently in the history of religion and spirituality, in fact, that it is a part of what Aldous Huxley and others labelled 'the perennial philosophy'. Tolle was saying nothing new. But these reflections are often buried deep in ancient texts. I wanted to visit Tolle because he claimed to have experienced, at first hand, what this was all about. And he was willing to talk about it.

I had half assumed, perhaps even half hoped, that he might turn out to be a clichéd kind of guru, living in an ashram, fat and drunk on his own power, wearing elaborate robes and surrounded by adoring acolytes. It turned out, though, that he lived in a pleasant but slightly cramped top-floor apartment in a building in Vancouver, in Canada, just up the street from the campus of the University of British Columbia. He answered the door himself, stooping slightly. He was sixty now and birdlike, clad not in golden robes but in a strikingly unfashionable orange shirt and brown slacks. He indicated a leather armchair, on which I sat down, then seated himself on a sofa facing it, and waited for me to say something.

In Tolle's company, I soon learned, there was a lot of waiting. As on the benches of Russell Square, he seemed entirely comfortable with this, feeling no need to fill the silences, no pressure to move things along. I was less comfortable, because I couldn't think of anything sensible to say. Even 'How are you?', I had suddenly realised, was a potentially problematic opening question when the word 'you' – and what, exactly, that might mean – was the very thing I had come to discuss.

Few things seem so obvious, fundamental and undeniable as the self. Whatever uncertainties you might harbour about how to live – how to be happy, how to behave morally, what relationships to pursue, or what work to do – you probably retain the bedrock assumption that all these things are happening to an easily identifiable, single entity called you. This feels like such firm ground, in fact, that it forms the basis of what is arguably the most famous line in the history of Western philosophy: the seventeenth-century French philosopher René Descartes's dictum *Cogito ergo sum*: I think, therefore I am. There are very few aspects of our experience of being alive, Descartes realised, about which we can truly be certain. But we can be confident that we are us – that, in the most basic sense, we are who we take ourselves to be.

It is worth following Descartes's argument quite closely here. Imagine, he begins, an evil demon who is determined to play as many tricks on you as possible – a demon 'supremely powerful and cunning, [who] has devoted all his efforts to deceiving [you]'. How far could the demon's deceptions go? Don't forget, Descartes points out, that you rely for your entire understanding of the external world on your five senses: you can't know anything at all about what's going on outside your body unless you can touch, see, hear, smell, or taste it. And so, in principle, *everything* you think you know about that world might in fact be a breathtakingly detailed and convincing illusion, concocted by the evil demon. Looking out from inside your head, Descartes asks, how could you ever be completely certain that 'the sky, the air, the earth, colours, shapes, sounds and all external things' are not merely delusions, traps that the demon 'has laid for [your] credulity'? You might respond that such a scenario is absurdly unlikely, but Descartes is not concerned with its likelihood. He is employing the philosophical technique that came to be known as 'systematic doubt', attempting to isolate only that knowledge that he could regard as totally, unshakably certain.

Descartes's evil demon might go further still. (He is extremely evil, after all.) By sending the right sort of deceptive signals to your brain, he might even be responsible for your feeling that you possess a physical body. Maybe, in reality, you don't have a body. Maybe you're just a brain in a jar on a shelf in the demon's laboratory. How could you ever be sure? The parallels here with the 1999 movie *The Matrix* are not coincidental: that film is essentially a twentieth-century meditation on Descartes's seventeenth-century insights. 'A viewer of *The Matrix*', as the philosopher Christopher Grau puts it, 'is naturally led to wonder: how do I know I am not in the matrix? How do I know for sure the world is not a sophisticated charade, put forward by some superhuman intelligence in such a way that I cannot possibly detect the ruse?'

And yet despite all these possibilities for deception, there is exactly one thing and one thing only that cannot possibly be an illusion, Descartes maintains – and that is the fact that you are experiencing all this. Even the person who fears that he or she may be being fooled about literally everything else must know for sure that there is a 'him' or a 'her' who's being fooled. The demon couldn't fake that. 'The proposition "I think, therefore I am"', writes Descartes, 'is the first and most certain which presents itself to whoever conducts his thoughts in order.' You might not be able to know much with utter certainty. But you know that you are you. The sense of being you *can't* be an illusion – because 'you' is what's experiencing all these possibly illusory things in the first place. Somebody has to be there in order to be tricked.

Or do they? One of the first people to spot a potential flaw in this reasoning was a contemporary of Descartes, the French philosopher and priest Pierre Gassendi, who dedicated a significant part of his career to attempting – largely fruitlessly – to persuade Europe's intelligentsia that their star philosopher had got things badly wrong. Descartes's method of 'systematic doubt' had been intended to uproot every unwarranted assumption about the nature of experience. But hidden inside *Cogito ergo sum*, Gassendi argued, one final devilish assumption remained. Just because thinking is going on, that didn't mean Descartes was justified in concluding that thinking is being done by one particular unitary thinking agent – by an 'I'. As the German scientist Georg Lichtenberg would later phrase it, Descartes was entitled only to claim that 'thinking is occurring', not 'I think, therefore I am.'

It was the great Scottish philosopher David Hume, writing in the first half of the eighteenth century, who most vividly illustrated this hidden assumption, proposing a thought experiment of his own. Never mind systematic doubt, Hume suggested: instead, simply try turning your attention inwards, and trying to find this thing you call your self. Hume had made the attempt many times, he claimed, but he could never succeed. Instead of a self, all he ever found were specific processes: emotions, sensations, and thoughts. Where was the self that was feeling those emotions, sensing those sensations, and thinking those thoughts? Hume was stumped:

> For my part, when I enter most intimately into what I call myself, I always stumble on some particular perception or other, of heat or cold, light or shade, love or hatred, pain or pleasure. I can never catch myself at any time without a perception, and never can observe any thing but the perception. When my perceptions are remov'd for any time, as by sound sleep, so long I am insensible of myself, and may truly be said not to exist . . . If any one upon serious and unprejudic'd reflection, thinks he has a different notion of himself, I must confess I can reason no longer with him.

It isn't completely inconceivable, Hume concedes, that other people – possibly even all other people in the world, except him – do indeed have some kind of clearly identifiable, easily located self. The only interior world to which he has any direct access is David Hume's, so how could he ever hope to prove otherwise? But he doubts it. 'I may venture to affirm of the rest of mankind', he goes on, 'that they [too] are nothing but a bundle or collection of different perceptions, which succeed each other with an inconceivable rapidity, and are in perpetual flux and movement.'

Modern neuroscience has provided strong support for the suspicion that the self is not the 'thing' that we imagine it to be – that there is, in the words of the neuropsychologist Paul Broks, no 'centre in the brain where things do all come together'. One good illustration of this emerges from experiments involving patients with 'split brains' – people in whom the corpus callosum, which connects the left and right hemispheres of the brain, has been severed. As the psychologist Michael Gazzaniga has demonstrated, 'split-brain' people behave as if each of their hemispheres were its own independent self. In one study, the word 'walk' was projected only into the right side of a patient's brain. He got up and began to walk – but when asked why he had done so, the left side of his brain, responsible for language, quickly came up with a convincing reason: 'To get a Coke.' Each hemisphere seems capable of acting in those ways that we tend to associate with a 'self', casting doubt on the notion that there's any one region of the brain where such a thing might reside. The philosopher Julian Baggini points out that this isn't quite the same as saying that the self 'doesn't exist'; just because we may be a complex collection of things, instead of one simple thing, it doesn't follow that we are not real. A 'bundle of perceptions', to use Hume's phrase, is still a real bundle of perceptions. But the fact remains that we have been using a term and a concept – the self – that on closer inspection isn't at all what it seems.

Eckhart Tolle looked at me and blinked amiably.

'Thanks for sparing the time!' I began, a little hesitantly, before immediately berating myself for not remembering that 'time' was one of the things that Tolle claimed no longer to experience in a meaningful way. 'Time isn't precious at all,' he writes in *The Power of Now*, 'because it is an illusion.' Only the present, 'the now', is real.

More on this – ironically enough – later.

'It's really a pleasure,' he replied, blinking amiably again and waiting. This waiting and smiling and blinking was something I'd seen him do before, albeit at a distance. A few years previously,

Oprah Winfrey, while championing his books on her talk show, had enlisted him to take part in a ten-week online seminar video series, during which she repeatedly characterised him as a spiritual leader with the power to transform the consciousness of the planet. Tolle had just smiled and blinked. Winfrey seemed unnerved by his willingness to break one of the first rules of broadcasting: no long stretches of silence.

The voice in my head – the one that was, right at that moment, criticising me for still not having come up with a meaningful opening question – is something most of us notice only when we're stressed, as I definitely was. But the starting-point of Eckhart Tolle's philosophy – as he began to explain, once I'd finally phrased a question – is that we spend our whole lives in the company of such a voice. The voice judges and interprets reality, determines our emotional reactions, and chatters so constantly and so loudly that we come to identify with it: we imagine that we *are* the chattering stream of thinking. If you doubt this account of what it's like inside your mind, consider the possibility that this might be because you're too closely identified with the chatter to notice. 'There is this complete identification with the thoughts that go through your head,' Tolle said, his accent betraying a trace of his native Germany, when I asked him what he thought was the biggest barrier to happiness for most people. 'It's just a total absence of awareness, except for the thoughts that are continuously passing through your mind. It is the state of being so identified with the voices in your head' – and at this point he emitted a tight Germanic chuckle – 'that you think you *are* the voices in your head.'

In his book *A New Earth*, Tolle recounts an outwardly insignificant incident that occurred some months before his terrifying nocturnal experience in the Belsize Park bedsit. It was the first time he realised how closely identified he was with his thinking. At that time, he was studying in the central library of the University of London, and would travel there on the Underground each morning, shortly after rush hour:

> One time, a woman in her early thirties sat opposite me. I had seen her before a few times on that train. One could not help but notice her. Although the train was full, the seats on either side of her were unoccupied, the reason being, no doubt, that she appeared to be quite insane. She looked extremely tense, and talked to herself incessantly in a loud and angry voice. She was so absorbed in her thoughts that she was totally unaware, it seemed, of other people, or her surroundings . . . Her monologue went something like this: 'And then she said to me . . . so I said to her you are a liar . . . how dare you accuse me of . . . when you are the one who has always taken advantage of me . . . I trusted you and you betrayed my trust . . .'

The woman got off the train at Tolle's stop. Out of curiosity, he decided to follow her, until gradually he began to realise that she was heading for the university library, just like him. For Tolle, this was troubling. He was an ambitious and driven young graduate student who had come to think of academic research as a pinnacle of human activity, and of universities like his as being home to an élite class of accomplished, or at least aspiring, intellectuals. He remembered wondering: 'How could an insane person like her be part of this?'

> I was still thinking about her when I was in the men's room, prior to entering the library. As I was washing my hands, I

thought: 'I hope I don't end up like her.' The man next to me looked briefly in my direction, and I suddenly was shocked when I realised that I hadn't just thought those words, but mumbled them aloud. 'Oh, my God, I'm already like her,' I thought.

I squirmed when I first read this, recalling my own Stoic exercise in talking out loud on the London Underground. Back then, my intention had been to learn that I could tolerate embarrassment and live with the thought that other people might think me insane. Tolle was making a more radical point: that only a very thin line separates such 'insane' people from the rest of us. The main difference is that, most of the time, we non-insane people manage to keep our constant mental chatter inaudible to others.

It is when we identify with this inner chatter, Tolle suggests – when we come to think of it *as* us – that thinking becomes compulsive. We do it all the time, ceaselessly, and the idea that we might ever enjoy a respite from thinking never occurs to us. We come to see our thinking and our continuing to exist as people as one and the same thing. 'Not to be able to stop thinking is a dreadful affliction,' Tolle writes. 'But we don't realise this, because almost everybody is suffering from it. So it's considered normal.' The sense of self that we construct from identifying with our thoughts is what Tolle calls the 'ego'. (Different thinkers use this term in very different ways.) And by definition, living in the service of the ego can never make us happy.

Why can the ego never bring happiness? Tolle's argument here echoes the Stoics, who concluded that our judgments about the world are the source of our distress. But he takes things further, suggesting that these judgments, along with all our other thoughts, are what we take ourselves to be. We're not only

distressed by our thoughts; we imagine that we *are* those
thoughts. The ego that results from this identification has a life
of its own. It sustains itself through dissatisfaction – through
the friction it creates against the present moment, by opposing
itself to what's happening, and by constantly projecting into the
future, so that happiness is always some other time, never now.
The ego, Tolle likes to say, thrives on drama, because compulsive
thinking can sink its teeth into drama. The ego also thrives on
focusing on the future, since it's much easier to think compulsively about the future than about the present. (It's really quite
tricky, when you try it, to think compulsively about right now.)
If all this is correct, we have inadvertently sentenced ourselves
to unhappiness. Compulsive thinking is what we take to be the
core of our being – and yet compulsive thinking relies on our
feeling dissatisfied.

The way out of this trap is not to stop thinking – thinking, Tolle
agrees, is exceedingly useful – but to *disidentify* from thoughts: to
stop taking your thoughts to be you, to realise, in the words of *The
Power of Now*, that 'you are not your mind'. We should start using
the mind as a tool, he argues, instead of letting the mind use us,
which is the normal state of affairs. When Descartes said 'I think,
therefore I am,' he had not discovered 'the most fundamental truth',
Tolle insists; instead, he had given expression to 'the most basic
error'.

What Tolle claimed had happened to him with such force that
night in his bedsit was precisely a disidentification from thinking.
At the time, he had just graduated with a first-class master's degree
in languages and history, and was preparing for a doctorate. 'I'd
done well because I was motivated by fear of not being good
enough,' he remembered. 'So I worked very hard.' He saw himself
as an intellectual in the making, and was 'convinced that all the

answers to the dilemmas of human existence could be found
through the intellect – that is, by thinking'. But his intellectual
labours weren't making him happy – and this realisation made
him feel even worse. 'I lived in a state of almost continuous
anxiety,' he wrote. Gradually, and then not so gradually, the anxiety
was ratcheting up and up. Something had to give. And on that
night, shortly after his twenty-ninth birthday, it did:

> I woke up in the early hours with a feeling of absolute dread.
> I had woken up with such a feeling many times before, but
> this time it was more intense than it had ever been. The
> silence of the night, the vague outlines of the furniture in
> the dark room, the distant noise of a passing train – every-
> thing felt so alien, so hostile, and so utterly meaningless that
> it created in me a deep loathing of the world. The most
> loathsome thing of all, however, was my own existence . . .
> I could feel that a deep longing for annihilation, for non-
> existence, was now becoming much stronger than the
> instinctive desire to continue to live. 'I cannot live with
> myself much longer.' This was the thought that kept repeating
> itself in my mind.

'I cannot live with myself': the phrase is a cliché, but Tolle was
stopped dead by its implications. 'If I cannot live with myself,' he
remembered thinking, 'there must be two of me: the "I" and the
"self" that "I" cannot live with. Maybe, I thought, only one of
them is real. I was so stunned by this realisation that my mind
stopped. I was conscious, but there were no more thoughts.' And
then, before he knew it, it was morning – the morning that he
felt suffused with a feeling of 'uninterrupted deep peace and bliss'.
    What had happened, if his account is to be believed, was that he

no longer mistakenly believed he *was* his thinking; he saw himself, instead, as the witness to it. This is an experience you can easily taste for yourself by deliberately deciding to watch your own thinking. Sit like a cat at a mouse-hole, Tolle advises, waiting to see what your next thought will be. 'When you listen to a thought,' he explains, 'you are aware not only of the thought, but also of yourself as the witness of the thought. A new dimension of consciousness has come in. As you listen to the thought, you feel a conscious presence – your deeper self – behind or underneath the thought, as it were. The thought then loses its power over you, and quickly subsides, because you are no longer energising the mind through identification with it. This is the beginning of the end of involuntary and compulsive thinking.' We have all experienced something 'behind or underneath' thought, in those moments that thinking seems temporarily to fall away: when gasping in awe at beautiful scenery, after intense physical exercise, or while making love. The trick is to take that stance towards thinking all the time, even when you're thinking. If any this sounds familiar, it may be because it leads back to Buddhism. Watching your thoughts in this way is a form of meditation.

This is the point at which Tolle's outlook gets especially tricky for a sceptic to swallow. He seems to assume that when you stop identifying with your ego, you discover who you *really* are – that you discover your 'deeper self' or your 'true Being', which was hiding behind the fake self all along. But this kind of talk rightly makes more mainstream philosophers nervous. Just because you have succeeded in dismantling the conventional understanding of the self, it doesn't necessarily follow that you'll find the 'real' one. Perhaps we are just a 'bundle of perceptions', as Hume put it. Perhaps there is no 'deeper', 'truer' meaning to the notion of who we are. Once again, though, this isn't a question that we need to answer conclusively. Merely asking it is what matters. It is enough, for now, to enquire within: don't you feel a certain tranquility when you seek to become the witness to your thoughts, rather than identifying with them completely?

The optimism-focused, goal-fixated, positive-thinking approach to happiness is exactly the kind of thing the ego loves. Positive thinking is all about identifying with your thoughts, rather than disidentifying from them. And the 'cult of optimism' is all about looking forward to a happy or successful future, thereby reinforcing the message that happiness belongs to some other time than now. Schemes and plans for making things better fuel our dissatisfaction with the only place where happiness can ever be found – the present. 'The important thing,' Tolle told me, 'is not to be continuously lost in this mental projection away from now. Most humans are never fully present in the now, because unconsciously they believe that the next moment must be more important than this one. But then you miss your whole life, which is never not now.' Another staccato chuckle. 'And that's a revelation for some people. To realise that your whole life is only ever now. Many people suddenly realise that they have lived most of their life as if this were not true – as if the opposite were true.' Without noticing we're doing it, we treat the future as intrinsically more valuable than the present. And yet the future never seems to arrive.

Instead of seeking ways to solve your problems in the future, it can be illuminating to try asking yourself if you have any problems right now. The answer, unless you're currently in physical pain, is very likely to be no. Most problems, by definition, involve thoughts about how something might turn out badly in the future, whether in five minutes or in five years, or thoughts about things that happened in the past. It can be curiously difficult to identify any problems that afflict you at this very moment, in the present – and it is always the present.

Or consider the fraught topic of self-esteem. We tend to assume that having high self-esteem is a good thing, but some psychologists have long suspected that there might be something wrong with the whole notion – because it rests on the assumption of a unitary, easily identifiable self. Setting out to give your 'self' one universal positive rating may in fact be deeply perilous. The problem lies in the fact that you're getting into the self-rating game at all; implicitly, you're assuming that you are a single self that can be given a universal grade. When you rate your self highly, you actually *create* the possibility of rating your self poorly; you are reinforcing the notion that your self is something that can be 'good' or 'bad' in the first place. And this will always be a preposterous overgeneralisation. You have strengths and weaknesses; you behave in good ways and bad ways. Smothering all these nuances with a blanket notion of self-esteem is a recipe for misery. Inculcate high self-esteem in your children, claims Paul Hauck, a psychologist opposed to the concept of self-esteem, and you will be 'teaching them arrogance, conceit and superiority' – or alternatively, when their high self-esteem falters, 'guilt, depression, [and] feelings of inferiority and insecurity' instead. Better to drop the generalisations. Rate your individual acts as good or bad, if you like. Seek to perform as many good ones, and as few bad ones, as possible. But leave your self out of it.

One final implication of thinking about selfhood in this way – and arguably the most significant one – concerns the idea of selflessness. We know from personal experience, and now from decades of psychology studies, that helping other people is a far more reliable strategy for happiness than focusing solely on yourself. One of the more distasteful aspects of positive thinking – and of conventional approaches to happiness in general – is the way in which they seem to encourage self-absorption. Then again, 'selfless' approaches to happiness can lead us into a conceptual muddle: if you take on a weekly volunteering assignment, say, with the aim of becoming happier, are you being selfless at all? Do you have to make yourself *miserable* in order to be truly self-less? The questions go on and on. Perhaps the answer to all these conundrums isn't to act selfishly or selflessly, but to question the notion of the self on which those distinctions are based. Both 'selfish' and 'selfless' activities are liable to end up merely feeding the ego, which thrives on dissatisfaction. Loosen your grip on selfhood itself, Tolle argues, and you'll stand a far better chance of cultivating happiness – your own and other people's – without the distraction of ego.

It's quite possible that all this simply leaves you cold – that it fails to chime in any way with your own inner experience. If that's the case, there is one more angle from which it can be demonstrated that selfhood is not all that it seems. This argument takes the form of an extended thought experiment, which I've adapted here from the work of the self-styled 'spiritual entertainer' Alan Watts. A bearded, plummy-voiced Englishman who made his home on the West Coast of the United States, and who died in 1973, Watts didn't have any breakthrough insights of his own. He was a populariser, intent on explaining the philosophies of the East to the populations of the West. Few professional philosophers today would consider him worthy of their title. But his insights – which rely on no New Agery nor pseudoscience at all, just rigorous, rational thinking – may, in a surprisingly enjoyable way, warp your mind.

Watts begins with what seems like an utterly straightforward question: What do you take to be the boundary of yourself – the place where you end and where 'the rest of the world' that isn't you begins? For most of us, the answer, as he puts it, is that we think of ourselves as 'packages of skin'. It is the envelope of skin enclosing the physical body that defines the boundary of our selves.

You might spot one immediate problem with this. Sometimes, when we use the word 'me', we seem to be using a different definition – one in which 'me' refers not to the whole body, but only to something inside the head. According to this definition, the rest of the body isn't 'me' to the same degree as the head. Suppose your foot had to be amputated: would you consider that you had become less 'yourself'? (Probably not – but if your *head* had to be amputated, things would be remarkably different.) Already, then, we seem to have two rival definitions of precisely what physical matter we're referring to when we refer to 'me'. But let's stick with the 'packages of skin' definition for now.

Suppose you were to zoom in, using an ultra-powerful microscope, on a part of your left hand, until all that you were looking at was a tiny region of your index finger, and a tiny part of the air surrounding it. Given sufficient magnification, what you would see through the microscope would be nothing but a cacophony of molecules: some making up your finger and some making up the adjacent air. Which brings us to the next question – or really the same question, in rephrased form. What exactly is your rationale for drawing a boundary between some of these molecules and others, so as to define some of them as 'you', and some of them as the world outside you? At this magnification, it's readily apparent that all we're talking about is molecules, after all. What makes some of them so special as to count as 'you'?

One obvious answer that springs to mind has to do with conscious control. You seem to be able to choose to move your index finger, for example, in a way that simply doesn't apply to things outside your skin. Perhaps this, then, is why the skin boundary is so important: on one side of it, you have conscious control; on the other side of it, you don't. But Watts has a ready response to that. Do you really exert conscious control, he wonders, over your breathing? Do you actively and consciously pump the blood through your veins, or dispatch antibodies to fight viral infections? You don't: those things just happen. Even thinking itself – as I had come to understand so acutely at the Insight Meditation Society – isn't as voluntary as we might like to imagine. Most of the time, thinking just seems to happen.

Fair enough, you might reply; perhaps I shouldn't have said *conscious* control. Unconscious control is plainly part of it, too. Whether consciously or unconsciously, I control everything inside my skin, and nothing outside it. Except, of course, that's not true, either: you exert control over plenty of things that are outside your skin. Using the right tools, you can build a swimming pool in your back garden; using your powers of persuasion, you might persuade hundreds of thousands of people to depose a dictator. You might argue that this is different – that it's an *indirect* form of control, while the control that you exert over your limbs feels more direct. But Watts wouldn't let you get away with that objection, because it relies on circular reasoning: it presumes an answer to the very conundrum that we're engaged in trying to untangle. After all, the distinction between 'direct' control and 'indirect' control is defined by nothing more or less than where you draw the boundary between 'yourself' and the rest of the world. And it is exactly this boundary – and whether we truly have good reason for drawing it where we traditionally draw it – that is at issue.

By now, the awkwardness of your situation ought to be apparent. Whatever criterion you propose as the basis for drawing the boundary between 'you' and 'not you', there seems to be a counterargument which, at the very least, throws the matter into doubt. It is at this point that Watts reveals the most disorienting part of his argument. Encountering it for the first time – I speak from experience – can be a little like ambling to the top of a gentle hill only to discover that its brow is also the precipice of a sheer, high cliff, dropping down to crashing waves below.

The argument goes as follows: that no matter where you draw the boundary – even if we could agree on a place at which to draw it – you would not really be drawing a boundary in the conventional sense at all. Because (here it comes) the very notion of a boundary line depends on it having two sides. When you think about it, it doesn't make much sense to describe a boundary as something that keeps two things apart. It makes more sense to describe it as the place at which they meet – or, more accurately, the place at which *they are exactly the same thing*. The inside of the boundary relies for its very existence on the outside, and vice versa; they are, inextricably and by definition, part of the same whole. You simply can't have the peak of a wave without the trough, or darkness without light.

This is the insight behind the ancient Chinese symbol of yin and yang, but there is nothing religious or even especially 'spiritual' about it. It is merely the conclusion, Watts argues, to which rigorous thinking must lead. There cannot be a 'you' without an 'everything else', and attempting to think about one in isolation from the other makes no sense. Nor is this some vague, insipid, flowers-and-incense observation about how 'we are all one'. It holds true on every level, from the most abstract to the most concrete. Yes, it is true that you wouldn't be you without the relationships you're in or the community to which you belong. But you also wouldn't be you if it weren't for all the physical objects in the world that aren't you.

We spend our lives failing to realise this obvious truth, and thus anxiously seeking to fortify our boundaries, to build our egos and assert our superiority over others, as if we could separate ourselves from them, without realising that interdependence makes us what we are. 'Really,' Watts wrote, 'the fundamental, ultimate mystery – the only thing you need to know to understand the deepest metaphysical secrets – is this: that for every outside, there is an inside, and that for every inside, there is an outside, and although they are different, they go together.'

That phrase 'they are different' is important. The case being made here is not that boundaries don't exist – that the 'true' way to perceive the world would be as some big, boundary-less mess of stuff, like half-melted ice cream. The fact that 'you' and 'everything else' are intrinsically interconnected needn't mean you don't exist. Our sanity depends on maintaining a coherent sense of self, and on setting healthy boundaries between ourselves and others – and neither Alan Watts nor Eckhart Tolle wishes to imperil your sanity. Instead, the conclusion to which both their thinking leads is that the self is best thought of as some kind of a fiction, albeit an extremely useful one – and that realising this, instead of doing everything we can to deny it, might be the route to fulfilment.

Others have remarked on the way that Eckhart Tolle's quiet presence seems to burn up people's scepticism, and this applied to me, too. Reluctant though I was to admit it, he really did seem to exude a palpable stillness, which seeped into the corners of the small Vancouver apartment and eventually, by the end of an afternoon's conversation, into me. The silences that had felt so awkward when I arrived slowly became more tolerable, then actually enjoyable, as my compulsion to fill them with talking began to subside. For long stretches of seconds, Tolle blinked and smiled, and I found myself smiling comfortably back.

Yet, still, I couldn't quite bring myself to believe that his inner life was as marvellously tranquil as he claimed. When, I wondered, was the last time that he had become really irritated? 'I can't remember the last time it happened,' he replied. 'I think maybe it was . . . ' Earlier today? Yesterday? 'I think it was a few months ago,' he said, after a while. 'I remember that I was walking outside, and there was this big dog, and the owner wasn't controlling it – it was pestering a smaller dog. And I felt a wave of irritation. But [the irritation] doesn't stick around, because it is not perpetuated by thought activity. It only lasted moments.' In *The Power of Now*, Tolle writes admiringly of watching ducks in a pond near his home, and what happens when they get into a fight. They tussle, but then, the confrontation over, they flap their wings and ruffle their feathers, as if to shake off the memory of the encounter. Then they swim peacefully once more. Ducks bear no grudges. People, with egos, do. Indeed, when Tolle hits his stride, there is no human outrage afflicting the world that he is not willing to attribute to our efforts to defend and strengthen our egos. War, tyrannies, and injustices of all kinds stand exposed as little but the efforts of insecure egos to fortify themselves: to harden their boundaries, to separate themselves, and to impose upon the rest of the world the thought patterns on which they have come to imagine that their very lives – although, in reality, only their egos – depend.

When I finally rose to leave the apartment, I hesitated for a moment – for some reason, shaking Tolle's hand seemed inappropriately formal – when he suddenly stepped forward and enveloped me in a bear hug. Then I took the lift to the ground floor, called a taxi, and sat on the wrought-iron bench outside the building, waiting to be collected. I felt curiously light-headed and peaceful, and it occurred to me that it might not be such a bad thing to stay sitting on that bench, in the fading light, doing nothing in particular, for several more hours. But that wasn't an option. I – whatever *that* meant – had to get to the airport in time for my plane home.

6

The Safety Catch

The Hidden Benefits of Insecurity

Security is a kind of death, I think.
      – Tennessee Williams, 'The Catastrophe of Success'

ON 13 JANUARY 2002, during the edgy, watchful months following the terrorist attacks of 9/11, a pilot named Elwood Menear – 'Woodie', to his friends – arrived at Philadelphia's International Airport. The forty-six-year-old was due to fly a routine domestic journey to Minneapolis on behalf of his employer, US Airways, and he had no grounds for imagining that his name might soon be making the headlines alongside that weekend's other most memorable news story, which involved President Bush choking on a pretzel.

Security screening procedures at Philadelphia, in common with those across America and the rest of the world, were becoming progressively tighter. Less than a month previously, Richard Reid, the would-be 'shoe bomber', had been tackled and subdued on board a flight from Paris to Miami, thereby initiating the era of compulsory shoe-checking for all travellers. Pilots were not excused all these rigorous new checks, and when Woodie Menear's turn came, the security screener expressed concern about the presence of a pair of tweezers in his cabin baggage. As it happened, tweezers – unlike corkscrews or metal scissors, for example – were not on the list of forbidden items; Menear was not breaching regulations by trying to bring them on board. But the official paused just long enough to spark frustration on the part of the pilot, who, like his colleagues, had been growing ever more exasperated by each new restriction. This time it was too much. Menear did not explode in rage; he merely asked a sarcastic question. But it was one that would lead to his immediate arrest, a night in jail, his suspension by US Airways, and months of legal wranglings before he was finally acquitted of 'making terroristic threats' and permitted to return to his job.

'Why are you worried about tweezers,' Menear asked, 'when I could crash the plane?'

Given the time and the place, it was an idiotic thing to say. But the insight that it crystallised was anything but idiotic. As aviation security restrictions grew more and more intricate in the years after Menear's arrest – culminating in the 2006 European ban on all but the tiniest of quantities of liquids in carry-on luggage – critics grew more strident in pointing out that the logic behind the whole policy seemed flawed. It made sense, of course, to keep guns and other weapons out of aeroplane cabins. But those had been prohibited for years. Beyond that, the new rules seemed destined to cause great inconvenience for millions of innocent passengers while doing very little to eliminate the risks posed by a dedicated hijacker. What 9/11 had shown, these critics argued, was not that light-duty 'boxcutter' utility knives were the next frontier in terrorism. What it had shown was that a terrorist who had reconciled himself to suicide would always have the upper hand against people who were unwilling to die – no matter which specific objects had been banned.

Bruce Schneier, an American security consultant who is one of the fiercest opponents of the post-9/11 crackdown, has made a name – and a few enemies – for himself by explaining the many ways in which one could easily hijack or bomb an aeroplane today, in spite of all the new measures. Garottes, for example, can be improvised from fishing line or dental floss, while the snapped-off handle of a wheeled bag makes 'a pretty effective spear'. Alternatively, you could buy some steel epoxy glue from a hard-ware store: it comes in two tubes, one containing steel dust and the other containing hardener, which you could combine in-flight, and mould into a stubby steel knife, using a metal teaspoon as a handle. (Neither steel epoxy glue nor metal teaspoons are prohib-ited on planes – unlike, say, snow globes, which are banned under American regulations.) Schneier's point is not, of course, that wheeled bags and dental floss should be urgently added to the list of items forbidden in flight. It is that you cannot make air travel significantly safer by banning each new item that a terrorist thinks to use, or that you fear he might, unless you're willing to ban *every* item – and perhaps also to force passengers to be strapped into their seats, too, given that hijackers could always use their bare hands. Not long after the 9/11 attacks, a reporter asked Schneier whether any measures could be taken that might guarantee that such a tragedy would never happen again. Sure, Schneier replied: just ground all the planes.

'There are precisely two things that have made air travel safer since 9/11: locks on cockpit doors, and teaching passengers that they have to fight back,' Schneier told me. He is forty-nine and ponytailed, and speaks in the quiet tones of someone who is confident of the truth of his opinions, and not especially concerned about winning you over. 'You can argue that there's a third – sky marshals. But actually, once you tell people you have them, you don't really need them. It's the *idea* of sky marshals that makes us safer, not the marshals themselves.'

If what Schneier says is correct, then an obvious question follows: Why do governments continue to impose these expensive and time-consuming restrictions? Why carry on playing a cat-and-mouse game with terrorists, in which the terrorists will always be one step ahead? There are many possible answers to this question, having to do with the pressure that politicians and safety officials feel to show that they are doing something, and to impress those who elect them or pay their salaries. But at the root of it all, Schneier argues, is the fundamental human desire for a *feeling* of safety and security – even though this feeling may be only indirectly related, at best, to *being* more safe or secure. Schneier coined the term 'security theatre' to refer to all those measures that are designed primarily to increase the feeling of security, without actually making people more secure. Indeed, it is perfectly possible to argue – Schneier has often done so – that security theatre in fact makes us *less* secure. It swallows resources that might otherwise be expended on more effective anti-terrorism measures, such as intelligence-gathering, and it makes passengers and security staff less alert to the kinds of suspicious behaviour they ought to be noticing. After all, if everyone's luggage is being so scrupulously examined that even snow globes are being intercepted, it might be easy to assume that you could let your guard down.

Start to look at security through Bruce Schneier's eyes, and some of the ways in which society approaches the issue begin to appear profoundly ridiculous. In 2007, for example, Britain's then prime minister, Gordon Brown, announced a barrage of measures to beef up security at the nation's airports, railway stations, and other transport hubs, including the construction of blast-resistant barriers. A posting on Schneier's blog explained that the barriers would be constructed at Liverpool Lime Street, that city's primary rail station, but that they would not be constructed at less busy suburban commuter stations, a few miles along the same stretch of track. The blog post was headlined: 'UK Spends Billions to Force Rail Terrorists to Drive a Little Further'. Brown's announcement was a classic piece of security theatre: a costly way to make travellers *feel* safer – so long as they didn't reflect too closely on the details – while doing nothing to deter an even slightly diligent terrorist.

In this book so far, we have seen how some of the most basic doctrines that dominate our thinking about happiness fail to work because we struggle for them too strenuously. It's easy to see how Bruce Schneier's critique of air security bears a superficial resemblance to this argument: in reality, many of the things we believe make air travel more secure don't do so, or make things worse. But the connection goes deeper – because 'security' in the context of air travel is really only one facet of a much bigger question that brings us to the heart of the 'negative' approach to happiness. The desire for a feeling of security and safety doesn't only lead us into irrationality in the field of counterterrorism. It leads us into irrationality all the time.

As we'll see, a staggering proportion of human activity – in politics, business, and international relations, as much as in our personal lives – is motivated by the desire to feel safe and secure. And yet this quest to feel secure doesn't always lead to security, still less to happiness. It turns out to be an awkward truth about psychology that people who find themselves in what the rest of us might consider conditions of extreme insecurity – such as severe poverty – discover insights into happiness from which the rest of us could stand to learn. And if the most radical proponents of the 'negative path' are to be believed, in turning towards insecurity we may come to understand that security itself is a kind of illusion – and that we were mistaken, all along, about what it was we thought we were searching for.

It is easy to feel, these days, that we live in uniquely insecure times, and that things are only going to get worse. Several years ago, the 2020 Project, an initiative of the American intelligence services charged with making broad forecasts about the future, published a report with a chapter bluntly entitled 'Pervasive Insecurity'. By 2020, the project's analysts wrote, 'we foresee a more pervasive sense of insecurity, which may be as much based on psychological perception as physical threats.' Among the chief causes for anxiety, they predicted, would be 'concerns over job security', 'fears revolving around migration', 'terrorism and internal conflicts', and even 'conflicts among great powers'. And all of that was written some time before the financial collapse of the late 2000s, which brought a new wave of insecurity to millions.

Yet it is easy, too, to find evidence that people have *always* believed that they are living in times of unique insecurity. In 1951 – a relatively happy and prosperous moment, all things considered, after the deepest pain of the post-war recovery and before the worst of the Cold War – Alan Watts captured his era's sense of insecurity well. There was, he wrote, 'the feeling that we live in a time of unusual insecurity. In the past hundred years or so, many long-established traditions have broken down – traditions of family, and social life, of government, of the economic order, and of religious belief. As the years go by, there seem to be fewer and fewer rocks to which we can hold, fewer things which we can regard as absolutely right and true, and fixed for all time.' Then again, that was how plenty of people felt in 634 BC in Rome, as well, when they were convinced that the city was destined to collapse after 120 years of existence. It is how people have felt at countless points in history since then. Try searching Google's library of digitised manuscripts for the phrase 'these uncertain times', and you'll find that it occurs over and over, in hundreds of journals and books, in virtually every decade the database encompasses, reaching back to the seventeenth century. 'As a matter of fact,' Watts insisted, 'our age is no more insecure than any other. Poverty, disease, war, change and death are nothing new.'

So people have always wanted to feel more secure than they do. Yet as Bruce Schneier's work in the field of air security helps to demonstrate, there's an enormous pitfall waiting for us – because the strategies that are designed to bestow a *feeling* of security often don't actually leave us more secure. They may even have the opposite effect. 'Security is both a feeling and a reality,' as Schneier puts it, 'and they're not the same.'

The feeling and the reality of security diverge in specific and predictable ways. Much has been written in recent years about 'cognitive biases' – the ways in which our judgments about reality tend to depart from reality itself – and many of these help explain the chronic mistakes we make when it comes to security. For example, we habitually fear threats from other humans more than threats from the natural world. We fear threats that we can easily call vividly to mind more than those we find difficult to picture – the so-called availability bias. We fear situations in which we feel as though we have no control, such as flying as a passenger on an aeroplane, more than situations in which we feel as if we have control, such as when at the steering wheel of a car. No wonder, then, that we sometimes risk making ourselves less secure by chasing feelings of security. You're vastly more likely to be

killed as the result of a car crash than an air crash, and vastly
more likely to die of heart disease than at the hands of a violent
intruder. But if you react to news stories about air terrorism by
taking the car when you'd otherwise have taken a plane, or if you
spend time and energy protecting your home from attackers that
you could have spent on improving your diet, you'll be letting
your biases guide you towards a greater *feeling* of security at the
expense of your real safety.

Psychologists are not unanimous about why these biases should
have developed in the first place, but Schneier makes the plausible
argument that the explanation lies in evolution – specifically,
the discrepancy between the rate of evolutionary change and the
rate at which modern society has developed. Adopting the long
view of our species, across evolutionary time, it is easy to see that
these biases might once have served our survival well – but that
they fail us now because we confront situations for which they
were never intended. Some animals, surprised by a car's headlights,
may leap wildly from one side of the road to the other, in an
instinctive effort to throw off the predator, which doesn't work
when your predator is a 4 × 4. And 'like a squirrel whose predator-
evasion techniques fail when confronted by a car,' observes Schneier,
'or a passenger pigeon who finds that evolution prepared him to
survive the hawk but not the shotgun, our innate capabilities to
deal with risk fail when confronted with things such as modern
human society, technology, and the media.'

Take, for example, the availability bias. Caring more about those
threats that you can picture vividly might, long ago, have made
sense: the reason you could picture them vividly, most likely, was
because they occurred a few yards away, in the village where you
lived, and very recently. They really did pose a more serious risk,
so the bias was a useful shortcut for making an accurate threat

assessment. But if the reason that they are mentally 'available' to you today is that you're in the habit of watching a daily news bulletin, the very purpose of which is to scour the globe for the most lurid scenes of mayhem, you will be misled into focusing your worry on threats you don't actually face. Seeing a television report of a terrorist attack on foreign soil, you might abandon plans for an overseas holiday, in order to hang on to your feeling of safety – when, in truth, spending too much time sitting on the sofa watching television might pose a far greater threat to your survival.

If cognitive biases were the only problem with the quest for safety and security, the solution might be straightforward, if not necessarily easy to implement: it would simply be a matter of bearing the biases in mind and doing our best to adjust our behaviours accordingly. We would then avoid being misled by our evolved emotional responses; we'd achieve the protection from danger that we had been seeking, and perfect happiness would follow. Needless to say, it isn't that simple. The more radical possibility – the one that takes us to the core of the 'negative' approach to happiness – is that there might be something more fundamentally problematic about the goal of security; and that real happiness might be dependent on being willing to face, and to tolerate, insecurity and vulnerability.

This is a thorny topic. You'd have to be insane to argue that it was preferable to live in conditions of serious danger, or that a certain basic sense of psychological security isn't a healthy thing to possess. (The terminology creates additional confusion, since you could argue that anyone who is able calmly to tolerate feelings of insecurity and vulnerability must already be, by definition, rather secure to begin with.) But a recurring theme in the study of happiness is that many of the ways in which we try to feel 'safe' don't ultimately make us happy. We seek financial security, yet above a certain threshold level, more money doesn't translate into more happiness. We protect ourselves from physical danger by moving to safer neighbourhoods, or even locking ourselves inside gated communities, but the effects of such trends on community life have been demonstrated to have a negative effect on collective levels of happiness. We seek the fulfilment of strong romantic relationships and friendships, yet striving too hard to achieve security in such relationships stifles them; their flourishing depends on a certain degree of *not* being protected, of being open to experiences both negative and positive. It is possible to be similarly protected from terrorism, as Schneier said, so long as you are happy to shut down the possibility of air travel itself. What all these examples have in common is that achieving perfect security would run counter to our interests. We might think we want security more than anything, but when it comes down to it, we don't.

'To be vulnerable', argue the psychotherapists Hal and Sidra Stone, 'is to be without defensive armour, to be authentic and present . . . when we are able to feel our vulnerability, we are able to experience the full range of our reactions to the world around us.' The point, says Brené Brown, a professor of social work who has studied the psychological benefits of vulnerability, is that 'you can't selectively numb emotion. You can't say: here's the bad stuff; here's vulnerability, here's grief, here's shame, here's fear, here's disappointment: I don't want these.' In the end, the only way you can achieve protection from the negatives is by achieving protection from the positives, too – whereupon you realise that you didn't really want such protection at all. Or as C. S. Lewis put it, more poetically:

To love at all is to be vulnerable. Love anything and your heart will be wrung, and possibly broken. If you want to make sure of keeping it intact, you must give your heart to no-one, not even an animal. Wrap it carefully round with your hobbies and little luxuries; avoid all entanglements; lock it up safe in the casket or coffin of your selfishness. But in that casket – safe, dark, motionless, airless – it will change. It will not be broken; it will become unbreakable, impenetrable, irredeemable.

Becoming numb to negative emotions, Brown's research illustrates, doesn't even work as a way of protecting yourself from negative emotions themselves – for reasons that the Catholic monk and writer Thomas Merton expressed in his autobiography *The Seven Storey Mountain*. 'The truth that many people never understand', he wrote, 'is that the more you try to avoid suffering, the more you suffer, because smaller and more insignificant things begin to torture you, in proportion to your fear of being hurt.' Seen this way, it becomes clear that security-chasing is a large part of the problem with the 'cult of optimism'. Through positive thinking and related approaches, we seek the safety and solid ground of certainty, of knowing how the future will turn out, of a time in the future when we'll be ceaselessly happy and never have to fear negative emotions again. But in chasing all that, we close down the very faculties that permit the happiness we crave.

For the American Buddhist nun Pema Chödrön, insecurity is the essential nature of reality – and all our distress arises from trying to scramble to solid ground that doesn't actually exist. 'Becoming a Buddhist', she says, 'is about becoming homeless.' To turn to face reality is to see that we exist in a condition of 'fundamental groundlessness'. Yet most of us chronically 'scramble not to feel that groundlessness . . . my whole training [is] that there is no way to tie up those loose ends'. She goes on: 'You're never going to erase the groundlessness. You're never going to have a neat, sweet little picture with no messiness.' Chödrön's most famous book is entitled *When Things Fall Apart*, which makes it sound as though it might be a manual for getting back on a secure footing when things go catastrophically wrong. In fact, her point is that when things fall apart, however painful the experience, it's a good thing; the collapse of your apparent security represents a confrontation with life as it really is. 'Things are not permanent, they don't last, there is no final security,' she says. What makes us miserable is not this truth, but our efforts to escape it.

At this point, though, a weighty objection to all this might be troubling you in the same way that it troubled me. It's all very well for those of us who find ourselves in relatively comfortable situations to praise insecurity and vulnerability. We may be fortunate enough to live out our entire lives without encountering insecurity in its most acute forms. But what do you learn about happiness when insecurity really is the unavoidable background condition of your daily life?

It was a Sunday morning in January, cloudless and hot, and many of the residents of Africa's second-largest urban slum were dressed for church: the men in well-pressed suits, the women in dresses of fuchsia and bright green, children clutching Bibles. Here in the poorest part of Kibera – across the rubbish-strewn railway tracks that divided the slum proper from the rest of the Kenyan capital of Nairobi – it was a challenge to keep your church clothes clean as you picked your way along the muddy paths that passed for roads; in many places, the ground was composed of discarded plastic bags and other detritus. Between homes made from scraps of sheet metal and mud, chickens and dogs wandered through gullies that flowed with raw sewage.

Most of the churchgoers were heading up the hill to the big Africa Inland church, or across to the main Catholic one. There were numerous other tiny shop-front churches, too, hidden among the homes – dark one-room shacks in which a minister could be seen preaching to an audience of two or three, or playing hymns on a Casio keyboard. But in the opinion of Frankie Oluoch, a twenty-two-year-old resident of Kibera who spent his Sundays not worshipping but attending to his various business interests, these smaller churches were essentially scams. 'In Kibera, a church is a business,' he said, his easy smile tinged with cynicism. He was sitting on a tattered sofa in the shady main room of his mother's house in Kibera, drinking Coke from a glass bottle. 'A church is the easiest way to get money from the aid organisations. One day, you fill up your church with kids – somebody who's dirty, some-body who's not eating – and then the organisation comes and sees the church is full, and they take photos to show their spon-sors, and they give you money.' He chuckled. 'It's all about the photos, you know?'

In another part of Kibera, reached by pursuing still narrower paths, deeper into the slum, then rounding a bend past a health clinic, three Kiberan men were starting their work day at the goat-bone recycling facility. It was an open-air compound, arranged in straightforward fashion: a pile of newly cleaned goat bones on one side, various saws and grinding implements in the middle, and then, on the other side, the results of their labours: beer-bottle openers, necklaces and other trinkets, waiting to be transported to central Nairobi to be sold to tourists. A chunky battery-powered cassette recorder was playing classic rock, though if you listened you could hear singing from the church on the hill. The smell of *nyama choma*, or roasted goat meat, sizzling on an open grill nearby wafted through the workshop, masking the odour of sewage.

Commercially speaking, Sunday in Kibera was no different to any other day, and that meant it was busy. Past the bone workshop, past the street grills, down along an alley covered with blue plastic sheeting, a gateway marked the official entrance to the slum's vast market. But the boundary wasn't obvious, because the whole of Kibera felt like a market. Along every crater-ridden lane, merchants at makeshift tables sold radios, or pineapples, or baby clothes in fluorescent colours; the navigators of wheelbarrows piled with building materials or discarded electronics veered to the left and right to avoid collisions with other people, and other wheelbarrows.

Meanwhile, in an alley leading away from the market, past an establishment showing British Premier League football matches on a satellite television, a man who gave his name as George was at home, working out at the gym he had improvised in his tiny yard. His barbell was a repurposed iron pipe, with concrete poured into cylindrical water vats at each end, in place of weight plates. 'A hundred and fifty kilograms!' he claimed, when asked how much he was hefting above his massive shoulders, making the veins in his forehead pulse. His children craned their necks out from behind the cloth covering their home's main room, and laughed at him.

By the standards of someone from almost anywhere else, the conditions faced by Kibera's residents – who number anywhere from 170,000 to a million, according to competing population surveys – are almost unimaginably harsh. The slum has no running water and no electricity, except what its residents 'borrow' by clipping wires to the cables that run overhead, bringing power to Nairobi's better-off citizens. Sexual violence is rampant. Car-jackings and opportunistic murders are a weekly occurrence. With no proper sanitation, Kibera's primary means of disposing of human waste is what the slum-dwellers wryly refer to as 'flying toilets': the practice of defecating into a plastic bag, then flinging it as far from your own home as possible. Flying toilets add diarrhoea and typhoid fever to the neighbourhood's catalogue of woes, which also includes the fact that, according to some estimates, 20 per cent of the population is infected with HIV.

For all these reasons – and also because it is a conveniently short drive from central Nairobi, with its international airport and comfortable business hotels – Kibera has become a world-famous landmark of suffering. Prime ministers and presidents travel there for photo-opportunities; television news crews come regularly to gawp; and the slum has disproportionately become the focus of hundreds of aid groups, many of them religious, mostly from the United States and Europe. Their names reflect the sense of agonised desperation for which the name 'Kibera' has come to stand: the Fountain of Hope Initiative; Seeds of Hope; Shining Hope for Communities; the Kibera Hope Centre; Kibera in Need.

But ask Norbert Aluku, a lanky young social worker, born and raised in Kibera, if his childhood there was one of misery and suffering, and he will laugh at you in disbelief. 'Of course not! Because, at the end of the day, it's not about your conditions. It's about taking whatever you have and using it as best you can, together with your neighbours. In Kibera, it's only with your neighbours that you're going to get by.' Or ask Irene Mueni, who lives there too, and who speaks darkly of traumatising events in her childhood, yet who still says: 'Happiness is subjective. You can be happy in a slum, unhappy in a city. The things you need for happiness aren't the things you think you need.'

This is the difficult truth that strikes many visitors to Kibera, and they struggle for the words to express it, aware that it is open to misinterpretation. Bluntly, Kiberans just don't seem as unhappy or as depressed as one might have expected. 'It's clear that poverty has crippled Kibera,' observes Jean-Pierre Larroque, a documentary filmmaker who has spent plenty of time there, 'but it doesn't exactly induce the pity-inducing cry for help that NGOs, church missions, and charity groups would have you believe.' What you see instead, he notes, are 'streets bustling with industry'. Kibera feels not so much like a place of despair as a hotbed of entrepreneurialism.

This awkward realisation – that people living in extremely fragile circumstances seem surprisingly high-functioning and non-depressed – isn't applicable only to Kibera, of course. It's so familiar that it has become a cliché, especially regarding sub-Saharan Africa. And it is laden with problems: it coasts close to a number of distasteful generalisations, perhaps even to racism, as well as to poisonous myths about 'primitive' people, uncorrupted by modernity. It can lead to questionable political conclusions, too: if people who are suffering from severe poverty and poor health are so happy, certain commentators are inclined to suggest, perhaps they don't require outside support. And we cringe, surely rightly, when we hear well-heeled celebrities speak in rapt tones about the simple joys of having nothing – as when, for example, Coleen Rooney, television presenter and footballer's wife, told an interviewer: 'I find it so inspiring when you see people from poorer countries on TV: they just seem so happy with their lives, despite their lack of material things . . . in the future, I plan to visit somewhere like Africa.'

The problem with merely dismissing this entire outlook as wrong or misguided, though, is that it appears to be at least partly true. International surveys of happiness – including several reputable research projects such as the World Values Survey – have consistently found some of the world's poorest countries to be among the happiest. (Nigeria, where 92 per cent of the population lives on less than two dollars a day, has come in in first place.) Survey data from the Afrobarometer research project, which monitors more than a dozen African countries, including Kenya, has indicated 'unusual levels of optimism among the poorest and most insecure respondents' in those places. Certain specific measures, such as how optimistic parents feel about their children's futures, actually appear to be *inversely* correlated with wealth and education: the least privileged report feeling the most upbeat. According to mental health researchers, anxiety disorders and depression are far less common in poorer countries. (Their studies take into account the difference in likelihood of getting diagnosed.) In one recent review of mental health problems around the world, sub-Saharan Africa came bottom in terms of prevalence; the top positions were all occupied by richer, industrialised regions.

'Look, this is a thing that social scientists have often pointed out,' Norbert told me when I made my second visit to Kibera. We were sitting on folding chairs in the shade cast by his one-storey office building on the outskirts of the slum. 'Just because you have social problems, it doesn't mean you don't have happiness. Do richer people have fewer problems, really? We have politicians going to jail for corruption, and I really don't think they're happy compared to me. There are problems at every level. Like heart disease or blood pressure if you're stressed.' He shrugged. 'Isn't that obvious?'

This is a psychological phenomenon that stands in need of explanation. Even if there is some debate about the methodologies of international surveys of happiness; even if the impressions of

Jean-Pierre Larroque and others don't capture the whole picture – why is it that places such as Kibera aren't unequivocally at the *bottom* of every assessment of happiness levels every time? A multiplicity of answers has been advanced, and none of them are completely satisfying. One is simply that people's expectations are lower. A related one is based on the (true) observation that happiness is relative: people who aren't surrounded by examples of more pleasant lifestyles don't rank their own situation so poorly. The problem with these arguments is that they all too easily drift into the condescending suggestion that slum-dwellers don't know any better – that they are simply unaware that it might be possible to live with running water, functioning toilets, and lower rates of disease. But this is certainly not the case in Kibera, whose residents live shoulder-to-shoulder with Nairobi's fancier neighbourhoods; some of them have jobs as domestic workers there. The grand mansion of a senior Kenyan politician sits just a modest walk back up the road from the slum to Nairobi. In a girls' school in the heart of Kibera, five-year-olds learn to read beneath a giant photograph of Times Square; Hollywood movies on videotape are commonplace. Norbert Aluku had even coined a term – 'the thirst' – for the ambition he tried to instill in younger Kiberans precisely by taking them to better areas of Nairobi to show them what could be theirs. Not knowing any better, in this case at least, doesn't explain the mystery.

I don't have an answer to the puzzle, either. But it does become a little less mysterious when viewed in the context of the psychology of security and insecurity. We have seen how pursuing our desire for a feeling of security can lead us badly astray; and that vulnerability may be a precondition for the very things that bring the greatest happiness – strong social relationships above all. What the people of Kibera and others in similar situations all share is a lack of access to those things that the rest of us self-defeatingly try to use to quell our feelings of insecurity. The point is certainly not that it's better not to have money, say, than it is to have it. But it's surely undeniable that if you don't have it, it's much harder to overinvest emotionally in it. The same goes for prestigious jobs, material possessions, or impressive educational qualifications: when you have little chance of obtaining them, you won't be misled into thinking they bring more happiness than they do. More broadly, living in such desperate circumstances means that shutting out feelings of insecurity is not a viable option. You have to turn and face the reality of insecurity instead. The people of Kibera are vulnerable whether they like it or not.

One American working in Kibera, Paige Elenson, told me she'd been strongly affected by just this realisation. 'I hate all that romanticism – "Oh, they're so happy,"' she told me. 'In many ways, they're really not . . . but when you don't have access to the good clothes and the nice jobs, when you don't have any of that to hold on to, you have to let people know you through your way of being, not through what you're wearing, or your job title. You actually have to be kind to people if you want them to like you! You have to look into their eyes! We don't have that so much in the US, because it's, like, 'Look what I'm wearing; look what it says on my business card – I don't need to be nice to you'. So there is this vulnerability, which is another way of saying that there's less pretence. I don't know that that makes you happier, necessarily . . . But when there's less to latch onto – when there are choices you don't have – then it changes things. You have to cut the crap.'

Speaking of crap: One day in Kibera, Norbert took me to see a project he was associated with, which involved recycling human waste into marketable biogas. This offered a new solution to the problem of flying toilets. People would stop flinging bags of the stuff into the street, he figured, once they began to realise they could make money from it. It was typical Kiberan pragmatism, assisted in this case by an American aid group. When Norbert talked about the importance of working with your neighbours and of working with what you had, he wasn't speaking in saccharine clichés. The communal activities he was talking about included recycling human waste.

'Look,' said Frankie Oluoch, drinking Coke on his mother's sofa, when I asked him about all this, 'Kibera is not a good place. Big problems, and a million NGOs who don't do any good. Major, major problems. But you have to manage, because you have to. So you take what you have and you get on with it. And you can be happy like that, because happiness comes from your family and other people, and in making something better of yourself, and in new horizons . . . right? Why worry about something you don't have?'

Above all, living in a situation of such inherent insecurity, while very far from preferable, was *clarifying*. Nobody would envy it. But living with fewer illusions meant facing reality head-on. Not having the option of trying to protect yourself in counter-productive ways made for a resilience in the face of hardship that qualified, in the end, as a modest but extremely durable kind of happiness.

We have seen that security may not always be the benefit we imagine it to be, and that insecurity may be compatible with – or perhaps even, in some sense, conducive to – happiness. But an even more radical suggestion is that our search for security might be based on a fundamental misunderstanding – that security, in the famed words of Helen Keller, 'is mostly a superstition'. To understand the enormous implications of this idea, we need to return, a final time, to the work of Alan Watts.

Watts begins his slim 1951 treatise *The Wisdom of Insecurity* by pointing out that there is one overwhelming explanation for his era's feelings of insecurity: the progress of science. Fewer and fewer of us can convince ourselves, if we ever could, that we are headed for an afterlife of eternal bliss; or that there is a God watching out for us; or that the moral rules laid down by the Pope or the Archbishop of Canterbury are unquestionably the ones we ought to follow. 'It is simply self-evident', he writes, 'that during the past century the authority of science has taken the place of the authority of religion in the popular imagination, and that scepticism, at least in spiritual things, has become more general than belief.' Watts, it is true, was writing prior to the resurgence of fundamentalist Christianity in America. But he might well have viewed that development as an inevitable reaction to the very scientific dominance he was describing.

It should go without saying – and Watts very much agrees – that scientific enquiry has brought immeasurable benefits. But at the same time, it has left many feeling a spiritual void. By eliminating gods and the afterlife, the scientific picture of the universe seems to have sapped individual human lives of any special meaning; we fit in only as mere organisms, living out our brief lives for no reason and then perishing. This, he suggests, is the source of the ultimate insecurity, the one that underlies all the others. Yet retreating back under the comforting wing of the old, doctrinaire religions isn't an option for most of us; you can't re-convince yourself of claims that you know are untrue. Are we stuck, then, with the choice of living meaningless but scientifically truthful lives, or lives based on super-stition and self-deception? Watts insists that there is a third alterna-tive, and it's what the rest of his little book is about.

The starting-point for this argument is the observation that impermanence is the nature of the universe: that 'the only constant is change'. It was Heraclitus, living in the fifth and sixth centuries BC, who said that 'no man steps in the same river twice', and his contemporary Confucius, in China, who was supposed to have pointed at a stream and observed, 'It is always flowing, day and night'. People, animals, plants, communities, and civilisations all grow, change, and die: it is the most obvious fact in the world, and almost everybody, scientific or religious, agrees with it.

Yet for all the obviousness of this insight, Watts observes, we seem to live in a constant state of fighting against it, struggling to find security, permanence, fixity, and stability. His point is not to scold you to give up the struggle against impermanence – 'Calling a desire bad names', he writes, 'doesn't get rid of it.' Instead, he wants to make you see that it is an error of a fundamental kind. Attempting to fix change is a contradiction; you can no more fix change than you can make heat cold or green purple. 'There is a contradiction in wanting to be perfectly secure in a universe whose very nature is momentariness and fluidity,' he writes. Even discussing the subject, he points out, risks a similar contradiction, because it is in the nature of language to try to fix and define. And so the most fundamental characteristic of the universe is therefore the one about which it is most difficult to speak.

But it's worse than a mere contradiction – because what we are really doing when we attempt to achieve fixity in the midst of change, Watts argues, is trying to *separate* ourselves from all that change, trying to enforce a distinction between ourselves and the rest of the world. To seek security is to try to remove yourself from change, and thus from the thing that defines life. 'If I want to be secure, that is, protected from the flux of life,' Watts writes,

'I am wanting to be separate from life.' Which brings us to the crux of the matter: it is because we want to feel secure that we build up the fortifications of ego, in order to defend ourselves, but it is those very fortifications that create the feeling of insecurity: 'To be secure means to isolate and fortify the "I", but it is just this feeling of being an isolated "I" which makes me feel lonely and afraid.' This is a strikingly counterintuitive notion: appreciating it entails a mental shift similar to that moment when the famous optical illusion switches from resembling a beautiful young woman to an old witch. We build castle walls to keep out the enemy, but it is the building of the walls that causes the enemy to spring into existence in the first place. It's only because there are castle walls that there is anything to attack. 'The desire for security and the feeling of insecurity are the same thing,' concludes Watts. 'To hold your breath is to lose your breath. A society based on the quest for security is nothing but a breath-retention contest, in which everyone is as taut as a drum and as purple as a beet.' Even if we temporarily and partially achieve the feeling of security, he adds, it doesn't feel good. Life inside the castle walls proves lonely and isolating. 'We discover [not only] that there is no safety, [and] that seeking it is painful, [but] that when we imagine we have found it, we don't like it.'

To understand the final flourish that Watts has in store, think back to the end of the previous chapter, and the challenge it presented to our assumptions about the nature of the self. There, we confronted the fact that there seems to be no straightforward place at which to draw the line between 'self' and 'other' – and that the boundary itself, even if we settle on somewhere to draw it, is more of a meeting point than a dividing line. 'Self' and 'other' rely on each other for their very existence. If that's true, it follows that 'security' is a mistake – because it implies a notion of separate selfhood that doesn't make much sense. What does it even *mean* to separate yourself from an ecosystem that is, in fact, what constitutes you? The point is not to 'confront' insecurity, but to appreciate that *you are it*. Watts writes:

> To understand that there is no security is far more than to agree with the theory that all things change, more even than to observe the transitoriness of life. The notion of security is based on the feeling that there is something within us which is permanent, something which endures through all the days and changes of life. We are struggling to make sure of the permanence, continuity, and safety of this enduring core, this center and soul of our being, which we call 'I'. For this we think to be the real man – the thinker of our thoughts, the feeler of our feelings, the knower of our knowledge. We do not actually understand that there is no security until we realize that this 'I' does not exist.

This extraordinary passage, once you grasp the point – and it took me a while – explains in the most complete sense why our efforts to find happiness are so frequently sabotaged by 'ironic' effects, delivering the exact opposite of what we set out to gain. All positive thinking, all goalsetting and visualising and looking on the bright side, all trying to make things *go our way*, as opposed to some other way, is rooted in an assumption about the separateness of 'us' and those 'things'. But on closer inspection this assumption collapses. Trying to flee from insecurity to security, from uncertainty to certainty, is an attempt to find an exit from the very system that makes us who we are in the first place. We can influence the system of which we are a part, certainly. But if we are motivated by this misunderstanding about who we are, and what security is, we'll always risk going too far, trying too hard, in self-defeating ways. Watts concludes:

> The real reason why human life can be so utterly exasperating and frustrating is not because there are facts called death, pain, fear, or hunger. The madness of the thing is that when such facts are present, we circle, buzz, writhe, and whirl, trying to get the 'I' out of the experience . . . Sanity, wholeness and integration lie in the realization that we are not divided, that man and his present experience are one, and that no separate 'I' or mind can be found . . . [Life] is a dance, and when you are dancing, you are not intent on getting somewhere. The meaning and purpose of dancing is the dance.

This, then, is the deep truth about insecurity: it is another word for life. That doesn't mean it's not wise to protect yourself, as far as you can, from certain specific dangers. But it does mean that feeling secure and really living life are, in some ultimate sense, opposites. And that you can no more succeed in achieving perfect security than a wave could succeed in leaving the ocean.

7

The Museum of Failure

The Case for Embracing Your Errors

> You can't turn a sow's ear into a Veal Orloff. But you can
> do something very good with a sow's ear.
> — Julia Child

IN AN UNREMARKABLE BUSINESS park near the airport outside
the city of Ann Arbor, in Michigan, stands a poignant memorial
to humanity's shattered dreams. Not that you'd know it from the
outside. From the outside, it looks like a car dealership, because
that's what it was until 2001, when a company with the enigmatic
name of GfK Custom Research North America moved in. Even
when you get inside – which members of the public rarely do
– it takes a few moments for your eyes to adjust to what you're
seeing. There is no lobby or reception desk, no list of departments,
nobody waiting to greet you. Instead, you find yourself in what
appears to be a vast and haphazardly organised supermarket. It
contains no shoppers, but along every aisle the grey metal shelves
are crammed with tens of thousands of packages of food and
household products. There is something unusually cacophonous
about these displays, and soon enough, you work out the reason.

Unlike in a real supermarket, there is only one of each item; there are no uniform ranks of jars of pasta sauce, boxes of dishwasher detergent, or fizzy-drink cans. The more important point about the products on these shelves, though, is that many of them would be impossible to find in a real supermarket anyway. They are failures: products withdrawn from sale after a few weeks or months because almost nobody wanted to buy them. In the product-design business, GfK Custom Research's storehouse of fiascos has acquired the nickname of 'the museum of failed products'. It is consumer capitalism's graveyard – the shadow side to the relentlessly upbeat, success-focused culture of modern marketing. Or to put it less grandly: it's almost certainly the only place on the planet where you'll find Clairol's Touch of Yogurt shampoo, alongside Gillette's equally unpopular For Oily Hair Only, a few feet from a now-empty bottle of Pepsi A.M. Breakfast Cola (born 1989; died 1990). The museum is home to discontinued brands of caffeinated beer; to TV dinners branded with the logo of the toothpaste manufacturer Colgate; to self-heating soup cans that had a regrettable tendency to explode in customers' faces; and to packets of breath mints that had to be withdrawn from sale because they looked like the tiny packages of crack cocaine dispensed by America's street dealers. It is where microwavable scrambled eggs – pre-scrambled and packaged in a cardboard tube, with a pop-up mechanism for easier consumption in the car – go to die.

Laugh too hard at any of these products, though, and the museum's proprietor, an understatedly stylish GfK employee named Carol Sherry, will purse her lips and arch her eyebrows over her Dolce & Gabbana spectacles as if to chide you. And she will be only half joking. It is Sherry's job to act as chaperone to the product designers and other executives who pay significant sums for the right to inspect GfK's collection, and she treats the products in her care like disappointing yet still fundamentally lovable children. One bright December morning, giving me a tour of the building, she paused before a cream-coloured bottle of body lotion, and an expression close to sadness flickered across her face. 'Ah, yes, now, this,' she said fondly. 'Pulled very abruptly from the market. Unfortunately, it led to an increased risk of fungal infection.'

There is a Japanese term, *mono no aware*, that translates very roughly as 'the pathos of things'. It captures a kind of poignant melancholy at life's impermanence – that additional beauty imparted to cherry blossoms, or cloud formations, or human features, as a result of their inevitably fleeting time on earth. It is only stretching this concept slightly to suggest that Sherry feels the same way about, for example, the cartons of Morning Banana Juice in her care, or about Fortune Snookies, a short-lived line of fortune cookies for dogs. Every failure, the way she sees it, embodies its own sad story of sincere effort on the part of designers, marketers, salespeople and others. It is never far from her mind that real people had their mortgages, their car payments, and their family holidays riding on the success of Touch of Yogurt or Fortune Snookies. Or of Heublein Wine & Dine Dinners, a line of pre-prepared meals packaged with a half-sized bottle of cooking wine, which customers, understandably, assumed was meant for drinking. (Then they tasted the wine. And then they stopped buying Heublein Wine & Dine Dinners.)

'I feel really sorry for the developer on this one,' Sherry said, indicating the breath mints that inadvertently resembled crack. 'I mean, I've met the guy. Why would he ever have spent any time on the streets, in the drug culture? He did everything right, except go out on the streets to see if his product looked like drugs.' She shook her head. 'To me, it takes incredible courage to be a product developer. There are so many ways it could go wrong. These are real people, who get up every morning and sincerely want to do their best, and then, well . . . things happen.'

The museum of failed products was itself a kind of accident, albeit a happier one. Its creator, a now-retired marketing man named Robert McMath, merely intended to accumulate a 'reference library' of consumer products, not failures per se. Starting in the 1960s, he began purchasing and preserving a sample of every new item he could find. (He usually emptied out any perishable contents, to stop things getting disgusting.) Soon the collection outgrew his office in upstate New York and he was forced to move into a converted granary to accommodate it. Later, GfK – the initials are derived from the German name of its parent company – bought him out, moving the whole lot to Michigan. What McMath hadn't taken into account, he told me on the phone from his home in California, was the three-word truth that was to prove the making of his career: 'Most products fail.' According to some estimates, the failure rate is as high as 90 per cent. Simply by collecting new products indiscriminately, McMath had ensured that his hoard would come to consist overwhelmingly of unsuccessful ones. 'You know, I never really liked the term "museum of failed products",' he told me. 'But there it is. It stuck. There wasn't much I could do about it.'

I suspected him of being a little disingenuous about this, since all the evidence suggests that McMath revelled in his reputation as a guru of failure. In the early years, he was a fixture on the lecture circuit, and then on American cable television; David Letterman even interviewed him about what McMath was happy to refer to as his 'library of losers'. He wrote a marketing manual, *What Were They Thinking?*, devoted largely to poking fun at products such as Revlon's No Sweat antiperspirant and Look of

Buttermilk, a companion product to Clairol's Touch of Yogurt. (As McMath points out, you should never mention sweat when marketing anti-sweat products, because shoppers find it repulsive. It's entirely unclear, meanwhile, what the 'look of buttermilk' might be, let alone why you might wish your hair to sport it.) But Sherry seemed disapproving of the levity with which her predecessor had approached his work. 'Originally, yes, the hook with the media was that he was the owner of a museum of failures,' she sighed. 'But I think that's just a shame. It's human to point fingers and revel in someone else's misery, I guess. But I just feel very attached to everything in here.' She had a point. True, I laughed when I encountered Goff's Low Ash Cat Food, with its proud boast, 'contains only one point five per cent ash!' (As the journalist Neil Steinberg has noted, this is like marketing a line of hot dogs called Few Mouse Hairs.) Yet several people presumably invested months of their lives in creating that cat food. I hope they can look back and chuckle about it now. But who knows?

By far the most striking thing about the museum of failed products, though, has to do with the fact that it exists as a viable, profit-making business in the first place. You might have assumed that any consumer product manufacturer worthy of the name would have its own such collection, a carefully stewarded resource to help it avoid repeating errors its rivals had already made. Yet the executives arriving every week at Carol Sherry's door are evidence of how rarely this happens. Product developers are so focused on their next hoped-for success – and so unwilling to invest time or energy in thinking about their industry's past failures – that they only belatedly realise how much they need, and are willing to pay, to access GfK's collection. Most surprising of all is the fact that many of the designers who have found their way to the museum

of failed products, over the years, have come there in order
to examine – or, alternatively, have been surprised to discover –
products that *their own companies* had created and then abandoned.
These firms were apparently so averse to thinking about the
unpleasant business of failure that they had neglected even to keep
samples of their own disasters.

'Here's how it usually goes,' said McMath. 'A product will be
developed by a product manager, and it won't work out, and he'll
probably just keep a few in his bedroom closet, for sentimental
value, but then he'll eventually leave the company.' The product
may now no longer exist anywhere, except in the manager's
bedroom. Nor, of course, will he bring examples of his failures
to his next place of work: why voluntarily associate yourself with
misfires? 'People are inspired by success and achievement, and
marketing people are as human as anyone,' said Sherry. 'You want
to be able to tell a good story about your accomplishments.' It is
unlikely that many people at his former firm will want to dwell
on what went wrong, either. Failure simply isn't a topic on which
ambitious people wish to spend much of their time. At best, it's
just depressing; at worst, it feels somehow infectious – as if the
germs of disaster might infect your next project. Recall the message
of Dr Robert H. Schuller, at Get Motivated!, instructing his audience to cut the word 'impossible' out of their vocabularies and
to refuse to contemplate the possibility of failure. The very fact
that the consumer products industry needs a museum of failed
products indicates that many product designers and marketing
executives have done exactly that.

McMath turned a little coy when I asked him to tell me which
executives, specifically, had found themselves compelled to visit
his collection, tails between legs, to examine their own companies'
products, though after some pestering he let it be known that

some of them might have worked for a multinational beginning with 'P' and ending in 'rocter & Gamble'. But he did vividly remember one product design team who approached him with a plan to market two companion lines of sex-specific diapers, for boys and girls, with the padding configured differently in each. This turns out to have been an often-attempted, often-abandoned innovation: parents generally don't see the need, while retailers resent having to use up more shelf space in order to avoid running out of either kind. It was with glee that Robert McMath ushered the designers to an aisle in his collection to show them not only that their idea had already been tried – but that it had been their own firm that had tried it.

Failure is everywhere. It's just that most of the time we would rather avoid confronting that fact.

Failure, and our fraught relationship to it, is a theme that has been playing in the background of much of this book so far. It is the thing that the culture of positive thinking strives at all costs to avoid, so it should come as little surprise that it should be so central to an alternative approach to happiness. The Stoic technique of negative visualisation is, precisely, about turning towards the possibility of failure. The critics of goalsetting are effectively proposing a new attitude towards failure, too, since an improvisational, trial-and-error approach necessarily entails being frequently willing to fail. The spiritual ruminations of Eckhart Tolle and Alan Watts, meanwhile, point to an even deeper kind of failure: the ultimate – and ultimately liberating – failure of the ego's efforts to maintain its separation and security.

But it is also worth considering the subject of failure directly, in order to see how the desperate efforts of the 'cult of optimism' to avoid it are so often counterproductive, and how we might be better off learning to embrace it. The first reason to turn towards failure is that our efforts not to think about failure leave us with a severely distorted understanding of what it takes to be successful. The second is that an openness to the emotional experience of failure can be a stepping-stone to a much richer kind of happiness than can be achieved by focusing only on success. It has become fashionable, in some circles, to insist upon the importance of 'embracing failure': no autobiography of a high-profile entrepreneur or politician or inventor is complete without several passages in which the author attributes his or her success to a willingness to fail. (Sir Richard Branson is a repeat offender in this regard.) But truly embracing failure entails a shift in perspective far greater than what most such figures mean when they pay lip-service to the notion. And in any case, heeding only the advice of the successful is a big part of the problem.

Our resistance to thinking about failure is especially curious in light of the fact that failure is so ubiquitous. 'Failure is the distinguishing feature of corporate life,' writes the economist Paul Ormerod, at the start of his book *Why Most Things Fail*, but in this sense corporate life is merely a microcosm of the whole of life. Evolution itself is driven by failure; we think of it as a matter of survival and adaptation, but it makes equal sense to think of it as a matter of not surviving and not adapting. Or perhaps more sense: of all the species that have ever existed, after all, fewer than 1 per cent of them survive today. The others failed. On an individual level, too, no matter how much success you may experience in life, your eventual story – no offence intended – will be one of failure. Your bodily organs will fail, and you'll die.

Yet though failure is ubiquitous, psychologists have long recognised that we find this notion appalling, and that we will go to enormous lengths to avoid thinking about it. At its pathological extreme, this fear of failure is known as 'kakorrhaphiophobia', the symptoms of which can include heart palpitations, hyperventilation and dizziness. Few of us suffer so acutely. But as we'll see, this may only be because we are so naturally skilled at 'editing out' our failures, in order to retain a memory of our actions that is vastly more flattering than the reality. Like product managers with failures stuffed into a bedroom closet, we will do anything to tell a success-based story of our lives. This leads, among other consequences, to the entertaining psychological phenomenon known as 'illusory superiority'. This mental glitch explains why, for example, the vast majority of people tell researchers that they consider themselves to be in the top 50 per cent of safe drivers – even though they couldn't possibly all be.

Like many commentators concerned about our reluctance to confront failure, Robert McMath likes to argue that we should behave 'more like scientists'. The implication is that scientists, unlike the rest of us, must by necessity learn to become more comfortable with failure. Professional scientists, not surprisingly, tend to share this flattering view. The goal of every good scientist is discovering the truth, so he can't be picky about whether the results of his experiments confirm or undermine his hypotheses. Scientific research involves devising a hypothesis, testing it, and then dealing with whatever results you obtain – even if they ruin your hopes of a prize-winning breakthrough. Right? Actually, maybe not. A fascinating series of studies of working scientists, conducted by the Irish-born researcher Kevin Dunbar, presents a very different picture – and confirms just how deeply and universally human the tendency to avoid confronting failure really is. Scientists, it transpires, may be just as bad as everyone else.

Dunbar negotiated access to four leading molecular biology

laboratories and began observing the work that was conducted there. For months, he videotaped interviews and recorded the weekly lab meetings at which researchers discussed their findings. (This kind of examination of what scientists do on a day-to-day basis is rare, not least because scientists themselves frequently dismiss it as irrelevant.) Dunbar's first discovery was that the researchers encountered failure all the time. 'If you're a scientist and you're doing an experiment,' he said later, 'about half the experiments that you do actually turn out wrong.' For whatever reason – faulty procedures or a flawed hypothesis – the results obtained did not mesh with the conclusions towards which the scientists believed they were advancing. As one of Dunbar's subjects put it in a meeting, describing yet another failure: 'I saw the results, and I wanted to throw myself off a bridge.'

Things got more interesting when Dunbar examined how the researchers responded to this deluge of failure. As he explained in an interview with *Wired* magazine, their reactions followed a predictable sequence. First, a scientist would blame his equipment or techniques – suspecting that a measuring device must be malfunctioning, or that he himself had made a stupid mistake. If the problem couldn't be explained away so easily, the researcher would then repeat the experiment, sometimes several times, in hopes that the anomaly would vanish. And if that didn't work, he would often simply put the experiment aside. Laboratories are busy places; scientists are overworked; there are vastly more potential avenues for research than could ever be pursued, and so researchers have to make choices about what they will focus on next. Consistently, Kevin Dunbar found, they chose to neglect their inexplicable results, focusing on their successes and avoiding dwelling upon their failures.

Using brain imaging, Dunbar has examined the part of the

human brain that seems most implicated in screening out failure: the dorsolateral prefrontal cortex, or DLPFC. This region plays a crucial role in filtering out irrelevant or unwanted incoming information, which is essential if you want to concentrate, say, on a single conversation at a noisy cocktail party. (People with damaged DLPFCs experience difficulty with such tasks.) But a similar filtering process appears to be triggered when we are presented with information that violates our expectations, even when it is far from irrelevant. In one experiment, Dunbar showed videos to an audience of physics students in which two objects of different sizes, dropped from the top of a tower, appeared to behave in defiance of the laws of gravity: they fell at different speeds. Physics students know that's not what really happens, and their DLPFCs lit up – much more so than was the case in viewers of the videos who weren't so familiar with this law of physics. Dunbar's hunch is that the physics students' brains were reacting to the unwanted, clearly inexplicable information by attempting to delete it from their awareness.

Back in Ann Arbor, at the museum of failed products, it wasn't hard to imagine how a similar aversion to confronting failure might have been responsible for the very existence of many of the products lining its shelves. Each one must have made it through a series of meetings at which nobody realised that the product was doomed. Perhaps nobody wanted to contemplate the prospect of failure; perhaps someone did, but didn't want to bring it up for discussion. Even if the product's likely failure was recognised, Robert McMath explained, those responsible for marketing it might well have responded by ploughing *more* money into it. This is a common reaction when a product looks like it's going to be a lemon, since with a big enough marketing spend, a marketing manager can at least guarantee a few sales, sparing the company total humiliation. By the time reality sets in, McMath notes in *What Were They Thinking?*, it is quite possible that 'the executives will have been promoted to another brand, or recruited by another company'. Thanks to a collective unwillingness to face up to failure, more money will have been invested in the doomed product, and little energy will have been dedicated to examining what went wrong. Everyone involved will have conspired – perhaps without realising what they're doing – never to think or speak of it again.

The first big problem with our reluctance to think about or analyse failure – whether our own or other people's – is that it leads to an utterly distorted picture of the causes of success. Some years ago, a management theorist from Oxford University named Jerker Denrell was attending an academic conference in Stockholm, in his native Sweden, and sitting through the kind of speech that can make it hard to stay awake. Up at the podium, a fellow researcher was explaining his findings about the personality traits of highly successful entrepreneurs. According to several new case studies, the speaker announced, high achievers demonstrated two key characteristics: they were willing to persevere in the face of setbacks, and they possessed enough charisma to convince others to follow them. All of which is boringly obvious, and it is easy to imagine eyelids across the conference hall beginning to droop. But Denrell found himself paying attention. The speech he was hearing, he realised, embodied an error that he had been encountering for some time; he had just never heard it so clearly expressed. It was a mistake so basic that it threatened to undermine a large proportion of his colleagues' work.

It may well be true that successful entrepreneurs possess

perseverance and leadership skills, of course. What is less obvious – and much less boring – is what the speaker neglected to mention: that those traits are likely to be the characteristics of extremely *unsuccessful* people, too. 'Think about it,' Denrell observed afterwards. 'Incurring large losses requires both persistence . . . and the ability to persuade others to pour their money down the drain.' People without much perseverance or charisma are more likely to end up in the middle, experiencing neither great success nor great failure. (If you never stick at anything and if you can't persuade others to follow you, you may never lead an army of like-minded souls to a stunning victory – but neither will you lead them off a cliff.) It seems entirely likely that the very successful and the very unsuccessful might actually have rather similar personalities. The only indisputable difference between the two is that the very unsuccessful are much, much less frequently interviewed by management scholars who are studying the causes of success. They are, after all, failures. Even if researchers *wanted* to interview them – which, by and large, they don't – it is hard to imagine how they might track them down in significant numbers. Success happens in public; indeed, achieving celebrity is part of many people's definition of what constitutes success. Failure is occasionally spectacular at first, but people who fail dwell largely in obscurity.

This problem, which is known as 'survivor bias' or the 'undersampling of failure', is already extremely familiar in many areas of scholarship and of life. Most of us grasp it intuitively in certain contexts, of which the canonical example is gambling. We know, deep down, not to conclude that if we have enjoyed a winning streak at the roulette table, we must possess some magical ability to predict the behaviour of the roulette wheel. We understand that winning at roulette is a matter of chance, and that probability dictates that winning streaks will sometimes occur. Losing streaks are more common, of course. It's just that they don't tend to cause any intrigued whispering around the casino. You never hear about all the men and women who *didn't* break the bank at Monte Carlo.

The speech that Jerker Denrell heard in Stockholm was one glaring example of how our conversations about success are always falling foul of the undersampling of failure. But there are countless others. Take the bestselling book *The Millionaire Next Door*, by the American researcher Thomas Stanley. This purports to be a research-based portrait of the millionaire personality, and though the jacket describes its conclusions as 'surprising', they really aren't. The typical millionaire, Stanley reveals, is disciplined and driven, street-smart but not necessarily intellectual, and frugal to the point of tight-fistedness. *The Millionaire Next Door*, its publishers claim, 'shattered one of contemporary America's most firmly held myths: that wealthy individuals belong to an elite group of the highly educated and exceedingly lucky, who often inherit their money and spend it on lavish purchases and pampered lifestyles'. The implication throughout – and surely the explanation for the book's commercial success – is that if you, too, were to become self-disciplined, street-smart and frugal, you too could make a million. Except that, knowing what we know about survivor bias, that doesn't necessarily follow at all. Judging by his own account of his research, Stanley spent no time whatsoever studying the personalities of those who had tried but failed to become millionaires, or those to whom the notion had never occurred. (To be fair, he does mention people who made a fortune but didn't manage to hold on to their money.) And so he has few grounds for concluding that frugality or self-discipline – or any other trait, for that matter – is part of the recipe for becoming a millionaire. Others who were equally frugal or self-disciplined might have come nowhere near millionairehood.

'Suppose you look at successful chief executives and you find they all brush their teeth,' Denrell told me. 'Well, you realise that this isn't a thing unique to chief executives, because everybody brushes their teeth. You know this, because you brush your teeth, too. So you dismiss it. But say they have some strange trait that you don't have much experience of. Well, it will seem to you that this is something that explains their success. It seems to make sense, after all.' And it feels intuitively right to be focusing on the successful, not on the failures: 'If you want to learn how to fly, you look at birds; you don't look at cockroaches.' But focusing solely on success leads us badly astray.

One of the more peculiar consequences of the survivor bias is the way that it casts doubt not only on the work of scholars who study success, but on the explanations that successful people themselves give – and may sincerely believe – for their own achievements. Bookshops are stuffed with autobiographical volumes of advice such as the one released in 2006 by the multi-millionaire publisher Felix Dennis, entitled *How to Get Rich: The Distilled Wisdom of One of Britain's Wealthiest Self-Made Entrepreneurs.* Dennis's book is far less annoying than most such works, thanks largely to his disarming sense of humour about being worth £700 million, and his refreshing honesty about how much he enjoys the yachts and Caribbean holidays and Michelin-starred food that his lifestyle affords him. And yet, beneath the bragging, his book conveys a similar message to many of the others: to make a fortune, you need stubbornness, a lack of regard for what other people think of you, and a willingness to take risks. Those qualities, Dennis suggests, made him what he is. To which Jerker Denrell might respond: how could he possibly know? Dennis, obviously, has lived only one life, and has no experience of an alternative one, culminating in financial failure, with which to compare it. Perhaps thousands of others exhibited the same determination, cheekiness, and pluck, but got nowhere. Maybe not. Maybe Dennis's ascent was due to dumb luck, or to some other personality trait, so that he actually succeeded in spite of his stubbornness or fondness for risks. His self-diagnosis may be correct, of course; it's just that he isn't automatically in a better position than anyone else to say.

Dennis's focus on risk-taking raises an intriguing additional point, which is that the willingness to fail is *itself* one of the personality traits we may come to overvalue as a result of survivor bias. This is the problem with homilies such as those of Richard Branson, who writes: 'Being unafraid of failure is, I believe, one of the most important qualities of a champion.' He may be right about the importance of not fearing failure, but then again, you don't hear speeches or read autobiographies by people who were unafraid of failure and then did indeed simply fail. A willingness to fail might not be associated with success at all; alternatively, as Denrell points out, a willingness to court failure by taking big risks might be correlated with both great success and great failure. The definition of a 'big risk', after all, is that it carries a significant likelihood of things not working out.

A parallel insight arises from Denrell's research into media commentators who make predictions about the future course of the economy. The ones who made the most extreme, headline-grabbing predictions, Denrell and his colleague Christina Fang concluded, were just as likely to prove astonishingly wrong as astonishingly right. They weren't better forecasters; they just made riskier forecasts – while the media, which trumpeted their predictions and praised them when they were vindicated by events, rarely followed up on their failed forecasts. This is something you might wish to consider before relying on such commentators when choosing where to invest your money.

It is worth bearing in mind, moreover, that virtually any advice about how to succeed, in life or work, is at constant risk of being undermined by survivor bias. We ignore or avoid failure so habitually that we rarely stop to consider all the people who may have followed any set of instructions for happiness or success – including those advanced in these pages – but then failed to achieve the result.

This is probably as good a time as any to tell you about my pubic louse.

I acquired the louse – just the one, though it was exceptionally large – in February 2001, at Greenwich in east London, at the site of the Millennium Dome, Britain's fabled monument to the dawn of the year 2000. The story of the dome is, notoriously, one of failure after failure: a financial catastrophe, a disaster in terms of visitor numbers, and the undoing of several prominent politicians' careers. By early 2001, the Millennium Experience, the exhibition that had occupied the interior of the 365-metre-wide marquee for the previous year, had ended. I had been sent, as a newspaper reporter, to witness the auction of the dome's contents, by means of which its now-bankrupt operators hoped to recover some fraction of their lost millions. I had been given £100 of my employer's petty cash, in order to make a purchase for the purposes of entertaining journalism. The serious money, it was clear, was going to be spent on the company's computers, its high-tech lighting rigs and catering equipment, but everything was up for grabs – including the exhibits that had dominated the Dome's fourteen 'zones', dedicated to such topics as Body, Mind, Faith, Work, Money and Play. The Body Zone was a giant replica of a human body – bigger, we had often been told, than the Statue of Liberty – through which visitors (although not enough of them) had walked. Demonstrating an audacious refusal to flinch from the unpalatable realities of their subject, the body's designers had equipped it with several mechanised pubic lice. With my £100, I bought one. The others went to an antiques dealer from Surrey, who told me he planned to use them to scare his wife and children. A man must have a hobby.

A dome employee named Geoff came to help me extract my louse from the storeroom. 'It's a bit sad, really,' he said, with what seemed to be real emotion. 'I used to work with this guy.' I took the creature to the processing desk, as required, where another worker took it from me and handed me a slip of paper. I wouldn't be able to take it off the premises, she explained, until the auction was completed, in a few days' time. Rules were rules.

I returned to the office, louseless and in a reflective mood. The auction had felt like a public admission of the dome's defeat, and thus an appropriate end to the whole saga: sad, but also funny, and above all fitting. The sorry story of the dome is probably best encapsulated by Dan Howland, an expert on fairgrounds and amusement parks, who expresses it as follows in a monograph entitled *Dome and Domer*:

From the moment it opened, it was clear that the Millennium Dome would be one of the grandest and most spectacular failures in exposition history. It was unpopular with both press and public, inaccessible, ill-conceived, poorly planned, mismanaged, and just generally dull. So much money was spent on the dome, and so much more shovelled in as the debacle continued, that Labour prime minister Tony Blair found his career hanging in the balance, while other Labour officials found their careers hanging in tatters. The story of the Millennium Dome is a tale of honest mistakes, bad design, hubris, stupidity, greed, corruption – but above all, it's a tale of something so monumentally awful that it takes on a sort of soggy grandeur.

There is no need to rehearse each of these missteps here. Among the more famous lowlights were the New Year's Eve 1999 opening ceremony, when thousands of invited guests, including influential politicians and national newspaper editors, were forced to shiver outdoors for hours before being funnelled through the dome's hopelessly inadequate number of metal detectors; the bomb threat that almost forced the building's evacuation that night; and the attempted heist, later that year, during which a team of thieves smashed their way inside with a digger and got halfway through executing the robbery of the world's second-largest flawless diamond, which they believed was inside. (Technically, this may not count as a low point for the dome, since the heist was thwarted; an informant had alerted the police, who had replaced the diamond with a replica, and were lying in wait.) The problems had started much earlier, though: in the years approaching the Millennium, many of the project's senior employees and consultants had resigned, and several chief executives had been fired. One of them subsequently told a parliamentary committee that the dome's highest-level staff had been on the verge of nervous breakdowns as 2000 approached, forcing him to hire a team of counsellors. The dome was so vast, we'd been informed, that it could hold 18,000 double-decker London buses. But the consensus among commentators seemed to be that ordering a large quantity of double-decker buses might have been a much better use of the more than £800 million that the project swallowed up.

The Millennium Dome, in other words, could hardly have been more of a catastrophe. And yet it also illustrated the extraordinary power of failure to bring people closer together. The atmosphere at the auction was surprisingly convivial – reflecting not just the schadenfreude of journalists, but an attitude that seemed to have accompanied the tale of the dome from the very beginning: a sort of affectionate popular embrace of the endeavour in all its haplessness. 'It's a souvenir of a national disaster,' one attendee at the auction told me, explaining his presence there. 'It's a very British thing to do, isn't it?' In the months following the auction, as politicians and commentators debated what should become of the now-empty dome, the columnist Ros Coward ably captured this bittersweet British fondness for its failure. This was not joy at the misfortune of others so much as a perverse pride in belonging to the nation whose failure the dome had been:

> The dome has a clear brand, and that brand is Disaster. It cries out to be exploited as a grand folly, an emblem of muddle, hype and plain foolishness with enormous entertainment potential . . . We've become fond of the building we love to hate, the great folly, with all the entertainment it has provided stumbling from crisis to disaster . . . Something about it chimes with the British character. We're good at disasters, at not taking ourselves seriously and delighting when things go magnificently and foolishly wrong . . . This is the key to its future. It should become a museum of disasters and follies, a history of doomed projects or unfortunate accidents.

That never happened, of course. These days, the dome is the O2 arena, a concert venue that occasionally plays host to stadium-sized motivational seminars.

A few days after the auction, I returned to Greenwich to collect my pubic louse, but it was nowhere to be found. The dome employee who helped me look for it was apologetic, but not surprised. Even in attempting to sell off its contents, the dome proved a failure. Over the next few years, I received sporadic letters from the accountants PricewaterhouseCoopers, who were handling the bankruptcy, implying that one day – presumably after more important creditors had been recompensed – I might get my newspaper's £100 back.

I'm still waiting.

This half-embrace of failure, as Coward suggests, is something the British like to think of as distinctly British. We celebrate Captain Scott's failed and fatal effort to be first to the South Pole; we cherish the spirit of the Dunkirk evacuation more than the triumph of victory. 'To all those who have written terrible books on success,' wrote the (British) journalist Stephen Pile in his 1979 bestseller (in Britain) *The Book of Heroic Failures*, 'I dedicate this terrible book on how it's perfectly all right to be incompetent . . . because I am, and so is everyone I know.' To citizens of the success-oriented United States, the fondness for failure can seem like a more generally European eccentricity, frequently attributed to the end of empire. 'Musing over failure is not a particularly American activity,' writes the journalist Neil Steinberg. 'Sure, it's big in Europe, where every nation, at one time or another, has had a lock on greatness, only to fritter it away smothering monster palaces in gold leaf and commissioning jeweled Fabergé eggs by the dozen. England had her empire; Spain, her Armada; France, her Napoleon; Germany, its unspeakable zenith. Even Belgium had a moment of glory – though, true, things haven't been quite the same since the death of Charles the Bold in 1477. For those nations, remembering and bitterly analyzing greatness are [just] about their only connection to it anymore. Why do you think they have all those pubs and outdoor cafés?'

But we should not write off the embrace of failure as a culturally specific quirk; in the context of the 'negative path' to happiness, there is more to say. We have seen already how a willingness to fail and to analyse past failures can be crucial to understanding achievement and success. But a more deeply counterintuitive possibility is that there is happiness to be found in embracing failure *as* failure, not just as a path to success – that welcoming it might simply feel better than perpetually struggling to avoid it.

There is an openness and honesty in failure, a down-to-earth confrontation with reality that is lacking at the higher altitudes of success. To achieve something impressive – as might have happened had the dome ever become, as Tony Blair predicted, 'a beacon to the world' – is necessarily to erect a kind of barrier between yourself and everyone else. To be impressed by something, meanwhile, implies feeling yourself to be in the presence of something different from, and better than, yourself. Failure, by contrast, collapses these boundaries, demonstrating the fallibility of those who might otherwise try to present themselves as immune to defeat. It cuts people down to human size. The vulnerability revealed by failure can nurture empathy and communality. Do you feel more or less connection to the people who ran the dome to learn that they had been on the brink of emotional collapse? The answer, surely, is more. Had the dome been a triumphant success, it would have been unthinkable for a reporter to have had the conversations I found myself having with its employees, who would have been uptight and wary, instructed not to communicate with the media except in ways that might burnish the brand. 'Psychologically, I suppose, it's healthy,' said one security guard, who was keeping watch over four life-sized mannequins in surgical dress that would eventually sell for £320. 'We've come to the funeral, we've buried the body, and we're grieving.' Failure is a relief. At last you can say what you think.

Still, it can be exceptionally hard to adopt this attitude towards your own failures. As Christopher Kayes's notion of 'goalodicy' suggests, we too often make our goals into parts of our identities, so that failure becomes an attack on who we are. Or, as Albert Ellis understood, we alight upon some desired outcome – being happily married, for example, or finding fulfilling work – and elevate it into one we feel we *must* attain, so that failing at it becomes not just sad but catastrophic. To use the Buddhist language of attach-ment and non-attachment, we become attached to success.

All these counterproductive ways of thinking about failure manifest themselves most acutely in the phenomenon of perfec-tionism. This is one of those traits that many people seem secretly, or not so secretly, proud to possess, since it hardly seems like a character flaw – yet perfectionism, at bottom, is a fear-driven striving to avoid the experience of failure at all costs. At its extremes, it is an exhausting and permanently stressful way to live. (There is a greater correlation between perfectionism and suicide, research suggests, than between feelings of hopelessness and suicide.) To fully embrace the experience of failure, not merely to tolerate it as a stepping-stone to success, is to abandon this constant straining never to put a foot wrong. It is to relax. 'Downfall', writes the American Zen Buddhist Natalie Goldberg, 'brings us to the ground, facing the nitty-gritty, things as they are with no glitter. Success cannot last forever. Everyone's time runs out.' She goes on: 'Achievement solidifies us. Believing we are invincible, we want more and more.' To see and feel things as they really are, 'we have to crash. Only then can we drop through to a more authentic self. Zen transmits its legacy from this deeper place. It is a different kind of failure: the Great Failure, a boundless surrender. Nothing to hold on to, and nothing to lose.'

Fortunately, it may be possible to cultivate some of this attitude towards failure without reaching the rarefied heights of Buddhist enlightenment. The work of the Stanford University psychologist Carol Dweck suggests that our experiences of failure are influenced overwhelmingly by the implicit beliefs we hold about the nature of talent and ability – and that we can, perhaps quite easily, nudge ourselves in the direction of a more healthy outlook.

Each of us can be placed somewhere on a continuum, Dweck argues, depending on our 'implicit view' – or unspoken attitude – about what talent is and where it comes from. Those with a 'fixed theory' assume that ability is innate; those with an 'incremental theory' believe that it evolves through challenge and hard work. If you're the kind of person who struggles mightily to avoid the experience of failure, it's likely that you reside near the 'fixed' end of Dweck's continuum. 'Fixed theory' people tend to approach challenges as occasions on which they are called upon to demonstrate their innate abilities, and so they find failure especially horrifying: to them, it's a sign that they tried to show how good they were, but didn't measure up. The classic example of a person with a 'fixed theory' is the young sports star who is encouraged to think of himself as a 'natural' – but who then fails to put in sufficient practice to realise his potential. If talent is innate, his unspoken reasoning goes, then why bother?

'Incremental theory' people are different. Because they think of abilities as emerging through tackling challenges, the experience of failure has a completely different meaning for them: it's evidence that they are stretching themselves to their current limit. If they weren't, they wouldn't fail. The relevant analogy here is with weight training; muscles grow by being pushed to the limits of their current capacity, where fibres tear and reheal. Among weightlifters, 'training to failure' isn't an admission of defeat – it's a strategy.

Happily, Dweck's studies indicate that we are not saddled for life with one mindset rather than another. A little confusingly, the 'fixed' mindset is not itself fixed, but can be shifted towards the 'incremental' end of the continuum. Some people manage to alter their outlook simply by being introduced to the 'fixed' versus 'incremental' distinction. Alternatively, it's worth trying to recall it when failure strikes: next time you flunk an exam or mishandle a social situation, consider that it is happening only because you're pushing at the limits of your present abilities – and therefore, over the long run, improving them. Should you wish to encourage an incremental outlook rather than a fixed one in your children, Dweck advises, take care to praise them for their effort rather than for their intelligence. Focusing on the latter is likely to exacerbate a fixed mindset, making them more reluctant to risk encountering failure in the future. The incremental mindset is the one most likely to lead to success – but a more profound point is that possessing an incremental outlook is a happier way to be, even if it *never* results in any particularly outstanding success. It allows you to abandon the stressful and tiring struggle of perfectionism. It's a win-win proposition, for which the only precondition is a heartfelt willingness to lose.

Interestingly, we may once have been much more willing to think about failure in this way. Prior to the nineteenth century, the historian Scott Sandage has argued, it was rare to hear the word 'failure' applied to an individual. Certain ventures, such as an attempt to run for office or to start a company, might prove to be failures – but the individual behind such an undertaking would be described as having 'made a failure', not as *being* one. To have made a failure could be depressing, no doubt, and even sometimes catastrophic. But it was not an across-the-board condemnation of an entire human life.

To research his fascinating book *Born Losers*, Sandage had to find creative ways around the survivor bias, which ensures that it is usually only tales of success that find their way into historical archives. Cleverly, he had the idea of using begging letters sent to the oil magnate John D. Rockefeller in the late 1800s. Poring over these and other sources solidified Sandage's hunch that the idea that a *person* could be 'a failure' had sprung directly from the growth of entrepreneurial capitalism over this period. One crucial development, he argues, was the emergence of credit rating agencies, whose role was to sit in judgment upon individuals seeking loans from banks, helping the banks determine the risk they would be taking by making the loan. In a society increasingly dominated by business, a bad credit rating could all too easily come to be seen as a verdict condemning a whole person – and it is from the language of credit rating, Sandage notes, that we take several modern idioms for describing someone's moral worth, such as 'good-for-nothing' and 'first-rate'. Failure, he writes, became transformed from a bump in the road of life to the place at which 'the story stops'. From the middle of the nineteenth century onwards, failure started to be thought of 'not merely [as] a cataclysm that adds to the plot of your life, but [as] something that stops your life cold, because you lose a sense of your future'.

Failure, in short, came to be seen as a kind of death. The message of the most radical proponents of the embrace of failure, like Natalie Goldberg, is that it is the exact opposite: the route to a far more vivid, raw, and acutely experienced way of being alive.

Most of the conventionally successful people who champion the benefits of embracing failure are making a much less radical claim than Goldberg's; they are talking about learning to tolerate failure only as a means to their eventual success. A rare exception is J. K. Rowling, the stratospherically successful author of the *Harry Potter* novels, who in 2008 gave a now-famous graduation speech at Harvard University on the subject of failure. Of course, it is impossible to know for sure how Rowling would feel about failure if it hadn't been followed, in her case, by spectacular success. But she conveyed the distinct impression that she would have felt the same about it even if she had remained obscure, poor, and creatively unfulfilled. Her words chime with many of the insights of the Stoics, the Buddhists, and others into the benefits of negativity, and they are worth quoting at length:

I think it fair to say that by any conventional measure, a mere seven years after my graduation day, I had failed on an epic scale. An exceptionally short-lived marriage had imploded, and I was jobless, a lone parent, and as poor as it is possible to be in modern Britain without being homeless. The fears that my parents had had for me, and that I had had for myself, had both come to pass, and by every usual standard, I was the biggest failure I knew. Now, I am not going to stand here and tell you that failure is fun. That period of my life was a dark one, and I had no idea there was going to be what the press has since represented as a fairytale resolution. I had no idea how far the tunnel extended . . . so why do I talk about the benefits of failure?

Simply because failure meant a stripping away of the inessential. I stopped pretending to myself that I was anything other than what I was, and began to direct all my energy into finishing the only work that mattered to me . . . I was set free, because my greatest fear had been realised, and I was still alive. [Failure] gave me an inner security that I had never attained by passing examinations . . . Such knowledge is a true gift, for all that it is painfully won, and it has been worth more than any qualification I ever earned.

Memento Mori

Death as a Way of Life

If I had my life over I should form the habit of nightly composing myself to thoughts of death. I would practice, as it were, the remembrance of death . . . without an ever-present sense of death, life is insipid. You might as well live on the whites of eggs.

 – Inspector Mortimer in Muriel Spark's *Memento Mori*

AT ONE POINT DURING the course of the 200,000-line Indian spiritual epic the *Mahabharata*, the warrior-prince Yudhisthira is being cross-questioned about the meaning of existence by a nature spirit on the banks of a lake, which is the sort of thing that happens in the *Mahabharata* all the time. 'What is the most wondrous thing in the world?', the spirit wants to know. Yudhisthira's reply has become one of the poem's best-known lines: 'The most wondrous thing in the world is that although, every day, innumerable creatures go to the abode of Death, still man thinks that he is immortal.'

'Wondrous' is a good way of putting it. Again and again, we have seen how merely not wanting to think certain thoughts or to feel certain emotions isn't sufficient to eliminate them. That's why nobody ever wins Daniel Wegner's 'white bear challenge', why self-help affirmations often make people feel worse, and why confronting worst-case scenarios is almost always preferable to trying to pretend they couldn't happen. But mortality seems a baffling exception to this rule. Death is everywhere, unavoidable, and uniquely terrifying. Yet as long as it's not impinging on us immediately – through recent bereavement, or a life-threatening illness, or a narrowly survived accident – many of us manage to avoid all thoughts of our own mortality for months, even years, at a time. The more you reflect on this, the stranger it seems. We are perfectly capable of feeling acute self-pity about more minor predicaments, at home or at work, on a daily basis. Yet the biggest predicament of all goes by, for the most part, not consciously worried about. 'At bottom,' wrote Freud – sweepingly, as usual, but in this case persuasively – 'no one believes in his own death.'

This apparent nonchalance in the face of mortality looks stranger still in light of the fact that we *do* talk about death, all the time, yet somehow without ever really talking about it. Who reads those magazine features listing 'a hundred things to do before you die' – places to travel, foods to eat, albums to hear – and pays any real attention to the 'before you die' part? If you did, your reaction might well be a cry of existential despair: 'Why bother, if I'm just going to die in the end anyway?' (And existential despair, needless to say, is not the response a magazine editor usually wishes to evoke among readers.) We're captivated by fictional tales of murder, but the 'murder' in a murder mystery rarely has much to do with the realities of death. Even real deaths in news reports can trigger horror, sympathy, or outrage without once prompting the viewer to reflect that the same basic fate, in a few decades at most, awaits him too. The idea of choosing to think about our own mortality, in a personal sense, as a matter of daily conversation, strikes us as hilarious – the joke on which, for example, much of the humour in Woody Allen's 1975 movie *Love and Death* rests:

> BORIS: Nothingness. Non-existence. Black emptiness.
> SONJA: What did you say?
> BORIS: Oh, I was just planning my future.

One of the most persuasive explanations of this psychological puzzle remains the one put forward in 1973 by Ernest Becker, in his magnum opus *The Denial of Death*. (Another death-fixated Woody Allen character, Alvy Singer, uses a copy to woo the titular heroine of *Annie Hall*.) Becker was born in Massachusetts in 1924; as a drafted soldier he encountered the worst realities of death while still a young man, helping to liberate a Nazi concentration camp by the time he had turned twenty-one. The lack of serious thought we give to mortality, for Becker, is no accident or over-sight: it is precisely *because* death is so terrifying and significant, he argues, that we don't think about it. 'The idea of death, the fear of it, haunts the human animal like nothing else,' his book begins. But the consequence is that we dedicate our lives to suppressing that fear, erecting vast psychological fortifications so that we can avoid confronting it. Indeed, an enormous proportion of all human activity, in Becker's view, is 'designed largely to avoid the fatality of death, to overcome it by denying in some way that it is the final destiny of man'.

We are able to sustain this denial, he explains, because we possess both a physical self and a symbolic one. And while it is inevitable that the physical self will perish, the symbolic self – the one that exists in our minds – is quite capable of convincing itself that it is immortal. The evidence of this is all around us; in fact, it's so ubiquitous that you might miss it. In Becker's view, all religions, all political movements and national identities, all business ventures, all charitable activity and all artistic pursuits are nothing but 'immortality projects', desperate efforts to break free of death's gravitational pull. We long to think of ourselves not as mortal humans but as immortal 'heroes'. Society itself is essentially a 'codified hero system' – a structure of customs, traditions and laws that we have designed to help us feel part of something bigger, and longer-lasting, than a mere human life. Thanks to our symbol-making capacities, he writes, 'The single organism can expand into dimensions of worlds and times without moving a physical limb; it can take eternity into itself, even as it gaspingly dies.' From this perspective, it isn't only conventionally religious people who depend on the notion of an afterlife. All normally adjusted people, religious or not, unconsciously do so – and 'every society is thus a "religion", whether it thinks so or not'. For Becker, mental illness is a malfunctioning of the internal death-denial machinery. Depressed people are depressed because they try but repeatedly fail to shield themselves, as others manage to do, from the truth that they are not, in reality, cosmically significant heroes – and that pretty soon they're going to die.

Immortality projects may be the cause of plenty of good things – great architecture, great literature, great acts of philanthropy, great civilisations – but in Becker's view they are simultaneously the cause of the worst things, too. Our urge to think of ourselves as heroes doesn't discriminate: it helps explain why we compete in sports or politics or commerce, but also why we fight wars. War represents the ultimate clashing of rival immortality projects: if my sense of immortality relies on my nation's triumph, and yours upon yours, we'll fight longer and harder than if we were seeking only territory or power. 'Making a killing in business or in the battlefield', writes the philosopher Sam Keen, paraphrasing Becker, 'frequently has less to do with economic need or political reality than with the need for assuring ourselves that we have achieved something of lasting worth . . . [Human conflicts] are life-and-death struggles – my gods against your gods, my immortality project against your immortality project.' In other words, we will fight so hard to preserve our symbolic immortality that we will sacrifice our physical lives. In order to deny death, we will die. Even worse, we will deny that this is what we are doing, until the point at which we can deny it no longer. 'One of the main reasons that it is so easy to march men off to war', Becker observes, bleakly, 'is that deep down, each of them feels sorry for the man next to him who will die. Each protects himself in this fantasy until the shock that he is bleeding.'

If Becker is right, the 'wondrous' fact that we behave as if we're immortal isn't so wondrous after all. You don't *fail* to think about your mortality. Rather, your life is one relentless attempt to avoid doing so – a struggle so elemental that, unlike in the case of the 'white bear challenge', for much of the time you succeed.

A few years after *The Denial of Death* became a bestseller, several experimentally minded psychologists realised that Becker's speculations (and, powerful as they were, they were just speculations) could easily be subjected to a more scientific test. If Becker is correct that we spend our lives fiercely but subconsciously trying to evade thoughts of our own death, it ought to follow that people who are explicitly *reminded* of their mortality – who are, in the language of psychology experiments, 'primed' to think about it – would instinctively fight back, by clinging ever harder to their death-denying beliefs and behaviours. This is the hunch underlying the field known evocatively as 'terror management theory', which over

the last two decades has generated numerous persuasive examples
of just how deeply the denial of death affects us.

One typical set of terror management experiments, at Rutgers
University in New Jersey, in 2003, unfolded as follows. First, the
participants were fed a banal cover story about why they had
been invited to take part – the study, they were informed, concerned 'the relationship between personality attributes and opinions about social issues'. Mortality wasn't mentioned. Then they
were asked to fill out some lengthy and largely mundane question-
naires, which were identical for each participant except when it
came to two specific questions. For one set of respondents, those
questions were about something mundane, too: their television-
watching habits. For the others – described as the 'mortality
salience' group – the questions focused on death. One was: 'Please
briefly describe the emotions that the thought of your own death
arouses in you.' The other question demanded that respondents
'jot down, as specifically as you can, what you think will happen
to you as you physically die, and once you are physically dead.'

Then came a second exercise, which was the study's real point.
Participants were asked to read a short essay that expressed strong
support for the foreign policies of George Bush, then to decide
how far they agreed with it. 'Personally,' read the essay, 'I endorse
the actions of President Bush and the members of his administration who have taken bold action in Iraq. I appreciate our
President's wisdom regarding the need to remove Saddam Hussein
from power . . . We need to stand behind our President and not
be distracted by citizens who are less than patriotic.'

Again and again, in terror management experiments, people
who have been shifted into this condition of 'mortality salience'
– prompted to think about death – demonstrate markedly
different attitudes from those who haven't. Their responses to

questions lend weight to the hypothesis that they are grasping hold of their immortality projects much more firmly than usual, in reaction against being reminded that they will die. Christians show more negativity towards Jews. Moralistic people become more moralistic. Where money is involved, people become less willing to share or to trust, and more eager to hoard whatever wealth they can. And at Rutgers in 2003, when asked how far they shared the views of the essay about President Bush, people in a state of 'mortality salience' were significantly more willing to endorse its author's fighting talk. Other studies have shown a similar preference, in conditions of mortality salience, for author-itarian personalities over 'relationship-oriented' ones. It seems clear that Bush benefited greatly from mortality salience effects in the real world as well. The terrorist attacks on 11 September 2001 would have functioned like an extreme version of the death questions on a terror-management questionnaire, startling anyone who heard the news into the realisation that they, too, could go into the office one ordinary morning and die. 'It is [fear] that makes people so willing to follow brash, strong-looking dema-gogues with tight jaws and loud voices,' wrote Becker – leaders 'who seem most capable of cleansing the world of the vague, the weak, the uncertain, the evil. Ah, to give oneself over to their direction – what calm, what relief.'

Mortality salience makes itself felt in numerous other, some-times unexpected ways. Experimental subjects who have been prompted to think about death demonstrate more intense reac-tions of disgust to discussions of human bodily waste. They agree more strongly with statements such as 'If I see someone vomit, it makes me sick to my stomach.' They are more likely to rank certain hypothetical scenarios as 'very disgusting', for example seeing maggots on a piece of meat. This response, researchers argue, shows that participants are struggling to buffer themselves against confronting reminders of their 'creatureliness' – of the fact that, like other animals, they are physically mortal. 'Disgust', one such paper states, enables 'humans to elevate themselves above other animals and thereby defend against death'. (This reaction to mortality, following Becker's logic, may also help explain some cultures' taboos against menstruating women, and why defecation and urination are generally done in private.) People in a condition of mortality salience, it transpires, are also more likely to be sympathetic to the theory of 'intelligent design', perhaps for similar reasons: if you can convince yourself that life didn't emerge meaninglessly from the primordial swamp, it's easier to feel that it won't end in meaningless extinction, either.

In view of all this, the argument that it could be *beneficial* to live with more daily consciousness of one's mortality might sound impractical at best. For one thing, Becker's argument seems to suggest that the denial of death is far too deep-rooted for us ever to hope to unseat it. Besides, if it is the motivation for all sorts of extraordinary human achievements, would you really even want to do so? Yet since the time of the ancient Greeks, certain radical thinkers have taken the position that a life suffused with an awareness of one's own mortality – as a matter of everyday habit, not just when direct encounters with death force our hand – might be a far richer kind of existence. It is also surely a more authentic one. Death *is* a fact of life, however hard we might try to deny it. In fact, the 'cult of optimism', with its focus on positivity at all costs, can itself be seen as a kind of 'immortality project' – one that promises a future vision of happiness and success so powerful and all-encompassing that it might somehow transcend death. Positive thinkers, it's true, do pay lip-service to mortality awareness, with their homilies about 'living each day as if it were your last'. But this is usually delivered as mere motivational advice, as a spur to get moving, to start realising your greatest ambitions. And if those ambitions are themselves simply more immortality projects, we have not really come any closer to living with an awareness of death.

Ernest Becker's appointment with mortality came tragically early: a year before *The Denial of Death* was published, he was diagnosed with colon cancer, at the age of forty-seven. Two years later, Sam Keen visited him, literally on his deathbed, in a hospital ward in Vancouver one rainy day in February 1974. Keen was there to conduct an interview with Becker for *Psychology Today*. 'Well,' Becker told him, 'now you'll have a chance to see whether I lived as I thought.' He had requested only a minimum of pain-killing medication, he explained, so as to remain 'clear' in his final inter-actions with his family, and in his dying. The denial of death might have structured all human civilisation, but it wasn't the best way, Becker believed, for an individual to deal with his own death. 'Gradually, reluctantly,' Keen wrote later, 'we are beginning to acknowledge that the bitter medicine [Becker] prescribes – contemplation of the horror of our own death – is, paradoxically, the tincture that adds sweetness to mortality.' The interview was published a month after their meeting, in March. A few days afterwards, Becker died.

It may be hard to swallow the idea that we should spend more time contemplating death, but there are some powerful and prag-matic arguments for doing so. Consider, for example, the Stoic technique of the 'premeditation of evils'. Death is going to happen, Seneca would say, and so it must be preferable to be mentally prepared for its approach, instead of shocked into the sudden realisation that it is imminent. In any case, our subconscious strivings not to think about death are never entirely successful: long before your own death becomes a probability, you'll occasionally find yourself in the grip of that middle-of-the-night panic so vividly captured by Philip Larkin in his poem 'Aubade': 'Unresting death, a whole day nearer now . . . Flashes afresh to hold and horrify.' Better, surely, to avoid such horror by normalising the prospect if possible.

But how to go about doing this? The denial of death isn't like most other problems, which weigh on us so heavily that we may eventually be driven to find a way to solve them. The whole problem is that, most of the time, it doesn't feel like a problem at all. Subconsciously assuming that you're immortal makes for a much easier existence, so long as you can keep it up. How, then, to fight this instinct and choose, as a matter of daily living, to confront death instead?

Solving this conundrum sounded like it might be a job for someone who was both a philosopher and a psychotherapist, and so in search of answers I turned to Lauren Tillinghast, a woman whose business cards and website described her as a 'philosophical counsellor'. She was part of a contemporary movement among philosophers who felt that they were returning the discipline to its Socratic roots, as a therapeutic practice intended to soothe the soul, not just an academic exercise in theory-spinning. Tillinghast did her fair share of such theorising; she'd published articles in philosophy journals with titles such as 'What Is an Attributive Adjective?' and 'The Classificatory Sense of "Art"'. But she also had a consulting office, in downtown Manhattan, a bright and neatly furnished room hidden inside an ageing office building that was home to a number of more conventional therapists, psychiatrists, and counsellors. She was in her early forties, and had the practised, friendly neutrality of a woman accustomed to listening non-judgmentally to other people's problems. She poured me some mint tea into a white china cup, ushered me to an armchair, and didn't flinch when I told her I wanted to talk about death – and, specifically, how one might learn to choose to live with greater awareness of one's mortality. 'Well, that's a pretty big topic,' she said. But we had to start somewhere, and we decided to begin with Epicurus.

The first step in trying to become more comfortable with your mortality involves attempting to reduce the terror induced by the mere thought of death. (If you can't manage that, you're unlikely to get much further.) Tillinghast explained that philosophers had often sought to achieve this by means of rational argument: if you can be persuaded that the fear of death is illogical, you're more likely to be able to let go of it. The ancient Greek philosopher Epicurus – a contemporary of Zeno of Citium, the original Stoic – had made one of the earliest attempts. Before him, the philosophical consensus on death, broadly speaking, was that it wasn't really final: the best argument for not being scared of it was that a glorious afterlife might follow. Epicurus's argument is the mirror-image of this. If life *doesn't* continue beyond death, he points out, that's an excellent reason not to be scared of it, either. 'Death is nothing to us,' he says, 'since when we are, death has not come, and when death has come, we are not.' You might fear a painful dying process. You might dread the pain of losing others to death; our focus here is not on the terrible pain of grief. But fearing being dead yourself makes no sense. Death spells the end of the experiencing subject, and thus the end of any capacity for experiencing the state we fear. Or as Einstein put it: 'The fear of death is the most unjustified of all fears, for there's no risk of accident to one who's dead.' The one great fear that governs our lives, from this perspective, stands exposed as a kind of error. It's as if, instead of imagining death, we had all along been imagining something more like being buried alive – deprived of all the benefits of existence, yet somehow still forced to experience the deprivation.

One powerful counterargument to this position is that our fear doesn't come from imagining death *wrongly*, but from the fact that we can't imagine it at all. That was roughly Freud's view of the matter: that what we call 'the fear of death' is really more of a horrified seizing-up in the face of something utterly inconceivable. But as the contemporary philosopher Thomas Nagel points out, there's something wrong with this argument, too – because there's nothing about 'unimaginable' states that is terrifying by definition. We can't imagine what it's like to be in a state of dreamless sleep, either, but we surrender to it every night, and very few of us do so with feelings of terror. 'People who are averse to death', Nagel notes drily, 'are not usually averse to unconsciousness.'

Epicurus has a second, connected point to make about the non-scariness of death, which has become known as the 'argument of symmetry'. Why do you fear the eternal oblivion of death, he wonders, if you don't look back with horror at the eternal oblivion before you were born – which, as far as you were concerned, was just as eternal, and just as much an oblivion? Vladimir Nabokov famously opens his memoir *Speak, Memory* with lines that drive this point home: 'The cradle rocks above an abyss, and common sense tells us that our existence is but a brief crack of light between two eternities of darkness. Although the two are identical twins, man, as a rule, views the prenatal abyss with much more calm than the one he is headed for.' If you weren't traumatised by not having yet been born, it seems logical not to worry about being traumatised by being dead. But of course, Tillinghast pointed out, 'it's not very useful, for most people, to point out that a fear is *illogical*. It doesn't make it go away.'

There's another problem with all these efforts to make *being dead* a less frightening prospect, which is this: who says that being dead is the problem in the first place? When we contemplate our own personal mortality, the real sting is surely that we're going to *stop being alive*, and lose all the benefits we enjoy as a result of living. 'People don't generally come to me because they fear the oblivion of being dead,' Tillinghast said. 'But the idea of everything that makes life *lifely* drawing to a close – well, that's a much greater source of anxiety.' It is true, of course, that you won't be around to *experience* being deprived of those benefits, so fearing that deprivation is arguably unjustifiable. But as Nagel argues, in an essay entitled simply 'Death', the fact that you shouldn't fear death doesn't mean that it isn't a bad thing. By way of analogy, he says, imagine an adult who suffers a severe brain injury and is reduced to the mental state of a three-year-old. He might be perfectly happy in his new condition, but nobody would disagree that something bad had still happened to the adult he once was. It makes no difference that the adult is no longer around. No matter how persuasive you find Epicurus's arguments against *fearing* death, it doesn't follow that death is not *bad*.

This distinction is crucial, because it begins to make sense of the idea that a greater degree of mortality awareness might be part of the recipe for happiness. For as long as you're terrified by the idea of your mortality, you can't really be expected to swallow Ernest Becker's 'bitter medicine' and voluntarily opt to spend more time thinking about your own death. On the other hand, trying to embrace death as a *good* thing would seem to be asking far too much of yourself. It might not necessarily even be desirable, since it could cause you to place less value on being alive. But coming to understand death as something that there is no reason to fear, yet which is still bad because of what it brings to an end, might be the ideal middle path. The argument is a thoroughly down-to-earth, pragmatic, and Stoic one: the more that you remain aware of life's finitude, the more you will cherish it, and the less likely you will be to fritter it away on distractions. 'Look at it like going to a really nice restaurant,' said Tillinghast. 'You take it as a fact that the meal isn't going to last forever. Never mind if that's the way it should be, or whether you feel like you're owed more meal, or you resent the fact that the meal isn't eternal. It's just the case that you have this one meal. So it would make sense, wouldn't it, to try to suck the marrow out of it? To focus on the flavours? To not let yourself be distracted by irritation at the fact that there's a woman at the next table wearing too much perfume?' The psychotherapist Irvin Yalom, in his book *Staring at the Sun*, points out that many of us live with the dim fear that on our deathbeds we'll come to regret how we spent our lives. Remembering our mortality moves us closer to the deathbed mindset from which such a judgment might be made – thus enabling us to spend our lives in ways that we're much less likely to come to regret.

Truly to confront your own mortality, Yalom argues, is to undergo an awakening – a total shift in perspective that fundamentally transforms how it feels to be alive. And it is not necessarily remotely pleasant. He recalls the reflections of one of his therapy patients, a woman in her early thirties: 'I suppose the strongest feelings came,' she told him, 'from realising that it would be *me* who will die – not some other entity, like Old-Lady-Me, or Terminally-Ill-and-Ready-to-Die me. I suppose I always thought of death obliquely, as something that *might* happen, rather than that would happen.' To make that switch, Yalom insists, is not merely to ratchet up the intensity with which you live, but to alter your relationship to life. It is a transformation he describes, borrowing the language of the philosopher Martin Heidegger, as a move from focusing on 'how things are' to the fact 'that things are' – on the sheer astonishing *is*-ness of existence.

This is the real distinction between mortality awareness as a way of life, on the one hand, and those clichéd slogans about 'living each day as if it were your last' on the other. The slogans may be motivational – a reminder to get down to the important stuff before it's too late. But Yalom is talking about a transformation that redefines what constitutes the 'important stuff'. When you really face mortality, the ultimate and unavoidable worst-case scenario, everything changes. 'All external expectations, all fear of embarrassment or failure – these things just fall away in the face of death, leaving only what is truly important,' Apple's founder Steve Jobs once said, in a speech that was speedily co-opted by several gurus of positive thinking, though in truth its message struck fatally at the heart of theirs. 'Remembering that you are going to die is the best way that I know to avoid the trap of thinking you have something to lose. You are already naked.'

Start thinking this way, Yalom points out, and it becomes a virtuous circle. Living more meaningfully will reduce your anxiety about the possibility of future regret at not having lived meaningfully – which will, in turn, keep sapping death of its power to induce anxiety. As he puts it, there is a positive correlation between the fear of death and the sense of unlived life. Live a life suffused with the awareness of its own finitude, and you can hope to finish it in something like the fashion that Jean-Paul Sartre hoped to die: 'quietly . . . certain that the last burst of my heart would be inscribed on the last page of my work, and that death would be taking only a dead man'.

After wrestling for a while with the ideas of Becker, Epicurus, Thomas Nagel and Irvin Yalom, I decided to take a trip to Mexico. I had suspected for some time that this would prove necessary if I was really going to understand the role of mortality awareness in daily life. I had often seen it claimed that Mexico had a unique attitude towards death. By common agreement, it was one of the few countries that still had an active tradition of *memento mori* – rituals and customs designed to encourage regular reflections on mortality – and, according to several recent international surveys, it was also one of the happiest; perhaps even the happiest or second happiest nation in the world, in fact, depending on the measures used. The most famous example of this attitude towards death is the annual celebration known as the Day of the Dead, when Mexicans toast those who have died – and death itself – with copious quantities of tequila, and bread in the shape of human remains; people build shrines in their homes, throng city squares, and conduct all-night vigils at the graves of deceased relatives. But this way of thinking runs deeper than a national holiday each November. As the celebrated Mexican essayist Octavio Paz writes, in his book *The Labyrinth of Solitude*: 'The word "death" is not pronounced in New York, in Paris, in London, because it burns the lips . . . the Mexican, in contrast, is familiar with death, jokes about it, caresses it, sleeps with it, celebrates it; it is one of his favorite toys and his most steadfast love.'

This more intimate relationship with mortality was not always so unusual. Such traditions date at least to ancient Rome. There, according to legend, generals who had been victorious in battle

would instruct a slave to follow behind as they paraded through
the streets; the slave's task was to keep repeating, for the general's
benefit, a warning against hubris: *memento mori*, 'remember you
shall die'. Much later, in Christian Europe, *memento mori* became
a staple of the visual arts: symbols of death appeared frequently
in still-life paintings, sometimes including skulls intended to
represent those of the artists' patrons. Public clocks featured
automata representing death, and sometimes the Latin slogan
'*Vulnerant omnes, ultima necat*' as a reminder of the effect of the
passing minutes: 'Every [hour] wounds, and the last one kills.'
The specific motivation for contemplating mortality differed from
era to era, and culture to culture. In the ancient world, it had
much to do with remembering to savour life as if it were a delicious meal, as Lauren Tillinghast had advised; for later Christians,
it was often more a case of remembering to behave well in antici-
pation of the final judgment.

I'd been especially intrigued to hear about one contemporary
example of death-awareness in Mexican daily life. Santa Muerte
was the name of a new religion (according to its followers) or a
Satanic cult (in the eyes of the Catholic Church) which worshipped
death itself – the figure known as La Santa Muerte, or Saint Death.
The movement had sprung up several decades ago in the toughest
neighbourhoods of Mexico City, among prostitutes and drug
dealers and the very poor – people for whom both the Mexican
government and the Catholic Church had failed to provide.
Instead, they prayed to Santa Muerte for protection from death,
for a gentle death, or sometimes for death to their enemies. Now,
as a result of immigration, Santa Muerte had spread to parts of
the United States; it was also said that some of Mexico's most
powerful businessmen and politicians kept secret death-shrines
at home. And although many of the followers of Saint Death

were law-abiding Mexicans – they had marched in the streets
to protest the government's attempts to characterise the movement as nothing but a band of criminals – it was nonetheless
true that it had become the religion of choice of the *narcotra-
ficantes*, the ruthless drug-smuggling gangs of Mexico's north.
At the movement's main shrine in the *barrio* of Tepito in Mexico
City – where a life-sized model of a skeleton, laden with jewel-
lery, stood in a glass case on a side-street – some of the country's most violent men came to leave offerings of dollar bills,
cigarettes, and marijuana. Whatever other significance the
movement had, being a follower of Santa Muerte seemed to
entail devoting oneself to an especially extreme form of *memento
mori* – to organising one's life around the omnipresence of
death. 'In a world of facts,' writes Paz, 'death is merely one
more fact. But since it is such a disagreeable fact, contrary to
all our concepts and to the very meaning of our lives, the
philosophy of progress . . . pretends to make it disappear, like
a magician palming a coin.' In Mexico, Santa Muerte was where
you turned if the circumstances of your life made this sleight-
of-hand impossible – if the constant fear of violent death
removed the option of ignoring your mortality.

I did visit Tepito during my time in Mexico, a few days before
the Day of the Dead itself, though it didn't prove the most
successful of assignments. I had been warned not to get there by
hailing a taxi from the street, because of the risk of kidnapping;
as a reporter, I have no real thirst for danger, and arguably I
shouldn't have gone at all. 'Foreigners for obvious reasons *never*
go to Tepito!', someone advised, in an internet forum that I probably shouldn't have consulted. 'Only idiots and the ignorant visit
Tepito,' warned someone else. A few days earlier, an armed gang
had gunned down six people on a street corner there, in the

middle of the day. In the newspapers, it was reported that the police had written off whole sections of it as too dangerous to bother trying to patrol. A filmmaker based in Mexico City, who'd made a documentary about Tepito, declined to accompany me there, citing safety concerns. And a restaurateur in a smarter part of the city had cheerily passed along what she claimed was a well-known saying: in Tepito, even the rats carried guns. My walk into Tepito was therefore, if nothing else, a pretty good exercise in *memento mori* for myself.

I set off from the heart of the city in the middle of the morning, through shopping streets and Mexico City's business district, then along bigger highways lined with scrappy, busy markets, until the streets grew narrower and the buildings smaller again, and I found myself in Tepito. The core of the neighbourhood was another cacophonous market – Tepito is notorious as a centre for the sale of counterfeit and stolen goods – but in my search for the Santa Muerte shrine I soon left the main roads and plunged into the deserted backstreets, where rats scuttled from towering piles of rubbish. I hurried past darkened doorways, growing nervous.

In the event, the scene at the shrine itself was festive. Around twenty people were waiting in an orderly line to pay their respects to the skeleton, which was resplendent in purple and orange necklaces and a lace shawl. Some carried their own, smaller statuettes, or bottles of spirits to leave as a gift; one or two blew cigar or cigarette smoke over the skeleton when they came to the front of the line, in what I later learned was a rite of spiritual cleansing. The devotees chatted and laughed – men and women, elderly women and muscular young men, some with newborn babies and toddlers in tow.

Having been unable to persuade a translator to come with me to the *barrio*, I was forced to rely on my terrible Spanish to start a conversation with a woman carrying a foot-high Death statue under her arm. Several other people in the line turned to stare.

She didn't want to talk. The atmosphere in my immediate vicinity quickly turned less festive. I was intruding. Besides, it was quite possible that some of those around me wouldn't want to talk to any reporter or any stranger: people came to Santa Muerte, according to the Mexican essayist Homero Aridjis, 'to ask her "protect me tonight because I am going to kidnap or assault somebody"'. It was a struggle to imagine a life in which death played quite so central a role. Then again, the great truth that was underlined by the scene at the shrine – where the generations mingled as they waited in line – was that death was a subject in which everyone had an inescapable interest.

As a pale, skinny Englishman, though, I was prominently out of place. And a muscular man in a black sleeveless vest, who seemed to be standing guard over the shrine, appeared to have noticed this. He glared at me. There was as much amusement as menace in his glare, since it was embarrassingly plain that I posed him no physical threat. Still, he tilted his head in such a way as to indicate the direction in which he believed I should now proceed: away from the shrine and back to the main street.

It was shortly after this that I made the decision to leave Tepito.

I had better luck on the Day of the Dead itself. (Celebrations begin on the last day of October, but the festival reaches its peak on 2 November.) Through a friend of a colleague, I'd made contact with a local retired taxi-driver named Francisco, who spoke decent English and had a sideline as a 'fixer' for journalists visiting Mexico City. At dusk, he pulled up outside my hotel in a severely battered grey van. 'It's a very safe car,' he said, beaming, though I hadn't asked, then added, 'My other car was in an accident – and now my brother cannot use his leg!' I didn't pursue the subject.

Francisco, as he'd explained to me on the phone a few days earlier, knew his way round the tiny settlements in the countryside outside the capital where the Day of the Dead was still *auténtico* – not commercialised or touristic but haunting and pure, and where villagers spent the entire night conducting vigils in local cemeteries, communing with the corpses of their relatives. It wasn't really in my interests to start quibbling about road safety.

In Mexico City, the official municipal celebrations were reaching their peak. The historical central square, the Zócalo, was packed with families strolling among carts selling bone-shaped bread and sugar skulls. People – adults and children – were everywhere dressed as death: boys as hollow-eyed vampires in stiff starched collars, women as 'La Catrina', the iconic Mexican image of death as a woman in a broad-brimmed hat. On many corners, there were altars to the dead, bedecked with papier-mâché skulls. Such traditions stretched back centuries, but they had been integrated into the life of a busy, modern city. In the offices of banks and insurance companies downtown, I'd been told, desks were often turned into altars. It was commonplace for colleagues to write comic poetry to each other, predicting the manner in which they might die.

But Francisco and I were headed away from the bustling squares, onto wide, chaotic highways – dodging stray dogs and suicidally piloted minibuses – and then, as night fell, on empty, unlit country lanes. 'You know,' Francisco said after we had passed another dimly illumined roadside statue of death, looming from the blackness, 'when I was a child, on this day, we would go from house to house, to make a joke about how each person was going to die. So if someone smokes too much, you brought him cigarettes, to make a joke about how he was going to die from too much smoking.' He smiled at the memory. 'Or if there was someone who lived in that house who had died from too much smoking, then you could bring cigarettes as a gift to remember him.'

'Didn't people get offended?'

'Offended?'

'You know. Insulted.'

'No, why?' He turned to look at me. 'I think that this is only in Mexico, though.'

He was largely right about that. Elsewhere in the Catholic world, 2 November is All Souls' Day, designated since the eighth century as an occasion for mournful remembrance of the dead. But when the *conquistadors* reached Mexico, in the fifteenth century, they encountered celebrations of death among the Mayan and Aztec populations far more elaborate than their own: the Aztecs honoured their 'lady of the dead', Mictecacihuatl, with a two-month festival of bonfires, dance and feasting. The colonists were determined to replace all this with something more sombre and more Christian. The Day of the Dead – with its strange mixture of Christianity and pre-Christian religions, mourning and humour – is a testament to the incompleteness of their victory.

There were cultures that took *memento mori* to even greater extremes. The sixteenth-century essayist Michel de Montaigne was fond of praising the ancient Egyptians – 'who in the height of their feasting and mirth, caused a dried skeleton of a man to be brought into the room, to serve as a memento to their guests'. (A writer's working space, Montaigne also believed, ought to have a good view of the cemetery; it tended to sharpen one's thinking.) And in the *Satipatthana Sutta*, one of the formative texts of Buddhism, the Buddha urges his monks to travel to charnel grounds in order to seek out – as objects upon which to meditate – one of the following:

. . . a corpse, one or two days old, swollen up, blue-black in colour, full of corruption; a corpse eaten by crows; a framework of bones, flesh hanging from it, bespattered with blood, held together by the sinews; bones, scattered in all directions, bleached and resembling shells; bones heaped together, after the lapse of years, weathered and crumbled to dust . . .

'Corpse practice', as it was known, was intended to lead the meditating monk to the realisation that – as the Buddha is supposed to have phrased it – 'This body of mine also has this nature, has this density, cannot escape it.'

Francisco and I drove on. Eventually, after a diversion to a tiny town to eat pork *chilaquiles* from a roadside stall, and to watch a procession of churchgoers bearing framed photographs of dead relatives, we arrived at his intended destination: the village of San Gregorio Atlapulco. It was chilly, and almost midnight. At first all I could see was an orange glow in the black sky; then, rounding a bend in the road, we came suddenly upon its source. The village cemetery was covered in hundreds of candles and blanketed everywhere in marigold petals, sending a soft orange light into the sky.

Francisco parked the van, and we walked into the cemetery. It took a moment for my eyes to adjust to what I was seeing. Many of the gravestones were only rough concrete slabs or stubby pieces of wood, but almost none were unattended. Next to each, sitting in folding chairs or cross-legged on the ground, were groups of two, three, or four people, sometimes more, holding murmured conversations and drinking tequila from paper cups. In one corner, a mariachi band in full costume strolled from grave to grave, serenading every headstone in turn. I stopped a woman who was carrying armfuls of rugs and chairs towards a nearby headstone, and asked what she was doing. 'Oh, it's my mother,' she said brightly, gesturing at the grave. 'We come every year.'

It would be entirely wrong to give the impression that the Day of the Dead – or Mexico's approach to *memento mori* in general, for that matter – represented any kind of shortcut around the inescapable and scarring realities of grief. The participants in the cemetery vigils were not, by and large, those still reeling from the impact of having recently been bereaved. The idea, in any case, was not to adopt a rictus grin in the face of death. That approach is surely the 'cult of optimism at its worst': it doesn't work, and even if it did, it wouldn't be an appropriate response to loss. The Day of the Dead is not an effort to remake something horrifying as something unproblematic; it is, precisely, a rejection of such binary categories. What was happening in the cemetery was *memento mori* at its most powerful – a ritual that neither repressed thoughts of death, nor sought, in the manner of an American or British Hallowe'en, to render it saccharine and harmless. It was about letting death seep back into life.

'In our tradition,' observes the writer Victor Landa, who was raised in Mexico, 'people die three deaths. The first is when our bodies cease to function; when our hearts no longer beat of their own accord, when our gaze no longer has depth or weight, when the space we occupy slowly loses its meaning. The second death comes when the body is lowered into the ground . . . the third death, the most definitive death, is when there is no one left alive to remember us.' Death was omnipresent that night in the cemetery, and yet – precisely as a consequence of that – the third kind of death was absent. An entire town was remembering. And remembering, too, their own mortality, which differed from their dead relatives' only in the sense that it had not claimed them yet.

You need not engage in cemetery vigils to practise *memento mori*, however. You can start much smaller. The psychologist Russ Harris suggests a simple exercise: imagine you are eighty years old – assuming you're not eighty already, that is; if you are, you'll have to pick an older age – and then complete the sentences 'I wish I'd spent more time on . . . ' and 'I wish I'd spent less time on . . .'. This turns out to be a surprisingly effective way to achieve mortality awareness in short order. Things fall into place. It becomes far easier to follow Lauren Tillinghast's advice – to figure out what, specifically, you might do in order to focus on life's flavours, so as to improve your chances of reaching death having lived life as fully and as deeply as possible.

This kind of smaller habit may actually be the most powerful form of *memento mori*. For it is precisely through such mundane and unassuming rituals that we can best hope to enfold an awareness of death into the daily rhythms of life, and thus achieve something of Epicurus's calm rationality in the face of mortality. What lingered in my mind for months after Mexico, in any case, was not the loud celebration of death, though I had seen some of that in central Mexico City. Instead, it was the sense I had absorbed, in San Gregorio Atlapulco, of relaxing alongside mortality, of comfortably coexisting with it, of the companionship of life and death.

Before we left the village that night, some time before two in the morning, I noticed an elderly woman sitting alone on a folding chair near one of the cemetery's boundary walls. She was wrapped in a shawl and appeared to be talking softly to a headstone.

Tentatively, I approached her. Interrupting felt wrong, but she wasn't hostile; smiling, she nodded at the ledge beside the grave, inviting me to sit. So I sat.

The strains of the mariachi band drifted over from the other side of the cemetery. Some families, I noticed, had built small wood fires to keep warm; a few feet away, Francisco clapped his arms around himself in an effort to generate heat. I looked out over the cemetery, strewn with marigolds and crowded with huddled figures. Beyond its edges, no lights illuminated the blackness, but inside, the fires and the hundreds of flickering candles lent the night a kind of cosiness, despite the chill. The musicians carried on playing. Death was in the air, and all was well.

Negative Capability

IN DECEMBER 1817, THE poet John Keats, then twenty-two years old, went to see the annual Christmas pantomime at the Theatre Royal, in London's Drury Lane. Also in attendance was his friend, the critic Charles Wentworth Dilke, and as they strolled home, the two men fell into conversation – about writing, and specifically about the nature of literary genius. Somewhere between the theatre in Soho and his home in Hampstead, Keats was struck by a realisation, which he set down several days later in a letter to his brothers. That letter records what one Keats biographer has called 'a touchstone moment' in the history of literature:

> I had not a dispute but a disquisition, with Dilke on various subjects; several things dove-tailed in my mind, and at once it struck me what quality went to form a Man of Achievement, especially in Literature, and which Shakespeare possessed so enormously: I mean Negative Capability, that is, when a man is capable of being in uncertainties, mysteries, doubts, without any irritable reaching after fact and reason . . .

There is something both awe-inspiring and perhaps faintly irritating about a twenty-two-year-old not only capable of such insights, but capable of having them so casually, on the way home from the pantomime. For Keats, such observations had always come effortlessly and frequently, as in some sense they needed to; three years later, he was dead. He thought so little of 'negative capability', in fact, that he never used the phrase in writing again, thereby generously providing future literary scholars with the opportunity to write entire books dedicated to unpicking what he might have meant.

At this point in our journey along the negative path to happiness, however, the outline of what he was saying ought at least to sound familiar. Sometimes the most valuable of all talents is to be able *not* to seek resolution; to notice the craving for completeness or certainty or comfort, and *not* to feel compelled to follow where it leads. Keats thought this addiction to certainty and completion was Dilke's biggest flaw, and the poet's verdict on his friend neatly encapsulates a theme we've encountered many times already: 'He will never come at a truth so long as he lives,' Keats wrote, 'because he is always trying at it.' It was the trying – the 'irritable reaching' – that was the whole problem.

More loosely defined, 'negative capability' is really just another term for living in accordance with the 'backwards law' – and it might be a good label to describe the chief talent I kept discovering among the people I encountered in the course of researching this book. What they all shared was this same turn of mind, which I came to visualise as a sort of graceful mental dance step: a willingness to adopt an oblique stance towards one's own inner life; to pause and take a step back; to turn to face what others might flee from; and to realise that the shortest apparent route to a positive mood is rarely a sure path to a more profound kind of happiness. The phrase 'negative capability' also helps to clarify a subtle double meaning in the word 'negative'. It refers both to a set of skills that involve 'not-doing', as opposed to doing – a negative kind of capability – as well as to the fact that this skill involves confronting negative (as in 'unpleasant') thoughts, emotions, and situations.

The point here is not that negative capability is always superior to the positive kind. Optimism is wonderful; goals can sometimes be useful; even positive thinking and positive visualisation have their benefits. The problem is that we have developed the habit of chronically overvaluing positivity and the skills of 'doing' in how we think about happiness, and that we chronically under-value negativity and the 'not-doing' skills, such as resting in uncertainty or getting friendly towards failure. To use an old cliché of therapy-speak, we spend too much of our lives seeking 'closure'. Even those of us who mock such clichés are often motivated by a craving to put an end to uncertainty and anxiety, whether by convincing ourselves that the future is bright, or by resigning ourselves despondently to the expectation that it won't be. What we need more of, instead, is what the psychologist Paul Pearsall called 'openture'. Yes, this is an awkward neologism. But its very awkwardness is a reminder of the spirit that it expresses, which includes embracing imperfection and easing up on the search for neat solutions.

The various approaches we have explored here frequently contradict each other on the level of details; sometimes they seem so intrinsically paradoxical as practically to contradict themselves. But in this broader sense, they all embody 'negative capability'. For the Stoics, the realisation that we can often choose not to be distressed by events, even if we can't choose events themselves, is the foundation of tranquility. For the Buddhists, a willingness to observe the 'inner weather' of your thoughts and emotions is the key to understanding that they need not dictate your actions. Each of these is a different way of resisting the 'irritable reaching' after better circumstances or better thoughts and feelings. But negative capability need not involve embracing an ancient philosophical or religious tradition. It is also the skill you're exhibiting when you move forward with a project – or with life – in the absence of sharply defined goals; when you dare to inspect your failures; when you stop trying to eliminate feelings of insecurity; or when you put aside 'motivational' techniques in favour of actually getting things done.

You might choose, of course, to dedicate your life to Stoicism, like Keith Seddon in his wizard's cottage in Watford; you might undergo a completely life-transforming experience in the manner of Eckhart Tolle. But you can also treat these ideas as a toolkit, from which tools can be borrowed as necessary. Anyone can become somewhat Stoic, or a bit more Buddhist, or practise *memento mori* a little more frequently; unlike far too many self-help schemes, which purport to be comprehensive guides to life, the negative path to happiness isn't an all-or-nothing affair. True negative capability entails moderation and balance and refraining from too much effortful struggling – including in the practice of negative capability. 'Proficiency and the results of proficiency', wrote Aldous Huxley, 'come only to those who have learned the paradoxical art of doing and not doing, of combining relaxation with activity, of letting go as a person in order that the immanent and transcendent Unknown Quantity may take hold.'

And the end result of all of this? The chief benefit of 'openture', Paul Pearsall claimed, is not certitude or even calm or comfort as we normally think of them, but rather the 'strange, excited comfort [of] being presented with, and grappling with, the tremendous mysteries life offers'. Ultimately, what defines the 'cult of optimism' and the culture of positive thinking – even in its most mystically tinged, New Age forms – is that it abhors a mystery. It seeks to make things certain, to make happiness permanent and final. And yet this kind of happiness – even if you do manage to achieve it – is shallow and unsatisfying. The greatest benefit of negative capability—the true power of negative thinking—is that it lets the mystery back in.

One of the worst things about being a motivational speaker, or any other kind of advocate for the power of positive thinking, must be the constant pressure to seem upbeat: if anyone ever catches you scowling, or stressed, or feeling sorry for yourself – all very normal occurrences for anybody, of course – it threatens to undermine everything you stand for. Becoming an advocate for the power of negative thinking, as I gradually did, holds no such hazard. Bad moods are permitted. Still, the ultimate purpose of all these adventures in negativity was supposed to be happiness. So you'd be entitled to wonder whether the philosophies and psychological techniques I encountered actually made me any happier – and which of them, after all the travelling and the reporting was over, retained a place in my life. Did the negative path to happiness really work? To answer that question with a simple yes or no, or to offer up a list of ten surefire tips for negative-thinking success, would be to violate the ethos of the thing. 'Openture' surely demands that we resist such tempting certainties. But I can offer an interim status report.

I did not make it a regular habit to humiliate myself on public transport systems in major cities. Nor did I relocate to rural Mexico to live a life infused with death. So far I haven't even

been on another silent meditation retreat since my week in
Massachusetts. But in numerous smaller ways, a modest degree
of negative capability has become my daily practice. Few days
now go by without some occasion on which I'll deploy what I
have come to think of as the 'Stoic pause' – which is all that it
takes to remember that it's my judgment about the infuriating
colleague, or the heavy traffic, or the burned food, that is the
cause of my distress, not the situation itself. Even five or ten
minutes' *vipassana* meditation, meanwhile, which I manage most
mornings, is sufficient to feel as if I've applied a squirt of WD-40
to my mental machinery: for the rest of the day, problematic
thoughts and emotions slip by with far less friction. Eckhart Tolle's
deceptively simple-sounding question – 'Do you have a problem
right now?' – is a marvellous antidote to low-level stress. And I
certainly could never have finished writing this book without
Shoma Morita's insight that there's no need to 'get motivated' (or
Get Motivated!) before you get on and act. In friendships and in
my relationship with my girlfriend, I came to understand more
deeply that happiness and vulnerability are often the same thing.
And at least once a week, I have reason to call to mind Albert
Ellis's distinction between a very bad outcome and an absolutely
terrible one. Imagining worst-case scenarios is one of my greatest
sources of solace in life, actually. When you really try to answer,
rationally and in detail, the question 'What's the worst that could
happen?', the answer is sometimes pretty bad. But it is finitely
bad, rather than infinitely terrifying, so there is always a chance
of coping with it. Or at least I think there is. I'm acutely aware
that, during the time I spent exploring this perspective on life,
no great tragedies befell me, and my family and friends largely
thrived. Like a good Stoic, I tried to stay conscious of that, so as
to derive happiness from feeling gratitude for my good fortune.

But for me personally, the real test of these philosophies may lie in the future.

Already, though, I can see that where these techniques ultimately lead is to somewhere beyond 'techniques', to a different definition of happiness itself. The real revelation of the 'negative path' was not so much the path as the destination. Embracing negativity as a technique, in the end, really makes sense only if the happiness you're aiming for is one that can accommodate negative as well as positive emotions. The aforementioned Paul Pearsall, inventor of 'openture', spent a large part of his life waging a lonely battle of which John Keats would surely have approved: to get the concept of 'awe' accepted by the psychological establishment as one of the primary human emotions, alongside such standards as love, joy, anger, fear, and sadness. 'Unlike all the other emotions,' he argued, awe 'is all of our feelings rolled up into one intense one. You can't peg it as just happy, sad, afraid, angry, or hopeful. Instead, it's a matter of experiencing all these feelings and yet, paradoxically, experiencing no clearly identifiable, or at least any easily describable, emotion.' Awe, he writes, 'is like trying to assemble a complex jigsaw puzzle with pieces missing. There's never any closure in an awe-inspired life, only constant acceptance of the mysteries of life. We're never allowed to know when this fantastic voyage might end ... but that's part of the life-disorienting chaos that makes this choice so thrillingly difficult.' Which seems, to me, as good a description as any of a happiness that is worthy of the name. This kind of happiness has nothing to do with the easy superficialities of positive thinking – with the grinning insistence on optimism at all costs, or the demand that success be guaranteed. It involves much more difficulty – and also much more authenticity – than that.

The negative path to happiness, then, is a different kind of path. But it is also a path to a different kind of destination. Or maybe it makes more sense to say that the path is the destination? These things are excruciatingly hard to put into words, and the spirit of negative capability surely dictates that we do not struggle too hard to do so. 'A good traveller has no fixed plans,' says the Chinese sage Lao Tzu, 'and is not intent upon arriving.' There could be no better way to make the journey.

Acknowledgements

Writing this book afforded me many opportunities to test its arguments by confronting uncertainty, anxiety, the prospect of failure, and occasionally blind terror. I am grateful that I didn't have to rely on positive-thinking affirmations to deal with this, but benefited instead from the skills and time of some extraordinary people. I thank above all my remarkably Stoical editors, Nick Davies at Canongate and Mitzi Angel at Faber and Faber, whose talents vastly improved the text. Among many to whom I'm grateful at Canongate and FSG are Jamie Byng, Cate Cannon, Jaz Lacey-Campbell, Norah Perkins, Octavia Reeve, Angela Robertson and Jeff Seroy.

To say that I am indebted to my agent, Claire Conrad, and to her colleague Tina Bennett in New York, would be a comical understatement; their guidance and encouragement has been indispensable. Thanks to everyone at Janklow & Nesbit.

As well as all the named interviewees, I thank the following people for advice, contacts, comments on chapters, or places to write: Cyntia Barrera, Tor Butler-Cole, Jeremy Chatzky, Clar Ni Chonghaile, Catherine Crawford, Joanna Ebenstein, Kenneth Folk, Jeffy Gibbins, Julia Greenberg, Debbie Joffe-Ellis, Solana Larsen,

Jeff Mikkelson, Mac Montandon, Salvador Oguín and Joanna Tuckman. At a particularly nerve-wracking point in the process of writing this book, I was hugely fortunate to join the community at Brooklyn Creative League, without which I might never have completed it. At *The Guardian,* for assistance or forbearance in differing measures, I thank Emma Cook, Janine Gibson, Clare Margetson, Emily Wilson and Becky Gardiner. Ian Katz doesn't really do forbearance, but I'm grateful to him for much else.

Since this book grew initially from the topics explored in my column for *Guardian Weekend* magazine, its ultimate source, as with so many ideas, is the mind of Merope Mills, the magazine's editor. Others deserving of much thanks include Esther Addley, Anne Bernstein and my friends from York, of whom I'll unfairly single out here Adam Ormond, Rurik Bradbury, Abigail Gibson, Daniel Weyman, Sally Weyman, Rachael Burnett and Robin Parmiter. Emma Brockes continued her indispensable service as outboard brain, and was much more help than any motivational seminar.

I'm by no means sure that it was a wise happiness strategy on the part of Heather Chaplin to decide to embrace this project as wholeheartedly as she did, but it made an incalculable difference. For this and many other reasons I am ridiculously lucky to know her.

Notes

Some of the interviews in this book were originally conducted in the course of reporting assignments for *The Guardian*. In a small number of other cases, scenes have been compressed or dialogue reconstructed from memory.

1: On Trying Too Hard to Be Happy

3   *has been accused of denying access to reporters . . . Lowe denies the charge:* See Eric Anderson, 'Media Barred from Get Motivated! Seminar, at Least for Now', Albany *Times Union* blog 'The Buzz', 21 July 2009; and Tamara Lowe's comment, at blog.timesunion.com/business/media-barred-from -get-motivated-seminar-at-least-for-now/

5   *has filed for bankruptcy:* See Rebecca Cathcart, 'Crystal Cathedral Files for Bankruptcy', *New York Times*, 18 October 2010.

5   *increased economic growth does not necessarily make for happier societies:* This is an endlessly contested subject, with rival psychologists and economists constantly doing battle, and as ever it rests on contentious definitions of happiness. But one of the very biggest and most up-to-date reviews of the data, which found an absence of correlation in the long term between economic growth and improved wellbeing, is Richard Easterlin et al., 'The Happiness–Income Paradox Revisited', *Proceedings of the National Academy of Sciences* 107 (2010): 22463–8.

5   *increased personal income . . . doesn't make for happier people:* See previous note; and see also Daniel Kahneman et al., 'Would You Be Happier If You Were Richer? A Focusing Illusion', *Science* 312 (2006): 1908–10. And perhaps more to the point, it certainly seems to be the case that if you *set out* to

achieve material goals, you'll be less happy than those with other priorities: see Carol Nickerson et al., 'Zeroing in on the Dark Side of the American Dream', *Psychological Science* 14 (2003): 531–6.

5   *Nor does better education:* See for example Robert Witter et al., 'Education and Subjective Well-Being: A Meta-Analysis', *Educational Evaluation and Policy Analysis* 6 (1984): 165–73.

5   *Nor does an increased choice of consumer products:* The canonical resource on this is Barry Schwartz, *The Paradox of Choice* (New York: Ecco, 2003).

5   *Nor do bigger and fancier homes:* Robert H. Frank, 'How Not to Buy Happiness', *Daedalus* 133 (2004): 69–79.

5   *research strongly suggests they aren't usually much help:* One example is Gerald Haeffel, 'When Self-Help Is No Help: Traditional Cognitive Skills Training Does Not Prevent Depressive Symptoms in People Who Ruminate', *Behaviour Research and Therapy* 48 (2010): 152–7. To be fair, studies have shown some specific self-help books to have a beneficial effect, notably *Feeling Good* by David Burns – see Eric Stice et al., 'Randomized Trial of a Brief Depression Prevention Program: An Elusive Search for a Psychosocial Placebo Control Condition', *Behaviour Research and Therapy* 45 (2007): 863–76.

5   *the 'eighteen-month rule':* For more on this, see Steve Salerno, *Sham: How the Self-Help Movement Made America Helpless* (New York: Crown, 2005).

6   *venting your anger doesn't get rid of it:* Brad Bushman, 'Does Venting Anger Feed or Extinguish the Flame? Catharsis, Rumination, Distraction, Anger, and Aggressive Responding', *Personality and Social Psychology Bulletin* 28 (2002): 724–31.

9   *'when you try to stay on the surface of the water . . .':* Both quotations from Alan Watts, *The Wisdom of Insecurity* (New York: Vintage, 1951), 9.

9   *'the harder we try . . .':* Aldous Huxley, *Complete Essays 1939–1956* (Lanham, Maryland: Ivan R. Dee, 2002), 225.

9   *the 'cult of optimism', as the philosopher Peter Vernezze calls it:* Peter Vernezze, *Don't Worry, Be Stoic* (Lanham, Maryland: University Press of America, 2005): xx.

13 *one typical transcript:* Daniel Wegner, *White Bears and Other Unwanted Thoughts* (New York: Guilford Press, 1989), 3.

13 *he explained in one paper:* Daniel Wegner, 'How to Think, Say or Do Precisely the Worst Thing for Any Occasion', *Science* 325 (2009): 48.

14 *'Metacognition . . . occurs when thought takes itself as an object':* Wegner, *White Bears and Other Unwanted Thoughts*, 44.

14 *'Metathoughts are instructions . . .':* Ibid., 54.

15   *when experimental subjects are told of an unhappy event:* Ibid., 128–9; see
     also Daniel Wegner et al., 'Ironic Processes in the Mental Control of
     Mood and Mood-Related Thought', *Journal of Personality and Social
     Psychology* 65 (1993): 1093–1104.

15   *patients who were suffering from panic disorders:* Chris Adler et al.,
     'Relaxation-Induced Panic (RIP): When Resting Isn't Peaceful', *Integrative
     Psychiatry* 5 (1987): 94–100.

15   *Bereaved people who make the most effort to avoid feeling grief:* Wegner,
     White Bears and Other Unwanted Thoughts, 9, in reference to Erich
     Lindemann, 'Symptomatology and Management of Acute Grief', *American
     Journal of Psychiatry* 101 (1944): 141–8.

15   *people instructed not to think about sex:* Wegner, *White Bears and Other
     Unwanted Thoughts,* 149, in reference to Barclay Martin, 'Expression and
     Inhibition of Sex Motive Arousal in College Males', *Journal of Abnormal
     and Social Psychology* 68 (1964): 307–12.

16   *An additional twist was revealed in 2009:* Joanne Wood et al., 'Positive Self-
     Statements: Power for Some, Peril for Others', *Psychological Science* 20
     (2009): 860–6.

19   *'To the extent that positive thinking had become a business in itself':* Barbara
     Ehrenreich, *Bright-Sided* (New York: Metropolitan, 2009), 12.

21   *'There are lots of ways of being miserable':* Edith Wharton, 'The Last
     Asset', in *The Collected Stories of Edith Wharton* (New York: Carroll & Graf,
     2003), 65.

22   *'doing the presumably sensible thing is counterproductive':* Steven Hayes,
     'Hello Darkness: Discovering Our Values by Confronting Our Fears',
     Psychotherapy Networker 31 (2007): 46–52.

2: What Would Seneca Do?

25   *a speech he gave to executives of the investment bank Merrill Lynch:* See Jeanne
     Pugh, 'The Eternal Optimist', *St. Petersburg Times,* 8 June 1985.

26   *Healthy and happy people . . . generally have a less accurate, overly optimistic
     grasp:* The classic study on 'depressive realism' is Lauren Alloy and Lyn
     Abramson, 'Judgment of Contingency in Depressed and Nondepressed
     Students: Sadder but Wiser?', *Journal of Experimental Psychology* 108 (1979):
     441–85.

27   *a particularly high-achieving week at work:* Heather Barry Kappes and
     Gabriele Oettingen, 'Positive Fantasies about Idealized Futures Sap Energies',
     Journal of Experimental and Social Psychology 47 (2011): 719–29.

27   *Oettingen had some of the participants rendered mildly dehydrated:* Ibid.

29 *writes the scholar of Stoicism William Irvine:* In *A Guide to the Good Life: The Ancient Art of Stoic Joy* (New York: Oxford, 2008), Kindle edition.

30 *'Things do not touch the soul':* Marcus Aurelius, *The Meditations,* Book IV, Trans. George Long; electronic text available at classics.mit.edu/Antoninus /meditations.html

32 *'the single most valuable technique':* In William Irvine, *A Guide to the Good Life.*

33 *'Whenever you grow attached to something':* Quoted in William Stephens, 'Epictetus on How the Stoic Sage Loves', at puffin.creighton.edu/phil /Stephens/OSAP%20Epictetus%20on%20Stoic%20Love.htm

35 *'Set aside a certain number of days':* Moral Epistles to Lucilius, Trans. Richard Gummere (Cambridge: Harvard University Press, 1917), 119.

38 *'Constantly regard the universe as one living being':* Marcus Aurelius, *Meditations,* Book IV.

40 *'Never have I trusted Fortune':* Seneca, *The Consolation of Helvia,* Trans. Moses Hadas (New York: Norton, 1968), 111–12.

41 *'Do not despise death':* Marcus Aurelius, *Meditations,* Book IX.

42 *'The cucumber is bitter? Put it down':* Marcus Aurelius, *Meditations,* Book VIII; the translation here is by Arthur Loat Farquharson (Oxford: Clarendon, 1944).

44 *America's psychologists had voted him the second most influential:* See Michael Kaufman, 'Albert Ellis, Influential Figure in Modern Psychology, Dies at 93', *New York Times,* 24 July 2007.

45 *'Whereupon thirty got up and walked away':* Myrtle Heery, 'An Interview with Albert Ellis', www.psychotherapy.net/interview/Albert_Ellis

46 *'Nobody took out a stiletto':* Ibid.

47 *'because . . . when you insist that an undesirable event is awful':* Albert Ellis, *How to Make Yourself Happy and Remarkably Less Disturbable* (Atascadero, California: Impact, 1999), 60.

3: The Storm Before the Calm

51 *immediately collapse onto the ground:* This anecdote comes from Rick Fields, *How the Swans Came to the Lake: A Narrative History of Buddhism in America* (Boston: Shambhala, 1992), 252.

52 *'Fall, hands a-clasped':* See Jack Kerouac, *Pomes All Sizes* (San Francisco: City Lights, 1992), 96.

52 *one Kerouac biographer:* Ann Charters, *Kerouac: A Biography* (New York: Macmillan, 1994), 219.

62 *'One realises . . . that one's brain is constantly chattering':* J. Krishnamurti,

'Dialogue at Los Alamos', March 1984; available at www.jkrishnamurti.org
/krishnamurti-teachings/print.php?tid=1588&chid=1285

64   *a series of experiments conducted in 2009*: For details, and for Fadel Zeidan's
     comments, see University of North Carolina at Charlotte release, 'Brief
     Training in Meditation May Help Manage Pain, Study Shows', at www
     .sciencedaily.com/releases/2009/11/091110065909.htm, and Fadel Zeidan et
     al., 'The Effects of Brief Mindfulness Meditation Training on Experimentally
     Induced Pain', *The Journal of Pain* 11 (2010): 199–209.

65   *In a related experiment by Zeidan's team:* See Fadel Zeidan et al., 'Brain
     Mechanisms Supporting the Modulation of Pain by Mindfulness Meditation',
     Journal of Neuroscience 31 (2011): 5540–8.

67   *'If we get the right emotion'*: From a talk at the TED conference by Tony
     Robbins, viewable online at www.ted.com/talks/tony_robbins_asks_why
     _we_do_what_we_do.html

68   *The author Julie Fast:* See Julie Fast, *Get It Done When You're Depressed*
     (New York: Alpha Books, 2008).

69   *'Inspiration is for amateurs'*: Quoted in Julie Burstein and Kurt Andersen,
     Spark: How Creativity Works (New York: HarperCollins, 2011), 13.

70   *'People . . . think that they should'*: Shoma Morita, *Morita Therapy and the
     True Nature of Anxiety-Based Disorders*, Trans. Akihisa Kondo (Albany:
     State University of New York Press, 1998), 53.

70   *'Many western therapeutic methods focus'*: See James Hill, 'Morita Therapy',
     at www.moritaschool.com/content/morita-therapy.

73   *'Clear mind is like the full moon in the sky'*: Stephen Mitchell, Ed., *Dropping
     Ashes on the Buddha: The Teaching of Zen Master Seung Sahn* (New York:
     Grove, 1994), 51–2.

4: Goal Crazy

75   *In 1996, a twenty-eight-year-old from Indiana*: My account of Christopher
     Kayes's travels, his account of the 1996 Everest disaster, and his interpreta-
     tion of the 1963 Everest study, along with quotes from Ed Viesturs, James
     Lester, Beck Weathers and others are drawn from an interview with Kayes
     and from his fascinating book *Destructive Goal Pursuit: The Mount Everest
     Disaster* (New York: Palgrave Macmillan, 2006).

80   *a largely forgotten psychology study:* My primary source is Christopher
     Kayes, *Destructive Goal Pursuit*, but the study in question is detailed in
     James Leste, 'Wrestling with the Self on Mount Everest', *Journal of
     Humanistic Psychology* 23 (1983): 31–41.

84   *a journalist from the technology magazine* Fast Company: Lawrence Tabak,

'If Your Goal Is Success, Don't Consult These Gurus', *Fast Company*, 18 December 2007.

85 *'Consider any individual at any period of his life'*: Alexis de Tocqueville, *Democracy in America*, Vol. 2, Trans. George Lawrence (New York: HarperCollins, 2007), 369.

86 *The psychologist Dorothy Rowe argues:* In Tim Lott, 'Why Uncertainty Is Good for You', *The Sunday Times*, 24 May 2009.

87 *Here are the words of one blogger:* See David Cain, 'How to Get Comfortable Not Knowing', at www.raptitude.com/2009/06/how-to-get-comfortable-not-knowing

87 *the economist Colin Camerer and three of his colleagues:* Colin Camerer et al., 'Labor Supply of New York City Cabdrivers: One Day at a Time', *Quarterly Journal of Economics* 112 (1997): 407–41.

89 *a 2009 paper with a heavy-handed pun for its title:* Lisa Ordóñez et al., 'Goals Gone Wild: The Systematic Side Effects of Over-Prescribing Goal Setting', *Academy of Management Perspectives* 23 (2009): 6–16.

90 *One illuminating example of the problem:* My account of GM's 'twenty-nine' campaign is drawn from Sean Cole, 'It's Not Always Good to Create Goals', from the website of the American Public Media radio show Marketplace, accessible at www.marketplace.org/topics/life/its-not-always-good-create-goals, and Drake Bennett, 'Ready, Aim . . . Fail', *Boston Globe*, 15 March 2009.

91 *Edwin Locke and Gary Latham's response:* Edwin Locke and Gary Latham, 'Has Goal Setting Gone Wild, or Have Its Attackers Abandoned Good Scholarship?', *Academy of Management Perspectives* 23 (2009): 17–23.

93 *'When we try to pick out any thing by itself':* John Muir, *My First Summer in the Sierra* (New York: Houghton Mifflin, 1911), 211.

93 *'The continued existence of complex interactive systems':* Gregory Bateson, *Steps to an Ecology of Mind* (Chicago: University of Chicago Press, 1972), 124.

94 *'I'm not sure if my goals drove me':* Steve Shapiro, *Goal-Free Living* (Hoboken, New Jersey: Wiley, 2006), xii.

95 *In survey research he commissioned:* Steve Shapiro, *Goal-Free Living*, v.

96 *A few years ago, the researcher Saras Sarasvathy:* Information and quotations about effectuation come primarily from Leigh Buchanan, 'How Great Entrepreneurs Think', *Inc. Magazine*, February 2011; and the website www.effectuation.org.

99 *'The quest for certainty blocks the search for meaning':* Erich Fromm, *Man for Himself* (New York: Macmillan, 1947), 45.

99 *'To be a good human':* In Bill Moyers, *A World of Ideas* (New York: Doubleday, 1989), 448.

5: Who's There?

102 *'a slow movement at first'*: All quotations from Eckhart Tolle are drawn either from my meeting with him or from his books *The Power of Now* and *A New Earth*. See Oliver Burkeman, 'The Bedsit Epiphany', *Guardian*, 11 April 2009; Eckhart Tolle, *The Power of Now* (Novato, California: New World Library, 1999) and *A New Earth* (New York: Dutton, 2005).

105 *'supremely powerful and cunning'*: This and following quotes are from René Descartes, *Meditations on First Philosophy*, Trans. Michael Moriarty (Oxford: Oxford University Press, 2008), 16.

106 *'A viewer of* The Matrix': Christopher Grau, Ed., *Philosophers Explore the Matrix* (New York: Oxford University Press, 2005), 13.

108 *'For my part, when I enter most intimately'*: David Hume, *An Enquiry Concerning Human Understanding and Selections from a Treatise of Human Nature*, Ed. Thom Chittom (New York: Barnes and Noble, 2004), 200.

108 no *'centre in the brain'*: Quoted in Julian Baggini, 'The Blurred Reality of Humanity', *Independent*, 21 March 2011.

109 *As the psychologist Michael Gazzaniga has demonstrated*: See Michael Gazzaniga, *The Ethical Brain* (New York: HarperCollins, 2006), 149.

117 *claims Paul Hauck*: Paul Hauck, *Overcoming the Rating Game: Beyond Self-Love, Beyond Self-Esteem* (Louisville, Kentucky: Westminster John Knox Press, 1992), 46.

118 *adapted here from the work of . . . Alan Watts*: All quotations from Alan Watts, *The Wisdom of Insecurity* (New York: Vintage, 1951).

6: The Safety Catch

127 *'a pretty effective spear'*: All quotations from Bruce Schneier come from my interview with him and from his essay 'The Psychology of Security'. See Oliver Burkeman, 'Heads in the Clouds', *Guardian*, 1 December 2007; and Bruce Schneier, 'The Psychology of Security', accessible at www.schneier.com/essay-155.html

130 *the 2020 Project . . . published a report*: See www.dni.gov/nic/NIC_global trend2020_s4.html

130 *'the feeling that we live in a time of unusual insecurity'*: Alan Watts, *The Wisdom of Insecurity* (New York: Vintage, 1951), 14.

131 *'As a matter of fact'*: Ibid., 15.

134 *'To be vulnerable . . . is to be without defensive armour'*: Quoted in Susan Schwartz Senstad, 'The Wisdom of Vulnerability'; available at voicedialogue.org/articles-b/Wisdom_Of_Vulnerability.pdf

134 *'You can't selectively numb emotion'*: From a talk at the TED conference by Brené Brown, viewable online at www.ted.com/talks/brene_brown_on _vulnerability.html

135 *'To love at all is to be vulnerable'*: Quoted in Vincent Genovesi, *In Pursuit of Love: Catholic Morality and Human Sexuality* (Collegeville, Minneapolis: Liturgical Press, 1996), 28.

135 *'The truth that many people never understand'*: Thomas Merton, *The Seven Storey Mountain* (New York: Harcourt, 1948), 91.

135 *'Becoming a Buddhist'*: Quoted in Helen Tworkov, 'No Right, No Wrong: An Interview with Pema Chödrön', *Tricycle*, Fall 1993.

136 *'Things are not permanent'*: Ibid.

140 *'It's clear that poverty has crippled Kibera'*: From Jean-Pierre Larroque, 'Of Crime and Camels', blog post at mediaforsocialchange.org/blog/of-crime -and-camels/ 22 July 2001

140 *'I find it so inspiring when you see people'*: See 'Colleen "Inspired" by Poor People', unbylined article at www.metro.co.uk/showbiz/22368-coleen -inspired-by-poor-people

141 *International surveys of happiness:* All World Values Survey data is accessible at www.worldvaluessurvey.org. Also see, for example, 'Nigeria Tops Happiness Survey', unbylined BBC News article, 2 October 2003, at news .bbc.co.uk/2/hi/3157570.stm

141 *Survey data from the Afrobarometer project:* A good overview of this research is Carol Graham and Matthew Hoover, 'Poverty and Optimism in Africa: Adaptation or Survival?', prepared for the Gallup Positive Psychology Summit, October 2006, accessible at www.brookings.edu/views/papers /graham/20061005ppt.pdf

141 *According to mental health researchers:* The study is by the World Health Organization World Mental Health Survey Consortium, entitled 'Prevalence, Severity, and Unmet Need for Treatment of Mental Disorders in the World Health Organization World Mental Health Surveys', and was reported in 'Global Study Finds Mental Illness Widespread', unbylined Associated Press report, 7 July 2004.

145 *'It is simply self-evident'*: Alan Watts, *The Wisdom of Insecurity*, 16.

7: The Museum of Failure

155 *As the journalist Neil Steinberg has noted:* Neil Steinberg, *Complete and Utter Failure* (New York: Doubleday, 1994), 31.

159 *'top 50 per cent of safe drivers'*: Ola Svenson, 'Are We All Less Risky and More Skillful Than Our Fellow Drivers?', *Acta Psychologica* 47 (1981): 143–8.

159 *A fascinating series of studies of working scientists:* See, for example, Kevin Dunbar, 'Scientific Creativity' from *The Encyclopedia of Creativity,* Ed. Steven Pritzker and Mark Runco (Waltham, Massachusetts: Academic Press, 1999): 1379–84; available at www.utsc.utoronto.ca/~dunbarlab /pubpdfs/DunbarCreativityEncyc99.pdf

160 *'If you're a scientist and you're doing an experiment':* From a PopTech conference talk by Kevin Dunbar, 'Kevin Dunbar on Unexpected Science', accessible online at poptech.org/popcasts/kevin_dunbar_on_unexpected _science

160 *As he explained in an interview with* Wired: See Jonah Lehrer, 'Accept Defeat: The Neuroscience of Screwing Up', *Wired,* January 2010.

163 *'Think about it':* All quotations from Jerker Denrell are from my interview with him or from Jerker Denrell, 'Vicarious Learning, Undersampling of Failure, and the Myths of Management', *Organization Science* 2003 (14): 227–43; and Jerker Denrell, 'Selection Bias and the Perils of Benchmarking', *Harvard Business Review,* April 2005.

166 *research into media commentators who make predictions:* Jerker Denrell and Christina Fang, 'Predicting the Next Big Thing: Success as a Signal of Poor Judgment', *Management Science* 56 (2010): 1653–67; see also Joe Keohane, 'That Guy Who Called the Big One? Don't Listen to Him', *Boston Globe,* 9 January 2011.

170 *'The dome has a clear brand':* Ros Coward, 'Wonderful, Foolish Dome', *Guardian,* 12 March 2001.

171 *'Musing over failure is not a particularly American activity':* Neil Steinberg, *Complete and Utter Failure,* 3.

173 *'Downfall . . . brings us to the ground':* Natalie Goldberg, *The Great Failure* (New York: HarperCollins, 2005), 1–2.

8: Memento Mori

180 *"At bottom . . . no one believes':* Sigmund Freud, *Reflections on War and Death* (New York: Moffat Yard, 1918), Google Books digitised version, 41.

183 *'Making a killing in business':* Sam Keen, Foreword to Ernest Becker, *The Denial of Death* (New York: Free Press, 1973), Kindle edition.

184 *One typical set of terror management experiments:* The Rutgers experiments are Mark Landau et al., 'Deliver Us from Evil: The Effects of Mortality Salience and Reminders of 9/11 on Support for President George W. Bush', *Personal and Social Psychology Bulletin* 30 (2004): 1136–50.

185 *Christians show more negativity towards Jews:* Jeff Greenberg et al., 'Evidence for Terror Management Theory II: The Effect of Mortality Salience on

Reactions to Those Who Threaten or Bolster the Cultural Worldview', *Journal of Personality and Social Psychology* 58 (1990): 308–18.

185 *Moralistic people become more moralistic:* Abram Rosenblatt et al., 'Evidence for Terror Management Theory: I. The Effects of Mortality Salience on Reactions to Those Who Violate or Uphold Cultural Values', *Journal of Personality and Social Psychology* 57 (1989): 681–90.

185 *more intense reactions of disgust:* Jamie Goldenberg et al., 'I Am *Not* an Animal: Mortality Salience, Disgust, and the Denial of Human Creatureliness', *Journal of Experimental Psychology* 130 (2001): 427–35.

186 *one such paper states:* Ibid.

186 *sympathetic to the theory of 'intelligent design':* Jessica Tracy et al., 'Death and Science: The Existential Underpinnings of Belief in Intelligent Design and Discomfort with Evolution', *PLoS One* 6 (2011): e17349.

187 *'Well,' Becker told him:* See Sam Keen, 'How a Philosopher Dies'; available online at samkeen.com/interviews-by-sam/interviews-by-sam/earnest -becker-how-a-philosopher-dies/

187 *'Gradually, reluctantly':* Sam Keen, Foreword to Ernest Becker, *The Denial of Death.*

190 *as the contemporary philosopher Thomas Nagel points out:* All Nagel quotations are from 'Death' in *Mortal Questions* (New York: Cambridge University Press, 1979), 1–10.

193 *Jean-Paul Sartre:* Quoted in Irvin Yalom, *Staring at the Sun* (San Francisco: Jossey-Bass, 2008), Kindle edition.

194 *also one of the happiest:* Two examples are an Ipsos Global survey that put Mexico third, detailed in 'World Is Happier Place Than in 2007 – Poll', unbylined report, Reuters, 10 February 2012; and the 2010 findings of the Happiness Barometer project, sponsored by the Coca-Cola Company in association with Complutense University of Madrid, which put Mexico in first place: see www.thecoca-colacompany.com/presscenter/happiness_barometer.pdf

198 *'to ask her to "protect me tonight . . ."':* Quoted in Elizabeth Fullerton, 'Booming Death Cult Draws Mexican Gangsters, Police', Reuters, 13 May 2004.

202 *'In our tradition':* Quoted in Judy King, 'Los Dias de los Muertos', in *Mexico Connect,* accessible at www.mexconnect.com/articles/1427-los-dias-de-los -muertos-the-days-of-the-dead

Epilogue: Negative Capability

205 *'a touchstone moment':* Steven Edward Jones, *Satire and Romanticism* (New York: Palgrave Macmillan, 2000), 196.

205 *'I had not a dispute but a disquisition':* Quoted ibid., 195–6.

206 *'He will never come at a truth'*: Quoted in Jacob Wigod, 'Negative Capability and Wise Passiveness', *PMLA* 67 (1952): 383–90.

207 *'openture'*: All Paul Pearsall quotations are from *Awe: The Delights and Dangers of Our Eleventh Emotion* (Deerfield Beach, Florida: Health Communications, 2007).

208 *'Proficiency and the results of proficiency'* Aldous Huxley, *Complete Essays 1939–1956* (Lanham, Maryland: Ivan R. Dec, 2002), 225.

212 *'A good traveller has no fixed plans'*: Lao-tzu, *Tao Te Ching: A New English Version*, translated by Stephen Mitchell (New York: HarperPerennial, 1991), 27.

Index

LOOK HOMEWARD, ANGEL

LOOK HOMEWARD,
ANGEL

A Story of the Buried Life

by

THOMAS WOLFE

With An Introduction

by MAXWELL E. PERKINS

CHARLES SCRIBNER'S SONS

New York

ACKNOWLEDGMENT

The essay on Thomas Wolfe by Maxwell E. Perkins is reprinted
from the *Harvard Library Bulletin*, Vol. I, No. 3 (Autumn
1947), by permission of the President and Fellows of Harvard
College.

TO A. B.

"Then, as all my soules bee,
Emparadis'd in you, (in whom alone
I understand, and grow and see,)
The rafters of my body, bone
Being still with you, the Muscle, Sinew, and Veine,
Which tile this house, will come againe."

THOMAS WOLFE[1]

When in the spring of 1947 William B. Wisdom, of New Orleans, presented to the Harvard College Library his distinguished collection of Thomas Wolfe, it was at once apparent that the person above all others to provide an introduction to it was Maxwell E. Perkins, '07, of Charles Scribner's Sons, editor of Wolfe's first novels, and allied to Wolfe by the closest ties of profession and of friendship. Mr. Perkins gladly consented to prepare an article; he was engaged upon it at his sudden death on 17 June 1947. Although the article was to have been expanded by another three thousand words, with a more detailed discussion of Wolfe as a person, as it stands it has the effect of a self-contained statement. It is published as the last writing of Maxwell Perkins and as an expression of the memorial which he planned to compose to Thomas Wolfe.

I think that there is not in any one place so nearly complete a collection of an author's writings and records as that of Thomas Wolfe's now in the Harvard Library. When he died on that sad day in September 1938, when war was impending, or soon after that, I learned that I was his executor and that he had actually left little—as he would have thought, and as it seemed then—besides his manuscripts. It was my obligation to dispose of them to the advantage of his beneficiaries and his memory, and though the times were bad, and Wolfe had not then been recognized as what he now is, I could have sold them commercially, piecemeal, through dealers, for more money than they ever brought. I was determined that this literary estate should remain a unit, available to

---

[1] The article is printed in the form received from Mr. Perkins's secretary two days after his death, with some slight modifications in punctuation and with the addition of a title. [Note by the Editor of the *Harvard Library Bulletin*.]

writers and students, and I tried to sell it as such; but at that time, with war clouds gathering and soon bursting, I could find no adequate buyer.

Then Aline Bernstein, to whom Wolfe had given the manuscript of *Look Homeward, Angel,* sold it by auction for the relief of her people in misfortune, on the understanding that it would be given to Harvard. Not long after that William B. Wisdom, who had recognized Wolfe as a writer of genius on the publication of the *Angel,* and whose faith in him had never wavered, offered to purchase all of his manuscripts and records. He had already accumulated a notable collection of Wolfiana. His correspondence showed me that he thought as I did—that the point of supreme importance was that these records and writings should not be scattered to the four winds, that they be kept intact. And so the whole great packing case of material—letters, bills, documents, notebooks and manuscripts—went to him on the stipulation, which I never need have asked for, that he would will it all to one institution. Since *Look Homeward, Angel* was already in Harvard, since Tom Wolfe had loved the reading room of the Library where, as he so often told me, he devoured his hundreds of books and spent most of his Harvard years, Mr. Wisdom made a gift of all this to Harvard. And there it now is.

Though I had worked as an editor with Thomas Wolfe on two huge manuscripts, *Look Homeward, Angel* and *Of Time and the River,* I was astonished on that Spring evening of 1935 when Tom, about to sail for England, brought to our house on East 49th Street, because Scribner's was closed, the huge packing case containing all his literary material. Tom and I and the taxi man carried it in and set it down. Then Tom said to the man, 'What is your name?' He said, 'Lucky.' 'Lucky!' said Tom—I think it was perhaps an Americanization of some Italian name—and grasped his hand. It seemed a good omen. We three had done something together. We were together for that moment. We all shook hands. But for days, that huge packing case blocked our hall, until I got it removed to Scribner's.

The first time I heard of Thomas Wolfe I had a sense of foreboding. I who love the man say this. Every good thing that comes is accompanied by trouble. It was in 1928 when Madeleine Boyd, a literary agent, came in. She talked of several manuscripts which did not much interest me, but frequently interrupted herself to tell of a wonderful novel about an American boy. I several times said to her, 'Why don't you bring it in here, Madeleine?' and she seemed to evade the question. But finally she said, 'I will bring it, if you promise to read every word of it.' I did promise, but she told me other things that made me realize that Wolfe was a turbulent spirit, and that we were in for turbulence. When the manuscript came, I was fascinated by the first scene where Eugene's father, Oliver W. Gant, with his brother, two little boys, stood by a roadside in Pennsylvania and saw a division of Lee's Army on the march to Gettysburg.

But then there came some ninety-odd pages about Oliver Gant's life in Newport News, and Baltimore, and elsewhere. All this was what Wolfe had heard, and had no actual association with which to reconcile it, and it was inferior to the first episode, and in fact to all the rest of the book. I was turned off to other work and gave the manuscript to Wallace Meyer, thinking, 'Here is another promising novel that probably will come to nothing.' Then Meyer showed me that wonderful night scene in the cafe where Ben was with the Doctors, and Horse Hines, the undertaker, came in. I dropped everything and began to read again, and all of us were reading the book simultaneously, you might say, including John Hall Wheelock, and there never was the slightest disagreement among us as to its importance.

After some correspondence between me and Wolfe, and between him and Madeleine Boyd, from which we learned how at the October Fair in Germany he had been almost beaten to death—when I realized again that we had a Moby Dick to deal with—Wolfe arrived in New York and stood in the doorway of my boxstall of an office leaning against the door jamb. When I looked up and saw his wild hair and bright countenance—although he was so altogether different physically—I thought of Shelley. *He* was fair, but his hair was wild, and his face was bright and his head disproportionately small.

We then began to work upon the book and the first thing we did, to give it unity, was to cut out that wonderful scene it began with and the ninety-odd pages that followed, because it seemed to me, and he agreed, that the whole tale should be unfolded through the memories and senses of the boy, Eugene, who was born in Asheville. We both thought that the story was compassed by that child's realization; that it was life and the world as he came to realize them. When he had tried to go back into the life of his father before he arrived in Asheville, without the inherent memory of events, the reality and the poignance were diminished—but for years it was on my conscience that I had persuaded Tom to cut out that first scene of the two little boys on the roadside with Gettysburg impending.

And then what happened? In *Of Time and the River* he brought the scene back to greater effect when old Gant was dying on the gallery of the hospital in Baltimore and in memory recalled his olden days. After that occurred I felt much less anxiety in suggesting cuts: I began then to realize that nothing Wolfe wrote was ever lost, that omissions from one book were restored in a later one. An extreme example of this is the fact that the whole second half of *The Web and the Rock* was originally intended to be the concluding episode in *Of Time and the River*. But most, and perhaps almost all, of those early incidents of Gant's life were worked into *The Web and the Rock* and *You Can't Go Home Again*.

I had realized, for Tom had prefaced his manuscript with a statement to that effect, that *Look Homeward, Angel* was autobiographical, but I had come to think of it as being so in the sense that *David Copperfield* is, or *War and Peace,* or *Pendennis*. But when we were working together, I suddenly saw that it was often almost literally autobiographical—that these people in it were his people. I am sure my face took on a look of alarm, and Tom saw it and he said, 'But Mr. Perkins, you don't understand. I think these people are *great* people and that they should be told about.' He was right. He had written a great book, and it had to be taken substantially as it was. And in truth, the extent of cutting in that book has somehow come to be greatly exaggerated. Really, it was more a matter of reorganization. For instance, Tom had that wonderful episode when Gant came back from his far-wandering and rode in early morning on the trolley car through the town and heard about who had died and who had been born and saw all the scenes that were so familiar to Tom or Eugene, as the old trolley rumbled along. This was immediately followed by an episode of a similar kind where Eugene, with his friends, walked home from school through the town of Asheville. That was presented in a Joycean way, but it was the same sort of thing—some one going through the town and through his perceptions revealing it to the reader. By putting these episodes next to each other the effect of each was diminished, and I think we gave both much greater value by separating them. We did a great deal of detailed cutting, but it was such things as that I speak of that constituted perhaps the greater part of the work.

Of Time and the River was a much greater struggle for Tom. Eventually, I think it was on Thanksgiving Day 1933, he brought me in desperation about two feet of typescript. The first scene in this was the platform of the railroad station in Asheville when Eugene was about to set out for Harvard, and his family had come to see him off. It must have run to about 30,000 words and I cut it to perhaps 10,000 and showed it to Tom. He approved it. When you are waiting for a train to come in, there is suspense. Something is going to happen. You must, it seemed to me, maintain that sense of suspense and you can't to the extent of 30,000 words. There never was any cutting that Tom did not agree to. He knew that cutting was necessary. His whole impulse was to utter what he felt and he had no time to revise and compress.

So then we began a year of nights of work, including Sundays, and every cut, and change, and interpolation, was argued about and about. The principle that I was working on was that this book, too, got its unity and its form through the senses of Eugene, and I remember how, if I had had my way, we should, by sticking to that principle, have lost one of the most wonderful episodes Wolfe ever wrote—the death of Gant. One night we agreed that certain transitions should be written in, but instead of doing them Wolfe brought on the next night some five thousand words about Eugene's sister in Asheville when her father was ill, and a doctor there and a nurse. I said, 'Tom, this is all outside the story, and you know it. Eugene was not there, he was in Cambridge; all of this was outside his perception and knowledge at the time.' Tom agreed with me, but the next night, he brought me another five thousand words or so which got up into the death of Gant. And then I realized I was wrong, even if right in theory. What he was doing was too good to let any rule of form impede him.

It is said that Tolstoy never willingly parted with the manuscript of *War and Peace*. One could imagine him working on it all through his life. Certainly Thomas Wolfe never willingly parted from the proofs of *Of Time and the River*. He sat brooding over them for weeks in the Scribner library and not reading. John Wheelock read them and we sent them to the printer and told Tom it had been done. I could believe that otherwise he might have clung to them to the end.

He dedicated that book to me in most extravagant terms. I never saw the dedication until the book was published and though I was most grateful for it, I had forebodings when I heard of his intention. I think it was that dedication that threw him off his stride and broke his magnificent scheme. It gave shallow people the impression that Wolfe could not function as a writer without collaboration, and one critic even used some such phrases as, 'Wolfe and Perkins—Perkins and Wolfe, what way is that to write a novel.' Nobody with the slightest comprehension of the nature of a writer could accept such an assumption. No writer could possibly tolerate the assumption, which perhaps Tom almost himself did, that he was dependent as a writer upon anyone else. He had to prove to himself and to the world that this was not so.

And that was the fundamental reason that he turned to another publisher. If he had not—but by the time he did it was plain that he had to tell, in the medium of fiction and through the transmutation of his amazing imagination, the story of his own life—he never would have broken his own great plan by distorting Eugene Gant into George Webber. That was a horrible mistake. I think Edward Aswell, of Harper & Brothers, agrees with me in this, but when the manuscript that came to form *The Web and the Rock* and *You Can't Go Home Again* got to him to work on, and in some degree to me, as Wolfe's executor, Tom was dead, and things had to be taken as they were.

The trouble began after the publication of *Of Time and the River,* which the reviewers enormously praised—but many of them asserted that Wolfe could only write about himself, that he could not see the world or anything objectively, with detachment—that he was always autobiographical. Wolfe was extremely sensitive to criticism, for all his tremendous faith in his genius as an obligation put upon him to fulfill. One day when I lived on East 49th Street near Second Avenue, and he on First Avenue, just off the corner of 49th, I met him as I was going home. He said he wanted to talk to me, as we did talk every evening about that time, and we went into the Waldorf. He referred to the criticisms against him, and said that he wanted to write a completely objective, unautobiographical book, and that it would show how strangely different everything is from what a person expects it to be. One might say that he was thinking of the theme that has run through so many great books, such as *Pickwick Papers* and *Don Quixote,* where a man, young or old, goes hopefully out into the world slap into the face of outrageous reality. He was going to put on the title page what was said by Prince Andrei, in *War and Peace,* after his first battle, when the praise fell upon those who had done nothing and blame almost fell upon one who had done everything. Prince Andrei, who saved the battery commander who most of all had held back the French from the blame that Little Tushin would have accepted, walked out with him into the night. Then as Tushin left, Tolstoy said, 'Prince Andrei looked up at the stars and sighed; everything was so different from what he thought it was going to be.'

Tom was in a desperate state. It was not only what the critics said that made him wish to write objectively, but that he knew that what he had written had given great pain even to those he loved the most. The conclusion of our talk was that if he could write such an objective book on this theme within a year, say, to the extent of perhaps a hundred thousand words, it might be well to do it. It was this that turned him to George Webber, but once he began on that he really and irresistibly resumed the one story he was destined to write, which was that of himself, or Eugene Gant.

And so, the first half of *The Web and the Rock,* of which there is only a typescript, is a re-telling in different terms of *Look Homeward, Angel.* Wolfe was diverted from his natural purpose—and even had he lived, what could have been done? Some of his finest writing is that first half of *The Web and the Rock.* Could anybody have just tossed it out?

But if Tom had held to his scheme and completed the whole story of his life as transmuted into fiction through his imagination, I think the accusation that he had no sense of form could not have stood. He wrote one long story, 'The Web of Earth,' which had perfect form, for all its intricacy. I remember saying to him, 'Not one word of this should be changed.' One might say that as his own physical dimensions were huge so was his conception of a book. He had one book to write about a vast, sprawling, turbulent land—America—as perceived by Eugene Gant. Even when he was in Europe, it was of America he thought. If he had not been diverted and had lived to complete it, I think it would have had the form that was suited to the subject.

His detractors say he could only write about himself, but all that he wrote of was transformed by his imagination. For instance, in *You Can't Go Home Again* he shows the character Foxhall Edwards at breakfast. Edwards's young daughter enters 'as swiftly and silently as a ray of light.' She is very shy and in a hurry to get to school. She tells of a theme she has written on Walt Whitman and what the teacher said of Whitman. When Edwards urges her not to hurry and makes various observations, she says, 'Oh, Daddy, you're so funny!' What Tom did was to make one unforgettable little character out of three daughters of Foxhall Edwards.

He got the ray of light many years ago when he was with me in my house in New Canaan, Connecticut, and one daughter, at the age of about eight or ten, came in and met this gigantic stranger. After she was introduced she fluttered all about the room in her embarrassment, but radiant, like a sunbeam. Then Tom was present when another daughter, in Radcliffe, consulted me about a paper she was writing on Whitman, but he put this back into her school days. The third, of which he composed a single character, was the youngest, who often did say, partly perhaps, because she was not at ease when Tom was there, 'Oh, Daddy, you're so silly.' That is how Tom worked. He created something new and something meaningful through a transmutation of what he saw, heard, and realized.

I think no one could understand Thomas Wolfe who had not seen or properly imagined the place in which he was born and grew up. Asheville, North Carolina, is encircled by mountains. The trains wind in and out through labyrinths of passes. A boy of Wolfe's imagination imprisoned there could think that what was beyond was all wonderful—different from what it was where there was not for him enough of anything. Whatever happened, Wolfe would have been what he was. I remember on the day of his death saying to his sister Mabel that I thought it amazing in an American family that one of the sons who wanted to be a writer should have been given the support that was given Tom, and that they all deserved great credit for that. She said it didn't matter, that nothing could have prevented Tom from doing what he did.

That is true, but I think that those mountainous walls which his imagination vaulted gave him the vision of an America with which his books are fundamentally concerned. He often spoke of the artist in America—how the whole color and character of the country was completely new—never interpreted; how in England, for instance, the writer inherited a long accretion of accepted expression from which he could start. But Tom would say—and he had seen the world—'who has ever made you know the color of an American box car?' Wolfe was in those mountains—he tells of the train whistles at night—the trains were winding their way out into the great world where it seemed to the boy there was everything desirable, and vast, and wonderful.

It was partly that which made him want to see everything, and read everything, and experience everything, and say everything. There was a night when he lived on First Avenue that Nancy Hale, who lived on East 49th Street near Third Avenue, heard a kind of chant, which grew louder. She got up and looked out of the window at two or three in the morning and there was the great figure of Thomas Wolfe, advancing in his long country-man's stride, with his swaying black raincoat, and what he was chanting was, 'I wrote ten thousand words today—I wrote ten thousand words today.'

Tom must have lived in eight or nine different parts of New York and Brooklyn for a year or more. He knew in the end every aspect of the City —he walked the streets endlessly—but he was not a city man. The city fascinated him but he did not really belong in it and was never satisfied to live in it. He was always thinking of America as a whole and planning trips to some part that he had not yet seen, and in the end taking them. His various quarters in town always looked as if he had just moved in, to camp for awhile. This was partly because he really had no interest in possessions of any kind, but it was also because he was in his very nature a Far Wanderer, bent upon seeing all places, and his rooms were just necessities into which he never settled. Even when he was there his mind was not. He needed a continent to range over, actually and in imagination. And his place was all America. It was with America he was most deeply concerned and I believe he opened it up as no other writer ever did for the people of his time and for the writers and artists and poets of tomorrow. Surely he had a thing to tell us.

MAXWELL E. PERKINS

TO THE READER

This is a first book, and in it the author has written of experience which is now far and lost, but which was once part of the fabric of his life. If any reader, therefore, should say that the book is "autobiographical" the writer has no answer for him: it seems to him that all serious work in fiction is autobiographical—that, for instance, a more autobiographical work than "Gulliver's Travels" cannot easily be imagined.

This note, however, is addressed principally to those persons whom the writer may have known in the period covered by these pages. To these persons, he would say what he believes they understand already: that this book was written in innocence and nakedness of spirit, and that the writer's main concern was to give fulness, life, and intensity to the actions and people in the book he was creating. Now that it is to be published, he would insist that this book is a fiction, and that he meditated no man's portrait here.

But we are the sum of all the moments of our lives—all that is ours is in them: we cannot escape or conceal it. If the writer has used the clay of life to make his book, he has only used what all men must, what none can keep from using. Fiction is not fact, but fiction is fact selected and understood, fiction is fact arranged and charged with purpose. Dr. Johnson remarked that a man would turn over half a library to make a single book: in the same way, a novelist may turn over half the people in a town to make a single figure in his novel. This is not the whole method but the writer believes it illustrates the whole method in a book that is written from a middle distance and is without rancour or bitter intention.

PART ONE

. . . a stone, a leaf, an unfound door; of a stone, a leaf, a door. And of all the forgotten faces.

Naked and alone we came into exile. In her dark womb we did not know our mother's face; from the prison of her flesh have we come into the unspeakable and incommunicable prison of this earth.

Which of us has known his brother? Which of us has looked into his father's heart? Which of us has not remained forever prison-pent? Which of us is not forever a stranger and alone?

O waste of loss, in the hot mazes, lost, among bright stars on this most weary unbright cinder, lost! Remembering speechlessly we seek the great forgotten language, the lost lane-end into heaven, a stone, a leaf, an unfound door. Where? When?

O lost, and by the wind grieved, ghost, come back again.

1

A destiny that leads the English to the Dutch is strange enough; but one that leads from Epsom into Pennsylvania, and thence into the hills that shut in Altamont over the proud coral cry of the cock, and the soft stone smile of an angel, is touched by that dark miracle of chance which makes new magic in a dusty world.

Each of us is all the sums he has not counted: subtract us into nakedness and night again, and you shall see begin in Crete four thousand years ago the love that ended yesterday in Texas.

The seed of our destruction will blossom in the desert, the alexin of our cure grows by a mountain rock, and our lives are haunted by a Georgia slattern, because a London cutpurse went unhung. Each moment is the fruit of forty thousand years. The minute-winning days, like flies, buzz home to death, and every moment is a window on all time.

This is a moment:

An Englishman named Gilbert Gaunt, which he later changed to Gant (a concession probably to Yankee phonetics), having come to Baltimore from Bristol in 1837 on a sailing vessel, soon let the profits of a public house which he had purchased roll down his improvident gullet. He wandered westward into Pennsylvania, eking out a dangerous living by matching fighting cocks against the champions of country barnyards, and often escaping after a night spent in a village jail, with his champion dead on the field of battle, without the clink of a coin in his pocket, and sometimes with the print of a farmer's big knuckles on his reckless face. But he always escaped, and coming at length among the Dutch at harvest time he was so touched by the plenty of their land that he cast out his anchors there. Within a year he married a rugged young widow with a tidy farm who like all the other Dutch had been charmed by his air of travel, and his grandiose speech, particularly when he did Hamlet in the manner of the great Edmund Kean. Every one said he should have been an actor.

The Englishman begot children—a daughter and four sons—lived easily and carelessly, and bore patiently the weight of his wife's harsh but honest tongue. The years passed, his bright somewhat staring eyes grew dull and bagged, the tall Englishman walked with a gouty shuffle: one morning when she came to nag him out of sleep she found him dead of an apoplexy. He left five children, a mortgage and—in his strange darks eyes which now stared bright and open—something that had not died: a passionate and obscure hunger for voyages.

So, with this legacy, we leave this Englishman and are concerned here-after with the heir to whom he bequeathed it, his second son, a boy named Oliver. How this boy stood by the roadside near his mother's farm, and saw the dusty Rebels march past on their way to Gettysburg, how his cold eyes darkened when he heard the great name of Virginia, and how the year the war had ended, when he was still fifteen, he had walked along a street in Baltimore, and seen within a little shop smooth granite slabs of death, carved lambs and cherubim, and an angel poised upon cold phthisic feet, with a smile of soft stone idiocy—this is a longer tale. But I know that his cold and shallow eyes had darkened with the obscure and passion-ate hunger that had lived in a dead man's eyes, and that had led from Fenchurch Street past Philadelphia. As the boy looked at the big angel with the carved stipe of lilystalk, a cold and nameless excitement possessed him. The long fingers of his big hands closed. He felt that he wanted, more than anything in the world, to carve delicately with a chisel. He wanted to wreak something dark and unspeakable in him into cold stone. He wanted to carve an angel's head.

Oliver entered the shop and asked a big bearded man with a wooden mallet for a job. He became the stone cutter's apprentice. He worked in that dusty yard five years. He became a stone cutter. When his apprentice-ship was over he had become a man.

He never found it. He never learned to carve an angel's head. The dove, the lamb, the smooth joined marble hands of death, and letters fair and fine—but not the angel. And of all the years of waste and loss—the riotous years in Baltimore, of work and savage drunkenness, and the theatre of Booth and Salvini, which had a disastrous effect upon the stone cutter, who memorized each accent of the noble rant, and strode muttering through the streets, with rapid gestures of the enormous talking hands—these are blind steps and gropings of our exile, the painting of our hunger as, remembering speechlessly, we seek the great forgotten language, the lost lane-end into heaven, a stone, a leaf, a door. Where? When?

He never found it, and he reeled down across the continent into the

Reconstruction South—a strange wild form of six feet four with cold uneasy eyes, a great blade of nose, and a rolling tide of rhetoric, a preposterous and comic invective, as formalized as classical epithet, which he used
seriously, but with a faint uneasy grin around the corners of his thin
wailing mouth.

He set up business in Sydney, the little capital city of one of the middle
Southern states, lived soberly and industriously under the attentive eye of
a folk still raw with defeat and hostility, and finally, his good name
founded and admission won, he married a gaunt tubercular spinstress, ten
years his elder, but with a nest egg and an unshakable will to matrimony.
Within eighteen months he was a howling maniac again, his little business
went smash while his foot stayed on the polished rail, and Cynthia, his
wife—whose life, the natives said, he had not helped to prolong—died
suddenly one night after a hemorrhage.

So, all was gone again—Cynthia, the shop, the hard-bought praise of
soberness, the angel's head—he walked through the streets at dark, yelling
his pentameter curse at Rebel ways, and all their indolence; but sick with
fear and loss and penitence, he wilted under the town's reproving stare,
becoming convinced, as the flesh wasted on his own gaunt frame, that
Cynthia's scourge was doing vengeance now on him.

He was only past thirty, but he looked much older. His face was yellow
and sunken; the waxen blade of his nose looked like a beak. He had long
brown mustaches that hung straight down mournfully.

His tremendous bouts of drinking had wrecked his health. He was thin
as a rail and had a cough. He thought of Cynthia now, in the lonely and
hostile town, and he became afraid. He thought he had tuberculosis and
that he was going to die.

So, alone and lost again, having found neither order nor establishment
in the world, and with the earth cut away from his feet, Oliver resumed
his aimless drift along the continent. He turned westward toward the great
fortress of the hills, knowing that behind them his evil fame would not be
known, and hoping that he might find in them isolation, a new life, and
recovered health.

The eyes of the gaunt spectre darkened again, as they had in his youth.

All day, under a wet gray sky of October, Oliver rode westward across
the mighty state. As he stared mournfully out the window at the great raw
land so sparsely tilled by the futile and occasional little farms, which
seemed to have made only little grubbing patches in the wilderness, his

heart went cold and leaden in him. He thought of the great barns of Pennsylvania, the ripe bending of golden grain, the plenty, the order, the clean thrift of the people. And he thought of how he had set out to get order and position for himself, and of the rioting confusion of his life, the blot and blur of years, and the red waste of his youth.

By God! he thought. I'm getting old! Why here?

The grisly parade of the spectre years trooped through his brain. Suddenly, he saw that his life had been channelled by a series of accidents: a mad Rebel singing of Armageddon, the sound of a bugle on the road, the mule-hoofs of the army, the silly white face of an angel in a dusty shop, a slut's pert wiggle of her hams as she passed by. He had reeled out of warmth and plenty into this barren land: as he stared out the window and saw the fallow unworked earth, the great raw lift of the Piedmont, the muddy red clay roads, and the slattern people gaping at the stations—a lean farmer gangling above his reins, a dawdling negro, a gap-toothed yokel, a hard sallow woman with a grimy baby—the strangeness of destiny stabbed him with fear. How came he here from the clean Dutch thrift of his youth into this vast lost earth of rickets?

The train rattled on over the reeking earth. Rain fell steadily. A brakeman came draftily into the dirty plush coach and emptied a scuttle of coal into the big stove at the end. High empty laughter shook a group of yokels sprawled on two turned seats. The bell tolled mournfully above the clacking wheels. There was a droning interminable wait at a junction-town near the foot-hills. Then the train moved on again across the vast rolling earth.

Dusk came. The huge bulk of the hills was foggily emergent. Small smoky lights went up in the hillside shacks. The train crawled dizzily across high trestles spanning ghostly hawsers of water. Far up, far down, plumed with wisps of smoke, toy cabins stuck to bank and gulch and hillside. The train toiled sinuously up among gouged red cuts with slow labor. As darkness came, Oliver descended at the little town of Old Stockade where the rails ended. The last great wall of the hills lay stark above him. As he left the dreary little station and stared into the greasy lamplight of a country store, Oliver felt that he was crawling, like a great beast, into the circle of those enormous hills to die.

The next morning he resumed his journey by coach. His destination was the little town of Altamont, twenty-four miles away beyond the rim of the great outer wall of the hills. As the horses strained slowly up the mountain road Oliver's spirit lifted a little. It was a gray-golden day in late October, bright and windy. There was a sharp bite and sparkle in the mountain air: the range soared above him, close, immense, clean, and barren. The trees rose gaunt and stark: they were almost leafless. The sky was full of windy white rags of cloud; a thick blade of mist washed slowly around the rampart of a mountain.

Below him a mountain stream foamed down its rocky bed, and he could see little dots of men laying the track that would coil across the hill toward Altamont. Then the sweating team lipped the gulch of the mountain, and, among soaring and lordly ranges that melted away in purple mist, they began the slow descent toward the high plateau on which the town of Altamont was built.

In the haunting eternity of these mountains, rimmed in their enormous cup, he found sprawled out on its hundred hills and hollows a town of four thousand people.

There were new lands. His heart lifted.

This town of Altamont had been settled soon after the Revolutionary War. It had been a convenient stopping-off place for cattledrovers and farmers in their swing eastward from Tennessee into South Carolina. And, for several decades before the Civil War, it had enjoyed the summer patronage of fashionable people from Charleston and the plantations of the hot South. When Oliver first came to it it had begun to get some reputation not only as a summer resort, but as a sanitarium for tuberculars. Several rich men from the North had established hunting lodges in the hills, and one of them had bought huge areas of mountain land and, with an army of imported architects, carpenters and masons, was planning the greatest country estate in America—something in limestone, with pitched slate roofs, and one hundred and eighty-three rooms. It was modelled on the chateau at Blois. There was also a vast new hotel, a sumptuous wooden barn, rambling comfortably upon the summit of a commanding hill.

But most of the population was still native, recruited from the hill and country people in the surrounding districts. They were Scotch-Irish mountaineers, rugged, provincial, intelligent, and industrious.

Oliver had about twelve hundred dollars saved from the wreckage of Cynthia's estate. During the winter he rented a little shack at one edge of the town's public square, acquired a small stock of marbles, and set up business. But he had little to do at first save to think of the prospect of his death. During the bitter and lonely winter, while he thought he was dying, the gaunt scarecrow Yankee that flapped muttering through the streets became an object of familiar gossip to the townspeople. All the people at his boarding-house knew that at night he walked his room with great caged strides, and that a long low moan that seemed wrung from his bowels quivered incessantly on his thin lips. But he spoke to no one about it.

And then the marvellous hill Spring came, green-golden, with brief spurting winds, the magic and fragrance of the blossoms, warm gusts of balsam. The great wound in Oliver began to heal. His voice was heard in the land once more, there were purple flashes of the old rhetoric, the ghost of the old eagerness.

One day in April, as with fresh awakened senses, he stood before his shop, watching the flurry of life in the square, Oliver heard behind him the voice of a man who was passing. And that voice, flat, drawling, complacent, touched with sudden light a picture that had lain dead in him for twenty years.

"Hit's a comin'! Accordin' to my figgers hit's due June 11, 1886."

Oliver turned and saw retreating the burly persuasive figure of the prophet he had last seen vanishing down the dusty road that led to Gettysburg and Armageddon.

"Who is that?" he asked a man.

The man looked and grinned.

"That's Bacchus Pentland," he said. "He's quite a character. There are a lot of his folks around here."

Oliver wet his great thumb briefly. Then, with a thin grin, he said: "Has Armageddon come yet?"

"He's expecting it any day now," said the man.

Then Oliver met Eliza. He lay one afternoon in Spring upon the smooth leather sofa of his little office, listening to the bright piping noises in the Square. A restoring peace brooded over his great extended body. He thought of the loamy black earth with its sudden young light of flowers, of the beaded chill of beer, and of the plumtree's dropping blossoms. Then he heard the brisk heel-taps of a woman coming down among the marbles, and he got hastily to his feet. He was drawing on his well brushed coat of heavy black just as she entered.

"I tell you what," said Eliza, pursing her lips in reproachful banter, "I wish I was a man and had nothing to do but lie around all day on a good easy sofa."

"Good afternoon, madam," said Oliver with a flourishing bow. "Yes," he said, as a faint sly grin bent the corners of his thin mouth, "I reckon you've caught me taking my constitutional. As a matter of fact I very rarely lie down in the daytime, but I've been in bad health for the last year now, and I'm not able to do the work I used to."

He was silent a moment; his face drooped in an expression of hangdog dejection. "Ah, Lord! I don't know what's to become of me!"

"Pshaw!" said Eliza briskly and contemptuously. "There's nothing wrong with you in my opinion. You're a big strapping fellow, in the prime of life. Half of it's only imagination. Most of the time we think we're sick it's all in the mind. I remember three years ago I was teaching school in Hominy Township when I was taken down with pneumonia. Nobody ever expected to see me come out of it alive but I got through it somehow; I well remember one day I was sitting down—as the fellow says, I reckon I was convalescin'; the reason I remember is Old Doctor Fletcher had just been and when he went out I saw him shake his head at my cousin Sally. 'Why Eliza, what on earth,' she said, just as soon as he had gone, 'he tells me you're spitting up blood every time you cough; you've got consumption as sure as you live.' 'Pshaw,' I said. I remember I laughed just as big as you please, determined to make a big joke of it all; I just thought to myself, I'm not going to give into it, I'll fool them all yet; 'I don't believe a word of it' (I said)," she nodded her head smartly at him, and pursed her lips, "'and besides, Sally' (I said) 'we've all got to go some time, and there's no use worrying about what's going to happen. It may come tomorrow, or it may come later, but it's bound to come to all in the end'."

"Ah Lord!" said Oliver, shaking his head sadly. "You hit the nail on the head that time. A truer word was never spoken."

Merciful God! he thought, with an anguished inner grin. How long is this to keep up? But she's a pippin as sure as you're born. He looked appreciatively at her trim erect figure, noting her milky white skin, her black-brown eyes, with their quaint child's stare, and her jet black hair drawn back tightly from her high white forehead. She had a curious trick of pursing her lips reflectively before she spoke; she liked to take her time, and came to the point after interminable divagations down all the lane-ends of memory and overtone, feasting upon the golden pageant of all she had ever said, done, felt, thought, seen, or replied, with egocentric delight.

Then, while he looked, she ceased speaking abruptly, put her neat gloved hand to her chin, and stared off with a thoughtful pursed mouth.

"Well," she said after a moment, "if you're getting your health back and spend a good part of your time lying around you ought to have something to occupy your mind." She opened a leather portmanteau she was carrying and produced a visiting card and two fat volumes. "My name," she said portentously, with slow emphasis, "is Eliza Pentland, and I represent the Larkin Publishing Company."

She spoke the words proudly, with dignified gusto. Merciful God! A book-agent! thought Gant.

"We are offering," said Eliza, opening a huge yellow book with a fancy design of spears and flags and laurel wreaths, "a book of poems called *Gems of Verse for Hearth and Fireside* as well as *Larkin's Domestic Doctor and Book of Household Remedies,* giving directions for the cure and prevention of over five hundred diseases."

"Well," said Gant, with a faint grin, wetting his big thumb briefly, "I ought to find one that I've got out of that."

"Why, yes," said Eliza, nodding smartly, "as the fellow says, you can read poetry for the good of your soul and Larkin for the good of your body."

"I like poetry," said Gant, thumbing over the pages, and pausing with interest at the section marked *Songs of the Spur and Sabre.* "In my boyhood I could recite it by the hour."

He bought the books. Eliza packed her samples, and stood up looking sharply and curiously about the dusty little shop.

"Doing any business?" she said.

"Very little," said Oliver sadly. "Hardly enough to keep body and soul together. I'm a stranger in a strange land."

"Pshaw!" said Eliza cheerfully. "You ought to get out and meet more people. You need something to take your mind off yourself. If I were you, I'd pitch right in and take an interest in the town's progress. We've got everything here it takes to make a big town—scenery, climate, and natural resources, and we all ought to work together. If I had a few thousand dollars I know what I'd do,"—she winked smartly at him, and began to speak with a curiously masculine gesture of the hand—forefinger extended, fist loosely clenched. "Do you see this corner here—the one you're on? It'll double in value in the next few years. Now, here!" she gestured before her with the loose masculine gesture. "They're going to run a street through there some day as sure as you live. And when they do—" she pursed her lips reflectively, "that property is going to be worth money."

She continued to talk about property with a strange meditative hunger. The town seemed to be an enormous blueprint to her: her head was stuffed uncannily with figures and estimates—who owned a lot, who sold it, the sale-price, the real value, the future value, first and second mortgages, and so on. When she had finished, Oliver said with the emphasis of strong aversion, thinking of Sydney:

"I hope I never own another piece of property as long as I live—save a house to live in. It is nothing but a curse and a care, and the tax-collector gets it all in the end."

Eliza looked at him with a startled expression, as if he had uttered a damnable heresy.

"Why, say! That's no way to talk!" she said. "You want to lay something by for a rainy day, don't you?"

"I'm having my rainy day now," he said gloomily. "All the property I need is eight feet of earth to be buried in."

Then, talking more cheerfully, he walked with her to the door of the shop, and watched her as she marched primly away across the square, holding her skirts at the curbs with ladylike nicety. Then he turned back among his marbles again with a stirring in him of a joy he thought he had lost forever.

The Pentland family, of which Eliza was a member, was one of the strangest tribes that ever came out of the hills. It had no clear title to the name of Pentland: a Scotch-Englishman of that name, who was a mining engineer, the grandfather of the present head of the family, had come into the hills after the Revolution, looking for copper, and lived there for several years, begetting several children by one of the pioneer women. When he disappeared the woman took for herself and her children the name of Pentland.

The present chieftain of the tribe was Eliza's father, the brother of the prophet Bacchus, Major Thomas Pentland. Another brother had been killed during the Seven Days. Major Pentland's military title was honestly if inconspicuously earned. While Bacchus, who never rose above the rank of Corporal, was blistering his hard hands at Shiloh, the Major, as commander of two companies of Home Volunteers, was guarding the stronghold of the native hills. This stronghold was never threatened until the closing days of the war, when the Volunteers, ambuscaded behind convenient trees and rocks, fired three volleys into a detachment of Sherman's stragglers, and quietly dispersed to the defense of their attendant wives and children.

The Pentland family was as old as any in the community, but it had always been poor, and had made few pretenses to gentility. By marriage, and by intermarriage among its own kinsmen, it could boast of some connection with the great, of some insanity, and a modicum of idiocy. But because of its obvious superiority, in intelligence and fibre, to most of the mountain people it held a position of solid respect among them.

The Pentlands bore a strong clan-marking. Like most rich personalities in strange families their powerful group-stamp became more impressive because of their differences. They had broad powerful noses, with fleshy deeply scalloped wings, sensual mouths, extraordinarily mixed of delicacy and coarseness, which in the process of thinking they convolved with astonishing flexibility, broad intelligent foreheads, and deep flat cheeks, a trifle hollowed. The men were generally ruddy of face, and their typical stature was meaty, strong, and of middling height, although it varied into gangling cadaverousness.

Major Thomas Pentland was the father of a numerous family of which Eliza was the only surviving girl. A younger sister had died a few years before of a disease which the family identified sorrowfully as "poor Jane's scrofula." There were six boys: Henry, the oldest, was now thirty, Will was twenty-six, Jim was twenty-two, and Thaddeus, Elmer and Greeley were, in the order named, eighteen, fifteen, and eleven. Eliza was twenty-four.

The four oldest children, Henry, Will, Eliza, and Jim, had passed their childhood in the years following the war. The poverty and privation of these years had been so terrible that none of them ever spoke of it now, but the bitter steel had sheared into their hearts, leaving scars that would not heal.

The effect of these years upon the oldest children was to develop in them an insane niggardliness, an insatiate love of property, and a desire to escape from the Major's household as quickly as possible.

"Father," Eliza had said with ladylike dignity, as she led Oliver for the first time into the sitting-room of the cottage, "I want you to meet Mr. Gant."

Major Pentland rose slowly from his rocker by the fire, folded a large knife, and put the apple he had been peeling on the mantel. Bacchus looked up benevolently from a whittled stick, and Will, glancing up from his stubby nails which he was paring as usual, greeted the visitor with a birdlike nod and wink. The men amused themselves constantly with pocket knives.

Major Pentland advanced slowly toward Gant. He was a stocky fleshy man in the middle fifties, with a ruddy face, a patriarchal beard, and the thick complacent features of his tribe.

"It's W. O. Gant, isn't it?" he asked in a drawling unctuous voice.

"Yes," said Oliver, "that's right."

"From what Eliza's been tellling me about you," said the Major, giving the signal to his audience, "I was going to say it ought to be L. E. Gant."

The room sounded with the fat pleased laughter of the Pentlands.

"Whew!" cried Eliza, putting her hand to the wing of her broad nose. "I'll vow, father! You ought to be ashamed of yourself."

Gant grinned with a thin false painting of mirth.

The miserable old scoundrel, he thought. He's had that one bottled up for a week.

"You've met Will before," said Eliza.

"Both before and aft," said Will with a smart wink.

When their laughter had died down, Eliza said: "And this—as the fellow says—is Uncle Bacchus."

"Yes, sir," said Bacchus beaming, "as large as life an' twice as sassy."

"They call him Back-us everywhere else," said Will, including them all in a brisk wink, "but here in the family we call him Behind-us."

"I suppose," said Major Pentland deliberately, "that you've served on a great many juries?"

"No," said Oliver, determined to endure the worst now with a frozen grin. "Why?"

"Because," said the Major looking around again, "I thought you were a fellow who'd done a lot of *courtin'*."

Then, amid their laughter, the door opened, and several of the others came in—Eliza's mother, a plain worn Scotchwoman, and Jim, a ruddy porcine young fellow, his father's beardless twin, and Thaddeus, mild, ruddy, brown of hair and eye, bovine, and finally Greeley, the youngest, a boy with lapping idiot grins, full of strange squealing noises at which they laughed. He was eleven, degenerate, weak, scrofulous, but his white moist hands could draw from a violin music that had in it something unearthly and untaught.

And as they sat there in the hot little room with its warm odor of mellowing apples, the vast winds howled down from the hills, there was a roaring in the pines, remote and demented, the bare boughs clashed. And as they peeled, or pared, or whittled, their talk slid from its rude jocularity to death and burial: they drawled monotonously, with evil hunger, their gossip of destiny, and of men but newly lain in the earth. And as their talk wore on, and Gant heard the spectre moan of the wind, he was entombed in loss and darkness, and his soul plunged downward in the pit of night, for he saw that he must die a stranger—that all, all but these triumphant Pentlands, who banqueted on death—must die.

And like a man who is perishing in the polar night, he thought of the rich meadows of his youth: the corn, the plum tree, and ripe grain. Why here? O lost!

2

Oliver married Eliza in May. After their wedding trip to Philadelphia, they returned to the house he had built for her on Woodson Street. With his great hands he had laid the foundations, burrowed out deep musty cellars in the earth, and sheeted the tall sides over with smooth trowellings of warm brown plaster. He had very little money, but his strange house grew to the rich modelling of his fantasy: when he had finished he had something which leaned to the slope of his narrow uphill yard, something with a high embracing porch in front, and warm rooms where one stepped up and down to the tackings of his whim. He built his house close to the quiet hilly street; he bedded the loamy soil with flowers; he laid the short walk to the high veranda steps with great square sheets of colored marble; he put a fence of spiked iron between his house and the world.

Then, in the cool long glade of yard that stretched four hundred feet behind the house he planted trees and grape vines. And whatever he touched in that rich fortress of his soul sprang into golden life: as the years passed, the fruit trees—the peach, the plum, the cherry, the apple— grew great and bent beneath their clusters. His grape vines thickened into brawny ropes of brown and coiled down the high wire fences of his lot, and hung in a dense fabric, upon his trellises, roping his domain twice around. They climbed the porch end of the house and framed the upper windows in thick bowers. And the flowers grew in rioting glory in his yard—the velvet-leaved nasturtium, slashed with a hundred tawny dyes, the rose, the snowball, the redcupped tulip, and the lily. The honeysuckle drooped its heavy mass upon the fence; wherever his great hands touched the earth it grew fruitful for him.

For him the house was the picture of his soul, the garment of his will. But for Eliza it was a piece of property, whose value she shrewdly appraised, a beginning for her hoard. Like all the older children of Major Pentland she had, since her twentieth year, begun the slow accretion of land: from the savings of her small wage as teacher and book-agent, she had already purchased one or two pieces of earth. On one of these, a small lot at the edge of the public square, she persuaded him to build a shop. This he did with his own hands, and the labor of two negro men: it was a two-story shack of brick, with wide wooden steps, leading down to the square from a marble porch. Upon this porch, flanking the wooden doors, he placed some marbles; by the door, he put the heavy simpering figure of an angel.

But Eliza was not content with his trade: there was no money in death. People, she thought, died too slowly. And she foresaw that her brother Will, who had begun at fifteen as helper in a lumber yard, and was now the owner of a tiny business, was destined to become a rich man. So she persuaded Gant to go into partnership with Will Pentland: at the end of a year, however, his patience broke, his tortured egotism leaped from its restraint, he howled that Will, whose business hours were spent chiefly in figuring upon a dirty envelope with a stub of a pencil, paring reflectively his stubby nails, or punning endlessly with a birdlike wink and nod, would ruin them all. Will therefore quietly bought out his partner's interest, and moved on toward the accumulation of a fortune, while Oliver returned to isolation and his grimy angels.

The strange figure of Oliver Gant cast its famous shadow through the town. Men heard at night and morning the great formula of his curse to Eliza. They saw him plunge to house and shop, they saw him bent above his marbles, they saw him mould in his great hands—with curse, and howl, with passionate devotion—the rich texture of his home. They laughed at his wild excess of speech, of feeling, and of gesture. They were silent before the maniac fury of his sprees, which occurred almost punctually every two months, and lasted two or three days. They picked him foul and witless from the cobbles, and brought him home—the banker, the policeman, and a burly devoted Swiss named Jannadeau, a grimy jeweller who rented a small fenced space among Gant's tombstones. And always they handled him with tender care, feeling something strange and proud and glorious lost in that drunken ruin of Babel. He was a stranger to them: no one—not even Eliza—ever called him by his first name. He was—and remained thereafter—"Mister" Gant.

And what Eliza endured in pain and fear and glory no one knew. He breathed over them all his hot lion-breath of desire and fury: when he was drunk, her white pursed face, and all the slow octopal movements of her temper, stirred him to red madness. She was at such times in real danger from his assault: she had to lock herself away from him.

For from the first, deeper than love, deeper than hate, as deep as the unfleshed bones of life, an obscure and final warfare was being waged between them. Eliza wept or was silent to his curse, nagged briefly in retort to his rhetoric, gave like a punched pillow to his lunging drive—and slowly, implacably had her way. Year by year, above his howl of protest, he did not know how, they gathered in small bits of earth, paid the hated taxes, and put the money that remained into more land. Over the wife, over the mother, the woman of property, who was like a man, walked slowly forth.

In eleven years she bore him nine children of whom six lived. The first, a girl, died in her twentieth month, of infant cholera; two more died at birth. The others outlived the grim and casual littering. The oldest, a boy, was born in 1885. He was given the name of Steve. The second, born fifteen months later, was a girl—Daisy. The next, likewise a girl—Helen—came three years later. Then, in 1892, came twins—boys—to whom Gant, always with a zest for politics, gave the names of Grover Cleveland and Benjamin Harrison. And the last, Luke, was born two years later, in 1894.

Twice, during this period, at intervals of five years, Gant's periodic spree lengthened into an unbroken drunkenness that lasted for weeks. He was caught, drowning in the tides of his thirst. Each time Eliza sent him away to take a cure for alcoholism at Richmond. Once, Eliza and four of her children were sick at the same time with typhoid fever. But during a weary convalescence she pursed her lips grimly and took them off to Florida.

Eliza came through stolidly to victory. As she marched down these enormous years of love and loss, stained with the rich dyes of pain and pride and death, and with the great wild flare of his alien and passionate life, her limbs faltered in the grip of ruin, but she came on, through sickness and emaciation, to victorious strength. She knew there had been glory in it: insensate and cruel as he had often been, she remembered the enormous beating color of his life, and the lost and stricken thing in him which he would never find. And fear and a speechless pity rose in her when at times she saw the small uneasy eyes grow still and darken with the foiled and groping hunger of old frustration. O lost!

3

In the great processional of the years through which the history of the Gants was evolving, few years had borne a heavier weight of pain, terror, and wretchedness, and none was destined to bring with it more conclusive events than that year which marked the beginning of the twentieth century. For Gant and his wife, the year 1900, in which one day they found themselves, after growing to maturity in another century—a transition which must have given, wherever it has happened, a brief but poignant loneliness to thousands of imaginative people—had coincidences, too striking to be unnoticed, with other boundaries in their lives.

In that year Gant passed his fiftieth birthday: he knew he was half as old as the century that had died, and that men do not often live as long as centuries. And in that year, too, Eliza, big with the last child she would ever have, went over the final hedge of terror and desperation and, in the opulent darkness of the summer night, as she lay flat in her bed with her hands upon her swollen belly, she began to design her life for the years when she would cease to be a mother.

In the already opening gulf on whose separate shores their lives were founded, she was beginning to look, with the infinite composure, the tremendous patience which waits through half a lifetime for an event, not so much with certain foresight, as with a prophetic, brooding instinct. This quality, this almost Buddhistic complacency which, rooted in the fundamental structure of her life, she could neither suppress nor conceal, was the quality he could least understand, that infuriated him most. He was fifty: he had a tragic consciousness of time—he saw the passionate fulness of his life upon the wane, and he cast about him like a senseless and infuriate beast. She had perhaps a greater reason for quietude than he, for she had come on from the cruel openings of her life, through disease, physical weakness, poverty, the constant imminence of death and misery: she had lost her first child, and brought the others safely through each succeeding plague; and now, at forty-two, her last child

17

stirring in her womb, she had a conviction, enforced by her Scotch superstition, and the blind vanity of her family, which saw extinction for others but not for itself, that she was being shaped to a purpose.

As she lay in her bed, a great star burned across her vision in the western quarter of the sky; she fancied it was climbing heaven slowly. And although she could not have said toward what pinnacle her life was moving, she saw in the future freedom that she had never known, possession and power and wealth, the desire for which was mixed inextinguishably with the current of her blood. Thinking of this in the dark, she pursed her lips with thoughtful satisfaction, unhumorously seeing herself at work in the carnival, taking away quite easily from the hands of folly what it had never known how to keep.

"I'll get it!" she thought, "I'll get it. Will has it! Jim has it. And I'm smarter than they are." And with regret, tinctured with pain and bitterness, she thought of Gant:

"Pshaw! If I hadn't kept after him he wouldn't have a stick to call his own to-day. What little we have got I've had to fight for; we wouldn't have a roof over our heads; we'd spend the rest of our lives in a rented house"—which was to her the final ignominy of shiftless and improvident people.

And she resumed: "The money he squanders every year in licker would buy a good lot: we could be well-to-do people now if we'd started at the very beginning. But he's always hated the very idea of owning anything: couldn't bear it, he told me once, since he lost his money in that trade in Sydney. If I'd been there, you can bet your bottom dollar there'd been no loss. Or, it'd be on the other side," she added grimly.

And lying there while the winds of early autumn swept down from the Southern hills, filling the black air with dropping leaves, and making, in intermittent rushes, a remote sad thunder in great trees, she thought of the stranger who had come to live in her, and of that other stranger, author of so much woe, who had lived with her for almost twenty years. And thinking of Gant, she felt again an inchoate aching wonder, recalling the savage strife between them, and the great submerged struggle beneath, founded upon the hatred and the love of property, in which she did not doubt of her victory, but which baffled her, foiled her.

"I'll vow!" she whispered. "I'll vow! I never saw such a man!"

Gant, faced with the loss of sensuous delight, knowing the time had come when all his Rabelaisian excess in eating, drinking, and loving must come under the halter, knew of no gain that could compensate him for the loss of libertinism; he felt, too, the sharp ache of regret, feeling that

he had possessed powers, had wasted chances, such as his partnership
with Will Pentland, that might have given him position and wealth. He
knew that the century had gone in which the best part of his life had
passed; he felt, more than ever, the strangeness and loneliness of our
little adventure upon the earth: he thought of his childhood on the Dutch
farm, the Baltimore days, the aimless drift down the continent, the
appalling fixation of his whole life upon a series of accidents. The
enormous tragedy of accident hung like a gray cloud over his life. He
saw more clearly than ever that he was a stranger in a strange land
among people who would always be alien to him. Strangest of all, he
thought, was this union, by which he had begotten children, created a life
dependent on him, with a woman so remote from all he understood.

He did not know whether the year 1900 marked for him a beginning
or an ending; but with the familiar weakness of the sensualist, he
resolved to make it an ending, burning the spent fire in him down to a
guttering flame. In the first half of the month of January, still penitently
true to the New Year's reformation, he begot a child: by Spring, when
it was evident that Eliza was again pregnant, he had hurled himself into
an orgy to which even a notable four months' drunk in 1896 could offer
no precedent. Day after day he became maniacally drunk, until he fixed
himself in a state of constant insanity: in May she sent him off again to
a sanitarium at Piedmont to take the "cure," which consisted simply in
feeding him plainly and cheaply, and keeping him away from alcohol
for six weeks, a regime which contributed no more ravenously to his
hunger than it did to his thirst. He returned, outwardly chastened, but
inwardly a raging furnace, toward the end of June: the day before he
came back, Eliza, obviously big with child, her white face compactly set,
walked sturdily into each of the town's fourteen saloons, calling up the
proprietor or the bar-man behind his counter, and speaking clearly
and loudly in the sodden company of bar clientry:

"See here: I just came in to tell you that Mr. Gant is coming back
to-morrow, and I want you all to know that if I hear of any of you
selling him a drink, I'll put you in the penitentiary."

The threat, they knew, was preposterous, but the white judicial face,
the thoughtful pursing of the lips, and the right hand, which she held
loosely clenched, like a man's, with the forefinger extended, emphasizing
her proclamation with a calm, but somehow powerful gesture, froze
them with a terror no amount of fierce excoriation could have produced.
They received her announcement in beery stupefaction, muttering at
most a startled agreement as she walked out.

"By God," said a mountaineer, sending a brown inaccurate stream toward a cuspidor, "she'll do it, too. That woman means business."

"Hell!" said Tim O'Donnel, thrusting his simian face comically above his counter, "I wouldn't give W. O. a drink now if it was fifteen cents a quart and we was alone in a privy. Is she gone yet?"

There was vast whisky laughter.

"Who is she?" some one asked.

"She's Will Pentland's sister."

"By God, she'll do it then," cried several; and the place trembled again with their laughter.

Will Pentland was in Loughran's when she entered. She did not greet him. When she had gone he turned to a man near him, prefacing his remark with a birdlike nod and wink: "Bet you can't do that," he said.

Gant, when he returned, and was publicly refused at a bar, was wild with rage and humiliation. He got whisky very easily, of course, by sending a drayman from his steps, or some negro, in for it; but, in spite of the notoriety of his conduct, which had, he knew, become a classic myth for the children of the town, he shrank at each new advertisement of his behaviour; he became, year by year, more, rather than less, sensitive to it, and his shame, his quivering humiliation on mornings after, product of rasped pride and jangled nerves, was pitiable. He felt bitterly that Eliza had with deliberate malice publicly degraded him: he screamed denunciation and abuse at her on his return home.

All through the summer Eliza walked with white boding placidity through horror—she had by now the hunger for it, waiting with terrible quiet the return of fear at night. Angered by her pregnancy, Gant went almost daily to Elizabeth's house in Eagle Crescent, whence he was delivered nightly by a band of exhausted and terrified prostitutes into the care of his son Steve, his oldest child, by now pertly free with nearly all the women in the district, who fondled him with good-natured vulgarity, laughed heartily at his glib innuendoes, and suffered him, even, to slap them smartly on their rumps, making for him roughly as he skipped nimbly away.

"Son," said Elizabeth, shaking Gant's waggling head vigorously, "don't you carry on, when you grow up, like the old rooster here. But he's a nice old boy when he wants to be," she continued, kissing the bald spot on his head, and deftly slipping into the boy's hand the wallet Gant had, in a torrent of generosity, given to her. She was scrupulously honest.

The boy was usually accompanied on these errands by Jannadeau and Tom Flack, a negro hack-man, who waited in patient constraint outside the latticed door of the brothel until the advancing tumult within announced that Gant had been enticed to depart. And he would go, either struggling clumsily and screaming eloquent abuse at his suppliant captors, or jovially acquiescent, bellowing a wanton song of his youth along the latticed crescent, and through the supper-silent highways of the town.

> "Up in that back room, boys,
> Up in *that* back room,
> All among the fleas and bugs,
> I pit-tee your sad doom."

Home, he would be cajoled up the tall veranda stairs, enticed into his bed; or, resisting all compulsion, he would seek out his wife, shut usually in her room, howling taunts at her, and accusations of unchastity, since there festered in him dark suspicion, fruit of his age, his wasting energy. Timid Daisy, pale from fright, would have fled to the neighboring arms of Sudie Isaacs, or to the Tarkintons; Helen, aged ten, even then his delight, would master him, feeding spoonfuls of scalding soup into his mouth, and slapping him sharply with her small hand when he became recalcitrant.

"You *drink* this! You better!"

He was enormously pleased: they were both strung on the same wires. Again, he was beyond all reason. Extravagantly mad, he built roaring fires in his sitting-room, drenching the leaping fire with a can of oil; spitting exultantly into the answering roar, and striking up, until he was exhausted, a profane chant, set to a few recurrent bars of music, which ran, for forty minutes, somewhat like this:

> "O-ho—Goddam,
> Goddam, Goddam,
> O-ho—Goddam,
> Goddam—Goddam."

—adopting usually the measure by which clock-chimes strike out the hour.

And outside, strung like apes along the wide wires of the fence, Sandy and Fergus Duncan, Seth Tarkinton, sometimes Ben and Grover themselves, joining in the glee of their friends, kept up an answering chant:

> "Old man Gant
> Came home drunk!
> Old man Gant
> Came home drunk!"

Daisy, from a neighbor's sanctuary, wept in shame and fear. But Helen, small thin fury, held on relentlessly: presently he would subside into a chair, and receive hot soup and stinging slaps with a grin. Upstairs Eliza lay, white-faced and watchfully.

So ran the summer by. The last grapes hung in dried and rotten clusters to the vines; the wind roared distantly; September ended.

One night the dry doctor, Cardiac, said: "I think we'll be through with this before to-morrow evening." He departed, leaving in the house a middle-aged country woman. She was a hard-handed practical nurse.

At eight o'clock Gant returned alone. The boy Steve had stayed at home for ready dispatch at Eliza's need; for the moment the attention was shifted from the master.

His great voice below, chanting obscenities, carried across the neighborhood: as she heard the sudden wild roar of flame up the chimney, shaking the house in its flight, she called Steve to her side, tensely: "Son, he'll burn us all up!" she whispered.

They heard a chair fall heavily below, his curse; they heard his heavy reeling stride across the dining-room and up the hall; they heard the sagging creak of the stair-rail as his body swung against it.

"He's coming!" she whispered, "He's coming! Lock the door, son!" The boy locked the door.

"Are you there?" Gant roared, pounding the flimsy door heavily with his great fist. "Miss Eliza: are you there?" howling at her the ironical title by which he addressed her at moments like this.

And he screamed a sermon of profanity and woven invective:—

"Little did I reck," he began, getting at once into the swing of preposterous rhetoric which he used half furiously, half comically, "little did I reck the day I first saw her eighteen bitter years ago, when she came wriggling around the corner at me like a snake on her belly—[a stock epithet which from repetition was now heart-balm to him]—little did I reck that—that—that it would come to this," he finished lamely. He waited quietly, in the heavy silence, for some answer, knowing that she lay in her white-faced calm behind the door, and filled with the old choking fury because he knew she would not answer.

"Are you there? I say, are you there, woman?" he howled, barking his big knuckles in a furious bombardment.

There was nothing but the white living silence.

"Ah me! Ah me!" he sighed with strong self-pity, then burst into forced snuffling sobs, which furnished a running accompaniment to his denunciation. "Merciful God!" he wept, "it's fearful, it's awful, it's croo-el. What have I ever done that God should punish me like this in my old age?"

There was no answer.

"Cynthia! Cynthia!" he howled suddenly, invoking the memory of his first wife, the gaunt tubercular spinstress whose life, it was said, his conduct had done nothing to prolong, but whom he was fond of supplicating now, realizing the hurt, the anger he caused to Eliza by doing so. "Cynthia! O Cynthia! Look down upon me in my hour of need! Give me succour! Give me aid! Protect me against this fiend out of Hell!"

And he continued, weeping in heavy snuffling burlesque: "O-boo-hoo-hoo! Come down and save me, I beg of you, I entreat you, I implore you, or I perish."

Silence answered.

"Ingratitude, more fierce than brutish beasts," Gant resumed, getting off on another track, fruitful with mixed and mangled quotation. "You will be punished, as sure as there's a just God in heaven. You will all be punished. Kick the old man, strike him, throw him out on the street: he's no good any more. He's no longer able to provide for the family—send him over the hill to the poorhouse. That's where he belongs. Rattle his bones over the stones. Honor thy father that thy days may be long. Ah, Lord!

> " 'Look, in this place ran Cassius' dagger through;
> See what a rent the envious Casca made;
> Through this the well-beloved Brutus stabbed;
> And, as he plucked his cursèd steel away,
> Mark how the blood of Cæsar followed it—' "

"Jeemy," said Mrs. Duncan at this moment to her husband, "ye'd better go over. He's loose agin, an' she's wi' chile."

The Scotchman thrust back his chair, moved strongly out of the ordered ritual of his life, and the warm fragrance of new-baked bread.

At the gate, outside Gant's, he found patient Jannadeau, fetched down by Ben. They spoke matter-of-factly, and hastened up the steps as they heard a crash upstairs, and a woman's cry. Eliza, in only her night-dress, opened the door:

"Come quick!" she whispered. "Come quick!"

"By God, I'll kill her," Gant screamed, plunging down the stairs at greater peril to his own life than to any other. "I'll kill her now, and put an end to my misery."

He had a heavy poker in his hand. The two men seized him; the burly jeweller took the poker from his hand with quiet strength.

"He cut his head on the bed-rail, mama," said Steve descending. It was true: Gant bled.

"Go for your Uncle Will, son. Quick!" He was off like a hound.

"I think he meant it that time," she whispered.

Duncan shut the door against the gaping line of neighbors beyond the gate.

"Ye'll be gettin' a cheel like that, Mrs. Gant."

"Keep him away from me! Keep him away!" she cried out strongly.

"Aye, I will that!" he answered in quiet Scotch.

She turned to go up the stairs, but on the second step she fell heavily to her knees. The country nurse, returning from the bathroom, in which she had locked herself, ran to her aid. She went up slowly then between the woman and Grover. Outside Ben dropped nimbly from the low eave on to the lily beds: Seth Tarkinton, clinging to fence wires, shouted greetings.

Gant went off docilely, somewhat dazed, between his two guardians: as his huge limbs sprawled brokenly in his rocker, they undressed him. Helen had already been busy in the kitchen for some time: she appeared now with boiling soup.

Gant's dead eyes lit with recognition as he saw her.

"Why baby," he roared, making a vast maudlin circle with his arms, "how are you?" She put the soup down; he swept her thin body crushingly against him, brushing her cheek and neck with his stiff-bristled mustache, breathing upon her the foul rank odor of rye whisky.

"Oh, he's cut himself!" the little girl thought she was going to cry.

"Look what they did to me, baby," he pointed to his wound and whimpered.

Will Pentland, true son of that clan who forgot one another never, and who saw one another only in times of death, pestilence, and terror, came in.

"Good evening, Mr. Pentland," said Duncan.

"Jus' tolable," he said, with his bird-like nod and wink, taking in both men good-naturedly. He stood in front of the fire, paring meditatively at his blunt nails with a dull knife. It was his familiar gesture when in company: no one, he felt, could see what you thought about anything, if you pared your nails.

The sight of him drew Gant instantly from his lethargy: he remembered the dissolved partnership; the familiar attitude of Will Pentland, as he stood before the fire, evoked all the markings he so heartily loathed in the clan—its pert complacency, its incessant punning, its success.

"Mountain Grills!" he roared. "Mountain Grills! The lowest of the low! The vilest of the vile!"

"Mr. Gant! Mr. Gant!" pleaded Jannadeau.

"What's the matter with you, W.O.?" asked Will Pentland, looking up innocently from his fingers. "Had something to eat that didn't agree with you?"—he winked pertly at Duncan, and went back to his fingers.

"Your miserable old father," howled Gant, "was horsewhipped on the public square for not paying his debts." This was a purely imaginative insult, which had secured itself as truth, however, in Gant's mind, as had so many other stock epithets, because it gave him heart-cockle satisfaction.

"Horsewhipped upon his public square, was he?" Will winked again, unable to resist the opening. "They kept it mighty quiet, didn't they?" But behind the intense good-humored posture of his face, his eyes were hard. He pursed his lips meditatively as he worked upon his fingers.

"But I'll tell you something about him, W. O.," he continued after a moment, with calm but boding judiciousness. "He let his wife die a natural death in her own bed. He didn't try to kill her."

"No, by God!" Gant rejoined. "He let her starve to death. If the old woman ever got a square meal in her life she got it under my roof. There's one thing sure: she could have gone to Hell and back, twice over, before she got it from old Tom Pentland, or any of his sons."

Will Pentland closed his blunt knife and put it in his pocket.

"Old Major Pentland never did an honest day's work in his life," Gant yelled, as a happy afterthought.

"Come now, Mr. Gant!" said Duncan reproachfully.

"Hush! Hush!" whispered the girl fiercely, coming before him closely with the soup. She thrust a smoking ladle at his mouth, but he turned his head away to hurl another insult. She slapped him sharply across the mouth.

"You *drink* this!" she whispered. And grinning meekly as his eyes rested upon her, he began to swallow soup.

Will Pentland looked at the girl attentively for a moment, then glanced at Duncan and Jannadeau with a nod and wink. Without saying another word, he left the room, and mounted the stairs. His sister lay quietly extended on her back.

"How do you feel, Eliza?" The room was heavy with the rich odor of mellowing pears; an unaccustomed fire of pine sticks burned in the grate: he took up his place before it, and began to pare his nails.

"Nobody knows—nobody knows," she began, bursting quickly into a rapid flow of tears, "what I've been through." She wiped her eyes in a moment on a corner of the coverlid: her broad powerful nose, founded redly on her white face, was like flame.

"What you got good to eat?" he said, winking at her with a comic gluttony.

"There are some pears in there on the shelf, Will. I put them there last week to mellow."

He went into the big closet and returned in a moment with a large yellow pear; he came back to the hearth and opened the smaller blade of his knife.

"I'll vow, Will," she said quietly after a moment. "I've had all I can put up with. I don't know what's got into him. But you can bet your bottom dollar I won't stand much more of it. I know how to shift for myself," she said, nodding her head smartly. He recognized the tone.

He almost forgot himself: "See her, Eliza," he began, "if you were thinking of building somewhere, I"—but he recovered himself in time—"I'll make you the best price you can get on the material," he concluded. He thrust a slice of pear quickly into his mouth.

She pursed her mouth rapidly for some moments.

"No," she said. "I'm not ready for that yet, Will. I'll let you know." The loose wood-coals crumbled on the hearth.

"I'll let you know," she said again. He clasped his knife and thrust it in a trousers pocket.

"Good night, Eliza," he said. "I reckon Pett will be in to see you. I'll tell her you're all right."

He went down the stairs quietly, and let himself out through the front door. As he descended the tall veranda steps, Duncan and Jannadeau came quietly down the yard from the sitting-room.

"How's W. O.?" he asked.

"Ah, he'll be all right now," said Duncan cheerfully. "He's fast asleep."

"The sleep of the righteous?" asked Will Pentland with a wink.

The Swiss resented the implied jeer at his Titan. "It is a gread bitty," began Jannadeau in a low guttural voice, "that Mr. Gant drinks. With his mind he could go far. When he's sober a finer man doesn't live."

"When he's sober?" said Will, winking at him in the dark. "What about when he's asleep."

"He's all right the minute Helen gets hold of him," Mr. Duncan remarked in his rich voice. "It's wonderful what that little girl can do to him."

"Ah, I tell you!" Jannadeau laughed with guttural pleasure. "That little girl knows her daddy in and out."

The child sat in the big chair by the waning sitting-room fire: she read until the flames had died to coals—then quietly she shovelled ashes on them. Gant, fathoms deep in slumber, lay on the smooth leather sofa against the wall. She had wrapped him well in a blanket; now she put a pillow on a chair and placed his feet on it. He was rank with whisky stench; the window rattled as he snored.

Thus, drowned in oblivion, ran his night; he slept when the great pangs of birth began in Eliza at two o'clock; slept through all the patient pain and care of doctor, nurse, and wife.

4

The baby was, to reverse an epigram, an unconscionable time in getting born; but when Gant finally awoke just after ten o'clock next morning, whimpering from tangled nerves, and the quivering shame of dim remembrance, he heard, as he drank the hot coffee Helen brought to him, a loud, long lungy cry above.

"Oh, my God, my God," he groaned. And he pointed toward the sound. "Is it a boy or a girl?"

"I haven't seen it yet, papa," Helen answered. "They won't let us in. But Doctor Cardiac came out and told us if we were good he might bring us a little boy."

There was a terrific clatter on the tin roof, the scolding country voice of the nurse: Steve dropped like a cat from the porch roof to the lily bed outside Gant's window.

"Steve, you damned scoundrel," roared the manor-lord with a momentary return to health, "what in the name of Jesus are you doing?"

The boy was gone over the fence.

"I seen it! I seen it!" his voice came streaking back.

"I seen it too!" screamed Grover, racing through the room and out again in simple exultancy.

"If I catch you younguns on this roof agin," yelled the country nurse aloft, "I'll take your hide off you."

Gant had been momentarily cheered when he heard that his latest heir was a male; but he walked the length of the room now, making endless plaint.

"Oh my God, my God! Did this have to be put upon me in my old age? Another mouth to feed! It's fearful, it's awful, it's croo-el," and he began to weep affectedly. Then, realizing presently that no one was near enough to be touched by his sorrow, he paused suddenly and precipitated himself toward the door, crossing the dining-room, and, going up the hall, making loud lament:

"Eliza! My wife! Oh, baby, say that you forgive me!" He went up the stairs, sobbing laboriously.

"Don't you let him in here!" cried the object of this prayer sharply with quite remarkable energy.

"Tell him he can't come in now," said Cardiac, in his dry voice, to the nurse, staring intently at the scales. "We've nothing but milk to drink, anyway," he added.

Gant was outside.

"Eliza, my wife! Be merciful, I beg of you. If I had known——"

"Yes," said the country nurse opening the door rudely, "if the dog hadn't stopped to lift his leg he'd a-caught the rabbit! You get away from here!" And she slammed it violently in his face.

He went downstairs with hang-dog head, but he grinned slyly as he thought of the nurse's answer. He wet his big thumb quickly on his tongue.

"Merciful God!" he said, and grinned. Then he set up his caged lament.

"I think this will do," said Cardiac, holding up something red, shiny, and puckered by its heels, and smacking it briskly on its rump, to liven it a bit.

The heir apparent had, as a matter of fact, made his debut completely equipped with all appurtenances, dependences, screws, cocks, faucets, hooks, eyes, nails, considered necessary for completeness of appearance, harmony of parts, and unity of effect in this most energetic, driving, and competitive world. He was the complete male in miniature, the tiny acorn from which the mighty oak must grow, the heir of all ages, the inheritor of unfulfilled renown, the child of progress, the darling of the budding Golden Age and, what's more, Fortune and her Fairies, not content with well-nigh smothering him with these blessings of time and family, saved him up carefully until Progress was rotten-ripe with glory.

"Well, what are you going to call it?" inquired Dr. Cardiac, referring thus, with shocking and medical coarseness, to this most royal imp.

Eliza was better tuned to cosmic vibrations. With a full, if inexact, sense of what portended, she gave to Luck's Lad the title of Eugene, a name which, beautifully, means "well born," but which, as any one will be able to testify, does not mean, has never meant, "well bred."

This chosen incandescence, to whom a name had already been given, and from whose centre most of the events in this chronicle must be seen, was borne in, as we have said, upon the very spear-head of history. But perhaps, reader, you have already thought of that? You *haven't?* Then let us refresh your historical memory.

By 1900, Oscar Wilde and James A. McNeill Whistler had almost finished saying the things they were reported as saying, and that Eugene was destined to hear, twenty years later; most of the Great Victorians had died before the bombardment began; William McKinley was up for a second term, the crew of the Spanish navy had returned home in a tugboat.

Abroad, grim old Britain had sent her ultimatum to the South Africans in 1899; Lord Roberts ("Little Bobs," as he was known affectionately to his men) was appointed commander-in-chief after several British reverses; the Transvaal Republic was annexed to Great Britain in September 1900, and formally annexed in the month of Eugene's birth. There was a Peace Conference two years later.

Meanwhile, what was going on in Japan? I will tell you: the first parliament met in 1891, there was a war with China in 1894-95, Formosa was ceded in 1895. Moreover, Warren Hastings had been impeached and tried; Pope Sixtus the Fifth had come and gone; Dalmatia had been subdued by Tiberius; Belisarius had been blinded by Justinian; the wedding and funeral ceremonies of Wilhelmina Charlotte Caroline of Brandenburg-Ansbach and King George the Second had been solemnized, while those of Berengaria of Navarre to King Richard the First were hardly more than a distant memory; Diocletian, Charles the Fifth, and Victor Amadeus of Sardinia, had all abdicated their thrones; Henry James Pye, Poet Laureate of England, was with his fathers; Cassiodorus, Quintilian, Juvenal, Lucretius, Martial, and Albert the Bear of Brandenburg had answered the last great roll-call; the battles of Antietam, Smolensko, Drumclog, Inkerman, Marengo, Cawnpore, Killiecrankie, Sluys, Actium, Lepanto, Tewkesbury, Brandywine, Hohenlinden, Salamis, and the Wilderness had been fought both by land and by sea; Hippias had been expelled from Athens by the Alcæmonidæ and the Lacedæmonians; Simonides, Menander, Strabo, Moschus, and Pindar had closed their earthly accounts; the beatified Eusebius, Athanasius, and Chrysostom had gone to their celestial niches; Menkaura had built the Third Pyramid; Aspalta had led victorious armies; the remote Bermudas, Malta, and the Windward Isles had been colonized. In addition, the Spanish Armada had been defeated; President Abraham Lincoln assassinated, and the Halifax Fisheries Award had given $5,500,000 to Britain for twelve-year fishing privileges. Finally, only thirty or forty million years before, our earliest ancestors had crawled out of the primeval slime; and then, no doubt, finding the change unpleasant, crawled back in again.

Such was the state of history when Eugene entered the theatre of human events in 1900.

We would give willingly some more extended account of the world his life touched during the first few years, showing, in all its perspectives and implications, the meaning of life as seen from the floor, or from the crib, but these impressions are suppressed when they might be told, not through any fault of intelligence, but through lack of muscular control, the powers of articulation, and because of the recurring waves of loneliness, weariness, depression, aberration, and utter blankness which war against the order in a man's mind until he is three or four years old.

Lying darkly in his crib, washed, powdered, and fed, he thought quietly of many things before he dropped off to sleep—the interminable sleep that obliterated time for him, and that gave him a sense of having missed forever a day of sparkling life. At these moments, he was heartsick with weary horror as he thought of the discomfort, weakness, dumbness, the infinite misunderstanding he would have to endure before he gained even physical freedom. He grew sick as he thought of the weary distance before him, the lack of co-ordination of the centres of control, the undisciplined and rowdy bladder, the helpless exhibition he was forced to give in the company of his sniggering, pawing brothers and sisters, dried, cleaned, revolved before them.

He was in agony because he was poverty-stricken in symbols: his mind was caught in a net because he had no words to work with. He had not even names for the objects around him: he probably defined them for himself by some jargon, reinforced by some mangling of the speech that roared about him, to which he listened intently day after day, realizing that his first escape must come through language. He indicated as quickly as he could his ravenous hunger for pictures and print: sometimes they brought him great books profusely illustrated, and he bribed them desperately by cooing, shrieking with delight, making extravagant faces, and doing all the other things they understood in him. He wondered savagely how they would feel if they knew what he really thought: at other times he had to laugh at them and at their whole preposterous comedy of errors as they pranced around for his amusement, waggled their heads at him, tickled him roughly, making him squeal violently against his will. The situation was at once profoundly annoying and comic: as he sat in the middle of the floor and watched them enter, seeing the face of each transformed by a foolish leer, and hearing their voices become absurd and sentimental whenever they addressed him, speaking to him words which he did not yet understand, but which he saw they were mangling in the preposterous hope of rendering intelligible that which has been previously mutilated, he had to laugh at the fools, in spite of his vexation.

And left alone to sleep within a shuttered room, with the thick sunlight printed in bars upon the floor, unfathomable loneliness and sadness crept through him: he saw his life down the solemn vista of a forest aisle, and he knew he would always be the sad one: caged in that little round of skull, imprisoned in that beating and most secret heart, his life must always walk down lonely passages. Lost. He understood that men were forever strangers to one another, that no one ever comes really to know any one, that imprisoned in the dark womb of our mother, we come to life without having seen her face, that we are given to her arms a stranger, and that, caught in that insoluble prison of being, we escape it never, no matter what arms may clasp us, what mouth may kiss us, what heart may warm us. Never, never, never, never, never.

He saw that the great figures that came and went about him, the huge leering heads that bent hideously into his crib, the great voices that rolled incoherently above him, had for one another not much greater understanding than they had for him: that even their speech, their entire fluidity and ease of movement were but meagre communicants of their thought or feeling, and served often not to promote understanding, but to deepen and widen strife, bitterness, and prejudice.

His brain went black with terror. He saw himself an inarticulate stranger, an amusing little clown, to be dandled and nursed by these enormous and remote figures. He had been sent from one mystery into another: somewhere within or without his consciousness he heard a great bell ringing faintly, as if it sounded undersea, and as he listened, the ghost of memory walked through his mind, and for a moment he felt that he had almost recovered what he had lost.

Sometimes, pulling himself abreast the high walls of his crib, he glanced down dizzily at the patterns of the carpet far below; the world swam in and out of his mind like a tide, now printing its whole sharp picture for an instant, again ebbing out dimly and sleepily, while he pieced the puzzle of sensation together bit by bit, seeing only the dancing fire-sheen on the poker, hearing then the elfin clucking of the sun-warm hens, somewhere beyond in a distant and enchanted world. Again, he heard their morning-wakeful crowing clear and loud, suddenly becoming a substantial and alert citizen of life; or, going and coming in alternate waves of fantasy and fact, he heard the loud, faery thunder of Daisy's parlor music. Years later, he heard it again, a door opened in his brain: she told him it was Paderewski's "Minuet."

His crib was a great woven basket, well mattressed and pillowed within; as he grew stronger, he was able to perform extraordinary acrobatics in it, tumbling, making a hoop of his body, and drawing himself easily and strongly erect: with patient effort he could worm over the side on to the floor. There, he would crawl on the vast design of the carpet, his eyes intent upon great wooden blocks piled chaotically on the floor. They had belonged to his brother Luke: all the letters of the alphabet, in bright multi-colored carving, were engraved upon them.

Holding them clumsily in his tiny hands, he studied for hours the symbols of speech, knowing that he had here the stones of the temple of language, and striving desperately to find the key that would draw order and intelligence from this anarchy. Great voices soared far above him, vast shapes came and went, lifting him to dizzy heights, depositing him with exhaustless strength. The bell rang under the sea.

One day when the opulent Southern Spring had richly unfolded, when the spongy black earth of the yard was covered with sudden, tender grass, and wet blossoms, the great cherry tree seethed slowly with a massive gem of amber sap, and the cherries hung ripening in prodigal clusters, Gant took him from his basket in the sun on the high front porch, and went with him around the house by the lily bed, taking him back under trees singing with hidden birds, to the far end of the lot.

Here the earth was unshaded, dry, clotted by the plough. Eugene knew by the stillness that it was Sunday: against the high wire fence there was the heavy smell of hot dock-weed. On the other side, Swain's cow was wrenching the cool coarse grass, lifting her head from time to time, and singing in her strong deep voice her Sunday exuberance. In the warm washed air, Eugene heard with absolute clearness all the brisk backyard sounds of the neighborhood, he became acutely aware of the whole scene, and as Swain's cow sang out again, he felt the flooded gates in him swing open. He answered "Moo!" phrasing the sound timidly but perfectly, and repeating it confidently in a moment when the cow answered.

Gant's delight was boundless. He turned and raced back toward the house at the full stride of his legs. And as he went, he nuzzled his stiff mustache into Eugene's tender neck, mooing industriously and always getting an answer.

"Lord a' mercy!" cried Eliza, looking from the kitchen window as he raced down the yard with breakneck strides, "He'll kill that child yet."

And as he rushed up the kitchen steps—all the house, save the upper side was off the ground—she came out on the little latticed veranda, her hands floury, her nose stove-red.

"Why, what on earth are you doing, Mr. Gant?"

"Moo-o-o! He said 'Moo-o-o!' Yes he did!" Gant spoke to Eugene rather than to Eliza.

Eugene answered him immediately: he felt it was all rather silly, and he saw he would be kept busy imitating Swain's cow for several days, but he was tremendously excited, nevertheless, feeling now that that wall had been breached.

Eliza was likewise thrilled, but her way of showing it was to turn back to the stove, hiding her pleasure, and saying: "I'll vow, Mr. Gant. I never saw such an idiot with a child."

Later, Eugene lay wakefully in his basket on the sitting-room floor, watching the smoking dishes go by in the eager hands of the combined family, for Eliza at this time cooked magnificently, and a Sunday dinner was something to remember. For two hours since their return from church, the little boys had been prowling hungrily around the kitchen: Ben, frowning proudly, kept his dignity outside the screen, making excursions frequently through the house to watch the progress of cookery; Grover came in and watched with frank interest until he was driven out; Luke, his broad humorous little face split by a wide exultant smile, rushed through the house, squealing exultantly:

> "Weenie, weedie, weeky
> Weenie, weedie, weeky,
> Weenie, weedie, weeky,
> Wee, Wee, Wee."

He had heard Daisy and Josephine Brown doing Cæsar together, and his chant was his own interpretation of Cæsar's brief boast: "Veni, Vidi, Vici."

As Eugene lay in his crib, he heard through the open door the dining-room clatter, the shrill excitement of the boys, the clangor of steel and knife as Gant prepared to carve the roast, the repetition of the morning's great event told over and over without variation, but with increasing zest.

"Soon," he thought, as the heavy food fragrance floated in to him, "I shall be in there with them." And he thought lusciously of mysterious and succulent food.

All through the afternoon upon the veranda Gant told the story, summoning the neighbors and calling upon Eugene to perform. Eugene heard clearly all that was said that day: he was not able to answer, but he saw now that speech was imminent.

Thus, later, he saw the first two years of his life in brilliant and isolated flashes. His second Christmas he remembered vaguely as a period of great festivity: it accustomed him to the third when it came. With the miraculous habitude children acquire, it seemed that he had known Christmas forever.

He was conscious of sunlight, rain, the leaping fire, his crib, the grim jail of winter: the second Spring, one warm day, he saw Daisy go off to school up the hill: it was the end of the noon recess, she had been home for lunch. She went to Miss Ford's School For Girls; it was a red brick residence on the corner at the top of the steep hill: he watched her join Eleanor Duncan just below. Her hair was braided in two long hanks down her back: she was demure, shy, maidenly, a timid and blushing girl; but he feared her attentions to him, for she bathed him furiously, wreaking whatever was explosive and violent beneath her placidity upon his hide. She really scrubbed him almost raw. He howled piteously. As she climbed the hill, he remembered her. He saw she was the same person.

He passed his second birthday with the light growing. Early in the following Spring he became conscious of a period of neglect: the house was deadly quiet; Gant's voice no longer roared around him, the boys came and went on stealthy feet. Luke, the fourth to be attacked by the pestilence, was desperately ill with typhoid: Eugene was intrusted almost completely to a young slovenly negress. He remembered vividly her tall slattern figure, her slapping lazy feet, her dirty white stockings, and her strong smell, black and funky. One day she took him out on the side porch to play: it was a young Spring morning, bursting moistly from the thaw of the earth. The negress sat upon the side-steps and yawned while he grubbed in his dirty little dress along the path, and upon the lily bed. Presently, she went to sleep against the post. Craftily, he wormed his body through the wide wires of the fence, into the cindered alley that wound back to the Swains', and up to the ornate wooden palace of the Hilliards.

They were among the highest aristocracy of the town: they had come from South Carolina, "near Charleston," which in itself gave them at that time a commanding prestige. The house, a huge gabled structure of walnut-brown, which gave the effect of many angles and no plan, was built upon the top of the hill which sloped down to Gant's; the level ground on top before the house was tenanted by lordly towering oaks. Below, along the cindered alley, flanking Gant's orchard, there were high singing pines.

Mr. Hilliard's house was considered one of the finest residences in the town. The neighborhood was middle-class, but the situation was magnificent, and the Hilliards carried on in the grand manner, lords of the castle who descended into the village, but did not mix with its people. All of their friends arrived by carriage from afar; every day punctually at two o'clock, an old liveried negro drove briskly up the winding alley behind two sleek brown mares, waiting under the carriage entrance at the side until his master and mistress should come out. Five minutes later they drove out, and were gone for two hours.

This ritual, followed closely from his father's sitting-room window, fascinated Eugene for years after: the people and the life next door were crudely and symbolically above him.

He felt a great satisfaction that morning in being at length in Hilliard's alley: it was his first escape, and it had been made into a forbidden and enhaloed region. He grubbed about in the middle of the road, disappointed in the quality of the cinders. The booming courthouse bell struck eleven times.

Now, exactly at three minutes after eleven every morning, so unfailing and perfect was the order of this great establishment, a huge gray horse trotted slowly up the hill, drawing behind him a heavy grocery wagon, musty, spicy, odorous with the fine smells of grocery-stores and occupied exclusively by the Hilliard victuals, and the driver, a young negro man who, at three minutes past eleven every morning, according to ritual, was comfortably asleep. Nothing could possibly go wrong: the horse could not have been tempted even by a pavement of oats to betray his sacred mission. Accordingly he trotted heavily up the hill, turned ponderously into the alley ruts, and advanced heavily until, feeling the great circle of his right forefoot obstructed by some foreign particle, he looked down and slowly removed his hoof from what had recently been the face of a little boy.

Then, with his legs carefully straddled, he moved on, drawing the wagon beyond Eugene's body, and stopping. Both negroes awoke simultaneously; there were cries within the house, and Eliza and Gant rushed out of doors. The frightened negro lifted Eugene, who was quite unconscious of his sudden return to the stage, into the burly arms of Doctor McGuire, who cursed the driver eloquently. His thick sensitive fingers moved swiftly around the bloody little face and found no fracture.

He nodded briefly at their desperate faces: "He's being saved for Congress," said he. "You have bad luck and hard heads, W. O."

"You Goddamned black scoundrel," yelled the master, turning with violent relief upon the driver. "I'll put you behind the bars for this." He thrust his great length of hands through the fence and choked the negro, who mumbled prayers, and had no idea what was happening to him, save that he was the centre of a wild commotion.

The negro girl, blubbering, had fled inward.

"This looks worse than it is," observed Dr. McGuire, laying the hero upon the lounge. "Some hot water, please." Nevertheless, it took two hours to bring him round. Every one spoke highly of the horse.

"He had more sense than the nigger," said Gant, wetting his thumb.

But all this, as Eliza knew in her heart, was part of the plan of the Dark Sisters. The entrails had been woven and read long since: the frail shell of skull which guarded life, and which might have been crushed as easily as a man breaks an egg, was kept intact. But Eugene carried the mark of the centaur for many years, though the light had to fall properly to reveal it.

When he was older, he wondered sometimes if the Hilliards had issued from their high place when he had so impiously disturbed the order of the manor. He never asked, but he thought not: he imagined them, at the most, as standing superbly by a drawn curtain, not quite certain what had happened, but feeling that it was something unpleasant, with blood in it.

Shortly after this, Mr. Hilliard had a "No-Trespassing" sign staked up in the lot.

5

Luke got well after cursing doctor, nurse, and family for several weeks: it was stubborn typhoid.

Gant was now head of a numerous family, which rose ladderwise from infancy to the adolescent Steve—who was eighteen—and the maidenly Daisy. She was seventeen and in her last year at high school. She was a timid, sensitive girl, looking like her name—Daisy-ish industrious and thorough in her studies: her teachers thought her one of the best students they had ever known. She had very little fire, or denial in her; she responded dutifully to instructions; she gave back what had been given to her. She played the piano without any passionate feeling for the music; but she rendered it honestly with a beautiful rippling touch. And she practised hours at a time.

It was apparent, however, that Steve was lacking in scholarship. When he was fourteen, he was summoned by the school principal to his little office, to take a thrashing for truancy and insubordination. But the spirit of acquiescence was not in him: he snatched the rod from the man's hand, broke it, smote him solidly in the eye, and dropped gleefully eighteen feet to the ground.

This was one of the best things he ever did: his conduct in other directions was less fortunate. Very early, as his truancy mounted, and after he had been expelled, and as his life hardened rapidly in a defiant viciousness, the antagonism between the boy and Gant grew open and bitter. Gant recognized perhaps most of his son's vices as his own: there was little, however, of his redeeming quality. Steve had a piece of tough suet where his heart should have been.

Of them all, he had had very much the worst of it. Since his childhood he had been the witness of his father's wildest debauches. He had not forgotten. Also, as the oldest, he was left to shift for himself while Eliza's attention focussed on her younger children. She was feeding Eugene at her breast long after Steve had taken his first two dollars to the ladies of Eagle Crescent.

He was inwardly sore at the abuse Gant heaped on him; he was not insensitive to his faults, but to be called a "good-for-nothing bum," "a worthless degenerate," "a pool-room loafer," hardened his outward manner of swagger defiance. Cheaply and flashily dressed, with peg-top yellow shoes, flaring striped trousers, and a broad-brimmed straw hat with a colored band, he would walk down the avenue with a preposterous lurch, and a smile of strained assurance on his face, saluting with servile cordiality all who would notice him. And if a man of property greeted him, his lacerated but overgrown vanity would seize the crumb, and he would boast pitifully at home: "They all know Little Stevie! He's got the respect of all the big men in this town, all right, all right! Every one has a good word for Little Stevie except his own people. Do you know what J. T. Collins said to me to-day?"

"What say? Who's that? Who's that?" asked Eliza with comic rapidity, looking up from her darning.

"J. T. Collins—that's who! He's only worth about two hundred thousand. 'Steve,' he said, just like that, 'if I had your brains' "—He would continue in this way with moody self-satisfaction, painting a picture of future success when all who scorned him now would flock to his standard.

"Oh, yes," said he, "they'll all be mighty anxious then to shake Little Stevie's hand."

Gant, in a fury, gave him a hard beating when he had been expelled from school. He had never forgotten. Finally, he was told to go to work and support himself: he found desultory employment as a soda-jerker, or as delivery boy for a morning paper. Once, with a crony, Gus Moody, son of a foundry-man, he had gone off to see the world. Grimy from vagabondage they had crawled off a freight-train at Knoxville, Tennessee, spent their little money on food, and in a brothel, and returned, two days later, coal-black but boastful of their exploit.

"I'll vow," Eliza fretted, "I don't know what's to become of that boy." It was the tragic flaw of her temperament to get to the vital point too late: she pursed her lips thoughtfully, wandered off in another direction, and wept when misfortune came. She always waited. Moreover, in her deepest heart, she had an affection for her oldest son, which, if it was not greater, was at least different in kind from what she bore for the others. His glib boastfulness, his pitiable brag, pleased her: they were to her indications of his "smartness," and she often infuriated her two studious girls by praising them. Thus, looking at a specimen of his handwriting, she would say:

"There's one thing sure: he writes a better hand than any of the rest of you, for all your schooling."

Steve had early tasted the joys of the bottle, stealing, during the days when he was a young attendant of his father's debauch, a furtive swallow from the strong rank whisky in a half-filled flask: the taste nauseated him, but the experience made good boasting for his fellows.

At fifteen, he had found, while smoking cigarettes with Gus Moody, in a neighbor's barn, a bottle wrapped in an oats sack by the worthy citizen, against the too sharp examination of his wife. When the man had come for secret potation some time later, and found his bottle half-empty, he had grimly dosed the remainder with Croton oil: the two boys were nauseously sick for several days.

One day, Steve forged a check on his father. It was some days before Gant discovered it: the amount was only three dollars, but his anger was bitter. In a pronouncement at home, delivered loudly enough to publish the boy's offense to the neighborhood, he spoke of the penitentiary, of letting him go to jail, of being disgraced in his old age—a period of his life at which he had not yet arrived, but which he used to his advantage in times of strife.

He paid the check, of course, but another name—that of "forger"—was added to the vocabulary of his abuse. Steve sneaked in and out of the house, eating his meals alone for several days. When he met his father little was said by either: behind the hard angry glaze of their eyes, they both looked depthlessly into each other; they knew that they could withhold nothing from each other, that the same sores festered in each, the same hungers and desires, the same crawling appetites polluted their blood. And knowing this, something in each of them turned away in grievous shame.

Gant added this to his tirades against Eliza; all that was bad in the boy his mother had given him.

"Mountain Blood! Mountain Blood!" he yelled. "He's Greeley Pentland all over again. Mark my words," he continued, after striding feverishly about the house, muttering to himself and bursting finally into the kitchen, "mark my words, he'll wind up in the penitentiary."

And, her nose reddened by the spitting grease, she would purse her lips, saying little, save, when goaded, to make some return calculated to infuriate and antagonize him.

"Well, maybe if he hadn't been sent to every dive in town to pull his daddy out, he would turn out better."

"You lie, Woman! By God, you lie!" he thundered magnificently but illogically.

Gant drank less: save for a terrifying spree every six or eight weeks, which bound them all in fear for two or three days, Eliza had little to complain of on this score. But her enormous patience was wearing very thin because of the daily cycle of abuse. They slept now in separate rooms upstairs: he rose at six or six-thirty, dressed and went down to build the fires. As he kindled a blaze in the range, and a roaring fire in the sitting-room, he muttered constantly to himself, with an occasional oratorical rise and fall of his voice. In this way he composed and polished the flood of his invective: when the demands of fluency and emphasis had been satisfied he would appear suddenly before her in the kitchen, and deliver himself without preliminary, as the grocer's negro entered with pork chops or a thick steak:

"Woman, would you have had a roof to shelter you to-day if it hadn't been for me? Could you have depended on your worthless old father, Tom Pentland, to give you one? Would Brother Will, or Brother Jim give you one? Did you ever hear of them giving any one anything? Did you ever hear of them caring for anything but their own miserable hides? Did you? Would any of them give a starving beggar a crust of bread? By God, no!

Not even if he ran a bakery shop! Ah me! 'Twas a bitter day for me when I first came into this accursed country: little did I know what it would lead to. Mountain Grills! Mountain Grills!" and the tide would reach its height.

At times, when she tried to reply to his attack, she would burst easily into tears. This pleased him: he liked to see her cry. But usually she made an occasional nagging retort: deep down, between their blind antagonistic souls, an ugly and desperate war was being waged. Yet, had he known to what lengths these daily assaults might drive her, he would have been astounded: they were part of the deep and feverish discontent of his spirit, the rooted instinct to have an object for his abuse.

Moreover, his own feeling for order was so great that he had a passionate aversion for what was slovenly, disorderly, diffuse. He was goaded to actual fury at times when he saw how carefully she saved bits of old string, empty cans and bottles, paper, trash of every description: the mania for acquisition, as yet an undeveloped madness in Eliza, enraged him.

"In God's name!" he would cry with genuine anger. "In God's name! Why don't you get rid of some of this junk?" And he would move destructively toward it.

"No you don't, Mr. Gant!" she would answer sharply. "You never know when those things will come in handy."

It was, perhaps, a reversal of custom that the deep-hungering spirit of quest belonged to the one with the greatest love of order, the most pious regard for ritual, who wove into a pattern even his daily tirades of abuse, and that the sprawling blot of chaos, animated by one all-mastering desire for possession, belonged to the practical, the daily person.

Gant had the passion of the true wanderer, of him who wanders from a fixed point. He needed the order and the dependence of a home—he was intensely a family man: their clustered warmth and strength about him was life. After his punctual morning tirade at Eliza, he went about the rousing of the slumbering children. Comically, he could not endure feeling, in the morning, that he was the only one awake and about.

His waking cry, delivered by formula, with huge comic gruffness from the foot of the stairs, took this form:

"Steve! Ben! Grover! Luke! You damned scoundrels: get up! In God's name, what will become of you! You'll never amount to anything as long as you live."

He would continue to roar at them from below as if they were wakefully attentive above.

"When I was your age, I had milked four cows, done all the chores, and walked eight miles through the snow by this time."

Indeed, when he described his early schooling, he furnished a landscape that was constantly three feet deep in snow, and frozen hard. He seemed never to have attended school save under polar conditions.

And fifteen minutes later, he would roar again: "You'll never amount to anything, you good-for-nothing bums! If one side of the wall caved in, you'd roll over to the other."

Presently now there would be the rapid thud of feet upstairs, and one by one they would descend, rushing naked into the sitting-room with their clothing bundled in their arms. Before his roaring fire they would dress.

By breakfast, save for sporadic laments, Gant was in something approaching good humor. They fed hugely: he stoked their plates for them with great slabs of fried steak, grits fried in egg, hot biscuits, jam, fried apples. He departed for his shop about the time the boys, their throats still convulsively swallowing hot food and coffee, rushed from the house at the warning signal of the mellow-tolling final nine-o'clock school bell.

He returned for lunch—dinner, as they called it—briefly garrulous with the morning's news; in the evening, as the family gathered in again, he returned, built his great fire, and launched his supreme invective, a ceremony which required a half hour in composition, and another three-quarters, with repetition and additions, in delivery. They dined then quite happily.

So passed the winter. Eugene was three; they bought him alphabet books, and animal pictures, with rhymed fables below. Gant read them to him indefatigably: in six weeks he knew them all by memory.

Through the late winter and spring he performed numberless times for the neighbors: holding the book in his hands he pretended to read what he knew by heart. Gant was delighted: he abetted the deception. Every one thought it extraordinary that a child should read so young.

In the Spring Gant began to drink again; his thirst withered, however, in two or three weeks, and shamefacedly he took up the routine of his life. But Eliza was preparing for a change.

It was 1904; there was in preparation a great world's exposition at Saint Louis: it was to be the visual history of civilization, bigger, better, and greater than anything of its kind ever known before. Many of the Altamont people intended to go: Eliza was fascinated at the prospect of combining travel with profit.

"Do you know what?" she began thoughtfully one night, as she laid down the paper, "I've a good notion to pack up and go."

"Go? Go where?"

"To Saint Louis," she answered. "Why, say—if things work out all right, we might simply pull out and settle down there." She knew that the suggestion of a total disruption of the established life, a voyage to new lands, a new quest of fortune fascinated him. It had been talked of years before when he had broken his partnership with Will Pentland.

"What do you intend to do out there? How are the children going to get along?"

"Why, sir," she began smugly, pursing her lips thoughtfully, and smiling cunningly, "I'll simply get me a good big house and drum up a trade among the Altamont people who are going."

"Merciful God, Mrs. Gant!" he howled tragically, "you surely wouldn't do a thing like that. I beg you not to."

"Why, pshaw, Mr. Gant, don't be such a fool. There's nothing wrong in keeping boarders. Some of the most respectable people in this town do it." She knew what a tender thing his pride was: he could not bear to be thought incapable of the support of his family—one of his most frequent boasts was that he was "a good provider." Further, the residence of any one under his roof not of his blood and bone sowed the air about with menace, breached his castle walls. Finally, he had a particular revulsion against lodgers: to earn one's living by accepting the contempt, the scorn, and the money of what he called "cheap boarders" was an almost unendurable ignominy.

She knew this but she could not understand his feeling. Not merely to possess property, but to draw income from it was part of the religion of her family, and she surpassed them all by her willingness to rent out a part of her home. She alone, in fact, of all the Pentlands was willing to relinquish the little moated castle of home; the particular secrecy and privacy of their walls she alone did not seem to value greatly. And she was the only one of them that wore a skirt.

Eugene had been fed from her breast until he was more than three years old: during the winter he was weaned. Something in her stopped; something began.

She had her way finally. Sometimes she would talk to Gant thoughtfully and persuasively about the World's Fair venture. Sometimes, during his evening tirades, she would snap back at him using the project as a threat. Just what was to be achieved she did not know. But she felt it was a beginning for her. And she had her way finally.

Gant succumbed to the lure of new lands. He was to remain at home: if all went well he would come out later. The prospect, too, of release for a time excited him. Something of the old thrill of youth touched him. He was left behind, but the world lurked full of unseen shadows for a lonely man. Daisy was in her last year at school: she stayed with him. But it cost him more than a pang or two to see Helen go. She was almost fourteen.

In early April, Eliza departed, bearing her excited brood about her, and carrying Eugene in her arms. He was bewildered at this rapid commotion, but he was electric with curiosity and activity.

The Tarkintons and Duncans streamed in: there were tears and kisses. Mrs. Tarkinton regarded her with some awe. The whole neighborhood was a bit bewildered at this latest turn.

"Well, well—you never can tell," said Eliza, smiling tearfully and enjoying the sensation she had provided. "If things go well we may settle down out there."

"You'll come back," said Mrs. Tarkinton with cheerful loyalty. "There's no place like Altamont."

They went to the station in the street-car: Ben and Grover gleefully sat together, guarding a big luncheon hamper. Helen clutched nervously a bundle of packages. Eliza glanced sharply at her long straight legs and thought of the half-fare.

"Say," she began, laughing indefinitely behind her hand, and nudging Gant, "she'll have to scrooch up, won't she? They'll think you're mighty big to be under twelve," she went on, addressing the girl directly.

Helen stirred nervously.

"We shouldn't have done that," Gant muttered.

"Pshaw!" said Eliza, "No one will ever notice her."

He saw them into the train, disposed comfortably by the solicitous Pullman porter.

"Keep your eye on them, George," he said, and gave the man a coin. Eliza eyed it jealously.

He kissed them all roughly with his mustache, but he patted his little girl's bony shoulders with his great hand, and hugged her to him. Something stabbed sharply in Eliza.

They had an awkward moment. The strangeness, the absurdity of the whole project, and the monstrous fumbling of all life, held them speechless.

"Well," he began, "I reckon you know what you're doing."

"Well, I tell you," she said, pursing her lips, and looking out the window, "you don't know what may come out of this."

He was vaguely appeased. The train jerked, and moved off slowly. He kissed her clumsily.

"Let me know as soon as you get there," he said, and he strode swiftly down the aisle.

"Good-by, good-by," cried Eliza, waving Eugene's small hand at the long figure on the platform. "Children," she said, "wave good-by to your papa." They all crowded to the window. Eliza wept.

Eugene watched the sun wane and redden on a rocky river, and on the painted rocks of Tennessee gorges: the enchanted river wound into his child's mind forever. Years later, it was to be remembered in dreams tenanted with elvish and mysterious beauty. Stilled in great wonder, he went to sleep to the rhythmical pounding of the heavy wheels.

They lived in a white house on the corner. There was a small plot of lawn in front, and a narrow strip on the side next to the pavement. He realized vaguely that it was far from the great central web and roar of the city—he thought he heard some one say four or five miles. Where was the river?

Two little boys, twins, with straight very blond heads, and thin, mean faces, raced up and down the sidewalk before the house incessantly on tricycles. They wore white sailor-suits, with blue collars, and he hated them very much. He felt vaguely that their father was a bad man who had fallen down an elevator shaft, breaking his legs.

The house had a back yard, completely enclosed by a red board fence. At the end was a red barn. Years later, Steve, returning home, said: "That section's all built up out there now." Where?

One day in the hot barren back yard, two cots and mattresses had been set up for airing. He lay upon one luxuriously, breathing the hot mattress, and drawing his small legs up lazily. Luke lay upon the other. They were eating peaches.

A fly grew sticky on Eugene's peach. He swallowed it. Luke howled with laughter.

"Swallowed a fly! Swallowed a fly!"

He grew violently sick, vomited, and was unable to eat for some time. He wondered why he had swallowed the fly when he had seen it all the time.

The summer came down blazing hot. Gant arrived for a few days, bringing Daisy with him. One night they drank beer at the Delmar Gardens. In the hot air, at a little table, he gazed thirstily at the beaded foaming stein: he would thrust his face, he thought, in that chill foam and drink deep of happiness. Eliza gave him a taste; they all shrieked at his bitter surprised face.

Years later he remembered Gant, his mustache flecked with foam, quaffing mightily at the glass: the magnificent gusto, the beautiful thirst inspired in him the desire for emulation, and he wondered if all beer were bitter, if there were not a period of initiation into the pleasures of this great beverage.

Faces from the old half-forgotten world floated in from time to time. Some of the Altamont people came and stayed at Eliza's house. One day, with sudden recollective horror he looked up into the brutal shaven face of Jim Lyda. He was the Altamont sheriff; he lived at the foot of the hill below Gant. Once, when Eugene was past two, Eliza had gone to Piedmont as witness in a trial. She was away two days; he was left in care of Mrs. Lyda. He had never forgotten Lyda's playful cruelty the first night.

Now, one day, this monster appeared again, by devilish sleight, and Eugene looked up into the heavy evil of his face. Eugene saw Eliza standing near Jim; and as the terror in the small face grew, Jim made as if to put his hand violently upon her. At his cry of rage and fear, they both laughed: for a blind moment or two Eugene for the first time hated her: he was mad, impotent with jealousy and fear.

At night the boys, Steve, Ben, and Grover, who had been sent out at once to seek employment by Eliza, returned from the Fair Grounds, chattering with the lively excitement of the day's bustle. Sniggering furtively, they talked suggestively about the Hoochy-Koochy: Eugene understood it was a dance. Steve hummed a monotonous, suggestive tune, and writhed sensually. They sang a song; the plaintive distant music haunted him. He learned it:

> "Meet me in Saint—Lou—iss, loo—ee,
> Meet me at the Fair,
> If you see the boys and girlies,
> Tell them I'll be there.
> We will dance the Hoochy-Koochy—"

and so on.

Sometimes, lying on a sunny quilt, Eugene grew conscious of a gentle peering face, a soft caressing voice, unlike any of the others in kind and quality, a tender olive skin, black hair, sloeblack eyes, exquisite, rather sad, kindliness. He nuzzled his soft face next to Eugene's, fondled and embraced him. On his brown neck he was birth-marked with a raspberry: Eugene touched it again and again with wonder. This was Grover—the gentlest and saddest of the boys.

Eliza sometimes allowed them to take him on excursions. Once, they made a voyage on a river steamer: he went below and from the side-openings looked closely upon the powerful yellow snake, coiling slowly and resistlessly past.

The boys worked on the Fair Grounds. They were call-boys at a place called the Inside Inn. The name charmed him: it flashed constantly through his brain. Sometimes his sisters, sometimes Eliza, sometimes the boys pulled him through the milling jungle of noise and figures, past the rich opulence and variety of the life of the Fair. He was drugged in fantasy as they passed the East India tea-house, and as he saw tall turbaned men who walked about within and caught for the first time, so that he never forgot, the slow incense of the East. Once in a huge building roaring with sound, he was rooted before a mighty locomotive, the greatest monster he had ever seen, whose wheels spun terrifically in grooves, whose blazing furnaces, raining hot red coals into the pit beneath, were fed incessantly by two grimed fire-painted stokers. The scene burned in his brain like some huge splendor out of Hell: he was appalled and fascinated by it.

Again, he stood at the edge of the slow, terrific orbit of the Ferris Wheel, reeled down the blaring confusion of the midway, felt his staggering mind converge helplessly into all the mad phantasmagoria of the carnival; he heard Luke's wild story of the snake-eater, and shrieked in agony when they threatened to take him in.

Once Daisy, yielding to the furtive cat-cruelty below her mild placidity, took him with her through the insane horrors of the scenic railway; they plunged bottomlessly from light into roaring blackness, and as his first yell ceased with a slackening of the car, rolled gently into a monstrous lighted gloom peopled with huge painted grotesques, the red maws of fiendish heads, the cunning appearances of death, nightmare, and madness. His unprepared mind was unrooted by insane fear: the car rolled downward from one lighted cavern to another, and as his heart withered to a pea, he heard from the people about him loud gusty laughter, in which his sister joined. His mind, just emerging from the unreal wilderness of childish fancy, gave way completely in this Fair, and he was paralyzed by the conviction, which often returned to him in later years, that his life was a fabulous nightmare and that, by cunning and conspirate artifice, he had surrendered all his hope, belief, and confidence to the lewd torture of demons masked in human flesh. Half-sensible, and purple with gasping terror, he came out finally into the warm and practical sunlight.

His last remembrance of the Fair came from a night in early autumn: with Daisy again he sat upon the driver's seat of a motor bus, listening for the first time to the wonder of its labored chugging, as they rolled, through ploughing sheets of rain, around the gleaming roads, and by the Cascades, pouring their water down before a white building jewelled with ten thousand lights.

The summer had passed. There was the rustling of autumn winds, a whispering breath of departed revelry: carnival was almost done.

And now the house grew very still: he saw his mother very little, he did not leave the house, he was in the care of his sisters, and he was constantly admonished to silence.

One day Gant came back a second time. Grover was down with typhoid.

"He said he ate a pear at the Fair grounds," Eliza repeated the story for the hundredth time. "He came home and complained of feeling sick. I put my hand on his head and he was burning up. 'Why, child,' I said, 'what on earth——?'"

Her black eyes brightened in her white face: she was afraid. She pursed her lips and spoke hopefully.

"Hello, son," said Gant, casually entering the room; his heart shrivelled as he saw the boy.

Eliza pursed her lips more and more thoughtfully after each visit the doctor made; she seized every spare crumb of encouragement and magnified it, but her heart was sick. Then one night, tearing away the mask suddenly, she came swiftly from the boy's room.

"Mr. Gant," she said in a whisper, pursing her lips. She shook her white face at him silently as if unable to speak. Then, rapidly, she concluded: "He's gone, he's gone, he's gone!"

Eugene was deep in midnight slumber. Some one shook him, loosening him slowly from his drowsiness. Presently he found himself in the arms of Helen, who sat on the bed holding him, her morbid stricken little face fastened on him. She spoke to him distinctly and slowly in a subdued voice, charged somehow with a terrible eagerness:

"Do you want to see Grover?" she whispered. "He's on the cooling board."

He wondered what a cooling board was; the house was full of menace. She bore him out into the dimly lighted hall, and carried him to the rooms at the front of the house. Behind the door he heard low voices. Quietly she opened it; the light blazed brightly on the bed. Eugene looked, horror swarmed like poison through his blood. Behind the little wasted shell that lay there he remembered suddenly the warm brown face, the soft eyes, that once had peered down at him: like one who has been mad, and suddenly recovers reason, he remembered that forgotten face he had not seen in weeks, that strange bright loneliness that would not return. O lost, and by the wind grieved, ghost, come back again.

Eliza sat heavily on a chair, her face bent sideways on her rested hand. She was weeping, her face contorted by the comical and ugly grimace that is far more terrible than any quiet beatitude of sorrow. Gant comforted her awkwardly but, looking at the boy from time to time, he went out into the hall and cast his arms forth in agony, in bewilderment.

The undertakers put the body in a basket and took it away.

"He was just twelve years and twenty days old," said Eliza over and over, and this fact seemed to trouble her more than any other.

"You children go and get some sleep now," she commanded suddenly and, as she spoke, her eye fell on Ben who stood puzzled and scowling, gazing in with his curious old-man's look. She thought of the severance of the twins; they had entered life within twenty minutes of each other; her heart was gripped with pity at the thought of the boy's loneliness. She wept anew. The children went to bed. For some time Eliza and Gant continued to sit alone in the room. Gant leaned his face in his powerful hands. "The best boy I had," he muttered. "By God, he was the best of the lot."

And in the ticking silence they recalled him, and in the heart of each was fear and remorse, because he had been a quiet boy, and there were many, and he had gone unnoticed.

"I'll never be able to forget his birthmark," Eliza whispered, "Never, never."

Then presently each thought of the other; they felt suddenly the horror and strangeness of their surroundings. They thought of the vine-wound house in the distant mountains, of the roaring fires, the tumult, the cursing, the pain, of their blind and tangled lives, and of blundering destiny which brought them here now in this distant place, with death, after the carnival's close.

Eliza wondered why she had come: she sought back through the hot and desperate mazes for the answer:

"If I had known," she began presently, "if I had known how it would turn out——"

"Never mind," he said, and he stroked her awkwardly. "By God!" he added dumbly after a moment. "It's pretty strange when you come to think about it."

And as they sat there more quietly now, swarming pity rose in them—not for themselves, but for each other, and for the waste, the confusion, the groping accident of life.

Gant thought briefly of his four and fifty years, his vanished youth, his diminishing strength, the ugliness and badness of so much of it; and he had the very quiet despair of a man who knows the forged chain may not be unlinked, the threaded design unwound, the done undone.

"If I had known. If I had known," said Eliza. And then: "I'm sorry." But he knew that her sorrow at that moment was not for him or for herself, or even for the boy whom idiot chance had thrust in the way of pestilence, but that, with a sudden inner flaming of her clairvoyant Scotch soul, she had looked cleanly, without pretense for the first time, upon the inexorable tides of Necessity, and that she was sorry for all who had lived, were living, or would live, fanning with their prayers the useless altar flames, suppliant with their hopes to an unwitting spirit, casting the tiny rockets of their belief against remote eternity, and hoping for grace, guidance, and delivery upon the spinning and forgotten cinder of this earth. O lost.

They went home immediately. At every station Gant and Eliza made restless expeditions to the baggage-car. It was gray autumnal November: the mountain forests were quilted with dry brown leaves. They blew about the streets of Altamont, they were deep in lane and gutter, they scampered dryly along before the wind.

The car ground noisily around the curve at the hill-top. The Gants descended: the body had already been sent on from the station. As Eliza came slowly down the hill, Mrs. Tarkinton ran from her house sobbing. Her eldest daughter had died a month before. The two women gave loud cries as they saw each other, and rushed together.

In Gant's parlor, the coffin had already been placed on trestles, the neighbors, funeral-faced and whispering, were assembled to greet them. That was all.

6

The death of Grover gave Eliza the most terrible wound of her life: her courage was snapped, her slow but powerful adventure toward freedom was abruptly stopped. Her flesh seemed to turn rotten when she thought of the distant city and the Fair: she was appalled before the hidden adversary who had struck her down.

With her desperate sadness she encysted herself within her house and her family, reclaimed that life she had been ready to renounce, lived laborious days and tried to drink, in toil, oblivion. But the dark lost face gleamed like a sudden and impalpable faun within the thickets of memory: she thought of the mark on his brown neck and wept.

During the grim winter the shadows lifted slowly. Gant brought back the roaring fires, the groaning succulent table, the lavish and explosive ritual of the daily life. The old gusto surged back in their lives.

And, as the winter waned, the interspersed darkness in Eugene's brain was lifted slowly, days, weeks, months began to emerge in consecutive brightness; his mind came from the confusion of the Fair: life opened practically.

Secure and conscious now in the guarded and sufficient strength of home, he lay with well-lined belly before the roasting vitality of the fire, poring insatiably over great volumes in the bookcase, exulting in the musty odor of the leaves, and in the pungent smell of their hot hides. The books he delighted in most were three huge calf-skin volumes called *Ridpath's History of the World*. Their numberless pages were illustrated with hundreds of drawings, engravings, wood-cuts: he followed the progression of the centuries pictorially before he could read. The pictures of battle delighted him most of all. Exulting in the howl of the beaten wind about the house, the thunder of great trees, he committed himself to the dark storm, releasing the mad devil's hunger all men have in them, which lusts for darkness, the wind, and incalculable speed. The past unrolled to him in separate and enormous visions; he built unending legends upon the pictures of the kings of Egypt, charioted swiftly by soaring horses, and something infinitely old and recollective seemed to awaken in him as he looked on fabulous monsters, the twined beards and huge beast-bodies of Assyrian kings, the walls of Babylon. His brain swarmed with pictures— Cyrus directing the charge, the spear-forest of the Macedonian phalanx, the splintered oars, the numberless huddle of the ships at Salamis, the feasts of Alexander, the terrific melee of the knights, the shattered lances, the axe and the sword, the massed pikemen, the beleaguered walls, the scaling ladders heavy with climbing men hurled backward, the Swiss who flung his body on the lances, the press of horse and foot, the gloomy forests of Gaul and Cæsarean conquests. Gant sat farther away, behind him, swinging violently back and forth in a stout rocker, spitting clean and powerful spurts of tobacco-juice over his son's head into the hissing fire.

Or again, Gant would read to him with sonorous and florid rhetoric passages from Shakespeare, among which he heard most often Marc Antony's funeral oration, Hamlet's soliloquy, the banquet scene in

Macbeth, and the scene between Desdemona and Othello before he strangles her. Or, he would recite or read poetry, for which he had a capacious and retentive memory. His favorites were: "O why should the spirit of mortal be proud" ("Lincoln's favorite poem," he was fond of saying); " 'We are lost,' the captain shouted, As he staggered down the stairs"; "I remember, I remember, the house where I was born"; "Ninety and nine with their captain, Rode on the enemy's track, Rode in the gray light of morning, Nine of the ninety came back"; "The boy stood on the burning deck"; and "Half a league, half a league, half a league onward."

Sometimes he would get Helen to recite "Still sits the schoolhouse by the road, a ragged beggar sunning; Around it still the sumachs grow, and blackberry vines are running."

And when she had told how grasses had been growing over the girl's head for forty years, and how the gray-haired man had found in life's harsh school how few hated to go above him, because, you see, they love him, Gant would sigh heavily, and say with a shake of his head:

"Ah me! There was never a truer word spoken than that."

The family was at the very core and ripeness of its life together. Gant lavished upon it his abuse, his affection, and his prodigal provisioning. They came to look forward eagerly to his entrance, for he brought with him the great gusto of living, of ritual. They would watch him in the evening as he turned the corner below with eager strides, follow carefully the processional of his movements from the time he flung his provisions upon the kitchen table to the re-kindling of his fire, with which he was always at odds when he entered, and on to which he poured wood, coal and kerosene lavishly. This done, he would remove his coat and wash himself at the basin vigorously, rubbing his great hands across his shaven, tough-bearded face with the cleansing and male sound of sand-paper. Then he would thrust his body against the door jamb and scratch his back energetically by moving it violently to and fro. This done, he would empty another half can of kerosene on the howling flame, lunging savagely at it, and muttering to himself.

Then, biting off a good hunk of powerful apple tobacco, which lay ready to his use on the mantel, he would pace back and forth across his room fiercely, oblivious of his grinning family who followed these ceremonies with exultant excitement, as he composed his tirade. Finally, he would burst in on Eliza in the kitchen, plunging to the heart of denunciation with a mad howl.

His turbulent and undisciplined rhetoric had acquired, by the regular convention of its usage, something of the movement and directness of classical epithet: his similes were preposterous, created really in a spirit of vulgar mirth, and the great comic intelligence that was in the family—down to the youngest—was shaken daily by it. The children grew to await his return in the evening with a kind of exhilaration. Indeed, Eliza herself, healing slowly and painfully her great hurt, got a certain stimulation from it; but there was still in her a fear of the periods of drunkenness, and latently, a stubborn and unforgiving recollection of the past.

But, during that winter, as death, assaulted by the quick and healing gaiety of children, those absolute little gods of the moment, lifted itself slowly out of their hearts, something like hopefulness returned to her. They were a life unto themselves—how lonely they were they did not know, but they were known to every one and friended by almost no one. Their status was singular—if they could have been distinguished by caste, they would probably have been called middle-class, but the Duncans, the Tarkintons, all their neighbors, and all their acquaintances throughout the town, never drew in to them, never came into the strange rich color of their lives, because they had twisted the design of all orderly life, because there was in them a mad, original, disturbing quality which they did not suspect. And companionship with the elect—those like the Hilliards—was equally impossible, even if they had had the gift or the desire for it. But they hadn't.

Gant was a great man, and not a singular one, because singularity does not hold life in unyielding devotion to it.

As he stormed through the house, unleashing his gathered bolts, the children followed him joyously, shrieking exultantly as he told Eliza he had first seen her "wriggling around the corner like a snake on her belly," or, as coming in from freezing weather he had charged her and all the Pentlands with malevolent domination of the elements.

"We will freeze," he yelled, "we will freeze in this hellish, damnable, cruel and God-forsaken climate. Does Brother Will care? Does Brother Jim care? Did the Old Hog, your miserable old father, care? Merciful God! I have fallen into the hands of fiends incarnate, more savage, more cruel, more abominable than the beasts of the field. Hellhounds that they are, they will sit by and gloat at my agony until I am done to death."

He paced rapidly about the adjacent wash-room for a moment, muttering to himself, while grinning Luke stood watchfully near.

"But they can eat!" he shouted, plunging suddenly at the kitchen door. "They can eat—when some one else will feed them. I shall never forget the Old Hog as long as I live. Cr-unch, Cr-unch, Cr-unch,"—they were all exploded with laughter as his face assumed an expression of insane gluttony, and as he continued, in a slow, whining voice intended to represent the speech of the late Major: " 'Eliza, if you don't mind I'll have some more of that chicken,' when the old scoundrel had shovelled it down his throat so fast we had to carry him away from the table."

As his denunciation reached some high extravagance the boys would squeal with laughter, and Gant, inwardly tickled, would glance around slyly with a faint grin bending the corners of his thin mouth. Eliza herself would laugh shortly, and then exclaim roughly: "Get out of here! I've had enough of your goings-on for one night."

Sometimes, on these occasions, his good humor grew so victorious that he would attempt clumsily to fondle her, putting one arm stiffly around her waist, while she bridled, became confused, and half-attempted to escape, saying: "Get away! Get away from me! It's too late for that now." Her white embarrassed smile was at once painful and comic: tears pressed closely behind it. At these rare, unnatural exhibitions of affection, the children laughed with constraint, fidgeted restlessly, and said: "Aw, papa, don't."

Eugene, when he first noticed an occurrence of this sort, was getting on to his fifth year: shame gathered in him in tangled clots, aching in his throat; he twisted his neck about convulsively, smiling desperately as he did later when he saw poor buffoons or mawkish scenes in the theatre. And he was never after able to see them touch each other with affection, without the same inchoate and choking humiliation: they were so used to the curse, the clamor, and the roughness, that any variation into tenderness came as a cruel affectation.

But as the slow months, gummed with sorrow, dropped more clearly, the powerful germinal instinct for property and freedom began to re-awaken in Eliza, and the ancient submerged struggle between their natures began again. The children were growing up—Eugene had found play-mates—Harry Tarkinton and Max Isaacs. Her sex was a fading coal.

Season by season, there began again the old strife of ownership and taxes. Returning home, with the tax-collector's report in his hand, Gant would be genuinely frantic with rage.

"In the name of God, Woman, what are we coming to? Before another year we'll all go to the poorhouse. Ah, Lord! I see very well where it will all end. I'll go to the wall, every penny we've got will go into the pockets of those accursed swindlers, and the rest will come under the sheriff's hammer. I curse the day I was ever fool enough to buy the first stick. Mark my words, we'll be living in soup-kitchens before this fearful, this awful, this hellish and damnable winter is finished."

She would purse her lips thoughtfully as she went over the list, while he looked at her with a face of strained agony.

"Yes, it does look pretty bad," she would remark. And then: "It's a pity you didn't listen to me last summer, Mr. Gant, when we had a chance of trading in that worthless old Owenby place for those two houses on Carter Street. We could have been getting forty dollars a month rent on them ever since."

"I never want to own another foot of land as long as I live," he yelled. "It's kept me a poor man all my life, and when I die they'll have to give me six feet of earth in Pauper's Field." And he would grow broodingly philosophic, speaking of the vanity of human effort, the last resting-place in earth of rich and poor, the significant fact that we could "take none of it with us," ending perhaps with "Ah me! It all comes to the same in the end, anyway."

Or, he would quote a few stanzas of Gray's *Elegy*, using that encyclopædia of stock melancholy with rather indefinite application:

"—Await alike th' inevitable hour,
    The paths of glory lead but to the grave."

But Eliza sat grimly on what they had.

Gant, for all his hatred of land ownership, was proud of living under his own shelter, and indeed proud in the possession of anything that was sanctified by his usage,' and that gave him comfort. He would have liked ready and unencumbered affluence—the possession of huge sums of money in the bank and in his pocket, the freedom to travel grandly, to go before the world spaciously. He liked to carry large sums of money in his pocket, a practice of which Eliza disapproved, and for which she reprimanded him frequently. Once or twice, when he was drunk, he had been robbed: he would brandish a roll of bills about under the stimulation of whisky, and dispense large sums to his children—ten, twenty, fifty dollars to each, with maudlin injunctions to "take it all! Take it all, God damn it!" But next day he was equally assiduous in his demands for its return: Helen usually collected it from the sometimes unwilling fingers of the boys. She would give it to him next day. She was fifteen or sixteen years old, and almost six feet high: a tall thin girl, with large hands and feet, big-boned, generous features, behind which the hysteria of constant excitement lurked.

The bond between the girl and her father grew stronger every day:

she was nervous, intense, irritable, and abusive as he was. She adored him. He had begun to suspect that this devotion, and his own response to it, was a cause more and more of annoyance to Eliza, and he was inclined to exaggerate and emphasize it, particularly when he was drunk, when his furious distaste for his wife, his obscene complaint against her, was crudely balanced by his maudlin docility to the girl.

And Eliza's hurt was deeper because she knew that just at this time, when her slightest movement goaded him, did what was most rawly essential in him reveal itself. She was forced to keep out of his way, lock herself in her room, while her young daughter victoriously subdued him.

The friction between Helen and Eliza was often acute: they spoke sharply and curtly to each other, and were painfully aware of the other's presence in cramped quarters. And, in addition to the unspoken rivalry over Gant, the girl was in the same way, equally, rasped by the temperamental difference of Eliza—driven to fury at times by her slow, mouth-pursing speech, her placidity, the intonations of her voice, the deep abiding patience of her nature.

They fed stupendously. Eugene began to observe the food and the seasons. In the autumn, they barrelled huge frosty apples in the cellar. Gant bought whole hogs from the butcher, returning home early to salt them, wearing a long work-apron, and rolling his sleeves half up his lean hairy arms. Smoked bacons hung in the pantry, the great bins were full of flour, the dark recessed shelves groaned with preserved cherries, peaches, plums, quinces, apples, pears. All that he touched waxed in rich pungent life: his Spring gardens, wrought in the black wet earth below the fruit trees, flourished in huge crinkled lettuces that wrenched cleanly from the loamy soil with small black clots stuck to their crisp stocks; fat red radishes; heavy tomatoes. The rich plums lay bursted on the grass; his huge cherry trees oozed with heavy gum jewels; his apple trees bent with thick green clusters. The earth was spermy for him like a big woman.

Spring was full of cool dewy mornings, spurting winds, and storms of intoxicating blossoms, and in this enchantment Eugene first felt the mixed lonely ache and promise of the seasons.

In the morning they rose in a house pungent with breakfast cookery, and they sat at a smoking table loaded with brains and eggs, ham, hot biscuit, fried apples seething in their gummed syrups, honey, golden butter, fried steak, scalding coffee. Or there were stacked batter-cakes, rum-colored molasses, fragrant brown sausages, a bowl of wet cherries, plums, fat juicy bacon, jam. At the mid-day meal, they ate heavily: a huge hot roast of beef, fat buttered lima-beans, tender corn smoking on the cob, thick red slabs of sliced tomatoes, rough savory spinach, hot yellow corn-bread, flaky biscuits, a deep-dish peach and apple cobbler spiced with cinnamon, tender cabbage, deep glass dishes piled with preserved fruits—cherries, pears, peaches. At night they might eat fried steak, hot squares of grits fried in egg and butter, pork-chops, fish, young fried chicken.

For the Thanksgiving and Christmas feasts four heavy turkeys were bought and fattened for weeks: Eugene fed them with cans of shelled corn several times a day, but he could not bear to be present at their executions, because by that time their cheerful excited gobbles made echoes in his heart. Eliza baked for weeks in advance: the whole energy of the family focussed upon the great ritual of the feast. A day or two before, the auxiliary dainties arrived in piled grocer's boxes—the magic of strange foods and fruits was added to familiar fare: there were glossed sticky dates, cold rich figs, cramped belly to belly in small boxes, dusty raisins, mixed nuts—the almond, pecan, the meaty nigger-toe, the walnut, sacks of assorted candies, piles of yellow Florida oranges, tangerines, sharp, acrid, nostalgic odors.

Seated before a roast or a fowl, Gant began a heavy clangor on his steel and carving knife, distributing thereafter Gargantuan portions to each plate. Eugene feasted from a high chair by his father's side, filled his distending belly until it was drum-tight, and was permitted to stop eating by his watchful sire only when his stomach was impregnable to the heavy prod of Gant's big finger.

"There's a soft place there," he would roar, and he would cover the scoured plate of his infant son with another heavy slab of beef. That their machinery withstood this hammer-handed treatment was a tribute to their vitality and Eliza's cookery.

Gant ate ravenously and without caution. He was immoderately fond of fish, and he invariably choked upon a bone while eating it. This happened hundreds of times, but each time he would look up suddenly with a howl of agony and terror, groaning and crying out strongly while a half-dozen hands pounded violently on his back.

"Merciful God!" he would gasp finally, "I thought I was done for that time."

"I'll vow, Mr. Gant," Eliza was vexed. "Why on earth don't you watch what you're doing? If you didn't eat so fast you wouldn't always get choked."

The children, staring, but relieved, settled slowly back in their places.

He had a Dutch love of abundance: again and again he described, the great stored barns, the groaning plenty of the Pennsylvanians.

On his journey to California, he had been charmed in New Orleans by the cheapness and profusion of tropical fruits: a peddler offered him a great bunch of bananas for twenty-five cents, and Gant had taken them at once, wondering desperately later, as they moved across the continent, why, and what he was going to do with them.

7

This journey to California was Gant's last great voyage. He made it two years after Eliza's return from St. Louis, when he was fifty-six years old. In the great frame was already stirring the chemistry of pain and death. Unspoken and undefined there was in him the knowledge that he was at length caught in the trap of life and fixity, that he was being borne under in this struggle against the terrible will that wanted to own the earth more than to explore it. This was the final flare of the old hunger that had once darkened in the small gray eyes, leading a boy into new lands and toward the soft stone smile of an angel.

And he returned from nine thousand miles of wandering, to the bleak bare prison of the hills on a gray day late in winter.

In the more than eight thousand days and nights of this life with Eliza, how often had he been wakefully, soberly and peripatetically conscious of the world outside him between the hours of one and five A. M.? Wholly, for not more than nineteen nights—one for the birth of Leslie, Eliza's first daughter; one for her death twenty-six months later, cholera infantis; one for the death of Major Tom Pentland, Eliza's father, in May, 1902; one for the birth of Luke; one, on the train westbound to Saint Louis, en route to Grover's death; one for the death in the Playhouse (1893) of Uncle Thaddeus Evans, an aged and devoted negro; one, with Eliza, in the month of March, 1897, as deathwatch to the corpse of old Major Isaacs; three at the end of the month of July, 1897, when it was thought that Eliza, withered to a white sheeting of skin upon a bone frame, must die of typhoid; again in early April, 1903, for Luke, typhoid death near; one for the death of Greeley Pentland, aged twenty-six, congenial scrofulous tubercular, violinist, Pentlandian punster, petty check-forger, and six weeks' jailbird; three nights, from the eleventh to the fourteenth of January, 1905, by the rheumatic cruci-fixion of his right side, participant in his own grief, accuser of himself and his God; once in February, 1896, as deathwatch to the remains of Sandy Duncan, aged eleven; once in September, 1895, penitentially alert and shamefast in the City "calaboose"; in a room of the Keeley Institute at Piedmont, North Carolina, June 7, 1896; on March 17, 1906, between Knoxville, Tennessee, and Altamont, at the conclusion of a seven weeks' journey to California.

How looked the home-earth then to Gant the Far-Wanderer? Light crept grayly, melting on the rocky river, the engine smoke streaked out on dawn like a cold breath, the hills were big, but nearer, nearer than he thought. And Altamont lay gray and withered in the hills, a bleak mean wintry dot. He stepped carefully down in squalid Toytown, noting that everything was low, near, and shrunken as he made his Gulliverian entry. He had a roof-and-gulley high conviction; with careful tucked-in elbows he weighted down the heated Toytown street-car, staring painfully at the dirty pasteboard *pebbledash* of the Pisgah Hotel, the brick and board cheap warehouses of Depot Street, the rusty clapboard flimsiness of the Florence (Railway Men's) Hotel, quaking with beef-fed harlotry.

So small, so small, so small, he thought. I never believed it. Even the hills here. I'll soon be sixty.

His sallow face, thin-flanked, was hang-dog and afraid. He stared wistful-sullenly down at the rattan seat as the car screeched round into the switch at the cut and stopped; the motorman, smoke-throated, slid the door back and entered with his handle. He closed the door and sat down yawning.

"Where you been, Mr. Gant?"

"California," said Gant.

"Thought I hadn't seen you," said the motorman.

There was a warm electric smell and one of hot burnt steel.

But two months dead! But two months dead! Ah, Lord! So it's come to this. Merciful God, this fearful, awful, and damnable climate. Death, death! Is it too late? A land of life, a flower land. How clear the green clear sea was. And all the fishes swimming there. Santa Catalina. Those in the East should always go West. How came I here? Down, down—always down, did I know where? Baltimore, Sydney—In God's name, why? The little boat glass-bottomed, so you could look down. She lifted up her skirts as she stepped down. Where now? A pair of pippins.

"Jim Bowles died while you were gone, I reckon," said the motorman.

"What!" howled Gant. "Merciful God!" he clucked mournfully downward. "What did he die of?" he asked.

"Pneumonia," said the motorman. "He was dead four days after he was took down."

"Why, he was a big healthy man in the prime of life," said Gant. "I was talking to him the day before I went away," he lied, convincing himself permanently that this was true. "He looked as if he had never known a day's sickness in his life."

"He went home one Friday night with a chill," said the motorman, "and the next Tuesday he was gone."

There was a crescent humming on the rails. With his thick glove finger he pushed away a clearing in the window-coated ice scurf and looked smokily out on the raw red cut-bank. The other car appeared abruptly at the end of the cut and curved with a skreeking jerk into the switch.

"No, sir," said the motorman, sliding back the door, "you never know who'll go next. Here to-day and gone to-morrow. Hit gits the big 'uns first sometimes."

He closed the door behind him and jerkily opened three notches of juice. The car ground briskly off like a wound toy.

In the prime of life, thought Gant. Myself like that some day. No, for others. Mother almost eighty-six. Eats like a horse, Augusta wrote. Must send her twenty dollars. Now in the cold clay, frozen. Keep till Spring. Rain, rot, rain. Who got the job? Brock or Saul Gudger? Bread out of my mouth. Do me to death—the stranger. Georgia marble, sandstone base, forty dollars.

> "A gracious friend from us is gone,
>   A voice we loved is fled,
> But faith and memory lead us on:
>   He lives; he is not dead."

Four cents a letter. Little enough, God knows, for the work you do. My letters the best. Could have been a writer. Like to draw too. And all of mine! I would have heard if anything—he would have told me. I'll never go that way. All right above the waist. If anything happens it will be down below. Eaten away. Whisky holes through all your guts. Pictures in Cardiac's office of man with cancer. But several doctors have to agree on it. Criminal offense if they don't. But, if worst comes to worst—all that's out-

side. Get it before it gets up in you. Still live. Old man Haight had a flap
in his belly. Ladled it out in a cup. McGuire—damned butcher. But he can
do anything. Cut off a piece here, sew it on there. Made the Hominy man
a nose with a piece of shinbone. Couldn't tell it. Ought to be possible. Cut
all the strings, tie them up again. While you wait. Sort of job for
McGuire—rough and ready. They'll do it some day. After I'm gone.
Things standing thus, unknown—but kill you maybe. Bull's too big. Soon
now the Spring. You'd die. Not big enough. All bloody in her brain. Full
filling fountains of bull-milk. Jupiter and what's-her-name.

But westward now he caught a glimpse of Pisgah and the western
range. It was more spacious there. The hills climbed sunward to the sun.
There was width to the eye, a smoking sun-hazed amplitude, the world
convoluting and opening into the world, hill and plain, into the west. The
West for desire, the East for home. To the east the short near mile-away
hills reeked protectively above the town. Birdseye, Sunset. A straight plume
of smoke coiled thickly from Judge Buck Sevier's smut-white clapboard
residence on the decent side of Pisgah Avenue, thin smoke-wisps rose from
the nigger shacks in the ravine below. Breakfast. Fried brains and eggs
with streaky rashers of limp bacon. Wake, wake, wake, you mountain
grills! Sleeps she yet, wrapped dirtily in three old wrappers in stale, airless
yellow-shaded cold. The chapped hands sick-sweet glycerined. Gum-headed
bottles, hairpins, and the bits of string. No one may enter now. Ashamed.
   A paper-carrier, number 7, finished his route on the corner of Vine
Street, as the car stopped, turned eastwards now from Pisgah Avenue
toward the town core. The boy folded, bent, and flattened the fresh sheets
deftly, throwing the block angularly thirty yards upon the porch of Shields
the jeweller; it struck the boarding and bounded back with a fresh plop.
Then he walked off with fatigued relief into time toward the twentieth
century, feeling gratefully the ghost-kiss of absent weight upon his now
free but still leaning right shoulder.
   About fourteen, thought Gant. That would be Spring of 1864. The
mule camp at Harrisburg. Thirty a month and keep. Men stank worse than
mules. I was in third bunk on top. Gil in second. Keep your damned dirty
hoof out of my mouth. It's bigger than a mule's. That was the man. If it
ever lands on you, you bastard, you'll think it is a mule's, said Gil. Then
they had it. Mother made us go. Big enough to work, she said. Born at the
heart of the world, why here? Twelve miles from Gettysburg. Out of the
South they came. Stove-pipe hats they had stolen. No shoes. Give me a
drink, son. That was Fitzhugh Lee. After the third day we went over.

Devil's Den. Cemetery Ridge. Stinking piles of arms and legs. Some of it done with meat-saws. Is the land richer now? The great barns bigger than the houses. Big eaters, all of us. I hid the cattle in the thicket. Belle Boyd, the Beautiful Rebel Spy. Sentenced to be shot four times. Took the despatches from his pocket while they danced. Probably a little chippie.

Hog-chitlins and hot cracklin' bread. Must get some. The whole hog or none. Always been a good provider. Little I ever had done for me.

The car still climbing, mounted the flimsy cheap-boarded brown-gray smuttiness of Skyland Avenue.

America's Switzerland. The Beautiful Land of the Sky. Jesus God! Old Bowman said he'll be a rich man some day. Built up all the way to Pasadena. Come on out. Too late now. Think he was in love with her. No matter. Too old. Wants her out there. No fool like—White bellies of the fish. A spring somewhere to wash me through. Clean as a baby once more. New Orleans, the night Jim Corbett knocked out John L. Sullivan. The man who tried to rob me. My clothes and my watch. Five blocks down Canal Street in my nightgown. Two A.M. Threw them all in a heap— watch landed on top. Fight in my room. Town full of crooks and pick-pockets for prizefight. Make good story. Policeman half hour later. They come out and beg you to come in. Frenchwomen. Creoles. Beautiful Creole heiress. Steamboat race. Captain, they are gaining. I will not be beaten. Out of wood. Use the bacon she said proudly. There was a terrific explosion. He got her as she sank the third time and swam to shore. They powder in front of the window, smacking their lips at you. For old men better maybe. Who gets the business there? Bury them all above ground. Water two feet down. Rots them. Why not? All big jobs. Italy. Carrara and Rome. Yet Brutus is an hon-or-able man. What's a Creole? French and Spanish. Has she any nigger blood? Ask Cardiac?

The car paused briefly at the car-shed, in sight of its stabled brothers. Then it moved reluctantly past the dynamic atmosphere of the Power and Light Company, wheeling bluntly into the gray frozen ribbon of Hatton Avenue, running gently up hill near its end into the frore silence of the Square.

Ah, Lord! Well do I remember. The old man offered me the whole piece for $1,000 three days after I arrived. Millionaire to-day if——

The car passed the Tuskegee on its eighty-yard climb into the Square. The fat slick worn leather-chairs marshalled between a fresh-rubbed gleam-ing line of brass spittoons squatted massively on each side of the entry door, before thick sheets of plate-glass that extended almost to the side-walks with indecent nearness.

Many a fat man's rump upon the leather. Like fish in a glass case.

Travelling man's wet chewed cigar, spit-limp on his greasy lips. Staring at all the women. Can't look back long. Gives advantage.

A negro bellboy sleepily wafted a gray dust-cloth across the leather. Within, before the replenished crackle-dance of the wood-fire, the night-clerk sprawled out in the deep receiving belly of a leather divan.

The car reached the Square, jolted across the netting of north-south lines, and came to a halt on the north side, facing east. Scurfing a patch away from the glazed window, Gant looked out. The Square in the wan-gray frozen morning walled round him with frozen unnatural smallness. He felt suddenly the cramped mean fixity of the Square: this was the one fixed spot in a world that writhed, evolved, and changed constantly in his vision, and he felt a sick green fear, a frozen constriction about his heart because the centre of his life now looked so shrunken. He got very definitely the impression that if he flung out his arms they would strike against the walls of the mean three-and-four-story brickbuilt buildings that flanked the Square raggedly.

Anchored to earth at last, he was hit suddenly by the whole cumulation of sight and movement, of eating, drinking, and acting that had gathered in him for two months. The limitless land, wood, field, hill, prairie, desert, mountain, the coast rushing away below his eyes, the ground that swam before his eyes at stations, the remembered ghosts of gumbo, oysters, huge Frisco seasteaks, tropical fruits swarmed with the infinite life, the cease-less pullulation of the sea. Here only, in his unreal-reality, this unnatural vision of what he had known for twenty years, did life lose its movement, change, color.

The Square had the horrible concreteness of a dream. At the far south-eastern edge he saw his shop: his name painted hugely in dirty scaly white across the brick near the roof: W. O. Gant—Marbles, Tombstones, Cemetery Fixtures. It was like a dream of hell, when a man finds his own name staring at him from the Devil's ledger; like a dream of death, when he who comes as mourner finds himself in the coffin, or as witness to a hanging, the condemned upon the scaffold.

A sleepy negro employed at the Manor Hotel clambered heavily up and slumped into one of the seats reserved for his race at the back. In a moment he began to snore gently through his blubbered lips.

At the east end of the Square, Big Bill Messler, with his vest half-unbuttoned over his girdled paunch-belly, descended slowly the steps of the City Hall, and moved soundingly off with country leisure along the cold-metallic sidewalk. The fountain, ringed with a thick bracelet of ice, played at quarter-strength a sheening glut of ice-blue water.

Cars droned separately into their focal positions; the carmen stamped their feet and talked smokily together; there was a breath of beginning life. Beside the City Hall, the firemen slept above their wagons: behind the bolted door great hoofs drummed woodenly.

A dray rattled across the east end of the Square before the City Hall, the old horse leaning back cautiously as he sloped down into the dray market by the oblique cobbled passage at the southeast that cut Gant's shop away from the market and "calaboose." As the car moved eastward again, Gant caught an angular view of Niggertown across this passage. The settlement was plumed delicately with a hundred tiny fumes of smoke.

The car sloped swiftly now down Academy Street, turned, as the upper edge of the negro settlement impinged steeply from the valley upon the white, into Ivy Street, and proceeded north along a street bordered on one side by smutty pebble-dash cottages, and on the other by a grove of lordly oaks, in which the large quaking plaster pile of old Professor Bowman's deserted School for Young Ladies loomed desolately, turning and stopping at the corner, at the top of the Woodson Street hill, by the great wintry, wooden, and deserted barn of the Ivy Hotel. It had never paid.

Gant kneed his heavy bag before him down the passage, depositing it for a moment at the curbing before he descended the hill. The unpaved frozen clay fell steeply and lumpily away. It was steeper, shorter, nearer than he thought. Only the trees looked large. He saw Duncan come out on his porch, shirtsleeved, and pick up the morning paper. Speak to him later. Too long now. As he expected, there was a fat coil of morning smoke above the Scotchman's chimney, but none from his own.

He went down the hill, opening his iron gate softly, and going around to the side entrance by the yard, rather than ascend the steep veranda steps. The grape vines, tough and barren, writhed about the house like sinewy ropes. He entered the sitting-room quietly. There was a strong odor of cold leather. Cold ashes were strewn thinly in the grate. He put his bag down and went back through the wash-room into the kitchen. Eliza, wearing one of his old coats, and a pair of fingerless woollen gloves, poked among the embers of a crawling little fire.

"Well, I'm back," Gant said.

"Why, what on earth!" she cried as he knew she would, becoming flustered and moving her arms indeterminately. He laid his hand clumsily on her shoulder for a moment. They stood awkwardly without movement. Then he seized the oil-can, and drenched the wood with kerosene. The flame roared up out of the stove.

"Mercy, Mr. Gant," cried Eliza, "you'll burn us up!"

But, seizing a handful of cut sticks and the oil-can, he lunged furiously toward the sitting-room.

As the flame shot roaring up from the oiled pine sticks, and he felt the fire-full chimney-throat tremble, he recovered joy. He brought back the width of the desert; the vast yellow serpent of the river, alluvial with the mined accretions of the continent; the rich vision of laden ships, masted above the sea-walls, the world-nostalgic ships, bearing about them the filtered and concentrated odors of the earth, sensual negroid rum and molasses, tar, ripening guavas, bananas, tangerines, pineapples in the warm holds of tropical boats, as cheap, as profuse, as abundant as the lazy equatorial earth and all its women; the great names of Louisiana, Texas, Arizona, Colorado, California; the blasted fiend-world of the desert, and the terrific boles of trees, tunnelled for the passage of a coach; water that fell from a mountain-top in a smoking noiseless coil, internal boiling lakes flung skywards by the punctual respiration of the earth, the multi-tudinous torture in form of granite oceans, gouged depthlessly by canyons, and iridescent with the daily chameleon-shift beyond man, beyond nature, of terrific colors, below the un-human iridescence of the sky.

Eliza, still excited, recovering speech, followed him into the sitting-room, holding her chapped gloved hands clasped before her stomach while she talked.

"I was saying to Steve last night, 'It wouldn't surprise me if your papa would come rolling in at any minute now'—I just had a feeling, I don't know what you'd call it," she said, her face plucked inward by the sudden fabrication of legend, "but it's pretty strange when you come to think of it. I was in Garret's the other day ordering some things, some vanilla extract, soda and a pound of coffee when Aleck Carter came up to me. 'Eliza,' he said, 'when's Mr. Gant coming back—I think I may have a job for him?' 'Why, Aleck,' I said, 'I don't much expect him before the first of April.' Well, sir, what do you know—I had no sooner got out on the street—I suppose I must have been thinking of something else, because I remember Emma Aldrich came by and hollered to me and I didn't think to answer her until she had gone on by, so I called out just as big as you please to her, 'Emma!'— the thing flashed over me all of a sudden—I was just as sure of it as I'm standing here—'what do you think? Mr. Gant's on his way back home'."

Jesus God! thought Gant. It's begun again.

Her memory moved over the ocean-bed of event like a great octopus, blindly but completely feeling its way into every seacave, rill, and estuary, focussed on all she had done, felt and thought, with sucking Pentlandian intentness, for whom the sun shone, or grew dark, rain fell, and mankind came, spoke, and died, shifted for a moment in time out of its void into the Pentlandian core, pattern and heart of purpose.

Meanwhile, as he laid big gleaming lumps of coal upon the wood, he muttered to himself, his mind ordering in a mounting sequence, with balanced and climactic periods, his carefully punctuated rhetoric.

Yes, musty cotton, baled and piled under long sheds of railway sidings; and odorous pine woodlands of the level South, saturated with brown faery light, and broken by the tall straight leafless poles of trees; a woman's leg below an elegantly lifted skirt mounting to a carriage in Canal Street (French or Creole probably); a white arm curved reaching for a window shade, French-olive faces window-glimmering, the Georgia doctor's wife who slept above him going out, the unquenchable fish-filled abundance of the unfenced, blue, slow cat-slapping lazy Pacific; and the river, the all-drinking, yellow, slow-surging snake that drained the continent. His life was like that river, rich with its own deposited and onward-borne agglutinations, fecund with its sedimental accretions, filled exhaustlessly by life in order to be more richly itself, and this life, with the great purpose of a river, he emptied now into the harbor of his house, the sufficient haven of himself, for whom the gnarled vines wove round him thrice, the earth burgeoned with abundant fruit and blossom, the fire burnt madly.

"What have you got for breakfast?" he said to Eliza.

"Why," she said, pursing her lips meditatively, "would you like some eggs?"

"Yes," said he, "with a few rashers of bacon and a couple of pork sausages."

He strode across the dining-room and went up the hall.

"Steve! Ben! Luke! You damned scoundrels!" he yelled. "Get up!"

Their feet thudded almost simultaneously upon the floor.

"Papa's home!" they shrieked.

Mr. Duncan watched butter soak through a new-baked roll. He looked through his curtain angularly down, and saw thick acrid smoke biting heavily into the air above Gant's house.

"He's back," said he, with satisfaction.

So, at the moment looking, Tarkinton of the paints said: "W. O.'s back."

Thus came he home, who had put out to land westward, Gant the Far-Wanderer.

8

Eugene was loose now in the limitless meadows of sensation: his sensory equipment was so complete that at the moment of perception of a single thing, the whole background of color, warmth, odor, sound, taste established itself, so that later, the breath of hot dandelion brought back the grass-warm banks of Spring, a day, a place, the rustling of young leaves, or the page of a book, the thin exotic smell of tangerine, the wintry bite of great apples; or, as with *Gulliver's Travels,* a bright windy day in March, the spurting moments of warmth, the drip and reek of the earth-thaw, the feel of the fire.

He had won his first release from the fences of home—he was not quite six, when, of his own insistence, he went to school. Eliza did not want him to go, but his only close companion, Max Isaacs, a year his senior, was going, and there was in his heart a constricting terror that he would be left alone again. She told him he could not go: she felt, somehow, that school began the slow, the final loosening of the cords that held them together, but as she saw him slide craftily out the gate one morning in September and run at top speed to the corner where the other little boy was waiting, she did nothing to bring him back. Something taut snapped in her; she remembered his furtive backward glance, and she wept. And she did not weep for herself, but for him: the hour after his birth she had looked in his dark eyes and had seen something that would brood there eternally, she knew, unfathomable wells of remote and intangible loneliness: she knew that in her dark and sorrowful womb a stranger had come to life, fed by the lost communications of eternity, his own ghost, haunter of his own house, lonely to himself and to the world. O lost.

Busy with the ache of their own growing-pains, his brothers and sisters had little time for him: he was almost six years younger than Luke, the youngest of them, but they exerted over him the occasional small cruelties, petty tormentings by elder children of a younger, interested and excited by the brief screaming insanity of his temper when, goaded and taunted

66

from some deep dream, he would seize a carving knife and pursue them, or batter his head against the walls.

They felt that he was "queer"—the other boys preached the smug cowardice of the child-herd, defending themselves, when their persecutions were discovered, by saying they would make a "real boy" of him. But there grew up in him a deep affection for Ben who stalked occasionally and softly through the house, guarding even then with scowling eyes, and surly speech, the secret life. Ben was a stranger: some deep instinct drew him to his child-brother, a portion of his small earnings as a paper-carrier he spent in gifts and amusement for Eugene, admonishing him sullenly, cuffing him occasionally, but defending him before the others.

Gant, as he watched his brooding face set for hours before a firelit book of pictures, concluded that the boy liked books, more vaguely, that he would make a lawyer of him, send him into politics, see him elected to the governorship, the Senate, the presidency. And he unfolded to him time after time all the rude American legendry of the country boys who became great men because they were country boys, poor boys, and hard-working farm boys. But Eliza thought of him as a scholar, a learned man, a professor, and with that convenient afterthought that annoyed Gant so deeply, but by which she firmly convinced herself, she saw in this book-brooder the fruit of her own deliberate design.

"I read every moment I could get the chance the summer before he was born," she said. And then, with a complacent and confidential smile which, Gant knew, always preceded some reference to her family, she said: "I tell you what: it may all come out in the Third Generation."

"The Third Generation be Goddamned!" answered Gant furiously.

"Now, I want to tell you," she went on thoughtfully, speaking with her forefinger, "folks have always said that his grandfather would have made a fine scholar if——"

"Merciful God!" said Gant, getting up suddenly and striding about the room with an ironical laugh. "I might have known that it would come to this! You may be sure," he exclaimed in high excitement, wetting his thumb briefly on his tongue, "that if there's any credit to be given I won't get it. Not from you! You'd rather die than admit it! No, but I'll tell you what you will do! You'll brag about that miserable old freak who never did a hard day's work in his life."

"Now, I wouldn't be so sure of that if I were you," Eliza began, her lips working rapidly.

"Jesus God!" he cried, flinging about the room with his customary indifference to reasoned debate. "Jesus God! What a travesty! A travesty on Nature! Hell hath no fury like a woman scorned!" he exclaimed, indefinitely but violently, and then as he strode about, he gave way to loud, bitter, forced laughter.

Thus, pent in his dark soul, Eugene sat brooding on a fire-lit book, a stranger in a noisy inn. The gates of his life were closing him in from their knowledge, a vast aerial world of fantasy was erecting its fuming and insubstantial fabric. He steeped his soul in streaming imagery, rifling the book-shelves for pictures and finding there such treasures as *With Stanley in Africa,* rich in the mystery of the jungle, alive with combat, black battle, the hurled spear, vast snake-rooted forests, thatched villages, gold and ivory; or Stoddard's *Lectures,* on whose slick heavy pages were stamped the most-visited scenes of Europe and Asia; a Book of Wonder, with enchanting drawings of all the marvels of the age—Santos Dumont in his balloon, liquid air poured from a kettle, all the navies of the earth lifted two feet from the water by an ounce of radium (Sir William Crookes), the building of the Eiffel Tower, the Flatiron Building, the stick-steered automobile, the submarine. After the earthquake in San Francisco there was a book describing it, its cheap green cover lurid with crumbling towers, shaken spires, toppling many-storied houses plunging into the splitting flame-jawed earth. And there was another called *Palaces of Sin,* or *The Devil in Society,* purporting to be the work of a pious millionaire, who had drained his vast fortune in exposing the painted sores that blemish the spotless-seeming hide of great position, and there were enticing pictures showing the author walking in a silk hat down a street full of magnificent palaces of sin.

Out of this strange jumbled gallery of pictures the pieced-out world was expanding under the brooding power of his imagination: the lost dark angels of the Doré "Milton" swooped into cavernous Hell beyond this upper earth of soaring or toppling spires, machine wonder, maced and mailed romance. And, as he thought of his future liberation into this epic world, where all the color of life blazed brightest far away from home, his heart flooded his face with lakes of blood.

He had heard already the ringing of remote church bells over a country-side on Sunday night; had listened to the earth steeped in the brooding of dark, and the million-noted little night things; and he had heard thus the far retreating wail of a whistle in a distant valley, and faint thunder on the rails; and he felt the infinite depth and width of the golden world in the brief seductions of a thousand multiplex and mixed mysterious odors and sensations, weaving, with a blinding interplay and aural explosions, one into the other.

He remembered yet the East India Tea House at the Fair, the sandal-wood, the turbans, and the robes, the cool interior and the smell of India tea; and he had felt now the nostalgic thrill of dew-wet mornings in Spring, the cherry scent, the cool clarion earth, the wet loaminess of the garden, the pungent breakfast smells and the floating snow of blossoms. He knew the inchoate sharp excitement of hot dandelions in young Spring grass at noon; the smell of cellars, cobwebs, and built-on secret earth; in July, of watermelons bedded in sweet hay, inside a farmer's covered wagon; of cantaloupe and crated peaches; and the scent of orange rind, bitter-sweet, before a fire of coals. He knew the good male smell of his father's sitting-room; of the smooth worn leather sofa, with the gaping horse-hair rent; of the blistered varnished wood upon the hearth; of the heated calf-skin bindings; of the flat moist plug of apple tobacco, stuck with a red flag; of wood-smoke and burnt leaves in October; of the brown tired autumn earth; of honey-suckle at night; of warm nasturtiums; of a clean ruddy farmer who comes weekly with printed butter, eggs and milk; of fat limp underdone bacon and of coffee; of a bakery-oven in the wind; of large deep-hued stringbeans smoking-hot and seasoned well with salt and butter; of a room of old pine boards in which books and carpets have been stored, long closed; of Concord grapes in their long white baskets.

Yes, and the exciting smell of chalk and varnished desks; the smell of heavy bread-sandwiches of cold fried meat and butter; the smell of new leather in a saddler's shop, or of a warm leather chair; of honey and of unground coffee; of barrelled sweet-pickles and cheese and all the fragrant compost of the grocer's; the smell of stored apples in the cellar, and of orchard-apple smells, of pressed-cider pulp; of pears ripening on a sunny shelf, and of ripe cherries stewing with sugar on hot stoves before preserv-ing; the smell of whittled wood, of all young lumber, of sawdust and shav-ings; of peaches stuck with cloves and pickled in brandy; of pine-sap, and green pine-needles; of a horse's pared hoof; of chestnuts roasting, of bowls of nuts and raisins; of hot cracklin, and of young roast pork; of butter and cinnamon melting on hot cand:ed yams.

Yes, and of the rank slow river, and of tomatoes rotten on the vine; the smell of rain-wet plums and boiling quinces; of rotten lily-pads; and of foul weeds rotting in green marsh scum; and the exquisite smell of the South, clean but funky, like a big woman; of soaking trees and the earth after heavy rain.

Yes, and the smell of hot daisy-fields in the morning; of melted puddling-iron in a foundry; the winter smell of horse-warm stables and smoking dung; of old oak and walnut; and the butcher's smell of meat, of strong slaughtered lamb, plump gouty liver, ground pasty sausages, and red beef; and of brown sugar melted with slivered bitter chocolate; and of crushed mint leaves, and of a wet lilac bush; of magnolia beneath the heavy moon, of dogwood and laurel; of an old caked pipe and Bourbon rye, aged in kegs of charred oak; the sharp smell of tobacco; of carbolic and nitric acids; the coarse true smell of a dog; of old imprisoned books; and the cool fern-smell near springs; of vanilla in cake-dough; and of cloven ponderous cheeses.

Yes, and of a hardware store, but mostly the good smell of nails; of the developing chemicals in a photographer's dark-room; and the young-life smell of paint and turpentine; of buckwheat batter and black sorghum; and of a negro and his horse, together; of boiling fudge; the brine smell of pickling vats; and the lush undergrowth smell of southern hills; of a slimy oyster-can, of chilled gutted fish; of a hot kitchen negress; of kerosene and linoleum; of sarsaparilla and guavas; and of ripe autumn persimmons; and the smell of the wind and the rain; and of the acrid thunder; of cold starlight, and the brittle-bladed frozen grass; of fog and the misted winter sun; of seed-time, bloom, and mellow dropping harvest.

And now, whetted intemperately by what he had felt, he began, at school, in that fecund romance, the geography, to breathe the mixed odors of the earth, sensing in every squat keg piled on a pier-head a treasure of golden rum, rich port, fat Burgundy; smelling the jungle growth of the tropics, the heavy odor of plantations, the salt-fish smell of harbors, voyaging in the vast, enchanting, but unperplexing world.

Now the innumerable archipelago had been threaded, and he stood, firm-planted, upon the unknown but waiting continent.

He learned to read almost at once, printing the shapes of words immediately with his strong visual memory; but it was weeks later before he learned to write, or even to copy, words. The ragged spume and wrack of fantasy and the lost world still floated from time to time through his clear schoolday morning brain, and although he followed accurately all the other instruction of his teacher, he was walled in his ancient unknowing world when they made letters. The children made their sprawling alphabets below a line of models, but all he accomplished was a line of jagged wavering spear-points on his sheet, which he repeated endlessly and rapturously, unable to see or understand the difference.

"I have learned to write," he thought.

Then, one day, Max Isaacs looked suddenly, from his exercise, on Eugene's sheet, and saw the jagged line.

"That ain't writin'," said he.

And clubbing his pencil in his warted grimy hand, he scrawled a copy of the exercise across the page.

The line of life, that beautiful developing structure of language that he saw flowing from his comrade's pencil, cut the knot in him that all instruction failed to do, and instantly he seized the pencil, and wrote the words in letters fairer and finer than his friend's. And he turned, with a cry in his throat, to the next page, and copied it without hesitation, and the next, the next. They looked at each other a moment with that clear wonder by which children accept miracles, and they never spoke of it again.

"That's writin' now," said Max. But they kept the mystery caged between them.

Eugene thought of this event later; always he could feel the opening gates in him, the plunge of the tide, the escape; but it happened like this one day at once. Still midget-near the live pelt of the earth, he saw many things that he kept in fearful secret, knowing that revelation would be punished with ridicule. One Saturday in Spring, he stopped with Max Isaacs above a deep pit in Central Avenue where city workmen were patching a broken watermain. The clay walls of their pit were much higher than their heads; behind their huddled backs there was a wide fissure, a window in the earth which opened on some dark subterranean passage. And as the boys looked, they gripped each other suddenly, for past the fissure slid the flat head of an enormous serpent; passed, and was followed by a scaled body as thick as a man's; the monster slid endlessly on into the deep earth and vanished behind the working and unwitting men. Shaken with fear they went away, they talked about it then and later in hushed voices, but they never revealed it.

He fell now easily into the School-Ritual; he choked his breakfast with his brothers every morning, gulped scalding coffee, and rushed off at the ominous warning of the final bell, clutching a hot paper-bag of food, already spattered hungrily with grease blots. He pounded along after his brothers, his heart hammering in his throat with excitement and, as he raced into the hollow at the foot of the Central Avenue hill, grew weak with nervousness, as he heard the bell ringing itself to sleep, jerking the slatting rope about in its dying echoes.

Ben, grinning evilly and scowling, would thrust his hand against the small of his back and rush him screaming, but unable to resist the plunging force behind, up the hill.

In a gasping voice he would sing the morning song, coming in pantingly on the last round of a song the quartered class took up at intervals:

> "—Merrily, merrily, merrily, merrily,
> Life is but a dream."

Or, in the frosty Autumn mornings:

> "Waken, lords and ladies gay,
> On the mountain dawns the day."

Or the Contest of the West Wind and the South Wind. Or the Miller's Song:

> "I envy no man, no, not I,
> And no one envies me."

He read quickly and easily; he spelled accurately. He did well with figures. But he hated the drawing lesson, although the boxes of crayons and paints delighted him. Sometimes the class would go into the woods, returning with specimens of flowers and leaves—the bitten flaming red of the maple, the brown pine comb, the brown oak leaf. These they would paint; or in Spring a spray of cherry-blossom, a tulip. He sat reverently before the authority of the plump woman who first taught him: he was terrified lest he do anything common or mean in her eyes.

The class squirmed: the little boys invented tortures or scrawled obscenities to the little girls. And the wilder and more indolent seized every chance of leaving the room, thus: "Teacher, may I be excused?" And they would go out into the lavatory, sniggering and dawdling about restlessly.

He could never say it, because it would reveal to her the shame of nature. Once, deathly sick, but locked in silence and dumb nausea, he had vomited finally upon his cupped hands.

He feared and hated the recess periods, trembled before the brawling confusion of the mob and the playground, but his pride forbade that he skulk within, or secrete himself away from them. Eliza had allowed his hair to grow long; she wound it around her finger every morning into fat Fauntleroy curls; the agony and humiliation it caused him was horrible, but she was unable or unwilling to understand it, and mouth-pursingly thoughtful and stubborn to all solicitation to cut it. She had the garnered curls of Ben, Grover, and Luke stored in tiny boxes: she wept sometimes when she saw Eugene's, they were the symbol of his babyhood to her, and her sad heart, so keen in marking departures, refused to surrender them. Even when his thick locks had become the luxuriant colony of Harry Tarkinton's lice, she would not cut them: she held his squirming body between her knees twice a day and ploughed his scalp with a fine-toothed comb.

As he made to her his trembling passionate entreaties, she would smile with an affectation of patronizing humor, make a bantering humming noise in her throat, and say: "Why, say—you can't grow up yet. You're my baby." Suddenly baffled before the yielding inflexibility of her nature, which could be driven to action only after incessant and maddening prods, Eugene, screaming-mad with helpless fury, would understand the cause of Gant's frenzy.

At school, he was a desperate and hunted little animal. The herd, infallible in its banded instinct, knew at once that a stranger had been thrust into it, and it was merciless at the hunt. As the lunch-time recess came, Eugene, clutching his big grease-stained bag, would rush for the playground pursued by the yelping pack. The leaders, two or three big louts of advanced age and deficient mentality, pressed closely about him, calling out suppliantly, "You know me, 'Gene. You know me"; and still racing for the far end, he would open his bag and hurl to them one of his big sandwiches, which stayed them for a moment, as they fell upon its possessor and clawed it to fragments, but they were upon him in a moment more with the same yelping insistence, hunting him down into a corner of the fence, and pressing in with outstretched paws and wild entreaty. He would give them what he had, sometimes with a momentary gust of fury, tearing away from a greedy hand half of a sandwich and devouring it. When they saw he had no more to give, they went away.

The great fantasy of Christmas still kept him devout. Gant was his unwearied comrade; night after night in the late autumn and early winter, he would scrawl petitions to Santa Claus, listing interminably the gifts he wanted most, and transmitting each, with perfect trust, to the roaring chimney. As the flame took the paper from his hand and blew its charred ghost away with a howl, Gant would rush with him to the window, point to the stormy northern sky, and say: "There it goes! Do you see it?"

He saw it. He saw his prayer, winged with the stanch convoying winds, borne northward to the rimed quaint gables of Toyland, into frozen merry Elfland: heard the tiny silver anvil-tones, the deep-lunged laughter of the little men, the stabled cries of aerial reindeer. Gant saw and heard

He was liberally dowered with bright-painted gimcracks upon Christthem, too.

mas Day; and in his heart he hated those who advocated "useful" gifts.
Gant bought him wagons, sleds, drums, horns—best of all, a small fireman's ladder wagon: it was the wonder, and finally the curse, of the
neighborhood. During his unoccupied hours, he lived for months in the
cellar with Harry Tarkinton and Max Isaacs: they strung the ladders on
wires above the wagon, so that, at a touch, they would fall in accurate
stacks. They would pretend to doze in their quarters, as firemen do, would
leap to action suddenly, as one of them imitated the warning bell: "Clang-
a-lang-a-lang." Then, quite beyond reason, Harry and Max yoked in a
plunging team, Eugene in the driver's seat, they would leap out through
the narrow door, gallop perilously to a neighbor's house, throw up ladders,
open windows, effect entries, extinguish imaginary flames, and return
oblivious to the shrieking indictment of the housewife.

For months they lived completely in this fantasy, modelling their actions
on those of the town's firemen, and on Jannadeau, who was the assistant
chief, child-proud over it: they had seen him, at the sound of the alarm,
rush like a madman from his window in Gant's shop, leaving the spattered
fragments of a watch upon his desk, and arriving at his duty just as the
great wagon hurtled at full speed into the Square. The firemen loved to
stage the most daring exhibitions before the gaping citizenry; helmeted
magnificently, they hung from the wagons in gymnastic postures, one man
holding another over rushing space, while number two caught in mid-air
the diving heavy body of the Swiss, who deliberately risked his neck as he
leaped for the rail. Thus, for one rapturous moment they stood poised
triangularly over rocking speed: the spine of the town was chilled
ecstatically.

And when the bells broke through the drowning winds at night, his
demon rushed into his heart, bursting all cords that held him to the earth,
promising him isolation and dominance over sea and land, inhabitation of
the dark: he looked down on the whirling disk of dark forest and field,
sloped over singing pines upon a huddled town, and carried its grated
guarded fires against its own roofs, swerving and pouncing with his
haltered storm upon their doomed and flaming walls, howling with thin
laughter above their stricken heads and, fiend-voiced, calling down the
bullet wind.

Or, holding in fief the storm and the dark and all the black powers of
wizardry, to gaze, ghoul-visaged, through a storm-lashed windowpane,
briefly planting unutterable horror in grouped and sheltered life; or, no
more than a man, but holding, in your more than mortal heart, demoniac
ecstasy, to crouch against a lonely storm-swept house, to gaze obliquely
through the streaming glass upon a woman, or your enemy, and while still

exulting in your victorious dark all-seeing isolation, to feel a touch upon your shoulder, and to look, haunter-haunted, pursuer-pursued, into the green corrupted hell-face of malignant death.

Yes, and a world of bedded women, fair glimmers in the panting darkness, while winds shook the house, and he arrived across the world between the fragrant columns of delight. The great mystery of their bodies groped darkly in him, but he had found there, at the school, instructors to desire—the hair-faced louts of Doubleday. They struck fear and wonder into the hearts of the smaller, gentler boys, for Doubleday was that infested region of the town-grown mountaineers, who lurked viciously through the night, and came at Hallowe'en to break the skulls of other gangs in rock warfare.

There was a boy named Otto Krause, a cheese-nosed, hair-faced, inch-browed German boy, lean and swift in the legs, hoarse-voiced and full of idiot laughter, who showed him the gardens of delight. There was a girl named Bessie Barnes, a black-haired, tall, bold-figured girl of thirteen years who acted as model. Otto Krause was fourteen, Eugene was eight: they were in the third grade. The German boy sat next to him, drew obscenities on his books, and passed his furtive scrawled indecencies across the aisle to Bessie.

And the nymph would answer with a lewd face, and a contemptuous blow against her shapely lifted buttock, a gesture which Otto considered as good as a promise, and which tickled him into hoarse sniggers.

Bessie walked in his brain.

In their furtive moments at school, he and Otto amused each other by drawing obscenities in their geographies, bestowing on the representations of tropical natives sagging breasts and huge organs. And they composed on tiny scraps of paper dirty little rhymes about teachers and principal. Their teacher was a gaunt red-faced spinster, with fierce glaring eyes: Eugene thought always of the soldier and the tinder and the dogs he had to pass, with eyes like saucers, windmills, the moon. Her name was Miss Groody, and Otto, with the idiot vulgarity of little boys, wrote of her:

> "Old Miss Groody
> Has Good Toody."

And Eugene, directing his fire against the principal, a plump, soft, foppish young man whose name was Armstrong, and who wore always a carnation in his coat, which, after whipping an offending boy, he was accustomed to hold delicately between his fingers, sniffing it with sensitive nostrils and lidded eyes, produced in the first rich joy of creation scores of rhymes, all to the discredit of Armstrong, his parentage, and his relations with Miss Groody.

He was obsessed; he spent the entire day now in the composition of poetry—all bawdy variations of a theme. And he could not bring himself to destroy them. His desk was stuffed with tiny crumpled balls of writing: one day, during the geography lesson, the woman caught him. His bones turned to rubber as she bore down on him glaring, and took from the concealing pages of his book the paper on which he had been writing. At recess she cleared his desk, read the sequence, and, with boding quietness, bade him to see the principal after school.

"What does it mean? What do you reckon it means?" he whispered dryly to Otto Krause.

"Oh, you'll ketch it now!" said Otto Krause, laughing hoarsely.

And the class tormented him slily, rubbing their bottoms when they caught his eye, and making grimaces of agony.

He was sick through to his guts. He had a loathing of physical humiliation which was not based on fear, from which he never recovered. The brazen insensitive spirit of the boys he envied but could not imitate: they would howl loudly under punishment, in order to mitigate it, and they were vaingloriously unconcerned ten minutes later. He did not think he could endure being whipped by the fat young man with the flower: at three o'clock, white-faced, he went to the man's office.

Armstrong, slit-eyed and thin lipped, began to swish the cane he held in his hand through the air as Eugene entered. Behind him, smoothed and flatted on his desk, was stacked the damning pile of rhymed insult.

"Did you write these?" he demanded, narrowing his eyes to little points in order to frighten his victim.

"Yes," said Eugene.

The principal cut the air again with his cane. He had visited Daisy several times, had eaten at Gant's plenteous board. He remembered very well.

"What have I ever done to you, son, that you should feel this way?" he said, with a sudden change of whining magnanimity.

"N-n-nothing," said Eugene.

"Do you think you'll ever do it again?" said he, becoming ominous again.

"N-no, sir," Eugene answered, in the ghost of a voice.

"All right," said God, grandly, throwing away his cane. "You can go."
His legs found themselves only when he had reached the playground.

But oh, the brave autumn and the songs they sang; harvest, and the
painting of a leaf; and "half-holiday to-day"; and "up in the air so high";
and the other one about the train—"the stations go whistling past"; the
mellow days, the opening gates of desire, the smoky sun, the dropping
patter of dead leaves.

"Every little snowflake is different in shape from every other."

"Good grashus! *All* of them, Miss Pratt?"

"All of the little snowflakes that ever were. Nature never repeats herself."

"Aw!"

Ben's beard was growing: he had shaved. He tumbled Eugene on the
leather sofa, played with him for hours, scraped his stubble chin against
the soft face of his brother. Eugene shrieked.

"When you can do that you'll be a man," said Ben.

And he sang softly, in his thin humming ghost's voice:

> "The woodpecker pecked at the schoolhouse door,
> He pecked and he pecked till his pecker got sore.
> The woodpecker pecked at the schoolhouse bell,
> He pecked and he pecked till his pecker got well."

They laughed—Eugene with rocking throatiness, Ben with a quiet
snicker. He had aqueous gray eyes, and a sallow bumpy skin. His head
was shapely, the forehead high and bony. His hair was crisp, maple-brown.
Below his perpetual scowl, his face was small, converging to a point: his
extraordinarily sensitive mouth smiled briefly, flickeringly, inwardly—like
a flash of light along a blade. And he always gave a cuff instead of a
caress: he was full of pride and tenderness.

9

Yes, and in that month when Prosperpine comes back, and Ceres' dead heart rekindles, when all the woods are a tender smoky blur, and birds no bigger than a budding leaf dart through the singing trees, and when odorous tar comes spongy in the streets, and boys roll balls of it upon their tongues, and they are lumpy with tops and agated marbles; and there is blasting thunder in the night, and the soaking millionfooted rain, and one looks out at morning on a stormy sky, a broken wrack of cloud; and when the mountain boy brings water to his kinsmen laying fence, and as the wind snakes through the grasses hears far in the valley below the long wail of the whistle, and the faint clangor of a bell; and the blue great cup of the hills seems closer, nearer, for he had heard an inarticulate promise: he has been pierced by Spring, that sharp knife.

And life unscales its rusty weathered pelt, and earth wells out in tender exhaustless strength, and the cup of a man's heart runs over with dateless expectancy, tongueless promise, indefinable desire. Something gathers in the throat, something blinds him in the eyes, and faint and valorous horns sound through the earth.

The little girls trot pigtailed primly on their dutiful way to school; but the young gods loiter: they hear the reed, the oatenstop, the running goathoofs in the spongy wood, here, there, everywhere: they dawdle, listen, fleetest when they wait, go vaguely on to their one fixed home, because the earth is full of ancient rumor and they cannot find the way. All of the gods have lost the way.

But they guarded what they had against the barbarians. Eugene, Max, and Harry ruled their little neighborhood: they made war upon the negroes and the Jews, who amused them, and upon the Pigtail Alley people, whom they hated and despised. Catlike they prowled about in the dark promise of night, sitting at times upon a wall in the exciting glare of the corner lamp, which flared gaseously, winking noisily from time to time.

Or, crouched in the concealing shrubbery of Gant's yard, they waited for romantic negro couples climbing homewards, jerking by a cord, as their victims came upon the spot, a stuffed black snake-appearing stocking. And the dark was shrill with laughter as the loud rich comic voices stammered, stopped, and screamed.

Or they stoned the cycling black boy of the markets, as he swerved down gracefully into an alley. Nor did they hate them: clowns are black. They had learned, as well, that it was proper to cuff these people kindly, curse them cheerfully, feed them magnanimously. Men are kind to a faithful wagging dog, but he must not walk habitually upon two legs. They knew that they must "take nothin' off a nigger," and that the beginnings of argument could best be scotched with a club and a broken head. Only, you couldn't break a nigger's head.

They spat joyously upon the Jews. Drown a Jew and hit a nigger.

The boys would wait on the Jews, follow them home shouting "Goose Grease! Goose Grease!" which, they were convinced, was the chief staple of Semitic diet; or with the blind acceptance of little boys of some traditional, or mangled, or imaginary catchword of abuse, they would yell after their muttering and tormented victim: "Veeshamadye Veeshamadye!" confident that they had pronounced the most unspeakable, to Jewish ears, of affronts.

Eugene had no interest in pogroms, but it was a fetich with Max. The chief object of their torture was a little furtive-faced boy, whose name was Isaac Lipinski. They pounced cattishly at him when he appeared, harried him down alleys, over fences, across yards, into barns, stables, and his own house; he moved with amazing speed and stealth, escaping fantastically, teasing them to the pursuit, thumbing his fingers at them, and grinning with wide Kike constant derision.

Or, steeped catlike in the wickedness of darkness, adrift in the brooding promise of the neighborhood, they would cluster silently under a Jew's home, grouped in a sniggering huddle as they listened to the rich excited voices, the throaty accentuation of the women; or convulsed at the hysterical quarrels which shook the Jew-walls almost nightly.

Once, shrieking with laughter, they followed a running fight through the streets between a young Jew and his father-in-law, in which each was pursued and pummelled, or pursuing and pummelling; and on the day when Louis Greenberg, a pale Jew returned from college, had killed himself by drinking carbolic acid, they stood curiously outside the dingy wailing house, shaken by sudden glee as they saw his father, a bearded orthodox old Jew, clothed in rusty, greasy black, and wearing a scarred derby, approach running up the hill to his home, shaking his hands in the air, and wailing rhythmically:

"Oi, yoi yoi yoi yoi,
Oi yoi yoi yoi yoi,
Oi yoi yoi yoi yoi."

But the whiteheaded children of Pigtail Alley they hated without humor, without any mitigation of a most bitter and alienate hate. Pigtail Alley was a muddy rut which sprawled down hill off the lower end of Woodson Street, ending vaguely in the rank stench of a green-scummed marsh bottom. On one side of this vile road there was a ragged line of whitewashed shacks, inhabited by poor whites, whose children were almost always whitehaired, and who, snuff-mouthed bony women, and tobacco-jawed men, sprawled stupidly in the sun-stench of their rude wide-boarded porches. At night a smoky lamp burned dismally in the dark interiors, there was a smell of frying cookery and of unclean flesh, strident rasping shrews' cries, the drunken maniacal mountain drawl of men: a scream and a curse.

Once, in the cherry time, when Gant's great White Wax was loaded with its clusters, and the pliant and enduring boughs were dotted thickly by the neighbor children, Jews and Gentiles alike, who had been herded under the captaincy of Luke, and picked one quart of every four for their own, one of these white-haired children had come doubtfully, mournfully, up the yard.

"All right, son," Luke, who was fifteen, called out in his hearty voice. "Get a basket and come on up."

The child came up the gummed trunk like a cat: Eugene rocked from the slender spiral topmost bough, exulting in his lightness, the tree's resilient strength, and the great morning-clarion fragrant backyard world. The Alley picked his bucket with miraculous speed, skinned spryly to the ground and emptied it into the heaping pan, and was halfway up the trunk again when his gaunt mother streaked up the yard toward him.

"You, Reese," she shrilled, "what're you doin' hyar?" She jerked him roughly to the ground and cut across his brown legs with a switch. He howled.

"You git along home," she ordered, giving him another cut.

She drove him along, upbraiding him in her harsh voice, cutting him sharply with the switch from moment to moment when, desperate with pride and humiliation, he slackened his retreat to a slow walk, or balked mulishly, howling again, and speeding a few paces on his short legs, when cut by the switch.

The treed boys sniggered, but Eugene, who had seen the pain upon the gaunt hard face of the woman, the furious pity of her blazing eyes, felt something open and burst stabbingly in him like an abscess.

"He left his cherries," he said to his brother.

Or, they jeered Loney Shytle, who left a stale sharp odor as she passed, her dirty dun hair covered in a wide plumed hat, her heels out of her dirty white stockings. She had caused incestuous rivalry between her father and her brother, she bore the scar of her mother's razor in her neck, and she walked, in her rundown shoes, with the wide stiff-legged hobble of disease.

One day as they pressed round a trapped alley boy, who backed slowly, fearfully, resentfully into a reeking wall, Willie Isaacs, the younger brother of Max, pointing with sniggering laughter, said:

"His mother takes in washin'."

And then, almost bent double by a soaring touch of humor, he added: "His mother takes in washin' from an ole nigger."

Harry Tarkinton laughed hoarsely. Eugene turned away indefinitely, craned his neck convulsively, lifted one foot sharply from the ground.

"She don't!" he screamed suddenly into their astounded faces. "She don't!"

Harry Tarkinton's parents were English. He was three or four years older than Eugene, an awkward, heavy, muscular boy, smelling always of his father's paints and oils, coarse-featured, meaty sloping jaw and a thick catarrhal look about his nose and mouth. He was the breaker of visions; the proposer of iniquities. In the cool thick evening grass of Gant's yard one sunset, he smashed forever, as they lay there talking, the enchantment of Christmas; but he brought in its stead the smell of paint, the gaseous ripstink, the unadorned, sweating, and imageless passion of the vulgar. But Eugene couldn't follow his barn-yard passion: the strong hen-stench, the Tarkintonian paint-smell, and the rank-mired branch-smell which mined under the filthy shambles of the backyard, stopped him.

Once, in the deserted afternoon, as he and Harry plundered through the vacant upper floor of Gant's house, they found a half-filled bottle of hair-restorer.

"Have you any hairs on your belly?" said Harry.

Eugene hemmed; hinted timidly at shagginess; confessed. They undid their buttons, smeared oily hands upon their bellies, and waited through rapturous days for the golden fleece.

"Hair makes a man of you," said Harry.

More often, as Spring deepened, he went now to Gant's shop on the Square. He loved the scene: the bright hill-cooled sun, the blown sheets of spray from the fountain, the garrulous firemen emerging from the winter, the lazy sprawling draymen on his father's wooden steps, snaking their whips deftly across the pavement, wrestling in heavy horseplay, Jannadeau in his dirty fly-specked window prying with delicate monocled intentness into the entrails of a watch, the reeking mossiness of Gant's fantastical brick shack, the great interior dustiness of the main room in front, sagging with gravestones—small polished slabs from Georgia, blunt ugly masses of Vermont granite, modest monuments with an urn, a cherub figure, or a couchant lamb, ponderous fly-specked angels from Carrara in Italy which he bought at great cost, and never sold—they were the joy of his heart.

Behind a wooden partition was his ware-room, layered with stonedust—coarse wooden trestles on which he carved inscriptions, stacked tool-shelves filled with chisels, drills, mallets, a pedalled emery wheel which Eugene worked furiously for hours, exulting in its mounting roar, piled sandstone bases, a small heat-blasted cast-iron stove, loose piled coal and wood.

Between the workroom and the ware-room, on the left as one entered, was Gant's office, a small room, deep in the dust of twenty years, with an old-fashioned desk, sheaves of banded dirty papers, a leather sofa, a smaller desk layered with round and square samples of marble and granite. The dirty window, which was never opened, looked out on the sloping market Square, pocketed obliquely off the public Square, and filled with the wagons of draymen and county peddlers, and on the lower side on a few Poor White houses and on the warehouse and office of Will Pentland.

Eugene would find his father, leaning perilously on Jannadeau's dirty glass showcase, or on the creaking little fence that marked him off, talking politics, war, death, and famine, denouncing the Democrats, with references to the bad weather, taxation, and soup-kitchens that attended their administration, and eulogizing all the acts, utterances, and policies of Theodore Roosevelt. Jannadeau, guttural, judiciously reasonable, statistically argumentative, would consult, in all disputed areas, his library—a greasy edition of the World Almanac, three years old, saying, triumphantly, after a moment of dirty thumbing: "Ah—just as I thought: the municipal taxation of Milwaukee under Democratic administration in 1905 was $2.25 the hundred, the lowest it had been in years. I cannot imagine why the total revenue is not given." And he would argue with animation, picking his nose with his blunt black fingers, his broad yellow face breaking into flaccid creases, as he laughed gutturally at Gant's unreason.

"And you may mark my words," proceeded Gant, as if he had never been interrupted, and had heard no dissenting judgment, "if they get in again we'll have soup-kitchens, the banks will go to the wall, and your guts will grease your backbone before another winter's over."

Or, he would find his father in the workroom, bending over a trestle, using the heavy wooden mallet with delicate care, as he guided the chisel through the mazes of an inscription. He never wore work-clothes; he worked dressed in well brushed garments of heavy black, his coat removed, and a long striped apron covering all his front. As Eugene saw him, he felt that this was no common craftsman, but a master, picking up his tools briefly for a *chef-d'oeuvre*.

"He is better at this than any one in all the world," Eugene thought, and his dark vision burned in him for a moment, as he thought that his father's work would never, as men reckon years, be extinguished, but that when that great skeleton lay powdered in earth, in many a tangled undergrowth, in the rank wilderness of forgotten churchyards, these letters would endure.

And he thought with pity of all the grocers and brewers and clothiers who had come and gone, with their perishable work a forgotten excrement, or a rotted fabric; or of plumbers, like Max's father, whose work rusted under ground, or of painters, like Harry's, whose work scaled with the seasons, or was obliterated with newer brighter paint; and the high horror of death and oblivion, the decomposition of life, memory, desire, in the huge burial-ground of the earth stormed through his heart. He mourned for all the men who had gone because they had not scored their name upon a rock, blasted their mark upon a cliff, sought out the most imperishable objects of the world and graven there some token, some emblem that utterly they might not be forgotten.

Again, Eugene would find Gant moving with bent strides across the depth of the building, tearing madly along between the sentinel marbles that aisled the ware-room, muttering, with hands gripped behind him, with ominous ebb and flow. Eugene waited. Presently, when he had shuttled thus across his shop some eighty times, he would leap, with a furious howl, to his front door, storming out upon the porch, and delivering his Jeremiad to the offending draymen:

"You are the lowest of the low, the vilest of the vile. You lousy good-for-nothing bums: you have brought me to the verge of starvation, you have frightened away the little business that might have put bread in my mouth, and kept the wolf from my door. By God, I hate you, for you stink a mile off. You low degenerates, you accursed reprobates; you would steal the pennies from a dead man's eyes, as you have from mine, fearful, awful, and bloodthirsty mountain grills that you are!"

He would tear back into the shop muttering, to return almost at once, with a strained pretense at calmness, which ended in a howl:

"Now I want to tell you: I give you fair warning once and for all. If I find you on my steps again, I'll put you all in jail."

They would disperse sheepishly to their wagons, flicking their whips aimlessly along the pavements.

"By God, somethin's sure upset the ole man."

An hour later, like heavy buzzing flies, they would drift back settling from nowhere on the broad steps.

As he emerged from the shop into the Square, they would greet him cheerfully, with a certain affection.

" 'Day, Mr. Gant."

"Good day, boys," he would answer kindly, absently. And he would be away with his gaunt devouring strides.

As Eugene entered, if Gant were busy on a stone, he would say gruffly, "Hello, son," and continue with his work, until he had polished the surface of the marble with pumice and water. Then he would take off his apron, put on his coat, and say, to the dawdling, expectant boy: "Come on. I guess you're thirsty."

And they would go across the Square to the cool depth of the drugstore, stand before the onyx splendor of the fountain, under the revolving wooden fans, and drink chill gaseous beverages, limeade so cold it made the head ache, or foaming ice-cream soda, which returned in sharp delicious belches down his tender nostrils.

Eugene, richer by twenty-five cents, would leave Gant then, and spend the remainder of the day in the library on the Square. He read now rapidly and easily; he read romantic and adventurous novels, with a tearing hunger. At home he devoured Luke's piled shelves of five-cent novels: he was deep in the weekly adventures of *Young Wild West,* fantasied in bed at night of virtuous and heroic relations with the beautiful Arietta, followed Nick Carter, through all the mazes of metropolitan crime, Frank Merriwell's athletic triumphs, Fred Fearnot, and the interminable victories of *The Liberty Boys of '76* over the hated Redcoats.

He cared not so much for love at first as he did for material success: the straw figures of women in boys' books, something with hair, dancing eyes, and virtuous opinions, impeccably good and vacant, satisfied him completely: they were the guerdon of heroism, something to be freed from villainy on the nick by a blow or a shot, and to be enjoyed along with a fat income.

At the library he ravaged the shelves of boys' books, going unweariedly through all the infinite monotony of the Algers—*Pluck and Luck, Sink or Swim, Grit, Jack's Ward, Jed the Poor-house Boy*—and dozens more. He gloated over the fat money-getting of these books (a motif in boys' books that has never been sufficiently recognized); all of the devices of fortune, the loose rail, the signalled train, the rich reward for heroism; or the full wallet found and restored to its owner; or the value of the supposedly worthless bonds; or the discovery of a rich patron in the city, sunk so deeply into his desires that he was never after able to quench them.

And all the details of money—the value of the estate usurped by the scoundrelly guardian and his caddish son, he feasted upon, reckoning up the amount of income, if it were not given, or if it were, dividing the annual sum into monthly and weekly portions, and dreaming on its purchasing power. His desires were not modest—no fortune under $250,000 satisfied him: the income of $100,000 at six per cent would pinch one, he felt, from lavishness; and if the reward of virtue was only twenty thousand dollars, he felt bitter chagrin, reckoning life insecure, and comfort a present warmth.

He built up a constant exchange of books among his companions, borrowing and lending in an intricate web, from Max Isaacs, from "Nosey" Schmidt, the butcher's son, who had all the rich adventures of the *Rover Boys;* he ransacked Gant's shelves at home, reading translations of the *Iliad* and the *Odyssey* at the same time as *Diamond Dick, Buffalo Bill,* and the Algers, and for the same reason; then, as the first years waned and the erotic gropings became more intelligible, he turned passionately to all romantic legendry, looking for women in whom blood ran hotly, whose breath was honey, and whose soft touch a spurting train of fire.

And in this pillage of the loaded shelves, he found himself wedged firmly into the grotesque pattern of Protestant fiction which yields the rewards of Dionysus to the loyal disciples of John Calvin, panting and praying in a breath, guarding the plumtree with the altar fires, outdoing the pagan harlot with the sanctified hussy.

Aye, thought he, he would have his cake and eat it too—but it would be a wedding-cake. He was devout in his desire to be a good man; he would bestow the accolade of his love upon nothing but a Virgin; he would marry himself to none but a Pure Woman. This, he saw from the books, would cause no renunciation of delight, for the good women were physically the most attractive.

He had learned unknowingly what the exquisite voluptuary finds, after weary toil, much later—that no condition of life is so favorable to his enjoyment as that one which is rigidly conventionalized. He had all the passionate fidelity of a child to the laws of the community: all the filtered deposit of Sunday Morning Presbyterianism had its effect.

He entombed himself in the flesh of a thousand fictional heroes, giving his favorites extension in life beyond their books, carrying their banners into the gray places of actuality, seeing himself now as the militant young clergyman, arrayed, in his war on slum conditions, against all the moneyed hostility of his fashionable church, aided in his hour of greatest travail by the lovely daughter of the millionaire tenement owner, and winning finally a victory for God, the poor, and himself.

. . . They stood silently a moment in the vast deserted nave of Saint Thomas'. Far in the depth of the vast church Old Michael's slender hands pressed softly on the organ-keys. The last rays of the setting sun poured in a golden shaft down through the western windows, falling for a moment, in a cloud of glory, as if in benediction, on Mainwaring's tired face.

"I am going," he said presently.

"Going?" she whispered. "Where?"

The organ music deepened.

"Out there," he gestured briefly to the West. "Out there—among His people."

"Going?" She could not conceal the tremor of her voice. "Going? Alone?"

He smiled sadly. The sun had set. The gathering darkness hid the suspicious moisture in his gray eyes.

"Yes, alone," he said. "Did not One greater than I go out alone some nineteen centuries ago?"

"Alone? Alone?" A sob rose in her throat and choked her.

"But before I go," he said, after a moment, in a voice which he strove in vain to render steady, "I want to tell you—" He paused a moment, struggling for mastery of his feelings.

"Yes?" she whispered.

"—That I shall never forget you, little girl, as long as I live. Never." He turned abruptly to depart.

"No, not alone! You shall not go alone!" she stopped him with a sudden cry.

He whirled as if he had been shot.

"What do you mean? What do you mean?" he cried hoarsely.

"Oh, can't you see! Can't you see!" She threw out her little hands imploringly, and her voice broke.

"Grace! Grace! Dear heaven, do you mean it!"

"You silly man! Oh, you dear blind foolish boy! Haven't you known for ages—since the day I first heard you preach at the Murphy Street settlement?"

He crushed her to him in a fierce embrace; her slender body yielded to his touch as he bent over her; and her round arms stole softly across his broad shoulders, around his neck, drawing his dark head to her as he planted hungry kisses on her closed eyes, the column of her throat, the parted petal of her fresh young lips.

"Forever," he answered solemnly. "So help me God."

The organ music swelled now into a triumphant pæan, filling with its exultant melody the vast darkness of the church. And as Old Michael cast his heart into the music, the tears flowed unrestrained across his withered cheeks, but smilingly happily through his tears, as dimly through his old eyes he saw the two young figures enacting again the age-old tale of youth and love, he murmured,

"I am the resurrection and the life, Alpha and Omega, the first and the last, the beginning and the end" . . .

Eugene turned his wet eyes to the light that streamed through the library windows, winked rapidly, gulped, and blew his nose heavily. Ah, yes! Ah, yes!

. . . The band of natives, seeing now that they had no more to fear, and wild with rage at the losses they had suffered, began to advance slowly toward the foot of the cliff, led by Taomi, who, dancing with fury, and hideous with warpaint, urged them on, exhorting them in a shrill voice.

Glendenning cursed softly under his breath as he looked once more at the empty cartridge belts, then grimly, as he gazed at the yelling horde below, slipped his two remaining cartridges into his Colt.

"For us?" she said, quietly. He nodded.

"It is the end?" she whispered, but without a trace of fear.

Again he nodded, and turned his head away for a moment. Presently he lifted his gray face to her.

"It is death, Veronica," he said, "and now I may speak."

"Yes, Bruce," she answered softly.

It was the first time he had ever heard her use his name, and his heart thrilled to it.

"I love you, Veronica," he said. "I have loved you ever since I found your almost lifeless body on the beach, during all the nights I lay outside your tent, listening to your quiet breathing within, love you most of all now in this hour of death when the obligation to keep silence no longer rests upon me."

"Dearest, dearest," she whispered, and he saw her face was wet with tears. "Why didn't you speak? I have loved you from the first."

She leaned toward him, her lips half-parted and tremulous, her breathing short and uncertain, and as his bare arms circled her fiercely their lips met in one long moment of rapture, one final moment of life and ecstasy, in which all the pent longing of their lives found release and consummation now at this triumphant moment of their death.

A distant reverberation shook the air. Glendenning looked up quickly, and rubbed his eyes with astonishment. There, in the island's little harbor were turning slowly the lean sides of a destroyer, and even as he looked, there was another burst of flame and smoke, and a whistling five-inch shell burst forty yards from where the natives had stopped. With a yell of mingled fear and baffled rage, they turned and fled off toward their canoes. Already, a boat, manned by the lusty arms of a blue-jacketed crew, had put off from the destroyer's side, and was coming in toward shore.

"Saved! We are saved!" cried Glendenning, and leaping to his feet he signalled the approaching boat. Suddenly he paused.

"Damn!" he muttered bitterly. "Oh, damn!"

"What is it, Bruce?" she asked.

He answered her in a cold harsh voice.

"A destroyer has just entered the harbor. We are saved, Miss Mullins. Saved!" And he laughed bitterly.

"Bruce! Dearest! What is it? Aren't you glad? Why do you act so strangely? We shall have all our life together."

"Together?" he said, with a harsh laugh. "Oh no, Miss Mullins. I know my place. Do you think old J. T. Mullins would let his daughter marry Bruce Glendenning, international vagabond, jack of all trades, and good at none of them? Oh no. That's over now, and it's good-by. I suppose," he said, with a wry smile, "I'll hear of your marriage to some Duke or Lord, or some of those foreigners some day. Well, good-by, Miss Mullins. Good luck. We'll both have to go our own way, I suppose." He turned away.

"You foolish boy! You dear bad silly boy!" She threw her arms around his neck, clasped him to her tightly, and scolded him tenderly. "Do you think I'll ever let you leave me now?"

"Veronica," he gasped. "Do you *mean* it?"

She tried to meet his adoring eyes, but couldn't: a rich wave of rosy red mantled her cheek, he drew her rapturously to him and, for the second time, but this time with the prophecy of eternal and abundant life before them, their lips met in sweet oblivion. . . .

Ah, me! Ah, me! Eugene's heart was filled with joy and sadness—with sorrow because the book was done. He pulled his clotted handkerchief from his pocket and blew the contents of his loaded heart into it in one mighty, triumphant and ecstatic blast of glory and sentiment. Ah, me! Good old Bruce-Eugene.

Lifted, by his fantasy, into a high interior world, he scored off briefly and entirely all the grimy smudges of life: he existed nobly in a heroic world with lovely and virtuous creatures. He saw himself in exalted circumstances with Bessie Barnes, her pure eyes dim with tears, her sweet lips tremulous with desire: he felt the strong handgrip of Honest Jack, her brother, his truehearted fidelity, the deep eternal locking of their brave souls, as they looked dumbly at each other with misty eyes, and thought of the pact of danger, the shoulder-to-shoulder drive through death and terror which had soldered them silently but implacably.

Eugene wanted the two things all men want: he wanted to be loved, and he wanted to be famous. His fame was chameleon, but its fruit and triumph lay at home, among the people of Altamont. The mountain town had for him enormous authority: with a child's egotism it was for him the centre of the earth, the small but dynamic core of all life. He saw himself winning Napoleonic triumphs in battle, falling, with his fierce picked men, like a thunderbolt upon an enemy's flank, trapping, hemming, and annihilating. He saw himself as the young captain of industry, dominant, victorious, rich; as the great criminal-lawyer bending to his eloquence a charmed court—but always he saw his return from the voyage wearing the great coronal of the world upon his modest brows.

The world was a phantasmal land of faery beyond the misted hem of the hills, a land of great reverberations, of genii-guarded orchards, wine-dark seas, chasmed and fantastical cities from which he would return into this substantial heart of life, his native town, with golden loot.

He quivered deliciously to temptation—he kept his titillated honor secure after subjecting it to the most trying inducements: the groomed beauty of the rich man's wife, publicly humiliated by her brutal husband, defended by Bruce-Eugene, and melting toward him with all the pure ardor of her lonely and womanly heart, pouring the sad measure of her life into his sympathetic ears over the wineglasses of her candled, rich, but intimate table. And as, in the shaded light, she moved yearningly toward him, sheathed plastically in her gown of rich velvet, he would detach gently the round arms that clung about his neck, the firm curved body that stuck gluily to his. Or the blonde princess in the fabulous Balkans, the empress of gabled Toyland, and the Doll Hussars—he would renounce, in a great scene upon the frontiers, her proffered renunciation, drinking eternal farewell on her red mouth, but wedding her to himself and to the citizenship of freedom when revolution had levelled her fortune to his own.

But, steeping himself in ancient myths, where the will and the deed were not thought darkly on, he spent himself, quilted in golden meadows, or in the green light of woods, in pagan love. Oh to be king, and see a fruity wide-hipped Jewess bathing on her roof, and to possess her; or a cragged and castled baron, to execute *le droit de seigneur* upon the choicest of the enfeoffed wives and wenches, in a vast chamber loud with the howling winds and lighted by the mad dancing flames of great logs!

But even more often, the shell of his morality broken to fragments by his desire, he would enact the bawdy fable of school-boys, and picture himself in hot romance with a handsome teacher. In the fourth grade his teacher was a young, inexperienced, but well-built woman, with carrot-colored hair, and full of reckless laughter.

He saw himself, grown to the age of potency, a strong, heroic, brilliant boy, the one spot of incandescence in a backwoods school attended by snag-toothed children and hair-faced louts. And, as the mellow autumn ripened, her interest in him would intensify, she would "keep him in" for imaginary offenses, setting him, in a somewhat confused way, to do some task, and gazing at him with steady yearning eyes when she thought he was not looking.

He would pretend to be stumped by the exercise: she would come eagerly and sit beside him, leaning over so that a few fine strands of carrot-colored hair brushed his nostrils, and so that he might feel the firm warmth of her white-waisted arms, and the swell of her tight-skirted thighs. She would explain things to him at great length, guiding his fingers with her own warm, slightly moist hand, when he pretended not to find the place; then she would chide him gently, saying tenderly:

"Why are you such a bad boy?" or softly: "Do you think you're going to be better after this?"

And he, simulating boyish, inarticulate coyness, would say: "Gosh, Miss Edith, I didn't mean to do nothin'."

Later, as the golden sun was waning redly, and there was nothing in the room but the smell of chalk and the heavy buzz of the old October flies, they would prepare to depart. As he twisted carelessly into his overcoat, she would chide him, call him to her, arrange the lapels and his necktie, and smooth out his tousled hair, saying:

"You're a good-looking boy. I bet all the girls are wild about you."

He would blush in a maidenly way and she, bitten with curiosity, would press him:

"Come on, now. Who's your girl?"

"I haven't got one, honest, Miss Edith."

"You don't want one of these silly little girls, Eugene," she would say, coaxingly. "You're too good for them—you're a great deal older than your years. You need the understanding a mature woman can give you."

And they would walk away in the setting sun, skirting the pine-fresh woods, passing along the path red with maple leaves, past great ripening pumpkins in the fields, and under the golden autumnal odor of persimmons.

She would live alone with her mother, an old deaf woman, in a little cottage set back from the road against a shelter of lonely singing pines, with a few grand oaks and maples in the leaf-bedded yard.

Before they came to the house, crossing a field, it would be necessary to go over a stile; he would go over first, helping her down, looking ardently at the graceful curve of her long, deliberately exposed, silk-clad leg.

As the days shortened, they would come by dark, or under the heavy low-hanging autumnal moon. She would pretend to be frightened as they passed the woods, press in to him and take his arm at imaginary sounds, until one night, crossing the stile, boldly resolved upon an issue, she would pretend difficulty in descending, and he would lift her down in his arms. She would whisper:

"How strong you are, Eugene." Still holding her, his hand would shift under her knees. And as he lowered her upon the frozen clotted earth, she would kiss him passionately, again and again, pressing him to her, caressing him, and under the frosted persimmon tree fulfilling and yielding herself up to his maiden and unfledged desire.

"That boy's read books by the hundreds," Gant boasted about the town. "He's read everything in the library by now."

"By God, W. O., you'll have to make a lawyer out of him. That's what he's cut out for." Major Liddell spat accurately, out of his high cracked voice, across the pavement, and settled back in his chair below the library windows, smoothing his stained white pointed beard with a palsied hand. He was a veteran.

10

But this freedom, this isolation in print, this dreaming and unlimited time of fantasy, was not to last unbroken. Both Gant and Eliza were fluent apologists for economic independence: all the boys had been sent out to earn money at a very early age.

"It teaches a boy to be independent and self-reliant," said Gant, feeling he had heard this somewhere before.

"Pshaw!" said Eliza. "It won't do them a bit of harm. If they don't learn now, they won't do a stroke of work later on. Besides, they can earn their own pocket money." This, undoubtedly, was a consideration of the greatest importance.

Thus, the boys had gone out to work, after school hours, and in the vacations, since they were very young. Unhappily, neither Eliza nor Gant were at any pains to examine the kind of work their children did, contenting themselves vaguely with the comfortable assurance that all work which earned money was honest, commendable, and formative of character.

By this time Ben, sullen, silent, alone, had withdrawn more closely than ever into his heart: in the brawling house he came and went, and was remembered, like a phantom. Each morning at three o'clock, when his fragile unfurnished body should have been soaked in sleep, he got up under the morning stars, departed silently from the sleeping house, and went down to the roaring morning presses and the inksmell that he loved, to begin the delivery of his route. Almost without consideration by Gant and Eliza he slipped quietly away from school after the eighth grade, took on extra duties at the paper's office and lived, in sufficient bitter pride, upon his earnings. He slept at home, ate perhaps one meal a day there, loping home gauntly at night, with his father's stride, thin long shoulders, bent prematurely by the weight of the heavy paper bag, pathetically, hungrily Gantian.

He bore encysted in him the evidence of their tragic fault: he walked alone in the darkness, death and the dark angels hovered, and no one saw him. At three-thirty in the morning, with his loaded bag beside him, he sat with other route boys in a lunch room, with a cup of coffee in one hand and a cigarette in the other, laughing softly, almost noiselessly, with his flickering exquisitely sensitive mouth, his scowling gray eyes.

At home he spent hours quietly absorbed in his life with Eugene, playing with him, cuffing him with his white hard hands from time to time, establishing with him a secret communication to which the life of the family had neither access nor understanding. From his small wages he gave the boy sums of spending-money, bought him expensive presents on his birthdays, at Christmas, or some special occasion, inwardly moved and pleased when he saw how like Mæcenas he seemed to Eugene, how deep and inexhaustible to the younger boy were his meagre resources. What he earned, all the history of his life away from home, he kept in jealous secrecy.

"It's nobody's business but my own. By God, I'm not asking any of you for anything," he said, sullenly and irritably, when Eliza pressed him curiously. He had a deep scowling affection for them all: he never forgot their birthdays, he always placed where they might find it, some gift, small, inexpensive, selected with the most discriminating taste. When, with their fervent over-emphasis, they went through long ecstasies of admiration, embroidering their thanks with florid decorations, he would jerk his head sideways to some imaginary listener, laughing softly and irritably, as he said:

"Oh for God's sake! Listen to this, won't you!"

Perhaps, as pigeon-toed, well creased, brushed, white-collared, Ben loped through the streets, or prowled softly and restlessly about the house, his dark angel wept, but no one else saw, and no one knew. He was a stranger, and as he sought through the house, he was always aprowl to find some entrance into life, some secret undiscovered door—a stone, a leaf,—that might admit him into light and fellowship. His passion for home was fundamental, in that jangled and clamorous household his sullen and contained quiet was like some soothing opiate on their nerves: with quiet authority, white-handed skill, he sought about repairing old scars, joining with delicate carpentry old broken things, prying quietly about a short-circuited wire, a defective socket.

"That boy's a born electrical engineer," said Gant. "I've a good notion to send him off to school." And he would paint a romantic picture of the prosperity of Mr. Charles Liddell, the Major's worthy son, who earned thousands by his electrical wizardry, and supported his father. And he would reproach them bitterly, as he dwelt on his own merit and the worthlessness of his sons:

"Other men's sons support their fathers in their old age—not mine! Not mine! Ah Lord—it will be a bitter day for me when I have to depend on one of mine. Tarkinton told me the other day that Rafe has given him five dollars a week for his food ever since he was sixteen. Do you think I could look for such treatment from one of mine? Do you? Not until Hell freezes over—and not then!" And he would refer to the hardships of his own youth, cast out, so he said, to earn his living, at an age which varied, according to his temper, at from six to eleven years, contrasting his poverty to the luxury in which his own children wallowed.

"No one ever did anything for me," he howled. "But everything's been done for you. And what gratitude do I get from you? Do you ever think of the old man who slaves up there in his cold shop in order to give you food and shelter? Do you? Ingratitude, more fierce than brutish beasts!" Remorseful food stuck vengefully in Eugene's throat.

Eugene was initiated to the ethics of success. It was not enough that a man work, though work was fundamental; it was even more important that he make money—a great deal if he was to be a great success—but at least enough to "support himself." This was for both Gant and Eliza the base of worth. Of so and so, they might say:

"He's not worth powder enough to kill him. He's never been able to support himself," to which Eliza, but not Gant, might add:

"He hasn't a stick of property to his name." This crowned him with infamy.

In the fresh sweet mornings of Spring now, Eugene was howled out of bed at six-thirty by his father, descended to the cool garden, and there, assisted by Gant, filled small strawberry baskets with great crinkled lettuces, radishes, plums, and green apples—somewhat later, with cherries. With these packed in a great hamper, he would peddle his wares through the neighborhood, selling them easily and delightfully, in a world of fragrant morning cookery, at five or ten cents a basket. He would return home gleefully with empty hamper in time for breakfast: he liked the work, the smell of gardens, of fresh wet vegetables; he loved the romantic structure of the earth which filled his pocket with chinking coins.

He was permitted to keep the money of his sales, although Eliza was annoyingly insistent that he should not squander it, but open a bank account with it with which, one day, he might establish himself in business, or buy a good piece of property. And she bought him a little bank, into which his reluctant fingers dropped a portion of his earnings, and from which he got a certain dreary satisfaction from time to time by shaking it close to his ear and dwelling hungrily on all the purchasable delight that was locked away from him in the small heavy bullion-chinking vault. There was a key, but Eliza kept it.

But, as the months passed, and the sturdy child's body of his infancy lengthened rapidly to some interior chemical expansion, and he became fragile, thin, pallid, but remarkably tall for his age, Eliza began to say: "That boy's big enough to do a little work."

Every Thursday afternoon now during the school months, and thence until Saturday, he was sent out upon the streets to sell *The Saturday Evening Post,* of which Luke held the local agency. Eugene hated the work with a deadly sweltering hatred; he watched the approach of Thursday with sick horror.

Luke had been the agent since his twelfth year: his reputation for salesmanship was sown through the town; he came with wide grin, exuberant vitality, wagging and witty tongue, hurling all his bursting energy into an insane extraversion. He lived absolutely in event: there was in him no secret place, nothing withheld and guarded—he had an instinctive horror of all loneliness.

He wanted above all else to be esteemed and liked by the world, and the need for the affection and esteem of his family was desperately essential. The fulsome praise, the heartiness of hand and tongue, the liberal display of sentiment were as the breath of life to him: he was overwhelmingly insistent in the payment of drinks at the fountain, the bringer-home of packed ice-cream for Eliza, and of cigars to Gant and, as Gant gave publication to his generosity, the boy's need for it increased—he built up an image of himself as the Good Fellow, witty, unselfish, laughed at but liked by all—as Big-Hearted Unselfish Luke. And this was the opinion people had of him.

Many times in the years that followed, when Eugene's pockets were empty, Luke thrust a coin roughly and impatiently in them, but, hard as the younger boy's need might be, there was always an awkward scene—painful, embarrassed protestations, a distressful confusion because Eugene, having accurately and intuitively gauged his brother's hunger for gratitude and esteem, felt sharply that he was yielding up his independence to a bludgeoning desire.

He had never felt the slightest shame at Ben's bounty: his enormously sensitized perception had told him long since that he might get the curse of annoyance, the cuff of anger, from his brother, but that past indulgences would not be brandished over him, and that even the thought of having bestowed gifts would give Ben inward shame. In this, he was like Ben: the thought of a gift he made, with its self-congratulatory implications, made him writhe.

Thus, before he was ten, Eugene's brooding spirit was nettled in the complexity of truth and seeming. He could find no words, no answers to the puzzles that baffled and maddened him: he found himself loathing that which bore the stamp of virtue, sick with weariness and horror at what was considered noble. He was hurled, at eight years, against the torturing paradox of the ungenerous-generous, the selfish-unselfish, the noble-base, and unable to fathom or define those deep springs of desire in the human spirit that seek public gratification by virtuous pretension, he was made wretched by the conviction of his own sinfulness.

There was in him a savage honesty, which exercised an uncontrollable domination over him when his heart or head were deeply involved. Thus, at the funeral of some remote kinsman, or of some acquaintance of the family, for whom he had never acquired any considerable affection, he would grow bitterly shamefast if, while listening to the solemn drone of the minister, or the sorrowful chanting of the singers, he felt his face had assumed an expression of unfelt and counterfeited grief: as a consequence he would shift about matter-of-factly, cross his legs, gaze indifferently at the ceiling, or look out of the window with a smile, until he was conscious his conduct had attracted the attention of people, and that they were looking on him with disfavor. Then, he felt a certain grim satisfaction as if, although having lost esteem, he had recorded his life.

But Luke flourished hardily in all the absurd mummery of the village: he gave heaping weight to every simulation of affection, grief, pity, good-will, and modesty—there was no excess that he did not underscore heavily, and the world's dull eye read him kindly.

He spun himself outward with ceaseless exuberance: he was genuinely and whole-heartedly involved. There was in him no toilsome web that might have checked him, no balancing or restraining weight—he had enormous energy, hungry gregariousness, the passion to pool his life.

In the family, where a simple brutal tag was enough for the appraisal of all fine consciences, Ben went simply as "the quiet one," Luke as the

generous and unselfish one, Eugene as the "scholar." It served. The
generous one, who had never in all his life had the power to fasten his
mind upon the pages of a book, or the logic of number, for an hour
together, resented, as he see-sawed comically from one leg to another,
stammering quaintly, whistling for the word that stuck in his throat,
the brooding abstraction of the youngest.

"Come on, this is no time for day-dreaming," he would stammer
ironically. "The early bird catches the worm—it's time we went out
on the street."

And although his reference to day-dreams was only part of the axiomatic
mosaic of his speech, Eugene was startled and confused, feeling that his
secret world, so fearfully guarded, had been revealed to ridicule. And
the older boy, too, smarting from his own dismal performances at school,
convinced himself that the deep inward turning of the spirit, the brooding
retreat into the secret place, which he recognized in the mysterious
hypnotic power of language over Eugene, was not only a species of
indolence, for the only work he recognized was that which strained at
weight or sweated in the facile waggery of the tongue, but that it was
moreover the indulgence of a "selfish" family-forgetting spirit. He was
determined to occupy alone the throne of goodness.

Thus, Eugene gathered vaguely but poignantly, that other boys of his
age were not only self-supporting, but had for years kept their decrepit
parents in luxury by their earnings as electrical engineers, presidents of
banks, or members of Congress. There was, in fact, no excess of suggestion
that Gant did not use upon his youngest son—he had felt, long since,
the vibration to every tremor of feeling of the million-noted little instru-
ment, and it pleased him to see the child wince, gulp, tortured with
remorse. Thus, while he piled high with succulent meat the boy's platter,
he would say sentimentally:

"I tell you what: there are not many boys who have what you have.
What's going to become of you when your old father's dead and gone?"
And he would paint a ghastly picture of himself lying cold in death,
lowered forever into the damp rot of the earth, buried, forgotten—
an event which, he hinted sorrowfully, was not remote.

"You'll remember the old man, then," he would say. "Ah, Lord! You
never miss the water till the well goes dry," noting with keen pleasure
the inward convulsion of the childish throat, the winking eyes, the
tense constricted face.

"I'll vow, Mr. Gant," Eliza bridled, also pleased, "you oughtn't to do
that to the child."

Or, he would speak sadly of "Little Jimmy," a legless little boy whom he had often pointed out to Eugene, who lived across the river from Riverside, the amusement park, and around whom he had woven a pathetic fable of poverty and orphanage which was desperately real now to his son. When Eugene was six, Gant had promised him carelessly a pony for Christmas, without any intention of fulfilling his promise. As Christmas neared he had begun to speak touchingly of "Little Jimmy," of the countless advantages of Eugene's lot and, after a mighty struggle, the boy had renounced the pony, in a scrawled message to Elfland, in favor of the cripple. Eugene never forgot: even when he had reached manhood the deception of "Little Jimmy" returned to him, without rancor, without ugliness, only with pain for all the blind waste, the stupid perjury, the thoughtless dishonor, the crippling dull deceit.

Luke parroted all of his father's sermons, but earnestly and witlessly, without Gant's humor, without his chicanery, only with his sentimentality. He lived in a world of symbols, large, crude, and gaudily painted, labelled "Father," "Mother," "Home," "Family," "Generosity," "Honor," "Unselfishness," made of sugar and molasses, and gummed glutinously with tear-shaped syrup.

"He's one good boy," the neighbors said.

"He's the cutest thing," said the ladies, who were charmed by his stutter, his wit, his good nature, his devout attendance on them.

"That boy's a hustler. He'll make his mark," said all the men in town.

And it was as the smiling hustler that he wanted to be known. He read piously all the circulars the Curtis Publishing Company sent to its agents: he posed himself in the various descriptive attitudes that were supposed to promote business—the proper manner of "approach," the most persuasive manner of drawing the journal from the bag, the animated description of its contents, in which he was supposed to be steeped as a result of his faithful reading—"the good salesman," the circulars said, "should know in and out the article he is selling"—a knowledge that Luke avoided, but which he replaced with eloquent invention of his own.

The literal digestion of these instructions resulted in one of the most fantastic exhibitions of print-vending ever seen: fortified by his own unlimited cheek, and by the pious axioms of the exhortations that "the good salesman will never take no for his answer," that he should "stick to his prospect" even if rebuffed, that he should "try to get the customer's psychology," the boy would fall into step with an unsuspecting pedestrian, open the broad sheets of *The Post* under the man's nose, and in a torrential harangue, sown thickly with stuttering speech, buffoonery, and ingratiation, delivered so rapidly that the man could neither accept nor reject the magazine, hound him before a grinning public down the length of a street, backing him defensively into a wall, and taking from the victim's eager fingers the five-cent coin that purchased his freedom.

"Yes, sir. Yes, sir," he would begin in a sonorous voice, dropping wide-leggedly into the "prospect's" stride. "This week's edition of *The Saturday Evening Post,* five cents, only a nickel, p-p-p-purchased weekly by t-t-two million readers. In this week's issue you have eighty-six pages of f-f-fact and fiction, to say n-n-nothing of the advertisements. If you c-c-c-can't read you'll get m-m-more than your money's worth out of the p-p-pictures. On page 13 this week, we have a very fine article, by I-I-I-Isaac F. Marcosson, the f-f-f-famous traveller and writer on politics; on page 29, you have a story by Irvin S. Cobb, the g-g-g-greatest living humorist, and a new story of the prize-ring by J-J-Jack London. If you b-b-bought it in a book, it'd c-c-cost you a d-d-dollar-and-a-half."

He had, besides these chance victims, an extensive clientry among the townsfolk. Swinging briskly and cheerily down the street, full of greetings and glib repartee, he would accost each of the grinning men by a new title, in a rich stammering tenor voice:

"Colonel, how are you! Major—here you are, a week's reading hot off the press. Captain, how's the boy?"

"How are you, son?"

"Couldn't be better, General—slick as a puppy's belly!"

And they would roar with wheezing, red-faced, Southern laughter:

"By God, he's a good 'un. Here, son, give me one of the damn things. I don't want it, but I'll buy it just to hear you talk."

He was full of pungent and racy vulgarity: he had, more than any of the family, a Rabelaisian earthiness that surged in him with limitless energy, charging his tongue with unpremeditated comparisons, Gargantuan metaphors. Finally, he wet the bed every night in spite of Eliza's fretting complaints: it was the final touch of his stuttering, whistling, cheerful, vital, and comic personality—he was Luke, the unique, Luke, the incomparable: he was, in spite of his garrulous and fidgeting nervousness, an intensely likable person—and he really had in him a bottomless well of affection. He wanted bounteous praise for his acts, but he had a deep, genuine kindliness and tenderness.

Every week, on Thursday, in Gant's dusty little office, he would gather the grinning cluster of small boys who bought *The Post* from him, and harangue them before he sent them out on their duties:

"Well, have you thought of what you're going to tell them yet? You know you can't sit around on your little tails and expect them to look you up. Have you got a spiel worked out yet? How do you approach 'em, eh?" he said, turning fiercely to a stricken small boy. "Speak up, speak up, G-G-G-God-damn it—don't s-s-stand there looking at me. Haw!" he said, laughing with sudden wild idiocy, "look at that face, won't you?"

Gant surveyed the proceedings from afar with Jannadeau, grinning.

"All right, Christopher Columbus," continued Luke, goodhumoredly, "What do you tell 'em, son?"

The boy cleared his throat timidly: "Mister, do you want to buy a copy of *The Saturday Evening Post?*"

"Oh, twah-twah," said Luke, with mincing delicacy, as the boys sniggered, "sweet twah-twah! Do you expect them to buy with a spiel like that? My God, where are your brains? Sail into them. Tackle them, and don't take no for an answer. Don't ask them if they *want* to buy. Dive into them: 'Here you are, sir—hot off the press.' Jesus Christ," he yelled, looking at the distant court-house clock with sudden fidget, "we should have been out an hour ago. Come on—don't stand there: here are your papers. How many do you want, you little Kike?"—for he had several Jews in his employ: they worshipped him and he was very fond of them— he liked their warmth, richness, humor.

"Twenty."

"Twenty!" he yelled. "You little loafer—you'll t-t-take fifty. G-g-go on, you c-c-can sell 'em all this afternoon. By G-G-God, papa," he said, pointing to the Jews, as Gant entered the office, "it l-l-looks like the Last S-S-Supper, don't it? All right!" he said, smacking across the buttocks a small boy who had bent for his quota. "Don't stick it in my face." They shrieked with laughter. "Dive in to them now. Don't let 'em get away from you." And, laughing and excited, he would send them out into the streets.

To this kind of employment and this method of exploitation Eugene was now initiated. He loathed the work with a deadly, an inexplicable loathing. But something in him festered deeply at the idea of disposing of his wares by the process of making such a wretched little nuisance of himself that riddance was purchased only at the price of the magazine. He writhed with shame and humiliation, but he stuck desperately to his task, a queer curly-headed passionate little creature, who raced along by the side of an astonished captive, pouring out of his dark eager face a hurricane of language. And men, fascinated somehow by this strange eloquence from a little boy, bought.

Sometimes the heavy paunch-bellied Federal judge, sometimes an attorney, a banker would take him home, bidding him to perform for their wives, the members of their families, giving him twenty-five cents when he was done, and dismissing him. "What do you think of that!" they said.

His first and nearest sales made, in the town, he would make the long circle on the hills and in the woods along the outskirts, visiting the tubercular sanitariums, selling the magazines easily and quickly—"like hot cakes" as Luke had it—to doctors and nurses, to white unshaven, sensitive-faced Jews, to the wisp of a rake, spitting his rotten lungs into a cup, to good-looking young women who coughed slightly from time to time, but who smiled at him from their chairs, and let their warm soft hands touch his slightly as they paid him.

Once, at a hillside sanitarium, two young New York Jews had taken him to the room of one of them, closed the door behind him, and assaulted him, tumbling him on the bed, while one drew forth a pocket knife and informed him he was going to perform a caponizing operation on him. They were two young men bored with the hills, the town, the deadly regime of their treatment, and it occurred to him years later that they had concocted the business, days ahead, in their dull lives, living for the excitement and terror they would arouse in him. His response was more violent than they had bargained for: he went mad with fear, screamed, and fought insanely. They were weak as cats, he squirmed out of their grasp and off the bed cuffing and clawing tigerishly, striking and kicking them with blind and mounting rage. He was released by a nurse who unlocked the door and led him out into the sunlight, the two young consumptives, exhausted and frightened, remaining in their room. He was nauseated by fear and by the impacts of his fists on their leprous bodies.

But the little mound of nickels and dimes and quarters chinked pleasantly in his pockets: leg-weary and exhausted he would stand before a gleaming fountain burying his hot face in an iced drink. Sometimes conscience-tortured, he would steal an hour away from the weary streets and go into the library for a period of enchantment and oblivion: he was often discovered by his watchful and bustling brother, who drove him out to his labor again, taunting and spurring him into activity.

"Wake up! You're not in Fairyland. Go after them."

Eugene's face was of no use to him as a mask: it was a dark pool in which every pebble of thought and feeling left its circle—his shame, his distaste for his employment was obvious, although he tried to conceal it: he was accused of false pride, told that he was "afraid of a little honest work," and reminded of the rich benefits he had received from his big-hearted parents.

He turned desperately to Ben. Sometimes Ben, loping along the streets of the town, met him, hot, tired, dirty, wearing his loaded canvas bag, scowled fiercely at him, upbraided him for his unkempt appearance, and took him into a lunch-room for something to eat—rich foaming milk, fat steaming kidney-beans, thick apple-pie.

Both Ben and Eugene were by nature aristocrats. Eugene had just begun to feel his social status—or rather his lack of one; Ben had felt it for years. The feeling at bottom might have resolved itself simply into a desire for the companionship of elegant and lovely women: neither was able, nor would have dared, to confess this, and Eugene was unable to confess that he was susceptible to the social snub, or the pain of caste inferiority: any suggestion that the companionship of elegant people was preferable to the fellowship of a world of Tarkintons, and its blousy daughters, would have been hailed with heavy ridicule by the family, as another indication of false and undemocratic pride. He would have been called "Mr. Vanderbilt" or "the Prince of Wales."

Ben, however, was not to be intimidated by their cant, or deceived by their twaddle. He saw them with bitter clarity, answered their pretensions with soft mocking laughter, and a brief nod upwards and to the side to the companion to whom he communicated all his contemptuous observation—his dark satiric angel: "Oh, my God! Listen to that, won't you?"

There was behind his scowling quiet eyes, something strange and fierce and unequivocal that frightened them: besides, he had secured for himself the kind of freedom they valued most—the economic freedom—and he spoke as he felt, answering their virtuous reproof with fierce quiet scorn.

One day, he stood, smelling of nicotine, before the fire, scowling darkly at Eugene who, grubby and tousled, had slung his heavy bag over his shoulder, and was preparing to depart.

"Come here, you little bum," he said. "When did you wash your hands last?" Scowling fiercely, he made a sudden motion as if to strike the boy, but he finished instead by re-tying, with his hard delicate hands, his tie.

"In God's name, mama," he burst out irritably to Eliza, "haven't you got a clean shirt to give him? You know, he ought to have one every month or so."

"What do you mean? What do you mean?" said Eliza with comic rapidity, looking up from a basket of socks she was darning. "I gave him that one last Tuesday."

"You little thug!" he growled, looking at Eugene with a fierce pain in his eyes. "Mama, for heaven's sake, why don't you send him to the barber's and get that lousy hair cut off? By God, I'll pay for it, if you don't want to spend the money."

She pursed her lips angrily and continued to darn. Eugene looked at him dumbly, gratefully. After Eugene had gone, the quiet one smoked moodily for a time, drawing the fragrant smoke in long gulps down into his thin lungs. Eliza, recollective and hurt at what had been said, worked on.

"What are you trying to do with your kid, mama?" he said in a hard quiet voice, after a silence. "Do you want to make a tramp out of him?"

"What do you mean? What do you mean?"

"Do you think it's right to send him out on the streets with every little thug in town?"

"Why, I don't know what you're talking about, boy," she said impatiently. "It's no disgrace for a boy to do a little honest work, and no one thinks so."

"Oh, my God," he said to the dark angel. "Listen to that!"

Eliza pursed her lips without speaking for a time.

"Pride goeth before a fall," she said after a moment. "Pride goeth before a fall."

"I can't see that that makes much difference to us," said he. "We've got no place to fall to."

"I consider myself as good as any one," she said, with dignity. "I hold my head up with any one I meet."

"Oh, my God," Ben said to his angel. "You don't meet any one. I don't notice any of your fine brothers or their wives coming to see you."

This was true, and it hurt. She pursed her lips.

"No mama," he continued after a moment's pause, "you and the Old Man have never given a damn what we've done so long as you thought you might save a nickel by it."

"Why, I don't know what you're talking about, boy," she answered. "You talk as if you thought we were Rich Folks. Beggars can't be choosers."

"Oh, my God," he laughed bitterly. "You and the Old Man like to make out you're paupers, but you've a sock full of money."

"I don't know what you mean," she said angrily.

"No," he said, with his frequent negative beginning, after a moody silence, "there are people in this town without a fifth what we've got who get twice as much out of it. The rest of us have never had anything, but I don't want to see the kid made into a little tramp."

There was a long silence. She darned bitterly, pursing her lips frequently, hovering between quiet and tears.

"I never thought," she began after a long pause, her mouth tremulous with a bitter hurt smile, "that I should live to hear such talk from a son of mine. You had better watch out," she hinted darkly, "a day of reckoning cometh. As sure as you live, as sure as you live. You will be repaid threefold for your unnatural," her voice sank to a tearful whisper, "your *unnatural* conduct!" She wept easily.

"Oh, my God," answered Ben, turning his lean, gray, bitter, bumpy face up toward his listening angel. "Listen to that, won't you?"

11

Eliza saw Altamont not as so many hills, buildings, people: she saw it in the pattern of a gigantic blueprint. She knew the history of every piece of valuable property—who bought it, who sold it, who owned it in 1893, and what it was now worth. She watched the tides of traffic cannily; she knew by what corners the largest number of people passed in a day or an hour; she was sensitive to every growing-pain of the young town, gauging from year to year its growth in any direction, and deducing the probable direction of its future expansion. She judged distances critically, saw at once where the beaten route to an important centre was stupidly circuitous, and looking in a straight line through houses and lots, she said:

"There'll be a street through here some day."

Her vision of land and population was clear, crude, focal—there was nothing technical about it: it was extraordinary for its direct intensity. Her instinct was to buy cheaply where people would come; to keep out of pockets and *culs de sac,* to buy on a street that moved toward a centre, and that could be given extension.

Thus, she began to think of Dixieland. It was situated five minutes from the public square, on a pleasant sloping middleclass street of small homes and boarding-houses. Dixieland was a big cheaply constructed frame house of eighteen or twenty drafty high-ceilinged rooms: it had a rambling, unplanned, gabular appearance, and was painted a dirty yellow. It had a pleasant green front yard, not deep but wide, bordered by a row of young deep-bodied maples: there was a sloping depth of one hundred and ninety feet, a frontage of one hundred and twenty. And Eliza, looking toward the town, said: "They'll put a street behind there some day."

In winter, the wind blew howling blasts under the skirts of Dixieland:

its back end was built high off the ground on wet columns of rotting brick. Its big rooms were heated by a small furnace which sent up, when charged with fire, a hot dry enervation to the rooms of the first floor, and a gaseous but chill radiation to those upstairs.

The place was for sale. Its owner was a middle-aged horse-faced gentleman whose name was the Reverend Wellington Hodge: he had begun life favorably in Altamont as a Methodist minister, but had run foul of trouble when he began to do double service to the Lord God of Hosts and John Barleycorn—his evangelical career came to an abrupt ending one winter's night when the streets were dumb with falling snow. Wellington, clad only in his winter heavies, made a wild sortie from Dixieland at two in the morning, announcing the kingdom of God and the banishment of the devil, in a mad marathon through the streets that landed him panting but victorious in front of the Post Office. Since then, with the assistance of his wife, he had eked out a hard living at the boarding-house. Now, he was spent, disgraced, and weary of the town.

Besides, the sheltering walls of Dixieland inspired him with horror—he felt that the malign influence of the house had governed his own disintegration. He was a sensitive man, and his promenades about his estate were checked by inhibited places: the cornice of the long girdling porch where a lodger had hanged himself one day at dawn, the spot in the hall where the consumptive had collapsed in a hemorrhage, the room where the old man cut his throat. He wanted to return to his home, a land of fast horses, wind-bent grass, and good whisky—Kentucky. He was ready to sell Dixieland.

Eliza pursed her lips more and more thoughtfully, went to town by way of Spring Street more and more often.

"That's going to be a good piece of property some day," she said to Gant.

He made no complaint. He felt suddenly the futility of opposing an implacable, an inexorable desire.

"Do you want it?" he said.

She pursed her lips several times: "It's a good buy," she said.

"You'll never regret it as long as you live, W. O.," said Dick Gudger, the agent.

"It's her house, Dick," said Gant wearily. "Make out the papers in her name."

She looked at him.

"I never want to own another piece of property as long as I live," said

Gant. "It's a curse and a care, and the tax-collector gets all you have in the end."

Eliza pursed her lips and nodded.

She bought the place for seventy-five hundred dollars. She had enough money to make the first payment of fifteen hundred. The balance was to be paid in installments of fifteen hundred dollars a year. This she knew she had to pay chiefly from the earnings of the house.

In the young autumn when the maples were still full and green, and the migratory swallows filled secretly the trees with clamor, and swooped of an evening in a black whirlwind down, drifting at its funnel end, like dead leaves, into their chosen chimney, Eliza moved into Dixieland. There was clangor, excitement, vast curiosity in the family about the purchase, but no clear conception of what had really happened. Gant and Eliza, although each felt dumbly that they had come to a decisive boundary in their lives, talked vaguely about their plans, spoke of Dixieland evasively as "a good investment," said nothing clearly. In fact, they felt their approaching separation instinctively: Eliza's life was moving by a half-blind but inevitable gravitation toward the centre of its desire—the exact meaning of her venture she would have been unable to define, but she had a deep conviction that the groping urge which had led her so blindly into death and misery at Saint Louis had now impelled her in the right direction. Her life was on the rails.

And however vaguely, confusedly, and casually they approached this complete disruption of their life together, the rooting up of their clamorous home, when the hour of departures came, the elements resolved themselves immutably and without hesitation.

Eliza took Eugene with her. He was the last tie that bound her to all the weary life of breast and cradle; he still slept with her of nights; she was like some swimmer who ventures out into a dark and desperate sea, not wholly trusting to her strength and destiny, but with a slender cord bound to her which stretches still to land.

With scarcely a word spoken, as if it had been known anciently and forever, Helen stayed with Gant.

The time for Daisy's marriage was growing near: she had been sought by a tall middle-aged shaven life-insurance agent, who wore spats, collars of immaculate starchiness˙ five inches in height, who spoke with an unctuous and insane croon, chortling gently in his throat from time to time for no reason at all. His name was Mr. McKissem, and she had screwed up enough courage, after an arduous siege, to refuse him, upon the private grounds of insanity.

She had promised herself to a young South Carolinian, who was connected rather vaguely with the grocery trade. His hair was parted in the middle of his low forehead, his voice was soft, drawling, amiable, his manner hearty and insistent, his habits large and generous. He brought Gant cigars on his visits, the boys large boxes of assorted candies. Every one felt that he had favorable prospects.

As for the others—Ben and Luke only—they were left floating in limbo; for Steve, since his eighteenth year, had spent most of his life away from home, existing for months by semi-vagabondage, scrappy employment, and small forgeries upon his father, in New Orleans, Jacksonville, Memphis, and reappearing to his depressed family after long intervals by telegraphing that he was desperately sick or, through the intermediacy of a crony who borrowed the title of "doctor" for the occasion, that he was dying, and would come home in a box if he was not sent for in the emaciated flesh.

Thus, before he was eight, Eugene gained another roof and lost forever the tumultuous, unhappy, warm centre of his home. He had from day to day no clear idea where the day's food, shelter, lodging was to come from, although he was reasonably sure it would be given: he ate wherever he happened to hang his hat, either at Gant's or at his mother's; occasionally, although infrequently, he slept with Luke in the sloping, alcoved, gabled back room, rude with calcimine, with the high drafty steps that slanted to the kitchen porch, with the odor of old stacked books in packing-cases, with the sweet orchard scents. There were two beds; he exulted in his unaccustomed occupancy of an entire mattress, dreaming of the day of manlike privacy. But Eliza did not allow this often: he was riven into her flesh.

Forgetful of him during the day's press, she summoned him at night over the telephone, demanding his return, and upbraiding Helen for keeping him. There was a bitter submerged struggle over him between Eliza and her daughter: absorbed in the management of Dixieland for days, she would suddenly remember his absence from meals, and call for him angrily across the phone.

"Good heavens, mama," Helen would answer irritably. "He's your child, not mine. I'm not going to see him starve."

"What do you mean? What do you mean? He ran off while dinner was on the table. I've got a good meal fixed for him here. H-m! A *good* meal."

Helen put her hand over the mouthpiece, making a face at him as he stood catlike and sniggering by, burlesquing the Pentland manner, tone, mouthing.

"H-m! Why, law me, child, yes—it's *good* soup."

He was convulsed silently.

And then aloud: "Well, it's your own lookout, not mine. If he doesn't want to stay up there, I can't help it."

When he returned to Dixieland, Eliza would question him with bitter working lips; she would prick at his hot pride in an effort to keep him by her.

"What do you mean by running off to your papa's like that? If I were you, I'd have too much pride for that. I'd be a-sha-a-med!" Her face worked with a bitter hurt smile. "Helen can't be bothered with you. She doesn't want you around."

But the powerful charm of Gant's house, of its tacked and added whimsy, its male smell, its girdling rich vines, its great gummed trees, its roaring internal seclusiveness, the blistered varnish, the hot calfskin, the comfort and abundance, seduced him easily away from the great chill tomb of Dixieland, particularly in winter, since Eliza was most sparing of coal.

Gant had already named it "The Barn"; in the morning now, after his heavy breakfast at home, he would swing gauntly toward town by way of Spring Street, composing en route the invective that he had formerly reserved to his sitting-room. He would stride through the wide chill hall of Dixieland, bursting in upon Eliza, and two or three negresses, busy preparing the morning meal for the hungry boarders who rocked energetically upon the porch. All of the objections, all of the abuse that had not been uttered when she bought the place, were vented now.

"Woman, you have deserted my bed and board, you have made a laughing stock of me before the world, and left your children to perish. Fiend that you are, there is nothing that you would not do to torture, humiliate and degrade me. You have deserted me in my old age; you have left me to die alone. Ah, Lord! It was a bitter day for us all when your gloating eyes first fell upon this damnable, this awful, this murderous and bloody Barn. There is no ignominy to which you will not stoop if you think it will put a nickel in your pocket. You have fallen so low not even your own brothers will come near you. 'Nor beast, nor man hath fallen so far.'"

And in the pantries, above the stove, into the dining-room, the rich voices of the negresses chuckled with laughter.

"Dat man sho' can tawk!"

Eliza got along badly with the negroes. She had all the dislike and distrust for them of the mountain people. Moreover, she had never been used to service, and she did not know how to accept or govern it graciously. She nagged and berated the sullen negro girls constantly, tortured by the thought that they were stealing her supplies and her furnishings, and dawdling away the time for which she paid them. And she paid them reluctantly, dribbling out their small wages a coin or two at a time, nagging them for their laziness and stupidity.

"What have you been doing all this time? Did you get those back rooms done upstairs?"

"No'm," said the negress sullenly, slatting flatfootedly down the kitchen.

"I'll vow," Eliza fretted. "I never saw such a good-for-nothing shiftless darkey in my life. You needn't think I'm going to pay you for wasting your time."

This would go on throughout the day. As a result, Eliza would often begin the day without a servant: the girls departed at night muttering sullenly, and did not appear the next morning. Moreover, her reputation for bickering pettiness spread through the length and breadth of Niggertown. It became increasingly difficult for her to find any one at all who would work for her. Completely flustered when she awoke to find herself without help, she would immediately call Helen over the telephone, pouring her fretful story into the girl's ears and entreating assistance:

"I'll declare, child, I don't know what I'm going to do. I could wring that worthless nigger's neck. Here I am left all alone with a house full of people."

"Mama, in heaven's name, what's the matter? Can't you keep a nigger in the house? Other people do. What do you do to them, anyway?"

But, fuming and irritable, she would leave Gant's and go to her mother's, serving the tables with large heartiness, nervous and animated good-humor. All the boarders were very fond of her: they said she was a fine girl. Every one did. There was a spacious and unsparing generosity about her, a dominant consuming vitality, which ate at her poor health, her slender supply of strength, so that her shattered nerves drew her frequently toward hysteria, and sometimes toward physical collapse. She was almost six feet tall: she had large hands and feet, thin straight legs, a big-boned generous face, with the long full chin slightly adroop, revealing her big gold-traced upper teeth. But, in spite of this gauntness, she did not look hard-featured or raw-boned. Her face was full of heartiness and devotion, sensitive, whole-souled, hurt, bitter, hysterical, but at times transparently radiant and handsome.

It was a spiritual and physical necessity for her to exhaust herself in service for others, and it was necessary for her to receive heavy slatherings of praise for that service, and especially necessary that she feel her efforts had gone unappreciated. Even at the beginning, she would become almost frantic reciting her grievances, telling the story of her service to Eliza in a voice that became harsh and hysterical:

"Let the least little thing go wrong and she's at the phone. It's not my place to go up there and work like a nigger for a crowd of old cheap boarders. You know that, don't you? *Don't* you?"

"Yes'm," said Eugene, meekly serving as audience.

"But she'd die rather than admit it. Do you ever hear her say a word of thanks? Do I get," she said laughing suddenly, her hysteria crossed for the moment with her great humor, "do I get so much as 'go-to-hell' for it?"

"*No!*" squealed Eugene, going off in fits of idiot laughter.

"Why, law me, child. H-m! Yes. It's *good* soup," said she, touched with her great earthy burlesque.

He tore his collar open, and undid his trousers, sliding to the floor in an apoplexy of laughter.

"Sdop! Sdop! You're g-g-gilling me!"

"H-m! Why, law me! Yes," she continued, grinning at him as if she hoped to succeed.

Nevertheless, whether Eliza was servantless or not, she went daily at dinner, the mid-day meal, to help at table, and frequently at night when Gant and the boys ate with Eliza instead of at home. She went because of her deep desire to serve, because it satisfied her need for giving more than was returned, and because, in spite of her jibes, along with Gant, at the Barn, and the "cheap boarders," the animation of feeding, the clatter of plates, the braided clamor of their talk, stimulated and excited her.

Like Gant, like Luke, she needed extension in life, movement, excitement: she wanted to dominate, to entertain, to be the life of the party. On small solicitation, she sang for the boarders, thumping the cheap piano with her heavy accurate touch, and singing in her strong, vibrant, somewhat hard soprano a repertory of songs classical, sentimental, and comic. Eugene remembered the soft cool nights of summer, the assembled boarders and "I Wonder Who's Kissing Her Now," which Gant demanded over and over; "Love Me and the World Is Mine"; "Till the Sands of the Desert Grow Cold"; "Dear Old Girl, the Rob-*bin* Sings Above You"; "The End of a Perfect Day"; and "Alexander's Rag-Time Band," which Luke had practised in a tortured house for weeks, and sung with thunderous success in the High School Minstrels.

Later, in the cool dark, Gant, rocking violently, would hold forth on the porch, his great voice carrying across the quiet neighborhood, as he held the charmed boarders by his torrential eloquence, his solution of problems of state, his prejudiced but bold opinion upon current news.

"—And what did *we* do, gentlemen? We sank their navy in an action that lasted only twenty minutes, stormed at by shot and shell, Teddy and his Rough Riders took the hill at Santiago—it was all over, as you well know, in a few months. We had declared war with no thought of ulterior gain; we came because the indignation of a *great* people had been aroused at the oppression of a smaller one, and then, with a magnanimity well worthy the greatest people of the face of the earth, we paid our defeated enemy twenty millions of dollars. Ah, Lord! That was magnanimity indeed! You don't think any other nation would have done that, do you?"

"No, sir," said the boarders emphatically.

They didn't always agree with his political opinions—Roosevelt was the faultless descendant of Julius Cæsar, Napoleon Bonaparte, and Abraham Lincoln—but they felt he had a fine head and would have gone far in politics.

"That man should have been a lawyer," said the boarders.

And yet, there was surging into these chosen hills the strong thrust of the world, like a kissing tide, which swings lazily in with a slapping glut of waters, and recoils into its parent crescent strength, to be thrown farther inward once again.

It was an element of Eliza's primitive and focal reasoning that men and women withered by the desert would seek an oasis, that those who were thirsty would seek water, and that those panting on the plains would look into the hills for comfort and relief. She had that bull's-eye accuracy which has since been celebrated, when plum-picking's over, under the name of "vision."

The streets, ten years before raw clay, were being paved: Gant went into frenzies over the paving assessments, cursed the land, the day of his birth, the machinations of Satan's children. But Eugene followed the wheeled casks of boiling tar; watched the great roller, a monster that crushed him in night-mares, powder the layered rock; felt, as he saw the odorous pressed tongue of pavement lengthen out, a swelling ecstasy.

From time to time, a stilted Cadillac gasped cylindrically up the hill past Dixieland: Eugene said a spell, as it faltered, for its success—Jim Sawyer, a young blood, came for Miss Cutler, the Pittsburgh beauty: he opened a door behind in the fat red belly. They got in.

Sometimes, when Eliza awoke to find her servants gone, he was sent down into Niggertown to capture a new one: in that city of rickets he searched into their fetid shacks, past the slow stench of little rills of mire and sewage, in fetid cellars, through all the rank labyrinth of the hill-sprawled settlement. He came, in the hot sealed dungeons of their rooms, to know the wild grace of their bodies, thrown upon a bed, their rich laughter, their smell of the jungle tropics stewed in with frying cookery and a boiling wash.

"Do you want a job?"

"Whose little boy are you?"

"Mrs. Eliza Gant's."

Silence. Presently: "Dere's a gal up de street at Mis' Cawpening's who's lookin' fo' wuk. *You* go see *huh.*"

Eliza watched them with a falcon's eye for thefts. Once, with a detective, she searched a departed girl's room in Niggertown, finding there sheets, towels, spoons that had been stolen from her. The girl went to the penitentiary for two years. Eliza loved the commotion of law, the smell and tension of the courts. Whenever she could go to law she did so: she delighted in bringing suit against people, or in having suit brought against her. She always won.

When her boarders defaulted payments she seized their belongings triumphantly, delighting particularly in eleventh-hour captures at the railway station, with the aid of an obedient constabulary, and ringed by the attentive offal of the town.

Eugene was ashamed of Dixieland. And he was again afraid to express his shame. As with *The Post,* he felt thwarted, netted, trapped. He hated the indecency of his life, the loss of dignity and seclusion, the surrender to the tumultuous rabble of the four walls which shield us from them. He felt, rather than understood, the waste, the confusion, the blind cruelty of their lives—his spirit was stretched out on the rack of despair and bafflement as there came to him more and more the conviction that their lives could not be more hopelessly distorted, wrenched, mutilated, and perverted away from all simple comfort, repose, happiness, if they set themselves deliberately to tangle the skein, twist the pattern. He choked with fury: he thought of Eliza's slow speech, her endless reminiscence, her maddening lip-pursing, and turned white with constricted rage.

He saw plainly by this time that their poverty, the threat of the poor-house, the lurid references to the pauper's grave, belonged to the insensate mythology of hoarding; anger smouldered like a brand in him at their sorry greed. There was no place sacred unto themselves, no place fixed for their own inhabitation, no place proof against the invasion of the boarders.

As the house filled, they went from room to little room, going successively down the shabby scale of their lives. He felt it would hurt them, coarsen them: he had even then an intense faith in food, in housing, in comfort—he felt that a civilized man must begin with them; he knew that wherever the spirit had withered, it had not withered because of food and plumbing.

As the house filled, in the summer season, and it was necessary to wait until the boarders had eaten before a place could be found for him, he walked sullenly about beneath the propped back porch of Dixieland, savagely exploring the dark cellar, or the two dank windowless rooms which Eliza rented, when she could, to negresses.

He felt now the petty cruelty of village caste. On Sunday for several years, he had bathed, brushed, arrayed his anointed body in clean underwear and shirting and departed, amid all the pleasurable bustle of Sunday morning, for the Presbyterian Sunday School. He had by this time been delivered from the instruction of the several spinsters who had taught his infant faith the catechism, the goodness of God, and the elements of celestial architecture. The five-cent piece which formerly he had yielded up reluctantly, thinking of cakes and ale, he now surrendered more gladly, since he usually had enough left over for cold gaseous draughts at the soda-fountain.

In the fresh Sunday morning air he marched off with brisk excitement to do duty at the altars, pausing near the church where the marshalled ranks of the boys' military school split cleanly into regimented Baptists, Methodists, Presbyterians.

The children assembled in a big room adjacent to the church, honey-combed to right and left with small classrooms, which they entered after the preliminary service was finished. They were exhorted from the platform by the superintendent, a Scotch dentist with a black-gray beard, fringed by a small area of embalmed skin, whose cells, tissues, and chemical juices seemed to have been fixed in a state of ageless suspension, and who looked no older from one decade to another.

He read the text, or the parable of the day's study, commented on it with Cæsarean dryness and concision, and surrendered the service to his assistant, a shaven, spectacled, Wilsonian-looking man, also Scotch, who smiled with cold affection at them over his high shiny collar, and led them through the verses of a hymn, heaving up his arms and leering at them encouragingly, as they approached the chorus. A sturdy spinstress thumped heavily upon a piano which shook like a leaf.

Eugene liked the high crystal voices of the little children, backed by the substantial marrow of the older boys and girls, and based on the strong volume of the Junior and Senior Baraccas and Philatheas. They sang:

"Throw out the lifeline, throw out the lifeline,
Someone is sinking to-day-ee"—

on the mornings when the collection went for missionary work. And they sang:

"Shall we gather at the river,
The bew-tee-ful, the bew-tee-ful r-hiver."

He liked that one very much. And the noble surge of "Onward, Christian Soldiers."

Later, he went into one of the little rooms with his class. The sliding doors rumbled together all around; presently there was a quiet drone throughout the building.

He was now in a class composed entirely of boys. His teacher was a tall white-faced young man, bent and thin, who was known to all the other boys as secretary of the Y.M.C.A. He was tubercular; but the boys admired him because of his former skill as a baseball and basketball player. He spoke in a sad, sugary, whining voice; he was oppressively Christ-like; he spoke to them intimately about the lesson of the day, asking them what it might teach them in their daily lives, in acts of obedience and love to their parents and friends, in duty, courtesy, and Christian charity. And he told them that when they were in doubt about their conduct they should ask themselves what Jesus would say: he spoke of Jesus often in his melancholy, somewhat discontented voice— Eugene became vaguely miserable as he talked, thinking of something soft, furry, with a wet tongue.

He was nervous and constrained: the other boys knew one another intimately—they lived on, or in the neighborhood of, Montgomery Avenue, which was the most fashionable street in town. Sometimes, one of them said to him, grinning: "Do you want to buy *The Saturday Evening Post,* Mister?"

Eugene, during the week, never touched the lives of any of them, even in a remote way. His idea of their eminence was grossly exaggerated; the town had grown rapidly from a straggling village—it had few families as old as the Pentlands, and, like all resort towns, its caste system was liquidly variable, depending chiefly upon wealth, ambition, and boldness.

Harry Tarkinton and Max Isaacs were Baptists, as were most of the people, the Scotch excepted, in Gant's neighborhood. In the social scale the Baptists were the most populous and were considered the most common: their minister was a large plump man with a red face and a white vest, who reached great oratorical effects, roaring at them like a lion, cooing at them like a dove, introducing his wife into the sermon frequently for purposes of intimacy and laughing, in a programme which the Episcopalians, who held the highest social eminence, and the Presbyterians, less fashionable, but solidly decent, felt was hardly chaste. The Methodists occupied the middle ground between vulgarity and decorum.

This starched and well brushed world of Sunday morning Presbyterianism, with its sober decency, its sense of restraint, its suggestion of quiet wealth, solid position, ordered ritual, seclusive establishment, moved him deeply with its tranquillity. He felt concretely his isolation from it, he entered it from the jangled disorder of his own life once a week, looking at it, and departing from it, for years, with the sad heart of a stranger. And from the mellow gloom of the church, the rich distant organ, the quiet nasal voice of the Scotch minister, the interminable prayers, and the rich little pictures of Christian mythology which he had collected as a child under the instruction of the spinsters, he gathered something of the pain, the mystery, the sensuous beauty of religion, something deeper and greater than this austere decency.

12

It was the winter, and the sullen dying autumn that he hated most at Dixieland—the dim fly-specked lights, the wretched progress about the house in search of warmth, Eliza untidily wrapped in an old sweater, a dirty muffler, a cast-off man's coat. She glycerined her cold-cracked hands. The chill walls festered with damp: they drank in death from the atmosphere: a woman died of typhoid, her husband came quickly out into the hall and dropped his hands. They were Ohio people.

Upstairs, upon a sleeping porch, a thin-faced Jew coughed through the interminable dark.

"In heaven's name, mama," Helen fumed, "why do you take them in? Can't you see he's got the bugs?"

"Why, no-o," said Eliza, pursing her lips. "He said he only had a little bronchial trouble. I asked him about it, and he laughed just as big as you please: 'Why, Mrs. Gant,' he said—" and there would follow an endless anecdote, embellished with many a winding rivulet. The girl raged: it was one of Eliza's basic traits to defend blindly whatever brought her money.

The Jew was a kind man. He coughed gently behind his white hand and ate bread fried in battered egg and butter. Eugene developed a keen appetite for it: innocently he called it "Jew Bread" and asked for more. Lichenfels laughed gently, coughed—his wife was full of swart rich laughter. The boy did small services for him: he gave him a coin from week to week. He was a clothier from a New Jersey town. In the Spring he went to a sanitarium; he died there later.

In the winter a few chill boarders, those faces, those personalities which become mediocre through repetition, sat for hours before the coals of the parlor hearth, rocking interminably, dull of voice and gesture, as hideously bored with themselves and Dixieland, no doubt, as he with them.

He liked the summers better. There came slow-bodied women from the hot rich South, dark-haired white-bodied girls from New Orleans, corn-haired blondes from Georgia, nigger-drawling desire from South Carolina. And there was malarial lassitude, tinged faintly with yellow, from Missis-sippi but with white biting teeth. A red-faced South Carolinian, with nicotined fingers, took him daily to the baseball games; a lank yellow planter, malarial from Mississippi, climbed hill, and wandered through the fragrant mountain valleys with him; of nights he heard the rich laughter of the women, tender and cruel, upon the dark porches, heard the florid throat-tones of the men; saw the yielding stealthy harlotry of the South— the dark seclusion of their midnight bodies, their morning innocence. Desire, with bloody beak, tore at his heart like jealous virtue: he was moral for that which was denied him.

Of mornings he stayed at Gant's with Helen playing ball with Buster Isaacs, a cousin of Max, a plump jolly little boy who lived next door; summoned later by the rich incense of Helen's boiling fudge. She sent him to the little Jewish grocery down the street for the sour relishes she liked so well: tabled in mid-morning they ate sour pickles, heavy slabs of ripe tomatoes, coated with thick mayonnaise, amber percolated coffee, fig-newtons and ladyfingers, hot pungent fudge pebbled with walnuts and coated fragrantly with butter, sandwiches of tender bacon and cucumber, iced belchy soft-drinks.

His trust in her Gantian wealth was boundless: this rich store of delight came from inexhaustible resources. Warm lively hens cackled cheerfully throughout the morning neighborhood; powerful negroes brought dripping ice in iron talons from their smoking wagons; he stood beneath their droning saws and caught the flying ice-pulp in his hands; he drank in the combined odor of their great bodies together with the rich compost of the refrigeration, and the sharp oiliness of the dining-room linoleum; and in the horsehair walnut parlor at mid-day, good with the mellow piano-smell and the smell of stale varnished wood, she played for him, and made him sing: "William Tell," "My Heart at Thy Sweet Voice," "The Song Without Words," "*Celeste Aïda*," "The Lost Chord," her long throat lean and tendoned as her vibrant voice rang out.

She took insatiable delight in him, stuffing him with sour and sugared relishes, tumbling him, in a random moment of her restless activity, upon Gant's lounge, and pinioning him while she slapped his squirming face sharply with her big hand.

Sometimes, frantic with some swift tangle of her nerves, she would attack him viciously, hating him for his dark brooding face, his full scalloped underlip, his deep absorption in a dream. Like Luke, and like Gant, she sought in the world ceaseless entertainment for her restless biting vitality: it infuriated her to see other people seek absorption within themselves—she hated him at times when, her own wires strumming, she saw his dark face brooding over a book or on some vision. She would tear the book from his hands, slap him, and stab him with her cruel savage tongue. She would pout out her lip, goggle her face about stupidly on a drooping neck, assume an expression of dopey idiocy, and pour out on him the horrible torrent of her venom.

"You little freak—wandering around with your queer dopey face. You're a regular little Pentland—you funny little freak, you. Everybody's laughing at you. Don't you know that? Don't you? We're going to dress you up as a girl, and let you go around like that. You haven't got a drop of Gant blood in you—papa's practically said as much—you're Greeley all over again; you're queer. Pentland queerness sticking out all over you."

Sometimes her sweltering and inchoate fury was so great that she threw him on the floor and stamped on him.

He did not mind the physical assault so much as he did the poisonous hatred of her tongue, insanely clever in fashioning the most wounding barbs. He went frantic with horror, jerked unexpectedly from Elfland into Hell, he bellowed madly, saw his bountiful angel change in a moment to a snake-haired fury, lost all his sublime faith in love and goodness. He rushed at the wall like an insane little goat, battered his head screaming again and again, wished desperately that his constricted and overloaded heart would burst, that something in him would break, that somehow, bloodily, he might escape the stifling prisonhouse of his life.

This satisfied her desire; it was what deeply she had wanted—she had found purging release in her savage attack upon him, and now she could drain herself cleanly in a wild smother of affection. She would seize him, struggling and screaming, in her long arms, plaster kisses all over his red mad face, soothing him with hearty flattery addressed in the third person:

"Why, he didn't think I meant it, did he? Didn't he know I was only joking? Why, he's strong as a little bull, isn't he? He's a regular little giant, that's what he is. Why, he's perfectly wild, isn't he? His eyes popping out of his head. I thought he was going to knock a hole in the wall.—Yes, ma'am. Why, law me, yes, child. It's *good* soup," resorting to her broad mimicry in order to make him laugh. And he would laugh against his will between his sobs, in a greater torture because of this agony of affection and reconciliation than because of the abuse.

Presently, when he had grown quiet, she would send him off to the store for pickles, cakes, cold bottled drinks; he would depart with red eyes, his cheeks furrowed dirtily by his tears, wondering desperately as he went down the street why the thing had happened, and drawing his foot sharply off the ground and craning his neck convulsively as shame burnt in him.

There was in Helen a restless hatred of dullness, respectability. Yet she was at heart a severely conventional person, in spite of her occasional vulgarity, which was merely a manifestation of her restless energy, a very naïve, a childishly innocent person about even the simple wickedness of the village. She had several devoted young men on her list—plain, harddrinking country types: one, a native, lean, red-faced, alcoholic, a city surveyor, who adored her; another, a strapping florid blond from the Tennessee coal fields; another, a young South Carolinian, townsman of her older sister's fiancé.

These young men—Hugh Parker, Jim Phelps, and Joe Cathcart, were innocently devoted; they liked her tireless and dominant energy, the eager monopoly of her tongue, her big sincerity and deep kindliness. She played and sang for them—threw all her energy into entertaining them. They brought her boxes of candy, little presents, were divided jealously among themselves, but united in their affirmation that she was "a fine girl."

And she would get Jim Phelps and Hugh Parker to bring her a drink of whisky as well: she had begun to depend on small potations of alcohol for the stimulus it gave her fevered body—a small drink was enough to operate electrically in her blood: it renewed her, energized her, gave her a temporary and hectic vitality. Thus, although she never drank much at a time and showed, beyond the renewed vitality and gaiety, no sign of intoxication, she nibbled at the bottle.

"I'll take a drink whenever I can get it," she said.

She liked, almost invariably, young fast women. She liked the hectic pleasure of their lives, the sense of danger, their humor and liberality. She was drawn magnetically to all the wedded harlotry, which, escaping the Sunday discipline of a Southern village, and the Saturday lust of sodden husbands, came gaily to Altamont in summer. She liked people who, as she said, "didn't mind taking a little drink now and then."

She liked Mary Thomas, a tall jolly young prostitute who came from Kentucky: she was a manicurist in an Altamont Hotel.

"There are two things I want to see," said Mary, "a rooster's you-know-what and a hen's what-is-it." She was full of loud compelling laughter. She had a small room with a sleeping porch, at the front of the house upstairs. Eugene brought her some cigarettes once: she stood before the window in a thin petticoat, her feet wide apart, her long sensual legs outlined against the light.

Helen wore her dresses, hats, and silk stockings. Sometimes they drank together. And, with humorous sentimentality, she defended her.

"Well, she's no hypocrite. That's one thing sure. She doesn't care who knows it." Or,

"She's no worse than a lot of your little goody-goodies, if the truth's known. She's only more open about it."

Or again, irritated at some implied criticism of her own friendliness with the girl, she would say angrily:

"What do you know about her? You'd better be careful how you talk about people. You'll get into trouble about it some day."

Nevertheless, she was scrupulous in her public avoidance of the girl and, illogically, in a moment of unreasoning annoyance she would attack Eliza:

"Why do you keep such people in your house, mama? Every one in town knows about her. Your place is getting the reputation of a regular chippyhouse all over town."

Eliza pursed her lips angrily:

"I don't pay any attention to them," she said. "I consider myself as good as any one. I hold my head up, and I expect every one else to do like-wise. You don't catch me associating with them."

It was part of her protective mechanism. She pretended to be proudly oblivious to any disagreeable circumstance which brought her in money. As a result, by that curious impalpable advertisement which exists among easy women, Dixieland became known to them—they floated casually in— the semi-public, clandestine prostitutes of a tourist town.

Helen had drifted apart from most of her friends of high school days—

the hard-working plain-faced Genevieve Pratt, daughter of a schoolmaster, "Teeney" Duncan, Gertrude Brown. Her companions now were livelier, if somewhat more vulgar, young women—Grace Deshaye, a plumber's daughter, an opulent blonde; Pearl Hines, daughter of a Baptist saddle-maker: she was heavy of body and face, but she had a powerful rag-time singing voice.

Her closest companion, however, was a girl whose name was Nan Gudger: she was a brisk, slender, vital girl, with a waist so tightly corsetted that a man's hands might go around it. She was the trusted, accurate, infallible bookkeeper of a grocery store. She contributed largely to the support of her family—a mother whom Eugene looked upon with sick flesh, because of the heavy goitre that sagged from her loose neck; a crippled sister who moved about the house by means of crutches and the propulsive strength of her powerful shoulders; and two brothers, hulking young thugs of twenty and eighteen years, who always bore upon their charmed bodies fresh knife-wounds, blue lumps and swellings, and other marks of their fights in poolroom and brothel. They lived in a two-story shack of rickety lumber on Clingman Street: the women worked uncomplainingly in the support of the young men. Eugene went here with Helen often: she liked the vulgarity, the humor, the excitement of their lives—and it amused her particularly to listen to Mary's obscene earthy conversation.

Upon the first of every month, Nan and Mary gave to the boys a portion of their earnings, for pocket money and for their monthly visit to the women of Eagle Crescent.

"Oh, *surely* not, Mary? Good heavens!" said Helen with eager unbelief.

"Why, hell yes, honey," said Mary, grinning her coarse drawl, taking her snuff-stick out of the brown corner of her mouth, and holding it in her strong hand. "We always give the boys money fer a woman once a month."

"Oh, *no!* You're joking," Helen said, laughing.

"Good God, child, don't you know *that?*" said Mary, spitting inaccurately at the fire, "Hit's good fer their health. They'd git sick if we didn't."

Eugene began to slide helplessly toward the floor. He got an instant panorama of the whole astonishing picture of humor and solemn superstition—the women contributing their money, in the interests of sanitation and health, to the debauches of the two grinning hairy nicotined young louts.

"What're you laughin' at, son?" said Mary, gooching him roughly in the ribs, as he lay panting and prostrate. "You ain't hardly out of didies yet."

She had all the savage passion of a mountaineer: crippled, she lived in the coarse heat of her brothers' lust. They were crude, kindly, ignorant, and murderous people. Nan was scrupulously respectable and well-mannered: she had thick negroid lips that turned outward, and hearty tropical laughter. She replaced the disreputable furniture of the house by new shiny Grand Rapids chairs and tables. There was a varnished book-case, forever locked, stored with stiff sets of unread books—*The Harvard Classics,* and a cheap encyclopædia.

When Mrs. Selborne first came to Dixieland from the hot South she was only twenty-three but she looked older. Ripeness with her was all: she was a tall heavy-bodied blonde, well kept and elegant. She moved leisurely with a luxurious sensual swing of the body: her smile was tender and full of vague allurement, her voice gentle, her sudden laughter, bubbling out of midnight secrecy, rich and full. She was one of several handsome and bacchic daughters of a depleted South Carolinian of good family; she had married at sixteen a red heavy man who came and went from her incomparable table, eating rapidly and heartily, muttering, when pressed, a few shy-sullen words, and departing to the closed leather-and-horse smell of his little office in the livery-stable he owned. She had two children by him, both girls: she moved with wasted stealth around all the quiet slander of a South Carolina mill-town, committing adultery carefully with a mill owner, a banker, and a lumber man, walking circumspectly with her tender blonde smile by day past all the sly smiles of town and trade, knowing that the earth was mined below her feet, and that her name, with clerk and merchant, was a sign for secret laughter. The natives, the men in particular, treated her with even more elaborate respect than a woman is usually given in a Southern town, but their eyes, behind the courteous unctions of their masks, were shiny with invitation.

Eugene felt when he first saw her, and knew about her, that she would never be caught and always known. His love for her was desperate. She was the living symbol of his desire—the dim vast figure of love and maternity, ageless and autumnal, waiting, corn-haired, deep-breasted, blonde of limb, in the ripe fields of harvest—Demeter, Helen, the ripe exhaustless and renewing energy, the cradling nurse of weariness and disenchantment. Below the thrust of Spring, the sharp knife, the voices of the young girls in the darkness, the sharp inchoate expectancies of youth, his deep desire burned inextinguishably: something turned him always to the older women.

When Mrs. Selborne first came to Dixieland her oldest child was seven years old, her youngest five. She received a small check from her husband every week, and a substantial one from the lumber man. She brought a negro girl with her: she was lavish in her dispensations to the negress, and to her children: this wastefulness, ease of living, and her rich seductive laughter fascinated Helen, drew her to the older woman.

And, at night, as Eugene listened to the low sweet voice of the woman, heard the rich sensual burst of her laughter, as she sat in the dark porch with a commercial traveller or some merchant in the town, his blood grew bitter with the morality of jealousy: he withered with his hurt, thought of her little sleeping children, and, with a passionate sense of fraternity, of her gulled husband. He dreamed of himself as the redemptive hero, saving her in an hour of great danger, making her penitent with grave reproof, accepting purely the love she offered.

In the morning, he breathed the seminal odor of her fresh bathed body as she passed him, gazed desperately into the tender sensuality of her face and, with a sense of unreality, wondered what change darkness wrought in this untelling face.

Steve returned from New Orleans after a year of vagabondage. The old preposterous swagger, following the ancient whine, reappeared as soon as he felt himself safely established at home again.

"Stevie doesn't have to work," said he. "He's smart enough to make the others work for him." This was his defiance to his record of petty forgeries against Gant: he saw himself as a clever swindler although he had never had courage to swindle any one except his father. People were reading the Get-Rich-Quick Wallingford stories: there was an immense admiration for this romantic criminal.

Steve was now a young man in the first twenties. He was somewhat above the middle height, bumpy of face and sallow of skin, with a light pleasing tenor voice. Eugene had a feeling of disgust and horror whenever his oldest brother returned: he knew that those who were physically least able to defend themselves, which included Eliza and himself, would bear the brunt of his whining, petty bullying, and drunken obscenity. He did not mind the physical abuse so much as he did its cowardly stealth, weakness, and slobbering reconciliations.

Once, Gant, making one of his sporadic efforts to get his son fixed in employment, had sent him out to a country graveyard to put up a small monument. Eugene was sent along. Steve worked steadily in the hot sun for an hour, growing more and more irritable because of the heat, the rank weedy stench of the graveyard, and his own deep antipathy to work. Eugene waited intensely for the attack he knew was coming.

"What are you standing there for?" screamed Big Brother at length, looking up in an agony of petulance. He struck sharply at the boy's shin with a heavy wrench he held in his hand, knocking him to the ground, and crippling him for the moment. Immediately, he was palsied, not with remorse, but with fear that he had injured him badly and would be discovered.

"You're not hurt, are you, buddy? You're not hurt?" he began in a quivering voice, putting his unclean yellow hands upon Eugene. And he made the effort at reconciliation Eugene so dreaded, whimpering, blowing his foul breath upon his brother's cringing flesh, and entreating him to say nothing of the occurrence when he went home. Eugene became violently nauseated: the stale odor of Steve's body, the clammy and unhealthy sweat that stank with nicotine, the touch of his tainted flesh filled him with horror.

There still remained, however, in the cast and carriage of his head, in his swagger walk, the ghost of his ruined boyishness: women were sometimes attracted to him. It was his fortune, therefore, to secure Mrs. Selborne for his mistress the first summer she came to Dixieland. At night her rich laughter welled up from the dark porch, they walked through the quiet leafy streets, they went to Riverside together, walking beyond the lights of the carnival into the dark sandy paths by the river.

But, as her friendship with Helen ripened, as she saw the revulsion of the Gants against their brother, and as she began to see what damage she had already done to herself by her union with this braggart who had brandished her name through every poolroom in town as a tribute to his own power, she cast him off, quietly, implacably, tenderly. When she returned now, summer by summer, she met with her innocent and unwitting smile all of his obscene innuendoes, his heavily suggestive threats, his bitter revelations behind her back. Her affection for Helen was genuine, but it was also, she felt, strategic and useful. The girl introduced her to handsome young men, gave parties and dances at Gant's and Eliza's for her, was really a partner in her intrigues, assuring her of privacy, silence, and darkness, and defending her angrily when the evil whispering began.

"What do you know about her? You don't know what she does. You'd better be careful how you talk about her. She's got a husband to defend her, you know. You'll get your head shot off some day." Or, more doubtfully:

"Well, I don't care what they say, I like her. She's mighty sweet. After all, what can we say about her for sure? No one can *prove* anything on her."

And in the winters now she made short visits to the South Carolina town where Mrs. Selborne lived, returning with an enthusiastic description of her reception, the parties "in her honor," the food, the lavish entertainment. Mrs. Selborne lived in the same town as Joe Gambell, the young clerk to whom Daisy was engaged. He was full of sly hints about the woman, but before her his manner was obsequious, confused, reverential, and he accepted without complaint the presents of food and clothing which she sent him after their marriage.

Daisy had been married in the month of June following Eliza's purchase of Dixieland: the wedding was arranged on a lavish scale, and took place in the big dining-room of the house. Gant and his two older sons grinned sheepishly in unaccustomed evening dress, the Pentlands, faithful in their attendance at weddings and funerals, sent gifts and came. Will and Pett gave a heavy set of carving steels.

"I hope you always have something to use them on," said Will, flensing his hand, and winking at Joe Gambell.

Eugene remembered weeks of frantic preparation, dress fittings, rehearsals, the hysteria of Daisy, who stared at her nails until they went blue, and the final splendor of the last two days—the arriving gifts, the house, unnaturally cheerful with rich carpets and flowers, the perilous moment when their lives joined, the big packed dining-room, the droning interminable Scotch voice of the Presbyterian minister, the mounting triumph of the music when the grocery clerk got his bride. Later, the confusion, the greetings, the hysteria of the women. Daisy sobbing uncontrollably in the arms of a distant cousin, Beth Pentland, who had come up with her hearty red husband, the owner of a chain of small groceries in a South Carolina town, bringing gifts and a giant watermelon, and whose own grief was enhanced by the discovery, after the wedding, that the dress she had worked on weeks in advance she had put on, in her frenzy, wrong side out.

Thus Daisy passed more or less definitely out of Eugene's life, although he was to see her briefly on visits, but with decreasing frequency, in the years that followed. The grocery clerk was making the one daring gesture of his life: he was breaking away from the cotton town, in which all the years of his life had been passed, and from the long lazy hours of grocery clerks, the languorous gossip of lank cotton farmers and townsmen, to which he had been used. He had found employment as a commercial traveller for a food products company: his headquarters was to be in Augusta, Georgia, but he was to travel into the far South.

This rooting up of his life, this adventure into new lands, the effort to improve his fortune and his state, was his wedding gift to his wife—a bold one, but imperilled already by distrust, fear, and his peasant suspicion of new scenes, new faces, new departures, of any life that differed from that of his village.

"There's no place like Henderson," said he, with complacent and annoying fidelity, referring to that haven of enervation, red clay, ignorance, slander, and superstition, in whose effluent rays he had been reared.

But he went to Augusta, and began his new life with Daisy in a lodging house. She was twenty-one, a slender, blushing girl who played the piano beautifully, accurately, academically, with a rippling touch, and no imagination. Eugene could never remember her very well.

In the early autumn after her marriage, Gant made the journey to Augusta, taking Eugene with him. The inner excitement of both was intense; the hot wait at the sleepy junction of Spartanburg, the ride in the dilapidated day coaches of the branch line that ran to Augusta, the hot baked autumnal land, rolling piedmont and pine woods, every detail of the landscape they drank in with thirsty adventurous eyes. Gant's roving spirit was parched for lack of travel: for Eugene, Saint Louis was a faint unreality, but there burned in him a vision of the opulent South, stranger even than his passionate winter nostalgia for the snow-bound North, which the drifted but short-lived snows in Altamont, the seizure of the unaccustomed moment for sledding and skating on the steep hills awakened in him with a Northern desire, a desire for the dark, the storm, the winds that roar across the earth and the triumphant comfort of warm walls which only a Southerner perhaps can know.

And he saw the town of Augusta first not in the drab hues of reality, but as one who bursts a window into the faery pageant of the world, as one who has lived in prison, and finds life and the earth in rosy dawn, as one who has lived in all the fabulous imagery of books, and finds in a journey only an extension and verification of it—so did he see Augusta, with the fresh washed eyes of a child, with glory, with enchantment.

They were gone two weeks. He remembered chiefly the brown stains of the recent flood, which had flowed through the town and inundated its lower floors, the broad main street, the odorous and gleaming drugstore, scented to him with all the spices of his fancy, the hills and fields

of Aiken, in South Carolina, where he sought vainly for John D. Rockefeller, a legendary prince who, he heard, went there for sport, marvelling
that two States could join imperceptibly, without visible markings, and
the cotton gin where he saw the great press mash the huge raw bales cleanly
into tight bundles half their former size.

Once, some children on the street had taunted him because of his long
hair, and he had fallen into a cursing fury; once, in a rage at some quarrel
with his sister, he set off on a world adventure, walking furiously for
hours down a country road by the river and cotton fields, captured finally
by Gant who sought for him in a hired rig.

They went to the theatre: it was one of the first plays he had seen.
The play was a biblical one, founded on the story of Saul and Jonathan,
and he whispered to Gant from scene to scene the trend of coming events
—a precocity which pleased his father mightily, and to which he referred
for months.

Just before they came home, Joe Gambell, in a fit of concocted petulance,
resigned his position, and announced that he was returning to Henderson.
His adventure had lasted three months.

13

In the years that followed, up to his eleventh or twelfth year when he
could no longer travel on half fares, Eugene voyaged year by year into
the rich mysterious South. Eliza, who, during her first winter at Dixieland,
had been stricken by severe attacks of rheumatism, induced partly by
kidney trouble, which caused her flesh to swell puffily, and which was
diagnosed by the doctor as Bright's Disease, began to make extensive,
although economical, voyages into Florida and Arkansas in search of
health and, rather vaguely, in search of wealth.

She always spoke hopefully of the possibility of opening a boarding-
house at some tropical winter resort, during the seasons there and in
Altamont. In winter now, she rented Dixieland for a few months, sometimes for a year, although she really had no intention of allowing the

place to slip through her fingers during the profitable summer season: usually, she let the place go, more or less deliberately, to some unscrupulous adventuress of lodging houses, good for a month's or two months' rent, but incapable of the sustained effort that would support it for a longer time. On her return from her journey, with rents in arrears, or with some other violation of the contract as an entering wedge, Eliza would surge triumphantly into battle, making a forced entrance with police, plain-clothes men, warrants, summonses, writs, injunctions, and all the other artillery of legal warfare, possessing herself forcibly, and with vindictive pleasure, of her property.

But she turned always into the South—the North for her was a land which she threatened often to explore, but which secretly she held in suspicion: there was in her no deep animosity because of an old war, her feeling was rather one of fear, distrust, alienation—the "Yankee" to whom she humorously referred was foreign and remote. So, she turned always into the South, the South that burned like Dark Helen in Eugene's blood, and she always took him with her. They still slept together.

His feeling for the South was not so much historic as it was of the core and desire of dark romanticism—that unlimited and inexplicable drunkenness, the magnetism of some men's blood that takes them into the heart of the heat, and beyond that, into the polar and emerald cold of the South as swiftly as it took the heart of that incomparable romanticist who wrote *The Rime of the Ancient Mariner,* beyond which there is nothing. And this desire of his was unquestionably enhanced by all he had read and visioned, by the romantic halo that his school history cast over the section, by the whole fantastic distortion of that period where people were said to live in "mansions," and slavery was a benevolent institution, conducted to a constant banjo-strumming, the strewn largesses of the colonel and the shuffle-dance of his happy dependents, where all women were pure, gentle, and beautiful, all men chivalrous and brave, and the Rebel horde a company of swagger, death-mocking cavaliers. Years later, when he could no longer think of the barren spiritual wilderness, the hostile and murderous intrenchment against all new life—when their cheap mythology, their legend of the charm of their manner, the aristocratic culture of their lives, the quaint sweetness of their drawl, made him writhe—when he could think of no return to their life and its swarming superstition without weariness and horror, so great was his fear of the legend, his fear of their antagonism, that he still pretended the most fanatic devotion to them, excusing his Northern residence on grounds of necessity rather than desire.

Finally, it occurred to him that these people had given him nothing, that neither their love not their hatred could injure him, that he owed them nothing, and he determined that he would say so, and repay their insolence with a curse. And he did.

So did his boundaries stretch into enchantment—into fabulous and solitary wonder broken only by Eliza's stingy practicality, by her lack of magnificence in a magnificent world, by the meals of sweet rolls and milk and butter in an untidy room, by the shoe boxes of luncheon carried on the trains and opened in the diner, after a lengthy inspection of the menu had led to the ordering of coffee, by the interminable quarrels over price and charges in almost every place they went, by her commands to him to "scrooch up" when the conductor came through for the tickets, for he was a tall lank boy, and his half-fare age might be called to question.

She took him to Florida in the late winter following Gant's return from Augusta: they went to Tampa first, and, a few days later, to Saint Petersburg. He plowed through the loose deep sand of the streets, fished interminably with jolly old men at the end of the long pier, devoured a chest full of dime novels that he found in the rooms she had rented in a private house. They left abruptly, after a terrific quarrel with the old Cracker who ran the place, who thought himself tricked out of the best part of a season's rent, and hurried off to South Carolina on receipt of a hysterical message from Daisy which bade her mother to "come at once." They arrived in the dingy little town, which was sticky with wet clay, and clammy with rain, in late March: Daisy's first child, a boy, had been born the day before. Eliza, annoyed at what she considered the useless disruption of her holiday, quarrelled bitterly with her daughter a day or two after her arrival, and departed for Altamont with the declaration, which Daisy ironically applauded, that she would never return again. But she did.

The following winter she went to New Orleans at the season of the Mardi Gras, taking her youngest with her. Eugene remembered the huge cisterns for rain-water, in the back yard of Aunt Mary's house, the heavy window-rattling thunder of Mary's snores at night, and the vast pageantry of carnival on Canal Street: the storied floats, the smiling beauties, the marching troops, the masks grotesque and fantastical. And once more he saw ships at anchor at the foot of Canal Street; and their tall keels looked over on the street behind the sea walls; and in the cemeteries all the graves were raised above the ground "because," said Oll, Gant's nephew, "the water rots 'em."

And he remembered the smells of the French market, the heavy fragrance of the coffee he drank there, and the foreign Sunday gaiety of the city's life—the theatres open, the sound of hammer and saw, the gay festivity of crowds. He visited the Boyles, old guests at Dixieland, who lived in the old French quarter, sleeping at night with Frank Boyle in a vast dark room lighted dimly with tapers: they had as cook an ancient negress who spoke only French, and who returned from the Market early in the morning bearing a huge basket loaded with vegetables, tropical fruits, fowls, meats. She cooked strange delicious food that he had never tasted before—heavy gumbo, garnished steaks, sauced fowls.

And he looked upon the huge yellow snake of the river, dreaming of its distant shores, the myriad estuaries lush with tropical growth that fed it, all the romantic life of plantation and canefields that fringed it, of moonlight, of dancing darkies on the levee, of slow lights on the gilded river boat, and the perfumed flesh of black-haired women, musical wraiths below the phantom drooping trees.

They had but shortly returned from Mardi Gras when, one howling night in winter, as he lay asleep at Gant's, the house was wakened by his father's terrible cries. Gant had been drinking heavily, day after fearful day. Eugene had been sent in the afternoons to his shop to fetch him home, and at sundown, with Jannadeau's aid, had brought him, behind the negro's spavined horse, roaring drunk to his house. There followed the usual routine of soup-feeding, undressing, and holding him in check until Doctor McGuire arrived, thrust his needle deeply into Gant's stringy arm, left sleeping-powders, and departed. The girl was exhausted; Gant himself had ravaged his strength, and had been brought down by two or three painful attacks of rheumatism.

Now, he awoke in the dark, possessed by his terror and agony, for the whole right side of his body was paralyzed by such pain as he did not know existed. He cursed and supplicated God alternately in his pain and terror. For days doctor and nurse strove with him, hoping that the leaping inflammation would not strike at his heart. He was gnarled, twisted, and bent with a savage attack of inflammatory rheumatism. As soon as he had recovered sufficiently to travel, he departed, under Helen's care, for Hot Springs. Almost savagely, she drove all other assistance from him, devoting every minute of the day to his care: they were gone six weeks—occasionally post-cards and letters describing a life of hotels, mineral baths, sickness and lameness, and the sport of the blooded rich, came to add new colors to Eugene's horizon: when they returned Gant was able again to walk, the rheumatism had been boiled from his limbs, but his right hand, gnarled and stiff, was permanently crippled. He was never again able to close it, and there was something strangely chastened in his manner, a gleam of awe and terror in his eyes.

But the union between Gant and his daughter was finally consummated. Before Gant lay, half-presaged, a road of pain and terror which led on to death, but as his great strength dwindled, palsied, broke along that road, she went with him inch by inch, welding beyond life, beyond death, beyond memory, the bond that linked them.

"I'd have died if it hadn't been for that girl," he said over and over. "She saved my life. I couldn't get along without her." And he boasted again and again of her devotion and loyalty, of the expenses of his journey, of the hotels, the wealth, the life they both had seen.

And, as the legend of Helen's goodness and devotion grew, and his dependence upon her got further advertisement, Eliza pursed her lips more and more thoughtfully, wept sometimes into the spitting grease of a pan, smiled, beneath her wide red nose, a smile tremulous, bitter, terribly hurt.

"I'll show them," she wept. "I'll show them." And she rubbed thoughtfully at a red itching patch that had appeared during the year upon the back of her left hand.

She went to Hot Springs in the winter that followed. They stopped at Memphis for a day or two: Steve was at work there in a paint store; he slipped quickly in and out of saloons, as he took Eugene about the city, leaving the boy outside for a moment while he went "in here to see a fellow"—a "fellow" who always sent him forth, Eugene thought, with an added impetuosity to his swagger.

Dizzily they crossed the river: at night he saw the small bleared shacks of Arkansas set in malarial fields.

Eliza sent him to one of the public schools of Hot Springs: he plunged heavily into the bewildering new world—performed brilliantly, and won the affection of the young woman who taught him, but paid the penalty of the stranger to all the hostile and banded little creatures of the class. Before his first month was out, he had paid desperately for his ignorance of their customs.

Eliza boiled herself out at the baths daily; sometimes, he went along with her, leaving her with a sensation of drunken independence, while he went into the men's quarters, stripping himself in a cool room, entering thence a hot one lined with couches, shutting himself in a steam-closet

where he felt himself momently dwindling into the raining puddle of
sweat at his feet, to emerge presently on trembling legs and to be rolled
and kneaded about magnificently in a huge tub by a powerful grinning
negro. Later, languorous, but with a feeling of deep purification, he lay
out on one of the couches, victoriously his own man in a man's world.
They talked from couch to couch, or walked pot-belliedly about, sashed
coyly with bath towels—malarial Southerners with malarial drawls,
paunch-eyed alcoholics, purple-skinned gamblers, and broken down prize-
fighters. He liked the smell of steam and of the sweaty men.

Eliza sent him out on the streets at once with *The Saturday Evening
Post*.

"It won't hurt you to do a little light work after school," said she. And
as he trudged off with his sack slung from his neck, she would call
after him:

"Spruce up, boy! Spruce up! Throw your shoulders back. Make folks
think you're somebody." And she gave him a pocketful of printed cards,
which bore this inscription:

SPEND YOUR SUMMERS AT

DIXIELAND

In Beautiful Altamont,

America's Switzerland.

Rates Reasonable—Both Transient and Tourist.

Apply Eliza E. Gant, Prop.

"You've got to help me drum up some trade, if we're to live, boy," she
said again, with the lip-pursing, mouth-tremulous jocularity that was
coming to wound him so deeply, because he felt it was only an obvious
mask for a more obvious insincerity.

He writhed as he saw himself finally a toughened pachyderm in Eliza's
world—sprucing up confidently, throwing his shoulders back proudly,
making people "think he was somebody" as he cordially acknowledged an
introduction by producing a card setting forth the joys of life in Altamont
and at Dixieland, and seized every opening in social relations for the
purpose of "drumming up trade." He hated the jargon of the profession,
which she had picked up somewhere long before, and which she used
constantly with such satisfaction—smacking her lips as she spoke of

"transients," or of "drumming up trade." In him, as in Gant, there was a silent horror of selling for money the bread of one's table, the shelter of one's walls, to the guest, the stranger, the unknown friend from out the world; to the sick, the weary, the lonely, the broken, the knave, the harlot, and the fool.

Thus, lost in the remote Ozarks, he wandered up Central Avenue, fringed on both sides by the swift-sloping hills, for him, by the borders of enchantment, the immediate portals of a land of timeless and never-ending faery. He drank endlessly the water that came smoking from the earth, hoping somehow to wash himself clean from all pollution, beginning his everlasting fantasy of the miraculous spring, or the bath, neck-high, of curative mud, which would draw out of a man's veins each drop of corrupted blood, dry up in him a cancerous growth, dwindle and absorb a cyst, remove all scorbutic blemishes, scoop and suck and thread away the fibrous slime of all disease, leaving him again with the perfect flesh of an animal.

And he gazed for hours into the entrances of the fashionable hotels, staring at the ladies' legs upon the verandas, watching the great ones of the land at their recreations, thinking, with a pang of wonder, that here were the people of Chambers, of Phillips, of all the society novelists, leading their godlike lives in flesh, recording their fiction. He was deeply reverential before the grand manner of these books, particularly before the grand manner of the English books: there people loved, but not as other people, elegantly; their speech was subtle, delicate, exquisite; even in their passions there was no gross lust or strong appetite—they were incapable of the vile thoughts or the meaty desire of common people. As he looked at the comely thighs of the young women on horses, fascinated to see their shapely legs split over the strong good smell of a horse, he wondered if the warm sinuous vibration of the great horse-back excited them, and what their love was like. The preposterous elegance of their manner in the books awed him: he saw seduction consummated in kid gloves, to the accompaniment of subtle repartee. Such thoughts, when he had them, filled him with shame at his own baseness—he imagined for these people a love conducted beyond all the laws of nature, achieving the delight of animals or of common men by the electrical touch of a finger, the flicker of an eye, the intonation of a phrase—exquisitely and incorruptibly.

And as they looked at his remote fabulous face, more strange now that its thick fringing curls had been shorn, they bought of him, paying him several times his fee, with the lazy penitence of wasters.

Great fish within the restaurant windows swam in glass wells—eels coiled snakily, white-bellied trout veered and sank: he dreamed of strange rich foods within.

And sometimes men returned in carriages from the distant river, laden with great fish, and he wondered if he would ever see that river. All that lay around him, near but unexplored, filled him with desire and longing.

And later, again, along the sandy coast of Florida, with Eliza, he wandered down the narrow lanes of Saint Augustine, raced along the hard packed beach of Daytona, scoured the green lawns of Palm Beach, before the hotels, for cocoanuts, which Eliza desired as souvenirs, filling a brown tow sack with them and walking, with the bag hung from his shoulders, down the interminable aisles of the Royal Poinciana or the Breakers, target of scorn, and scandal, and amusement from slave and prince; or traversed the spacious palm-cool walks that cut the peninsula, to see, sprawled in the sensual loose sand the ladies' silken legs, the brown lean bodies of the men, the long seaplunges in the unending scroll-work of the emerald and infinite sea, which had beat in his brain from his father's shells, which had played at his mountain heart, but which never, until now, had he seen. Through the spattered sunlight of the palms, in the smooth walks, princess and lord were wheeled: in latticed bar-rooms, droning with the buzzing fans, men drank from glacéd tall glasses.

Or again, they came to Jacksonville, lived there for several weeks near Pett and Greeley; he studied under a little crippled man from Harvard, going to lunch with his teacher at a buffet, where the man consumed beer and pretzels. Eliza protested the tuition when she left: the cripple shrugged his shoulders, took what she had to offer. Eugene twisted his neck about, and lifted his foot from the ground.

Thus did he see first, he the hill-bound, the sky-girt, of whom the mountains were his masters, the fabulous South. The picture of flashing field, of wood, and hill, stayed in his heart forever: lost in the dark land, he lay the night-long through within his berth, watching the shadowy and phantom South flash by, sleeping at length, and waking suddenly, to see cool lakes in Florida at dawn, standing quietly as if they had waited from eternity for this meeting; or hearing, as the train in the dark hours of morning slid into Savannah, the strange quiet voices of the men upon the platform, the boding faint echoes of the station, or seeing, in pale dawn, the phantom woods, a rutted lane, a cow, a boy, a drab, dull-eyed against a cottage door, glimpsed, at this moment of rushing time, for which all life had been aplot, to flash upon the window and be gone.

The commonness of all things in the earth he remembered with a strange familiarity—he dreamed of the quiet roads, the moonlit woodlands, and he thought that some day he would come to them on foot, and find them there unchanged, in all the wonder of recognition. They had existed for him anciently and forever.

Eugene was almost twelve years old.

PART TWO

14

The plum-tree, black and brittle, rocks stiffly in winter wind. Her million little twigs are frozen in spears of ice. But in the Spring, lithe and heavy, she will bend under her great load of fruit and blossoms. She will grow young again. Red plums will ripen, will be shaken desperately upon the tiny stems. They will fall bursted on the loamy warm wet earth; when the wind blows in the orchard the air will be filled with dropping plums; the night will be filled with the sound of their dropping, and a great tree of birds will sing, burgeoning, blossoming richly, filling the air also with warm-throated plum-dropping bird-notes.

The harsh hill-earth has moistly thawed and softened, rich soaking rain falls, fresh-bladed tender grass like soft hair growing sparsely streaks the land.

My Brother Ben's face, thought Eugene, is like a piece of slightly yellow ivory; his high white head is knotted fiercely by his old man's scowl; his mouth is like a knife, his smile the flicker of light across a blade. His face is like a blade, and a knife, and a flicker of light: it is delicate and fierce, and scowls beautifully forever, and when he fastens his hard white fingers and his scowling eyes upon a thing he wants to fix, he sniffs with sharp and private concentration through his long pointed nose. Thus women, looking, feel a well of tenderness for his pointed, bumpy, always scowling face: his hair shines like that of a young boy—it is crinkled and crisp as lettuce.

Into the April night-and-morning streets goes Ben. The night is brightly pricked with cool and tender stars. The orchard stirs leafily in the short fresh wind. Ben prowls softly out of the sleeping house. His thin bright face is dark within the orchard. There is a smell of nicotine and shoe leather under the young blossoms. His pigeon-toed tan shoes ring musically up the empty streets. Lazily slaps the water in the fountain on the Square; all the firemen are asleep—but Big Bill Merrick, the brave cop, hogjowled and red, leans swinishly over mince-pie and coffee in Uneeda Lunch. The warm good ink-smell beats in rich waves into the street: a whistling train howls off into the Springtime South.

By the cool orchards in the dark the paper-carriers go. The copper legs of negresses in their dark dens stir. The creek brawls cleanly.

A new one, Number 6, heard boys speak of Foxy:

"Who's Foxy?" asked Number 6.

"Foxy's a bastard, Number 6. Don't let him catch you."

"The bastard caught me three times last week. In the Greek's every time. Why can't they let us eat?"

Number 3 thought of Friday morning—he had the Niggertown route. "How many—3?"

"One hundred and sixty-two."

"How many Dead Heads you got, son?" said Mr. Randall cynically. "Do you ever try to collect from them?" he added, thumbing through the book.

"He takes it out in Poon-Tang," said Foxy, grinning. "A week's subscription free for a dose."

"What you got to say about it?" asked Number 3 belligerently. "You've been knocking down on them for six years."

"Jazz 'em all if you like," said Randall, "but get the money. Ben, I want you to go round with him Saturday."

Ben laughed silently and cynically into the air:

"Oh, my God!" he said. "Do you expect me to check up on the little thug? He's been knocking down on you for the last six months."

"All right! All right!" said Randall, annoyed. "That's what I want you to find out."

"Oh, for God's sake, Randall," said Ben contemptuously, "he's got niggers on that book who've been dead for five years. That's what you get for keeping every little crook that comes along."

"If you don't get a move on, 3, I'll give your route to another boy," said Randall.

"Hell, get another boy. I don't care," said Number 3, toughly.

"Oh, for God's sake! Listen to this, won't you?" said Ben, laughing thinly and nodding to his angel, indicating Number 3 with a scowling jerk of his head.

"Yes, listen to this, won't you! That's what I said," Number 3 answered pugnaciously.

"All right, little boy. Run on and deliver your papers now, before you get hurt," said Ben, turning his scowl quietly upon him and looking at him blackly for a moment. "Ah, you little crook," he said with profound loathing, "I have a kid brother who's worth six like you."

Spring lay strewn lightly like a fragrant gauzy scarf upon the earth; the night was a cool bowl of lilac darkness, filled with fresh orchard scents.

Gant slept heavily, rattling the loose window-sash with deep rasping snores; with short explosive thunders, ripping the lilac night, 36 began to climb Saluda. She bucked helplessly like a goat, her wheels spun furiously on the rails, Tom Cline stared seriously down into the milky boiling creek, and waited. She slipped, spun, held, ploughed slowly up, like a straining mule, into the dark. Content, he leaned far out the cab and looked: the starlight glimmered faintly on the rails. He ate a thick sandwich of cold buttered fried meat, tearing it raggedly and glueily staining it under his big black fingers. There was a smell of dogwood and laurel in the cool slow passage of the world. The cars clanked humpily across the spur; the switchman, bathed murkily in the hot yellow light of his perilous bank-edged hut, stood sullen at the switch.

Arms spread upon his cab-sill, chewing thoughtfully, Tom, goggle-eyed, looked carefully down at him. They had never spoken. Then in silence he turned and took the milk-bottle, half full of cold coffee, that his fireman offered him. He washed his food down with the large easy gurgling swallows of a bishop.

At 18 Valley Street, the red shack-porch, slime-scummed with a greasy salve of yellow negroid mud, quaked rottenly. Number 3's square-folded ink-fresh paper struck flat against the door, falling on its edge stiffly to the porch like a block of light wood. Within, May Corpening stirred nakedly, muttering as if doped and moving her heavy copper legs, in the fetid bed-warmth, with the slow noise of silk.

Harry Tugman lit a Camel, drawing the smoke deep into his powerful ink-stained lungs as he watched the press run down. His bare arms were heavy-muscled as his presses. He dropped comfortably into his pliant creaking chair and tilted back, casually scanning the warm pungent sheet. Luxurious smoke steamed slowly from his nostrils. He cast the sheet away.

"Christ!" he said. "What a makeup!"

Ben came down stairs, moody, scowling, and humped over toward the ice-box.

"For God's sake, Mac," he called out irritably to the Make-up Man, as he scowled under the lifted lid, "don't you ever keep anything except root-beer and sour milk?"

"What do you want, for Christ's sake?"

"I'd like to get a Coca-Cola once in a while. You know," he said bitingly, "Old Man Candler down in Atlanta is still making it."

Harry Tugman cast his cigarette away.

"They haven't got the news up here yet, Ben," said he. "You'll have to wait till the excitement over Lee's surrender has died down. Come on," he said abruptly, getting up, "let's go over to the Greasy Spoon."

He thrust his big head down into the deep well of the sink, letting the lukewarm water sluice refreshingly over his broad neck and blue-white sallow night-time face, strong, tough, and humorous. He soaped his hands with thick slathering suds, his muscles twisting slowly like big snakes.

He sang in his powerful quartette baritone:

> "Beware! Beware! Beware!
> Many brave hearts lie asleep in the deep,
> So beware! Bee-ware!"

Comfortably they rested in the warm completed exhaustion of the quiet press-room: upstairs the offices, bathed in green-yellow light, sprawled like men relaxed after work. The boys had gone to their routes. The place seemed to breathe slowly and wearily. The dawn-sweet air washed coolly over their faces. The sky was faintly pearled at the horizon.

Strangely, in sharp broken fragments, life awoke in the lilac darkness. Clop-clopping slowly on the ringing street, Number Six, Mrs. Goulderbilt's powerful brown mare, drew inevitably on the bottle-clinking cream-yellow wagon, racked to the top with creamy extra-heavy high-priced milk. The driver was a fresh-skinned young countryman, richly odorous with the smell of fresh sweat and milk. Eight miles, through the starlit dewy fields and forests of Biltburn, under the high brick English lodgegate, they had come into the town.

At the Pisgah Hotel, opposite the station, the last door clicked softly; the stealthy footfalls of the night ceased; Miss Bernice Redmond gave the negro porter eight one-dollar bills and went definitely to bed with the request that she be not disturbed until one o'clock; a shifting engine slatted noisily about in the yard; past the Biltburn crossing Tom Cline whistled with even, mournful respirations. By this time Number 3 had delivered 142 of his papers; he had only to ascend the rickety wooden stairs of the Eagle Crescent bank to finish the eight houses of the Crescent. He looked anxiously across the hill-and-dale-sprawled negro settlement to the eastern rim: behind Birdseye Gap the sky was pearl-gray—the stars looked drowned. Not much time left, he thought. He had a blond meaty face, pale-colored and covered thickly with young blond hair. His jaw was long and fleshy: it sloped backward. He ran his tongue along his full cracked underlip.

A 1910 model, four-cylinder, seven-pasesnger Hudson, with mounting steady roar, shot drunkenly out from the station curbing, lurched into the level negro-sleeping stretch of South End Avenue, where the firemen had their tournaments, and zipped townward doing almost fifty. The station quietly stirred in its sleep: there were faint reverberating noises under the empty sheds; brisk hammer-taps upon car wheels, metallic heel-clicks in the tiled waiting-room. Sleepily a negress slopped water on the tiles, with languid sullen movement pushing a gray sopping rag around the floor.

It was now five-thirty. Ben had gone out of the house into the orchard at three twenty-five. In another forty minutes Gant would waken, dress, and build the morning fires.

"Ben," said Harry Tugman, as they walked out of the relaxed office, "if Jimmy Dean comes messing around my press-room again they can get some one else to print their lousy sheet. What the hell! I can get a job on the *Atlanta Constitution* whenever I want it."

"Did he come down to-night?" asked Ben.

"Yes," said Harry Tugman, "and he got out again. I told him to take his little tail upstairs."

"Oh, for God's sake!" said Ben. "What did he say?"

"He said, '*I'm* the editor! I'm the editor of this paper!' 'I don't give a good goddam,' I said, 'If you're the President's snotrag. If you want any paper to-day keep out of the press-room.' And believe me, he went!"

In cool blue-pearl darkness they rounded the end of the Post Office and cut diagonally across the street to Uneeda Lunch No. 3. It was a small beanery, twelve feet wide, wedged in between an optician's and a Greek shoe parlor.

Within, Dr. Hugh McGuire sat on a stool patiently impaling kidney beans, one at a time, upon the prongs of his fork. A strong odor of corn

whisky soaked the air about him. His thick skilful butcher's hands, hairy
on the backs, gripped the fork numbly. His heavy-jowled face was blotted
by large brown patches. He turned round and stared owlishly as Ben
entered, fixing the wavering glare of his bulbous red eyes finally upon him.

"Hello, son," he said in his barking kindly voice, "what can I do for
you?"

"Oh, for God's sake," said Ben laughing contemptuously, and jerking
his head toward Tugman. "Listen to this, won't you?"

They sat down at the lower end. At this moment, Horse Hines, the
undertaker, entered, producing, although he was not a thin man, the effect
of a skeleton clad in a black frock coat. His long lantern mouth split
horsily in a professional smile displaying big horse teeth in his white
heavily starched face.

"Gentlemen, gentlemen," he said for no apparent reason, rubbing his
lean hands briskly as if it was cold. His palm-flesh rattled together like
old bones.

Coker, the Lung Shark, who had not ceased to regard McGuire's bean-
hunt with sardonic interest, now took the long cigar out of his devil's head
and held it between his stained fingers as he tapped his companion.

"Let's get out," he grinned quietly, nodding toward Horse Hines. "It
will look bad if we're seen together here."

"Good morning, Ben," said Horse Hines, sitting down below him. "Are
all the folks well?" he added, softly.

Sideways Ben looked at him scowling, then jerked his head back to the
counterman, with a fast bitter flicker of his lips.

"Doctor," said Harry Tugman with servile medicine-man respect, "what
do you charge to operate?"

"Operate what?" McGuire barked presently, having pronged a kidney
bean.

"Why—appendicitis," said Harry Tugman, for it was all he could
think of.

"Three hundred dollars when we go into the belly," said McGuire. He
coughed chokingly to the side.

"You're drowning in your own secretions," said Coker with his yellow
grin. "Like Old Lady Sladen."

"My God!" said Harry Tugman, thinking jealously of lost news. "When
did she go?"

"To-night," said Coker.

"God, I'm sorry to hear that," said Harry Tugman, greatly relieved.

"I've just finished laying the old lady out," said Horse Hines gently. "A bundle of skin and bones." He sighed regretfully, and for a moment his boiled eye moistened.

Ben turned his scowling head around with an expression of nausea.

"Joe," said Horse Hines with merry professionalism, "give me a mug of that embalming fluid." He thrust his horsehead indicatively at the coffee urn.

"Oh, for God's sake," Ben muttered in terms of loathing. "Do you ever wash your damned hands before you come in here?" he burst out irritably.

Ben was twenty. Men did not think of his age.

"Would you like some cold pork, son?" said Coker, with his yellow malicious grin.

Ben made a retching noise in his throat, and put his hand upon his stomach.

"What's the matter, Ben?" Harry Tugman laughed heavily and struck him on the back.

Ben got off the stool, took his coffee mug and the piece of tanned mince pie he had ordered, and moved to the other side of Harry Tugman. Every one laughed. Then he jerked his head toward McGuire with a quick frown.

"By God, Tug," he said. "They've got us cornered."

"Listen to him," said McGuire to Coker. "A chip off the old block, isn't he? I brought that boy into the world, saw him through typhoid, got the old man over seven hundred drunks, and I've been called eighteen different kinds of son of a bitch for my pains ever since. But let one of 'em get a belly ache," he added proudly, "and you'll see how quick they come running to me. Isn't that right, Ben?" he said, turning to him.

"Oh, listen to this!" said Ben, laughing irritably and burying his peaked face in his coffee mug. His bitter savor filled the place with life, with tenderness, with beauty. They looked on him with drunken, kindly eyes— at his gray scornful face and the lonely demon flicker of his smile.

"And I tell you something else," said McGuire, ponderously wheeling around on Coker, "if one of them's got to be cut open, see who gets the job. What about it, Ben?" he asked.

"By God, if you ever cut me open, McGuire," said Ben, "I'm going to be damned sure you can walk straight before you do."

"Come on, Hugh," said Coker, prodding McGuire under his shoulder. "Stop chasing those beans around the plate. Crawl off or fall off that damned stool—I don't care which."

McGuire, drunkenly lost in revery, stared witlessly down at his bean plate and sighed.

"Come on, you damned fool," said Coker, getting up, "you've got to operate in forty-five minutes."

"Oh, for God's sake," said Ben, lifting his face from the stained mug, "who's the victim? I'll send flowers."

". . . all of us sooner or later," McGuire mumbled puffily through his puff-lips. "Rich and poor alike. Here to-day and gone to-morrow. Doesn't matter . . . doesn't matter at all."

"In heaven's name," Ben burst out irritably to Coker. "Are you going to let him operate like that? Why don't you shoot them instead?"

Coker plucked the cigar from his long malarial grinning face:

"Why, he's just getting hot, son," said he.

Nacreous pearl light swam faintly about the hem of the lilac darkness; the edges of light and darkness were stitched upon the hills. Morning moved like a pearl-gray tide across the fields and up the hill-flanks, flowing rapidly down into the soluble dark.

At the curb now, young Dr. Jefferson Spaugh brought his Buick roadster to a halt, and got out, foppishly drawing off his gloves and flicking the silk lapels of his dinner jacket. His face, whisky-red, was highboned and handsome; his mouth was straightlipped, cruel, and sensual. An inherited aura of mountain-cornfield sweat hung scentlessly but telepathically about him; he was a smartened-up mountaineer with country-club and University of Pennsylvania glossings. Four years in Philly change a man.

Thrusting his gloves carelessly into his coat, he entered. McGuire slid bearishly off his stool and gazed him into focus. Then he made beckoning round-arm gestures with his fat hands.

"Look at it, will you," he said. "Does any one know what it is?"

"It's Percy," said Coker. "You know Percy Van der Gould, don't you?"

"I've been dancing all night at the Hilliards," said Spaugh elegantly. "Damn! These new patent-leather pumps have ruined my feet." He sat upon a stool, and elegantly displayed his large country feet, indecently broad and angular in the shoes.

"What's he been doing?" said McGuire doubtfully, turning to Coker for enlightenment.

"He's been dancing all night at the Hilliards," said Coker in a mincing voice.

McGuire shielded his bloated face coyly with his hand.

"O crush me!" he said, "I'm a grape! Dancing at the Hilliards, were you, you damned Mountain Grill. You've been on a Poon-Tang Picnic in Niggertown. You can't load that bunk on us."

Bull-lunged, their laughter filled the nacreous dawn.

"Patent-leather pumps!" said McGuire. "Hurt his feet. By God, Coker, the first time he came to town ten years ago he'd never been curried above the knees. They had to throw him down to put shoes on him."

Ben laughed thinly to the Angel.

"A couple of slices of buttered toast, if you please, not too brown," said Spaugh delicately to the counterman.

"A mess of hog chitlings and sorghum, you mean, you bastard. You were brought up on salt pork and cornbread."

"We're getting too low and coarse for him, Hugh," said Coker. "Now that he's got drunk with some of the best families, he's in great demand socially. He's so highly thought of that he's become the official midwife to all pregnant virgins."

"Yes," said McGuire, "he's their friend. He helps them out. He not only helps them out, he helps them in again."

"What's wrong with that?" said Spaugh. "We ought to keep it in the family, oughtn't we?"

Their laughter howled out into the tender dawn.

"This conversation is getting too rough for me," said Horse Hines banteringly as he got off his stool.

"Shake hands with Coker before you go, Horse," said McGuire. "He's the best friend you've ever had. You ought to give him royalties."

The light that filled the world now was soft and otherworldly like the light that fills the sea-floors of Catalina where the great fish swim. Flat-footedly, with kidney-aching back, Patrolman Leslie Roberts all unbuttoned slouched through the submarine pearl light and paused, gently agitating his club behind him, as he turned his hollow liverish face toward the open door.

"Here's your patient," said Coker softly, "the Constipated Cop."

Aloud, with great cordiality, they all said: "How are you, Les?"

"Oh, tolable, tolable," said the policeman mournfully. As draggled as his mustaches, he passed on, hocking into the gutter a slimy gob of phlegm.

"Well, good morning, gentlemen," said Horse Hines, making to go.

"Remember what I told you, Horse. Be good to Coker, your best friend." McGuire jerked a thumb toward Coker.

Beneath his thin joviality Horse Hines was hurt.

"I do remember," said the undertaker gravely. "We are both members of honorable professions: in the hour of death when the storm-tossed ship puts into its haven of rest, we are the trustees of the Almighty."

"Why, Horse!" Coker exclaimed, "this is eloquence!"

"The sacred rites of closing the eyes, of composing the limbs, and of preparing for burial the lifeless repository of the departed soul is our holy mission; it is for us, the living, to pour balm upon the broken heart of Grief, to soothe the widow's ache, to brush away the orphan's tears; it is for us, the living, to highly resolve that——"

"——Government of the people, for the people, and by the people," said Hugh McGuire.

"Yes, Horse," said Coker, "you are right. I'm touched. And what's more, we do it all for nothing. At least," he added virtuously, "I never charge for soothing the widow's ache."

"What about embalming the broken heart of Grief?" asked McGuire.

"I said *balm*," Horse Hines remarked coldly.

"Say, Horse," said Harry Tugman, who had listened with great interest, "didn't you make a speech with all that in it last summer at the Undertakers' Convention?"

"What's true then is true now," said Horse Hines bitterly, as he left the place.

"Jesus!" said Harry Tugman, "we've got him good and sore. I thought I'd bust a gut, doc, when you pulled that one about embalming the broken heart of Grief."

At this moment Dr. Ravenel brought his Hudson to a halt across the street before the Post Office, and walked over rapidly, drawing his gauntlets off. He was bareheaded; his silver aristocratic hair was thinly rumpled; his surgical gray eyes probed restlessly below the thick lenses of his spectacles. He had a famous, calm, deeply concerned face, shaven, ashen, lean, lit gravely now and then by humor.

"Oh Christ!" said Coker. "Here comes Teacher!"

"Good morning, Hugh," he said as he entered. "Are you going into training again for the bughouse?"

"Look who's here!" McGuire roared hospitably. "Dead-eye Dick, the literary sawbones, whose private collection of gallstones is the finest in the world. When d'jew get back, son?"

"Just in time, it seems," said Ravenel, holding a cigarette cleanly between his long surgical fingers. He looked at his watch. "I believe you have a little engagement at the Ravenel hospital in about half an hour. Is that right?"

"By God, Dick, you're always right," McGuire yelled enthusiastically. "What'd you tell 'em up there, boy?"

"I told them," said Dick Ravenel, whose affection was like a flower that grew behind a wall, "that the best surgeon in America when he was sober was a lousy bum named Hugh McGuire who was always drunk."

"Now wait, wait. Hold on a minute!" said McGuire, holding up his thick hand. "I protest, Dick. You meant well, son, but you got that mixed up. You mean the best surgeon in America when he's not sober."

"Did you read one of your papers?" said Coker.

"Yes," said Dick Ravenel. "I read one on carcinoma of the liver."

"How about one on pyorrhea of the toe-nails?" said McGuire. "Did you read that one?"

Harry Tugman laughed heavily, not wholly knowing why. McGuire belched into the silence loudly and was witlessly adrift for a moment.

"Literature, literature, Dick," he returned portentously. "It's been the ruin of many a good surgeon. You read too much, Dick. Yon Cassius hath a lean and hungry look. You know too much. The letter killeth the spirit, you know. Me—Dick, did you ever know me to take anything out that I didn't put back? Anyway, don't I always leave 'em something to go on with? I'm no scholar, Dick. I've never had your advantages. I'm a self-made butcher. I'm a carpenter, Dick. I'm an interior decorator. I'm a mechanic, a plumber, an electrician, a butcher, a tailor, a jeweller. I'm a jewel, a gem, a diamond in the rough, Dick. I'm a practical man. I take out their works, spit upon them, trim off the dirty edges, and send them on their way again. I economize, Dick; I throw away everything I can't use, and use everything I throw away. Who made the Pope a tailbone from his knuckle? Who made the dog howl? Aha—that's why the governor looks so young. We are filled up with useless machinery, Dick. Efficiency, economy, power! Have you a Little Fairy in your Home? You haven't! Then let the Gold Dust Twins do the work! Ask Ben—he knows!"

"O my God!" laughed Ben thinly, "listen to that, won't you?"

Two doors below, directly before the Post Office, Pete Mascari rolled upward with corrugated thunder the shutters of his fruit shop. The pearl light fell coolly upon the fruity architecture, on the pyramided masonry of spit-bright winesaps, the thin sharp yellow of the Florida oranges, the purple Tokays, sawdust-bedded. There was a stale fruity odor from the shop of ripening bananas, crated apples, and the acrid tang of powder; the windows are filled with Roman candles, crossed rockets, pinwheels, squat green Happy Hooligans, and multilating Jack Johnsons, red cannoncrackers, and tiny acrid packets of crackling spattering firecrackers. Light fell a moment on the ashen corpsiness of his face and on the liquid Sicilian poison of his eyes.

"Don' pincha da grape. Pinch da banan'!"

A street-car, toy-green with new Spring paint, went squareward.

"Dick," said McGuire more soberly, "take the job, if you like."

Ravenel shook his head.

"I'll stand by," said he. "I won't operate. I'm afraid of one like this. It's your job, drunk or sober."

"Removing a tumor from a woman, ain't you?" said Coker.

"No," said Dick Ravenel, "removing a woman from a tumor."

"Bet you it weighs fifty pounds, if it weighs an ounce," said McGuire with sudden professional interest.

Dick Ravenel winced ever so slightly. A cool spurt of young wind, clean as a kid, flowed by him. McGuire's meaty shoulders recoiled burlily as if from the cold shock of water. He seemed to waken.

"I'd like a bath," he said to Dick Ravenel, "and a shave." He rubbed his hand across his blotched hairy face.

"You can use my room, Hugh, at the hotel," said Jeff Spaugh, looking at Ravenel somewhat eagerly.

"I'll use the hospital," he said.

"You'll just have time," said Ravenel.

"In God's name, let's get a start on," he cried impatiently.

"Did you see Kelly do this one at Hopkins?" asked McGuire.

"Yes," said Dick Ravenel, "after a very long prayer. That's to give power to his elbow. The patient died."

"Damn the prayers!" said McGuire. "They won't do much good to this one. She called me a low-down lickered-up whisky-drinking bastard last night: if she still feels like that she'll get well."

"These mountain women take a lot of killing," said Jeff Spaugh sagely.

"Do you want to come along?" McGuire asked Coker.

"No, thanks. I'm getting some sleep," he answered. "The old girl took a hell of a time. I thought she'd never get through dying."

They started to go.

"Ben," said McGuire, with a return to his former manner, "tell the Old Man I'll beat hell out of him if he doesn't give Helen a rest. Is he staying sober?"

"In heaven's name, McGuire, how should I know?" Ben burst out irritably. "Do you think that's all I've got to do—watching your licker-heads?"

"That's a great girl, boy," said McGuire sentimentally. "One in a million."

"Hugh, for God's sake, come on," cried Dick Ravenel.

The four medical men went out into the pearl light. The town emerged from the lilac darkness with a washed renascent cleanliness. All the world seemed as young as Spring. McGuire walked across to Ravenel's car, and sank comfortably with a sense of invigoration into the cool leathers. Jeff Spaugh plunged off violently with a ripping explosion of his engine and a cavalier wave of his hand.

Admiringly Harry Tugman's face turned to the slumped burly figure of Hugh McGuire.

"By God!" he boasted, "I bet he does the damnedest piece of operating you ever heard of."

"Why, hell," said the counterman loyally, "he ain't worth a damn until he's got a quart of corn licker under his belt. Give him a few drinks and he'll cut off your damned head and put it on again without your knowing it."

As Jeff Spaugh roared off Harry Tugman said jealously: "Look at that bastard. Mr. Vanderbilt. He thinks he's hell, don't he? A big pile of bull. Ben, do you reckon he was really out at the Hilliards to-night?"

"Oh for God's sake," said Ben irritably, "how the hell should I know! What difference does it make?" he added furiously.

"I guess Little Maudie will fill up the column to-morrow with some of her crap," said Harry Tugman. " 'The Younger Set,' she calls it! Christ! It goes all the way from every little bitch old enough to wear drawers, to Old Man Redmond. If Saul Gudger belongs to the Younger Set, Ben, you and I are still in the third grade. Why, hell, yes," he said with an air of conviction to the grinning counterman, "he was bald as a pig's knuckle when the Spanish American War broke out."

The counterman laughed.

Foaming with brilliant slapdash improvisation Harry Tugman declaimed:

"Members of the Younger Set were charmingly entertained last night at a dinner dance given at Snotwood, the beautiful residence of Mr. and Mrs. Clarence Firkins, in honor of their youngest daughter, Gladys, who made her debutt this season. Mr. and Mrs. Firkins, accompanied by their daughter, greeted each of the arriving guests at the threshhold in a manner reviving the finest old traditions of Southern aristocracy, while Mrs. Firkins' accomplished sister, Miss Catherine Hipkiss, affectionately known to members of the local younger set as Roaring Kate, supervised the checking of overcoats, evening wraps, jock-straps, and jewelry.

"Dinner was served promptly at eight o'clock, followed by coffee and Pluto Water at eight forty-five. A delicious nine-course collation had been prepared by Artaxerxes Papadopolos, the well-known confectioner and caterer, and proprietor of the Bijou Café for Ladies and Gents.

"After first-aid and a thorough medical examination by Dr. Jefferson Reginald Alfonso Spaugh, the popular *gin*-ecologist, the guests adjourned to the Ball Room where dance music was provided by Zeke Buckner's Upper Hominy Stringed Quartette, Mr. Buckner himself officiating at the trap drum and tambourine.

"Among those dancing were the Misses Aline Titsworth, Lena Ginster, Ophelia Legg, Gladys Firkins, Beatrice Slutsky, Mary Whitesides, Helen Shockett, and Lofta Barnes.

"Also the Messrs. I. C. Bottom, U. B. Freely, R. U. Reddy, O. I. Lovett, Cummings Strong, Sansom Horney, Preston Updyke, Dows Wicket, Petti-grew Biggs, Otis Goode, and J. Broad Stern."

Ben laughed noiselessly, and bent his pointed face into the mug again. Then, he stretched his thin arms out, extending his body sensually up-ward, and forcing out in a wide yawn the night-time accumulation of weariness, boredom, and disgust.

"Oh-h-h-h my God!"

Virginal sunlight crept into the street in young moteless shafts. At this moment Gant awoke.

He lay quietly on his back for a moment in the pleasant yellow-shaded dusk of the sitting-room, listening to the rippling flutiness of the live piping birdy morning. He yawned cavernously and thrust his right hand scratching into the dense hairthicket of his breast.

The fast cackle-cluck of sensual hens. Come and rob us. All through the night for you, master. Rich protesting yielding voices of Jewesses. Do it, don't it. Break an egg in them.

Sleepless, straight, alert, the counterpane moulded over his gaunt legs, he listened to the protesting invitations of the hens.

From the warm dust, shaking their fat feathered bodies, protesting but satisfied they staggered up. For me. The earth too and the vine. The moist new earth cleaving like cut pork from the plough. Or like water from a ship. The spongy sod spaded cleanly and rolled back like flesh. Or the earth loosened and hoed gently around the roots of the cherry trees. The earth receives my seed. For me the great lettuces. Spongy and full of sap now like a woman. The thick grapevine—in August the heavy clustered grapes—How there? Like milk from a breast. Or blood through a vein. Fattens and plumps them.

All through the night the blossoms dropping. Soon now the White Wax. Green apples end of May. Isaacs' June Apple hangs half on my side. Bacon and fried green apples.

With sharp whetted hunger he thought of breakfast. He threw the sheet back cleanly, swung in an orbit to a sitting position and put his white somewhat phthisic feet on the floor. Standing up tenderly, he walked over to his leather rocker and put on a pair of clean white-footed socks. Then he pulled his nightgown over his head, looking for a moment in the dresser mirror at his great boned structure, the long stringy muscles of his arms, and his flat-meated hairy chest. His stomach sagged paunchily. He thrust his white flaccid calves quickly through the shrunken legs of a union suit, stretched it out elasticly with a comfortable widening of his shoulders and buttoned it. Then he stepped into his roomy sculpturally heavy trousers and drew on his soft-leathered laceless shoes. Crossing his suspender braces over his shoulders, he strode into the kitchen and had a brisk fire of oil and pine snapping in the range within three minutes. He was stimulated and alive in all the fresh wakefulness of the Spring morning.

Through Birdseye Gap, in the dewy richness of Lunn's Cove, Judge Webster Tayloe, the eminent, prosperous, and aristocratic corporation counsel (retired, but occasional consultations), rose in the rich walnut twilight of his bedchamber, noted approvingly, through the black lenses of the glasses that gave his long, subtle, and contemptuous face its final advantage over the rabble, that one of his country bumpkins was coming from the third pasture with a slopping pail of new milk, another was sharpening a scythe in the young glint of the sun, and another, emulating his more intelligent fellow, the horse, was backing a buggy slowly under the carriage shed.

Approvingly he watched his young mulatto son come over the lawn with lazy cat-speed, noting with satisfaction the grace and quickness of his movements, the slender barrel strength of his torso, his smallboned resiliency. Also the well-shaped intelligent head, the eager black eyes, the sensitive oval face, and the beautiful coprous olive of the skin. He was very like a better-class Spaniard. Quod potui perfeci. By this fusion, perhaps, men like men.

By the river the reed-pipes, the muse's temple, the sacred wood again. Why not? As in this cove. I, too, have lived in Arcady.

He took off his glasses for a moment and looked at the ptotic malevolence of his left eye, and the large harlequinesque wart in the cheek below it. The black glasses gave the suggestion that he was half-masked; they added a touch of unsearchable mystery to the subtle, sensual and disquieting intelligence of his face. His negro man appeared at this moment and told him his bath was ready. He drew the long thin nightgown over his freckled Fitzsimmons body and stepped vigorously into tepid water. Then for ten minutes he was sponged, scraped, and kneaded, upon a long table by the powerful plastic hands of the negro. He dressed in fresh laundered underwear and newly pressed clothes of black. He tied a black string carelessly below the wide belt of starched collar and buttoned across his straight long figure a frock coat that reached his knees. He took a cigarette from a box on his table and lighted it.

Bouncing tinnily down the coiling road that came through the Gap from the town, a flivver glinted momently through the trees. Two men were in it. His face hardened against it, he watched it go by his gates on the road with a scuffle of dust. Dimly he saw their lewd red mountain faces, and completed the image with sweat and corduroy. And in the town their city cousins. Brick, stucco, the white little eczema of Suburbia. Federated Half-Breeds of the World.

Into my Valley next with lawnmowers and front lawns. He ground out the life of the cigarette against an ashtray, and began a rapid window calculation of his horses, asses, kine, swine, and hens; the stored plenitude of his great barn, the heavy fruitage of his fields and orchards. A man came toward the house with a bucket of eggs in one hand and a bucket of butter in the other; each cake was stamped with a sheaf of wheat and wrapped loosely in clean white linen cloths. He smiled grimly: if attacked he could withstand a prolonged siege.

At Dixieland, Eliza slept soundly in a small dark room with a window opening on the uncertain light of the back porch. Her chamber was festooned with a pendant wilderness of cord and string; stacks of old newspapers and magazines were piled in the corners; and every shelf was loaded with gummed, labelled, half-filled medicine bottles. There was a smell in the air of mentholatum, Vick's Pneumonia Cure, and sweet glycerine. The negress arrived, coming under the built-up house and climbing lazily the steep tunnel of back steps. She knocked at the door.

"Who's there!" cried Eliza sharply, waking at once, and coming forward to the door. She wore a gray flannel nightgown over a heavy woollen undershirt that Ben had discarded: the pendant string floated gently to and fro as she opened the door, like some strange seamoss floating below the sea. Upstairs, in the small front room with the sleeping-porch, slept Miss Billie Edwards, twenty-four, of Missouri, the daring and masterful liontamer of Johnny L. Jones Combined Shows, then playing in the field on the hill behind the Plum Street School. Next to her, in the large airy room at the corner, Mrs. Marie Pert, forty-one, the wife of an itinerant and usually absent drug salesman, lay deep in the pit of alcoholic slumber. Upon each end of the mantel was a small snapshot in a silver frame—one of her absent daughter, Louise, eighteen, and one of Benjamin Gant, lying on the grass-bank in front of the house, propped on his elbow and wearing a wide straw hat that shaded all his face except his mouth. Also, in other chambers, front and back, Mr. Conway Richards, candy-wheel concessionaire with the Johnny L. Jones Combined Shows, Miss Lily Mangum, twenty-six, trained nurse, Mr. William H. Baskett, fifty-three, of Hattiesburg, Mississippi, cotton grower, banker, and sufferer from malaria, and his wife; in the large room at the head of the stairs Miss Annie Mitchell, nineteen, of Valdosta, Georgia, Miss Thelma Cheshire, twenty-one, of Florence, South Carolina, and Mrs. Rose Levin, twenty-eight, of Chicago, Illinois, all members of the chorus of "Molasses" Evans and His Broadway Beauties, booked out of Atlanta, Georgia, by the Piedmont Amusement Agency.

"O G-hirls! The Duke of Gorgonzola and the Count of Limburger are on their way here now. I want all you girls to be nice to them and to show them a good time when they arrive."

"You *bet* we will."

"And keep your eye on the little one—he's the one with all the money."

"I'll *say* we will. Hurrah, Hurrah, Hurrah!"

> "We are the girls that have the fun,
>   We're snappy and happy every one;
>   We're jolly and gay
>   And ready to play,
>   And that is why we say-ee——"

Behind a bill-plastered fence-boarding on upper Valley Street, opposite the Y. M. I. (colored), and in the very heart of the crowded amusement and commercial centre of Altamont's colored population, Moses Andrews, twenty-six, colored, slept the last great sleep of white and black. His pockets, which only the night before had been full of the money Saul Stein, the pawnbroker, had given him in exchange for certain articles which he had taken from the home of Mr. George Rollins, the attorney (as an 18-carat Waltham gold watch with a heavy chain of twined gold, the diamond engagement ring of Mrs. Rollins, three pairs of the finest silk stockings, and two pairs of gentlemen's under-drawers), were now empty, a half-filled bottle of Cloverleaf Bonded Kentucky Rye, with which he had retired behind the boards to slumber, lay unmolested in the flaccid grip of his left hand, and his broad black throat gaped cleanly open from ear to ear, as a result of the skilled razor-work of his hated and hating rival, Jefferson Flack, twenty-eight, who now lay peacefully, unsuspected and unsought, with their mutual mistress, Miss Molly Fiske, in her apartment on east Pine Street. Moses had been murdered in moonlight.

A starved cat walked softly along by the boards on Upper Valley: as the courthouse bell boomed out its solid six strokes, eight negro laborers, the bottoms of their overalls stiff with agglutinated cement, tramped by like a single animal, in a wedge, each carrying his lunch in a small lard bucket.

Meanwhile, the following events occurred simultaneously throughout the neighborhood.

Dr. H. M. McRae, fifty-eight, minister of the First Presbyterian Church, having washed his lean Scotch body, arrayed himself in stiff black and a boiled white shirt, and shaved his spare clean un-aging face, descended from his chamber in his residence on Cumberland Avenue, to his breakfast of oatmeal, dry toast, and boiled milk. His heart was pure, his mind upright, his faith and his life like a clean board scrubbed with sandstone. He prayed in thirty-minute prayers without impertinence for all men and the success of all good ventures. He was a white unwasting flame that shone through love and death; his speech rang out like steel with a steady passion.

In Dr. Frank Engel's Sanitarium and Turkish Bath Establishment on Liberty Street, Mr. J. H. Brown, wealthy sportsman and publisher of the *Altamont Citizen,* sank into dreamless sleep, after five minutes in the steam-closet, ten in the tub, and thirty in the dry-room, where he had submitted to the expert osteopathy of "Colonel" Andrews (as Dr. Engel's skilled negro masseur was affectionately known), from the soles of his gouty feet to the veinous silken gloss of his slightly purple face.

Across the street, at the corner of Liberty and Federal, and at the foot of Battery Hill, a white-jacketed negro sleepily restacked in boxes the scattered poker-chips that covered the centre table in the upstairs centre room of the Altamont City Club. The guests, just departed, were Mr. Gilbert Woodcock, Mr. Reeves Stikeleather, Mr. Henry Pentland, Jr.,

Mr. Sidney Newbeck, of Cleveland, Ohio (retired), and the aforementioned Mr. J. H. Brown.

"And, Jesus, Ben!" said Harry Tugman, emerging at this moment
from Uneeda No. 3, "I thought I'd have a hemorrhage when they pulled
the Old Man out of the closet. After all the stuff he printed about
cleaning up the town, too."

"It wouldn't surprise me if Judge Sevier had them raid him," said Ben.

"Why certainly, Ben," said Harry Tugman impatiently, "that's the idea,
but Queen Elizabeth was behind it. You don't think there's anything she
doesn't hear about, do you? So help me Jesus, you never heard a yap
out of him for a week. He was afraid to show his face out of the office."

At the Convent School of Saint Catherine's on Saint Clement's Road,
Sister Theresa, the Mother Superior, walked softly through the dormitory
lifting the window-shade beside each cot, letting the orchard cherry-apple
bloom come gently into the long cool glade of roseleaf sleeping girls.
Their breath expired gently upon their dewy half-opened mouths, light
fell rosily upon the pillowed curve of their arms, their slender young sides,
and the crisp pink buds of their breasts. At the other end of the room a
fat girl lay squarely on her back, her arms and legs outspread, and
snored solidly through blubbering lips. They had yet an hour of sleep.

From one of the little white tables between the cots Theresa picked up
an opened book incautiously left there the night before, read below her
gray mustache with the still inward smile of her great-boned face, its title
—*The Common Law*, by Robert W. Chambers—and gripping a pencil in
her broad earthstained hand, scrawled briefly in jagged male letters:
"Rubbish, Elizabeth—but see for yourself." Then, on her soft powerful
tread, she went downstairs, and entered her study, where Sister Louise
(French), Sister Mary (History), and Sister Bernice (Ancient Languages)
were waiting for the morning consultation. When they had gone, she sat
down to her desk and worked for an hour on the manuscript of that
book, modestly intended for school children, which has since celebrated her
name wherever the noble architecture of prose is valued—the great *Biology*.

Then the gong rang in the dormitory, she heard the high laughter of
young maidens, and rising saw, coming from the plum-tree by the wall, a
young nun, Sister Agnes, with blossoms in her arms.

Below, tree-hidden, in the Biltburn bottom, there was a thunder on the
rails, a wailing whistle cry.

Beneath the City Hall, in the huge sloping cellar, the market booths
were open. The aproned butchers swung their cleavers down on fresh

cold joints, slapping the thick chops on heavy sheets of mottled paper, and tossing them, roughly tied, to the waiting negro delivery-boys.

The self-respecting negro, J. H. Jackson, stood in his square vegetable-stall, attended by his two grave-faced sons, and his spectacled businesslike daughter. He was surrounded by wide slanting shelves of fruit and vegetables, smelling of the earth and morning—great crinkled lettuces, fat radishes still clotted damply with black loam, quill-stemmed young onions newly wrenched from gardens, late celery, spring potatoes, and the thin rinded citrous fruits of Florida.

Above him, Sorrell, the fish and oyster man, drew up from the depths of an enamelled ice-packed can dripping ladlefuls of oysters, pouring them into thick cardboard cartons. Wide-bellied heavy seafish—carp, trout, bass, shad—lay gutted in beds of ice.

Mr. Michael Walter Creech, the butcher, having finished his hearty breakfast of calves' liver, eggs and bacon, hot biscuits and coffee, made a sign to one of the waiting row of negro boys. The line sprang forward like hounds; he stopped them with a curse and a lifted cleaver. The fortunate youth who had been chosen then came forward and took the tray, still richly morselled with food and a pot half full of coffee. As he had to depart at this moment on a delivery, he put it down in the saw-dust at the end of the bench and spat copiously upon it in order to protect it from his scavenging comrades. Then he wheeled off, full of rich laughter and triumphant malice. Mr. Creech looked at his niggers darkly.

The town had so far forgotten Mr. Creech's own African blood (an eighth on his father's side, old Walter Creech, out of Yellow Jenny) that it was about ready to offer him political preferment; but Mr. Creech himself had not forgotten. He glanced bitterly at his brother, Jay, who, happily ignorant of hatred, that fanged poison which may taint even a brother's heart, was enthusiastically cleaving spare-ribs on the huge bole of his own table, singing meanwhile in a rich tenor voice the opening bars of "The Little Gray Home In The West":

> ". . . there are blue eyes that shine
> Just because they meet mine . . ."

Mr. Creech looked venomously at Jay's yellow jowls, the fat throbbing of his jaundiced throat, the crisp singed whorl of his hair.

By God, he thought in his anguish of spirit, he might be taken for a Mexican.

Jay's golden voice neared its triumph, breaking with delicate restraint, on the last note, into a high sweet falsetto which he maintained for more than twenty seconds. All of the butchers stopped working, several of them, big strong men with grown-up families dashed a tear out of their eyes.

The great audience was held spellbound. Not a soul stirred. Not even a dog or a horse stirred. As the last sweet note melted away in a gossamer tremolo, a silence profound as that of the tombs, nay, of death itself, betokened the highest triumph the artist is destined to know upon this earth. Somewhere in the crowd a woman sobbed and collapsed in a faint. She was immediately carried out by two Boy Scouts who happened to be present, and who administered first aid to her in the rest-room, one of them hastily kindling a crackling fire of pine boughs by striking two flints together, while the other made a tourniquet, and tied several knots in his handkerchief. Then pandemonium broke loose. Women tore the jewels from their fingers, ropes of pearls from their necks, chrysanthemums, hyacinths, tulips and daisies from their expensive corsages, while the fashionably-dressed men in the near-by stalls kept up a constant bombardment of tomatoes, lettuces, new potatoes, beef-tallow, pigs' knuckles, fish-heads, clams, loin-chops, and pork-sausages.

Among the stalls of the market, the boarding-house keepers of Altamont walked with spying bargain-hunting eyes and inquisitive nose. They were of various sizes and ages, but they were all stamped with the print of haggling determination and a pugnacious closure of the mouth. They pried in among the fish and vegetables, pinching cabbages, weighing onions, exfoliating lettuce-heads. You've got to keep your eye on people or they'll skin you. And if you leave things to a lazy shiftless nigger she'll waste more than she cooks. They looked at one another hardfaced—Mrs. Barrett of the Grosvenor at Mrs. Neville of Glen View; Mrs. Ambler of the Colonial at Miss Mamie Featherstone of Ravencrest; Mrs. Ledbetter of the Belvedere——

"I hear you're full up, Mrs. Coleman," said she inquiringly.

"O, I'm full up all the time," said Mrs. Coleman. "My people are all permanents, I don't want to fool with the transients," she said loftily.

"Well," said Mrs. Ledbetter acidly, "I could fill my house up at any time with lungers who call themselves something else, but I won't have them. I was saying the other day——"

Mrs. Michalove of Oakwood at Mrs. Jarvis of The Waverley; Mrs. Cowan of Ridgmont at——

The city is splendidly equipped to meet the demands of the great and steadily growing crowd of tourists that fill the Mountain Metropolis during the busy months of June, July, and August. In addition to eight hotels de luxe of the highest quality, there were registered at the Board of Trade

in 1911 over 250 private hotels, boarding-houses and sanitariums all
catering to the needs of those who come on missions of business, pleasure,
or health.

Stop their baggage at the station.

At this moment Number 3, having finished his route, stepped softly on
to the slime-scummed porch of the house on Valley Street, rapped gently
at the door, and opened it quietly, groping his way through black miasmic
air to the bed in which May Corpening lay. She muttered as if drugged
as he touched her, turned toward him, and sleepily awakened, drew him
down to her with heavied and sensual caress, yoked under her big coppery
arms. Tom Cline clumped greasily up the steps of his residence on Bartlett
Street, swinging his tin pail; Ben returned to the paper office with Harry
Tugman; and Eugene, in the back room on Woodson Street, waking
suddenly to Gant's powerful command from the foot of the stairs, turned
his face full into a momentary vision of roseflushed blue sky and tender
blossoms that drifted slowly earthward.

15

The mountains were his masters. They rimmed in life. They were the
cup of reality, beyond growth, beyond struggle and death. They were his
absolute unity in the midst of eternal change. Old haunt-eyed faces
glimmered in his memory. He thought of Swain's cow, St. Louis, death,
himself in the cradle. He was the haunter of himself, trying for a
moment to recover what he had been part of. He did not understand
change, he did not understand growth. He stared at his framed baby
picture in the parlor, and turned away sick with fear and the effort to
touch, retain, grasp himself for only a moment.

And these bodiless phantoms of his life appeared with terrible precision, with all the mad nearness of a vision. That which was five years
gone came within the touch of his hand, and he ceased at that moment
to believe in his own existence. He expected some one to wake him; he
would hear Gant's great voice below the laden vines, would gaze sleepily
from the porch into the rich low moon, and go obediently to bed. But still

there would be all that he remembered before that and what if—Cause flowed ceaselessly into cause.

He heard the ghostly ticking of his life; his powerful clairvoyance, the wild Scotch gift of Eliza, burned inward back across the phantom years, plucking out of the ghostly shadows a million gleams of light—a little station by the rails at dawn, the road cleft through the pineland seen at twilight, a smoky cabin-light below the trestles, a boy who ran among the bounding calves, a wisp-haired slattern, with snuff-sticked mouth, framed in a door, floury negroes unloading sacks from freight-cars on a shed, the man who drove the Fair Grounds bus at Saint Louis, a cool-lipped lake at dawn.

His life coiled back into the brown murk of the past like a twined filament of electric wire; he gave life, a pattern, and movement to these million sensations that Chance, the loss or gain of a moment, the turn of the head, the enormous and aimless impulsion of accident, had thrust into the blazing heat of him. His mind picked out in white living brightness these pinpoints of experience and the ghostliness of all things else became more awful because of them. So many of the sensations that returned to open haunting vistas of fantasy and imagining had been caught from a whirling landscape through the windows of the train.

And it was this that awed him—the weird combination of fixity and change, the terrible moment of immobility stamped with eternity in which, passing life at great speed, both the observer and the observed seem frozen in time. There was one moment of timeless suspension when the land did not move, the train did not move, the slattern in the doorway did not move, he did not move. It was as if God had lifted his baton sharply above the endless orchestration of the seas, and the eternal movement had stopped, suspended in the timeless architecture of the absolute. Or like those motion-pictures that describe the movements of a swimmer making a dive, or a horse taking a hedge—movement is petrified suddenly in mid-air, the inexorable completion of an act is arrested. Then, completing its parabola, the suspended body plops down into the pool. Only, these images that burnt in him existed without beginning or ending, without the essential structure of time. Fixed in no-time, the slattern vanished, fixed, without a moment of transition.

His sense of unreality came from time and movement, from imagining the woman, when the train had passed, as walking back into the house, lifting a kettle from the hearth embers. Thus life turned shadow, the living lights went ghost again. The boy among the calves. Where later? Where now?

I am, he thought, a part of all that I have touched and that has touched me, which, having for me no existence save that which I gave to it, became other than itself by being mixed with what I then was, and is now still otherwise, having fused with what I now am, which is itself a cumulation of what I have been becoming. Why here? Why there? Why now? Why then?

The fusion of the two strong egotisms, Eliza's inbrooding and Gant's expanding outward, made of him a fanatical zealot in the religion of Chance. Beyond all misuse, waste, pain, tragedy, death, confusion, unswerving necessity was on the rails; not a sparrow fell through the air but that its repercussion acted on his life, and the lonely light that fell upon the viscous and interminable seas at dawn awoke sea-changes washing life to him. The fish swam upward from the depth.

The seed of our destruction will blossom in the desert, the alexin of our cure grows by a mountain rock, and our lives are haunted by a Georgia slattern because a London cut-purse went unhung. Through Chance, we are each a ghost to all the others, and our only reality; through Chance, the huge hinge of the world, and a grain of dust; the stone that starts an avalanche, the pebble whose concentric circles widen across the seas.

He believed himself thus at the centre of life; he believed the mountains rimmed the heart of the world; he believed that from all the chaos of accident the inevitable event came at the inexorable moment to add to the sum of his life.

Against the hidden other flanks of the immutable hills the world washed like a vast and shadowy sea, alive with the great fish of his imagining. Variety, in this unvisited world, was unending, but order and purpose certain: there would be no wastage in adventure—courage would be regarded with beauty, talent with success, all merit with its true deserving. There would be peril, there would be toil, there would be struggle. But there would not be confusion and waste. There would not be groping. For collected Fate would fall, on its chosen moment, like a plum. There was no disorder in enchantment.

Spring lay abroad through all the garden of this world. Beyond the hills the land bayed out to other hills, to golden cities, to rich meadows, to deep forests, to the sea. Forever and forever.

Beyond the hills were the mines of King Solomon, the toy republics of Central America, and little tinkling fountains in a court; beyond, the moonlit roofs of Bagdad, the little grated blinds of Samarkand, the moonlit camels of Bythinia, the Spanish ranch-house of the Triple Z, and J. B. Montgomery and his lovely daughter stepping from their private car upon a western track; and the castle-haunted crags of Graustark; the fortune-yielding casino of Monte Carlo; and the blue eternal Mediterranean, mother of empires. And instant wealth ticked out upon a tape, and the first stage of the Eiffel Tower where the restaurant was, and Frenchmen setting fire to their whiskers, and a farm in Devon, white cream, brown ale, the winter's chimney merriment, and *Lorna Doone;* and the hanging gardens of Babylon, and supper in the sunset with the queens, and the slow slide of the barge upon the Nile, or the wise rich bodies of Egyptian women couched on moonlit balustrades, and the thunder of the chariots of great kings, and tomb-treasure sought at midnight, and the wine-rich chateau land of France, and calico warm legs in hay.

Upon a field in Thrace Queen Helen lay, her lovely body dappled in the sun.

Meanwhile, business had been fairly good. Eliza's earning power the first few years at Dixieland had been injured by her illnesses. Now, however, she had recovered, and had paid off the last installment on the house. It was entirely hers. The property at this time was worth perhaps $12,000. In addition she had borrowed $3,500 on a twenty-year $5,000 life insurance policy that had only two years more to run, and had made extensive alterations: she had added a large sleeping-porch upstairs, tacked on two rooms, a bath, and a hallway on one side, and extended a hallway, adding three bedrooms, two baths, and a water-closet, on the other. Downstairs she had widened the veranda, put in a large sun-parlor under the sleeping-porch, knocked out the archway in the dining-room, which she prepared to use as a big bedroom in the slack season, scooped out a small pantry in which the family was to eat, and added a tiny room beside the kitchen for her own occupancy.

The construction was after her own plans, and of the cheapest material: it never lost the smell of raw wood, cheap varnish, and flimsy rough plastering, but she had added eight or ten rooms at a cost of only $3,000. The year before she had banked almost $2,000—her bank account was almost $5,000. In addition, she owned jointly with Gant the shop on the Square, which had thirty feet of frontage, and was valued at $20,000, from which he got $65 a month in rent; $20 from Jannadeau, $25 from the McLean Plumbing Company in the basement, and $20 from the J. N. Gillespie Printing Co., which occupied all of the second story.

There were, besides, three good building-lots on Merrion Avenue valued at $2,000 apiece, or at $5,500 for all three; the house on Woodson Street valued at $5,000; 110 acres of wooded mountainside with a farm-house, several hundred peach, apple and cherry trees, and a few acres of arable ground for which Gant received $120 a year in rent, and which they valued at $50 an acre, $5,500; two houses, one on Carter Street, and one on Duncan, rented to railway people, for which they received $25 a month apiece, and which they valued together at $4,500; forty-eight acres of land two miles above Biltburn, and four from Altamont, upon the important Reynoldsville Road, which they valued at $210 an acre, or $10,000; three houses in Niggertown—one on lower Valley Street, one on Beaumont Crescent, just below the negro Johnson's big house, and one on Short Oak, valued at $600, $900, and $1,600 respectively, and drawing a room-rental of $8, $12, and $17 a month (total: $3,100 and $37 rental); two houses across the river, four miles away in West Altamont, valued at $2,750 and at $3,500, drawing a rental of $22 and $30 a month; three lots, lost in the growth of a rough hillside, a mile from the main highway through West Altamont, $500; and a house, unoccupied, object of Gantian anathema, on Lower Hatton Avenue, $4,500.

In addition, Gant held 10 shares, which were already worth $200 each ($2,000), in the newly organized Fidelity Bank; his stock of stones, monuments, and fly-specked angels represented an investment of $2,700, although he could not have sold them outright for so much; and he had about $3,000 deposited in the Fidelity, the Merchants, and the Battery Hill banks.

Thus, at the beginning of 1912, before the rapid and intensive development of Southern industry, and the consequent tripling of Altamont's population, and before the multiplication of her land values, the wealth of Gant and Eliza amounted to about $100,000, the great bulk of which was solidly founded in juicy well chosen pieces of property of Eliza's selection, yielding them a monthly rental of more than $200, which, added to their own earning capacities at the shop and Dixieland, gave them a combined yearly income of $8,000 or $10,000. Although Gant often cried out bitterly against his business and declared, when he was not attacking property, that he had never made even a bare living from his tombstones, he was rarely short of ready money: he usually had one or two small commissions from country people, and he always carried a well-filled purse, containing $150 or $200 in five- and ten-dollar bills, which he allowed

Eugene to count out frequently, enjoying his son's delight, and the feel of abundance.

Eliza had suffered one or two losses in her investments, led astray by a strain of wild romanticism which destroyed for the moment her shrewd caution. She invested $1,200 in the Missouri Utopia of a colonizer, and received nothing for her money but a weekly copy of the man's newspaper, several beautiful prospectuses of the look of things when finished, and a piece of clay sculpture, eight inches in height, showing Big Brother with his little sisters Jenny and Kate, the last with thumb in her mouth.

"By God," said Gant, who made savage fun of the proceeding, "she ought to have it on her nose."

And Ben sneered, jerking his head toward it, saying:

"There's her $1,200."

But Eliza was preparing to go on by herself. She saw that co-operation with Gant in the purchase of land was becoming more difficult each year. And with something like pain, something assuredly like hunger, she saw various rich plums fall into other hands or go unbought. She realized that in a very short time land values would soar beyond her present means. And she proposed to be on hand when the pie was cut.

Across the street from Dixieland was the Brunswick, a well-built red brick house of twenty rooms. The marble facings had been done by Gant himself twenty years before, the hardwood floors and oak timbering by Will Pentland. It was an ugly gabled Victorian house, the marriage gift of a rich Northerner to his daughter, who died of tuberculosis.

"Not a better built house in town," said Gant.

Nevertheless he refused to buy it with Eliza, and with an aching heart she saw it go to St. Greenberg, the rich junk-man, for $8,500. Within a year he had sold off five lots at the back, on the Yancy Street side, for $1,000 each, and was holding the house for $20,000.

"We could have had our money back by now three times over," Eliza fretted.

She did not have enough money at the time for any important investment. She saved and she waited.

Will Pentland's fortune at this time was vaguely estimated at from $500,000 to $700,000. It was mainly in property, a great deal of which was situated—warehouses and buildings—near the passenger depot of the railway.

Sometimes Altamont people, particularly the young men who loafed about Collister's drug-store, and who spent long dreamy hours estimating the wealth of the native plutocracy, called Will Pentland a millionaire. At this time it was a distinction in American life to be a millionaire. There were only six or eight thousand. But Will Pentland wasn't one. He was really worth only a half million.

Mr. Goulderbilt was a millionaire. He was driven into town in a big Packard, but he got out and went along the streets like other men.

One time Gant pointed him out to Eugene. He was about to enter a bank. "There he is," whispered Gant. "Do you see him?"

Eugene nodded, wagging his head mechanically. He was unable to speak. Mr. Goulderbilt was a small dapper man, with black hair, black clothes, and a black mustache. His hands and feet were small.

"He's got over $50,000,000," said Gant. "You'd never think it to look at him, would you?"

And Eugene dreamed of these money princes living in a princely fashion. He wanted to see them riding down a street in a crested coach around which rode a teetering guard of liveried outriders. He wanted their fingers to be heavily gemmed, their clothes trimmed with ermine, their women coroneted with flashing mosaics of amethyst, beryl, ruby, topaz, sapphire, opal, emerald, and wearing thick ropes of pearls. And he wanted to see them living in palaces of alabaster columns, eating in vast halls upon an immense creamy table from vessels of old silver—eating strange fabulous foods—swelling unctuous paps of a fat pregnant sow, oiled mushrooms, calvered salmon, jugged hare, the beards of barbels dressed with an exquisite and poignant sauce, carps' tongues, dormice and camels' heels, with spoons of amber headed with diamond and carbuncle, and cups of agate, studded with emeralds, hyacinths, and rubies—everything, in fact, for which Epicure Mammon wished.

Eugene met only one millionaire whose performances in public satisfied him, and he, unhappily, was crazy. His name was Simon.

Simon, when Eugene first saw him, was a man of almost fifty years. He had a strong, rather heavy figure of middling height, a lean brown face, with shadowy hollows across the cheeks, always closely shaven, but sometimes badly scarred by his gouging fingernails, and a long thin mouth that curved slightly downward, subtle, sensitive, lighting his whole face at times with blazing demoniac glee. He had straight abundant hair, heavily grayed, which he kept smartly brushed and flattened at the sides. His clothing was loose and well cut: he wore a dark coat above baggy gray flannels, silk shirt rayed with broad stripes, a collar to match, and a generous loosely knotted tie. His waistcoats were of a ruddy-brown chequered pattern. He had an appearance of great distinction.

Simon and his two keepers first came to Dixieland when difficulties with several of the Altamont hotels forced them to look for private quarters. The men took two rooms and a sleeping-porch, and paid generously.

"Why, pshaw!" said Eliza persuasively to Helen. "I don't believe there's a thing wrong with him. He's as quiet and well-behaved as you please."

At this moment there was a piercing yell upstairs, followed by a long peal of diabolical laughter. Eugene bounded up and down the hall in his exultancy and delight, producing little squealing noises in his throat. Ben, scowling, with a quick flicker of his mouth, drew back his hard white hand swiftly as if to cuff his brother. Instead, he jerked his head sideways to Eliza, and said with a soft, scornful laugh: "By God, mama, I don't see why you have to take them in. You've got enough of them in the family already."

"Mama, in heaven's name—" Helen began furiously. At this moment Gant strode in out of the dusk, carrying a mottled package of pork chops, and muttering rhetorically to himself. There was another long peal of laughter above. He halted abruptly, startled, and lifted his head. Luke, listening attentively at the foot of the stairs, exploded in a loud boisterous guffaw, and the girl, her annoyance changing at once to angry amusement, walked toward her father's inquiring face, and prodded him several times in the ribs.

"Hey?" he said startled. "What is it?"

"Miss Eliza's got a crazy man upstairs," she sniggered, enjoying his amazement.

"Jesus God!" Gant yelled frantically, wetting his big thumb swiftly on his tongue, and glancing up toward his Maker with an attitude of exaggerated supplication in his small gray eyes and the thrust of his huge bladelike nose. Then, letting his arms slap heavily at his sides, in a gesture of defeat, he began to walk rapidly back and forth, clucking his deprecation loudly. Eliza stood solidly, looking from one to another, her lips working rapidly, her white face hurt and bitter.

There was another long howl of mirth above. Gant paused, caught Helen's eye, and began to grin suddenly in an unwilling sheepish manner.

"God have mercy on us," he chuckled. "She'll have the place filled with all of Barnum's freaks the next thing you know."

At this moment, Simon, self-contained, distinguished and grave in his manner, descended the steps with Mr. Gilroy and Mr. Flannagan, his companions. The two guards were red in the face, and breathed stertorously as if from some recent exertion. Simon, however, preserved his habitual appearance of immaculate and well-washed urbanity.

"Good evening," he remarked suavely. "I hope I have not kept you waiting long." He caught sight of Eugene.

"Come here, my boy," he said very kindly.

"It's all right," remarked Mr. Gilroy, encouragingly. "He wouldn't hurt a fly."

Eugene moved into the presence.

"And what is your name, young man?" said Simon with his beautiful devil's smile.

"Eugene."

"That's a very fine name," said Simon. "Always try to live up to it." He thrust his hand carelessly and magnificently into his coat pocket, drawing out under the boy's astonished eyes, a handful of shining five and ten-cent pieces.

"Always be good to the birds, my boy," said Simon, and he poured the money into Eugene's cupped hands.

Every one looked doubtfully at Mr. Gilroy.

"Oh, that's all right!" said Mr. Gilroy cheerfully. "He'll never miss it. There's lots more where that came from."

"He's a mul-tye-millionaire," Mr. Flannagan explained proudly. "We give him four or five dollars in small change every morning just to throw away."

Simon caught sight of Gant for the first time.

"Look out for the Stingaree," he cried. "Remember the Maine."

"I tell you what," said Eliza laughing. "He's not so crazy as you think."

"That's right," said Mr. Gilroy, noting Gant's grin. "The Stingaree's a fish. They have them in Florida."

"Don't forget the birds, my friends," said Simon, going out with his companions. "Be good to the birds."

They became very fond of him. Somehow he fitted into the pattern of their life. None of them was uncomfortable in the presence of madness. In the flowering darkness of Spring, prisoned in a room, his satanic laughter burst suddenly out: Eugene listened, thrilled, and slept, unable to forget the smile of dark flowering evil, the loose pocket chinking heavily with coins.

Night, the myriad rustle of tiny wings. Heard lapping water of the inland seas.

—And the air will be filled with warm-throated plum-dropping bird-notes. He was almost twelve. He was done with childhood. As that Spring ripened he felt entirely, for the first time, the full delight of loneliness. Sheeted in his thin nightgown, he stood in darkness by the orchard window of the back room at Gant's, drinking the sweet air down, exulting in his isolation in darkness, hearing the strange wail of the whistle going west.

The prison walls of self had closed entirely round him; he was walled completely by the esymplastic power of his imagination—he had learned by now to project mechanically, before the world, an acceptable counterfeit of himself which would protect him from intrusion. He no longer went through the torment of the recess flight and pursuit. He was now in one of the upper grades of grammar school, he was one of the Big Boys. His hair had been cut when he was nine years old, after a bitter seige against Eliza's obstinacy. He no longer suffered because of the curls. But he had grown like a weed, he already topped his mother by an inch or two; his body was big-boned but very thin and fragile, with no meat on it; his legs were absurdly long, thin, and straight, giving him a curious scissored look as he walked with long bounding strides.

Stuck on a thin undeveloped neck beneath a big wide-browed head covered thickly by curling hair which had changed, since his infancy, from a light maple to dark brown-black, was a face so small, and so delicately sculptured, that it seemed not to belong to its body. The strangeness, the remote quality of this face was enhanced by its brooding fabulous concentration, by its passionate dark intensity, across which every splinter of thought or sensation flashed like a streak of light across a pool. The mouth was full, sensual, extraordinarily mobile, the lower lip deeply scooped and pouting. His rapt dreaming intensity set the face usually in an expression of almost sullen contemplation; he smiled, oftener than he laughed, inwardly, at some extravagant invention, or some recollection of the absurd, now fully appreciated for the first time. He did not open his lips to smile—there was a swift twisted flicker across his mouth. His thick heavily arched eyebrows grew straight across the base of his nose.

That Spring he was more alone than ever. Eliza's departure for Dixieland three or four years before, and the disruption of established life at Gant's, had begun the loosening of his first friendships with the neighborhood boys, Harry Tarkinton, Max Isaacs, and the others, and had now almost completely severed them. Occasionally he saw these boys again, occasionally he resumed again, at sporadic intervals, his association with them, but he now had no steady companionship, he had only a series of associations with children whose parents stayed for a time at Dixieland, with Tim O'Doyle, whose mother ran the Brunswick, with children here and there who briefly held his interest.

But he became passionately bored with them, plunged into a miasmic swamp of weariness and horror, after a time, because of the dullness and ugliness of their lives, their minds, their amusements. Dull people filled him with terror: he was never so much frightened by tedium in his own life as in the lives of others—his early distaste for Pett Pentland and her grim rusty aunts came from submerged memories of the old house on Central Avenue, the smell of mellow apples and medicine in the hot room, the swooping howl of the wind outside, and the endless monotone of their conversation on disease, death, and misery. He was filled with terror and anger against them because they were able to live, to thrive, in this horrible depression that sickened him.

Thus, the entire landscape, the whole physical background of his life, was now dappled by powerful prejudices of liking and distaste formed, God knows how, or by what intangible affinities of thought, feeling and connotation. Thus, one street would seem to him to be a "good street"—to exist in the rich light of cheerful, abundant, and high-hearted living; another, inexplicably, a "bad street," touching him somehow with fear, hopelessness, depression.

Perhaps the cold red light of some remembered winter's afternoon, waning pallidly over a playing-field, with all its mockery of Spring, while lights flared up smokily in houses, the rabble-rout of children dirtily went in to supper, and men came back to the dull but warm imprisonment of home, oil lamps (which he hated), and bedtime, clotted in him a hatred of the place which remained even when the sensations that caused it were forgotten.

Or, returning from some country walk in late autumn, he would come back from Cove or Valley with dewy nose, clotted boots, the smell of a mashed persimmon on his knee, and the odor of wet earth and grass on the palms of his hands, and with a stubborn dislike and suspicion of the scene he had visited, and fear of the people who lived there.

He had the most extraordinary love of incandescence. He hated dull lights, smoky lights, soft, or sombre lights. At night he wanted to be in rooms brilliantly illuminated with beautiful, blazing, sharp, poignant lights. After that, the dark.

He played games badly, although he took a violent interest in sports. Max Isaacs continued to interest him as an athlete long after he had ceased to interest him as a person. The game Max Isaacs excelled in was baseball. Usually he played one of the outfield positions, ranging easily about in his field, when a ball was hit to him, with the speed of a panther, making impossible catches with effortless grace. He was a terrific hitter, standing at the plate casually but alertly, and meeting the ball squarely with a level swinging smack of his heavy shoulders. Eugene tried vainly to imitate the precision and power of this movement, which drove the ball in a smoking arc out of the lot, but he was never able: he chopped down clumsily and blindly, knocking a futile bounder to some nimble baseman. In the field he was equally useless: he never learned to play in a team, to become a limb of that single animal which united telepathically in a concerted movement. He became nervous, highly excited, and erratic in team-play, but he spent hours alone with another boy, or, after the mid-day meal, with Ben, passing a ball back and forth.

He developed blinding speed, bending all the young suppleness of his long thin body behind the ball, exulting as it smoked into the pocket of the mitt with a loud smack, or streaked up with a sharp dropping curve. Ben, taken by surprise by a fast drop, would curse him savagely, and in a rage hurl the ball back into his thin gloved hand. In the Spring and Summer he went as often as he could afford it, or was invited, to the baseball games in the district league, a fanatic partisan of the town club and its best players, making a fantasy constantly of himself in a heroic game-saving rôle.

But he was in no way able to submit himself to the discipline, the hard labor, the acceptance of defeat and failure that make a good athlete; he wanted always to win, he wanted always to be the general, the heroic spear-head of victory. And after that he wanted to be loved. Victory and love. In all of his swarming fantasies Eugene saw himself like this—unbeaten and beloved. But moments of clear vision returned to him when all the defeat and misery of his life was revealed. He saw his gangling and absurd figure, his remote unpractical brooding face, too like a dark strange flower to arouse any feeling among his companions and his kin, he thought, but discomfort, bitterness, and mockery; he remembered, with a drained sick heart, the countless humiliations, physical and verbal, he had endured, at the hands of school and family, before the world, and as he thought, the horns of victory died within the wood, the battle-drums of triumph stopped, the proud clangor of the gongs quivered away in silence. His eagles had flown; he saw himself, in a moment of reason, as a madman playing Cæsar. He craned his head aside and covered his face with his hand.

16

The Spring grew ripe. There was at mid-day a soft drowsiness in the sun. Warm sporting gusts of wind howled faintly at the eaves; the young grass bent; the daisies twinkled.

He pressed his high knees uncomfortably against the bottom of his desk, grew nostalgic on his dreams. Bessie Barnes scrawled vigorously two rows away, displaying her long full silken leg. Open for me the gates of delight. Behind her sat a girl named Ruth, dark, with milk-white skin, eyes as gentle as her name, and thick black hair, parted in middle. He thought of a wild life with Bessie and of a later resurrection, a pure holy life, with Ruth.

One day, after the noon recess, they were marshalled by the teachers— all of the children in the three upper grades—and marched upstairs to the big assembly hall. They were excited, and gossiped in low voices as they went. They had never been called upstairs at this hour. Quite often the bells rang in the halls: they sprang quickly into line and were marched out in double files. That was fire drill. They liked that. Once they emptied the building in four minutes.

This was something new. They marched into the big room and sat down in blocks of seats assigned to each class: they sat with a seat between each of them. In a moment the door of the principal's office on the left—where little boys were beaten—was opened, and the principal came out. He walked around the corner of the big room and stepped softly up on the platform. He began to talk.

He was a new principal. Young Armstrong, who had smelled the flower so delicately, and who had visited Daisy, and who once had almost beaten Eugene because of the smutty rhymes, was gone. The new principal was older. He was about thirty-eight years old. He was a strong rather heavy man a little under six feet tall; he was one of a large family who had grown up on a Tennessee farm. His father was poor but he had helped his children to get an education. All this Eugene knew already, because the principal made long talks to them in the morning and said he had never had their advantages. He pointed to himself with some pride. And he urged the little boys, playfully but earnestly, to "be not like dumb driven cattle, be a hero in the strife." That was poetry, Longfellow.

The principal had thick powerful shoulders; clumsy white arms, knotted with big awkward country muscles. Eugene had seen him once hoeing in the schoolyard; each of them had been given a plant to set out. He got those muscles on the farm. The boys said he beat very hard. He walked with a clumsy stealthy tread—awkward and comical enough, it is true, but he could be up at a boy's back before you knew it. Otto Krause called him Creeping Jesus. The name stuck, among the tough crowd. Eugene was a little shocked by it.

The principal had a white face of waxen transparency, with deep flat cheeks like the Pentlands, a pallid nose, a trifle deeper in its color than his face, and a thin slightly-bowed mouth. His hair was coarse, black, and thick, but he never let it grow too long. He had short dry hands, strong, and always coated deeply with chalk. When he passed near by, Eugene got the odor of chalk and of the schoolhouse: his heart grew cold with excitement and fear. The sanctity of chalk and school hovered about the man's flesh. He was the one who could touch without being touched, beat without being beaten. Eugene had terrible fantasies of resistance, shuddering with horror as he thought of the awful consequences of fighting back: something like God's fist in lighting. Then he looked around cautiously to see if any one had noticed.

The principal's name was Leonard. He made long speeches to the children every morning, after a ten-minute prayer. He had a high sonorous countrified voice which often trailed off in a comical drawl; he got lost very easily in revery, would pause in the middle of a sentence, gaze absently off with his mouth half-open and an expression of stupefaction on his face, and return presently to the business before him, his mind still loose, with witless distracted laugh.

He talked to the children aimlessly, pompously, dully for twenty minutes every morning: the teachers yawned carefully behind their hands, the students made furtive drawings, or passed notes. He spoke to them of "the higher life" and of "the things of the mind." He assured them that they were the leaders of to-morrow and the hope of the world. Then he quoted Longfellow.

He was a good man, a dull man, a man of honor. He had a broad streak of coarse earthy brutality in him. He loved a farm better than anything in the world except a school. He had rented a big dilapidated house in a grove of lordly oaks on the outskirts of town: he lived there with his wife and his two children. He had a cow—he was never without a cow: he would go out at night and morning to milk her, laughing his vacant silly laugh, and giving her a good smacking kick in the belly to make her come round into position.

He was a heavy-handed master. He put down rebellion with good cornfield violence. If a boy was impudent to him he would rip him powerfully from his seat, drag his wriggling figure into his office, breathing stertorously as he walked along at his clumsy rapid gait, and saying roundly, in tones of scathing contempt: "Why, you young upstart, we'll just see who's master here. I'll just show you, my sonny, if I'm to be dictated to by every two-by-four whippersnapper who comes along." And once within the office, with the glazed door shut, he published the stern warning of his justice by the loud exertion of his breathing, the cutting swish of his rattan, and the yowls of pain and terror that he exacted from his captive.

He had called the school together that day to command it to write him a composition. The children sat, staring dumbly up at him as he made a rambling explanation of what he wanted. Finally he announced a prize. He would give five dollars from his own pocket to the student who wrote the best paper. That aroused them. There was a rustle of interest.

They were to write a paper on the meaning of a French picture called The Song of the Lark. It represented a French peasant girl, barefooted, with a sickle in one hand, and with face upturned in the morning-light of the fields as she listened to the bird-song. They were asked to describe what they saw in the expression of the girl's face. They were asked to tell what the picture meant to them. It had been reproduced in one of their readers. A larger print was now hung up on the platform for their inspection. Sheets of yellow paper were given them. They stared, thoughtfully masticating their pencils. Finally, the room was silent save for a minute scratching on paper.

The warm wind spouted about the eaves; the grasses bent, whistling gently.

Eugene wrote: "The girl is hearing the song of the first lark. She knows that it means Spring has come. She is about seventeen or eighteen years old. Her people are very poor, she has never been anywhere. In the winter she wears wooden shoes. She is making out as if she was going to whistle. But she doesn't let on to the bird that she has heard him. The rest of her people are behind her, coming down the field, but we do not see them. She has a father, a mother, and two brothers. They have worked hard all their life. The girl is the youngest child. She thinks she would

like to go away somewhere and see the world. Sometimes she hears the
whistle of a train that is going to Paris. She has never ridden on a train
in her life. She would like to go to Paris. She would like to have some fine
clothes, she would like to travel. Perhaps she would like to start life new
in America, the Land of Opportunity. The girl has had a hard time. Her
people do not understand her. If they saw her listening to the lark they
would poke fun at her. She has never had the advantages of a good education, her people are so poor, but she would profit by her opportunity if
she did, more than some people who have. You can tell by looking at her
that she's intelligent."

It was early in May; examinations came in another two weeks. He
thought of them with excitement and pleasure—he liked the period of
hard cramming, the long reviews, the delight of emptying out abundantly
on paper his stored knowledge. The big assembly room had about it the
odor of completion, of sharp nervous ecstasy. All through the summer it
would be drowsy-warm; if only here, alone, with the big plaster cast of
Minerva, himself and Bessie Barnes, or Miss—Miss—

"We want this boy," said Margaret Leonard. She handed Eugene's
paper over to her husband. They were starting a private school for boys.
That was what the paper had been for.

Leonard took the paper, pretended to read half a page, looked off
absently into eternity, and began to rub his chin reflectively, leaving a
slight coating of chalk-dust on his face. Then, catching her eye, he laughed
idiotically, and said: "Why, that little rascal! Huh? Do you suppose——?"

Feeling delightfully scattered, he bent over with a long suction of
whining laughter, slapping his knee and leaving a chalk print, making a
slobbering noise in his mouth.

"The Lord have mercy!" he gasped.

"Here! Never you mind about that," she said, laughing with tender
sharp amusement. "Pull yourself together and see this boy's people." She
loved the man dearly, and he loved her.

A few days later Leonard assembled the children a second time. He
made a rambling speech, the purport of which was to inform them that
one of them had won the prize, but to conceal the winner's name. Then,
after several divagations, which he thoroughly enjoyed, he read Eugene's
paper, announced his name, and called him forward.

Chalkface took chalkhand. The boy's heart thundered against his ribs.
The proud horns blared, he tasted glory.

Patiently, all through the summer, Leonard laid siege to Gant and Eliza.
Gant fidgeted, spoke shiftily, finally said:

"You'll have to see his mother." Privately he was bitterly scornful, roared the merits of the public school as an incubator of citizenship. The family was contemptuous. Private school! Mr. Vanderbilt! Ruin him for good!

Which made Eliza reflective. She had a good streak of snobbism. Mr. Vanderbilt? She was as good as any of them. They'd just see.

"Who are you going to have?" she asked. "Have you drummed any one up yet?"

Leonard mentioned the sons of several fashionable and wealthy people,— of Dr. Kitchen, the eye, ear, nose and throat man, Mr. Arthur, the corporation lawyer, and Bishop Raper, of the Episcopal diocese.

Eliza grew more reflective. She thought of Pett. She needn't give herself airs.

"How much are you asking?" she said.

He told her the tuition was one hundred dollars a year. She pursed her lips lingeringly before she answered.

"Hm-m!" she began, with a bantering smile, as she looked at Eugene. "That's a whole lot of money. You know," she continued with her tremulous smile, "as the darkey says, we're pore-folks."

Eugene squirmed.

"Well what about it, boy?" said Eliza banteringly. "Do you think you're worth that much money?"

Mr. Leonard placed his white dry hand upon Eugene's shoulders, affectionately sliding it down his back and across his kidneys, leaving white chalk prints everywhere. Then he clamped his meaty palm tightly around the slender bracelet of boy-arm.

"That boy's worth it," he said, shaking him gently to and fro. "Yes, sir!"

Eugene smiled painfully. Eliza continued to purse her lips. She felt a strong psychic relation to Leonard. They both took time.

"Say," she said, rubbing her broad red nose, and smiling slyly, "I used to be a school-teacher. You didn't know that, did you? But I didn't get any such prices as you're asking," she added. "I thought myself mighty lucky if I got my board and twenty dollars a month."

"Is that so, Mrs. Gant?" said Mr. Leonard with great interest. "Well, sir!" He began to laugh in a vague whine, pulling Eugene about more violently and deadening his arm under his crushing grip.

"Yes," said Eliza, "I remember my father—it was long before you were born, boy," she said to Eugene, "for I hadn't laid eyes on your papa—as the feller says, you were nothing but a dish-rag hanging out in heaven— I'd have laughed at any one who suggested marriage then—Well, I tell you what [she shook her head with a sad pursed deprecating mouth], we were mighty poor at the time, I can tell you.—I was thinking about it the other day—many's the time we didn't have food in the house for the next meal.—Well, as I was saying, your grandfather [addressing Eugene] came home one night and said—Look here, what about it?—Who do you suppose I saw to-day?—I remember him just as plain as if I saw him standing here—I had a feeling—[addressing Leonard with a doubtful smile] I don't know what you'd call it but it's pretty strange when you come to think about it, isn't it?—I had just finished helping Aunt Jane set the table—she had come all the way from Yancey County to visit your grandmother—when all of a sudden it flashed over me—mind you [to Leonard] I never looked out the window or anything but I knew just as well as I knew anything that he was coming—mercy I cried—here comes—why what on earth are you talking about, Eliza? said your grandma—I remember she went to the door and looked out down the path—there's no one there—He's acoming, I said—wait and see—Who? said your grandmother —Why, father, I said—he's carrying something on his shoulder—and sure enough—I had no sooner got the words out of my mouth than there he was just acoming it for all he was worth, up the path, with a tow-sack full of apples on his back—you could tell by the way he walked that he had news of some sort—well—sure enough—without stopping to say howdy-do—I remembered he began to talk almost before he got into the house—O father, I called out—you've brought the apples—it was the year after I had almost died of pneumonia—I'd been spitting up blood ever since—and having hemorrhages—and I asked him to bring me some apples —Well sir, mother said to him, and she looked mighty queer, I can tell you—that's the strangest thing I ever heard of—and she told him what had happened—Well, he looked pretty serious and said—Yes, I'll never forget the way he said it—I reckon she saw me. I wasn't there but I was thinking of being there and coming up the path at that very moment—I've got news for you he said—who do you suppose I saw to-day—why, I've no idea, I said—why old Professor Truman—he came rushing up to me in town and said, see here: where's Eliza—I've got a job for her if she wants it, teaching school this winter out on Beaverdam—why, pshaw, said your grandfather, she's never taught school a day in her life—and Professor Truman laughed just as big as you please and said never you mind about that—Eliza can do anything she sets her mind on—well sir, that's the way it all came about." High-sorrowful and sad, she paused for a moment, adrift, her white face slanting her life back through the aisled grove of years.

"Well, sir!" said Mr. Leonard vaguely, rubbing his chin, "You young rascal, you!" he said, giving Eugene another jerk, and beginning to laugh with narcissistic pleasure.

Eliza pursed her lips slowly.

"Well," she said, "I'll send him to you for a year." That was the way she did business. Tides run deep in Sargasso.

So, on the hairline of million-minded impulse, destiny bore down on his life again.

Mr. Leonard had leased an old pre-war house, set on a hill wooded by magnificent trees. It faced west and south, looking toward Biltburn, and abruptly down on South End, and the negro flats that stretched to the depot. One day early in September he took Eugene there. They walked across town, talking weightily of politics, across the Square, down Hatton Avenue, south into Church, and southwesterly along the bending road that ended in the schoolhouse on the abutting hill.

The huge trees made sad autumn music as they entered the grounds. In the broad hall of the squat rambling old house Eugene for the first time saw Margaret Leonard. She held a broom in her hands, and was aproned. But his first impression was of her shocking fragility.

Margaret Leonard at this time was thirty-four years old. She had borne two children, a son who was now six years old, and a daughter who was two. As she stood there, with her long slender fingers splayed about the broomstick, he noted, with a momentary cold nausea, that the tip of her right index finger was flattened out as if it had been crushed beyond healing by a hammer. But it was years before he knew that tuberculars sometimes have such fingers.

Margaret Leonard was of middling height, five feet six inches perhaps. As the giddiness of his embarrassment wore off he saw that she could not weigh more than eighty or ninety pounds. He had heard of the children. Now he remembered them, and Leonard's white muscular bulk, with a sense of horror. His swift vision leaped at once to the sexual relation, and something in him twisted aside, incredulous and afraid.

She had on a dress of crisp gray gingham, not loose or lapping round her wasted figure, but hiding every line in her body, like a draped stick.

As his mind groped out of the pain of impression he heard her voice and, still feeling within him the strange convulsive shame, he lifted his eyes to her face. It was the most tranquil and the most passionate face he had ever seen. The skin was sallow with a dead ashen tinge; beneath, the delicate bone-carving of face and skull traced itself clearly: the cadaverous tightness of those who are about to die had been checked. She had won her way back just far enough to balance carefully in the scales of disease and recovery. It was necessary for her to measure everything she did.

Her thin face was given a touch of shrewdness and decision by the straight line of her nose, the fine long carving of her chin. Beneath the sallow minutely pitted skin in her cheeks, and about her mouth, several frayed nerve-centres twitched from moment to moment, jarring the skin slightly without contorting or destroying the passionate calm beauty that fed her inexhaustibly from within. This face was the constant field of conflict, nearly always calm, but always reflecting the incessant struggle and victory of the enormous energy that inhabited her, over the thousand jangling devils of depletion and weariness that tried to pull her apart. There was always written upon her the epic poetry of beauty and repose out of struggle—he never ceased to feel that she had her hand around the reins of her heart, that gathered into her grasp were all the straining wires and sinews of disunion which would scatter and unjoint her members, once she let go. Literally, physically, he felt that, the great tide of valiance once flowed out of her, she would immediately go to pieces.

She was like some great general, famous, tranquil, wounded unto death, who, with his fingers clamped across a severed artery, stops for an hour the ebbing of his life—sends on the battle.

Her hair was coarse and dull-brown, fairly abundant, tinged lightly with gray: it was combed evenly in the middle and bound tightly in a knot behind. Everything about her was very clean, like a scrubbed kitchen board: she took his hand, he felt the firm nervous vitality of her fingers, and he noticed how clean and scrubbed her thin somewhat labor-worn hands were. If he noticed her emaciation at all now, it was only with a sense of her purification: he felt himself in union not with disease, but with the greatest health he had ever known. She made a high music in him. His heart lifted.

"This," said Mr. Leonard, stroking him gently across the kidneys, "is Mister Eugene Gant."

"Well, sir," she said, in a low voice, in which a vibrant wire was thrumming, "I'm glad to know you." The voice had in it that quality of quiet wonder that he had sometimes heard in the voices of people who had seen or were told of some strange event, or coincidence, that seemed to reach beyond life, beyond nature—a note of acceptance; and suddenly he knew that all life seemed eternally strange to this woman, that she looked directly into the beauty and the mystery and the tragedy in the hearts of men, and that he seemed beautiful to her.

Her face darkened with the strange passionate vitality that left no print, that lived there bodiless like life; her brown eyes darkened into black as if a bird had flown through them and left the shadow of its wings. She saw his small remote face burning strangely at the end of his long unfleshed body, she saw the straight thin shanks, the big feet turned awkwardly inward, the dusty patches on his stockings at the knees, and his thin wristy arms that stuck out painfully below his cheap ill-fitting jacket; she saw the thin hunched line of his shoulders, the tangled mass of hair—and she did not laugh.

He turned his face up to her as a prisoner who recovers light, as a man long pent in darkness who bathes himself in the great pool of dawn, as a blind man who feels upon his eyes the white core and essence of immutable brightness. His body drank in her great light as a famished castaway the rain: he closed his eyes and let the great light bathe him, and when he opened them again, he saw that her own were luminous and wet.

Then she began to laugh. "Why, Mr. Leonard," she said, "what in the world! He's almost as tall as you. Here, boy. Stand up here while I measure." Deft-fingered, she put them back to back. Mr. Leonard was two or three inches taller than Eugene. He began to whine with laughter.

"Why, the rascal," he said. "That little shaver."

"How old are you, boy?" she asked.

"I'll be twelve next month," he said.

"Well, what do you know about that!" she said wonderingly. "I tell you what, though," she continued. "We've got to get some meat on those bones. You can't go around like that. I don't like the way you look." She shook her head.

He was uncomfortable, disturbed, vaguely resentful. It embarrassed and frightened him to be told that he was "delicate"; it touched sharply on his pride.

She took him into a big room on the left that had been fitted out as a living-room and library. She watched his face light with eagerness as he saw the fifteen hundred or two thousand books shelved away in various places. He sat down clumsily in a wicker chair by the table and waited until she returned, bringing him a plate of sandwiches and a tall glass full of clabber, which he had never tasted before.

When he had finished, she drew a chair near to his, and sat down. She had previously sent Leonard out on some barnyard errands; he could be heard from time to time shouting in an authoritative country voice to his live stock.

"Well, tell me boy," she said, "what have you been reading?"

Craftily he picked his way across the waste land of printery, naming as his favorites those books which he felt would win her approval. As he had read everything, good and bad, that the town library contained, he was able to make an impressive showing. Sometimes she stopped him to question about a book—he rebuilt the story richly with a blazing tenacity of detail that satisfied her wholly. She was excited and eager—she saw at once how abundantly she could feed this ravenous hunger for knowledge, experience, wisdom. And he knew suddenly the joy of obedience: the wild ignorant groping, the blind hunt, the desperate baffled desire was now to be ruddered, guided, controlled. The way through the passage to India, that he had never been able to find, would now be charted for him. Before he went away she had given him a fat volume of nine hundred pages, shot through with spirited engravings of love and battle, of the period he loved best.

He was drowned deep at midnight in the destiny of the man who killed the bear, the burner of windmills and the scourge of banditry, in all the life of road and tavern in the Middle Ages, in valiant and beautiful Gerard, the seed of genius, the father of Erasmus. Eugene thought *The Cloister and the Hearth* the best story he had ever read.

The Altamont Fitting School was the greatest venture of their lives. All the delayed success that Leonard had dreamed of as a younger man he hoped to realize now. For him the school was independence, mastership, power, and, he hoped, prosperity. For her, teaching was its own exceeding great reward—her lyric music, her life, the world in which plastically she built to beauty what was good, the lord of her soul that gave her spirit life while he broke her body.

In the cruel volcano of the boy's mind, the little brier moths of his idolatry wavered in to their strange marriage and were consumed. One by one the merciless years reaped down his gods and captains. What had lived up to hope? What had withstood the scourge of growth and memory? Why had the gold become so dim? All of his life, it seemed, his blazing loyalties began with men and ended with images; the life he leaned on melted below his weight, and looking down, he saw he clasped a statue; but enduring, a victorious reality amid his shadow-haunted heart, she remained, who first had touched his blinded eyes with light, who nested his hooded houseless soul. She remained.

O death in life that turns our men to stone! O change that levels down our gods! If only one lives yet, above the cinders of the consuming years, shall not this dust awaken, shall not dead faith revive, shall we not see God again, as once in morning, on the mountain? Who walks with us on the hills?

17

Eugene spent the next four years of his life in Leonard's school. Against the bleak horror of Dixieland, against the dark road of pain and death down which the great limbs of Gant had already begun to slope, against all the loneliness and imprisonment of his own life which had gnawed him like hunger, these years at Leonard's bloomed like golden apples.

From Leonard he got little—a dry campaign over an arid waste of Latin prose: first, a harsh, stiff, unintelligent skirmishing among the rules of grammar, which frightened and bewildered him needlessly, and gave him for years an unhealthy dislike of syntax, and an absurd prejudice against the laws on which the language was built. Then, a year's study of the lean, clear precision of Caesar, the magnificent structure of the style—the concision, the skeleton certainty, deadened by the disjointed daily partition, the dull parsing, the lumbering *cliché* of pedantic translation:

"Having done all things that were necessary, and the season now being propitious for carrying on war, Caesar began to arrange his legions in battle array."

All the dark pageantry of war in Gaul, the thrust of the Roman spear through the shield of hide, the barbaric parleys in the forests, and the proud clangor of triumph—all that might have been supplied in the story of the great realist, by one touch of the transforming passion with which a great teacher projects his work, was lacking.

Instead, glibly, the wheels ground on into the hard rut of method and memory. March 12, last year—three days late. *Cogitata*. Neut. pl. of participle used as substantive. *Quo* used instead of *ut* to express purpose when comparative follows. Eighty lines for to-morrow.

They spent a weary age, two years, on that dull dog, Cicero. *De Senectute. De Amicitia*. They skirted Virgil because John Dorsey Leonard was a bad sailor—he was not at all sure of Virgilian navigation. He hated exploration. He distrusted voyages. Next year, he said. And the great names of Ovid, lord of the elves and gnomes, the Bacchic piper of *Amores,* or of Lucretius, full of the rhythm of tides. *Nox est perpetua.*

"Huh?" drawled Mr. Leonard, vacantly beginning to laugh. He was fingermarked with chalk from chin to crotch. Stephen ("Pap") Rheinhart leaned forward gently and fleshed his penpoint in Eugene Gant's left rump. Eugene grunted painfully.

"Why, no," said Mr. Leonard, stroking his chin. "A different sort of Latin."

"What sort?" Tom Davis insisted. "Harder than Cicero?"

"Well," said Mr. Leonard, dubiously, "different. A little beyond you at present."

"*—est perpetua. Una dormienda. Luna dies et nox.*"

"Is Latin poetry hard to read?" Eugene said.

"Well," said Mr. Leonard, shaking his head. "It's not easy. Horace—" he began carefully.

"He wrote Odes and Epodes," said Tom Davis. "What is an Epode, Mr. Leonard?"

"Why," said Mr. Leonard reflectively, "it's a form of poetry."

"Hell!" said "Pap" Rheinhart in a rude whisper to Eugene. "I knew that before I paid tuition."

Smiling lusciously, and stroking himself with gentle fingers, Mr. Leonard turned back to the lesson.

"Now let me see," he began.

"Who was Catullus?" Eugene shouted violently. Like a flung spear in his brain, the name.

"He was a poet," Mr. Leonard answered thoughtlessly, quickly, startled. He regretted.

"What sort of poetry did he write?" asked Eugene.

There was no answer.

"Was it like Horace?"

"No-o," said Mr. Leonard reflectively. "It wasn't exactly like Horace."

"What was it like?" said Tom Davis.

"Like your granny's gut," "Pap" Rheinhart toughly whispered.

"Why—he wrote on topics of general interest in his day," said Mr. Leonard easily.

"Did he write about being in love?" said Eugene in a quivering voice. Tom Davis turned a surprised face on him.

"Gre-a-at Day!" he exclaimed, after a moment. Then he began to laugh.

"He wrote about being in love," Eugene cried with sudden certain passion. "He wrote about being in love with a lady named Lesbia. Ask Mr. Leonard if you don't believe me."

They turned thirsty faces up to him.

"Why—no—yes—I don't know about all that," said Mr. Leonard, challengingly, confused. "Where'd you hear all this, boy?"

"I read it in a book," said Eugene, wondering where. Like a flung spear, the name.

—Whose tongue was fanged like a serpent, flung spear of ecstasy and passion.

Odi et amo: quare id faciam...

"Well, not altogether," said Mr. Leonard. "Some of them," he conceded.

...fortasse requiris. Nescio, sed fieri sentio et excrucior.

"Who was she?" said Tom Davis.

"Oh, it was the custom in those days," said Mr. Leonard carelessly. "Like Dante and Beatrice. It was a way the poet had of paying a compliment."

The serpent whispered. There was a distillation of wild exultancy in his blood. The rags of obedience, servility, reverential awe dropped in a belt around him.

"She was a man's wife!" he said loudly. "That's who she was."

Awful stillness.

"Why—here—who told you that?" said Mr. Leonard, bewildered, but considering matrimony a wild and possibly dangerous myth. "Who told you, boy?"

"What was she, then?" said Tom Davis pointedly.

"Why—not exactly," Mr. Leonard murmured, rubbing his chin.

"She was a Bad Woman," said Eugene. Then, most desperately, he added: "She was a Little Chippie."

"Pap" Rheinhart drew in his breath sharply.

"What's that, what's that, what's that?" cried Mr. Leonard rapidly when he could speak. Fury boiled up in him. He sprang from his chair. "What did you say, boy?"

But he thought of Margaret and looked down, with a sudden sense of palsy, into the white ruination of boy-face. Too far beyond. He sat down again, shaken.

—Whose foulest cry was shafted with his passion, whose greatest music flowered out of filth——.

> *"Nulla potest mulier tantum se dicere amatam*
> *Vere, quantum a me Lesbia amata mea es."*

"You should be more careful of your talk, Eugene," said Mr. Leonard gently.

"See here!" he exclaimed suddenly, turning with violence to his book. "This is getting no work done. Come on, now!" he said heartily, spitting upon his intellectual hands. "You rascals you!" he said, noting Tom Davis' grin. "I know what you're after—you want to take up the whole period."

Tom Davis' heavy laughter boomed out, mingling with his own whine.

"All right, Tom," said Mr. Leonard briskly, "page 43, section 6, line 15. Begin at that point."

At this moment the bell rang and Tom Davis' laughter filled the room.

Nevertheless, in charted lanes of custom, he gave competent instruction. He would perhaps have had difficulty in constructing a page of Latin prose and verse with which he had not become literally familiar by years of repetition. In Greek, certainly, his deficiency would have been even more marked, but he would have known a second aorist or an optative in the dark (if he had ever met it before). There were two final years of precious Greek: they read the *Anabasis*.

"What's the good of all this stuff?" said Tom Davis argumentatively.

Mr. Leonard was on sure ground here. He understood the value of the classics.

"It teaches a man to appreciate the Finer Things. It gives him the foundations of a liberal education. It trains his mind."

"What good's it going to do him when he goes to work?" said "Pap" Rheinhart. "It's not going to teach him how to grow more corn."

"Well—I'm not so sure of that," said Mr. Leonard with a protesting laugh. "I think it does."

"Pap" Rheinhart looked at him with a comical cock of the head. He had a wry neck, which gave his humorous kindly face a sidelong expression of quizzical maturity.

He had a gruff voice; he was full of rough kindly humor, and chewed tobacco constantly. His father was wealthy. He lived on a big farm in the Cove, ran a dairy and had a foundry in the town. They were unpretending people—German stock.

"Pshaw, Mr. Leonard," said "Pap" Rheinhart. "Are you going to talk Latin to your farmhands?"

"Egibus wantibus a peckibus of cornibus," said Tom Davis with sounding laughter. Mr. Leonard laughed with abstracted appreciation. The joke was his own.

"It trains the mind to grapple with problems of all sorts," he said.

"According to what you say," said Tom Davis, "a man who has studied Greek makes a better plumber than one who hasn't."

"Yes, sir," said Mr. Leonard, shaking his head smartly, "you know, I believe he does." He joined, pleased, with their pleasant laughter, a loose slobbering giggle.

He was on trodden ground. They engaged him in long debates: as he ate his lunch, he waved a hot biscuit around, persuasive, sweetly reasonable, exhaustively minute in an effort to prove the connection of Greek and groceries. The great wind of Athens had touched him not at all. Of the delicate and sensuous intelligence of the Greeks, their feminine grace, the constructive power and subtlety of their intelligence, the instability of their character, and the structure, restraint and perfection of their forms, he said nothing.

He had caught a glimpse, in an American college, of the great structure of the most architectural of languages: he felt the sculptural perfection of such a word as γυνάικος, but his opinions smelled of chalk, the classroom, and a very bad lamp—Greek was good because it was ancient, classic, and academic. The smell of the East, the dark tide of the Orient that flowed below, touched the lives of poet and soldier, with something perverse, evil, luxurious, was as far from his life as Lesbos. He was simply the mouthpiece of a formula of which he was assured without having a genuine belief.

καὶ κατὰ γῆν καὶ κατὰ θάλατταν.

The mathematics and history teacher was John Dorsey's sister Amy. She was a powerful woman, five feet ten inches tall, who weighed 185 pounds. She had very thick black hair, straight and oily, and very black eyes, giving a heavy sensuousness to her face. Her thick forearms were fleeced with light down. She was not fat, but she corsetted tightly, her powerful arms and heavy shoulders bulging through the cool white of her shirtwaists. In warm weather she perspired abundantly: her waists were stained below the arm-pits with big spreading blots of sweat; in the winter, as she warmed herself by the fire, she had about her the exiciting odor of chalk, and the strong good smell of a healthy animal. Eugene, passing down the wind-swept back porch one day in winter, looked in on her room just as her tiny niece opened the door to come out. She sat before a dancing coal-fire, after her bath, drawing on her stockings. Fascinated, he stared at her broad red shoulders, her big body steaming cleanly like a beast.

She liked the fire and the radiance of warmth: sleepily alert she sat by the stove, with her legs spread, sucking in the heat, her large earth strength more heavily sensuous than her brother's. Stroked by the slow heat-tingle she smiled slowly with indifferent affection on all the boys. No men came to see her: like a pool she was thirsty for lips. She sought no one. With lazy cat-warmth she smiled on all the world.

She was a good teacher of mathematics: number to her was innate. Lazily she took their tablets, worked answers lazily, smiling good-naturedly with contempt. Behind her, at a desk, Durand Jarvis moaned passionately to Eugene, and writhed erotically, gripping the leaf of his desk fiercely.

Sister Sheba arrived with her consumptive husband at the end of the second year—cadaver, flecked lightly on the lips with blood, seventy-three years old. They said he was forty-nine—sickness made him look old. He was a tall man, six feet three, with long straight mustaches, waxen and emaciated as a mandarin. He painted pictures—impressionist blobs—sheep on a gorsey hill, fishboats at the piers, with a warm red jumble of brick buildings in the background.

Old Gloucester Town, Marblehead, Cape Cod Folks, Captains Courageous—the rich salty names came reeking up with a smell of tarred rope, dry codheads rotting in the sun, rocking dories knee-deep in gutted fish, the strong loin-smell of the sea in harbors, and the quiet brooding vacancy of a seaman's face, sign of his marriage with ocean. How look the seas at dawn in Spring? The cold gulls sleep upon the wind. But rose the skies.

They saw the waxen mandarin walk shakily three times up and down the road. It was Spring, there was a south wind high in the big trees. He wavered along on a stick, planted before him with a blue phthisic hand. His eyes were blue and pale as if he had been drowned.

He had begotten two children by Sheba—girls. They were exotic tender blossoms, all black and milky white, as strange and lovely as Spring. The boys groped curiously.

"He must be a better man than he looks yet," said Tom Davis. "The little 'un's only two or three years old."

"He's not as old as he looks," said Eugene. "He looks old because he's been sick. He's only forty-nine."

"How do you know?" said Tom Davis.

"Miss Amy says so," said Eugene innocently.

"Pap" Rheinhart cocked his head on Eugene and carried his quid deftly on the end of his tongue to the other cheek.

"Forty-nine!" he said, "you'd better see a doctor, boy. He's as old as God."

"That's what she said," Eugene insisted doggedly.

"Why, of course she said it!" "Pap" Rheinhart replied. "You don't think they're going to let it out, do you? When they're running a school here."

"Son, you must be simple!" said Jack Candler who had not thought of it up to now.

"Hell, you're their Pet. They know you'll believe whatever they tell you," said Julius Arthur. "Pap" Rheinhart looked at him searchingly, then shook his head as if a cure was impossible. They laughed at his faith.

"Well, if he's so old," said Eugene, "why did old Lady Lattimer marry him?"

"Why, because she couldn't get any one else, of course," said "Pap" Rheinhart, impatient at this obtuseness.

"Do you suppose she has had to keep him up?" said Tom Davis curiously. Silently they wondered. And Eugene, as he saw the two lovely children fall like petals from their mother's heavy breast, as he saw the waxen artist faltering his last steps to death, and heard Sheba's strong voice leveling a conversation at its beginning, expanding in violent burlesque all of her opinions, was bewildered again before the unsearchable riddle—out of death, life, out of the coarse rank earth, a flower.

His faith was above conviction. Disillusion had come so often that it had awakened in him a strain of bitter suspicion, an occasional mockery, virulent, coarse, cruel, and subtle, which was all the more scalding because of his own pain. Unknowingly, he had begun to build up in himself a vast mythology for which he cared all the more deeply because he realized its untruth. Brokenly, obscurely, he was beginning to feel that it was not truth that men live for—the creative men—but for falsehood. At times his devouring, unsated brain seemed to be beyond his governance: it was a frightful bird whose beak was in his heart, whose talons tore unceasingly at his bowels. And this unsleeping demon wheeled, plunged, revolved about an object, returning suddenly, after it had flown away, with victorious malice, leaving stripped, mean, and common all that he had clothed with wonder.

But he saw hopefully that he never learned—that what remained was the tinsel and the gold. He was so bitter with his tongue because his heart believed so much.

The merciless brain lay coiled and alert like a snake: it saw every gesture, every quick glance above his head, the shoddy scaffolding of all reception. But these people existed for him in a world remote from human error. He opened one window of his heart to Margaret, together they entered the sacred grove of poetry; but all dark desire, the dream of fair

forms, and all the misery, drunkenness, and disorder of his life at home
he kept fearfully shut. He was afraid they would hear. Desperately he
wondered how many of the boys had heard of it. And all the facts that
levelled Margaret down to life, that plunged her in the defiling stream of
life, were as unreal and horrible as a nightmare.

That she had been near death from tuberculosis, that the violent and
garrulous Sheba had married an old man, who had begotten two children
and was now about to die, that the whole little family, powerful in
cohesive fidelity, were nursing their great sores in privacy, building up
before the sharp eyes and rattling tongues of young boys a barrier of
flimsy pretense and evasion, numbed him with a sense of unreality.

Eugene believed in the glory and the gold.

He lived more at Dixieland now. He had been more closely bound to
Eliza since he began at Leonard's. Gant, Helen, and Luke were scornful
of the private school. The children were resentful of it—a little jealous.
And their temper was barbed now with a new sting. They would say:

"You've ruined him completely since you sent him to a private school."
Or, "He's too good to soil his hands now that he's quit the public school."

Eliza herself kept him sufficiently reminded of his obligation. She spoke
often of the effort she had to make to pay the tuition fee, and of her
poverty. She said, he must work hard, and help her all he could in his
spare hours. He should also help her through the summer and "drum up
trade" among the arriving tourists at the station.

"For God's sake! What's the matter with you?" Luke jeered. "You're
not ashamed of a little honest work, are you?"

This way, sir, for Dixieland. Mrs. Eliza E. Gant, proprietor. Just A
Whisper Off The Square, Captain. All the comforts of the Modern Jail.
Bisquits and home-made pies just like mother should have made but didn't.

That boy's a hustler.

At the end of Eugene's first year at Leonard's, Eliza told John Dorsey
she could no longer afford to pay the tuition. He conferred with Margaret
and, returning, agreed to take the boy for half price.

"He can help you drum up new prospects," said Eliza.

"Yes," Leonard agreed, "that's the very thing."

Ben bought a new pair of shoes. They were tan. He paid six dollars for
them. He always bought good things. But they burnt the soles of his
feet. In a scowling rage he loped to his room and took them off.

"Goddam it!" he yelled, and hurled them at the wall. Eliza came to the door.

"You'll never have a penny, boy, as long as you waste money the way you do. I tell you what, it's pretty bad when you think of it." She shook her head sadly with puckered mouth.

"O for God's sake!" he growled. "Listen to this! By God, you never hear me asking any one for anything, do you?" he burst out in a rage.

She took the shoes and gave them to Eugene.

"It would be a pity to throw away a good pair of shoes," she said. "Try 'em on, boy."

He tried them on. His feet were already bigger than Ben's. He walked about carefully and painfully a few steps.

"How do they feel?" asked Eliza.

"All right, I guess," he said doubtfully. "They're a little tight."

He liked their clean strength, the good smell of leather. They were the best shoes he had ever had.

Ben entered the kitchen.

"You little brute!" he said. "You've a foot like a mule." Scowling, he knelt and touched the straining leather at the toes. Eugene winced.

"Mama, for God's sake," Ben cried out irritably, "don't make the kid wear them if they're too small. I'll buy him a pair myself if you're too stingy to spend the money."

"Why, what's wrong with these?" said Eliza. She pressed them with her fingers. "Why, pshaw!" she said. "There's nothing wrong with them. All shoes are a little tight at first. It won't hurt him a bit."

But he had to give up at the end of six weeks. The hard leather did not stretch, his feet hurt more every day. He limped about more and more painfully until he planted each step woodenly as if he were walking on blocks. His feet were numb and dead, sore on the palms. One day, in a rage, Ben flung him down and took them off. It was several days before he began to walk with ease again. But his toes that had grown through boyhood straight and strong were pressed into a pulp, the bones gnarled, bent and twisted, the nails thick and dead.

"It does seem a pity to throw those good shoes away," sighed Eliza.

But she had strange fits of generosity. He didn't understand.

A girl came down to Altamont from the west. She was from Sevier, a mountain town, she said. She had a big brown body, and black hair and eyes of a Cherokee Indian.

"Mark my words," said Gant. "That girl's got Cherokee blood in her somewhere."

She took a room, and for days rocked back and forth in a chair before the parlor fire. She was shy, frightened, a little sullen—her manners were country and decorous. She never spoke unless she was spoken to.

Sometimes she was sick and stayed in bed. Eliza took her food then, and was extremely kind to her.

Day after day the girl rocked back and forth, all through the stormy autumn. Eugene could hear her large feet as rhythmically they hit the floor, ceaselessly propelling the rocker. Her name was Mrs. Morgan.

One day as he laid large crackling lumps upon the piled glowing mass of coals, Eliza entered the room. Mrs. Morgan rocked away stolidly. Eliza stood by the fire for a moment, pursing her lips reflectivly, and folding her hands quietly upon her stomach. She looked out the window at the stormy sky, the swept windy bareness of the street.

"I tell you what," she said, "it looks like a hard winter for the poor folks."

"Yes'm," said Mrs. Morgan sullenly. She kept on rocking.

Eliza was silent a moment longer.

"Where's your husband?" she asked presently.

"In Sevier," Mrs. Morgan said. "He's a railroad man."

"What's that, what's that?" said Eliza quickly, comically. "A railroad man, you say?" she inquired sharply.

"Yes'm."

"Well, it looks mighty funny to me he hasn't been in to see you," said Eliza, with enormous accusing tranquillity. "I'd call it a pretty poor sort of man who'd act like that."

Mrs. Morgan said nothing. Her tar-black eyes glittered in fireflame.

"Have you got any money?" said Eliza.

"No'm," said Mrs. Morgan.

Eliza stood solidly, enjoying the warmth, pursing her lips. "When do you expect to have your baby?" said Eliza suddenly.

Mrs. Morgan said nothing for a moment. She kept on rocking.

"In less'n a month now, I reckon," she answered.

She had been getting bigger week after week.

Eliza bent over and pulled her skirt up, revealing her leg to the knee, cotton-stockinged and lumpily wadded with her heavy flannels

"Whew!" she cried out coyly, noticing that Eugene was staring. "Turn your head, boy," she commanded, snickering and rubbing her finger along her nose. The dull green of rolled banknotes shone through her stockings. She pulled the bills out.

"Well, I reckon you'll have to have a little money," said Eliza, peeling off two tens, and giving them to Mrs. Morgan.

"Thank you, ma'am," said Mrs. Morgan, taking the money.

"You can stay here until you're able to work again," said Eliza. "I know a good doctor."

"Mama, in heaven's name," Helen fumed. "Where on earth do you get these people?"

"Merciful God!" howled Gant, "you've had 'em all—blind, lame, crazy, chippies and bastards. They all come here."

Neverthelesss, when he saw Mrs. Morgan now, he always made a profound bow, saying with the most florid courtesy:

"How do you do, madam?" Aside, to Helen, he said:

"I tell you what—she's a fine-looking girl."

"Hahahaha," said Helen, laughing in an ironic falsetto, and prodding him, "you wouldn't mind having her yourself, would you?"

"B'God," he said humorously, wetting his thumb, and grinning slyly at Eliza, "she's got a pair of pippins."

Eliza smiled bitterly into popping grease.

"Hm!" she said disdainfully. "I don't care how many he goes with. There's no fool like an old fool. You'd better not be too smart. That's a game two can play at."

"Hahahahaha!" laughed Helen thinly, "she's mad now."

Helen took Mrs. Morgan often to Gant's and cooked great meals for her. She also brought her presents of candy and scented soap from town.

They called in McGuire at the birth of the child. From below Eugene heard the quiet commotion in the upstairs room, the low moans of the woman, and finally a high piercing wail. Eliza, greatly excited, kept kettles seething with hot water constantly over the gas flame of the stove. From time to time she rushed upstairs with a boiling kettle, descending a moment later more slowly, pausing from step to step while she listened attentively to the sounds in the room.

"After all," said Helen, banging kettles about restlesly in the kitchen, "what do we know about her? Nobody can say she hasn't got a husband, can they? They'd better be careful! People have no right to say those things," she cried out irritably against unknown detractors.

It was night. Eugene went out on to the veranda. The air was frosty, clear, not very cool. Above the black bulk of the eastern hills, and in the great bowl of the sky, far bright stars were scintillant as jewels. The light burned brightly in neighborhood houses, as bright and as hard as if carved from some cold gem. Across the wide yard-spaces wafted the warm odor of hamburger steak and fried onions. Ben stood at the veranda rail, leaning upon his cocked leg, smoking with deep lung inhalations. Eugene went over and stood by him. They heard the wail upstairs. Eugene snickered, looking up at the thin ivory mask. Ben lifted his white hand sharply to strike him, but dropped it with a growl of contempt, smiling faintly. Far before them, on the top of Birdseye, faint lights wavered in the rich Jew's castle. In the neighborhood there was a slight mist of supper, and frost-far voices.

Deep womb, dark flower. The Hidden. The secret fruit, heart-red, fed by rich Indian blood. Womb-night brooding darkness flowering secretly into life.

Mrs. Morgan went away two weeks after her child was born. He was a little brown-skinned boy, with a tuft of elvish black hair, and very black bright eyes. He was like a little Indian. Before she left Eliza gave her twenty dollars.

"Where are you going?" she asked.

"I've got folks in Sevier," said Mrs. Morgan.

She went up the street carrying a cheap imitation-crocodile valise. At her shoulder the baby waggled his head, and looked merrily back with his bright black eyes. Eliza waved to him and smiled tremulously; she turned back into the house sniffling, with wet eyes.

Why did she come to Dixieland, I wonder? Eugene thought.

Eliza was good to a little man with a mustache. He had a wife and a little girl nine years old. He was a hotel steward; he was out of work and he stayed at Dixieland until he owed her more than one hundred dollars. But he split kindling neatly, and carried up coal; he did handy jobs of carpentry, and painted up rusty places about the house.

She was very fond of him; he was what she called "a good family man." She liked domestic people; she liked men who were house-broken. The little man was very kind and very tame. Eugene liked him because he made good coffee. Eliza never bothered him about the money. Finally, he got work at the Inn, and quarters there. He paid Eliza all he owed her.

Eugene stayed late at the school, returning in the afternoon at three or four o'clock. Sometimes it was almost dark when he came back to Dixieland. Eliza was fretful at his absences, and brought him his dinner crisped and dried from its long heating in the oven. There was a heavy vegetable soup thickly glutinous with cabbage, beans, and tomatoes, and covered on top with big grease blisters. There would also be warmed-over beef, pork or chicken, a dish full of cold lima beans, biscuits, slaw, and coffee.

But the school had become the centre of his heart and life—Margaret Leonard his spiritual mother. He liked to be there most in the afternoons when the crowd of boys had gone, and when he was free to wander about the old house, under the singing majesty of great trees, exultant in the proud solitude of that fine hill, the clean windy rain of the acorns, the tang of burning leaves. He would read wolfishly until Margaret discovered him and drove him out under the trees or toward the flat court behind Bishop Raper's residence at the entrance, which was used for basketball. Here, while the western sky reddened, he raced down toward the goal, passing the ball to a companion, exulting in his growing swiftness, agility, and expertness in shooting the basket.

Margaret Leonard watched his health jealously, almost morbidly, warning him constantly of the terrible consequences that followed physical depletion, the years required to build back what had once been thrown carelessly away.

"Look here, boy!" she would begin, stopping him in a quiet boding voice. "Come in here a minute. I want to talk to you."

Somewhat frightened, extremely nervous, he would sit down beside her.

"How much sleep have you been getting?" she asked.

Hopefully, he said nine hours a night. That should be about right.

"Well, make it ten," she commanded sternly. "See here, 'Gene, you simply can't afford to take chances with your health. Lordy, boy, I know what I'm talking about. I've had to pay the price, I tell you. You can't do anything in this world without your health, boy."

"But I'm all right," he protested desperately, frightened. "There's nothing wrong with me."

"You're not strong, boy. You've got to get some meat on your bones. I tell you what, I'm worried by those circles under your eyes. Do you keep regular hours?"

He did not: he hated regular hours. The excitement, the movement, the constant moments of crisis at Gant's and Eliza's had him keyed to their stimulation. The order and convention of domestic life he had never known. He was desperately afraid of regularity. It meant dullness and inanition to him. He loved the hour of midnight.

But obediently he promised her that he would be regular—regular in eating, sleeping, studying, and exercising.

But he had not yet learned to play with the crowd. He still feared, disliked and distrusted them.

He shrank from the physical conflict of boy life, but knowing her eye was upon him he plunged desperately into their games, his frail strength buffeted in the rush of strong legs, the heavy jar of strong bodies, picking himself up bruised and sore at heart to follow and join again the mill of the burly pack. Day after day to the ache of his body was added the ache and shame of his spirit, but he hung on with a pallid smile across his lips, and envy and fear of their strength in his heart. He parroted faithfully all that John Dorsey had to say about the "spirit of fair play," "sportsmanship," "playing the game for the game's sake," "accepting defeat or victory with a smile," and so on, but he had no genuine belief or understanding. These phrases were current among all the boys at the school— they had been made somewhat too conscious of them and, as he listened, at times the old, inexplicable shame returned—he craned his neck and drew one foot sharply off the ground.

And Eugene noted, with the old baffling shame again, as this cheap tableau of self-conscious, robust, and raucously aggressive boyhood was posed, that, for all the mouthing of phrases, the jargon about fair play and sportsmanship, the weaker, at Leonard's, was the legitimate prey of the stronger. Leonard, beaten by a boy in a play of wits, or in an argument for justice, would assert the righteousness of his cause by physical violence. These spectacles were ugly and revolting: Eugene watched them with sick fascination.

Leonard himself was not a bad man—he was a man of considerable character, kindliness, and honest determination. He loved his family, he stood up with some courage against the bigotry in the Methodist church, where he was a deacon, and at length had to withdraw because of his remarks on Darwin's theory. He was, thus, an example of that sad liberalism of the village—an advanced thinker among the Methodists, a bearer of the torch at noon, an apologist for the toleration of ideas that have been established for fifty years. He tried faithfully to do his duties as a teacher. But he was of the earth—even his heavy-handed violence was of the earth, and had in it the unconscious brutality of nature. Although he asserted his interest in "the things of the mind," his interest in the soil was much greater, and he had added little to his stock of information since leaving college. He was slow-witted and quite lacking in the sensitive intuitions of Margaret, who loved the man with such passionate fidelity, however, that she seconded all his acts before the world. Eugene had even heard her cry out in a shrill, trembling voice against a student who had answered her husband insolently: "Why, I'd slap his head off! That's what I'd do!" And the boy had trembled, with fear and nausea, to see her so. But thus, he knew, could love change one. Leonard thought his actions wise and good: he had grown up in a tradition that demanded strict obedience to the master, and that would not brook opposition to his rulings. He had learned from his father, a Tennessee patriarch who ran a farm, preached on Sundays, and put down rebellion in his family with a horse-whip and pious prayers, the advantages of being God! He thought little boys who resisted him should be beaten.

Upon the sons of his wealthiest and most prominent clients, as well as upon his own children, Leonard was careful to inflict no chastisement, and these young men, arrogantly conscious of their immunity, were studious in their insolence and disobedience. The son of the Bishop, Justin Raper, a tall thin boy of thirteen, with black hair, a thin dark bumpy face, and absurdly petulant lips, typed copies of a dirty ballad and sold them among the students at five cents a copy.

> "Madam, your daughter looks very fine,
>   Slapoon!
> Madam, your daughter looks very fine,
>   Slapoon!"

Moreover, Leonard surprised this youth one afternoon in Spring on the eastern flank of the hill, in the thick grass beneath a flowering dogwood, united in sexual congress with Miss Hazel Bradley, the daughter of a small grocer who lived below on Biltburn Avenue, and whose lewdness was already advertised in the town. Leonard, on second thought, did not go to the Bishop. He went to the Grocer.

"Well," said Mr. Bradley, brushing his long mustache reflectively away from his mouth, "you ought to put up a no-trespassin' sign."

The target of concentrated abuse, both for John Dorsey and the boys, was the son of a Jew. The boy's name was Edward Michalove. His father was a jeweller, a man with a dark, gentle floridity of manner and complexion. He had white delicate fingers. His counters were filled with old brooches, gemmed buckles, ancient incrusted watches. The boy had two sisters—large handsome women. His mother was dead. None of them looked Jewish: they all had a soft dark fluescence of appearance.

At twelve, he was a tall slender lad, with dark amber features, and the mincing effeminacy of an old maid. He was terrified in the company of other boys, all that was sharp, spinsterly, and venomous, would come protectively to the surface when he was ridiculed or threatened, and he would burst into shrill unpleasant laughter, or hysterical tears. His mincing walk, with the constant gesture of catching maidenly at the fringe of his coat as he walked along, his high husky voice, with a voluptuous and feminine current playing through it, drew upon him at once the terrible battery of their dislike.

They called him "Miss" Michalove; they badgered him into a state of constant hysteria, until he became an unpleasant snarling little cat, holding up his small clawed hands to scratch them with his long nails whenever they approached; they made him detestable, master and boys alike, and they hated him for what they made of him.

Sobbing one day when he had been kept in after school hours, he leaped up and rushed suddenly for the doors. Leonard, breathing stertorously, pounded awkwardly after him, and returned in a moment dragging the screaming boy along by the collar.

"Sit down!" yelled John Dorsey, hurling him into a desk. Then, his boiling fury unappeased, and baffled by fear of inflicting some crippling punishment on the boy, he added illogically: "Stand up!" and jerked him to his feet again.

"You young upstart!" he panted. "You little two-by-two whippersnapper! We'll just see, my sonny, if I'm to be dictated to by the like of you."

"Take your hands off me!" Edward screamed, in an agony of physical loathing. "I'll tell my father on you, old man Leonard, and he'll come down here and kick your big fat behind all over the lot. See if he don't."

Eugene closed his eyes, unable to witness the snuffing out of a young life. He was cold and sick about his heart. But when he opened his eyes again Edward, flushed and sobbing, was standing where he stood. Nothing had happened.

Eugene waited for God's visitation upon the unhappy blasphemer. He gathered, from the slightly open paralysis that had frozen John Dorsey's and Sister Amy's face, that they were waiting too.

Edward lived. There was nothing beyond this—nothing.

Eugene thought of this young Jew years later with the old piercing shame, with the riving pain by which a man recalls the irrevocable moment of some cowardly or dishonorable act. For not only did he join in the persecution of the boy—he was also glad at heart because of the existence of some one weaker than himself, some one at whom the flood of ridicule might be directed. Years later it came to him that on the narrow shoulders of that Jew lay a burden he might otherwise have borne, that that overladen heart was swollen with a misery that might have been his.

Mr. Leonard's "men of to-morrow" were doing nicely. The spirit of justice, of physical honor was almost unknown to them, but they were loud in proclaiming the letter. Each of them lived in a fear of discovery; each of them who was able built up his own defenses of swagger, pretense, and loud assertion—the great masculine flower of gentleness, courage, and honor died in a foul tangle. The great clan of go-getter was emergent in young boys—big in voice, violent in threat, withered and pale at heart— the "He-men" were on the rails.

And Eugene, encysted now completely behind the walls of his fantasy, hurled his physical body daily to defeat, imitated, as best he could, the speech, gesture, and bearing of his fellows, joined, by act or spirit, in the attack on those weaker than himself, and was compensated sometimes for his bruises when he heard Margaret say that he was "a boy with a fine spirit." She said it very often.

He was, fortunately, thanks to Gant and Eliza, a creature that was dominantly masculine in its sex, but in all his life, either at home or in school, he had seldom known victory. Fear he knew well. And so incessant, it seemed to him later, had been this tyranny of strength, that in his young wild twenties when his great boneframe was powerfully fleshed at last, and he heard about him the loud voices, the violent assertion, the empty threat, memory would waken in him a maniacal anger, and he would hurl the insolent intruding swaggerer from his path, thrust back the jostler, glare insanely into fearful surprised faces and curse them.

He never forgot the Jew; he always thought of him with shame. But it was many years before he could understand that that sensitive and feminine person, bound to him by the secret and terrible bonds of his own dishonor, had in him nothing perverse, nothing unnatural, nothing degenerate. He was as much like a woman as a man. That was all. There is no place among the Boy Scouts for the androgyne—it must go to Parnassus.

18

In the years that had followed Eliza's removal to Dixieland, by a slow inexorable chemistry of union and repellence, profound changes had occurred in the alignment of the Gants. Eugene had passed away from Helen's earlier guardianship into the keeping of Ben. This separation was inevitable. The great affection she had shown him when he was a young child was based not on any deep kinship of mind or body or spirit, but on her vast maternal feeling, something that poured from her in a cataract of tenderness and cruelty upon young, weak, plastic life.

The time had passed when she could tousle him on the bed in a smother of slaps and kisses, crushing him, stroking him, biting and kissing his young flesh. He was not so attractive physically—he had lost the round contours of infancy, he had grown up like a weed, his limbs were long and gangling, his feet large, his shoulders bony, and his head too big and heavy for the scrawny neck on which it sagged forward. Moreover, he sank deeper year by year into the secret life, a strange wild thing bloomed darkly in his face, and when she spoke to him his eyes were filled with the shadows of great ships and cities.

And this secret life, which she could never touch, and which she could never understand, choked her with fury. It was necessary for her to seize life in her big red-knuckled hands, to cuff and caress it, to fondle, love, and enslave it. Her boiling energy rushed outward on all things that lived in the touch of the sun. It was necessary for her to dominate and enslave, all her virtues—her strong lust to serve, to give, to nurse, to amuse—came from the imperative need for dominance over almost all she touched.

She was herself ungovernable; she disliked whatever did not yield to her governance. In his loneliness he would have yielded his spirit into bondage willingly if in exchange he might have had her love which so strangely he had forfeited, but he was unable to reveal to her the flowering ecstasies, the dark and incommunicable fantasies in which his life was bound. She hated secrecy; an air of mystery, a crafty but knowing reticence, or the unfathomable depths of other-wordliness goaded her to fury.

Convulsed by a momentary rush of hatred, she would caricature the pout of his lips, the droop of his head, his bounding kangaroo walk.

"You little freak. You nasty little freak. You don't even know who you are—you little bastard. You're not a Gant. Any one can see that. You haven't a drop of papa's blood in you. Queer one! Queer one! You're Greeley Pentland all over again."

She always returned to this—she was fanatically partisan, her hysterical superstition had already lined the family in embattled groups of those who were Gant and those who were Pentland. On the Pentland side, she placed Steve, Daisy, and Eugene—they were, she thought, the "cold and selfish ones," and the implication of the older sister and the younger brother with the criminal member of the family gave her an added pleasure. Her union with Luke was now inseparable. It had been inevitable. They were the Gants—those who were generous, fine, and honorable.

The love of Luke and Helen was epic. They found in each other the constant effervescence, the boundless extraversion, the richness, the loudness, the desperate need to give and to serve that was life to them. They exacerbated the nerves of each other, but their love was beyond grievance, and their songs of praise were extravagant.

"I'll criticise him if I like," she said pugnaciously. "I've got the right to. But I won't hear any one else criticise him. He's a fine generous boy—the finest one in this family. That's one thing sure."

Ben alone seemed to be without the grouping. He moved among them like a shadow—he was remote from their passionate fullblooded partisanship. But she thought of him as "generous"—he was, she concluded, a "Gant."

In spite of this violent dislike for the Pentlands, both Helen and Luke had inherited all Gant's social hypocrisy. They wanted above all else to put a good face on before the world, to be well liked and to have many friends. They were profuse in their thanks, extravagant in their praise, cloying in their flattery. They slathered it on. They kept their ill-temper, their nervousness, and their irritability for exhibition at home. And in the presence of any members of Jim or Will Pentland's family their manner was not only friendly, it was even touched slightly with servility. Money impressed them.

It was a period of incessant movement in the family. Steve had married a year or two before a woman from a small town in lower Indiana. She was thirty-seven years old, twelve years his senior, a squat heavy German with a big nose and a patient and ugly face. She had come to Dixieland one summer with another woman, a spinster of lifelong acquaintance, and allowed him to seduce her before she left. The winter following, her father, a small manufacturer of cigars, had died, leaving her $9,000 in insurance, his home, a small sum of money in the bank, and a quarter share in his business, which was left to the management of his two sons.

Early in Spring the woman, whose name was Margaret Lutz, returned to Dixieland. One drowsy afternoon Eugene found them at Gant's. The house was deserted save for them. They were sprawled out face downward, with their hands across each other's hips, on Gant's bed. They lay there silently, while he looked, in an ugly stupor. Steve's yellow odor filled the room. Eugene began to tremble with insane fury. The Spring was warm and lovely, the air brooded slightly in a flowering breeze, there was a smell of soft tar. He had come down to the empty house exultantly, tasting its delicious silence, the cool mustiness of indoors, and a solitary afternoon with great calf volumes. In a moment the world turned hag.

There was nothing that Steve touched that he did not taint.

Eugene hated him because he stunk, because all that he touched stunk, because he brought fear, shame, and loathing wherever he went; because his kisses were fouler than his curses, his whines nastier than his threats. He saw the woman's hair blown gently by the blubbered exhalations of his brother's foul breath.

"What are you doing there on papa's bed?" he screamed.

Steve rose stupidly and seized him by the arm. The woman sat up, dopily staring, her short legs widened.

"I suppose you're going to be a little Tattle-tale," said Steve, bludgeoning him with heavy contempt. "You're going to run right up and tell mama, aren't you?" he said. He fastened his yellow fingers on Eugene's arm.

"Get off papa's bed," said Eugene desperately. He jerked his arm away.

"You're not going to tell on us, buddy, are you?" Steve wheedled, breathing pollution in his face.

He grew sick.

"Let me go," he muttered. "No."

Steve and Margaret were married soon after. With the old sense of physical shame Eugene watched them descend the stairs at Dixieland each morning for breakfast. Steve swaggered absurdly, smiled complacently, and hinted at great fortune about the town. There was rumor of a quarter-million.

"Put it there, Steve," said Harry Tugman, slapping him powerfully upon the shoulder. "By God, I always said you'd get there."

Eliza smiled at swagger and boast, her proud, pleased, tremulous sad smile. The first-born.

"Little Stevie doesn't have to worry any longer," said he. "He's on Easy Street. Where are all the Wise Guys now who said 'I told you so'? They're all mighty glad to give Little Stevie a Big Smile and the Glad Hand when he breezes down the street. Every Knocker is a Booster now all right, all right."

"I tell you what," said Eliza with proud smiles, "he's no fool. He's as bright as the next one when he wants to be." Brighter, she thought.

Steve bought new clothes, tan shoes, striped silk shirts, and a wide straw hat with a red, white and blue band. He swung his shoulders in a wide arc as he walked, snapped his fingers nonchalantly, and smiled with elaborate condescension on those who greeted him. Helen was vastly annoyed and amused; she had to laugh at his absurd strut, and she had a great rush of feeling for Margaret Lutz. She called her "honey," felt her eyes mist warmly with unaccountable tears as she looked into the patient, bewildered, and slightly frightened face of the German woman. She took her in her arms and fondled her.

"That's all right, honey," she said, "you let us know if he doesn't treat you right. We'll fix him."

"Steve's a good boy," said Margaret, "when he isn't drinking. I've nothing to say against him when he's sober." She burst into tears.

"That awful, that awful curse," said Eliza, shaking her head sadly, "the curse of licker. It's been responsible for the ruination of more homes than anything else."

"Well, she'll never win any beauty prizes, that's one thing sure," said Helen privately to Eliza.

"I'll vow!" said Eliza.

"What on earth did he mean by doing such a thing!" she continued. "She's ten years older than he if she's a day."

"I think he's done pretty well, if you ask me," said Helen, annoyed. "Good heavens, mama! You talk as if he's some sort of prize. Every one in town knows what Steve is." She laughed ironically and angrily. "No, indeed! He got the best of the bargain. Margaret's a decent girl."

"Well," said Eliza hopefully, "maybe he's going to brace up now and make a new start. He's promised that he'd try."

"Well, I should hope so," said Helen scathingly. "I should hope so. It's about time."

Her dislike for him was innate. She had placed him among the tribe of the Pentlands. But he was really more like Gant than any one else. He was like Gant in all his weakness, with none of his cleanliness, his lean fibre, his remorse. In her heart she knew this and it increased her dislike for him. She shared in the fierce antagonism Gant felt toward his son. But her feeling was broken, as was all her feeling, by moments of friendliness, charity, tolerance.

"What are you going to do, Steve?" she asked. "You've got a family now, you know."

"Little Stevie doesn't have to worry any longer," he said, smiling easily. "He lets the others do the worrying." He lifted his yellow fingers to his mouth, drawing deeply at a cigarette.

"Good heavens, Steve," she burst out angrily. "Pull yourself together and try to be a man for once. Margaret's a woman. You surely don't expect her to keep you up, do you?"

"What business is that of yours, for Christ's sake?" he said in a high ugly voice. "Nobody's asked your advice, have they? All of you are against me. None of you had a good word for me when I was down and out, and now it gets your goat to see me make good." He had believed for years that he was persecuted—his failure at home he attributed to the malice, envy, and disloyalty of his family, his failure abroad to the malice and envy of an opposing force that he called "the world."

"No," he said, taking another long puff at the moist cigarette, "don't worry about Stevie. He doesn't need anything from any of you, and you don't hear him asking for anything. You see that, don't you?" he said, pulling a roll of banknotes from his pocket and peeling off a few twenties. "Well, there's lots more where that came from. And I'll tell you something else: Little Stevie will be right up there among the Big Boys soon. He's got a couple of deals coming off that'll show the pikers in this town where to get off. You get that, don't you?" he said.

Ben, who had been sitting on the piano stool all this time, scowling savagely at the keys, and humming a little recurrent tune to himself while he picked it out with one finger, turned now to Helen, with a sharp flicker of his mouth, and jerked his head sideways.

"I hear Mr. Vanderbilt's getting jealous," he said.

Helen laughed ironically, huskily.

"You think you're a pretty wise guy, don't you?" said Steve heavily. "But I don't notice it's getting you anywhere."

Ben turned his scowling eyes upon him, and sniffed sharply, unconsciously.

"Now, I hope you're not going to forget your old friends, Mr. Rockefeller," he said in his subdued, caressing ominous voice. "I'd like to be vice-president if the job's still open." He turned back to the keyboard—and searched with a hooked finger.

"All right, all right," said Steve. "Go ahead and laugh, both of you, if you think it's funny. But you notice that Little Stevie isn't a fifteen-dollar clerk in a newspaper office, don't you? And he doesn't have to sing in moving-picture shows, either," he added.

Helen's big-boned face reddened angrily. She had begun to sing in public with the saddlemaker's daughter.

"You'd better not talk, Steve, until you get a job and quit bumming around," she said. "You're a fine one to talk, hanging around pool-rooms and drug-stores all day on your wife's money. Why, it's absurd!" she said furiously.

"Oh for God's sake!" Ben cried irritably, wheeling around. "What do you want to listen to him for? Can't you see he's crazy?"

As the summer lengthened, Steve began to drink heavily again. His decayed teeth, neglected for years, began to ache simultaneously: he was wild with pain and cheap whisky. He felt that Eliza and Margaret were in some way responsible for his woe—he sought them out day after day when they were alone, and screamed at them. He called them foul names and said they had poisoned his system.

In the early hours of morning, at two or three o'clock, he would waken, and walk through the house weeping and entreating release. Eliza would send him to Spaugh at the hotel or to McGuire, at his residence, in Eugene's charge. The doctors, surly and half-awake, peeled back his shirt-sleeve and drove a needle with morphine deep in his upper arm. After that, he found relief and sleep again.

One night, at the supper hour, he returned to Dixieland, holding his tortured jaws between his hands. He found Eliza bending over the spitting grease of the red-hot stove. He cursed her for bearing him, he cursed her for allowing him to have teeth, he cursed her for lack of sympathy, motherly love, human kindliness.

Her white face worked silently above the heat.

"Get out of here," she said. "You don't know what you're talking about. It's that accursed licker that makes you so mean." She began to weep, brushing at her broad red nose with her hand.

"I never thought I'd live to hear such talk from a son of mine," she said. She held out her forefinger with the old powerful gesture.

"Now, I want to tell you," she said, "I'm not going to put up with you any longer. If you don't get out of here at once I'm going to call 38 and let them take you." This was the police station. It awoke unpleasant memories. He had spent the day in jail on two similar occasions. He became more violent than before, screamed a vile name at her, and made a motion to strike her. At this moment, Luke entered; he was on his way to Gant's.

The antagonism between the boy and his older brother was deep and deadly. It had lasted for years. Now, trembling with anger, Luke came to his mother's defense.

"You m-m-m-miserable d-d-d-degenerate," he stuttered, unconsciously falling into the swing of the Gantian rhetoric. "You ought to b-b-b-be horsewhipped."

He was a well grown and muscular young fellow of nineteen years, but too sensitive to all the taboos of brotherhood to be prepared for the attack Steve made on him. Steve drove at him viciously, smashing drunkenly at his face with both hands. He was driven gasping and blinded across the kitchen.

Wrong forever on the throne.

Somewhere, through fear and fury, Eugene heard Ben's voice humming unconcernedly, and the slow picked tune on the piano.

"Ben!" he screamed, dancing about and grasping a hammer.

Ben entered like a cat. Luke was bleeding warmly from the nose.

"Come on, come on, you big bastard," said Steve, exalted by his success, throwing himself into a fancy boxing posture. "I'll take you on now. You haven't got a chance, Ben," he continued, with elaborate pity. "You haven't got a chance, boy. I'll tear your head off with what I know."

Ben scowled quietly at him for a moment while he pranced softly about, proposing his fists in Police Gazette attitudes. Then, exploding suddenly in maniacal anger, the quiet one sprang upon the amateur pugilist with one bound, and flattened him with a single blow of his fist. Steve's head bounced upon the floor in a most comforting fashion. Eugene gave a loud shriek of ecstasy and danced about, insane with joy, while Ben, making little snarling noises in his throat, leaped on his brother's prostrate body and thumped his bruised skull upon the boards. There was a beautiful thoroughness about his wakened anger—it never made inquiries till later.

"Good old Ben," screamed Eugene, howling with insane laughter, "Good old Ben."

Eliza, who had been calling out loudly for help, the police, and the interference of the general public, now succeeded, with Luke's assistance, in checking Ben's assault, and pulling him up from his dazed victim. She wept bitterly, her heart laden with pain and sadness, while Luke, forgetful of his bloody nose, sorrowful and full of shame only because brother had struck brother, assisted Steve to his feet and brushed him off.

A terrible shame started up in each of them—they were unable to meet one another's gaze. Ben's thin face was very white; he trembled violently and, catching sight of Steve's bleared eyes for a moment, he made a retching noise in his throat, went over to the sink, and drank a glass of cold water.

"A house divided against itself cannot stand," Eliza wept.

Helen came in from town with a bag of warm bread and cakes.

"What's the matter?" she said, noting at once all that had happened.

"I don't know," said Eliza, her face working, shaking her head for several moments before she spoke. "It seems that the judgment of God is against us. There's been nothing but misery all my life. All I want is a little peace." She wept softly, wiping her weak bleared eyes with the back of her hand.

"Well, forget about it," said Helen quietly. Her voice was casual, weary, sad. "How do you feel, Steve?" she asked.

"I wouldn't make any trouble for any one, Helen," he said, with a maudlin whimper. "No! No!" he continued in a brooding voice, "They've never given Steve a chance. They're all down on him. They jumped on me, Helen. My own brothers jumped on me, sick as I am, and beat me up. It's all right. I'm going away somewhere and try to forget. Stevie doesn't hold any grudge against any one. He's not built that way. Give me your hand, buddy," he said, turning to Ben with nauseous sentimentality and extending his yellow fingers, "I'm willing to shake your hand. You hit me to-night, but Steve's willing to forget."

"Oh my God," said Ben, grasping his stomach. He leaned weakly across the sink and drank another glass of water.

"No. No." Steve began again. "Stevie isn't built——"

He would have continued indefinitely in this strain, but Helen checked him with weary finality.

"Well, forget about it," she said, "all of you. Life's too short."

Life was. At these moments, after battle, after all the confusion, antagonism, and disorder of their lives had exploded in a moment of strife, they gained an hour of repose in which they saw themselves with sad tranquillity. They were like men who, driving forward desperately at some mirage, turn, for a moment, to see their footprints stretching interminably away across the waste land of the desert; or I should say, they were like those who have been mad, and who will be mad again, but who see themselves for a moment quietly, sanely, at morning, looking with sad untroubled eyes into a mirror.

Their faces were sad. There was great age in them. They felt suddenly the distance they had come and the amount they had lived. They had a moment of cohesion, a moment of tragic affection and union, which drew them together like small jets of flame against all the senseless nihilism of life.

Margaret came in fearfully. Her eyes were red, her broad German face white and tearful. A group of excited boarders whispered in the hall.

"I'll lose them all now," Eliza fretted. "The last time three left. Over twenty dollars a week and money so hard to get. I don't know what's to become of us all." She wept again.

"Oh, for heaven's sake," said Helen impatiently. "Forget about the boarders once in a while."

Steve sank stupidly into a chair by the long table. From time to time he muttered sentimentally to himself. Luke, his face sensitive, hurt, ashamed around his mouth, stood by him attentively, spoke gently to him, and brought him a glass of water.

"Give him a cup of coffee, mama," Helen cried irritably. "For heaven's sake, you might do a little for him."

"Why here, here," said Eliza, rushing awkwardly to the gas range and lighting a burner. "I never thought—I'll have some in a minute."

Margaret sat in a chair on the other side of the disorderly table, leaning her face in her hand and weeping. Her tears dredged little gulches through the thick compost of rouge and powder with which she coated her rough skin.

"Cheer up, honey," said Helen, beginning to laugh. "Christmas is coming." She patted the broad German back comfortingly.

Ben opened the torn screen door and stepped out on the back porch. It was a cool night in the rich month of August; the sky was deeply pricked with great stars. He lighted a cigarette, holding the match with white trembling fingers. There were faint sounds from summer porches, the laughter of women, a distant throb of music at a dance. Eugene went and stood beside him: he looked up at him with wonder, exultancy, and with sadness. He prodded him half with fear, half with joy.

Ben snarled softly at him, made a sudden motion to strike him, but stopped. A swift light flickered across his mouth. He smoked.

Steve went away with the German woman to Indiana, where, at first, came news of opulence, fatness, ease, and furs (with photographs), later of brawls with her honest brothers, and talk of divorce, reunion and renascence. He gravitated between the two poles of his support, Margaret and Eliza, returning to Altamont every summer for a period of drugs and drunkenness that ended in a family fight, jail, and a hospital cure.

"Hell commences," howled Gant, "as soon as he comes home. He's a curse and a care, the lowest of the low, the vilest of the vile. Woman, you have given birth to a monster who will not rest until he has done me to death, fearful, cruel, and accursed reprobate that he is!"

But Eliza wrote her oldest son regularly, enclosed sums of money from time to time, and revived her hopes incessantly, against nature, against reason, against the structure of life. She did not dare to come openly to his defense, to reveal frankly the place he held in her heart's core, but she would produce each letter in which he spoke boastfully of his successes, or announced his monthly resurrection, and read them to an unmoved family. They were florid, foolish letters, full of quotation marks and written in a large fancy hand. She was proud and pleased at all their extravagances; his flowery illiteracy was another proof to her of his superior intelligence.

Dear Mama:

Yours of the 11th to hand and must say I was glad to know you were in "the land of the living" again as I had begun to feel it was a "long time between drinks" since your last. ("I tell you what," said Eliza, looking up and sniggering with pleasure, "he's no fool." Helen, with a smile that was half ribald, half annoyed, about her big mouth, made a face at Luke, and lifted her eyes patiently upward to God as Eliza continued. Gant leaned forward tensely with his head craned upward, listening carefully with a faint grin of pleasure.) Well, mama, since I last wrote you things have been coming my way and it now looks as if the "Prodigal Son" will come home some day in his own private car. ("Hey, what's that?" said Gant, and she read it again for him. He wet his thumb and looked about with a pleased grin. "Wh-wh-what's the matter?" asked Luke. "Has he b-b-bought the railroad?" Helen laughed hoarsely. "I'm from Missouri," she said.) It took me a long time to get started, mama, but things were breaking against me and all that little Stevie has ever asked from any one in this "vale of tears" is a fair chance. (Helen laughed her ironical husky falsetto. "All that little S-S-Stevie has ever asked," said Luke, reddening with annoyance, "is the whole g-g-g-goddam world with a few gold mines thrown in.) But now that I'm on my feet at last, mama, I'm going to show the world that I haven't forgotten those who stood by me in my "hour of need," and that the best friend a man ever had is his mother. ("Where's the shovel?" said Ben, snickering quietly.)

"That boy writes a good letter," said Gant appreciatively. "I'm damned if he's not the smartest one of the lot when he wants to be."

"Yes," said Luke angrily, "he's so smart that you'll b-b-believe any fairy tale he wants to tell you. B-b-b-but the one who's stuck by you through thick and thin gets no c-c-credit at all." He glanced meaningly at Helen. "It's a d-d-damn shame."

"Forget about it," she said wearily.

"Well," said Eliza thoughtfully, holding the letter in her folded hands and gazing away, "perhaps he's going to turn over a new leaf now. You never know." Lost in pleased revery she looked into vacancy, pursing her lips.

"I hope so!" said Helen wearily. "You've got to show me."

Privately: "You see how it is, don't you?" she said to Luke, mounting to hysteria. "Do I get any credit? Do I? I can work my fingers to the bone for them, but do I get so much as Go to Hell for my trouble? Do I?"

In these years Helen went off into the South with Pearl Hines, the saddlemaker's daughter. They sang together at moving-picture theatres in country towns. They were booked from a theatrical office in Atlanta.

Pearl Hines was a heavily built girl with a meaty face and negroid lips. She was jolly and vital. She sang ragtime and nigger songs with a natural passion, swinging her hips and shaking her breasts erotically.

"Here comes my da-dad-dy now
O pop, O pop, O-o pop."

They earned as much as $100 a week sometimes. They played in towns like Waycross, Georgia; Greenville, South Carolina; Hattiesburg, Mississippi, and Baton Rouge, Louisiana.

They brought with them the great armor of innocency. They were eager and decent girls. Occasionally the village men made cautious explorative insults, relying on the superstition that lives in small towns concerning "show girls." But generally they were well treated.

For them, these ventures into new lands were eager with promise. The vacant idiot laughter, the ribald enthusiasm with which South Carolina or Georgia countrymen, filling a theatre with the strong smell of clay and sweat, greeted Pearl's songs, left them unwounded, pleased, eager. They were excited to know that they were members of the profession; they bought *Variety* regularly, they saw themselves finally a celebrated high-salaried team on "big time" in great cities. Pearl was to "put over" the popular songs, to introduce the rag melodies with the vital rhythm of her dynamic meatiness, Helen was to give operatic dignity to the programme. In a respectful hush, bathed in a pink spot, she sang ditties of higher quality—Tosti's "Goodbye," "The End of a Perfect Day," and "The Rosary." She had a big, full, somewhat metallic voice: she had received training from her Aunt Louise, the splendid blonde who had lived in Altamont for several years after her separation from Elmer Pentland. Louise gave music lessons and enjoyed her waning youth with handsome young men. She was one of the ripe, rich, dangerous women that Helen liked. She had a little girl and went away to New York with the child when tongues grew fanged.

But she said: "Helen, that voice ought to be trained for grand opera."

Helen had not forgotten. She fantasied of France and Italy: the big crude glare of what she called "a career in opera," the florid music, the tiered galleries winking with gems, the torrential applause directed toward the full-blooded, dominant all-shadowing songsters struck up great anthems in her. It was a scene, she thought, in which she was meant to shine. And as the team of Gant and Hines (The Dixie Melody Twins) moved on their jagged circuit through the South, this desire, bright, fierce, and formless, seemed, in some way, to be nearer realization.

She wrote home frequently, usually to Gant. Her letters beat like great pulses; they were filled with the excitement of new cities, presentiments of abundant life. In every town they met "lovely people"—everywhere, in fact, good wives and mothers, and nice young men, were attracted hospitably to these two decent, happy, exciting girls. There was a vast decency, an enormous clean vitality about Helen that subjugated good people and defeated bad ones. She held under her dominion a score of young men—masculine, red-faced, hard-drinking and shy. Her relation to them was maternal and magistral, they came to listen and to be ruled; they adored her, but few of them tried to kiss her.

Eugene was puzzled and frightened by these lamb-like lions. Among men, they were fierce, bold, and combative; with her, awkward and timorous. One of them, a city surveyor, lean, highboned, alcoholic, was constantly involved in police-court brawls; another, a railroad detective, a large fair young man, split the skulls of negroes when he was drunk, shot several men, and was himself finally killed in a Tennessee gun-fight.

She never lacked for friends and protectors wherever she went. Occasionally, Pearl's happy and vital sensuality, the innocent gusto with which she implored

> "Some sweet old daddy
> Come make a fuss over me."

drew on village rakedom to false conjectures. Unpleasant men with wet cigars would ask them to have a convivial drink of corn whisky, call them "girley," and suggest a hotel room or a motorcar as a meeting-place. When this happened, Pearl was stricken into silence; helpless and abashed, she appealed to Helen.

And she, her large loose mouth tense and wounded at the corners, her eyes a little brighter, would answer:

"I don't know what you mean by that remark. I guess you've made a mistake about us." This did not fail to exact stammering apologies and excuses.

She was painfully innocent, temperamentally incapable of wholly be-lieving the worst about any one. She lived in the excitement of rumor and suggestion: it never seemed to her actually possible that the fast young women who excited her had, in the phrase she used, "gone the limit." She was skilled in gossip, and greedily attentive to it, but of the complex nastiness of village life she had little actual knowledge. Thus, with Pearl Hines, she walked confidently and joyously over volcanic crust, scenting only the odor of freedom, change, and adventure.

But this partnership came to an end. The intention of Pearl Hines' life was direct and certain. She wanted to get married, she had always wanted to get married before she was twenty-five. For Helen, the singing partner-ship, the exploration of new lands, had been a gesture toward freedom, an instinctive groping toward a centre of life and purpose to which she could fasten her energy, a blind hunger for variety, beauty, and inde-pendence. She did not know what she wanted to do with her life; it was probable that she would never control even partially her destiny: she would be controlled, when the time came, by the great necessity that lived in her. That necessity was to enslave and to serve.

For two or three years Helen and Pearl supported themselves by these tours, leaving Altamont during its dull winter lassitude, and returning to it in Spring, or in Summer, with money enough to suffice them until their next season.

Pearl juggled carefully with the proposals of several young men during this period. She had the warmest affection for a ball-player, the second baseman and manager of the Altamont team. He was a tough handsome young animal, forever hurling his glove down in a frenzy of despair during the course of a game, and rushing belligerently at the umpire. She liked his hard assurance, his rapid twang, his tanned lean body.

But she was in love with no one—she would never be—and caution told her that the life-risk on bush-league ball-players was very great. She married finally a young man from Jersey City, heavy of hand, hoof, and voice, who owned a young but flourishing truck and livery business.

Thus, the partnership of the Dixie Melody Twins was dissolved. Helen, left alone, turned away from the drear monotony of the small towns to the gaiety, the variety, and the slaking fulfilment of her desires, which she hoped somehow to find in the cities.

She missed Luke terribly. Without him she felt incomplete, unarmored. He had been enrolled in the Georgia School of Technology in Atlanta for two years. He was taking the course in electrical engineering, the whole direction of his life had been thus shaped by Gant's eulogies, years before, of the young electrical expert, Liddell. He was failing in his work—his mind had never been forced to the discipline of study. All purpose with him was broken by a thousand impulses: his brain stammered as did his tongue, and as he turned impatiently and irritably to the logarithm tables, he muttered the number of the page in idiot repetition, keeping up a constant wild vibration of his leg upon the ball of his foot.

His great commercial talent was salesmanship; he had superlatively that quality that American actors and men of business call "personality"—a wild energy, a Rabelaisian vulgarity, a sensory instinct for rapid and swingeing repartee, and a hypnotic power of speech, torrential, meaningless, mad, and evangelical. He could sell anything because in the jargon of salesmen, he could sell himself; and there was a fortune in him in the fantastic elasticity of American business, the club of all the queer trades, of wild promotions, where, amok with zealot rage, he could have chanted the yokels into delirium, and cut the buttons from their coats, doing every one, everything, and finally himself. He was not an electrical engineer— he was electrical energy. He had no gift for study—he gathered his un-riveted mind together and bridged with it desperately, but crumpled under the stress and strain of calculus and the mechanical sciences.

Enormous humor flowed from him like crude light. Men who had never known him seethed with strange internal laughter when they saw him, and roared helplessly when he began to speak. Yet, his physical beauty was astonishing. His head was like that of a wild angel—coils and whorls of living golden hair flashed from his head, his features were regular, generous, and masculine, illuminated by the strange inner smile of idiot ecstasy.

His broad mouth, even when stammering irritably or when nervousness clouded his face, was always cocked for laugher—unearthly, exultant, idiot laughter. There was in him demonic exuberance, a wild intelligence that did not come from the brain. Eager for praise, for public esteem, and expert in ingratiation, this demon possessed him utterly at the most unexpected moments, in the most decorous surroundings, when he was himself doing all in his power to preserve the good opinion in which he was held.

Thus, listening to an old lady of the church, who with all her power of persuasion and earnestness was unfolding the dogmas of Presbyterianism to him, he would lean forward in an attitude of exaggerated respectfulness and attention, one broad hand clinched about his knee, while he murmured gentle agreement to what she said:

"Yes? . . . Ye-e-es? . . . Ye-e-es? . . . Ye-e-es? . . . Is that right? . . . Ye-e-es?"

Suddenly the demonic force would burst in him. Insanely tickled at the cadences of his agreement, the earnest placidity and oblivion of the old woman, and the extravagant pretense of the whole situation, his face flooded with wild exultancy, he would croon in a fat luscious bawdily suggestive voice:

"Y-ah-s? . . . Y-a-h-s? . . . Y-ah-s? . . . Y-ah-s?"

And when at length too late she became aware of this drowning flood of demonic nonsense, and paused, turning an abrupt startled face to him, he would burst into a wild "Whah-whah-whah-whah" of laughter, beyond all reason, with strange throat noises, tickling her roughly in the ribs.

Often Eliza, in the midst of long, minutely replenished reminiscence, would grow conscious, while she was purse-lipped in revery, of this annihilating mockery, would slap at his hand angrily as he gooched her, and shake a pursed piqued face at him, saying, with a heavy scorn that set him off into fresh "whah-whahs": "I'll declare, boy! You act like a regular idiot," and then shaking her head sadly, with elaborate pity: "I'd be ash-a-amed! A-sha-a-med."

His quality was extraordinary; he had something that was a great deal better than most intelligence; he saw the world in burlesque, and his occasional answer to its sham, hypocrisy, and intrigue was the idiot devastation of "whah-whah!" But he did not possess his demon; it possessed him from time to time. If it had possessed him wholly, constantly, his life would have prevailed with astonishing honesty and precision. But when he reflected, he was a child—with all the hypocrisy, sentimentality and dishonest pretense of a child.

His face was a church in which beauty and humor were married—the strange and the familiar were at one in him. Men, looking at Luke, felt a start of recognition as if they saw something of which they had never heard, but which they had known forever.

Once or twice, during the Winter and Spring, while she was touring with Pearl Hines, Helen got into Atlanta to see him. In Spring they attended the week of Grand Opera. He would find employment for one night as a spearman in *Aïda* and pass the doorman for the remainder of the week with the assurance that he was "a member of the company—Lukio Gantio."

His large feet spread tightly out in sandals; behind the shingreaves his awkward calves were spined thickly with hair; a thick screw of hair writhed under the edge of his tin helmet, as he lofed in the wings, leaning comically on his spear, his face lit with exultancy.

Caruso, waiting his entrance, regarded him from time to time with a wide Wop smile.

"Wotta you call yourself, eh?" asked Caruso, approaching and looking him over.

"W-w-w-why," he said, "d-don't you know one of your s-s-s-soldiers when you see him?"

"You're one hell of a soldier," said Caruso.

"Whah-whah-whah!" Luke answered. With difficulty he restrained his prodding fingers.

In the summer now he returned to Altamont, finding employment with a firm of land-auctioneers, and assisting them at the sale of a tract or a parcel of lots. He moved about above the crowd in the bed of a wagon, exhorting them to bid, with his hand at the side of his mouth, in a harangue compounded of frenzy, passionate solicitation, and bawdry. The work intoxicated him. With wide grins of expectancy they crowded round the spokes. In a high throaty tenor he called to them:

"Step right up, gentlemen, lot number 17, in beautiful Homewood— we furnish the wood, you furnish the home. Now gentlemen, this handsome building-site has a depth of 179 feet, leaving plenty of room for garden and backhouse (grow your own corn cobs in beautiful Homewood) with a frontage of 114 feet on a magnificent new macadam road."

"Where is the road?" some one shouted.

"On the blueprint, of course, Colonel. You've got it all in black and white. Now, gentlemen, the opportunity of your lives is kicking you in the pants. Are you men of vision? Think what Ford, Edison, Napoleon Bonaparte, and Julius Caesar would do. Obey that impulse. You can't lose. The town is coming this way. Listen carefully. Do you hear it?

Swell. The new courthouse will be built on yonder hill, the undertaker and the village bakery will occupy handsome edifices of pressed brick just above you. Oyez, oyez, oyez. What am I offered? What am I offered? Own your own home in beautiful Homewood, within a cannonshot of all railway, automobile, and airplane connections. Running water abounds within a Washingtonian stone's throw and in all the pipes. Our caravans meet all trains. Gentlemen, here's your chance to make a fortune. The ground is rich in mineral resources—gold, silver, copper, iron, bituminous coal and oil, will be found in large quantities below the roots of all the trees."

"What about the bushes, Luke?" yelled Mr. Halloran, the dairy-lunch magnate.

"Down in the bushes, that is where she gushes," Luke answered amid general tumult. "All right, Major. You with the face. What am I offered? What am I offered?"

When there was no sale, he greeted incoming tourists at the station-curbing with eloquent invitations to Dixieland, rich, persuasive, dominant above all the soliciting babel of the car-drivers, negro hotel-porters, and boarding-house husbands.

"I'll give you a dollar apiece for every one you drum up," said Eliza.

"O that's all right." O modestly. Generously.

"He'd give you the shirt off his back," said Gant.

A fine boy. As she cooled from her labors in the summer night, he brought her little boxes of ice-cream from town.

He was a hustler: he sold patent washboards, trick potato-peelers, and powdered cockroach-poison from house to house. To the negroes he sold hair-oil guaranteed to straighten kinky hair, and religious lithographs, peopled with flying angels, white and black, and volant cherubs, black and white, sailing about the knees of an impartial and crucified Saviour, and subtitled "God Loves Them Both."

They sold like hot cakes.

Otherwise, he drove Gant's car—a 1913 five-passenger Ford, purchase of an inspired hour of madness, occupant now of half Gant's conversation, object of abuse, boast, and anathema. It was before every one owned a car. Gant was awed and terrified by his rash act, exalted at the splendor of his chariot, appalled at its expense. Each bill for gasoline, repairs, or equipment brought a howl of anguish from him; a puncture, a breakdown, a minor disorder caused him to circle about in maddened strides, cursing, praying, weeping.

"I've never had a moment's peace since I bought it," he howled. "Accursed and bloody monster that it is, it will not be content until it has sucked out my life-blood, sold the roof over my head, and sent me out to the pauper's grave to perish. Merciful God," he wept, "it's fearful, it's awful, it's cruel that I should be afflicted thus in my old age." Turning to his constrained and apologetic son abruptly, he said: "How much is the bill? Hey?" His eyes roved wildly in his head.

"D-d-d-don't get excited, papa," Luke answered soothingly, teetering from foot to foot, "it's only $8.92."

"Jesus God!" Gant screamed. "I'm ruined." Sobbing in loud burlesque sniffles, he began his caged pacing.

But it was pleasant at dusk or in the cool summer nights, with Eliza or one of his daughters beside him, and a fragrant weed between his pallid lips, to hinge his long body into the back seat, and ride out into the fragrant countryside, or through the long dark streets of town. At the approach of another car he cried out in loud alarm, by turns cursing and entreating his son to caution. Luke drove nervously, erratically, wildly— his stammering impatient hands and knees communicated their uneven fidget to the flivver. He cursed irritably, plunged in exacerbated fury at the brake, and burst out in an annoyed "tuh-tuh-tuh-tuh," when the car stalled.

As the hour grew late, and the streets silent, his madness swelled in him. Lipping the rim of a long hill street, tree-arched and leafy and shelving in even terraces, he would burst suddenly into insane laughter, bend over the wheel, and pull the throttle open, his idiot "whah-whahs" filling the darkness as Gant screamed curses at him. Down through the night they tore at murderous speed, the boy laughing at curse and prayer alike as they shot past the blind menace of street-crossings.

"You Goddamned scoundrel!" Gant yelled. "Stop, you mountain grill, or I'll put you in jail."

"Whah-whah."—His laughter soared to a crazy falsetto.

Daisy, arrived for a few weeks of summer coolness, quite blue with terror, would clutch the most recent of her annual arrivals to her breast, melodramatically, and moan:

"I beg of you, for the sake of my family, for the sake of my innocent motherless babes——"

"Whah-whah-whah!"

"He's a fiend out of hell," cried Gant, beginning to weep. "Cruel and criminal monster that he is, he will batter our brains out against a tree, before he's done." They whizzed with a perilous swerve by a car that, with a startled screech of its brakes, balked at the corner like a frightened horse.

"You damned thug!" Gant roared, plunging forward and fastening his great hands around Luke's throat. "Will you stop?"

Luke added another notch of blazing speed. Gant fell backward with a howl of terror.

On Sunday they made long tours into the country. Often they drove to Reynoldsville, twenty-two miles away. It was an ugly little resort, noisy with arriving and departing cars, with a warm stench of oil and gasoline heavy above its broad main street. But people were coming and going from several States: Southward they came up from South Carolina and Georgia, cotton-farmers, small tradesmen and their families in battered cars coated with red sandclay dust. They had a heavy afternoon dinner of fried chicken, corn, string-beans, and sliced tomatoes, at one of the big wooden boarding-house hotels, spent another hour in a drugstore over a chocolate nut-sundae, watched the summer crowd of fortunate tourists and ripe cool-skinned virgins flow by upon the wide sidewalk in thick pullulation, and returned again, after a brief tour of the town, on the winding immediate drop to the hot South. New lands.

Fluescent with smooth ripe curves, the drawling virgins of the South filled summer porches.

Luke was a darling. He was a dear, a fine boy, a big-hearted generous fellow, and just the cutest thing. Women liked him, laughed at him, pulled fondly the thick golden curls of his hair. He was sentimentally tender to children—girls of fourteen years. He had a grand romantic feeling for Delia Selborne, the oldest daughter of Mrs. Selborne. He bought her presents, was tender and irritable by turns. Once, at Gant's, on the porch under an August moon and the smell of ripening grapes, he caressed her while Helen sang in the parlor. He caressed her gently, leaned his head over her, and said he would like to lay it on her b-b-b-b-breast. Eugene watched them bitterly, with an inch of poison round his heart. He wanted the girl for himself: she was stupid, but she had the wise body and faint hovering smile of her mother. He wanted Mrs. Selborne more, he fantasied passionately about her yet, but her image lived again in Delia. As a result, he was proud, cold, scornful and foolish before them. They disliked him.

Enviously, with gnawn heart, he observed Luke's ministrations to Mrs. Selborne. His service was so devout, so extravagant that even Helen grew annoyed and occasionally jealous. And nightly, from a remote corner at Gant's or Eliza's, or from a parked automobile before the house, he heard her rich welling laughter, full of tenderness, surrender, and mystery. Sometimes, waiting in pitch darkness on the stairs at Eliza's, at one or two o'clock in the morning, he felt her pass him. As she touched him in the dark, she gave a low cry of terror; with an uncivil grunt he reassured her, and descended to bed with a pounding heart and burning face.

Ah, yes, he thought, with green morality, observing his brother throned in laughter and affection, you Big Fool, you—you're just a sucker! You show off and act big, my sonny, and spend your money bringing ice-cream for them—but what do you get out of it? How do you feel when she gets out of an automobile at two o'clock in the morning after grunting in the dark with some damned travelling-man, or with old Poxy Logan who's been keeping a nigger woman up for years. "May I p-p-p-put my head on your breast?" You make me sick, you damned fool. *She's* no better, only you don't know beans. She'll let you spend all your money on her and then she'll run off with some little pimp in an automobile for the rest of the night. Yes, that's so. Do you want to make anything out of it? You big bluff. Come out into the back yard. . . . I'll show you . . . take that . . . and that . . . and that . . .

Pumping his fists wildly, he fought his phantom into defeat and himself into exhaustion.

Luke had several hundred dollars saved from *The Saturday Evening Post* days, when he went off to school. He accepted very little money from Gant. He waited on tables, he solicited for college boarding-houses, he was the agent for a tailor who made Kippy Kampus Klothes. Gant boasted of these efforts. The town shifted its quid, nodded pertly, and spat, saying: "That boy'll make his mark."

Luke worked as hard for an education as any other self-made man. He made every sacrifice. He did everything but study.

He was an immense popular success, so very extra, so very Luky. The school sought and adored him. Twice, after football games, he mounted a hearse and made funeral orations over the University of Georgia.

But, in spite of all his effort, toward the end of his third year he was still a sophomore, with every prospect of remaining one. One day in Spring he wrote the following letter to Gant:

"The b-b-b-bastards who r-r-run this place have it in for me. I've been c-c-c-crooked good and proper. They take your hard-earned m-m-money here and skin you. I'm g-g-g-going to a real school."

He went to Pittsburgh and found work with the Westinghouse Electric Company. Three times a week at night he attended courses at the Carnegie Institute of Technology. He made friends.

The war had come. After fifteen months in Pittsburgh he moved on to

Dayton where he got employment at a boiler factory engaged in the fabrication of war materials.

From time to time, in summer for a few weeks, at Christmas for a few days, he returned to celebrate his holidays with his family. Always he brought Gant a suitcase stocked with beer and whisky. That boy was "good to his father."

19

One afternoon in the young summer, Gant leaned upon the rail, talking to Jannadeau. He was getting on to sixty-five, his erect body had settled, he stooped a little. He spoke of old age often, and he wept in his tirades now because of his stiffened hand. Soaked in pity, he referred to himself as "the poor old cripple who has to provide for them all."

The indolence of age and disintegration was creeping over him. He now rose a full hour later, he came to his shop punctually, but he spent long hours of the day extended on the worn leather couch of his office, or in gossip with Jannadeau, bawdy old Liddell, Cardiac, and Fagg Sluder, who had salted away his fortune in two big buildings on the Square and was at the present moment tilted comfortably in a chair before the fire department, gossiping eagerly with members of the ball club, whose chief support he was. It was after five o'clock, the game was over.

Negro laborers, grisly with a white coating of cement, sloped down past the shop on their way home. The draymen dispersed slowly, a slouchy policeman loafed down the steps of the city hall picking his teeth, and on the market side, from high grilled windows, there came the occasional howls of a drunken negress. Life buzzed slowly like a fly.

The sun had reddened slightly, there was a cool flowing breath from the hills, a freshening relaxation over the tired earth, the hope, the ecstasy of evening in the air. In slow pulses the thick plume of fountain rose, fell upon itself, and slapped the pool in lazy rhythms. A wagon rattled leanly over the big cobbles; beyond the firemen, the grocer Bradley wound up his awning with slow creaking revolutions.

Across the Square, at its other edge, the young virgins of the eastern part of town walked lightly home in chattering groups. They came to town at four o'clock in the afternoon, walked up and down the little avenue several times, entered a shop to purchase small justifications, and finally went into the chief drugstore, where the bucks of the town loafed and drawled in lazy alert groups. It was their club, their brasserie, the forum of the sexes. With confident smiles the young men detached themselves from their group and strolled back to booth and table.

"Hey theah! Wheahd you come from?"

"Move ovah theah, lady. I want to tawk to you."

Eyes as blue as Southern skies looked roguishly up to laughing gray ones, the winsome dimples deepened, and the sweetest little tail in dear old Dixie slid gently over on the polished board.

Gant spent delightful hours now in the gossip of dirty old men—their huddled bawdry exploded in cracked high wheezes on the Square. He came home at evening stored with gutter tidings, wetting his thumb and smiling slyly as he questioned Helen hopefully:

"She's no better than a regular little chippie—eh?"

"Ha-ha-ha-ha-," she laughed mockingly. "Don't you wish you knew?"

His age bore certain fruits, emoluments of service. When she came home in the evening with one of her friends, she presented the girl with jocose eagerness to his embrace. And, crying out paternally, "Why, bless her heart! Come kiss the old man," he planted bristling mustache kisses on their white throats, their soft lips, grasping the firm meat of one arm tenderly with his good hand and cradling them gently. They shrieked with throaty giggle-twiddles of pleasure because it tuh-tuh-tuh-tuh-*tickled* so.

"Ooh! Mr. Gant! Whah-whah-whah!"

"Your father's such a nice man," they said. "Such lovely manners."

Helen's eyes fed fiercely on them. She laughed with husky-harsh excitement.

"Hah-ha-ha! He likes that, doesn't he? It's too bad, old boy, isn't it? No more monkey business."

He talked with Jannadeau, while his fugitive eyes roved over the east end of the Square. Before the shop the comely matrons of the town came up from the market. From time to time they smiled, seeing him, and he bowed sweepingly. Such lovely manners.

"The King of England," he observed, "is only a figurehead. He doesn't begin to have the power of the President of the United States."

"His power is severely limited," said Jannadeau gutturally, "by custom but not by statute. In actuality he is still one of the most powerful monarchs in the world." His thick black fingers probed carefully into the viscera of a watch.

"The late King Edward for all his faults," said Gant, wetting his thumb, "was a smart man. This fellow they've got now is a nonentity and a nincompoop." He grinned faintly, craftily, with pleasure at the big words, glancing slily at the Swiss to see if they had told.

His uneasy eyes followed carefully the stylish carriage of "Queen" Elizabeth's well clad figure as she went down by the shop. She smiled pleasantly, and for a moment turned her candid stare upon smooth marble slabs of death, carved lambs and cherubim. Gant bowed elaborately.

"Good-evening, madam," he said.

She disappeared. In a moment she came back decisively and mounted the broad steps. He watched her approach with quickened pulses. Twelve years.

"How's the madam?" he said gallantly. "Elizabeth, I was just telling Jannadeau you were the most stylish woman in town."

"Well, that's mighty sweet of you, Mr. Gant," she said in her cool poised voice. "You've always got a word for every one."

She gave a bright pleasant nod to Jannadeau, who swung his huge scowling head ponderously around and muttered at her.

"Why, Elizabeth," said Gant, "you haven't changed an inch in fifteen years. I don't believe you're a day older."

She was thirty-eight and pleasantly aware of it.

"Oh, yes," she said laughing. "You're only saying that to make me feel good. I'm no chicken any more."

She had a pale clear skin, pleasantly freckled, carrot-colored hair, and a thin mouth live with humor. Her figure was trim and strong—no longer young. She had a great deal of energy, distinction, and elegance in her manner.

"How are all the girls, Elizabeth?" he asked kindly.

Her face grew sad. She began to pull her gloves off.

"That's what I came to see you about," she said. "I lost one of them last week."

"Yes," said Gant gravely, "I was sorry to hear of that."

"She was the best girl I had," said Elizabeth. "I'd have done anything in the world for her. We did everything we could," she added. "I've no regrets on that score. I had a doctor and two trained nurses by her all the time."

She opened her black leather handbag, thrust her gloves into it, and pulling out a small bluebordered handkerchief, began to weep quietly.

"Huh-huh-huh-huh-huh," said Gant, shaking his head. "Too bad, too bad, too bad. Come back to my office," he said. They went back and sat down. Elizabeth dried her eyes.

"What was her name?" he asked.

"We called her Lily—her full name was Lillian Reed."

"Why, I knew that girl," he exclaimed. "I spoke to her not over two weeks ago."

"Yes," said Elizabeth, "she went like that—one hemorrhage right after another, down here." She tapped her abdomen. "Nobody ever knew she was sick until last Wednesday. Friday she was gone." She wept again.

"T-t-t-t-t," he clucked regretfully. "Too bad, too bad. She was pretty as a picture."

"I couldn't have loved her more, Mr. Gant," said Elizabeth, "if she had been my own daughter."

"How old was she?" he asked

"Twenty-two," said Elizabeth, beginning to weep again.

"What a pity! What a pity!" he agreed. "Did she have any people?"

"No one who would do anything for her," Elizabeth said. "Her mother died when she was thirteen—she was born out here on the Beetree Fork—and her father," she added indignantly, "is a mean old bastard who's never done anything for her or any one else. He didn't even come to her funeral."

"He will be punished," said Gant darkly.

"As sure as there's a God in heaven," Elizabeth agreed, "he'll get what's coming to him in hell. The old bastard!" she continued virtuously, "I hope he rots!"

"You can depend upon it," he said grimly. "He will. Ah, Lord." He was silent a moment while he shook his head with slow regret.

"A pity, a pity," he muttered. "So young." He had the moment of triumph all men have when they hear some one has died. A moment, too, of grisly fear. Sixty-four.

"I couldn't have loved her more," said Elizabeth, "if she'd been one of my own. A young girl like that, with all her life before her."

"It's pretty sad when you come to think of it," he said. "By God, it is."

"And she was such a fine girl, Mr. Gant," said Elizabeth, weeping softly. "She had such a bright future before her. She had more opportunities than I ever had, and I suppose you know"—she spoke modestly—"what I've done."

"Why," he exclaimed, startled, "you're a rich woman, Elizabeth—damned if I don't believe you are. You own property all over town."

"I wouldn't say that," she answered, "but I've got enough to live on without ever doing another lick of work. I've had to work hard all my life. From now on I don't intend to turn my hand over."

She regarded him with a shy pleased smile, and touched a coil of her fine hair with a small competent hand. He looked at her attentively, noting with pleasure her firm uncorseted hips, moulded compactly into her tailored suit, and her cocked comely legs tapering to graceful feet, shod in neat little slippers of tan. She was firm, strong, washed, and elegant—a faint scent of lilac hovered over her: he looked at her candid eyes, lucently gray, and saw that she was quite a great lady.

"By God, Elizabeth," he said, "you're a fine-looking woman."

"I've had a good life," she said. "I've taken care of myself."

They had always known each other—since first they met. They had no excuses, no questions, no replies. The world fell away from them. In the silence they heard the pulsing slap of the fountain, the high laughter of bawdry in the Square. He took a book of models from the desk, and began to turn its slick pages. They showed modest blocks of Georgia marble and Vermont granite.

"I don't want any of those," she said impatiently. "I've already made up my mind. I know what I want."

He looked up surprised. "What is it?"

"I want the angel out front."

His face was shocked and unwilling. He gnawed the corner of his thin lip. No one knew how fond he was of the angel. Publicly he called it his White Elephant. He cursed it and said he had been a fool to order it. For six years it had stood on the porch, weathering, in all the wind and the rain. It was now brown and fly-specked. But it had come from Carrara in Italy, and it held a stone lily delicately in one hand. The other hand was lifted in benediction, it was poised clumsily upon the ball of one phthisic foot, and its stupid white face wore a smile of soft stone idiocy.

In his rages, Gant sometimes directed vast climaxes of abuse at the angel. "Fiend out of Hell!" he roared. "You have impoverished me, you have ruined me, you have cursed my declining years, and now you will crush me to death, fearful, awful, and unnatural monster that you are."

But sometimes when he was drunk he fell weeping on his knees before it, called it Cynthia, and entreated its love, forgiveness, and blessing for its sinful but repentant boy. There was laughter from the Square.

"What's the matter?" said Elizabeth. "Don't you want to sell it?"

"It will cost you a good deal, Elizabeth," he said evasively.

"I don't care," she answered, positively. "I've got the money. How much do you want?"

He was silent, thinking for a moment of the place where the angel stood. He knew he had nothing to cover or obliterate that place—it left a barren crater in his heart.

"All right," he said. "You can have it for what I paid for it—$420."

She took a thick sheaf of banknotes from her purse and counted the money out for him. He pushed it back.

"No. Pay me when the job's finished and it has been set up. You want some sort of inscription, don't you?"

"Yes. There's her full name, age, place of birth, and so on," she said, giving him a scrawled envelope. "I want some poetry, too—something that suits a young girl taken off like this."

He pulled his tattered little book of inscriptions from a pigeonhole, and thumbed its pages, reading her a quatrain here and there. To each she shook her head. Finally, he said:

"How's this one, Elizabeth?" He read:

> She went away in beauty's flower,
> Before her youth was spent;
> Ere life and love had lived their hour
> God called her, and she went.

> Yet whispers Faith upon the wind:
> No grief to her was given.
> She left *your* love and went to find
> A greater one in heaven.

"Oh, that's lovely—lovely," she said. "I want that one."

"Yes," he agreed, "I think that's the best one."

In the musty cool smell of his little office they got up. Her gallant figure reached his shoulder. She buttoned her kid gloves over the small pink haunch of her palms and glanced about her. His battered sofa filled one wall, the line of his long body was printed in the leather. She looked up at him. His face was sad and grave. They remembered.

"It's been a long time, Elizabeth," he said.

They walked slowly to the front through aisled marbles. Sentinelled just beyond the wooden doors, the angel leered vacantly down. Jannadeau drew his great head turtlewise a little further into the protective hunch of his burly shoulders. They went out on to the porch.

The moon stood already, like its own phantom, in the clear washed skies of evening. A little boy with an empty paper-delivery bag swung lithely by, his freckled nostrils dilating pleasantly with hunger and the fancied smell of supper. He passed, and for a moment, as they stood at the porch edge, all life seemed frozen in a picture: the firemen and Fagg Sluder had seen Gant, whispered, and were now looking toward him; a policeman, at the high side-porch of the Police Court, leaned on the rail and stared; at the near edge of the central grass-plot below the fountain, a farmer bent for water at a bubbling jet, rose dripping, and stared; from the Tax Collector's office, City Hall, upstairs, Yancey, huge, meaty, shirtsleeved, stared. And in that second the slow pulse of the fountain was suspended, life was held, like an arrested gesture, in photographic abeyance, and Gant felt himself alone move deathward in a world of seemings as, in 1910, a man might find himself again in a picture taken on the grounds of the Chicago Fair, when he was thirty and his mustache black, and, noting the bustled ladies and the derbied men fixed in the second's pullulation, remember the dead instant, seek beyond the borders for what was there (he knew); or as a veteran who finds himself upon his elbow near Ulysses Grant, before the march, in pictures of the Civil War, and sees a dead man on a horse; or I should say, like some completed Don, who finds himself again before a tent in Scotland in his youth, and notes a cricket-bat long lost and long forgotten, the face of a poet who has died, and young men and the tutor as they looked that Long Vacation when they read nine hours a day for "Greats."

Where now? Where after? Where then?

20

Gant, during these years in which Helen and Luke, the two for whom he felt the deepest affection, were absent a large part of the time, lived a splintered existence at home and at Eliza's. He feared and hated a lonely life, but habit was deeply rooted in him, and he was unwilling to exchange the well-used comfort of his own home for the bald wintriness of Eliza's. She did not want him. She fed him willingly enough, but his tirades and his nightly sojourns, both longer and more frequent now that his daughter was absent, annoyed her more than they ever had before.

"You have a place of your own," she cried fretfully. "Why don't you stay in it? I don't want you around making trouble."

"Send him on," he moaned bitterly. "Send him on. Over the stones rattle his bones, he's only a beggar that nobody owns. Ah, Lord! The old dray-horse has had its day. Its race is run. Kick him out: the old cripple can no longer provide them with victuals, and they will throw him on the junk-heap, unnatural and degenerate monsters that they are."

But he remained at Dixieland as long as there was any one to listen to him, and to the bleak little group of winter boarders he brought magic. They fed hungrily on all the dramatic gusto with which, lunging back and forth in the big rocker, before the blazing parlor fire, he told and retold the legends of his experience, taking, before their charmed eyes, an incident that had touched him romantically, and embellishing, weaving and building it up. A whole mythology grew up as, goggle-eyed, they listened:

General Fitzhugh Lee, who had reined up before the farmer boy and asked for a drink of water, now tossed off an oaken bucketful, questioned him closely concerning the best roads into Gettysburg, asked if he had seen detachments of the enemy, wrote his name down in a small book, and went off saying to his staff: "That boy will make his mark. It is impossible to defeat an enemy which breeds boys like that."

The Indians, whom he had passed amicably as he rode out into the New Mexican desert on a burro, seeking the ancient fort, now spurred after him with fell intent and wild scalping whoops. He rode furiously through mut-tering redskin villages, and found the protection of two cattlemen in the nick of time. The thief who had entered his room at dead of night in New Orleans, and picked up his clothes, and whom he had fought desperately upon the floor, he now pursued naked for seventeen blocks (not five) down Canal Street.

He went several times a week to the moving-picture shows, taking Eugene, and sitting, bent forward in hunched absorption, through two full performances. They came out at ten-thirty or eleven o'clock, on cold ringing pavements, into a world frozen bare—a dead city of closed shops, dressed windows, milliners' and clothiers' models posturing with waxen gaiety at congealed silence.

On the Square the slackened fountain dropped a fat spire of freezing water into its thickening rim of ice. In summer, a tall spire blown in blue sheets of spray. When they turned it down it wilted—that was like a foun-tain, too. No wind blew.

His eyes fixed on the clean concrete walk, Gant strode on, muttering dra-matically, composing a narrative of the picture. The cold steel of new sewing-machines glinted in dim light. The Singer building. Tallest in the world. The stitching hum of Eliza's machine. Needle through your finger before you know it. He winced. They passed the Sluder Building at the corner of the Square and turned left. Gets over $700 a month in office-rent from this alone. The window on the corner was filled with rubber syringes and thermos bottles. Drink Coca Cola. They say he stole the formula from old mountain woman. $50,000,000 now. Rats in the vats. Dope at Wood's better. Too weak here. He had recently acquired a taste for the beverage and drank four or five glasses a day.

D. Stern had his old shack on that corner twenty years before Fagg bought it. Belonged to Paston estate. Could have bought it for a song. Rich man now. D. moved to North Main now. The Jew's rich. Fortune out of winnies. They're hot, they're hot. In a broken pot. If I had a little time I'd make a little rhyme. Thirteen kids—she had one every year. As broad as she's long. They all get fat. Every one works. Sons pay father board. None of mine, I can assure you. The Jews get there.

The hunchback—what did they call him? One of Nature's Cruel Jests. Ah, Lord! What's become of old John Bunny? I used to like his pictures. Oh yes. Dead.

That pure look they have, at the end, when he kisses her, mused Eugene. Later—A Warmer Clime. Her long lashes curled down over her wet eyes, she was unable to meet his gaze. The sweet lips trembled with desire as, clasping her in a grip of steel, he bent down over her yielding body and planted hungry kisses on her mouth. When the purple canopy of dawn had been reft asunder by the rays of the invading sun. The Stranger. It wouldn't do to say the next morning. They have a thick coat of yellow paint all over their face. Meanwhile, in Old England. I wonder what they say to each other. They're a pretty tough lot, I suppose.

A swift thrust of conviction left him unperturbed. The other was better.

He thought of the Stranger. Steel-gray eyes. A steady face. An eighth of a second faster on the draw than any one else. Two-gun Bill Hart. Anderson of the Essanay. Strong quiet men.

He clapped his hand against his buttock with a sharp smack and shot the murderous forefinger at an ashcan, a lamp-post, and a barber-pole, with a snapping wrist. Gant, startled in composition, gave him a quick uneasy look. They walked on.

Came a day when Spring put forth her blossoms on the earth again. No, no—not that. Then all grew dark. Picture of a lily trampled on the earth. That means he bigged her. Art. Filled her with thee a baby fair. You can't go away now. Why? Because—because—her eyes dropped shyly, a slow flush mantled her cheek. He stared at her blankly for a moment, then his puzzled gaze—(O good!)—fell to the tiny object she was fingering nervously, with dawning comprehension. Blushing rosily, she tried to conceal the little jacket behind her. Grace! A great light broke on him! Do you mean it? She went to him with a cry, half laugh, half sob, and buried her burning face in his neck. You silly boy. Of course I mean it (you bastard!). The little dance girl. Smiling with wet lechery and manipulating his moist rope of cigar, Faro Jim shuffled a pack of cards slowly and fixed on her his vulturesque eye. A knife in his shiny boots, a small derringer and three aces up his ruffled sleeve, and suave murder in his heart. But the cold gray eyes of the Stranger missed nothing. Imperturbably he drank his Scotch, wheeled from the mirror with barking Colt just one-sixth of a second before the gambler could fire. Faro coughed and slid forward slowly upon the floor.

There was no sound now in the crowded room of the Triple Y. Men stood petrified. The face of Bad Bill and the two Mexicans had turned a dirty gray. Finally, the sheriff spoke, turning with awe from the still figure on the sawdust floor.

"By God, stranger!" he ejaculated, "I never knew the man lived who could beat Faro to the draw. What's yore name?"

"In the fam'ly Bible back home, pardner," the Stranger drawled, "it's Eugene Gant, but folks out here generally calls me The Dixie Ghost."

There was a slow gasp of wonder from the crowd.

"Gawd!" some one whispered. "It's the Ghost!"

As the Ghost turned coolly back to finish his interrupted drink, he found himself face to face with the little dancing girl. Two smoking globes of brine welled from the pellucid depths of her pure eyes and fell with a hot splash on his bronzed hand.

"How can I ever thank you!" she cried. "You have saved me from a fate far worse than death."

But the Ghost, who had faced death many times without a flicker of a lash, was unable to face something he saw now in a pair of big brown eyes. He took off his sombrero and twisted it shyly in his big hands.

"Why, that's all right, ma'am," he gulped awkwardly. "Glad to be of service to a lady any time."

By this time the two bartenders had thrown a table-cloth over Faro Bill, carried the limp body into the back room, and returned to their positions behind the bar. The crowd clustered about in little groups, laughing and talking excitedly, and in a moment, as the pianist began to hammer out a tune on the battered piano, broke into the measures of a waltz.

In the wild West of those days, passions were primitive, vengeance sudden, and retribution immediate.

Two dimples sentinelled a platoon of milk-white teeth.

"Won't you dance with me, Mr. Ghost?" she coaxed.

Thoughtfully he pondered on love's mystery. Pure but passionate. Appearances against her, 'tis true. The foul breath of slander. She worked in a bawdy-house but her heart was clean. Outside of that, what can one say against her? He thought pleasantly of murder. With child's eyes he regarded his extinct enemies. Men died violently but cleanly, in the movies. Bang-bang. Good-by, boys, I'm through. Through the head or heart—a clean hole, no blood. He had kept innocency. Do their guts or their brains come spilling out? Currant jelly where a face was, the chin shot off. Or down there that other—His arm beat the air like a wing: he writhed. If you lose that? Done, die. He clutched his throat in his anguish.

They bent down eastward along Academy Street, having turned right from the little caudal appendage that gave on the northeastern corner of the Square. The boy's mind flamed with bright streaming images, sharp as gems, mutable as chameleons. His life was the shadow of a shadow, a play within a play. He became the hero-actor-star, the lord of the cinema, and the lover of a beautiful movie-queen, as heroic as his postures, with a superior actuality for every make-believe. He was the Ghost and he who played the Ghost, the cause that minted legend into fact.

He was those heroes whom he admired, and the victor, in beauty, nobility, and sterling worth, over those whom he despised because they always triumphed and were forever good and pretty and beloved of women. He was chosen and beloved of a bevy of internationally renowned beauties, vampires and pure sweet girls alike, with fruity blondes in the lead, all contesting for his favors, and some of the least scrupulous resorting to underhand practices in order to win him. Their pure eyes turned up to him in everlasting close-ups: he feasted virtuously upon their proffered lips and, conflict over, murder sanctified, and virtue crowned, walked away with his siren into the convenient blaze of a constantly setting sun.

With burning sidelong face he looked quickly up at Gant, twisting his convulsive neck.

Across the street, a calcium glare from the corner light bathed coldly the new brick facade of the Orpheum Theatre. All This Week Gus Nolan and His Georgia Peaches. Also the Piedmont Comedy Four and Miss Bobbie Dukane.

The theatre was dark, the second show was over. They stared curiously across the street at the posters. In this cold silence where were the Peaches? At the Athens now, upon the Square. They always went there after. Gant looked at his watch. 11:12. Big Bill Messler outside swinging his club and watching them. On the counter stools a dozen bucks and ogling rakehells. I've got a car outside. Dalliance under difficulties. Later, the Genevieve on Liberty Street. They all stay there. Whisperings. Footfalls. Raided.

Girls from good families, some of them, I suppose, Gant thought.

Opposite the Baptist Church a hearse was drawn up before Gorham's Undertaking Parlors. A light burned dimly through the ferns. Who can that be? he wondered. Miss Annie Patton critically ill. She's past eighty. Some lunger from New York. A little Jew with a peaked face. Some one all the time. Await alike th' inevitable hour. Ah, Lord!

With loss of hunger, he thought of undertaking and undertakers, and in particular of Mr. Gorham. He was a man with blond hair and white eyebrows.

Waited to marry her when that rich young Cuban died, so they could take honeymoon to Havana.

They turned down Spring Street by the Baptist Church. This is really like a city of the dead, Eugene thought. The town, rimed with frost, lay frozen below the stars in a cataleptic trance. The animacy of life hung in abeyance. Nothing grew old, nothing decayed, nothing died. It was triumph over time. If a great demon snapped his fingers and stopped all life in the world for an instant that should be a hundred years, who would know the difference? Every man a Sleeping Beauty. If you're waking call me early, call me early, mother dear.

He tried to see life and movement behind the walls, and failed. He and Gant were all that lived. For a house betrays nothing: there may be murder behind its very quiet face. He thought that Troy should be like this—perfect, undecayed as the day when Hector died. Only they burned it. To find old cities as they were, unruined—the picture charmed him. The Lost Atlantis. Ville d'Ys. The old lost towns, seasunken. Great vacant ways, unrusted, echoed under his lonely feet; he haunted vast arcades, he pierced the atrium, his shoes rang on the temple flags.

Or to be, he lusciously meditated, left alone with a group of pretty women in a town whence all the other people had fled from some terror of plague, earthquake, volcano, or other menace to which he, quite happily, was immune. Lolling his tongue delicately, he saw himself loafing sy-baritically through first-class confectioners' and grocers' shops, gorging like an anaconda on imported dainties: exquisite small fish from Russia, France, and Sardinia; coal-black hams from England; ripe olives, brandied peaches, and liqueur chocolates. He would loot old cellars for fat Burgundies, crack the gold necks of earth-chilled bottles of Pol Roger against the wall, and slake his noonday thirst at the spouting bung of a great butt of *Münchener dunkels*. When his linen was soiled he would outfit himself anew with silk underwear and the finest shirtings; he would have a new hat every day in the week and new suits whenever he pleased.

He would occupy a new house every day, and sleep in a different bed every night, selecting the most luxurious residence ultimately for perma-nent occupancy, and bringing together in it the richest treasures of every notable library in the city. Finally, when he wanted a woman from the small group that remained and that spent its time in weaving new entice-ments for him, he would summons her by ringing out the number he had given her on the Court House bell.

He wanted opulent solitude. His dark vision burned on kingdoms under the sea, on windy castle crags, and on the deep elf kingdoms at the earth's core. He groped for the doorless land of faery, that illimitable haunted country that opened somewhere below a leaf or a stone. And no birds sing.

More practically, he saw for himself great mansions in the ground, grottoes buried in the deep heart of a hill, vast chambers of brown earth, sumptuously appointed with his bee-like plunder. Cool hidden cisterns would bring him air; from a peephole in the hillside he could look down on a winding road and see armed men seeking for him, or hear their thwarted gropings overhead. He would pull fat fish from subterranean pools, his great earth cellars would be stocked with old wine, he could loot the world of its treasures, including the handsomest women, and never be caught.

King Solomon's mines. She. Proserpine. Ali Baba. Orpheus and Eurydice. Naked came I from my mother's womb. Naked shall I return. Let the mothering womb of earth engulf me. Naked, a valiant wisp of man, in vast brown limbs engulfed.

They neared the corner above Eliza's. For the first time the boy noted that their pace had quickened, and that he had almost broken into a trot in order to keep up with Gant's awkward plunging strides.

His father was moaning softly with long quivering exhalations of breath, and he had one hand clasped over his pain. The boy spluttered idiotically with laughter. Gant turned a glance full of reproach and physical torture upon him.

"Oh-h-h-h-h! Merciful God," he whined, "it's hurting me."

Abruptly, Eugene was touched with pity. For the first time he saw plainly that great Gant had grown old. The sallow face had yellowed and lost its sinew. The thin mouth was petulant. The chemistry of decay had left its mark.

No, there was no return after this. Eugene saw now that Gant was dying very slowly. The vast resiliency, the illimitable power of former times had vanished. The big frame was breaking up before him like a beached ship. Gant was sick. He was old.

He had a disease that is very common among old men who have lived carelessly and lustily—enlargement of the prostate gland. It was not often in itself a fatal disease—it was more often one of the flags of age and death, but it was ugly and uncomfortable. It was generally treated successfully by surgery—the operation was not desperate. But Gant hated and feared the knife: he listened eagerly to all persuasions against it.

He had no gift for philosophy. He could not view with amusement and detachment the death of the senses, the waning of desire, the waxing of physical impotence. He fed hungrily, lewdly, on all news of seduction: his amusement had in it the eyes of eagerness, the hot breath of desire. He was incapable of the pleasant irony by which the philosophic spirit mocks that folly it is no longer able to enjoy.

Gant was incapable of resignation. He had the most burning of all lusts—the lust of memory, the ravenous hunger of the will which tries to waken what is dead. He had reached the time of life when he read the papers greedily for news of death. As friends and acquaintances died he shook his head with the melancholy hypocrisy of old men, saying: "They're all going, one by one. Ah, Lord! The old man will be the next." But he did not believe it. Death was still for the others, not for himself.

He grew old very rapidly. He began to die before their eyes—a quick age, and a slow death, impotent, disintegrating, horrible because his life had been so much identified with physical excess—huge drinking, huge eating, huge rioting debauchery. It was fantastic and terrible to see the great body waste. They began to watch the progress of his disease with something of the horror with which one watches the movements of a dog with a broken leg, before he is destroyed—a horror greater than that one feels when a man has a similar hurt, because a man may live without legs. A dog is all included in his hide.

His wild bombast was tempered now by senile petulance. He cursed and whined by intervals. At the dead of night he would rise, full of pain and terror, blaspheming vilely against his God at one moment, and frantically entreating forgiveness at the next. Through all this tirade ran the high quivering exhalation of physical pain—actual and undeniable.

"Oh-h-h-h-h! I curse the day I was born! . . . I curse the day I was given life by that bloodthirsty Monster up above . . . Oh-h-h-h-h! Jesus! I beg of you. I know I've been bad. Forgive me. Have mercy and pity upon me! Give me another chance, in Jesus' name . . . Oh-h-h-h-h!"

Eugene had moments of furious anger because of these demonstrations. He was angry that Gant, having eaten his cake, now howled because he had stomach-ache and at the same time begged for more. Bitterly he reflected that his father's life had devoured whatever had served it, and that few men had had more sensuous enjoyment, or had been more ruthless in their demands on others. He found these exhibitions, these wild denunciations and cowardly grovellings in propitiation of a God none of them paid any attention to in health, ugly and abominable. The constant meditation of both Gant and Eliza on the death of others, their morbid raking of the news for items announcing the death of some person known to them, their weird absorption with the death of some toothless hag who, galled by bedsores, at length found release after her eightieth year, while fire, famine, and slaughter in other parts of the world passed unnoticed by them, their extravagant superstition over what was local and unimportant, seeing the intervention of God in the death of a peasant, and the suspension of divine law and natural order in their own, filled him with choking fury.

But Eliza was in splendid condition now to ponder upon the death of others. Her health was perfect. She was in her middle fifties: she had grown triumphantly stronger after the diseases of the middle years. White, compact, a great deal heavier now than she had ever been, she performed daily tasks of drudgery in the maintenance of Dixieland, that would have floored a strong negro. She hardly ever got to bed before two o'clock in the morning, and was up again before seven.

She admitted her health grudgingly. She made the most of every ache, and she infuriated Gant by meeting every complaint with a corresponding account of her own disorders. When badgered by Helen because of her supposed neglect of the sick man or when the concentration of attention upon the invalid piqued her jealousy, she smiled with white tremulous bitterness, hinting darkly:

"He may not be the first to go. I had a premonition—I don't know what else you'd call it—the other day. I tell you what—it may not be long now—"

Her eyes bleared with pity—shaking her puckered mouth, she wept at her own funeral.

"Good heavens, mama!" Helen burst out furiously. "There's nothing wrong with you. Papa's a sick man! Don't you realize that?"

She didn't.

"Pshaw!" she said. "There's nothing much wrong with him. McGuire told me two men out of three have it after they're fifty."

His body as it sickened distilled a green bile of hatred against her crescent health. It made him mad to see her stand so strong. Murderous impotent, baffled—a maniacal anger against her groped for an outlet in him, sometimes exploding in a wild inchoate scream.

He yielded weakly to invalidism, he became tyrannous of attention, jealous of service. Her indifference to his health maddened him, created a morbid hunger for pity and tears. At times he got insanely drunk and tried to frighten her by feigning death, one time so successfully that Ben, bending over his rigid form in the hallway, was whitened with conviction.

"I can't feel his heart, mama," he said, with a nervous whicker of his lips.

"Well," she said, picking her language with deliberate choosiness, "the pitcher went to the well once too often. I knew it would happen sooner or later."

Through a slotted eye he glared murderously at her. Judicially, with placid folded hands, she studied him. Her calm eye caught the slow movement of a stealthy inhalation.

"You get his purse, son, and any papers he may have," she directed. "I'll call the undertaker."

With an infuriate scream the dead awakened.

"I thought that would bring you to," she said complacently.

He scrambled to his feet.

"You hell-hound!" he yelled. "You would drink my heart's blood. You are without mercy and without pity—inhuman and bloody monster that you are."

"Some day," Eliza observed, "you'll cry wolf-wolf once too often."

He went three times a week to Cardiac's office for treatment. The dry doctor had grown old; behind his dusty restraint, the prim authority of his manner, there was a deepening well of senile bawdry. He had a comfortable fortune, he cared little for his dwindling practice. He was still a brilliant bacteriologist: he spent hours over slides etched in flowering patterns of bacilli, and he was sought after by diseased prostitutes, to whom he rendered competent service.

He dissuaded the Gants from surgery. He was jealously absorbed in the treatment of Gant's disease, scoffed at operations, and insisted he could give adequate relief by manipulation of the affected parts and the use of the catheter.

The two men became devoted friends. The doctor gave up entire mornings to the treatment of Gant's disease. The consulting-room was filled with their sly laughter while scrofulous mountaineers glared dully at the pages of *Life* in the antechamber. As Gant sprawled out voluptuously on the table after his masseur had finished his work, he listened appreciatively to the secrets of light women, or to tidbits from books of pseudoscientific pornography, of which the doctor had a large number.

"You say," he demanded eagerly, "that the monks petitioned the archbishop?"

"Yes," said the doctor. "They suffered during the hot weather. He wrote 'granted' across the petition. Here's a photograph of the document." He held the book open in his clean parched fingers.

"Merciful God!" said Gant, staring. "I suppose it's pretty bad in those hot countries."

He licked his thumb, smiling lewdly to himself. The late Oscar Wilde, for instance.

21

During the first years of this illness Gant showed a diminished, but not a seriously impaired, energy. At first he had, under the doctor's treatment, periods of tranquillity when he almost believed himself well. There were also times when he became a whining dotard over night, lay indolently abed for days, and was flabbily acquiescent to his disorder. These climaxes usually came on the heels of a roaring spree. The saloons had been closed for years: the town had been one of the first to vote on "local option."

Gant had piously contributed his vote for purity. Eugene remembered the day, years before, when he went proudly with his father to the polls. The militant "drys" had agreed to advertise their vote by wearing a scrap of white silk in their lapels. That was for purity. The defiant wets wore "red."

Announced by violent trumpetings in the Protestant churches, the day of atonement dawned on a seasoned army of well drilled teetotalers. Those wets who had victoriously withstood the pressure of hearth and pulpit— their number (*aië, aië,*) was small—went to their death with the gallant swagger, and with the gleam of purloined honor, of men who are to die fighting most desperately against the engulfing mob.

They did not know how gallant was their cause: they knew only that they had stood against the will of a priest-ridden community—the most annihilating force in the village. They had never been told they stood for liberty; they stood rubily, stubbornly, with the strong brown smell of shame in their nostrils, for the bloodshot, malt-mouthed, red-nosed, loose-pursed Demon Rum. So, they came down with vine leaves in their hair, and a good fog of rye upon their breaths, and with brave set smiles around their determined mouths.

As they approached the polls, glancing, like surrounded knights, for an embattled brother, the church women of the town, bent like huntresses above the straining leash, gave the word to the eager children of the Sunday schools. Dressed all in white, and clutching firmly in their small hands the tiny stems of American flags, the pigmies, monstrous as only children can be when they become the witless mouths of slogans and crusades, charged hungrily, uttering their shrill cries, upon their Gulliver. "There he is, children. Go get him."

Swirling around the marked man in wild elves' dance, they sang with piping empty violence:

> "We are some fond mother's treasure,
>   Men and women of to-morrow,
> For a moment's empty pleasure
>   Would you give us lifelong sorrow?
>
> Think of sisters, wives, and mothers,
>   Of helpless babes in some low slum,
> Think not of yourself, but others,
>   Vote against the Demon Rum."

Eugene shuddered, and looked up at Gant's white emblem with coy pride. They walked happily by unhappy alcoholics, deltaed in foaming eddies of innocence, and smiling murderously down at some fond mother's treasure.

If they were mine I'd warm their little tails, they thought—privately.

Outside the corrugated walls of the warehouse, Gant paused for a moment to acknowledge the fervent congratulation of a group of ladies from the First Baptist Church: Mrs. Tarkinton, Mrs. Fagg Sluder, Mrs. C. M. McDonnel, and Mrs. W. H. (Pett) Pentland, who, heavily powdered, trailed her long skirt of gray silk with a musty rustle, and sneered elegantly down over her whaleboned collar. She was very fond of Gant.

"Where's Will?" he asked.

"Feathering the pockets of the licker interests, when he ought to be down here doing the Lord's Work," she replied with Christian bitterness. "Nobody but you knows what I've had to put up with, Mr. Gant. You've had to put up with the queer Pentland streak, in your own home," she added with lucid significance.

He shook his head regretfully, and stared sorrowfully at the gutter.

"Ah, Lord, Pett! We've been through the mill—both of us."

A smell of drying roots and sassafras twisted a sharp spiral from the warehouse into the thin slits of his nostrils.

"When the time comes to speak up for the right," Pett announced to several of the ladies, "you'll always find Will Gant ready to do his part."

With far-seeing statesmanship he looked westward toward Pisgah.

"Licker," he said, "is a curse and a care. It has caused the sufferings of untold millions—"

"Amen, Amen," Mrs. Tarkinton chanted softly, swaying her wide hips rhythmically.

"—it has brought poverty, disease, and suffering to hundreds of thousands of homes, broken the hearts of wives and mothers, and taken bread from the mouths of little orphaned children."

"Amen, brother."

"It has been," Gant began, but at this moment his uneasy eye lighted upon the broad red face of Tim O'Doyle and the fierce whiskered whiskiness of Major Ambrose Nethersole, two prominent publicans, who were standing near the entrance not six feet away and listening attentively.

"Go on!" Major Nethersole urged, with the deep chest notes of a bull-frog. "Go on, W. O., but for God's sake, don't belch!"

"Begod!" said Tim O'Doyle, wiping a tiny rill of tobacco juice from the thick simian corner of his mouth, "I've seen him start for the door and step through the windey. When we see him coming we hire two extra bottle openers. He used to give the barman a bonus to get up early."

"Pay no attention to them, ladies, I beg of you," said Gant scathingly. "They are the lowest of the low, the whisky-besotted dregs of humanity, who deserve to bear not even the name of men, so far have they retrograded backwards."

With a flourishing sweep of his slouch hat he departed into the warehouse.

"By God!" said Ambrose Nethersole approvingly. "It takes W. O. to tie a knot in the tail of the English language. It always did."

But within two months he moaned bitterly his unwetted thirst. For several years he ordered, from time to time, the alloted quota—a gallon of whisky every two weeks—from Baltimore. It was the day of the blind tiger. The town was mined thickly with them. Bad rye and moonshine corn were the prevailing beverages. He grew old, he was sick, he still drank.

A slow trickle of lust crawled painfully down the parched gulley of desire, and ended feebly in dry fumbling lechery. He made pretty young summer widows at Dixieland presents of money, underwear, and silk stockings, which he drew on over their shapely legs in the dusty gloom of his little office. Smiling with imperturbable tenderness, Mrs. Selborne thrust out her heavy legs slowly to swell with warm ripe smack his gift of flowered green-silk garters. Wetting his thumb with sly thin aftersmile, he told.

A grass widow, forty-nine, with piled hair of dyed henna, corseted breasts and hips architecturally protuberant in a sharp diagonal, meaty mottled arms, and a gulched face of leaden flaccidity puttied up brightly with cosmetics, rented the upstairs of Woodson Street while Helen was absent.

"She looks like an adventuress, hey?" said Gant hopefully.

She had a son. He was fourteen, with a round olive face, a soft white body, and thin legs. He bit his nails intently. His hair and eyes were dark, his face full of sad stealth. He was wise and made himself unobtrusively scarce at proper times.

Gant came home earlier. The widow rocked brightly on the porch. He. bowed sweepingly, calling her *Madam*. Coy-kittenish, she talked down at him, slogged against the creaking stair rail. She leered cosily at him. She came and went freely through his sitting-room, where he now slept. One evening, just after he had entered, she came in from the bathroom, scented lightly with the best soap, and beefily moulded into a flame-red kimono.

A handsome woman yet, he thought. Good evening, madam.

He got up from his rocker, put aside the crackling sheets of the evening paper (Republican), and unclipped his steel-rimmed glasses from the great blade of his nose.

She came over with sprightly gait to the empty hearth, clasping her wrapper tightly with veinous hands.

Swiftly, with a gay leer, she opened the garment, disclosing her thin legs, silkshod, and her lumpy hips, gaudily clothed in ruffled drawers of blue silk.

"Aren't they pretty?" she twittered invitingly but obscurely. Then, as he took an eager stride forward, she skipped away like a ponderous maenad soliciting Bacchic pursuit.

"A pair of pippins," he agreed, inclusively.

After this, she prepared breakfast for him. From Dixieland, Eliza surveyed them with a bitter eye. He had no talent for concealment. His visits morning and evening were briefer, his tongue more benevolent.

"I know what you're up to down there," she said. "You needn't think I don't."

He grinned sheepishly and wet his thumb. Her mouth worked silently at attempted speech for a moment. She speared a frying steak and flipped it over on its raw back, smiling vengefully in a mounting column of greasy blue vapor. He poked her clumsily with his stiff fingers; she shrieked a protest mixed of anger and amusement, and moved awkwardly out of his reach with bridling gait.

"Get away! I don't want you round me! It's too late for that." She laughed with nagging mockery.

"Don't you wish you could, though? I'll vow!" she continued, kneading her lips for several seconds in an effort to speak. "I'd be ashamed. Every one's laughing at you behind your back."

"You lie! By God, you lie!" he thundered magnificently, touched. Hammer-hurling Thor.

But he tired very quickly of his new love. He was weary, and frightened by his depletion. For a time he gave the widow small sums of money, and forgot the rent. He transferred to her his storming abuse, muttered ominously to himself in long aisle-pacings at his shop, when he saw that he had lost the ancient freedom of his house and saddled himself with a tyrannous hag. One evening he returned insanely drunk, routed her out of her chamber and pursued her unfrocked, untoothed, unputtied, with a fluttering length of kimono in her palsied hand, driving her finally into the yard beneath the big cherry tree, which he circled, howling, making frantic lunges for her as she twittered with fear, casting splintered glances all over the listening neighborhood as she put on the crumpled wrapper, hid partially the indecent jigging of her breasts, and implored succor. It did not come.

"You bitch!" he screamed. "I'll kill you. You have drunk my heart's-blood, you have driven me to the brink of destruction, and you gloat upon my misery, listening with fiendish delight to my death-rattle, bloody and unnatural monster that you are."

She kept the tree deftly between them and, when his attention was diverted for a moment to the flood of anathema, tore off on fear-quick feet, streetward to the haven of the Tarkintons' house. As she rested there, in Mrs. Tarkinton's consolatory arms, weeping hysterically and dredging gullies in her poor painted face, they heard his chaotic footsteps blundering within his house, the heavy crash of furniture, and his fierce curses when he fell.

"He'll kill himself! He'll kill himself!" she cried. "He doesn't know what he's doing. Oh, my God!" she wept. "I've never been talked to that way by any man in my life!"

Gant fell heavily within his house. There was silence. She rose fearfully.

"He's not a bad man," she whispered.

One morning in early summer, after Helen had returned, Eugene was wakened by scuffling feet and excited cries along the small boardwalk that skirted the house on its upper side and led to the playhouse, a musty little structure of pine with a single big room, which he could almost touch from the sloping roof that flowed about his gabled backroom window. The playhouse was another of the strange extravagancies of Gantian fancy: it had been built for the children when they were young. It had been for many years closed, it was a retreat of delight; its imprisoned air, stale and cool, was scented permanently with old pine boards, cased books, and dusty magazines.

For some weeks now it had been occupied by Mrs. Selborne's South Carolina cook, Annie, a plump comely negress of thirty-five, with a rich coppery skin. The woman had come into the mountains for the summer: she was a good cook and expected work at hotels or boarding-houses. Helen engaged her for five dollars a week. It was an act of pride.

That morning, Gant had wakened earlier and stared at his ceiling thoughtfully. He had risen, dressed, and wearing his leather slippers, walked softly back, along the boards, to the playhouse. Helen was roused by Annie's loud protests. Tingling with premonition she came down stairs, and found Gant wringing his hands and moaning as he walked up and down the washroom. Through the open doors she heard the negress complaining loudly to herself as she banged out drawers and slammed her belongings together.

"I ain't used to no such goins-on. I'se a married woman, I is. I ain't goin' to stay in dis house anothah minnit."

Helen turned furiously upon Gant and shook him.

"You rotten old thing, you!" she cried. "How dare you!"

"Merciful God!" he whined, stamping his foot like a child, and pacing up and down. "Why did this have to come upon me in my old age!" He began to sniffle affectedly. "Boo-hoo-hoo! O Jesus, it's fearful, it's awful, it's cruel that you should put this affliction on me." His contempt for reason was Parnassian. He accused God for exposing him; he wept because he had been caught.

Helen rushed out to the playhouse and with large gesture and hearty entreaty strove to appease outraged Annie.

"Come on, Annie," she coaxed. "I'll give you a dollar a week more if you stay. Forget about it!"

"No'm," said Annie stubbornly. "I cain't stay heah any longer. I'se afraid of dat man."

Gant paused in his distracted pacing from time to time long enough to cock an eager ear. At each iteration of Annie's firm refusals, he fetched out a deep groan and took up his lament again.

Luke, who had descended, had fidgeted about in a nervous prance from one large bare foot to another. Now he went to the door and looked out, bursting suddenly into a large Whah-Whah as he caught sight of the sullen respectability of the negress' expression. Helen came back into the house with an angry perturbed face.

"She'll tell this all over town," she announced.

Gant moaned in lengthy exhalations. Eugene, shocked at first, and frightened, flung madly across the kitchen linoleum in twisting leaps, falling catlike on his bare soles. He squealed ecstatically at Ben who loped in scowling, and began to snicker in short contemptuous fragments.

"And of course she'll tell Mrs. Selborne all about it, as soon as she goes back to Henderson," Helen continued.

"O my God!" Gant whined, "why was this put on me—"

"O gotohell! Gotohell!" she said comically, her wrath loosened suddenly by a ribald and exasperated smile. They howled.

"I shall dy-ee."

Eugene choked in faint hiccoughs and began to slide gently down the kitchen-washroom door jamb.

"Ah! you little idiot!" Ben snarled, lifting his white hand sharply. He turned away quickly with a flickering smile.

At this moment, Annie appeared on the walk outside the door, with a face full of grieved decorum.

Luke looked nervously and gravely from his father to the negress, fidgeting from one big foot to the other.

"I'se a married woman," said Anna. "I ain't used to nothin' like dis. I wants my money."

Luke blew up in an explosion of wild laughter.

"Whah-whah!" He pronged her larded ribs with scooped fingers. She moved away angrily, muttering.

Eugene lolled about feebly on the floor, kicking one leg out gently as if he had just been decapitated, and fumbling blindly at the neckband of his nightshirt. A faint clucking sound came at intervals from his wide-open mouth.

They laughed wildly, helplessly, draining into mad laughter all the welled and agglutinated hysteria that had gathered in them, washing out in a moment of fierce surrender all the fear and fatality of their lives, the pain of age and death.

Dying, he walked among them, whining his lament against God's lidless stare, gauging their laughter cautiously with uneasy prying eyes, a faint tickled grin playing craftily about his wailing mouth.

Roofing the deep tides, swinging in their embrace, rocked Eliza's life Sargassic, as when, at morning, a breath of kitchen air squirmed through her guarded crack of door, and fanned the pendant clusters of old string in floating rhythm. She rubbed the sleep gently from her small weak eyes, smiling dimly as she thought, unwakened, of ancient losses. Her worn fingers still groped softly in the bed beside her, and when she found it vacant, she awoke. Remembered. My youngest, my oldest, final bitter fruit, O dark of soul, O far and lonely, where? Remembered O his face! Death-son, partner of my peril, last coinage of my flesh, who warmed my flanks and nestled to my back. Gone? Cut off from me? When? Where?

The screen slammed, the market boy dumped ground sausage on the table, a negress fumbled at the stove. Awake now.

Ben moved quietly, but not stealthily, about, confessing and denying nothing. His thin laughter pierced the darkness softly above the droning creak of the wooden porch-swing. Mrs. Pert laughed gently, comfortingly. She was forty-three: a large woman of gentle manners, who drank a great deal. When she was drunk, her voice was soft, low, and fuzzy, she laughed uncertainly, mildly, and walked with careful alcoholic gravity. She dressed well: she was well fleshed, but not sensual-looking. She had good features, soft oaken hair, blue eyes, a little bleared. She laughed with a comfortable, happy chuckle. They were all very fond of her. Helen called her "Fatty."

Her husband was a drug salesman: he travelled through Tennessee, Arkansas, and Mississippi, and returned to Altamont for a fortnight every four months. Her daughter, Catherine, who was almost Ben's age, came to Dixieland for a few weeks each summer. She was a school-teacher in a public school in a Tennessee village. Ben squired both.

Mrs. Pert chuckled softly when she spoke to him, and called him "Old Ben." In the darkness he sat, talking a little, humming a little, laughing occasionally in his thin minor key, quietly, with a cigarette between his forked ivory fingers, drawing deeply. He would buy a flask of whisky and they would drink it very quietly. Perhaps they talked a little more. But they were never riotous. Occasionally, they would rise at midnight from the swing, and go out into the street, departing under leafy trees. They would not return during the night. Eliza, ironing out a great pile of rumpled laundry in the kitchen, would listen. Presently, she would mount the stairs, peer carefully into Mrs. Pert's room, and descend, her lips thoughtfully kneaded.

She had to speak these things to Helen. There was a strange defiant communion between them. They laughed or were bitter together.

"Why, of course," said Helen, impatiently, "I've known it all along." But she looked beyond the door curiously, her big gold-laced teeth half-shown in her open mouth, the child look of belief, wonder, scepticism, and hurt innocency in her big highboned face.

"Do you suppose he really does? Oh surely not mama. She's old enough to be his mother."

Across Eliza's white puckered face, thoughtful and reproving, a sly smile broke. She rubbed her finger under the broad wings of her nose to conceal it, and snickered.

"I tell you what!" she said. "He's a chip off the old block. His father over again," she whispered. "It's in the blood."

Helen laughed huskily, picking vaguely at her chin, and gazing out across the weedy garden.

"Poor old Ben!" she said, and her eyes, she did not know why, were sheeted with tears. "Well, 'Fatty's' a lady. I like her—I don't care who knows it," she added defiantly. "It's their business anyway. They're quiet about it. You've got to say that much for them."

She was silent a moment.

"Women are crazy about him," she said. "They like the quiet ones, don't they? He's a gentleman."

Eliza shook her head portentously for several moments.

"What do you think!" she whispered, and shook her pursed lips again. "Always ten years older at least."

"Poor old Ben!" Helen said again.

"The quiet one, the sad one. I tell you what!" Eliza shook her head, unable to speak. Her eyes too were wet.

They thought of sons and lovers: they drew closer in their communion, they drank the cup of their twin slavery as they thought of the Gant men who would always know hunger, the strangers on the land, the unknown farers who had lost their way. O lost!

The hands of women were hungry for his crisp hair. When they came to the paper office to insert advertisements they asked for him. Frowning gravely, he leaned upon the counter with feet crossed, reading, in a somewhat illiterate monotone, what they had written. His thin hairy wrists slatted leanly against his starched white cuffs, his strong nervous fingers, ivoried by nicotine, smoothed out the crumples. Scowling intently, he bent his fine head, erasing, arranging. Emphatic lady-fingers twitched. "How's that?" Answers vague-voiced, eyes tangled in crisp hair. "Oh, much better, thank you."

Wanted: frowning boy-man head for understanding fingers of mature and sympathetic woman. Unhappily married. Address Mrs. B. J. X., Box 74. Eight cents a word for one insertion. "Oh, [tenderly] thank you, Ben."

"Ben," said Jack Eaton, the advertising manager, thrusting his plump face into the city editor's office, "one of your harem's out there. She wanted to murder me when I tried to take it. See if she's got a friend."

"Oh, listen to this, won't you?" Ben snickered fiercely to the City Editor. "You missed your calling, Eaton. What you want is the endman's job with Honeyboy Evans."

Scowling, he cast the cigarette from his ivory hand, and loped out into the office. Eaton remained a moment to laugh with the City Editor. O rare Ben Gant!

Sometimes, returning late at night to Woodson Street, in the crowded summer season, he slept with Eugene in the front room upstairs where they had all been born. Propped high on pillows in the old cream-colored bed, painted gaily at head and foot with round medals of clustering fruit, he read aloud in a quiet puzzled voice, fumbling over pronunciation, the baseball stories of Ring Lardner. *You know me, Al.* Just outside the windows the flat veranda roof was still warm from its daytime exhalations of tar-calked tin. Rich cobwebbed grapes hung in packed clusters among the broad leaves. *I didn't raise my boy to be a southpaw. I've a good mind to give Gleason a sock in the eye.*

Ben read painfully, pausing a moment later to snicker. Thus, like a child, he groped intently at all meanings, with scowling studiousness. Women liked to see him scowl and study so. He was sudden only in anger, and in his quick communications with his angel.

22

Toward the beginning of Eugene's fourteenth year, when he had been a student at Leonard's for two years, Ben got work for him as a paper carrier. Eliza grumbled at the boy's laziness. She complained that she could get him to do little or nothing for her. In fact, he was not lazy, but he hated all the dreariness of boarding-house routine. Her demands on him were not heavy, but they were frequent and unexpected. He was depressed at the uselessness of effort in Dixieland, at the total erasure of all daily labor. If she had given him position, the daily responsibility of an ordered task, he could have fulfilled it with zeal. But her own method was much too random: she wanted to keep him on tap for an occasional errand, and he did not have her interest.

Dixieland was the heart of her life. It owned her. It appalled him. When she sent him to the grocer's for bread, he felt wearily that the bread would be eaten by strangers, that nothing out of the effort of their lives grew younger, better, or more beautiful, that all was erased in a daily wash of sewage. She sent him forth in the rank thicket of her garden to hoe out the swarming weeds that clustered about her vegetables, which flourished, as did all the earth, under her careless touch. He knew, as he chopped down in a weary frenzy, that the weeds would grow again in the hot sun-stench, that her vegetables—weeded or not—would grow fat and be fed to her boarders, and that her life, hers alone, would endure to something. As he looked at her, he felt the weariness and horror of time: all but her must die in a smothering Sargasso. Thus, flailing the clotted earth drunk-enly, he would be brought to suddenly by her piercing scream from the high back porch, and realize that he had destroyed totally a row of young bladed corn.

"Why, what on earth, boy!" she fretted angrily, peering down at him through a shelving confusion of wash-tubs, limp drying stockings, empty milk-bottles, murky and unwashed, and rusty lard-buckets. "I'll vow!" she said, turning to Mr. Baskett, the Hattiesburg cotton merchant, who grinned down malarially through his scraggly mustaches, "what am I going to do with him? He's chopped down every stock of corn in the row."

"Yes," Mr. Baskett said, peering over, "and missed every weed. Boy," he added judicially, "you need two months on a farm."

The bread that I fetch will be eaten by strangers. I carry coal and split up wood for fires to warm them. Smoke. *Fuimus fumus.* All of our life goes up in smoke. There is no structure, no creation in it, not even the smoky structure of dreams. Come lower, angel; whisper in our ears. We are passing away in smoke and there is nothing to-day but weariness to pay us for yesterday's toil. How may we save ourselves?

He was given the Niggertown route—the hardest and least profitable of all. He was paid two cents a copy for weekly deliveries, given ten per cent of his weekly collections, and ten cents for every new subscription. Thus, he was able to earn four or five dollars a week. His thin undeveloped body drank sleep with insatiable thirst, but it was now necessary for him to get up at half-past three in the morning with darkness and silence making an unreal humming in his drugged ears.

Strange aerial music came fluting out of darkness, or over his slow-wakening senses swept the great waves of symphonic orchestration. Fiend-voices, beautiful and sleep-loud, called down through darkness and light, developing the thread of ancient memory.

Staggering blindly in the whitewashed glare, his eyes, sleepcorded opened slowly as he was born anew, umbilically cut, from darkness.

Waken, ghost-eared boy, but into darkness. Waken, phantom, O into us. Try, try, O try the way. Open the wall of light. Ghost, ghost, who is the ghost? O lost. Ghost, ghost, who is the ghost? O whisper-tongued laughter. Eugene! Eugene! Here, O here, Eugene. Here, Eugene. The way is here, Eugene. Have you forgotten? The leaf, the rock, the wall of light. Lift up the rock, Eugene, the leaf, the stone, the unfound door. Return, return.

A voice, sleep-strange and loud, forever far-near, spoke.

Eugene!

Spoke, ceased, continued without speaking, to speak. In him spoke. Where darkness, son, is light. Try, boy, the word you know remember. In the beginning was the logos. Over the border the borderless green-forested land. Yesterday, remember?

Far-forested, a horn-note wound. Sea-forested, water-far, the grotted coral sea-far horn-note. The pillioned ladies witch-faced in bottle-green robes saddle-swinging. Merwomen unscaled and lovely in sea-floor colonnades. The hidden land below the rock. The flitting wood-girls growing into bark. Far-faint, as he wakened, they besought him with lessening whir. Then deeper song, fiend-throated, wind-shod. Brother, O brother! They shot down the brink of darkness, gone on the wind like bullets. O lost, and by the wind grieved, ghost, come back again.

He dressed and descended the stairs gently to the back porch. The cool air, charged with blue starlight, shocked his body into wakefulness, but as he walked townward up the silent streets, the strange ringing in his ears persisted. He listened like his own ghost, to his footsteps, heard from afar the winking flicker of the street-lamps, saw, from sea-sunk eyes, the town.

There sounded in his heart a solemn music. It filled the earth, the air, the universe; it was not loud, but it was omnipresent, and it spoke to him of death and darkness, and of the focal march of all who lived or had lived, converging on a plain. The world was filled with silent marching men: no word was spoken, but in the heart of each there was a common knowledge, the word that all men knew and had forgotten, the lost key opening the prison gates, the lane-end into heaven, and as the music soared and filled him, he cried: "I will remember. When I come to the place, I shall know."

Hot bands of light streamed murkily from the doors and windows of the office. From the press-room downstairs there was an ascending roar as the big press mounted to its capacity. As he entered the office and drank in the warm tides of steel and ink that soaked the air, he awoke suddenly, his light-drugged limbs solidifying with a quick shock, as would some aerial spirit, whose floating body corporealizes the instant it touches earth. The carriers, waiting in a boisterous line, filed up to the circulation manager's desk, depositing their collections, cold handfuls of greasy coin. Seated beneath a green-shaded light, he ran swiftly down their books, totalling up their figures and counting nickels, dimes, and pennies into little spooned trays of a drawer. Then he gave to each a scrawled order for his morning quota.

They ran downstairs, eager as whippets to be off, brandishing their slips at a sullen counter whose black fingers galloped accurately across the stiff ridges of a great sheaf. He allowed them two "extras." If the carrier was not scrupulous, he increased his number of spare copies by keeping on his book the names of a half-dozen discontinued subscribers. These surplus copies were always good for coffee and pie with the lunchman, or as tribute to a favorite policeman, fireman, or motorman.

In the press-pit Harry Tugman loafed under their stare comfortably, a fat trickle of cigarette smoke coiling from his nostrils. He glanced over the press with professional carelessness, displaying his powerful chest with its thick bush, which lay a dark blot under his sweat-wet under-shirt. An assistant pressman climbed nimbly among roaring pistons and cylinders, an oil-can and a bunch of waste in his hand. A broad river of white paper rushed constantly up from the cylinder and leaped into a mangling chaos of machinery whence it emerged a second later, cut, printed, folded and stacked, sliding along a board with a hundred others in a fattening sheaf.

Machine-magic! Why not men, like that? Doctor, surgeon, poet, priest— stacked, folded, printed.

Harry Tugman cast away his wet fragment of cigarette with a luxurious grimace. The carriers eyed him reverently. Once he had knocked a sub-pressman down for sitting in his chair. He was Boss. He got $55 a week. If he was not pleased he could get work at any time on the *New Orleans Times-Picayune*, the *Louisville Courier Journal*, the *Atlanta Constitution*, the *Knoxville Sentinel*, the *Norfolk Pilot*. He could travel.

In a moment more they were out on the streets, hobbling along rapidly under the accustomed weight of the crammed canvas bags.

He was most desperately afraid of failure. He listened with constricted face to Eliza's admonition.

"Spruce up, boy! Spruce up! Make them think you are somebody!"

He had little confidence in himself; he recoiled in advance from the humiliation of dismissal. He feared the sabre-cut of language, and before his own pride he drew back and was afraid.

For three mornings he accompanied the retiring carrier, gathering his mind to focal intensity while he tried to memorize each stereotyped movement of the delivery, tracing again and again the labyrinthine web of Niggertown, wreaking his plan out among the sprawled chaos of clay and slime, making incandescent those houses to which a paper was delivered, and forgetting the others. Years later, alone in darkness, when he had forgotten the twisted anarchy of that pattern, he still remembered a corner where he left his bag while he climbed a spur of hill, a bank down which he clambered to three rotting shacks, a high porched house into which accurately he shot his folded block of news.

The retiring carrier was a robust country boy of seventeen who had been given better employment at the paper office. His name was Jennings Ware. He was tough, good-humored, a little cynical, and he smoked a great many cigarettes. He was clothed in vitality and comfort. He taught his pupil when and where to expect the prying face of "Foxy," how to escape discovery under the lunchroom counter, and how to fold a paper and throw it with the speed and accuracy of a ball.

In the fresh pre-natal morning they began their route, walking down the steep hill of Valley Street into tropical sleep, past the stabled torpor of black sleepers, past all the illicit loves, the casual and innumerable adulteries of Niggertown. As the stiff block of paper thudded sharply on the flimsy porch of a shack, or smacked the loose boarding of a door, they were answered by a long sullen moan of discontent. They sniggered.

"Check this one off," said Jennings Ware, "if you can't collect next time. She owes for six weeks now."

"This one," he said, flipping a paper quietly on a door mat, "is good pay. They're good niggers. You'll get your money every Wednesday."

"There's a High Yaller in here," he said, hurling the paper against the door with a whizzing smack and smiling, as a young full-meated woman's yell of indignation answered, a thin devil's grin. "You can have that if you want it."

A wan smile of fear struggled across Eugene's mouth. Jennings Ware looked at him shrewdly, but did not press him. Jennings Ware was a good-hearted boy.

"She's a pretty good old girl," he said. "You've got a right to a few dead-heads. Take it out in trade."

They walked on down the dark unpaved street, folding papers rapidly during the intervals between delivery.

"It's a hell of a route," said Jennings Ware. "When it rains it's terrible. You'll go into mud up to your knees. And you can't collect from half the bastards." He hurled a paper viciously.

"But, oh man" he said, after a moment. "If you want Jelly Roll you've come to the right place. I ain't kidding you!"

"With—with niggers?" Eugene whispered, moistening his dry lips.

Jennings Ware turned his red satirical face on him.

"You don't see any Society Belles around here, do you?" he said.

"Are niggers good?" Eugene asked in a small dry voice.

"Boy!" The word blew out of Jennings Ware's mouth like an explosion. He was silent a moment.

"There ain't nothing better," he said.

At first, the canvas strap of the paper-bag bit cruelly across his slender shoulders. He strained against the galling weight that pulled him earthwards. The first weeks were like a warring nightmare: day after day he fought his way up to liberation. He knew all the sorrow of those who carry weight; he knew, morning by morning, the aerial ecstasy of release. As his load lightened with the progress of his route, his leaning shoulder rose with winged buoyancy, his straining limbs grew light: at the end of his labor his flesh, touched sensuously by fatigue, bounded lightly from the earth. He was Mercury chained by fardels, Ariel bent beneath a pack: freed, his wingshod feet trod brightness. He sailed in air. The rapier stars glinted upon his serfdom: dawn reddened on release. He was like a sailor drowned within the hold, who gropes to life and morning through a hatch; a diver twined desperately in octopal feelers, who cuts himself from death and mounts slowly from the sea-floor into light.

Within a month a thick hummock of muscle hardened on his shoulder: he bent jubilantly into his work. He had now no fear of failure. His heart lifted like a proud crested cock. He had been dropped among others without favor, and he surpassed them. He was a lord of darkness; he exulted in the lonely sufficiency of his work. He walked into the sprawled chaos of the settlement, the rifleman of news for sleeping men. His fast hands blocked the crackling sheet, he swung his lean arm like a whip. He saw the pale stars drown, and ragged light break open on the hills. Alone, the only man alive, he began the day for men, as he walked by the shuttered windows and heard the long denned snore of the tropics. He walked amid this close thick sleep, hearing again the ghostly ring of his own feet, and the vast orchestral music of darkness. As the gray tide of morning surged westward he awoke.

And Eugene watched the slow fusion of the seasons; he saw the royal processional of the months; he saw the summer light eat like a river into dark; he saw dark triumph once again; and he saw the minute-winning days, like flies, buzz home to death.

In summer, full day had come before he finished: he walked home in a world of wakenings. The first cars were grouped on the Square as he passed, their new green paint giving them the pleasant appearance of fresh toys. The huge battered cans of the milkmen glinted cleanly in the sun. Light fell hopefully upon the swarthy greasiness of George Chakales, nightman of the Athens Cafe. The Hellenic Dawn. And in Uneeda No. 1, upon the Square, Eugene sat, washing an egg-sandwich down with long swallows of pungent coffee, stooled in a friendly company of motormen, policemen, chauffeurs, plasterers, and masons. It was very pleasant, he felt, to complete one's work when all the world was beginning theirs. He went home under singing trees of birds.

In autumn, a late red moon rode low in the skies till morning. The air was filled with dropping leaves, there was a solemn thunder of great trees upon the hills; sad phantasmal whisperings and the vast cathedral music deepened in his heart.

In winter, he went down joyously into the dark howling wind, leaning his weight upon its advancing wall as it swept up a hill; and when in early Spring the small cold rain fell from the reeking sky he was content. He was alone.

He harried his deficient subscribers for payment, with a wild tenacity. He accepted their easy promises without question; he hunted them down in their own rooms, or in the rooms of a neighbor, he pressed so doggedly that, at length, sullenly or good-humoredly, they paid a part of their debt. This was more than any of his predecessors had accomplished, but he fretted nervously over his accounts until he found that he had become, for the circulation manager, the exemplar for indolent boys. As he dumped his desperately gathered pile of "chicken feed" upon the man's desk, his employer would turn accusingly to a delinquent boy, saying:

"Look at that! He does it every week! Niggers, too!"

His pallid face would flame with joy and pride. When he spoke to the great man his voice trembled. He could hardly speak.

As the wind yelled through the dark, he burst into maniacal laughter. He leaped high into the air with a scream of insane exultancy, burred in his throat idiot animal-squeals, and shot his papers terrifically into the flimsy boarding of the shacks. He was free. He was alone. He heard the howl of a train-whistle, and it was not so far away. In the darkness he flung his arm out to the man on the rails, his goggled brother with steel-steady rail-fixed eyes.

He did not shrink so much, beneath the menace of the family fist. He was more happily unmindful of his own unworthiness.

Assembled with three or four of the carriers in the lunchroom, he learned to smoke: in the sweet blue air of Spring, as he sloped down to his route, he came to know the beauty of Lady Nicotine, the delectable wraith who coiled into his brain, left her poignant breath in his young nostrils, her sharp kiss upon his mouth.

He was a sharp blade.

The Spring drove a thorn into his heart, it drew a wild cry from his lips. For it, he had no speech.

He knew hunger. He knew thirst. A great flame rose in him. He cooled his hot face in the night by bubbling water jets. Alone, he wept sometimes with pain and ecstasy. At home the frightened silence of his childhood was now touched with savage restraint. He was wired like a race-horse. A white atom of inchoate fury would burst in him like a rocket, and for a moment he would be cursing mad.

"What's wrong with him? Is it the Pentland crazy streak coming out?" Helen asked, seated in Eliza's kitchen.

Eliza moulded her lips portentously for some time, shaking her head slowly.

"Why," she said, with a cunning smile, "don't you know, child?"

His need for the negroes had become acute. He spent his afternoons after school combing restlessly through the celled hive of Niggertown. The rank stench of the branch, pouring its thick brown sewage down a bed of worn boulders, the smell of wood-smoke and laundry stewing in a black iron yard-pot, and the low jungle cadences of dusk, the forms that slid, dropped, and vanished, beneath a twinkling orchestration of small sounds. Fat ropes of language in the dusk, the larded sizzle of frying fish, the sad faint twanging of a banjo, and the stamp, far-faint, of heavy feet; voices Nilotic, river-wailing, and the greasy light of four thousand smoky lamps in shack and tenement.

From the worn central butte round which the colony swarmed; the panting voices of the Calvary Baptist Church mounted, in an exhausting and unceasing frenzy, from seven o'clock until two in the morning, in their wild jungle wail of sin and love and death. The dark was hived with flesh and mystery. Rich wells of laughter bubbled everywhere. The catforms slid. Everything was immanent. Everything was far. Nothing could be touched.

In this old witch-magic of the dark, he began to know the awful innocence of evil, the terrible youth of an ancient race; his lips slid back across his teeth, he prowled in darkness with loose swinging arms, and his eyes shone. Shame and terror, indefinable, surged through him. He could not face the question in his heart.

A good part of his subscription list was solidly founded among decent and laborious darkies—barbers, tailors, grocers, pharmacists, and ging-hamed black housewives, who paid him promptly on a given day each week, greeting him with warm smiles full of teeth, and titles of respect extravagant and kindly: "Mister," "Colonel," "General," "Governor," and so on. They all knew Gant.

But another part—the part in which his desire and wonder met—were "floaters," young men and women of precarious means, variable lives, who slid mysteriously from cell to cell, who peopled the night with their flitting stealth. He sought these phantoms fruitlessly for weeks, until he discovered that he might find them only on Sunday morning, tossed like heavy sacks across one another, in the fetid dark of a tenement room, a half-dozen young men and women, in a snoring exhaustion of whisky-stupor and sexual depletion.

One Saturday evening, in the fading red of a summer twilight, he returned to one of these tenements, a rickety three-story shack, that cropped its two lower floors down a tall clay bank at the western ledge, near the whites. Two dozen men and women lived here. He was on the search for a woman named Ella Corpening. He had never been able to find her: she was weeks behind in her subscriptions. But her door stood open to-night: a warm waft of air and cooking food came up to him. He descended the rotten steps that climbed the bank.

Ella Corpening sat facing the door in a rocking chair, purring lazily in the red glow of a little kitchen range, with her big legs stretched comfort-ably out on the floor. She was a mulatto of twenty-six years, a handsome woman of Amazonian proportions, with smooth tawny skin.

She was dressed in the garments of some former mistress: she wore a brown woollen skirt, patent-leather shoes with high suede tops pearl-buttoned, and gray silk hose. Her long heavy arms shone darkly through the light texture of a freshly laundered white shirtwaist. A lacing of cheap blue ribbon gleamed across the heavy curve of her breasts.

There was a bubbling pot of cabbage and sliced fat pork upon the stove.

"Paper boy," said Eugene. "Come to collect."

"Is you de boy?" drawled Ella Corpening with a lazy movement of her arm. "How much does I owe?"

"$1.20," he answered. He looked meaningfully at one extended leg, where, thrust in below the knee, a wadded bank-note gleamed dully.

"Dat's my rent money," she said. "Can't give you dat. Dollah-twenty!" She brooded. "Uh! Uh!" she grunted pleasantly. "Don't seem lak it ought to be dat much."

"It is, though," he said, opening his account book.

"It mus' is," she agreed, "if de book say so."

She meditated luxuriously for a moment.

"Does you collec' Sunday mawnin'?" she asked.

"Yes," he said.

"You come roun' in de mawnin'," she said hopefully. "I'll have some-thin' fo' yuh, sho. I'se waitin' fo' a white gent'man now. He's goin' gib me a dollah."

She moved her great limbs slowly, and smiled at him. Forked pulses beat against his eyes. He gulped dryly: his legs were rotten with excitement.

"What's—what's he going to give you a dollar for?" he muttered, barely audible.

"Jelly Roll," said Ella Corpening.

He moved his lips twice, unable to speak. She got up from her chair.

"What yo' want?" she asked softly. "Jelly Roll?"

"Want to see—to see!" he gasped.

She closed the door opening on the bank and locked it. The stove cast a grated glow from its open ashpan. There was a momentary rain of red cinders into the pit.

Ella Corpening opened the door beyond that, leading to another room. There were two dirty rumpled beds; the single window was bolted and covered by an old green shade. She lit a smoky little lamp, and turned the wick low.

There was a battered little dresser with a mottled glass, from which the blistered varnish was flaking. Over the screened hearth, on a low mantel, there was a Kewpie doll, sashed with pink ribbon, a vase with fluted edges and gilt flowers, won at a carnival, and a paper of pins. A calendar, also, by courtesy of the Altamont Coal and Ice Company, showing an Indian maid paddling her canoe down an alley of paved moonlight, and a religious motto in flowered scrollwork, framed in walnut: *God Loves Them Both*.

"What yo' want?" she whispered, facing him.

Far off, he listened to the ghost of his own voice.

"Take off your clothes."

Her skirt fell in a ring about her feet. She took off her starched waist. In a moment, save for her hose, she stood naked before him.

Her breath came quickly, her full tongue licked across her mouth.

"Dance!" he cried. "Dance!"

She began to moan softly, while an undulant tremor flowed through her great yellow body; her hips and her round heavy breasts writhed slowly in a sensual rhythm.

Her straight oiled hair fell across her neck in a thick shock. She extended her arms for balance, the lids closed over her large yellow eyeballs. She came near him. He felt her hot breath on his face, the smothering flood of her breasts. He was whirled like a chip in the wild torrent of her passion. Her powerful yellow hands gripped his slender arms round like bracelets. She shook him to and fro slowly, fastening him tightly against her pelt.

He strained back desperately against the door, drowning in her embrace.

"Get-'way nigger. Get-'way," he panted thickly.

Slowly she released him: without opening her eyes, moaning, she slid back as if he had been a young tree. She sang, in a wailing minor key, with unceasing iteration:

> "Jelly Roll! Je-e-e-ly Roll!"——

her voice falling each time to a low moan.

Her face, the broad column of her throat, and her deep-breasted torso were rilled with sweat. He fumbled blindly for the door, lunged across the outer room and, gasping, found his way into the air. Her chant, unbroken and undisturbed by his departure, followed him up the flimsy steps. He did not pause to get his breath until he came to the edge of the market square. Below him in the valley, across on the butte, the smoky lamps of Niggertown flared in the dusk. Faint laughter, rich, jungle-wild, welled up from hived darkness. He heard lost twangling notes, the measured thump of distant feet; beyond, above, more thin, more far than all, the rapid wail of sinners in a church.

23

’Εντεῦθεν ἐξελαύνει σταθμοὺς τρεῖς παρασάγγας πεντεκαίδεκα ἐπὶ τὸν Εὐφράτην ποταμὸν.

He did not tell the Leonards that he was working in the early morning. He knew they would oppose his employment, and that their opposition would manifest itself in the triumphant argument of lowered grades. Also, Margaret Leonard, he knew, would talk ominously of health undermined, of the promise of future years destroyed, of the sweet lost hours of morning sleep that could never be regained. He was really more robust now than he had ever been. He was heavier and stronger. But he sometimes felt a gnawing hunger for sleep: he grew heavy at mid-day, revived in the afternoon, but found it difficult to keep his sleepy brain fixed on a book after eight o'clock in the evening.

He learned little of discipline. Under the care of the Leonards he came even to have a romantic contempt for it. Margaret Leonard had the marvelous vision, of great people, for essences. She saw always the dominant color, but she did not always see the shadings. She was an inspired sentimentalist. She thought she "knew boys": she was proud of her knowledge of them. In fact, however, she had little knowledge of them. She would have been stricken with horror if she could have known the wild confusion of adolescence, the sexual nightmares of puberty, the grief, the fear, the shame in which a boy broods over the dark world of his desire. She did not know that every boy, caged in from confession by his fear, is to himself a monster.

She did not have knowledge But she had wisdom She found immediately a person's quality. Boys were her heroes, her little gods. She believed that the world was to be saved, life redeemed, by one of them. She saw the flame that burns in each of them, and she guarded it. She tried somehow to reach the dark gropings toward light and articulation, of the blunt, the stolid, the shamefast. She spoke a calm low word to the trembling racehorse, and he was still.

Thus, he made no confessions. He was still prison-pent. But he turned always to Margaret Leonard as toward the light: she saw the unholy fires that cast their sword-dance on his face, she saw the hunger and the pain, and she fed him—majestic crime!—on poetry.

Whatever of fear or shame locked them in careful silence, whatever decorous pretense of custom guarded their tongues, they found release in the eloquent symbols of verse. And by that sign, Margaret was lost to the good angels. For what care the ambassadors of Satan, for all the small fidelities of the letter and the word, if from the singing choir of earthly methodism we can steal a single heart—lift up, flame-tipped, one great lost soul to the high sinfulness of poetry?

The wine of the grape had never stained her mouth, but the wine of poetry was inextinguishably mixed with her blood, entombed in her flesh.

By the beginning of his fifteenth year Eugene knew almost every major lyric in the language. He possessed them to their living core, not in a handful of scattered quotations, but almost line for line. His thirst was drunken, insatiate: he added to his hoard entire scenes from Schiller's *Wilhelm Tell*, which he read by himself in German; the lyrics of Heine, and several folk songs. He committed to memory the entire passage in the *Anabasis*, the mounting and triumphal Greek which described the moment when the starving remnant of the Ten Thousand had come at length to the sea, and sent up their great cry, calling it by name. In addition, he memorized some of the sonorous stupidities of Cicero, because of the sound, and a little of Caesar, terse and lean.

The great lyrics of Burns he knew from music, from reading, or from hearing Gant recite them. But "Tam O'Shanter" Margaret Leonard read to him, her eyes sparkling with laughter as she read:

> "In hell they'll roast thee like a herrin'."

The shorter Wordsworth pieces he had read at grammar school. "My heart leaps up," "I wandered lonely as a cloud," and "Behold her, single in the field," he had known for years; but Margaret read him the sonnets and made him commit "The world is too much with us" to memory. Her voice trembled and grew low with passion when she read it.

He knew all the songs in Shakespeare's plays, but the two that moved him most were: "O mistress mine, where are you roaming?" which blew a far horn in his heart, and the great song from *Cymbeline*: "Fear no more the heat o' the sun." He had tried to read all the sonnets, and failed, because their woven density was too much for his experience, but he had read, and forgotten, perhaps half of them, and remembered a few which burned up from the page, strangely, immediately, like lamps for him.

Those that he knew were: "When, in the chronicle of wasted time," "To me, fair friend, you never can be old," "Let me not to the marriage of true minds," "The expense of spirit in a waste of shame," "When to the sessions of sweet silent thought," "Shall I compare thee to a summer's day?" "From you have I been absent in the spring," and "That time of year thou mayest in me behold," the greatest of all, which Margaret brought him to, and which shot through him with such electric ecstasy when he came to "Bare ruined choirs, where late the sweet birds sang," that he could hardly hold his course unbroken through the rest of it.

He read all the plays save *Timon, Titus Andronicus, Pericles, Coriolanus,* and *King John,* but the only play that held his interest from first to last was *King Lear.* With most of the famous declamatory passages he had been familiar, for years, by Gant's recitation, and now they wearied him. And all the wordy pinwheels of the clowns, which Margaret laughed at dutifully, and exhibited as specimens of the master's swingeing wit, he felt vaguely were very dull. He never had any confidence in Shakespeare's humor—his Touchstones were not only windy fools, but dull ones.

"For my part I had rather bear with you than bear you; yet I should bear no cross if I did bear you, for I think you have no money in your purse."

This sort of thing reminded him unpleasantly of the Pentlands. The Fool in "Lear" alone he thought admirable—a sad, tragic, mysterious fool. For the rest, he went about and composed parodies, which, with a devil's grin, he told himself would split the sides of posterity. Such as: "Aye, nuncle, an if Shrove Tuesday come last Wednesday, I'll do the capon to thy cock, as Tom O'Ludgate told the shepherd when he found the cowslips gone. Dost bay with two throats, Cerberus? Down, boy, down!"

The admired beauties he was often tired of, perhaps because he had heard them so often, and it seemed to him, moreover, that Shakespeare often spoke absurdly and pompously when he might better have spoken simply, as in the scene where, being informed by the Queen of the death of his sister by drowning, Laertes says:

> "Too much of water hast thou, poor Ophelia,
> And therefore I forbid my tears."

You really can't beat that (he thought). Aye, Ben! Would he had blotted a hundred! A thousand!

But he was deep in other passages which the elocutionist misses, such as the terrible and epic invocation of Edmund, in *King Lear,* drenched in evil, which begins:

> "Thou, Nature, art my goddess,"

and ends,

> "Now, gods, stand up for bastards."

It was as dark as night, as evil as Niggertown, as vast as the elemental winds that howled down across the hills: he chanted it in the black hours of his labor, into the dark and the wind. He understood; he exulted in its evil—which was the evil of earth, of illicit nature. It was a call to the unclassed; it was a cry for those beyond the fence, for rebel angels, and for all of the men who are too tall.

He knew nothing of the Elizabethan drama beyond Shakespeare's plays. But he very early came to know a little of the poetry of Ben Jonson, whom Margaret looked on as a literary Falstaff, condoning, with the familiar weakness of the schoolmarm, his Gargantuan excesses as a pardonable whimsy of genius.

She was somewhat academically mirthful over the literary bacchanalia, as a professor in a Baptist college smacks his lips appetizingly and beams ruddily at his classes when he reads of sack and porter and tankards foaming with the musty ale. All this is part of the liberal tradition. Men of the world are broadminded. Witness Professor Albert Thorndyke Firkins, of the University of Chicago, at the Falcon in Soho. Smiling bravely, he sits over a half-pint of bitter beer, in the company of a racing tout, a sway-backed barmaid, broad in the stern, with adjustable teeth, and three companionable tarts from Lisle street, who are making the best of two pints of Guinness. With eager impatience he awaits the arrival of G. K. Chesterton and E. V. Lucas.

"O rare Ben Jonson!" Margaret Leonard sighed with gentle laughter. "Ah, Lord!"

"My God, boy!" Sheba roared, snatching the suggested motif of conversation out of the air, and licking her buttered fingers noisily as she stormed into action. "God bless him!" Her hairy red face burned like clover, her veinous eyes were tearful bright. "God bless him, 'Gene! He was as English as roast beef and a tankard of musty ale!"

"Ah, Lord!" sighed Margaret. "He was a genius if ever there was one."

With misty eyes she gazed far off, a thread of laughter on her mouth. "Whee!" she laughed gently. "Old Ben!"

"And say, 'Gene!" Sheba continued, bending forward with a fat hand gripped upon her knee. "Do you know that the greatest tribute to Shakespeare's genius is from his hand?"

"Ah, I tell you, boy!" said Margaret, with darkened eyes. Her voice was husky. He was afraid she was going to weep.

"And yet the fools!" Sheba yelled. "The mean little two-by-two pusillanimous swill-drinking fools—"

"Whee!" gently Margaret moaned. John Dorsey turned his chalk-white face to the boy and whined with vacant appreciation, winking his head pertly. Ah absently!

"—for that's all they are, have had the effrontry to suggest that he was jealous."

"Pshaw!" said Margaret impatiently. "There's nothing in that."

"Why, they don't know what they're talking about!" Sheba turned a sudden grinning face upon him. "The little upstarts! It takes us to tell 'em, 'Gene," she said.

He began to slide floorwards out of the wicker chair. John Dorsey slapped his meaty thigh, and bent forward whining inchoately, drooling slightly at the mouth.

"The Lord a' mercy!" he wheezed, gasping.

"I was talking to a feller the other day," said Sheba, "a lawyer that you'd think might know a *little* something, and I used a quotation out of *The Merchant of Venice* that every schoolboy knows—'The quality of mercy is not strained.' The man looked at me as if he thought I was crazy!"

"Great heavens!" said Margaret in a still voice.

"I said, 'Look here, Mr. So-and-so, you may be a smart lawyer, you may have your million dollars that they say you have, but there are a lot of things you don't know yet. There are a lot of things money can't buy, my sonny, and one of them is the society of cult-shered men and women.'"

"Why, pshaw!" said Mr. Leonard. "What do these little whippersnappers know about the things of the mind? You might as well expect some ignorant darky out in the fields to construe a passage in Homer." He grasped a glass half full of clabber, on the table, and tilting it intently in his chalky fingers, spooned out a lumpy spilth of curds which he slid, quivering, into his mouth. "No, sir!" he laughed. "They may be Big Men on the tax collector's books, but when they try to associate with educated men and women, as the feller says, 'they—they—'" he began to whine, "'why, they just ain't nothin'.'"

"What shall it profit a man," said Sheba, "if he gain the whole world, and lose—"

"Ah, Lord!" sighed Margaret, shaking her smoke-dark eyes. "I tell you!"

She told him. She told him of the Swan's profound knowledge of the human heart, his universal and well-rounded characterization, his enormous humor.

"Fought a long hour by Shrewsbury clock!" She laughed. "The fat rascal! Imagine a man keeping the time!"

And, carefully: "It was the custom of the time, 'Gene. As a matter of fact, when you read some of the plays of his contemporaries you see how much purer he is than they are." But she avoided a word, a line, here and there. The slightly spotty Swan—muddied a little by custom. Then, too, the Bible.

The smoky candle-ends of time. Parnassus As Seen From Mount Sinai: Lecture with lantern-slides by Professor McTavish (D.D.) of Presbyterian College.

"And observe, Eugene," she said, "he never made vice attractive."

"Why didn't he?" he asked. "There's Falstaff."

"Yes," she replied, "and you know what happened to him, don't you?"

"Why," he considered, "he died!"

"You see, don't you?" she concluded, with triumphant warning.

I see, don't I? The wages of sin. What, by the way, are the wages of virtue? The good die young.

> Boo-hoo! Boo-hoo! Boo-hoo!
> I really feel so blue!
>   I was given to crime,
>   And cut off in my prime
> When only eighty-two.

"Then, note," she said, "how none of his characters stand still. You can see them grow, from first to last. No one is the same at the end as he was in the beginning."

In the beginning was the word. I am Alpha and Omega. The growth of Lear. He grew old and mad. There's growth for you.

This tin-currency of criticism she had picked up in a few courses at college, and in her reading. They were—are, perhaps, still—part of the glib jargon of pedants. But they did her no real injury. They were simply the things people said. She felt, guiltily, that she must trick out her teaching with these gauds: she was afraid that what she had to offer was not enough. What she had to offer was simply a feeling that was so profoundly right, so unerring, that she could no more utter great verse meanly than mean verse well. She was a voice that God seeks. She was the reed of demonic ecstasy. She was possessed, she knew not how, but she knew the moment of her possession. The singing tongues of all the world were wakened into life again under the incantation of her voice. She was inhabited. She was spent.

She passed through their barred and bolted boy-life with the direct stride of a spirit. She opened their hearts as if they had been lockets. They said: "Mrs. Leonard is sure a nice lady."

He knew some of Ben Jonson's poems, including the fine Hymn to Diana, "Queen and huntress, chaste and fair," and the great tribute to Shakespeare which lifted his hair at

> ". . . But call forth thundering Æschylus,
> Euripides and Sophocles to us."——

and caught at his throat at:

> "He was not for an age, but for all time!
> And all the Muses still were in their prime . . ."

The elegy to little Salathiel Pavy, the child actor, was honey from the lion's mouth. But it was too long.

Of Herrick, sealed of the tribe of Ben, he knew much more. The poetry sang itself. It was, he thought later, the most perfect and unfailing lyrical voice in the language—a clean, sweet, small, unfaltering note. It is done with the incomparable ease of an inspired child. The young men and women of our century have tried to recapture it, as they have tried to recapture Blake and, a little more successfully, Donne.

> Here a little child I stand
> Heaving up my either hand;
> Cold as paddocks though they be,
>
> Here I lift them up to Thee,
> For a benison to fall
> On our meat and on us all. Amen.

There was nothing beyond this—nothing that surpassed it in precision, delicacy, and wholeness.

Their names dropped musically like small fat bird-notes through the freckled sunlight of a young world: prophetically he brooded on the sweet lost bird-cries of their names, knowing they never would return. Herrick, Crashaw, Carew, Suckling, Campion, Lovelace, Dekker. O sweet content, O sweet, O sweet content!

He read shelves of novels: all of Thackeray, all the stories of Poe and Hawthorne, and Herman Melville's *Omoo* and *Typee,* which he found at Gant's. Of *Moby Dick* he had never heard. He read a half-dozen Coopers, all of Mark Twain, but failed to finish a single book of Howells or James.

He read a dozen of Scott, and liked best of all *Quentin Durward,* because the descriptions of food were as bountiful and appetizing as any he had ever read.

Eliza went to Florida again during his fourteenth year and left him to board with the Leonards. Helen was drifting, with crescent weariness and fear, through the cities of the East and Middle-West. She sang for several weeks in a small cabaret in Baltimore, she moved on to Philadelphia and thumped out popular tunes on a battered piano at the music counter of a five and ten cent store, with studious tongue out-thrust as she puzzled through new scores.

Gant wrote her faithfully twice a week—a blue but copious log of existence. Occasionally he enclosed small checks, which she saved, uncashed.

"Your mother," he wrote, "has gone off on another wild-goose chase to Florida, leaving me here alone to face the music, freeze, or starve. God knows what we'll all come to before the end of this fearful, hellish, and damnable winter, but I predict the poorhouse and soup-kitchens like we had in the Cleveland administration. When the Democrats are in, you may as well begin to count your ribs. The banks have no money, people are out of work. You can mark my words everything will go to the tax-collector under the hammer before we're done. The temperature was 7 above when I looked this morning, coal has gone up seventy-five cents a ton. The Sunny South. Keep off the grass said Bill Nye. Jesus God! I passed the Southern Fuel Co. yesterday and saw old Wagner at the window with a fiendish smile of gloatation on his face as he looked out on the sufferings of the widows and orphans. Little does he care if they all freeze. Bob Grady dropped dead Tuesday morning as he was coming out of the Citizen's Bank. I had known him twenty-five years. He'd never been sick a day in his life. All, all are gone, the old familiar faces. Old

Gant will be the next. I have been eating at Mrs. Sales' since your mother went away. You've never seen such a table as she keeps in your life—a profusion of fruits piled up in pyramids, stewed prunes, peaches, and preserves, big roasts of pork, beef, lamb, cold cuts of ham and tongue, and a half dozen vegetables in an abundance that beggars description. How in God's name she does it for thirty-five cents I don't know. Eugene is staying with the Leonards while your mother's away. I take him up to Sales' with me once or twice a week and give him a square meal. They look mighty serious when they see those long legs coming. God knows where he puts it all—he can eat more than any three people I ever saw. I suppose he gets pretty lean pickings at the school. He's got the lean and hungry Gant look. Poor child. He has no mother any more. I'll do the best I can for him until the smash comes. Leonard comes and brags about him every week. He says his equal is not to be found anywhere. Every one in town has heard of him. Preston Carr (who's sure to be the next governor) was talking to me about him the other day. He wants me to send him to the State university law school where he will make lifelong friends among the people of his own State, and then put him into politics. It's what I should have done. I'm going to give him a good education. The rest is up to him. Perhaps he'll be a credit to the name. You haven't seen him since he put on long pants. His mother picked out a beautiful suit at Moale's Christmas. He went down to Daisy's for Christmas and put them on. I bought him a cheap pair at the Racket Store for every-day wear. He can save the good ones for Sunday. Your mother has let the Old Barn to Mrs. Revell until she gets back. I went in the other day and found it warm for the first time in my life. She keeps the furnace going and she's not afraid to burn coal. I hardly ever see Ben from one week to another. He comes in and prowls around in the kitchen at one and two o'clock in the morning and I'm up and gone hours before he's awake. You can get nothing out of him—he never says a half-dozen words and if you ask him a civil question he cuts you off short. I see him down-town late at night sometimes with Mrs. P. They're thick as thieves together. I guess she's a bad egg. This is all for this time. John Duke was shot and killed by the house detective at the Whitstone hotel Sunday night. He was drunk and threatening to shoot every one. It's a sad thing for his wife. He left three children. She was in to see me to-day. He was well-liked by every one but a terror when he drank. My heart bled for her. She's a pretty little woman. Liquor has caused more misery than all the other evils in the world put together. I curse the day it was first invented. Enclosed find a small check to buy yourself a present. God knows what we're coming to. Aff. Your Father, W. O. Gant."

She saved carefully all his letters—written on his heavy slick business stationery in the huge Gothic sprawl of his crippled right hand.

In Florida, meanwhile, Eliza surged up and down the coast, stared thoughtfully at the ungrown town of Miami, found prices too high at Palm Beach, rents too dear at Daytona, and turned inland at length to Orlando, where, groved round with linked lakes and citrous fruits, the Pentlands waited her approach, Pett, with a cold lust of battle on her face, Will with a grimace of itching nervousness while he scaled stubbily at the flaky tetter of his hand.

24

With thick chalked fingers John Dorsey thoughtfully massaged his torso from loin to chin.

"Now, let me see," he whined with studious deliberation, "what he gives on this." He fumbled for the notes.

Tom Davis turned his reddening cheeks toward the window, a low sputter of laughter escaping from his screwed lips.

Guy Doak gazed solemnly at Eugene, with a forked hand stroking his grave pallid face.

"*Entgegen,*" said Eugene, in a small choked voice, "follows its object."

John Dorsey laughed uncertainly, and shook his head, still searching the notes.

"I'm not so sure of that," he said.

Their wild laughter leaped like freed hounds. Tom Davis hurled himself violently downward over his desk. John Dorsey looked up, adding uncertainly his absent falsetto mirth.

From time to time, in spite of himself, they taught him a little German, a language of which he had been quite happily ignorant. The lesson had become for them a daily hunger: they worked it over with mad intensity, speeding and polishing their translation in order to enjoy his bewilderment. Sometimes, deliberately, they salted their pages with glib false readings, sometimes they interpolated passages of wild absurdity, waiting exultantly for his cautious amendment of a word that did not exist.

"Slowly the moonlight crept up the chair in which the old man was sitting, reaching his knees, his breast, and finally,"—Guy Doak looked up slyly at his tutor, "giving him a good punch in the eye."

"No-o," said John Dorsey, rubbing his chin, "not exactly. 'Catching him squarely in the eye' gets the idiom better, I think."

Tom Davis thrust a mouthful of strange gurgling noises into his desk, and waited for the classic evasion. It came at once.

"Let me see," said John Dorsey, turning the pages, "what he gives on this."

Guy Doak scrawled a brief message across a crumpled wad and thrust it on Eugene's desk. Eugene read:

> "Gebe mir ein Stück Papier,
> Before I bust you on the ear."

He detached two slick sheets from his tablet, and wrote in answer:

> "Du bist wie eine bum-me."

They read sweet gluey little stories, fat German tear-gulps: *Immensee, Höher als die Kirche, Der Zerbrochene Krug.* Then, *Wilhelm Tell.* The fine lyrical measure of the opening song, the unearthly siren song to the fisher-boy, haunted them with its faery music. The heavy melodrama of some of the scenes was unhackneyed to them: they bent eagerly to the apple-shooting scene, and the escape by boat. As for the rest, it was, they wearily recognized, Great Literature. Mr. Schiller, they saw, was religiously impressed, like Patrick Henry, George Washington, and Paul Revere, with the beauties of Liberty. His embattled Swiss bounded ponderously from crag to crag, invoking it in windy speeches.

"The mountains," observed John Dorsey, touched, in a happy moment, by the genius of the place, "have been the traditional seat of Liberty."

Eugene turned his face toward the western ranges. He heard, far off, a whistle, a remote, thunder on the rails.

During this season of Eliza's absence he roomed with Guy Doak.

Guy Doak was five years his senior. He was a native of Newark, New Jersey: his speech was touched with Yankee nasality, his manner with Yankee crispness. His mother, a boarding-house mistress, had come to Altamont a year or two before to retrieve her health: she was tubercular, and spent part of the winter in Florida.

Guy Doak had a trim cocky figure of medium height, black hair, bright dark eyes, a pale, very smooth oval face, somehow suggestive, Eugene thought, of a fish's belly, with somewhat unhappily full jaws which made his lower features seem larger than his upper. He was foppishly neat in his dress. People called him a good-looking boy.

He made few friends. To the boys at Leonard's this Yankee was far more remote than the rich Cuban boy, Manuel Quevado, whose fat dark laughter and broken speech was all for girls. He belonged to a richer South, but they knew him.

Guy Doak had none of their floridity. He was lacking in their hearty violence. He did not laugh loudly. He had a sharp, bright, shallow mind, inflexibly dogmatic. His companions were bad Southern romantics, he was a false Yankee realist. They arrived, thus, by different means, at a common goal of superstition. Guy Doak had already hardened into the American city-dweller's mould of infantile cynicism. He was occasionally merry with the other boys in the classic manner of the city fellow with the yokels. He was wise. Above all, he was wise. It was safe to assume, he felt, that Truth was always on the scaffold, and Wrong forever on the throne. So far from being depressed by the slaughter of the innocents, the spectacle gave him much bitter amusement.

Outside of this, Guy Doak was a very nice fellow—sharp, obstinate, unsubtle, and pleased with his wit. They lived on the first floor at Leonard's: at night, by a roaring wood fire, they listened carefully to the great thunder of the trees, and to the stealthy creaking foot-steps of the master as he came softly down the stairs, and paused by their door. They ate at table with Margaret, John Dorsey, Miss Amy, the two children, John Dorsey, junior, nine, and Margaret, five, and two of Leonard's Tennessee nephews—Tyson Leonard, a ferret-faced boy of eighteen, foulmouthed and sly, and Dirk Barnard, a tall slender boy, seventeen, with a bumpy face, brown merry eyes, and a quick temper. At table they kept up a secret correspondence of innuendo and hidden movement, fleshing a fork in a grunting neighbor as John Dorsey said the blessing, and choking with smothered laughter. At night, they tapped messages on floor and ceiling, crept out for sniggering conventions in the windy dark hall, and fled to their innocent beds as John Dorsey stormed down on them.

Leonard was fighting hard to keep his little school alive. He had less than twenty students the first year, and less than thirty the second. From an income of not more than $3,000 he had to pay Miss Amy, who had left a high school position to help him, a small salary. The old house on its fine wooded hill was full of outmoded plumbing and drafty corridors: he had leased it at a small rental. But the rough usage of thirty boys demanded a considerable yearly restoration. The Leonards were fighting very stubbornly and courageously for their existence.

The food was scant and poor: at breakfast, a dish of blue, watery oatmeal, eggs and toast; at lunch, a thin soup, hot sour cornbread, and a vegetable boiled with a piece of fat pork; at dinner, hot biscuits, a small meat loaf, and creamed or boiled potatoes. No one was permitted coffee or tea, but there was an abundance of fresh creamy milk. John Dorsey always kept and milked his own cow. Occasionally there was a deep, crusted pie, hot, yolky muffins, or spicy gingerbread of Margaret's make. She was a splendid cook.

Often, at night, Guy Doak slid quietly out through the window on to the side porch, and escaped down the road under the concealing roar of the trees. He would return from town within two hours, crawling in exultantly with a bag full of hot frankfurter sandwiches coated thickly with mustard, chopped onion, and a hot Mexican sauce. With a crafty grin he unfoiled two five-cent cigars, which they smoked magnificently, with a sharp tang of daring, blowing the smoke up the chimney in order to thwart a possible irruption by the master. And Guy brought back, from the wind and the night, the good salt breath of gossip in street and store, news of the town, and the brave swagger of the drugstore gallants.

As they smoked and stuffed fat palatable bites of sandwich into their mouths, they would regard each other with pleased sniggers, carrying on thus an insane symphony of laughter:

"Chuckle, chuckle!—laugh of gloatation."

"Tee-hee, tee-hee, tee-hee! . . laugh of titterosity."

"Snuh-huh, snuh-huh, snuh-huh! . . laugh of gluttonotiousness."

The vigorous warmth of burning wood filled their room pleasantly: over their sheltered heads the dark gigantic wind howled through the earth. O sheltered love, nooked warmly in against this winter night. O warm fair women, whether within a forest hut, or by the town ledged high above the moaning seas, shot upon the wind, I come.

Guy Doak toyed gently at his belly with his right hand, and stroked his round chin slowly with his left.

"Now let me see," he whined, "what he gives on this."

Their laughter rang around the walls. Too late, they heard the aroused stealthy foot-falls of the master, creaking down the hall. Later—silence, the dark, the wind.

Miss Amy closed her small beautifully kept grade book, thrust her great arms upward, and yawned. Eugene looked hopefully at her and out along the playing court, reddened by the late sun. He was wild, uncontrollable, erratic. His mad tongue leaped out in class. He could never keep peace a full day. He amazed them. They loved him, and they punished him piously, affectionately. He was never released at the dismissal hour. He was always "kept in."

John Dorsey noted each whisper of disorder, or each failure in preparation, by careful markings in a book. Each afternoon he read the names of delinquents, amid a low mutter of sullen protest, and stated their penalties. Once Eugene got through an entire day without a mark. He stood triumphantly before Leonard while the master searched the record.

John Dorsey began to laugh foolishly; he gripped his hand affectionately around the boy's arm.

"Well, sir!" he said. "There must be a mistake. I'm going to keep you in on general principles."

He bent to a long dribbling suction of laughter. Eugene's wild eyes were shot with tears of anger and surprise. He never forgot.

Miss Amy yawned, and smiled on him with slow powerful affectionate contempt.

"Go on!" she said, in her broad, lazy accent. "I don't want to fool with you any more. You're not worth powder enough to blow you up."

Margaret came in, her face furrowed deeply between smoke-dark eyes, full of tender sternness and hidden laughter.

"What's wrong with the rascal?" she asked. "Can't he learn algebra?"

"He can learn!" drawled Miss Amy. "He can learn anything. He's lazy—that's what it is. Just plain lazy."

She smacked his buttock smartly with a ruler.

"I'd like to warm you a bit with this," she laughed, slowly and richly. "You'd learn then."

"Here!" said Margaret, shaking her head in protest. "You leave that boy alone. Don't look behind the faun's ears. Never mind about algebra, here. That's for poor folks. There's no need for algebra where two and two make five."

Miss Amy turned her handsome gypsy eyes on Eugene.

"Go on. I've seen enough of you." She made a strong weary gesture of dismissal.

Hatless, with a mad whoop, he plunged through the door and leaped the porch rail.

"Here, boy!" Margaret called. "Where's your hat?"

Grinning, he galloped back, picked up a limp rag of dirty green felt, and pulled it over his chaotic hair. Curly tufts stuck through the gaping crease-holes.

"Come here!" said Margaret gravely. Her nervous fingers pulled his frayed necktie around to the front, tugged down his vest, and buttoned his coat over tightly, while he peered at her with his strange devil's grin. Suddenly she trembled with laughter.

"Good heavens, Amy," she said. "Look at that hat."

Miss Amy smiled at him with indifferent sleepy cat-warmth.

"You want to fix yourself up, 'Gene," she said, "so the girls will begin to notice you."

He heard the strange song of Margaret's laughter.

"Can you see him out courting?" she said. "The poor girl would think she had a demon lover, sure."

> "As e'er beneath a waning moon was haunted
> By woman wailing for her demon lover."

His eyes burned on her face, flowing with dark secret beauty.

"Get along, you scamp!" she ordered.

He turned, and, crying fiercely in his throat, tore down the road with bounding strides.

All the dusk blurred in her eyes.

"Leave him alone!" she whispered to no one. "Leave him alone!"

A light wind of April fanned over the hill. There was a smell of burning leaves and rubble around the school. In the field on the hill flank behind the house a plowman drove his big horse with loose clanking traces around a lessening square of dry fallow earth. Gee, woa. His strong feet followed after. The big share bit cleanly down, cleaving a deep spermy furrow of moist young earth along its track.

John Dorsey Leonard stared fascinated out the window at the annual rejuvenation of the earth. Before his eyes the emergent nymph was scaling her hard cracked hag's pelt. The golden age returned.

Down the road a straggling queue of boys were all gone into the world of light. Wet with honest sweat, the plowman paused at the turn, and wiped the blue shirting of his forearm across his beaded forehead. Meanwhile, his intelligent animal, taking advantage of the interval, lifted with slow majesty a proud flowing tail, and added his mite to the fertility of the soil with three moist oaty droppings. Watching, John Dorsey grunted approvingly. They also serve who only stand and wait.

"Please, Mr. Leonard," said Eugene, carefully choosing his moment, "can I go?"

John Dorsey Leonard stroked his chin absently, and stared sightlessly at his book. Others abide our question, thou art free.

"Huh?" he purred vaguely. Then, with a high vacant snigger he turned suddenly, and said:

"You rascal, you! See if Mrs. Leonard wants you." He fastened his brutal grip with keen hunger into the boy's thin arm. April is the cruellest of months. Eugene winced, moved away, and then stood quietly, checked by memory of the old revolt from awe.

He found Margaret in the library reading to the children from *The Water Babies*.

"Mr. Leonard says to ask you if I can go?" he said.

And her eyes were darkened wholly.

"Yes, you scamp. Go on," she said. "Tell me, boy," she coaxed, softly, "can't you be a little bit better?"

"Yes'm," he promised, easily. "I'll try." Say not the struggle naught availeth.

She smiled at his high mettled prancing nervousness.

"In hell they'll roast thee like a herrin'," she said gently. "Get out of here."

He bounded away from the nunnery of the chaste breast and quiet mind.

As he leaped down the stairs into the yard he heard Dirk Barnard's lusty splashing bathtub solo. Sweet Thames, run softly till I end my song. Tyson Leonard, having raked into every slut's corner of nature with a thin satisfied grin, emerged from the barn with a cap full of fresh eggs. A stammering cackle of protest followed him from angry hens who found too late that men betray. At the barnside, under the carriage shed, "Pap" Rheinhart tightened the bellyband of his saddled brown mare, swinging strongly into the saddle, and with a hard scramble of hoofs, came up the hill, wheeled in behind the house, and drew up by Eugene.

"Jump on, 'Gene," he invited, patting the mare's broad rump. "I'll take you home."

Eugene looked up at him grinning.

"You'll take me nowhere," he said. "I couldn't sit down for a week last time."

"Pap" boomed with laughter.

"Why, pshaw, boy!" he said. "That was nothing but a gentle little dog-trot."

"Dog-trot your granny," said Eugene. "You tried to kill me."

"Pap" Rheinhart turned his wry neck down on the boy with grave dry humor.

"Come on," he said gruffly. "I'm not going to hurt you. I'll teach you how to ride a horse."

"Much obliged, Pap," said Eugene ironically. "But I'm thinking of using my tail a good deal in my old age. I don't want to wear it out while I'm young."

Pleased with them both, "Pap" Rheinhart laughed loud and deep, spat a brown quid back over the horse's crupper, and, digging his heels in smartly, galloped away around the house, into the road. The horse bent furiously to his work, like a bounding dog. With four-hooved thunder he drummed upon the sounding earth. *Quadrupedante putrem sonitu quatit ungula campum.*

At the two-posted entry, by the bishop's boundary, the departing students turned, split quickly to the sides, and urged the horseman on with shrill cries. "Pap" bent low, with loose-reined hands above the horse-mane, went through the gate like the whiz of a cross-bow. Then, he jerked the mare back on her haunches with a dusty skid of hoofs, and waited for the boys to come up.

"Hey!" With high bounding exultancy Eugene came down the road to join them. Without turning, stolid Van Yeats threw up his hand impatiently and greeted the unseen with a cheer. The others turned, welcoming him with ironical congratulation.

"'Highpockets,'" said "Doc" Hines, comically puckering his small tough face, "how'd you happen to git out on time?" He had an affected, high-pitched nigger drawl. When he spoke he kept one hand in his coat pocket, fingering a leather thong loaded with buckshot.

"J. D. had to do his spring plowing," said Eugene.

"Well, if it ain't ole Handsome," said Julius Arthur. He grinned squintly, revealing a mouthful of stained teeth screwed in a wire clamp. His face was covered with small yellow pustulate sores. How begot, how nourished?

"Shall we sing our little song for Handsome Hal?" said Ralph Rolls to his copesmate Julius. He wore a derby hat jammed over his pert freckled face. As he spoke he took a ragged twist of tobacco from his pocket and bit off a large chew with a rough air of relish.

"Want a chew, Jule?" he said.

Julius took the twist, wiped off his mouth with a loose male grin, and crammed a large quid into his cheek.

He brought me roots of relish sweet.

"Want one, Highpockets?" he asked Eugene, grinning.

I hate him that would upon the rack of this tough world stretch me out longer.

"Hell," said Ralph Rolls. "Handsome would curl up and die if he ever took a chew."

In Spring like torpid snakes my enemies awaken.

At the corner of Church Street, across from the new imitation Tudor of the Episcopal church, they paused. Above them, on the hill, rose the steeples of the Methodist and Presbyterian churches. Ye antique spires, ye distant towers!

"Who's going my way?" said Julius Arthur. "Come on, 'Gene. The car's down here. I'll take you home."

"Thanks, but I can't," said Eugene. "I'm going up-town." Their curious eyes on Dixieland when I get out.

"You going home, Villa?"

"No," said George Graves.

"Well, keep Hal out of trouble," said Ralph Rolls.

Julius Arthur laughed roughly and thrust his hand through Eugene's hair. "Old Hairbreadth Hal," he said. "The cutthroat from Saw-Tooth Gap!"

"Don't let 'em climb your frame, son," said Van Yeats, turning his quiet pleasant face on Eugene. "If you need help, let me know."

"So long, boys."

"So long."

They crossed the street, mixing in nimble horse-play, and turned down past the church along a sloping street that led to the garages. George Graves and Eugene continued up the hill.

"Julius is a good boy," said George Graves. "His father makes more money than any other lawyer in town."

"Yes," said Eugene, still brooding on Dixieland and his clumsy deceptions.

A street-sweeper walked along slowly uphill, beside his deep wedge-bodied cart. From time to time he stopped the big slow-footed horse and, sweeping the littered droppings of street and gutter into a pan, with a long-handled brush, dumped his collections into the cart. Let not Ambition mock their useful toil.

Three sparrows hopped deftly about three fresh smoking globes of horse-dung, pecking out tidbits with dainty gourmandism. Driven away by the approaching cart, they skimmed briskly over to the bank, with bright twitters of annoyance. One too like thee, tameless, and swift, and proud.

George Graves ascended the hill with a slow ponderous rhythm, staring darkly at the ground.

"Say, 'Gene!" he said finally. "I don't believe he makes that much."

Eugene thought seriously for a moment. With George Graves, it was necessary to resume a discussion where it had been left off three days before.

"Who?" he said, "John Dorsey? Yes, I think he does," he added, grinning.

"Not over $2,500, anyway," said George Graves gloomily.

"No—three thousand, three thousand!" he said, in a choking voice.

George Graves turned to him with a sombre, puzzled smile. "What's the matter?" he asked.

"O you fool! You damn fool!" gasped Eugene. "You've been thinking about it all this time."

George Graves laughed sheepishly, with embarrassment, richly.

From the top of the hill at the left, the swelling unction of the Methodist organ welled up remotely from the choir, accompanied by a fruity contralto voice, much in demand at funerals. Abide with me.

Most musical of mourners, weep again!

George Graves turned and examined the four large black houses, ascending on flat terraces to the church, of Paston Place.

"That's a good piece of property, 'Gene," he said. "It belongs to the Paston estate."

Fast falls the even-tide. Heaves the proud harlot her distended breast, in intricacies of laborious song.

"It will all go to Gil Paston some day," said George Graves with virtuous regret. "He's not worth a damn."

They had reached the top of the hill. Church Street ended levelly a block beyond, in the narrow gulch of the avenue. They saw, with quickened pulse, the little pullulation of the town.

A negro dug tenderly in the round loamy flowerbeds of the Presbyterian churchyard, bending now and then to thrust his thick fingers gently in about the roots. The old church, with its sharp steeple, rotted slowly, decently, prosperously, like a good man's life, down into its wet lichened brick. Eugene looked gratefully, with a second's pride, at its dark decorum, its solid Scotch breeding.

"I'm a Presbyterian," he said. "What are you?"

"An Episcopalian, when I go," said George Graves with irreverent laughter.

"To hell with these Methodists!" Eugene said with an elegant, disdainful face. "They're too damn common for us." God in three persons—blessed Trinity. "Brother Graves," he continued, in a fat well-oiled voice, "I didn't see you at prayer-meeting Wednesday night. Where in Jesus' name were you?"

With his open palm he struck George Graves violently between his meaty shoulders. George Graves staggered drunkenly with high resounding laughter.

"Why, Brother Gant," said he, "I had a little appointment with one of the Good Sisters, out in the cow-shed."

Eugene gathered a telephone pole into his wild embrace, and threw one leg erotically over its second foot-wedge. George Graves leaned his heavy shoulder against it, his great limbs drained with laughter.

There was a hot blast of steamy air from the Appalachian Laundry across the street and, as the door from the office of the washroom opened, they had a moment's glimpse of negresses plunging their wet arms into the liquefaction of their clothes.

George Graves dried his eyes. Laughing wearily, they crossed over.

"We oughtn't to talk like that, 'Gene," said George Graves reproachfully. "Sure enough! It's not right."

He became moodily serious rapidly. "The best people in this town are church members," he said earnestly. "It's a fine thing."

"Why?" said Eugene, with an idle curiosity.

"Because," said George Graves, "you get to know all the people who are worth a damn."

Worth being damned, he thought quickly. A quaint idea.

"It helps you in a business way. They come to know you and respect you. You won't get far in this town, 'Gene, without them. It pays," he added devoutly, "to be a Christian."

"Yes," Eugene agreed seriously, "you're right." To walk together to the kirk, with a goodly company.

He thought sadly of his lost sobriety, and of how once, lonely, he had walked the decent lanes of God's Scotch town. Unbidden they came again to haunt his memory, the shaven faces of good tradesmen, each leading the well washed kingdom of his home in its obedient ritual, the lean hushed smiles of worship, the chained passion of devotion, as they implored God's love upon their ventures, or delivered their virgin daughters into the holy barter of marriage. And from even deeper adyts of his brain there swam up slowly to the shores of his old hunger the great fish whose names he scarcely knew—whose names, garnered with blind toil from a thousand books, from Augustine, himself a name, to Jeremy Taylor, the English metaphysician, were brief evocations of scalded light, electric, phosphorescent, illuminating by their magic connotations the vast far depths of ritual and religion: They came—Bartholomew, Hilarius, Chrysostomos, Polycarp, Anthony, Jerome, and the forty martyrs of

Cappadocia who walked the waves—coiled like their own green shadows for a moment, and were gone.

"Besides," said George Graves, "a man ought to go anyway. Honesty's the best policy."

Across the street, on the second floor of a small brick three-story building that housed several members of the legal, medical, surgical, and dental professions, Dr. H. M. Smathers pumped vigorously with his right foot, took a wad of cotton from his assistant, Miss Lola Bruce, and thrusting it securely into the jaw of his unseen patient, bent his fashionable bald head intently. A tiny breeze blew back the thin curtains, and revealed him, white-jacketed, competent, drill in hand.

"Do you feel that?" he said tenderly.

"Wrogd gdo gurk!"

"Spit!" With thee conversing, I forget all time.

"I suppose," said George Graves thoughtfully, "the gold they use in people's teeth is worth a lot of money."

"Yes," said Eugene, finding the idea attractive, "if only one person in ten has gold fillings that would be ten million in the United States alone. You can figure on five dollars' worth each, can't you?"

"Easy!" said George Graves. "More than that." He brooded lusciously a moment. "That's a lot of money," he said.

In the office of the Rogers-Malone Undertaking Establishment the painful family of death was assembled, "Horse" Hines, tilted back in a swivel chair, with his feet thrust out on the broad window-ledge, chatted lazily with Mr. C. M. Powell, the suave silent partner. How sleep the brave, who sink to rest. Forget not yet.

"There's good money in undertaking," said George Graves. "Mr. Powell's well off."

Eugene's eyes were glued on the lantern face of "Horse" Hines. He beat the air with a convulsive arm, and sank his fingers in his throat.

"What's the matter?" cried George Graves.

"They shall not bury me alive," he said.

"You can't tell," George Graves said gloomily. "It's been known to happen. They've dug them up later and found them turned over on their faces."

Eugene shuddered. "I think," he suggested painfully, "they're supposed to take out your insides when they embalm you."

"Yes," said George Graves more hopefully, "and that stuff they use would kill you anyway. They pump you full of it."

With shrunken heart, Eugene considered. The ghost of old fear, that had been laid for years, walked forth to haunt him.

In his old fantasies of death he had watched his living burial, had foreseen his waking life-in-death, his slow, frustrated efforts to push away the smothering flood of earth until, as a drowning swimmer claws the air, his mute and stiffened fingers thrust from the ground a call for hands.

Fascinated, they stared through screen-doors down the dark central corridor, flanked by jars of weeping ferns. A sweet funereal odor of carnations and cedar-wood floated on the cool heavy air. Dimly, beyond a central partition, they saw a heavy casket, on a wheeled trestle, with rich silver handles and velvet coverings. The thick light faded there in dark.

"They're laid out in the room behind," said George Graves, lowering his voice.

To rot away into a flower, to melt into a tree with the friendless bodies of unburied men.

At this moment, having given to misery all he had (a tear), the very Reverend Father James O'Haley, S.J., among the faithless faithful only he, unshaken, unseduced, unterrified, emerged plumply from the chapel, walked up the soft aisle rug with brisk short-legged strides, and came out into the light. His pale blue eyes blinked rapidly for a moment, his plump uncreased face set firmly in a smile of quiet benevolence; he covered himself with a small well-kept hat of black velvet, and set off toward the avenue. Eugene shrank back gently as the little man walked past him: that small priestly figure in black bore on him the awful accolade of his great Mistress, that smooth face had heard the unutterable, seen the unknowable. In this remote outpost of the mighty Church, he was the standard-bearer of the one true faith, the consecrate flesh of God.

"They don't get any pay," said George Graves sorrowfully.

"How do they live, then?" Eugene asked.

"Don't you worry!" said George Graves, with a knowing smile.

"They get all that's coming to them. He doesn't seem to be starving, does he?"

"No," said Eugene, "he doesn't."

"He lives on the fat of the land," said George Graves. "Wine at every meal. There are some rich Catholics in this town."

"Yes," said Eugene. "Frank Moriarty's got a pot full of money that he made selling licker."

"Don't let them hear you," said George Graves, with a surly laugh. "They've got a family tree and a coat of arms already."

"A beer-bottle rampant on a field of limburger cheese, gules," said Eugene.

"They're trying to get the Princess Madeleine into Society," said George Graves.

"Hell fire!" Eugene cried, grinning. "Let's let her in, if that's all she wants. We belong to the Younger Set, don't we?"

"You may," said George Graves, reeling with laughter, "but I don't. I wouldn't be caught dead with the little pimps."

"Mr. Eugene Gant was the host last night at a hot wienie roast given to members of the local Younger Set at Dixieland, the beautiful old ancestral mansion of his mother, Mrs. Eliza Gant."

George Graves staggered. "You oughtn't to say that, 'Gene," he gasped. He shook his head reproachfully. "Your mother's a fine woman."

"During the course of the evening, the Honorable George Graves, the talented scion of one of our oldest and wealthiest families, the Chesterfield Graveses, ($10 a week and up), rendered a few appropriate selections on the jews-harp."

Pausing deliberately, George Graves wiped his streaming eyes, and blew his nose. In the windows of Bain's millinery store, a waxen nymph bore a confection of rakish plumes upon her false tresses, and extended her simpering fingers in elegant counterpoise. Hats For Milady. O that those lips had language.

At this moment, with a smooth friction of trotting rumps, the death-wagon of Rogers-Malone turned swiftly in from the avenue, and wheeled by on ringing hoofs. They turned curiously and watched it draw up to the curb.

"Another Redskin bit the dust," said George Graves.

Come, delicate death, serenely arriving, arriving.

"Horse" Hines came out quickly on long flapping legs, and opened the doors behind. In another moment, with the help of the two men on the driver's seat, he had lowered the long wicker basket gently, and vanished, quietly, gravely, into the fragrant gloom of his establishment.

As Eugene watched, the old fatality of place returned. Each day, he thought, we pass the spot where some day we must die; or shall I, too, ride dead to some mean building yet unknown? Shall this bright clay, the hill-bound, die in lodgings yet unbuilt? Shall these eyes, drenched with visions yet unseen, stored with the viscous and interminable seas at dawn, with the sad comfort of unfulfilled Arcadias, seal up their cold dead dreams upon a tick, as this, in time, in some hot village of the plains?

He caught and fixed the instant. A telegraph messenger wheeled vigorously in from the avenue with pumping feet, curved widely into the alley at his right, jerking his wheel up sharply as he took the curb and coasted down to the delivery boy's entrance. And post o'er land and ocean without rest. Milton, thou shouldst be living at this hour.

Descending the dark stairs of the Medical Building slowly, Mrs. Thomas Hewitt, the comely wife of the prominent attorney (of Arthur, Hewitt, and Grey), turned out into the light, and advanced slowly toward the avenue. She was greeted with flourishing gestures of the hat by Henry T. Merriman (Merriman and Merriman), and Judge Robert C. Allan, professional colleagues of her husband. She smiled and shot each quickly with a glance. Pleasant is this flesh. When she had passed they looked after her a moment. Then they continued their discussion of the courts.

On the third floor of the First National Bank building on the right hand corner, Fergus Paston, fifty-six, a thin lecherous mouth between iron-gray dundrearies, leaned his cocked leg upon his open window, and followed the movements of Miss Bernie Powers, twenty-two, crossing the street. Even in our ashes live their wonted fires.

On the opposite corner, Mrs. Roland Rawls, whose husband was manager of the Peerless Pulp Company (Plant No. 3), and whose father owned it, emerged from the rich seclusion of Arthur N. Wright, jeweller. She clasped her silver meshbag and stepped into her attendant Packard. She was a tall black-haired woman of thirty-three with a good figure: her face was dull, flat, and Mid-western.

"She's the one with the money," said George Graves. "He hasn't a damn thing. It's all in her name. She wants to be an opera singer."

"Can she sing?"

"Not worth a damn," said George Graves. "I've heard her. There's your chance, 'Gene. She's got a daughter about your age."

"What does she do?" said Eugene.

"She wants to be an actress," said George Graves, laughing throatily.

"You have to work too damn hard for your money," said Eugene.

They had reached the corner by the Bank, and now halted, indecisively, looking up the cool gulch of afternoon. The street buzzed with a light gay swarm of idlers: the faces of the virgins bloomed in and out like petals on a bough. Advancing upon him, an inch to the second, Eugene saw, ten feet away, the heavy paralyzed body of old Mr. Avery. He was a very great scholar, stone-deaf, and seventy-eight years old. He lived alone in a room above the Public Library. He had neither friends nor connections. He was a myth.

"Oh, my God!" said Eugene. "Here he comes!"

It was too late for escape.

Gasping a welcome, Mr. Avery bore down on him, with a violent shuffle of his feet and a palsied tattoo of his heavy stick which brought him over the intervening three yards in forty seconds.

"Well, young fellow," he panted, "how's Latin?"

"Fine," Eugene screamed into his pink ear.

"*Poeta nascitur, non fit,*" said Mr. Avery, and went off into a silent wheeze of laughter which brought on a fit of coughing strangulation. His eyes bulged, his tender pink skin grew crimson, he roared his terror out in a phlegmy rattle, while his goose-white hand trembled frantically for his handkerchief. A crowd gathered. Eugene quickly drew a dirty handkerchief from the old man's pocket, and thrust it into his hands. He tore up from his convulsed organs a rotting mass, and panted rapidly for breath. The crowd dispersed somewhat dejectedly.

George Graves grinned darkly. "That's too bad," he said. "You oughtn't to laugh, 'Gene." He turned away, gurgling.

"Can you conjugate?" gasped Mr. Avery. "Here's the way I learned:

> "*Amo, amas,*
> I love a lass.
> *Amat,*
> He loves her, too."

Quivering with tremors of laughter, he launched himself again. Because he could not leave them, save by the inch, they moved off several yards to the curb. Grow old along with me!

"That's a damn shame," said George Graves, looking after him and shaking his head. "Where's he going?"

"To supper," said Eugene.

"To supper!" said George Graves. "It's only four o'clock. Where does he eat?"

Not where he eats, but where he is eaten.

"At the Uneeda," said Eugene, beginning to choke. "It takes him two hours to get there."

"Does he go every day?" said George Graves, beginning to laugh.

"Three times a day," Eugene screamed. "He spends all morning going to dinner, and all afternoon going to supper."

A whisper of laughter came from their weary jaws. They sighed like sedge.

At this moment, dodging briskly through the crowd, with a loud and cheerful word for every one, Mr. Joseph Bailey, secretary of the Altamont Chamber of Commerce, short, broad, and ruddy, came by them with a hearty gesture of the hand:

"Hello, boys!" he cried. "How're they going?" But before either of them could answer, he had passed on, with an encouraging shake of his head, and a deep applauding *"That's* right."

"What's right?" said Eugene.

But before George Graves could answer, the great lung specialist, Dr. Fairfax Grinder, scion of one of the oldest and proudest families in Virginia, drove in viciously from Church Street, with his sinewy length of six feet and eight inches coiled tensely in the deep pit of his big Buick roadster. Cursing generally the whole crawling itch of Confederate and Yankee postwar rabbledom, with a few special parentheses for Jews and niggers, he drove full tilt at the short plump figure of Joe Zamschnick, men's furnishings ("Just a Whisper Off The Square").

Joseph, two yards away from legal safety, hurled himself with a wild scream headlong at the curb. He arrived on hands and knees, but under his own power.

"K-hurses!" said Eugene. "Foiled again."

'Twas true! Dr. Fairfax Grinder's lean bristled upper lip drew back over his strong yellow teeth. He jammed on his brakes, and lifted his car round with a complete revolution of his long arms. Then he roared away through scattering traffic, in a greasy blue cloud of gasoline and burnt rubber.

Joe Zamschnick frantically wiped his gleaming bald head with a silk handkerchief and called loudly on the public to bear witness.

"What's the matter with him?" said George Graves, disappointed. "He usually goes up on the sidewalk after them if he can't get them on the street."

On the other side of the street, attracting no more than a languid stare from the loafing natives, the Honorable William Jennings Bryan paused benevolently before the windows of the H. Martin Grimes Bookstore, allowing the frisking breeze to toy pleasantly with his famous locks. The tangles of Neaera's hair.

The Commoner stared carefully at the window display which included several copies of *Before Adam,* by Jack London. Then he entered, and selected a dozen views of Altamont and the surrounding hills.

"He may come here to live," said George Graves. "Dr. Doak's offered to give him a house and lot in Doak Park."

"Why?" said Eugene.

"Because the advertising will be worth a lot to the town," said George Graves.

A little before them, that undaunted daughter of desires, Miss Elizabeth Scragg, emerged from Woolworth's Five and Ten Cent Store, and turned up toward the Square. Smiling, she acknowledged the ponderous salute of

Big Jeff White, the giant half-owner of the Whitstone hotel, whose fortunes had begun when he had refused to return to his old comrade, Dickson Reese, the embezzling cashier, ninety thousand dollars of entrusted loot. Dog eat dog. Thief catch thief. It is not growing like a tree, in bulk doth make man better be.

His six-and-a-half-foot shadow flitted slowly before them. He passed, in creaking number twelves, a massive smooth-jowled man with a great paunch girdled in a wide belt.

Across the street again, before the windows of the Van W. Yeats Shoe Company, the Reverend J. Brooks Gall, Amherst ('61), and as loyal a Deke as ever breathed, but looking only sixty of his seventy-three years, paused in his brisk walk, and engaged in sprightly monologue, three of his fellow Boy Scouts—the Messrs. Lewis Monk, seventeen, Bruce Rogers, thirteen, and Malcolm Hodges, fourteen. None knew as well as he the heart of a boy. He, too, it seems, had once been one himself. Thus, as one bright anecdote succeeded, or suggested, a half-dozen others, they smiled dutifully, with attentive respect, below the lifted barrier of his bristly white mustache, into the gleaming rhyme of his false teeth. And, with rough but affectionate camaraderie, he would pause from time to time to say: "Old Male!" or "Old Bruce!" gripping firmly his listener's arm, shaking him gently. Pallidly, on restless feet, they smiled, plotting escape with slant-eyed stealth.

Mr. Buse, the Oriental rug merchant, came around the corner below them from Liberty Street. His broad dark face was wreathed in Persian smiles. I met a traveller from an antique land.

In the Bijou Cafe for Ladies and Gents, Mike, the counter man, leaned his hairy arms upon the marble slab, and bent his wrinkled inch of brow upon a week-old copy of *Atlantis*. Fride Chicken To-day with Sweet Potatos. Hail to thee, blithe spirit, bird thou never wert. A solitary fly darted swiftly about the greasy cover of a glass humidor, under which a leathery quarter of mince pie lay weltering. Spring had come.

Meanwhile, having completed twice their parade up and down the street from the Square to the post-office, the Misses Christine Ball, Viola Powell, Aline Rollins, and Dorothy Hazzard were accosted outside Wood's Drug Store by Tom French, seventeen, Roy Duncan, nineteen, and Carl Jones, eighteen.

"Where do you think you're going?" said Tom French, insolently.

Gayly, brightly, in unison, they answered:

"Hey—ee!"

"Hay's seven dollars a ton," said Roy Duncan, and immediately burst into a high cackle of laughter, in which all the others joined, merrily.

"You craz-ee!" said Viola Powell tenderly. Tell me, ye merchants' daughters, did ye see another creature fair and wise as she.

"Mr. Duncan," said Tom French, turning his proud ominous face upon his best friend, "I want you to meet a friend of mine, Miss Rollins."

"I think I've met this man somewhere before," said Aline Rollins. Another Splendor on his mouth alit.

"Yes," said Roy Duncan, "I go there often."

His small tight freckled impish face was creased again by his high cackle. All I could never be. They moved into the store, where drouthy neibors neibors meet, through the idling group of fountain gallants.

Mr. Henry Sorrell (It Can Be Done), and Mr. John T Howland (We Sell Lots and Lots of Lots), emerged, beyond Arthur N. Wright's, jeweller, from the gloomy dusk of the Gruner Building. Each looked into the subdivisions of the other's heart; their eyes kept the great Vision of the guarded mount as swiftly they turned into Church Street where Sorrell's Hudson was parked.

White-vested, a trifle paunchy, with large broad feet, a shaven moon of red face, and abundant taffy-colored hair, the Reverend John Smallwood, pastor of the First Baptist Church, walked heavily up the street, greeting his parishioners warmly, and hoping to see his Pilot face to face. Instead, however, he encountered the Honorable William Jennings Bryan, who was coming slowly out of the bookstore. The two close friends greeted each other affectionately, and, with a firm friendly laying on of hands, gave each to each the Christian aid of a benevolent exorcism.

"Just the man I was looking for," said Brother Smallwood. In silence, slowly, they shook hands for several seconds. Silence was pleased.

"That," observed the Commoner with grave humor, "is what I thought the Great American People said to me on three occasions." It was a favorite jest—ripe with wisdom, mellowed by the years, yet, withal, so characteristic of the man. The deep furrows of his mouth widened in a smile. Our master —famous, calm, and dead.

Passed, on catspaw rubber tread, from the long dark bookstore, Professor L. B. Dunn, principal of Graded School No. 3, Montgomery Avenue. He smiled coldly at them with a gimlet narrowing of his spectacled eyes. The tell-tale cover of *The New Republic* peeked from his pocket. Clamped under his lean and freckled arm were new library copies of *The Great Illusion,* by Norman Angell, and *The Ancient Grudge,* by Owen Wister. A lifelong advocate of a union of the two great English-speaking (sic) nations, making together irresistibly for peace, truth, and righteousness in a benevolent but firm authority over the less responsible elements of civilization, he passed, the Catholic man, pleasantly dedicated to the brave adventuring of minds and the salvaging of mankind. Ah, yes!

"And how are you and the Good Woman enjoying your sojourn in the Land of the Sky?" said the Reverend John Smallwood.

"Our only regret," said the Commoner, "is that our visit here must be measured by days and not by months. Nay, by years."

Mr. Richard Gorman, twenty-six, city reporter of *The Citizen,* strode rapidly up the street, with proud cold news-nose lifted. His complacent smile, hard-lipped, loosened into servility.

"Ah, there, Dick," said John Smallwood, clasping his hand affectionately, and squeezing his arm, "Just the man I was looking for. Do you know Mr. Bryan?"

"As fellow newspaper men," said the Commoner, "Dick and I have been close friends for—how many years is it, my boy?"

"Three, I think sir," said Mr. Gorman, blushing prettily.

"I wish you could have been here, Dick," said the Reverend Smallwood, "to hear what Mr. Bryan was saying about us. The good people of this town would be mighty proud to hear it."

"I'd like another statement from you before you go, Mr. Bryan," said Richard Gorman. "There's a story going the rounds that you may make your home with us in the future."

When questioned by a *Citizen* reporter, Mr. Bryan refused either to confirm or deny the rumor:

"I may have a statement to make later," he observed with a significant smile, "but at present I must content myself by saying that if I could have chosen the place of my birth, I could not have found a fairer spot than this wonderland of nature."

Earthly Paradise, thinks Commoner.

"I have travelled far in my day," continued the man who had been chosen three times by a great Party to contend for the highest honor within the gift of the people. "I have gone from the woods of Maine to the wave-washed sands of Florida, from Hatteras to Halifax, and from the summits of the Rockies to where Missouri rolls her turgid flood, but I have seen few spots that equal, and none that surpass, the beauty of this mountain Eden."

The reporter made notes rapidly.

The years of his glory washed back to him upon the rolling tides of rhetoric—the great lost days of the first crusade when the money barons trembled beneath the shadow of the Cross of Gold, and Bryan! Bryan! Bryan! Bryan! burned through the land like a comet. Ere I was old. 1896. Ah, woeful *ere,* which tells me youth's no longer here.

Foresees Dawn of New Era.

When pressed more closely by the reporter as to his future plans, Mr. Bryan replied:

"My schedule is completely filled, for months to come, with speaking engagements that will take me from one end of the country to the other, in the fight I am making for the reduction of the vast armaments that form the chief obstacle to the reign of peace on earth, good-will to men. After that, who knows?" he said, flashing his famous smile. "Perhaps I shall come back to this beautiful region, and take up my life among my good friends here as one who, having fought the good fight, deserves to spend the declining years of his life not only within sight, but within the actual boundaries, of the happy land of Canaan."

Asked if he could predict with any certainty the date of his proposed retirement, the Commoner answered characteristically with the following beautiful quotation from Longfellow:

> "When the war-drum throbbed no longer,
> And the battle-flags were furled
> In the Parliament of man,
> The Federation of the world."

The magic cell of music—the electric piano in the shallow tiled lobby of Altamont's favorite cinema, the Ajax, stopped playing with firm, tinny abruptness, hummed ominously for a moment, and without warning commenced anew. It's a long way to Tipperary. The world shook with the stamp of marching men.

Miss Margaret Blanchard and Mrs. C. M. McReady, the druggist's drugged wife who, by the white pitted fabric of her skin, and the wide bright somnolence of her eyes, on honey-dew had fed too often, came out of the theatre and turned down toward Wood's pharmacy.

To-day: Maurice Costello and Edith M. Storey in *Throw Out the Life-line,* a Vitagraph Release.

Goggling, his great idiot's head lolling on his scrawny neck, wearing the wide-rimmed straw hat that covered him winter and summer, Willie Goff, the pencil merchant, jerked past, with inward lunges of his crippled right foot. The fingers of his withered arm pointed stiffly toward himself, beckoning to him, and touching him as he walked with stiff jerking taps, in a terrible parody of vanity. A gaudy handkerchief with blue, yellow and crimson patterns hung in a riotous blot from his breast-pocket over his neatly belted gray Norfolk jacket, a wide loose collar of silk barred with red and orange stripes flowered across his narrow shoulders. In his lapel a huge red carnation. His thin face, beneath the jutting globular head, grinned constantly, glutting his features with wide, lapping, receding, returning, idiot smiles. For should he live a thousand years, he never will be out of humor. He burred ecstatically at the passers-by, who grinned fondly at him, and continued down to Wood's where he was greeted with loud cheers and laughter by a group of young men who loitered at the fountain's end. They gathered around him boisterously, pounding his back and drawing him up to the fountain. Pleased, he looked at them warmly, gratefully. He was touched and happy.

"What're you having, Willie?" said Mr. Tobias Pottle.

"Give me a dope," said Willie Goff to the grinning jerker, "a dope and lime."

Pudge Carr, the politician's son, laughed hilariously. "Want a dope and lime, do you, Willie?" he said, and struck him heavily on the back. His thick stupid face composed itself.

"Have a cigarette, Willie," he said, offering the package to Willie Goff.

"What's yours?" said the jerker to Toby Pottle.

"Give me a dope, too."

"I don't want anything," said Pudge Carr. Such drinks as made them nobly wild, not mad.

Pudge Carr held a lighted match to Willie's cigarette, winking slowly at Brady Chalmers, a tall, handsome fellow, with black hair, and a long dark face. Willie Goff drew in on his cigarette, lighting it with dry smacking lips. He coughed, removed the weed, and held it awkwardly between his thumb and forefinger, looking at it, curiously.

They sputtered with laughter, involved and lost in clouds of fume, and guzzling deep, the boor, the lackey, and the groom.

Brady Chalmers took Willie's colored handkerchief gently from his pocket and held it up for their inspection. Then he folded it carefully and put it back.

"What are you all dressed up about, Willie?" he said. "You must be going to see your girl."

Willie Goff grinned cunningly.

Toby Pottle blew a luxurious jet of smoke through his nostrils. He was twenty-four, carefully groomed, with slick blond hair, and a pink massaged face.

"Come on, Willie," he said, blandly, quietly, "you've got a girl, haven't you?"

Willie Goff leered knowingly; at the counter-end, Tim McCall, twenty-eight, who had been slowly feeding cracked ice from his cupped fist into his bloated whisky-fierce jowls, collapsed suddenly, blowing a bright rattling hail upon the marble ledge.

"I've got several," said Willie Goff. "A fellow's got to have a little Poon-Tang, hasn't he?"

Flushed with high ringing laughter, they smiled, spoke respectfully, uncovered before Miss Tot Webster, Miss Mary McGraw, and Miss Martha Cotton, older members of the Younger Set. They called for stronger music, louder wine.

"How do you do?"

"Aha! Aha!" said Brady Chalmers to Miss Mary McGraw. "Where were *you* that time?"

"*You'll* never know," she called back. It was between them—their little secret. They laughed knowingly with joy of possession.

"Come on back, Pudge," said Euston Phipps, their escort. "You too, Brady." He followed the ladies back—tall, bold, swagger—a young alcoholic with one sound lung. He was a good golfer.

Pert boys rushed from the crowded booths and tables to the fountain, coming up with a long slide. They shouted their orders rudely, nagging the swift jerkers glibly, stridently.

"All right, son. Two dopes and a mint limeade. Make it snappy."

"Do you work around here, boy?"

The jerkers moved in ragtime tempo, juggling the drinks, tossing scooped globes of ice-cream into the air and catching them in glasses, beating swift rhythms with a spoon.

Seated alone, with thick brown eyes above her straw regardant, Mrs. Thelma Jarvis, the milliner, drew, in one swizzling guzzle, the last beaded chain of linked sweetness long drawn out from the bottom of her glass. Drink to me only with thine eyes. She rose slowly, looking into the mirror of her open purse. Then, fluescent, her ripe limbs moulded in a dress of silk henna, she writhed carefully among the crowded tables, with a low rich murmur of contrition. Her voice was ever soft, gentle, and low—an excellent thing in a woman. The high light chatter of the tables dropped as she went by. For God's sake, hold your tongue and let me love! On amber undulant limbs she walked slowly up the aisle past perfume, stationery, rubber goods, and toilet preparations, pausing at the cigar counter to pay her check. Her round, melon-heavy breasts nodded their heads in slow but sprightly dance. A poet could not but be gay, in such a jocund company.

But—at the entrance, standing in the alcove by the magazine rack, Mr. Paul Goodson, of the Dependable Life, closed his long grinning dish-face abruptly, and ceased talking. He doffed his hat without effusiveness, as did his companion, Coston Smathers, the furniture man (you furnish the girl, we furnish the house). They were both Baptists.

Mrs. Thelma Jarvis turned her warm ivory stare upon them, parted her full small mouth in a remote smile, and passed, ambulant. When she had gone they turned to each other, grinning quietly. We'll be waiting at the river. Swiftly they glanced about them. No one had seen.

Patroness of all the arts, but particular sponsor for Music, Heavenly Maid, Mrs. Franz Wilhelm Von Zeck, wife of the noted lung specialist, and the discoverer of Von Zeck's serum, came imperially from the doors of the Fashion Mart, and was handed tenderly into the receiving cushions of her Cadillac by Mr. Louis Rosalsky. Benevolently but distantly she smiled down upon him: the white parchment of his hard Polish face was broken by a grin of cruel servility curving up around the wings of his immense putty-colored nose. Frau Von Zeck settled her powerful chins upon the coarse shelving of her Wagnerian breasts and, her ponderous gaze already dreaming on remote philanthropies, was charioted smoothly away from the devoted tradesman. *Nur wer die Sehnsucht kennt, weiss was Ich leide.*

Mr. Rosalsky returned into his store.

For the third time the Misses Mildred Shuford, Helen Pendergast, and Mary Catherine Bruce drove by, clustered together like unpicked cherries in the front seat of Miss Shuford's Reo. They passed, searching the pavements with eager, haughty eyes, pleased at their proud appearance. They turned up Liberty Street on their fourth swing round the circle. Waltz me around again, Willie.

"Do you know how to dance, George?" Eugene asked. His heart was full of bitter pride and fear.

"Yes," said George Graves absently, "a little bit. I don't like it." He lifted his brooding eyes.

"Say, 'Gene," he said, "how much do you think Dr. Von Zeck is worth?"

He answered Eugene's laughter with a puzzled sheepish grin.

"Come on," said Eugene. "I'll match you for a drink."

They dodged nimbly across the narrow street, amid the thickening afternoon traffic.

"It's getting worse all the time," said George Graves. "The people who laid the town out didn't have any vision. What's it going to be like, ten years from now?"

"They could widen the streets, couldn't they?" said Eugene.

"No. Not now. You'd have to move all the buildings back. Wonder how much it would cost?" said George Graves thoughtfully.

"And if we don't," Professor L. B. Dunn's precise voice sounded its cold warning, "their next move will be directed against us. You may yet live to see the day when the iron heel of militarism is on your neck, and the armed forces of the Kaiser do the goose-step up and down this street. When that day comes——"

"I don't put any stock in those stories," said Mr. Bob Webster rudely and irreverently. He was a small man, with a gray, mean face, violent and bitter. A chronic intestinal sourness seemed to have left its print upon his features. "In my opinion, it's all propaganda. Those Germans are too damn good for them, that's all. They're beginning to call for calf-rope."

"When that day comes," Professor Dunn implacably continued, "remember what I told you. The German government has imperialistic designs upon the whole of the world. It is looking to the day when it shall have all mankind under the yoke of Krupp and Kultur. The fate of civilization is hanging in the balance. Mankind is at the crossroads. I pray God it shall not be said that we were found wanting. I pray God that this free people may never suffer as little Belgium suffered, that our wives and daughters may not be led off into slavery or shame, our children maimed and slaughtered."

"It's not our fight," said Mr. Bob Webster. "I don't want to send my boys three thousand miles across the sea to get shot for those foreigners. If they come over here, I'll shoulder a gun with the best of them, but until they do they can fight it out among themselves. Isn't that right, Judge?" he said, turning toward the party of the third part, Judge Walter C. Jeter, of the Federal Circuit, who had fortunately been a close friend of Grover Cleveland. Ancestral voices prophesying war.

"Did you know the Wheeler boys?" Eugene asked George Graves. "Paul and Clifton?"

"Yes," said George Graves. "They went away and joined the French army. They're in the Foreign Legion."

"They're in the aviation part of it," said Eugene. "The Lafayette Eskydrill. Clifton Wheeler has shot down more than six Germans."

"The boys around here didn't like him," said George Graves. "They thought he was a sissy."

Eugene winced slightly at the sound of the word.

"How old was he?" he asked.

"He was a grown man," said George. "Twenty-two or three."

Disappointed, Eugene considered his chance of glory. (*Ich bin ja noch ein Kind.*)

"—But fortunately," continued Judge Walter C. Jeter deliberately, "we have a man in the White House on whose farseeing statesmanship we can safely rely. Let us trust to the wisdom of his leadership, obeying, in word and spirit, the principles of strict neutrality, accepting only as a last resort a course that would lead this great nation again into the suffering and tragedy of war, which," his voice sank to a whisper, "God forbid!"

Thinking of a more ancient war, in which he had borne himself gallantly, Colonel James Buchanan Pettigrew, head of the Pettigrew Military Academy (Est. 1789), rode by in his open victoria, behind an old negro driver and two well-nourished brown mares. There was a good brown smell of horse and sweat-cured leather. The old negro snaked his whip gently across the sleek trotting rumps, growling softly.

Colonel Pettigrew was wrapped to his waist in a heavy rug, his shoulders were covered with a gray Confederate cape. He bent forward, leaning his old weight upon a heavy polished stick, which his freckled hands gripped upon the silver knob. Muttering, his proud powerful old head turned shakily from side to side, darting fierce splintered glances at the drifting crowd. He was a very parfit gentil knight.

He muttered.

"Suh?" said the negro, pulling in on his reins, and turning around.

"Go on! Go on, you scoundrel!" said Colonel Pettigrew.

"Yes, suh," said the negro. They drove on.

In the crowd of loafing youngsters that stood across the threshold of Wood's pharmacy, Colonel Pettigrew's darting eyes saw two of his own cadets. They were pimply youths, with slack jaws and a sloppy carriage.

He muttered his disgust. Not the same! Not the same! Nothing the same! In his proud youth, in the only war that mattered, Colonel Pettigrew had marched at the head of his own cadets. There were 117, sir, all under nineteen. They stepped forward to a man . . . until not a single commissioned officer was left . . . 36 came back . . . since 1789 . . . it must go on! . . . 19, sir—all under one hundred and seventeen . . . must . . . go . . . on!

His sagging cheek-flanks trembled gently. The horses trotted out of sight around the corner, with a smooth-spoked rumble of rubber tires.

George Graves and Eugene entered Wood's pharmacy and stood up to the counter. The elder soda-jerker, scowling, drew a sopping rag across a puddle of slop upon the marble slab.

"What's yours?" he said irritably.

"I want a chock-lut milk," said Eugene.

"Make it two," added George Graves.

O for a draught of vintage that hath been cooled a long age in the deep-delvèd earth!

Yes. The enormous crime had been committed. And, for almost a year, Eugene had been maintaining a desperate neutrality. His heart, however, was not neutral. The fate of civilization, it appeared, hung in the balance.

The war had begun at the peak of the summer season. Dixieland was full. His closest friend at the time was a sharp old spinstress with frayed nerves, who had been for thirty years a teacher of English in a New York City public school. Day by day, after the murder of the Grand Duke, they watched the tides of blood and desolation mount through the world. Miss Crane's thin red nostrils quivered with indignation. Her old gray eyes were sharp with anger. The idea! The idea!

For, of all the English, none can show a loftier or more inspired love for Albion's Isle than American ladies who teach its noble tongue.

Eugene was also faithful. With Miss Crane he kept a face of mournful regret, but his heart drummed a martial tattoo against his ribs. The air was full of fifes and flutes; he heard the ghostly throbbing of great guns.

"We must be fair!" said Margaret Leonard. "We must be fair!" But her eyes darkened when she read the news of England's entry, and her throat was trembling like a bird's. When she looked up her eyes were wet.

"Ah, Lord!" she said. "You'll see things now."

"Little Bobs!" roared Sheba.

"God bless him! Did you see where he's going to take the field?"

John Dorsey Leonard laid down the paper, and bent over with high drooling laughter.

"Lord a'mercy!" he gasped. "Let the rascals come now!"

Ah, well—they came.

All through that waning summer, Eugene shuttled frantically from the school to Dixieland, unable, in the delirium of promised glory, to curb his prancing limbs. He devoured every scrap of news, and rushed to share it with the Leonards or Miss Crane. He read every paper he could lay his hands on, exulting in the defeats that were forcing the Germans back at every point. For, he gathered from this wilderness of print, things were going badly with the Huns. At a thousand points they fled squealing before English steel at Mons, fell suppliantly before the French charge along the Marne; withdrew here, gave way there, ran away elsewhere. Then, one morning, when they should have been at Cologne, they were lined up at the walls of Paris. They had run in the wrong direction. The world grew dark. Desperately, he tried to understand. He could not. By the extraordinary strategy of always retreating, the German army had arrived before Paris. It was something new in warfare. It was several years, in fact, before Eugene could understand that some one in the German armies had done some fighting.

John Dorsey Leonard was untroubled.

"You wait!" he said confidently. "You just wait, my sonny. That old fellow Joffer knows what he's about. This is just what he's been waiting for. Now he's got them where he wants them."

Eugene wondered for what subtle reason a French general might want a German army in Paris.

Margaret lifted her troubled eyes from the paper.

"It looks mighty serious," she said. "I tell you!" She was silent a moment, a torrent of passion rose up in her throat. Then she added in a low trembling voice: "If England goes, we all go."

"God bless her!" Sheba yelled.

"God bless her, 'Gene," she continued, tapping him on the knee. "When I stepped ashore on her dear old soil that time, I just couldn't help myself. I didn't care what any one thought. I knelt right down there in the dirt, and pretended to tie my shoe, but say, boy"—her bleared eyes glistened through her tears—"God bless her, I couldn't help it. Do you know what I did? I leaned over and kissed her earth." Large gummy tears rolled down her red cheeks. She was weeping loudly, but she went on. "I said: This is the earth of Shakespeare, and Milton, and John Keats and, by God, what's more, it's mine as well! God bless her! God bless her!"

Tears flowed quietly from Margaret Leonard's eyes. Her face was wet. She could not speak. They were all deeply moved.

"She won't go," said John Dorsey Leonard. "We'll have a word to say to that! She won't go! You wait!"

In Eugene's fantasy there burned the fixed vision of the great hands clasped across the sea, the flowering of green fields, and the developing convolutions of a faery London—mighty, elfin, old, a romantic labyrinth of ancient crowded ways, tall, leaning houses, Lucullan food and drink, and the mad imperial eyes of genius burning among the swarm of quaint originality.

As the war developed, and the literature of war-enchantment began to appear, Margaret Leonard gave him book after book to read. They were the books of the young men—the young men who fought to blot out the evil of the world with their blood. In her trembling voice she read to him Rupert Brooke's sonnet—"If I should die, think only this of me"—and she put a copy of Donald Hankey's *A Student in Arms* into his hand, saying:

"Read this, boy. It will stir you as you've never been stirred before. Those boys have seen the vision!"

He read it. He read many others. He saw the vision. He became a member of this legion of chivalry—young Galahad-Eugene—a spearhead of righteousness. He had gone a-Grailing. He composed dozens of personal memoirs, into which quietly, humorously, with fine-tempered English restraint, he poured the full measure of his pure crusading heart. Sometimes, he came through to the piping times of peace minus an arm, a leg, or an eye, diminished but ennobled; sometimes his last radiant words were penned on the eve of the attack that took his life. With glistening eyes, he read his own epilogue, enjoyed his post-mortem glory, as his last words were recorded and explained by his editor. Then, witness of his own martyrdom, he dropped two smoking tears upon his young slain body. *Dulce et decorum est pro patria mori.*

Ben loped along, scowling, by Wood's pharmacy. As he passed the idling group at the tiled entrance, he cast on them a look of sudden fierce contempt. Then he laughed quietly, savagely.

"Oh, my God!" he said.

At the corner, scowling, he waited for Mrs. Pert to cross from the Post Office. She came over slowly, reeling.

Having arranged to meet her later in the pharmacy, he crossed over, and turned angularly down Federal Street behind the Post Office. At the second entrance to the Doctors' and Surgeons' Building, he turned in, and began to mount the dark creaking stairs. Somewhere, with punctual developing monotony, a single drop of water was falling into the wet black basin of a sink. He paused in the wide corridor of the first floor to control the nervous thudding of his heart. Then he walked half-way down and entered the waiting-room of Dr. J. H. Coker. It was vacant. Frowning, he sniffed the air. The whole building was sharp with the clean nervous odor of antiseptics. A litter of magazines—*Life, Judge, The Literary Digest,* and

The American—on the black mission table, told its story of weary and distressed fumbling. The inner door opened and the doctor's assistant, Miss Ray, came out. She had on her hat. She was ready to depart.

"Do you want to see the doctor?" she asked.

"Yes," said Ben, "is he busy?"

"Come on in, Ben," said Coker, coming to the door. He took his long wet cigar from his mouth, grinning yellowly. "That's all for to-day, Laura. You can go."

"Good-bye," said Miss Laura Ray, departing.

Ben went into Coker's office. Coker closed the door and sat down at his untidy desk.

"You'll be more comfortable if you lie down on that table," he said grinning.

Ben gave the doctor's table a look of nausea.

"How many have died on that thing?" he asked. He sat down nervously in a chair by the desk, and lighted a cigarette, holding the flame to the charred end of cigar Coker thrust forward.

"Well, what can I do for you, son?" he asked.

"I'm tired of pushing daisies here," said Ben. "I want to push them somewhere else."

"What do you mean, Ben?"

"I suppose you've heard, Coker," said Ben quietly and insultingly, "that there's a war going on in Europe. That is, if you've learned to read the papers."

"No, I hadn't heard about it, son," said Coker, puffing slowly and deeply. "I read a paper—the one that comes out in the morning. I suppose they haven't got the news yet." He grinned maliciously. "What do you want, Ben?"

"I'm thinking of going to Canada and enlisting," said Ben. "I want you to tell me if I can get in."

Coker was silent a moment. He took the long chewed weed from his mouth and looked at it thoughtfully.

"What do you want to do that for, Ben?" he said.

Ben got up suddenly, and went to the window. He cast his cigarette away into the court. It struck the cement well with a small dry plop. When he turned around, his sallow face had gone white and passionate.

"In Christ's name, Coker," he said, "what's it all about? Are you able to tell me? What in heaven's name are we here for? You're a doctor—you ought to know something."

Coker continued to look at his cigar. It had gone out again.

"Why?" he said deliberately. "Why should I know anything?"

"Where do we come from? Where do we go to? What are we here for? What the hell is it all about?" Ben cried out furiously in a rising voice. He turned bitterly, accusingly, on the older man. "For God's sake, speak up, Coker. Don't sit there like a damned tailor's dummy. Say something, won't you?"

"What do you want me to say?" said Coker. "What am I? A mind-reader? A spiritualist? I'm your physician, not your priest. I've seen them born, and I've seen them die. What happens to them before or after, I can't say."

"Damn that!" said Ben. "What happens to them in between?"

"You're as great an authority on that as I am, Ben," said Coker. "What you want, son, is not a doctor, but a prophet."

"They come to you when they're sick, don't they?" said Ben. "'They all want to get well, don't they? You do your best to cure them, don't you?"

"No," said Coker. "Not always. But I'll grant that I'm supposed to. What of it?"

"You must all think that it's about something," said Ben, "or you wouldn't do it!"

"A man must live, mustn't he?" said Coker with a grin.

"That's what I'm asking you, Coker. Why must he?"

"Why," said Coker, "in order to work nine hours a day in a newspaper office, sleep nine hours, and enjoy the other six in washing, shaving, dressing, eating at the Greasy Spoon, loafing in front of Wood's, and occasionally taking the Merry Widow to see Francis X. Bushman. Isn't that reason enough for any man? If a man's hard-working and decent, and invests his money in the Building and Loan every week, instead of squandering it on cigarettes, coca-cola, and Kuppenheimer clothes, he may own a little home some day." Coker's voice sank to a hush of reverence. "He may even have his own car, Ben. Think of that! He can get in it, and ride, and ride, and ride. He can ride all over these damned mountains. He can be very, very happy. He can take exercise regularly in the Y. M. C. A. and think only clean thoughts. He can marry a good pure woman and have any number of fine sons and daughters, all of whom may be brought up in the Baptist, Methodist, or Presbyterian faiths, and given splendid courses in Economics, Commercial Law, and the Fine Arts, at the State university. There's plenty to live for, Ben. There's something to keep you busy every moment."

"You're a great wit, Coker," Ben said, scowling. "You're as funny as a crutch." He straightened his humped shoulders self-consciously, and filled his lungs with air.

"Well, what about it?" he asked, with a nervous grin. "Am I fit to go?"

"Let's see," said Coker deliberately, beginning to look him over. "Feet—pigeon-toed, but good arch." He looked at Ben's tan leathers closely.

"What's the matter, Coker?" said Ben. "Do you need your toes to shoot a gun with?"

"How're your teeth, son?"

Ben drew back his thin lips and showed two rows of hard white grinders. At the same moment, casually, swiftly, Coker prodded him with a strong yellow finger in the solar plexis. His distended chest collapsed; he bent over, laughing, and coughed dryly. Coker turned away to his desk and picked up his cigar.

"What's the matter, Coker?" said Ben. "What's the idea?"

"That's all, son. I'm through with you," said Coker.

"Well, what about it?" said Ben nervously.

"What about what?"

"Am I all right?"

"Certainly you're all right," said Coker. He turned with burning match. "Who said you weren't all right?"

Ben stared at him, scowling, with fear-bright eyes.

"Quit your kidding, Coker," he said. "I'm three times seven, you know. Am I fit to go?"

"What's the rush?" said Coker. "The war's not over yet. We may get into it before long. Why not wait a bit?"

"That means I'm not fit," said Ben. "What's the matter with me, Coker?"

"Nothing," said Coker carefully. "You're a bit thin. A little run down, aren't you, Ben? You need a little meat on those bones, son. You can't sit on a stool at the Greasy Spoon, with a cigarette in one hand and a cup of coffee in the other, and get fat."

"Am I all right or not, Coker?"

Coker's long death's-head widened in a yellow grin.

"Yes," he said. "You're all right, Ben. You're one of the most all right people I know."

Ben read the true answer in Coker's veined and weary eyes. His own were sick with fear. But he said bitingly:

"Thanks, Coker. You're a lot of help. I appreciate what you've done a lot. As a doctor, you're a fine first baseman."

Coker grinned. Ben left the office.

As he went out on the street he met Harry Tugman going down to the paper office.

"What's the matter, Ben?" said Harry Tugman. "Feeling sick?"

"Yes," said Ben, scowling at him. "I've just had a shot of 606."

He went up the street to meet Mrs. Pert.

26

In the autumn, at the beginning of his fifteenth year—his last year at Leonard's—Eugene went to Charleston on a short excursion. He found a substitute for his paper route.

"Come on!" said Max Isaacs, whom he still occasionally saw. "We're going to have a good time, son."

"Yeah, man!" said Malvin Bowden, whose mother was conducting the tour. "You can still git beer in Charleston," he added with a dissipated leer.

"You can go swimmin' in the ocean at the Isle of Palms," said Max Isaacs. Then, reverently, he added: "You can go to the Navy Yard an' see the ships."

He was waiting until he should be old enough to join the navy. He read the posters greedily. He knew all the navy men at the enlistment office. He had read all the booklets—he was deep in naval lore. He knew to a dollar the earnings of firemen, second class, of radio men, and of all kinds of C. P. O.'s.

His father was a plumber. He did not want to be a plumber. He wanted to join the navy and see the world. In the navy, a man was given good pay and a good education. He learned a trade. He got good food and good clothing. It was all given to him free, for nothing.

"H'm!" said Eliza, with a bantering smile. "Why, say, boy, what do you want to do that for? You're my baby!"

It had been years since he was. She smiled tremulously.

"Yes'm," said Eugene. "Can I go? It's only for five days. I've got the money." He thrust his hand into his pocket, feeling.

"I tell you what!" said Eliza, working her lips, smiling. "You may wish you had that money before this winter's over. You're going to need new shoes and a warm overcoat when the cold weather comes. You must be mighty rich. I wish I could afford to go running off on a trip like that."

295

"Oh, my God!" said Ben, with a short laugh. He tossed his cigarette into one of the first fires of the year.

"I want to tell you, son," said Eliza, becoming grave, "you've got to learn the value of a dollar or you'll never have a roof to call your own. I want you to have a good time, boy, but you musn't squander your money."

"Yes'm," said Eugene.

"For heaven's sake!" Ben cried. "It's the kid's own money. Let him do what he likes with it. If he wants to throw it out the damned window, it's his own business."

She clasped her hands thoughtfully upon her waist and stared away, pursing her lips.

"Well, I reckon it'll be all right," she said. "Mrs. Bowden will take good care of you."

It was his first journey to a strange place alone. Eliza packed an old valise carefully, and stowed away a box of sandwiches and eggs. He went away at night. As he stood by his valise, washed, brushed, excited, she wept a little. He was again, she felt, a little farther off. The hunger for voyages was in his face.

"Be a good boy," she said. "Don't get into any trouble down there." She thought carefully a moment, looking away. Then she went down in her stocking, and pulled out a five-dollar bill.

"Don't waste your money," she said. "Here's a little extra. You may need it."

"Come here, you little thug!" said Ben. Scowling, his quick hands worked busily at the boy's stringy tie. He jerked down his vest, slipping a wadded ten-dollar bill into Eugene's pocket. "Behave yourself," he said, "or I'll beat you to death."

Max Isaacs whistled from the street. He went out to join them.

There were six in Mrs. Bowden's party: Max Isaacs, Malvin Bowden, Eugene, two girls named Josie and Louise, and Mrs. Bowden. Josie was Mrs. Bowden's niece and lived with her. She was a tall beanpole of a girl with a prognathous mouth and stick-out grinning teeth. She was twenty. The other girl, Louise, was a waitress. She was small, plump, a warm brunette. Mrs. Bowden was a little sallow woman with ratty brown hair. She had brown worn-out eyes. She was a dressmaker. Her husband, a carpenter, had died in the Spring. There was a little insurance money. That was how she came to take the trip.

Now, by night, he was riding once more into the South. The day-coach was hot, full of the weary smell of old red plush. People dozed painfully, distressed by the mournful tolling of the bell, and the grinding halts. A baby wailed thinly. Its mother, a gaunt wisp-haired mountaineer, turned the back of the seat ahead, and bedded the child on a spread newspaper. Its wizened face peeked dirtily out of its swaddling discomfort of soiled jackets and pink ribbon. It wailed and slept. At the front of the car, a young hill-man, high-boned and red, clad in corduroys and leather leggings, shelled peanuts steadily, throwing the shells into the aisle People trod through them with a sharp masty crackle. The boys, bored, paraded restlessly to the car-end for water. There was a crushed litter of sanitary drinking-cups upon the floor, and a stale odor from the toilets.

The two girls slept soundly on turned seats. The small one breathed warmly and sweetly through moist parted lips.

The weariness of the night wore in upon their jaded nerves, lay upon their dry hot eyeballs. They flattened noses against the dirty windows, and watched the vast structure of the earth sweep past—clumped woodlands, the bending sweep of the fields, the huge flowing lift of the earth-waves, cyclic intersections bewildering—the American earth—rude, immeasurable, formless, mighty.

His mind was bound in the sad lulling magic of the car wheels. Clackety-clack. Clackety-clack. Clackety-clack. Clackety-clack. He thought of his life as something that had happened long ago. He had found, at last, his gateway to the lost world. But did it lie before or behind him? Was he leaving or entering it? Above the rhythm of the wheels he thought of Eliza's laughter over ancient things. He saw a brief forgotten gesture, her white broad forehead, a ghost of old grief in her eyes. Ben, Gant—their strange lost voices. Their sad laughter. They swam toward him through green walls of fantasy. They caught and twisted at his heart. The green ghost-glimmer of their faces coiled away. Lost. Lost.

"Let's go for a smoke," said Max Isaacs.

They went back and stood wedged for stability on the closed platform of the car. They lighted cigarettes.

Light broke against the east, in a murky rim. The far dark was eaten cleanly away. The horizon sky was barred with hard fierce strips of light. Still buried in night, they looked across at the unimpinging sheet of day. They looked under the lifted curtain at brightness. They were knifed sharply away from it. Then, gently, light melted across the land like dew. The world was gray.

The east broke out in ragged flame. In the car, the little waitress breathed deeply, sighed, and opened her clear eyes.

Max Isaacs fumbled his cigarette awkwardly, looked at Eugene, and grinned sheepishly with delight, craning his neck along his collar, and making a nervous grimace of his white fuzz-haired face. His hair was thick, straight, the color of taffy. He had blond eyebrows. There was much kindness in him. They looked at each other with clumsy tenderness. They thought of the lost years at Woodson Street. They saw with decent wonder their awkward bulk of puberty. The proud gate of the years swung open for them. They felt a lonely glory. They said farewell.

Charleston, fat weed that roots itself on Lethe wharf, lived in another time. The hours were days, the days weeks.

They arrived in the morning. By noon, several weeks had passed, and he longed for the day's ending. They were quartered in a small hotel on King Street—an old place above stores, with big rooms. After lunch, they went out to see the town. Max Isaacs and Malvin Bowden turned at once toward the Navy Yard. Mrs. Bowden went with them. Eugene was weary for sleep. He promised to meet them later.

When they had gone, he pulled off his shoes and took off his coat and shirt, and lay down to sleep in a big dark room, into which the warm sun fell in shuttered bars. Time droned like a sleepy October fly.

At five o'clock, Louise, the little waitress, came to wake him. She, too, had wanted to sleep. She knocked gently at the door. When he did not answer, she opened it quietly and came in, closing it behind her. She came to the side of the bed and looked at him for a moment.

"Eugene!" she whispered. "Eugene."

He murmured drowsily, and stirred. The little waitress smiled and sat down on the bed. She bent over him and tickled him gently in the ribs, chuckling to see him squirm. Then she tickled the soles of his feet. He wakened slowly, yawning, rubbing sleep from his eyes.

"What is it?" he said.

"It's time to go out there," she said.

"Out where?"

"To the Navy Yard. We promised to meet them."

"Oh, damn the Navy Yard!" he groaned. "I'd rather sleep."

"So would I!" she agreed. She yawned luxuriously, stretching her plump arms above her head. "I'm so sleepy. I could stretch out anywhere." She looked meaningly at the bed.

He wakened at once, sensuously alert. He lifted himself upon one elbow: a hot torrent of blood swarmed through his cheeks. His pulses beat thickly.

"We're all alone up here," said Louise smiling. "We've got the whole floor to ourselves."

"Why don't you lie down and take a nap, if you're still sleepy?" he asked. "I'll wake you up," he added, with gentle chivalry.

"I've got such a little room. It's hot and stuffy. That's why I got up," said Louise. "What a nice big room you've got!"

"Yes," he said. "It's a nice big bed, too." They were silent a waiting moment.

"Why don't you lie down here, Louise?" he said, in a low unsteady voice. "I'll get up," he added hastily, sitting up. "I'll wake you."

"Oh, no," she said, "I wouldn't feel right."

They were again silent. She looked admiringly at his thin young arms.

"My!" she said. "I bet you're strong."

He flexed his long stringy muscles manfully, and expanded his chest.

"My!" she said. "How old are you, 'Gene?"

He was just at his fifteenth year.

"I'm going on sixteen," he said. "How old are you, Louise?"

"I'm eighteen," she said. "I bet you're a regular heart-breaker, 'Gene. How many girls have you got?"

"Oh—I don't know. Not many," he said truthfully enough. He wanted to talk—he wanted to talk madly, seductively, wickedly. He would excite her by uttering, in grave respectful tones, honestly, matter-of-factly, the most erotic suggestions.

"I guess you like the tall ones, don't you?" said Louise. "A tall fellow wouldn't want a little thing like me, would he? Although," she said quickly, "you never know. They say opposites attract each other."

"I don't like tall girls," said Eugene. "They're too skinny. I like them about your size, when they've got a good build."

"Have I got a good build, 'Gene?" said Louise, holding her arms up and smiling.

"Yes, you have a pretty build, Louise—a fine build," said Eugene earnestly. "The kind I like."

"I haven't got a pretty face. I've got an ugly face," she said invitingly.

"You haven't got an ugly face. You have a pretty face," said Eugene firmly. "Anyway, the face doesn't matter much with me," he added, subtly.

"What do you like best, 'Gene?" Louise asked.

He thought carefully and gravely.

"Why," he said, "a woman ought to have pretty legs. Sometimes a woman has an ugly face, but a pretty leg. The prettiest legs I ever saw were on a High Yellow."

"Were they prettier than mine?" said the waitress, with an easy laugh.
She crossed her legs slowly and displayed her silk-shod ankle.

"I don't know, Louise," he said, staring critically. "I can't see enough."

"Is that enough?" she said, pulling her tight skirt above her calves.

"No," said Eugene.

"Is that?" she pulled her skirt back over her knees, and displayed her
plump thighs, gartered with a ruffled band of silk and red rosettes. She
thrust her small feet out, coyly turning the toes in.

"Lord!" said Eugene, staring with keen interest at the garter. "I never
saw any like that before. That's pretty." He gulped noisily. "Don't those
things hurt you, Louise?"

"Uh-uh," she said, as if puzzled, "why?"

"I should think they'd cut into your skin," he said. "I know mine do if I
wear them too tight. See."

He pulled up his trousers' leg and showed his young gartered shank,
lightly spired with hair.

Louise looked, and felt the garter gravely with a plump hand.

"Mine don't hurt me," she said. She snapped the elastic with a ripe
smack. "See!"

"Let me see," he said. He placed his trembling fingers lightly upon her
garter.

"Yes," he said unsteadily. "I see."

Her round young weight lay heavy against him, her warm young face
turned blindly up to his own. His brain reeled as if drunken, he dropped
his mouth awkwardly upon her parted lips. She sank back heavily on the
pillows. He planted dry and clumsy kisses upon her mouth, her eyes, in
little circles round her throat and face. He fumbled at the throat-hook of
her waist, but his fingers shook so violently that he could not unfasten it.
She lifted her smooth hands with a comatose gesture, and unfastened it
for him.

Then he lifted his beet-red face, and whispered tremulously, not knowing
well what he said:

"You're a nice girl, Louise. A pretty girl."

She thrust her pink fingers slowly through his hair, drew back his face
into her breasts again, moaned softly as he kissed her, and clutched his
hair in an aching grip. He put his arms around her and drew her to him.
They devoured each other with young wet kisses, insatiate, unhappy, trying
to grow together in their embrace, draw out the last distillation of desire in
a single kiss.

He lay sprawled, scattered and witless with passion, unable to collect and focus his heat. He heard the wild tongueless cries of desire, the inchoate ecstasy that knows no gateway of release. But he knew fear—not the social fear, but the fear of ignorance, of discovery. He feared his potency. He spoke to her thickly, wildly, not hearing himself speak.

"Do you want me to? Do you want me to, Louise?"

She drew his face down, murmuring:

"You won't hurt me, 'Gene? You wouldn't do anything to hurt me, honey? If anything happens—" she said drowsily.

He seized the straw of her suggestion.

"I won't be the first. I won't be the one to begin you. I've never started a a girl off," he babbled, aware vaguely that he was voicing an approved doctrine of chivalry. "See here, Louise!" he shook her—she seemed drugged. "You've got to tell me before—. I won't do *that!* I may be a bad fellow, but nobody can say I ever did that. Do you hear!" His voice rose shrilly; his face worked wildly; he was hardly able to speak.

"I say, do you hear? Am I the first one, or not? You've got to answer! Did you ever—before?"

She looked at him lazily. She smiled.

"No," she said.

"I may be bad, but I won't do that." He had become inarticulate; his voice went off into a speechless jargon. Gasping, stammering, with contorted and writhing face, he sought for speech.

She rose suddenly, and put her warm arms comfortingly around him. Soothing and caressing him, she drew him down on her breast. She stroked his head, and talked quietly to him.

"I know you wouldn't, honey. I know you wouldn't. Don't talk. Don't say anything. Why, you're all excited, dear. There. Why, you're shaking like a leaf. You're high-strung, honey. That's what it is. You're a bundle of nerves."

He wept soundlessly into her arm.

He became quieter. She smiled, and kissed him softly.

"Put on your clothes," said Louise. "We ought to get started if we're going out there."

In his confusion he tried to draw on a pair of Mrs. Bowden's cast-off pumps. Louise laughed richly, and thrust her fingers through his hair.

At the Navy Yard, they could not find the Bowdens nor Max Isaacs. A young sailor took them over a destroyer. Louise went up a railed iron ladder with an emphatic rhythm of her shapely thighs. She showed her legs. She stared impudently at a picture of a chorus lady, cut from the

Police Gazette. The young sailor rolled his eyes aloft with an expression of innocent debauchery. Then he winked heavily at Eugene.

The deck of the Oregon.

"What's that for?" said Louise, pointing to the outline in nails of Admiral Dewey's foot.

"That's where he stood during the fight," said the sailor.

Louise put her small foot within the print of the greater one. The sailor winked at Eugene. You may fire when you are ready, Gridley.

"She's a nice girl," said Eugene.

"Yeah," said Max Isaacs. "She's a nice lady." He craned his neck awkwardly, and squinted. "About how old is she?"

"She's eighteen," said Eugene.

Malvin Bowden stared at him.

"You're crazy!" said he. "She's twenty-one."

"No," said Eugene, "she's eighteen. She told me so."

"I don't care," said Malvin Bowden, "she's no such thing. She's twenty-one. I reckon I ought to know. My folks have known her for five years. She had a baby when she was eighteen."

"Aw!" said Max Isaacs.

"Yes," said Malvin Bowden, "a travelling man got her in trouble. Then he ran away."

"Aw!" said Max Isaacs. "Without marryin' her or anything?"

"He didn't do nothing for her. He ran away," said Malvin Bowden. "Her people are raising the kid now."

"Great Day!" said Max Isaacs slowly. Then, sternly, he added, "A man who'd do a thing like that ought to be shot."

"You're right!" said Malvin Bowden.

They loafed along the Battery, along the borders of ruined Camelot.

"Those are nice old places," said Max Isaacs. "They've been good houses in their day."

He looked greedily at wrought-iron gateways; the old lust of his childhood for iron-scraps awoke.

"Those are old Southern mansions," said Eugene, reverently.

The bay was still: there was a green stench of warm standing water.

"They've let the place run down," said Malvin. "It's no bigger now than it was before the Civil War."

No, sir, and, by heaven, so long as one true Southern heart is left alive to remember Appomattox, Reconstruction, and the Black parliaments, we will defend with our dearest blood our menaced, but sacred, traditions.

"They need some Northern capital," said Max Isaacs sagely. They all did.

An old woman, wearing a tiny bonnet, was led out on a high veranda from one of the houses, by an attentive negress. She seated herself in a porch rocker and stared blindly into the sun. Eugene looked at her sympathetically. She had probably not been informed by her loyal children of the unsuccessful termination of the war. United in their brave deception, they stinted themselves daily, reining in on their proud stomachs in order that she might have all the luxury to which she had been accustomed. What did she eat? The wing of a chicken, no doubt, and a glass of dry sherry. Meanwhile, all the valuable heirlooms had been pawned or sold. Fortunately, she was almost blind, and could not see the wastage of their fortune. It was very sad. But did she not sometimes think of that old time of the wine and the roses? When knighthood was in flower?

"Look at that old lady," whispered Malvin Bowden.

"You can *tell* she's a lady," said Max Isaacs. "I bet she's never turned her hand over."

"An old family," said Eugene gently. "The Southern aristocracy."

An old negro came by, fringed benevolently by white whiskers. A good old man—an ante-bellum darkey. Dear Lord, their number was few in these unhappy days.

Eugene thought of the beautiful institution of human slavery, which his slaveless maternal ancestry had fought so valiantly to preserve. Bress de Lawd, Marse! Ole Mose doan' wan' to be free niggah. How he goan' lib widout marse? He doan' wan' stahve wid free niggahs. Har, har, har!

Philanthropy. Pure philanthropy. He brushed a tear from his een.

They were going across the harbor to the Isle of Palms. As the boat churned past the round brick cylinder of Fort Sumter, Malvin Bowden said:

"They had the most men. If things had been even, we'd have beaten them."

"They didn't beat us," said Max Isaacs. "We wore ourselves out beating them."

"We were defeated," said Eugene, quietly, "not beaten."

Max Isaacs stared at him dumbly.

"Aw!" he said.

They left the little boat, and ground away toward the beach in a street-car. The land had grown dry and yellow in the enervation of the summer. The foliage was coated with dust: they rattled past cheap summer houses, baked and blistered, stogged drearily in the sand. They were small, flimsy, a multitudinous vermin—all with their little wooden sign of lodging. "The Ishkabibble," "Seaview," "Rest Haven," "Atlantic Inn,"—Eugene looked at them, reading with weariness the bleached and jaded humor of their names.

"There are a lot of boarding-houses in the world," said he.

A hot wind of beginning autumn rustled dryly through the long parched leaves of stunted palms. Before them rose the huge rusted spokes of a Ferris Wheel. St. Louis. They had reached the beach.

Malvin Bowden leaped joyously from the car.

"Last one in's a rotten egg!" he cried, and streaked for the bathhouse.

"Kings! I've got kings, son," yelled Max Isaacs. He held up his crossed fingers. The beach was bare: two or three concessions stood idly open for business. The sky curved over them, a cloudless blue burnished bowl. The sea offshore was glazed emerald: the waves rode heavily in, thickening murkily as they turned with sunlight and sediment to a beachy yellow.

They walked slowly down the beach toward the bathhouse. The tranquil, incessant thunder of the sea made in them a lonely music. Seawards, their eyes probed through the seething glare.

"I'm going to join the navy, 'Gene," said Max Isaacs. "Come on and go with me."

"I'm not old enough," said Eugene. "You're not, either."

"I'll be sixteen in November," said Max Isaacs defensively.

"That's not old enough."

"I'm going to lie to get in," said Max Isaacs. "They won't bother you. You can get in. Come on."

"No," said Eugene. "I can't."

"Why not?" said Max Isaacs. "What are you going to do?"

"I'm going to college," said Eugene. "I'm going to get an education and study law."

"You'll have lots of time," said Max Isaacs. "You can go to college when you come out. They teach you a lot in the navy. They give you a good training. You go everywhere."

"No," said Eugene. "I can't."

But his pulse throbbed as he listened to the lonely thunder of the sea. He saw strange dusky faces, palm frondage, and heard the little tinkling sounds of Asia. He believed in harbors at the end.

Mrs. Bowden's niece and the waitress came out on the next car. After his immersion he lay, trembling slightly under the gusty wind, upon the beach. A fine tang of salt was on his lips. He licked his clean young flesh.

Louise came from the bathhouse and walked slowly toward him. She came proudly, her warm curves moulded into her bathing-suit: her legs were covered with stockings of green silk.

Far out, beyond the ropes, Max Isaacs lifted his white heavy arms, and slid swiftly through a surging wall of green water. His body glimmered greenly for a moment; he stood erect wiping his eyes and shaking water from his ears.

Eugene took the waitress by the hand and led her into the water. She advanced slowly, with little twittering cries. An undulant surge rolled in deceptively, and rose suddenly to her chin, drinking her breath. She gasped and clung to him. Initiated, they bucked deliciously through a roaring wall of water, and, while her eyes were still closed, he caught her to him with young salty kisses.

Presently they came out, and walked over the wet strip of beach into the warm loose sand, bedding their dripping bodies gratefully in its warmth. The waitress shivered: he moulded sand over her legs and hips, until she was half buried. He kissed her, stilling his trembling lips upon her mouth.

"I like you! I like you a lot!" he said.

"What did they tell you about me?" she said. "Did they talk about me?"

"I don't care," he said. "I don't care about that. I like you."

"You won't remember me, honey, when you start going with the girls. You'll forget about me. Some day you'll see me, and you won't even know me. You won't recognize me. You'll pass without speaking."

"No," he said. "I'll never forget you, Louise. So long as I live."

Their hearts were filled with the lonely thunder of the sea. She kissed him. They were hill-born.

He returned in late September.

In October, Gant, with Ben and Helen, departed for Baltimore. The operation, too long deferred, was now inevitable. His disease had grown steadily worse. He had gone through a period of incessant pain. He was enfeebled. He was frightened.

Rising at night, he would rouse the sleeping house with his cries, commanding terror with his old magnificence.

"I see it! I see it! The knife! The knife! . . . Do you see its shadow? . . . There! There! There!"

With Boothian gusto he recoiled, pointing to invulnerable nothings.

"Do you see him standing there in the shadows? So you've come at last to take the old man with you? . . . There he stands—the Grim Reaper—as I always knew he would. Jesus, have mercy on my soul!"

Gant lay in a long cot in the Urological Institute at Johns Hopkins. Every day a cheerful little man came briskly in and looked at his chart. He talked happily and went away. He was one of the greatest surgeons in the country.

"Don't worry," said the nurse encouragingly, "the mortality's only four per cent. It used to be thirty. He's reduced it."

Gant groaned, and slipped his big hand into his daughter's vital grasp.

"Don't worry, old boy!" she said, "you're going to be as good as you ever were, after this."

She fed him with her life, her hope, her love. He was almost tranquil when they wheeled him in to his operation.

But the little gray-haired man looked, shook his head regretfully, and trimmed deftly.

"All right!" he said, four minutes later, to his assistant. "Close the wound."

Gant was dying of cancer.

Gant sat in a wheeled chair upon the high fifth-floor veranda, looking out through bright October air at the city spread far into the haze before him. He looked very clean, almost fragile. A faint grin of happiness and relief hovered about his thin mouth. He smoked a long cigar, with fresh-awakened senses.

"There," he said pointing, "is where I spent part of my boyhood. Old Jeff Streeter's hotel stood about there," he pointed.

"Dig down!" said Helen, grinning.

Gant thought of the years between, and the vexed pattern of fate. His life seemed strange to him.

"We'll go to see all those places when you get out of here. They're going to let you out of here, day after to-morrow. Did you know that? Did you know you're almost well?" she cried with a big smile.

"I'm going to be a well man after this," said Gant. "I feel twenty years younger!"

"Poor old papa!" she said. "Poor old papa!"

Her eyes were wet. She put her big hands on his face, and drew his head against her.

27

My Shakespeare, rise! He rose. The bard rose throughout the length and breadth of his brave new world. He was not for an age, but for all time. Then, too, his tercentenary happened only once—at the end of three hundred years. It was observed piously from Maryland to Oregon. Eighty-one members of the House of Representatives, when asked by literate journalists for their favorite lines, replied instantly with a quotation from Polonius: "This above all: to thine own self be true." The Swan was played, and pageanted, and essayed in every schoolhouse in the land.

Eugene tore the Chandos portrait from the pages of the *Independent* and nailed it to the calcimined wall of the back-room. Then, still full of the great echoing paean of Ben Jonson's, he scrawled below it in large trembling letters: "My Shakespeare, rise!" The large plump face—"as damned silly a head as ever I looked at"—stared baldly at him with goggle eyes, the goatee pointed ripe with hayseed vanity. But, lit by the presence, Eugene plunged back into the essay littered across his table.

He was discovered. In an unwise absence, he left the Bard upon the wall. When he returned, Ben and Helen had read his scrawl. Thereafter, he was called poetically to table, to the telephone, to go an errand.

"My Shakespeare, rise!"

With red resentful face, he rose.

"Will My Shakespeare pass the biscuit?" or, "Could I trouble My Shakespeare for the butter?" said Ben, scowling at him.

"My Shakespeare! My Shakespeare! Do you want another piece of pie?" said Helen. Then, full of penitent laughter, she added: "That's a shame! We oughtn't to treat the poor kid like that." Laughing, she plucked at her large straight chin, gazing out the window, and laughing absently—penitently, laughing.

But—"his art was universal. He saw life clearly and he saw it whole. He was an intellectual ocean whose waves touched every shore of thought. He was all things in one: lawyer, merchant, soldier, doctor, statesman. Men of science have been amazed by the depth of his learning. In *The Merchant of Venice*, he deals with the most technical questions of law with the skill of an attorney. In *King Lear*, he boldly prescribes sleep as a remedy for Lear's insanity. 'Sleep that knits up the ravell'd sleave of care.' Thus, he has foreseen the latest researches of modern science by almost three centuries. In his sympathetic and well-rounded sense of characterization, he laughs with, not at, his characters."

Eugene won the medal—bronze or of some other material even more enduring. The Bard's profile murkily indented. W. S. 1616-1916. A long and useful life.

The machinery of the pageant was beautiful and simple. Its author—Dr. George B. Rockham, at one time, it was whispered, a trouper with the Ben Greet players—had seen to that. All the words had been written by Dr. George B. Rockham, and all the words, accordingly, had been written for Dr. George B. Rockham. Dr. George B. Rockham was the Voice of History. The innocent children of Altamont's schools were the mute illustrations of that voice.

Eugene was Prince Hal. The day before the pageant his costume arrived from Philadelphia. At John Dorsey Leonard's direction he put it on. Then he came out sheepishly before John Dorsey on the school veranda, fingering his tin sword and looking somewhat doubtfully at his pink silk hose which came three quarters up his skinny shanks, and left exposed, below his doublet, a six-inch hiatus of raw thigh.

John Dorsey Leonard looked gravely.

"Here, boy," he said. "Let me see!"

He pulled strongly at the top of the deficient hose, with no result save to open up large runs in them. Then John Dorsey Leonard began to laugh. He slid helplessly down upon the porch rail, and bent over, palsied with silent laughter, from which a high whine, full of spittle, presently emerged.

"O-oh my Lord!" he gasped. "Egscuse me!" he panted, seeing the boy's angry face. "It's the funniest thing I ever—" at this moment his voice died of paralysis.

"I'll fix you," said Miss Amy. "I've got just the thing for you."

She gave him a full baggy clown's suit, of green linen. It was a relic of a Hallowe'en party; its wide folds were gartered about his ankles.

He turned a distressed, puzzled face toward Miss Amy.

"That's not right, is it?" he asked. "He never wore anything like this, did he?"

Miss Amy looked. Her deep bosom heaved with full contralto laughter. "Yes, that's right! That's fine!" she yelled. "He was like that, anyway. No one will ever notice, boy." She collapsed heavily into a wicker chair which widened with a protesting creak.

"Oh, Lord!" she groaned, wet-cheeked. "I don't believe I ever saw——"

The pageant was performed on the embowered lawns of the Manor House. Dr. George B. Rockham stood in a green hollow—a natural amphitheatre. His audience sat on the turf of the encircling banks. As the phantom cavalcade of poetry and the drama wound down to him, Dr. George B. Rockham disposed of each character neatly in descriptive pentameter verse. He was dressed in the fashion of the Restoration—a period he coveted because it understood the charms of muscular calves. His heavy legs bulged knottily below a coy fringe of drawer-ruffles.

. Eugene stood waiting on the road above, behind an obscuring wall of trees. It was rich young May. "Doc" Hines (Falstaff) waited beside him. His small tough face grinned apishly over garments stuffed with yards of wadding. Grinning, he smote himself upon his swollen paunch: the blow left a dropsical depression.

He turned, with a comical squint, on Eugene:

"Hal," said he, "you're a hell of a looking prince."

"You're no beauty, Jack," said Eugene.

Behind him, Julius Arthur (Macbeth), drew his sword with a flourish. "I challenge you, Hal," said he.

In the young shimmering light their tin swords clashed rapidly. Twittered with young bird-laughter, on bank and saddle sprawled, all of the Bard's *personæ*. Julius Arthur thrust swiftly, was warded, then, with loose grin, buried his brand suddenly in "Doc" Hines' receiving paunch. The company of the immortal shrieked happily.

Miss Ida Nelson, the assistant director, rushed angrily among them.

"Sh!" she hissed loudly. "Sh-h!" She was very angry. She had spent the afternoon hissing loudly.

Swinging gently in her side-saddle, Rosalind, on horseback, a ripe little beauty from the convent, smiled warmly at him. Looking, he forgot.

Below them, on the road, the crowded press loosened slowly, broke off in minute fragments, and disappeared into the hidden gulch of Dr. George Rockham's receiving voice. With fat hammy sonority he welcomed them.

But he had not come to Shakespeare. The pageant had opened with the Voices of Past and Present—voices a trifle out of harmony with the tenor of event—but necessary to the commercial success of the enterprise. These voices now moved voicelessly past—four frightened sales-ladies from Schwartzberg's, clad decently in cheese-cloth and sandals, who came by bearing the banner of their concern. Or, as the doctor's more eloquent iambics had it:

> "Fair Commerce, sister of the arts, thou, too,
> Shalt take thy lawful place upon our stage."

They came and passed: Ginsberg's—"the glass of fashion and the mould of form"; Bradley the Grocer—"when first Pomona held her fruity horn"; The Buick Agency—"the chariots of Oxus and of Ind."

Came, passed—like pageantry of mist on an autumnal stream.

Behind them, serried ranks of cherubim, the marshalled legions of Altamont's Sunday schools, each in white arrayed and clutching grimly in tiny hands two thousand tiny flags of freedom, God's small angels, and surely there for God knows what far-off event, began to move into the hollow. Their teachers nursed them gently into action, with tapping feet and palms.

"One, two, *three,* four. One, two, *three,* four. Quickly, children!"

A hidden orchestra, musical in the trees, greeted them, as they approached, with holy strains: the Baptists, with the simple doctrine of "It's the Old-time Religion"; the Methodists, with "I'll Be Waiting at the River"; the Presbyterians, with "Rock of Ages"; the Episcopalians, with "Jesus, Lover of My Soul"; and rising to lyrical climactic passion, the little Jews, with the nobly marching music of "Onward, Christian Soldiers."

They passed without laughter. There was a pause.

"Well, thank God for that!" said Ralph Rolls coarsely in a solemn quiet. The Bard's strewn host laughed, rustled noisily into line.

"Sh-h! Sh-h!" hissed Miss Ida Nelson.

"What the hell does she think she is?" said Julius Arthur, "a steam valve?"

Eugene looked attentively at the shapely legs of the page, Viola.

"Wow!" said Ralph Rolls, with his accustomed audibility. "Look who's here!"

She looked on them all with a pert impartial smile. But she never told her love.

Miss Ida Nelson caught the doctor's stealthy sign. Carefully, in slow twos, she fed them down to him.

The Moor of Venice (Mr. George Graves), turned his broad back upon their jibes, and lurched down with sullen-sheepish grin, unable to conceal the massive embarrassment of his calves.

"Tell him who you are, Villa," said Doc Hines. "You look like Jack Johnson."

The town, in its first white shirting of Spring, sat on the turfy banks, and looked down gravely upon the bosky little comedy of errors; the encircling mountains, and the gods thereon, looked down upon the slightly larger theatre of the town; and, figuratively, from mountains that looked down on mountains, the last stronghold of philosophy, the author of this chronicle looked down on everything.

"Here we go, Hal," said Doc Hines, nudging Eugene.

"Give 'em hell, son," said Julius Arthur. "You're dressed for the part."

"He looks it, you mean," said Ralph Rolls. "Boy, you'll knock 'em dead," he added with an indecent laugh.

They descended into the hollow, accompanied by a low but growing titter of amazement from the audience. Before them, the doctor had just disposed of Desdemona, who parted with a graceful obeisance. He was now engaged on Othello, who stood, bullish and shy, till his ordeal should finish. In a moment, he strode away, and the doctor turned to Falstaff, reading the man by his padded belly, briskly, with relief:

> "Now, Tragedy, begone, and to our dell
> Bring antic Jollity with cap and bells:
> Falstaff, thou prince of jesters, lewd old man
> Who surfeited a royal prince with mirth,
> And swayed a kingdom with his wanton quips——"

Embarrassed by the growing undertone of laughter, Doc Hines squinted around with a tough grin, gave a comical hitch to his padded figure, and whispered a hoarse aside to Eugene: "Hear that, Hal? I'm hell on wheels, ain't I?"

Eugene saw him depart in a green blur, and presently became aware that an unnatural silence had descended upon Doctor George B. Rockham. The Voice of History was, for the moment, mute. Its long jaw, in fact, had fallen ajar.

Dr. George B. Rockham looked wildly about him for succor. He rolled his eyes entreatingly upwards at Miss Ida Nelson. She turned her head away.

"Who are you?" he said hoarsely, holding a hairy hand carefully beside his mouth.

"Prince Hal," said Eugene, likewise hoarsely and behind his hand.

Dr. George B. Rockham staggered a little. Their speech had reached the stalls. But firmly, before the tethered chafing laughter, he began:

> "Friend to the weak and comrade of the wild,
> By folly sired to wisdom, dauntless Hal——"

Laughter, laughter unleashed and turbulent, laughter that rose flood by flood upon itself, laughter wild, earth-shaking, thunder-cuffing, drowned Dr. George B. Rockham and all he had to say. Laughter! Laughter! Laughter!

Helen was married in the month of June—a month sacred, it is said, to Hymen, but used so often for nuptials that the god's blessing is probably not infallible.

She had returned to Altamont in May, from her last singing engagement. She had beeen in Atlanta for the week of opera, and had come back by way of Henderson, where she had visited Daisy and Mrs. Selborne. There she had found her mate.

He was not a stranger to her. She had known him years before in Altamont, where he had lived for a short time as district agent for the great and humane corporation that employed him—the Federal Cash Register Company. Since that time he had gone to various parts of the country at his master's bidding, carrying with him his great message of prosperity and thrift. At the present time, he lived with his sister and his aged mother, whose ponderous infirmity of limb had not impaired her appetite, in a South Carolina town. He was devoted and generous to them both. And the Federal Cash Register Company, touched by his devotion to duty, rewarded him with a good salary. His name was Barton. The Bartons lived well.

Helen returned with the unexpectedness in which all returning Gants delighted. She came in on members of her family, one afternoon, in the kitchen at Dixieland.

"Hello, everybody!" she said.

"Well, for G-g-god's sake," said Luke after a moment. "Look who's here!"

They embraced heartily.

"Why, what on earth!" cried Eliza, putting her iron down on the board, and wavering on her feet, in an effort to walk in two directions at once. They kissed.

"I was just thinking to myself," said Eliza, more calmly, "that it wouldn't surprise me a bit if you should come walking in. I had a premonition, I don't know what else you'd call it——"

"Oh, my God!" groaned the girl, good-humoredly, but with a shade of annoyance. "Don't start that Pentland spooky stuff! It makes my flesh crawl."

She exchanged a glance of burlesque entreaty with Luke. Winking, he turned suddenly, and with an idiotic laugh, tickled Eliza sharply.

"Get away!" she shrieked.

He chortled madly.

"I'll declare, boy!" she said fretfully. "I believe you're crazy. I'll vow I do!"

Helen laughed huskily.

"Well," said Eliza, "how'd you leave Daisy and the children?"

"They're all right, I suppose," said Helen wearily. "Oh, my God! Deliver me!" she laughed. "You never saw such pests! I spent fifty dollars on them in toys and presents alone! You'd never think it from the thanks I get. Daisy takes it all as her due! Selfish! Selfish! Selfish!"

"For G-g-god's sake!" said Luke loyally.

She was one fine girl.

"I paid for everything I got at Daisy's, I can assure you!" she said, sharply, challengingly. "I spent no more time there than I had to. I was at Mrs. Selborne's nearly all the time. I had practically all my meals there."

Her need for independence had become greater; her hunger for dependents acute. Her denial of obligation to others was militant. She gave more than she received.

"Well, I'm in for it," she said presently, trying to mask her strong eagerness.

"In for what?" asked Luke.

"I've gone and done it at last," she said.

"Mercy!" shrieked Eliza. "You're not married, are you?"

"Not yet," said Helen, "but I will be soon."

Then she told them about Mr. Hugh T. Barton, the cash register salesman. She spoke loyally and kindly of him, without great love.

"He's ten years older than I am," she said.

"Well," said Eliza thoughtfully, moulding her lips. "They sometimes make the best husbands." After a moment, she asked: "Has he got any property?"

"No," said Helen, "they live up all he makes. They live in style, I tell you. There are two servants in that house all the time. The old lady doesn't turn her hand over."

"Where are you going to live?" said Eliza sharply. "With his folks?"

"Well, I should say not! I should say not!" said Helen slowly and emphatically. "Good heavens, mama!" she continued irritably. "I want a home of my own. Can't you realize that? I've been doing for others all my life. Now I'm going to let them do for me. I want no in-laws about. No, sir!" she said emphatically.

Luke bit his nails nervously.

"Well, he's g-g-getting a great g-g-girl," he said. "I hope he has sense enough to realize that."

Moved, she laughed bigly, ironically.

"I've got one booster, haven't I?" she said. She looked at him seriously with clear affectionate eyes. "Well, thanks, Luke. You're one of the lot that's always had the interests of the family at heart."

Her big face was for a moment tranquil and eager. A great calm lay there: the radiant decent beauty of dawn and rainwater. Her eyes were as luminous and believing as a child's. No evil dwelt in her. She had learned nothing.

"Have you told your papa?" said Eliza, presently.

"No," she said, after a pause, "I haven't."

They thought of Gant in silence, with wonder. Her going was a marvel.

"I have a right to my own life," said Helen angrily, as if some one disputed that right, "as much as any one. Good heavens, mama! You and papa have lived your lives—don't you know that? Do you think it's right that I should go on forever looking after him? Do you?" Her voice rose under the stress of hysteria.

"Why, no-o. I never said—" Eliza began, flustered and conciliatory.

"You've spent your life f-f-finking of others and not of yourself," said Luke. "That's the trouble. They don't appreciate it."

"Well, I'm not going to any longer. That's one thing sure! No, indeed! I want a home and some children. I'm going to have them!" she said defiantly. In a moment, she added tenderly:

"Poor old papa! I wonder what he's going to say?"

He said very little. The Gants, after initial surprise, moulded new events very quickly into the texture of their lives. Abysmal change widened their souls out in a brooding unconsciousness.

Mr. Hugh Barton came up into the hills to visit his affianced kin. He came, to their huge delight, lounging in the long racing chassis of a dusty brown 1911 Buick roadster. He came, in a gaseous coil, to the the roaring explosion of great engines. He descended, a tall, elegant figure, dyspeptic, lean almost to emaciation, very foppishly laundered and tailored. He looked the car over slowly, critically, a long cigar clamped in the corner of his saturnine mouth, drawing his gauntlets off deliberately. Then, in the same unhurried fashion, he removed from his

head the ten-gallon gray sombrero—the only astonishing feature of his
otherwise undebatable costume—and shook each long thin leg delicately
for a moment to straighten out the wrinkles. But there were none.
Then, deliberately, he came up the walk to Dixieland, where the Gants
were assembled. As he came, unhurried, he took the cigar from his
mouth calmly and held it in the fingers of his lean, hairy, violently
palsied hand. His thin black hair, fine spun, was fanned lightly from
its elegance by a wantoning breeze. He espied his betrothed and grinned,
with dignity, sardonically, with big nuggets of gold teeth. They greeted
and kissed.

"This is my mother, Hugh," said Helen.

Hugh Barton bent slowly, courteously, from his thin waist. He fastened
on Eliza a keen penetrating stare that discomposed her. His lips twisted
again in an impressive sardonic smile. Every one felt he was going
to say something very, very important.

"How do you do?" he asked, and took her hand.

Every one then felt that Hugh Barton had said something very, very
important.

With equal slow gravity he greeted each one. They were somewhat
awed by his lordliness. Luke, however, burst out uncontrollably:

"You're g-g-getting a fine girl, Mr. B-b-barton."

Hugh Barton turned on him slowly and fixed him with his keen
stare.

"I think so," he said gravely. His voice was deep, deliberate, with
an impressive rasp. He was selling himself.

In an awkward silence he turned, grinning amiably, on Eugene.

"Have a cigar?" he asked, taking three long powerful weeds from
his upper vest pocket, and holding them out in his clean twitching
fingers.

"Thanks," said Eugene with a dissipated leer, "I'll smoke a Camel."

He took a package of cigarettes from his pocket. Gravely, Hugh
Barton held a match for him.

"Why do you wear the big hat?" asked Eugene.

"Psychology," he said. "It makes 'em talk."

"I tell you what!" said Eliza, beginning to laugh. "That's pretty
smart, isn't it?"

"Sure!" said Luke. "That's advertising! It pays to advertise!"

"Yes," said Mr. Barton slowly, "you've got to get the other fellow's
psychology."

The phrase seemed to describe an action of modified assault and restrained pillage.

They liked him very much. They all went into the house.

Hugh Barton's mother was in her seventy-fourth year, but she had the strength of a healthy woman of fifty, and the appetite of two of forty. She was a powerful old lady, six feet tall, with the big bones of a man, and a heavy full-jawed face, sensuous and complacent, and excellently equipped with a champing mill of strong yellow horse-teeth. It was cake and pudding to see her at work on corn on the cob. A slight paralysis had slowed her tongue and thickened her speech a little, so that she spoke deliberately, with a ponderous enunciation of each word. This deformity, which she carefully hid, added to, rather than subtracted from, the pontifical weight of her opinions: she was an earnest Republican—in memory of her departed mate—and she took a violent dislike to any one who opposed her political judgment. When thwarted or annoyed in any way, the heavy benevolence of her face was dislodged by a thunder-cloud of petulance, and her wide pouting underlip rolled out like a window-shade. But, as she barged slowly along, one big hand gripping a heavy stick on which she leaned her massive weight, she was an impressive dowager.

"She's a lady—a real lady," said Helen proudly. "Any one can see that! She goes out with all the best people."

Hugh Barton's sister, Mrs. Genevieve Watson, was a sallow woman of thirty-eight years, tall, wren-like and emaciated, like her brother; dyspeptic, and very elegantly kept. The divorced Watson was conspicuous for his absence from all conversations: there was once or twice a heavy flutter around his name, a funereal hush, and a muttered suggestion of oriental debauchery.

"He was a beast," said Hugh Barton, "a low dog. He treated sister very badly."

Mrs. Barton wagged her great head with the slow but emphatic approval she accorded all her son's opinions.

"O-o-h!" she said. "He was a ter-rib-bul man."

He had, they inferred, been given to hellish practices. He had "gone after other women."

Sister Veve had a narrow discontented face, a metallic vivacity, an effusive cordiality. She was always very smartly dressed. She had somewhat vague connections in the real estate business; she spoke grandly of obscure affairs; she was always on the verge of an indefinite "Big Deal."

"I'm getting them lined up, brother," she would say with cheerful confidence. "Things are coming my way. J. D. came in to-day and said: 'Veve—you're the only woman in the world that can put this thing across. Go to it, little girl. There's a fortune in it for you.'" And so on.

Her conversation, Eugene thought, was not unlike Brother Steve's.

But their affection and loyalty for one another was beautiful. Its unaccustomed faith, its abiding tranquillity, puzzled and disturbed the Gants. They were touched indefinably, a little annoyed, because of it.

The Bartons came to Woodson Street two weeks before the wedding. Within three days after their arrival, Helen and old lady Barton were at odds. It was inevitable. The heat of the girl's first affection for Barton's family wore off very quickly: her possessive instinct asserted itself—she would halve no one's love, she would share with no other a place in the heart. She would own, she would possess completely. She would be generous, but she would be mistress. She would give. It was the law of her nature.

She began immediately, by force of this essential stress, to make out a case against the old woman.

Mrs. Barton, too, felt the extent of her loss. She wanted to be sure that Helen realized the extent of her acquisition of one of the latter-day saints.

Rocking ponderously in the dark on Gant's veranda, the old woman would say:

"You are get-ting a good boy, Hel-en." She would wag her powerful head from side to side, pugnaciously emphatic. "Though I do say it myself, you are get-ting one good boy, Hel-en. A bet-ter boy than Hugh does-ent live."

"Oh, I don't know!" said Helen, annoyed. "I don't think it's such a bad bargain for him either, you know. I think pretty well of myself, too." And she would laugh, huskily, heartily, trying in laughter to conceal her resentment, but visibly, to every eye but Mrs. Barton's, angered.

A moment later, on some pretext, she would be back into the house, where, with a face contorted by her rising hysteria, to Luke, Eugene, or any sympathetic audience, she would burst out:

"You heard that, didn't you? You heard that? You see what I've got to put up with, don't you? Do you see? Do you blame me for not wanting that damned old woman around? Do you? You see how she wants to run things, don't you? Do you see how she rubs it into me whenever she gets a chance? She can't bear to give him up. Of course not! He's her meal-ticket. They've bled him white. Why, even now, if it came to a question of choosing between us—" her face worked strongly. She could not continue. In a moment she quieted herself, and said decisively: "I suppose you know now why we're going to live away from them. You see, don't you? Do you blame me?"

"No'm," said Eugene, obedient after pumping.

"It's a d-d-damn shame!" said Luke loyally.

At this moment Mrs. Barton, kindly but authoritative, called from the veranda:

"Hel-en! Where are you, Hel-en?"

"O gotohell. Gotohell!" said Helen, in a comic undertone.

"Yes? What is it?" she called out sharply.

You see, don't you?

She was married at Dixieland, because she was having a big wedding. She knew a great many people.

As her wedding-day approached, her suppressed hysteria mounted. Her sense of decorum grew militant: she attacked Eliza bitterly for keeping certain dubious people in the house.

"Mama, in heaven's name! What do you mean by allowing such goings-on right in the face of Hugh and his people? What do you suppose they think of it? Have you no respect for my feelings? Good heavens, are you going to have the house full of chippies on the night of my wedding?" Her voice was high and cracked. She almost wept.

"Why, child!" said Eliza, with troubled face. "What do you mean? I've never noticed anything."

"Are you blind! Every one's talking about it! They're practically living together!" This last was a reference to a condition existing between a dissipated and alcoholic young man and a darkly handsome young woman, slightly tubercular.

To Eugene was assigned the task of digging this couple out of their burrow. He waited sternly outside the girl's room, watching the shadow dance at the door crack. At the end of the sixth hour, the besieged surrendered—the man came out. The boy—pallid, but proud of his trust— told the house-defiler that he must go. The young man agreed with cheerful alcoholism. He went at once.

Mrs. Pert was saved in the house-cleaning.

"After all," said Helen, "what do we know about her? They can say
what they like about Fatty. I like her."

Ferns, flowers, potted plants, presents and guests arriving. The long
nasal drone of the Presbyterian minister. The packed crowd. The triumphant booming of "The Wedding March."

A flashlight: Hugh Barton and his bride limply astare—frightened;
Gant, Ben, Luke, and Eugene, widely, sheepishly agrin; Eliza, high-
sorrowful and sad; Mrs. Selborne and a smile of subtle mystery; the
pert flower-girls; Pearl Hines' happy laughter.

When it was over, Eliza and her daughter hung in each other's arms,
weeping.

Eliza repeated over and over, from guest to guest:

> "A son is a son till he gets him a wife,
> But a daughter's a daughter all the days of her life."

She was comforted.

They escaped at length, wilted, from the thronging press of well-
wishing guests. White-faced, scared witless, Mr. and Mrs. Hugh Barton
got into a closed car. It was done! They would spend the night at the
Battery Hill. Ben had engaged the wedding-suite. To-morrow, a honeymoon to Niagara.

Before they went, the girl kissed Eugene with something of the old
affection.

"I'll see you in the Fall, honey. Come over as soon as you're settled."

For Hugh Barton was beginning life with his bride in a new place.
He was going to the capital of the State. And it had already been
determined, chiefly by Gant, that Eugene was going to the State
University.

But Hugh and Helen did not go honeymooning the next morning,
as they had planned. During the night, as she lay at Dixieland, old
Mrs. Barton was taken with a violent, a retching sickness. For once, her
massive digestive mechanism failed to meet the heavy demands she had
put upon it during the pre-nuptial banqueting. She came near death.

Hugh and Helen returned abruptly next morning to a scene of dismal
tinsellings and jaded lilies. Helen hurled her vitality into the sick woman's
care; dominant, furious, all-mastering, she blew back her life into her.

Within three days, Mrs. Barton was out of danger; but her complete recovery was slow, ugly, and painful. As the days lengthened out wearily, the girl became more and more bitter over her thwarted honeymoon. Rushing out of the sick-room, she would enter Eliza's kitchen with writhen face, unable to control her anger:

"That damned old woman! Sometimes I believe she did it on purpose. My God, am I to get no happiness from life? Will they never leave me alone? Urr-p! Urr-p!"—Her rough bacchic smile played loosely over her large unhappy face. "Mama, in God's name where does it all come from?" she said, grinning tearfully. "I do nothing but mop up after her. Will you please tell me how long it's going to last?"

Eliza laughed slyly, passing her finger under her broad nosewing.

"Why, child!" she said. "What in the world! I've never seen the like! She must have saved up for the last six months."

"Yes, sir!" said Helen, looking vaguely away, with a profane smile playing across her mouth, "I'd just like to know where the hell it all comes from. I've had everything else," she said, with a rough angry laugh, "I'm expecting one of her kidneys at any minute."

"Whew-w!" cried Eliza, shaken with laughter.

"Hel-en! Oh Hel'en!" Mrs. Barton's voice came feebly in to them.

"O gotohell!" said the girl, sotto-voce. "Urr-p! Urr-p!" She burst suddenly into tears: "Is it going to be like this always! I sometimes believe the judgment of God is against us all. Papa was right."

"Pshaw!" said Eliza, wetting her fingers, and threading a needle before the light. "I'd go on and pay no more attention to her. There's nothing wrong with her. It's all imagination!" It was Eliza's rooted conviction that most human ills, except her own, were "all imagination."

"Hel-en!"

"All right! I'm coming!" the girl cried cheerfully, turning an angry grin on Eliza as she went. It was funny. It was ugly. It was terrible.

It seemed, in fact, that papa was right, and that the chief celestial Cloud-Pusher, the often hymned, whom our bitter moderns have sometimes called "the ancient Jester"—had turned his frown upon their fortunes.

It began to rain—rain incessant, spouting, torrential rain, fell among the reeking hills, leaving grass and foliage drowned upon the slopes, starting the liquid avalanche of earth upon a settlement, glutting lean rocky mountain-streams to a foaming welter of yellow flood. It mined the yellow banks away with unheard droppings; it caved in hillsides; it drank the steep banked earth away below the rails, leaving them strung to their aerial ties across a gutted canyon.

There was a flood in Altamont. It swept down in a converging width from the hills, filling the little river, and foaming beyond its banks in a wide waste Mississippi. It looted the bottomlands of the river; it floated iron and wooden bridges from their piers as it might float a leaf; it brought ruin to the railway flats and all who dwelt therein.

The town was cut off from every communication with the world. At the end of the third week, as the waters slid back into their channels, Hugh Barton and his bride, crouched grimly in the great pit of the Buick, rode out through flooded roads, crawled desperately over ruined trestles, daring the irresistible wrath of water to achieve their wilted anti-climactic honeymoon.

"He will go where I send him or not at all," Gant spoke his final word, not loudly.

Thus, it was decided that Eugene must go to the State University.

Eugene did not want to go to the State University.

For two years he had romanced with Margaret Leonard about his future education. It was proposed that, in view of his youth, he should attend Vanderbilt (or Virginia) for two years, go to Harvard for two years more, and then, having arrived by easy stages at Paradise, "top things off" with a year or two at Oxford.

"Then," said John Dorsey Leonard, who talked enchantingly on the subject, between mouthfuls of clabber, "then, my sonny, a man may begin to say he's really 'cultsherd.' After that, of course," he continued with a spacious carelessness, "he may travel for a year or so."

But the Leonards were not yet ready to part with him.

"You're too young, boy," said Margaret Leonard. "Can't you persuade your father to wait another year? You're only a child in years, Eugene. You have all the time in the world." Her eyes darkened as she talked.

Gant would not be persuaded.

"He's old enough," he said. "When I was his age I had been earning my living for years. I'm getting old. I won't be here much longer. I want him to begin to make a name for himself before I die."

He refused stubbornly to consider any postponement. In his youngest son he saw the last hope of his name's survival in laurels—in the political laurels he so valued. He wanted his son to be a great and far-seeing statesman and a member of the Republican or Democratic party. His choice of a university was therefore a measure of political expediency, founded upon the judgment of his legal and political friends.

"He's ready to go," said Gant, "and he's going to the State University, and nowhere else. He'll be given as good an education there as he can get anywhere. Furthermore, he will make friends there who will stand by him the rest of his life." He turned upon his son a glance of bitter reproach. "There are very few boys who have had your chance," said he, "and you ought to be grateful instead of turning up your nose at it. Mark my words, you'll live to see the day when you'll thank me for sending you there. Now, I've given you my last word: you'll go where I send you or you'll go nowhere at all."

PART THREE

28

Eugene was not quite sixteen years old when he was sent away to the university. He was, at the time, over six feet and three inches tall, and weighed perhaps 130 pounds. He had been sick very little in his life, but his rapid growth had eaten sharply at his strength: he was full of a wild energy of mind and body that devoured him and left him exhausted. He tired very quickly.

He was a child when he went away: he was a child who had looked much on pain and evil, and remained a fantasist of the Ideal. Walled up in his great city of visions, his tongue had learned to mock, his lip to sneer, but the harsh rasp of the world had worn no grooving in the secret life. Again and again he had been bogged in the gray slough of factuality. His cruel eyes had missed the meaning of no gesture, his packed and bitter heart had sweltered in him like a hot ingot, but all his hard wisdom melted at the glow of his imagination. He was not a child when he reflected, but when he dreamt, he was; and it was the child and dreamer that governed his belief. He belonged, perhaps, to an older and simpler race of men: he belonged with the Mythmakers. For him, the sun was a lordly lamp to light him on his grand adventuring. He believed in brave heroic lives. He believed in the fine flowers of tenderness and gentleness he had little known. He believed in beauty and in order, and that he would wreak out their mighty forms upon the distressful chaos of his life. He believed in love, and in the goodness and glory of women. He believed in valiance, and he hoped that, like Socrates, he would do nothing mean or common in the hour of danger. He exulted in his youth, and he believed that he could never die.

Four years later, when he was graduated, he had passed his adolescence, the kiss of love and death burned on his lips, and he was still a child.

When it was at last plain that Gant's will was on this inflexible, Margaret Leonard had said, quietly:

"Well, then, go your ways, boy. Go your ways. God bless you."

She looked a moment at his long thin figure and turned to John Dorsey Leonard with wet eyes:

"Do you remember that shaver in knee-pants who came to us four years ago? Can you believe it?"

John Dorsey Leonard laughed quietly, with weary gentle relaxation. "What do you know about it?" he said.

When Margaret turned to him again her voice, low and gentle, was charged with the greatest passion he had ever heard in it.

"You are taking a part of our heart with you, boy. Do you know that?"

She took his trembling hand gently between her own lean fingers. He lowered his head and closed his eyelids tightly.

"Eugene," she continued, "we could not love you more if you were our own child. We wanted to keep you with us for another year, but since that cannot be, we are sending you out with our hopes pinned to you. Oh, boy, you are fine. There is no atom in you that is not fine. A glory and a chrism of bright genius rest upon you. God bless you: the world is yours."

The proud words of love and glory sank like music to his heart, evoking their bright pictures of triumph, and piercing him with the bitter shame of his concealed desires. Love bade him enter, but his soul drew back, guilty of lust and sin.

He tore his hand from her grasp, clinching, with the strangled cry of an animal, his convulsive throat.

"I can't!" he choked. "You mustn't think—" He could not go on; his life groped blindly to confessional.

Later, after he left her, her light kiss upon his cheek, the first she had ever given him, burned like a ring of fire.

That summer he was closer to Ben then ever before. They occupied the same room at Woodson Street. Luke had returned to the Westinghouse plant at Pittsburgh after Helen's marriage.

Gant still occupied his sitting-room, but the rest of the house he had rented to a sprightly gray-haired widow of forty. She looked after them beautifully, but she served Ben with an especial tenderness. At night, on the cool veranda, Eugene would find them below the ripening clusters, hear the quiet note of his brother's voice, his laugh, see the slow red arc of his cigarette in darkness.

The quiet one was more quiet and morose than he had ever been before: he stalked through the house scowling ferociously. All his conversation with Eliza was short and bitterly scornful; with Gant he spoke hardly at all. They had never talked together. Their eyes never met—a great shame, the shame of father and son, that mystery that goes down beyond motherhood, beyond life, that mysterious shame that seals the lips of all men, and lives in their hearts, had silenced them.

But to Eugene, Ben talked more freely than ever before. As they sat upon their beds at night, reading and smoking before they slept, all of the pain and bitterness of Benjamin Gant's life burst out in violent denunciation. He began to speak with slow sullen difficulty, halting over his words as he did when he read, but speaking more rapidly as his quiet voice became more passionate.

"I suppose they've told you how poor they are?" he began, tossing his cigarette away.

"Well," said Eugene, "I've got to go easy. I mustn't waste my money."

"Ah-h!" said Ben, making an ugly face. He laughed silently, with a thin and bitter contortion of his lips.

"Papa said that a lot of boys pay their own way through college by waiting on tables and so on. Perhaps I can do something like that."

Ben turned over on his side until he faced his brother, propping himself on his thin hairy forearm.

"Now listen, 'Gene," he said sternly, "don't be a damned little fool, do you hear? You take every damn cent you can get out of them," he added savagely.

"Well, I appreciate what they're doing. I'm getting a lot more than the rest of you had. They're doing a lot for me," said the boy.

"For *you,* you little idiot!" said Ben, scowling at him in disgust. "They're doing it all for themselves. Don't let them get away with that. They think you'll make good and bring a lot of credit to them some day. They're rushing you into it two years too soon, as it is. No, you take everything you can get. The rest of us never had anything, but I want to see you get all that's coming to you. My God!" he cried furiously. "Their money's doing no one any good rotting in the damned bank, is it? No, 'Gene, get all you can. When you get down there, if you find you need more to hold your own with the other boys, make the old man give it to you. You've never had a chance to hold your head up in your own home town, so make the most of your chances when you get away."

He lighted a cigarette and smoked in bitter silence for a moment. "To hell with it all!" he said. "What in God's name are we living for!"

Eugene's first year at the university was filled for him with loneliness, pain, and failure. Within three weeks of his matriculation, he had been made the dupe of a half-dozen classic jokes, his ignorance of all campus tradition had been exploited, his gullibility was a byword. He was the greenest of all green Freshmen, past and present: he had listened attentively to a sermon in chapel by a sophomore with false whiskers; he had prepared studiously for an examination on the contents of the college catalogue; and he had been guilty of the inexcusable blunder of making a speech of acceptance on his election, with fifty others, to the literary society.

And these buffooneries—a little cruel, but only with the cruelty of vacant laughter, and a part of the schedule of rough humor in an American college—salty, extravagant, and national—opened deep wounds in him, which his companions hardly suspected. He was conspicuous at once not only because of his blunders, but also because of his young wild child's face, and his great raw length of body, with the bounding scissor legs. The undergraduates passed him in grinning clusters: he saluted them obediently, but with a sick heart. And the smug smiling faces of his own classmen, the wiser Freshmen, complacently guiltless of his own mistakes, touched him at moments with insane fury.

"Smile and smile and s-mile—damn you!" he cursed through his grating teeth. For the first time in his life he began to dislike whatever fits too snugly in a measure. He began to dislike and envy the inconspicuous mould of general nature—the multitudinous arms, legs, hands, feet, and figures that are comfortably shaped for ready-made garments. And the prettily regular, wherever he found it, he hated—the vacantly handsome young men, with shining hair, evenly parted in the middle, with sure strong middling limbs meant to go gracefully on dancefloors. He longed to see them commit some awkward blunder—to trip and sprawl, to be flatulent, to lose a strategic button in mixed company, to be unconscious of a hanging shirt-tail while with a pretty girl. But they made no mistakes.

As he walked across the campus, he heard his name called mockingly from a dozen of the impartial windows, he heard the hidden laughter, and he ground his teeth. And at night, he stiffened with shame in his dark bed, ripping the sheet between his fingers as, with the unbalanced vision, the swollen egotism of the introvert, the picture of a crowded student-room, filled with the grinning historians of his exploits, burned in his brain. He strangled his fierce cry with a taloned hand. He wanted to blot out the shameful moment, unweave the loom. It seemed to him that his ruin was final, that he had stamped the beginning of his university life with folly that would never be forgotten, and that the best he could do would be to seek out obscurity for the next four years. He saw himself in his clown's trappings and thought of his former vision of success and honor with a lacerating self-contempt.

There was no one to whom he could turn: he had no friends. His conception of university life was a romantic blur, evoked from his reading and tempered with memories of Stover at Yale, Young Fred Fearnot, and jolly youths with affectionate linked arms, bawling out a cheer-song. No one had given him even the rudimentary data of the somewhat rudimentary life of an American university. He had not been warned of the general taboos. Thus, he had come greenly on his new life, unprepared, as he came ever thereafter on all new life, save for his opium visions of himself a stranger in Arcadias.

He was alone. He was desperately lonely.

But the university was a charming, an unforgettable place. It was situated in the little village of Pulpit Hill, in the central midland of the big State. Students came and departed by motor from the dreary tobacco town of Exeter, twelve miles away: the countryside was raw, powerful and ugly, a rolling land of field, wood, and hollow; but the university itself was buried in a pastoral wilderness, on a long tabling butte, which rose steeply above the country. One burst suddenly, at the hill-top, on the end of the straggling village street, flanked by faculty houses, and winding a mile in to the town centre and the university. The central campus sloped back and up over a broad area of rich turf, groved with magnificent ancient trees. A quadrangle of post-Revolutionary buildings of weathered brick bounded the upper end: other newer buildings, in the modern bad manner (the Pedagogic Neo-Greeky), were scattered around beyond the central design: beyond, there was a thickly forested wilderness. There was still a good flavor of the wilderness about the place—one felt its remoteness, its isolated charm. It seemed to Eugene like a provincial outpost of great Rome: the wilderness crept up to it like a beast.

Its great poverty, its century-long struggle in the forest, had given the university a sweetness and a beauty it was later to forfeit. It had the fine authority of provincialism—the provincialism of an older South. Nothing mattered but the State: the State was a mighty empire, a rich kingdom—there was, beyond, a remote and semi-barbaric world.

Few of the university's sons had been distinguished in the nation's life—there had been an obscure President of the United States, and a few

Cabinet members, but few had sought such distinction: it was glory enough to be a great man in one's State. Nothing beyond mattered very much.

In this pastoral setting a young man was enabled to loaf comfortably and delightfully through four luxurious and indolent years. There was, God knows, seclusion enough for monastic scholarship, but the rare romantic quality of the atmosphere, the prodigal opulence of Springtime, thick with flowers and drenched in a fragrant warmth of green shimmering light, quenched pretty thoroughly any incipient rash of bookishness. Instead, they loafed and invited their souls or, with great energy and enthusiasm, promoted the affairs of glee-clubs, athletic teams, class politics, fraternities, debating societies, and dramatic clubs. And they talked—always they talked, under the trees, against the ivied walls, assembled in their rooms, they talked—in limp sprawls—incessant, charming, empty Southern talk; they talked with a large easy fluency about God, the Devil, and philosophy, the girls, politics, athletics, fraternities and the girls— My God! how they talked!

"Observe," lisped Mr. Torrington, the old Rhodes Scholar (Pulpit Hill and Merton, '14), "observe how skilfully he holds suspense until the very end. Observe with what consummate art he builds up his climax, keeping his meaning hidden until the very last word." Further, in fact.

At last, thought Eugene, I am getting an education. This must be good writing, because it seems so very dull. When it hurts, the dentist says, it does you good. Democracy must be real, because it is so very earnest. It must be a certainty, because it is so elegantly embalmed in this marble mausoleum of language. Essays For College Men—Woodrow Wilson, Lord Bryce and Dean Briggs.

But there was no word here of the loud raucous voice of America, political conventions and the Big Brass Band, Tweed, Tammany, the Big Stick, lynching bees and black barbecue parties, the Boston Irish, and the damnable machinations of the Pope as exposed by the *Babylon Hollow Trumpet* (Dem.), the rape of the Belgian virgins, rum, oil, Wall Street and Mexico.

All that, Mr. Torrington would have said, was temporary and accidental. It was unsound.

Mr. Torrington smiled moistly at Eugene and urged him tenderly into a chair drawn intimately to his desk.

"Mr.—? Mr.—?—" he said, fumbling at his index cards.

"Gant," said Eugene.

"Ah, yes—Mr. Gant," he smiled his contrition. "Now—about your outside reading?" he began.

But what, thought Eugene, about my inside reading?

Did he like to read? Ah—that was good. He was so glad to hear it. The true university in these days, said Carlyle (he did hope Eugene like rugged old Thomas), was a collection of books.

"Yes, sir," said Eugene.

That, it seemed to him, was the Oxford Plan. Oh, yes—he had been there, three years, in fact. His mild eye kindled. To loaf along the High on a warm Spring day, stopping to examine in the bookseller's windows the treasures that might be had for so little. Then to Buol's or to a friend's room for tea, or for a walk in the meadows or Magdalen gardens, or to look down into the quad, at the gay pageant of youth below. Ah—Ah! A great place? Well—he'd hardly say that. It all depended what one meant by a great place. Half the looseness in thought—unfortunately, he fancied, more prevalent among American than among English youth—came from an indefinite exuberance of ill-defined speech.

"Yes, sir," said Eugene.

A great place? Well, he'd scarcely say that. The expression was typically American. Butter-lipped, he turned on the boy a smile of soft unfriendliness:

"It kills," he observed, "a man's useless enthusiasms."

Eugene whitened a little.

"That's fine," he said.

Now—let him see. Did he like plays—the modern drama? Excellent. They were doing some very interesting things in the modern drama. Barrie—oh, a charming fellow! What was that? Shaw!

"Yes, sir," said Eugene. "I've read all the others. There's a new book out."

"Oh, but really! My dear boy!" said Mr. Torrington with gentle amazement. He shrugged his shoulders and became politely indifferent. Very well, if he liked. Of course, he thought it rather a pity to waste one's time so when they were really doing some first-rate things. That was *just* the trouble, however. The appeal of a man like that was mainly to the unformed taste, the uncritical judgment. He had a flashy attraction for the immature. Oh, yes! Undoubtedly an amusing fellow. Clever—yes, but hardly significant. And—didn't he think—a trifle noisy? Or had he noticed that? Yes—there was to be sure an amusing Celtic strain, not without charm, but unsound. He was not in line with the best modern thought.

"I'll take the Barrie," said Eugene.

Yes, he rather thought that would be better.

"Well, good day. Mr.—Mr.—?—?" he smiled, fumbling again with his cards.

"Gant."

Oh yes, to be sure,—Gant. He held out his plump limp hand. He did hope Mr. Gant would call on him. Perhaps he'd be able to advise him on some of the little problems that, he knew, were constantly cropping up during the first year. Above all, he mustn't get discouraged.

"Yes, sir," said Eugene, backing feverishly to the door. When he felt the open space behind him, he fell through it, and vanished.

Anyway, he thought grimly, I've read all the damned Barries. I'll write the damned report for him, and damned well read what I damn well please.

God save our King and Queen!

He had courses besides in Chemistry, Mathematics, Greek, and Latin.

He worked hard and with interest at his Latin. His instructor was a tall shaven man, with a yellow saturnine face. He parted his scant hair cleverly in such a way as to suggest horns. His lips were always twisted in a satanic smile, his eyes gleamed sideward with heavy malicious humor. Eugene had great hopes of him. When the boy arrived, panting and breakfastless, a moment after the class had settled to order, the satanic professor would greet him with elaborate irony: "Ah there, Brother Gant! Just in time for church again. Have you slept well?"

The class roared its appreciation of these subtleties. And later, in an expectant pause, he would deepen his arched brows portentously, stare up mockingly under his bushy eyebrows at his expectant audience, and say, in a deep sardonic voice:

"And now, I am going to request Brother Gant to favor us with one of his polished and scholarly translations."

These heavy jibes were hard to bear because, of all the class, two dozen or more, Brother Gant was the only one to prepare his work without the aid of a printed translation. He worked hard on Livy and Tacitus, going over the lesson several times until he had dug out a smooth and competent reading of his own. This he was stupid enough to deliver in downright fashion, without hesitation, or a skilfully affected doubt here and there. For his pains and honesty he was handsomely rewarded by the Amateur Diabolist. The lean smile would deepen as the boy read, the man would lift his eyes significantly to the grinning class, and when it was over, he would say:

"Bravo, Brother Gant! Excellent! Splendid! You are riding a good pony—but a little too smoothly, my boy. You ride a little too well."

The class sniggered heavily.

When he could stand it no longer, he sought the man out one day after the class.

"See here, sir! See here!" he began in a voice choking with fury and exasperation. "Sir—I assure you—" he thought of all the grinning apes in the class, palming off profitably their stolen translations, and he could not go on.

The Devil's Disciple was not a bad man; he was only, like most men who pride themselves on their astuteness, a foolish one.

"Nonsense, Mr. Gant," said he kindly. "You don't think you can fool me on a translation, do you? It's all right with me, you know," he continued, grinning. "If you'd rather ride a pony than do your own work, I'll give you a passing grade—so long as you do it well."

"But—" Eugene began explosively.

"But I think it's a pity, Mr. Gant," said the professor, gravely, "that you're willing to slide along this way. See here, my boy, you're capable of doing first-rate work. I can see that. Why don't you make an effort? Why don't you buckle down and really study, after this?"

Eugene stared at the man, with tears of anger in his eyes. He sputtered but could not speak. But suddenly, as he looked down into the knowing leer, the perfect and preposterous injustice of the thing—like a caricature—overcame him: he burst into an explosive laugh of rage and amusement which the teacher, no doubt, accepted as confession.

"Well, what do you say?" he asked. "Will you try?"

"All right! Yes!" the boy yelled. "I'll try it."

He bought at once a copy of the translation used by the class. Thereafter, when he read, faltering prettily here and there over a phrase, until his instructor should come to his aid, the satanic professor listened gravely and attentively, nodding his head in approval from time to time, and saying, with great satisfaction, when he had finished: "Good, Mr. Gant. Very good. That shows what a little real work will do."

And privately, he would say: "You see the difference, don't you? I knew at once when you stopped using that pony. Your translation is not so smooth, but it's your own now. You're doing good work, my boy, and you're getting something out of it. It's worth it, isn't it?"

"Yes," said Eugene gratefully, "it certainly is——"

By far the most distinguished of his teachers this first year was Mr. Edward Pettigrew ("Buck") Benson, the Greek professor. Buck Benson was a little man in the middle-forties, a bachelor, somewhat dandified, but old-fashioned, in his dress. He wore wing collars, large plump cravats, and suede-topped shoes. His hair was thick, heavily grayed, beautifully kept. His face was courteously pugnacious, fierce, with large yellow bulging eyeballs, and several bulldog pleatings around the mouth. It was an altogether handsome ugliness.

His voice was low, lazy, pleasant, with an indolent drawl, but without changing its pace or its inflection he could flay a victim with as cruel a tongue as ever wagged, and in the next moment wipe out hostility, restore affection, heal all wounds by the same agency. His charm was enormous. Among the students he was the subject for comical speculation—in their myths, they made of him a passionate and sophisticated lover, and his midget cycle-car, which bounded like an overgrown toy around the campus, the scene of many romantic seductions.

He was a good Grecian—an elegant indolent scholar. Under his instruction Eugene began to read Homer. The boy knew little grammar—he had learned little at Leonard's—but, since he had had the bad judgment to begin Greek under some one other than Buck Benson, Buck Benson thought he knew even less than he did. He studied desperately, but the bitter dyspeptic gaze of the elegant little man frightened him into halting, timorous, clumsy performances. And as he proceeded, with thumping heart and tremulous voice, Buck Benson's manner would become more and more weary, until finally, dropping his book, he would drawl:

"Mister Gant, you make me so damned mad I could throw you out the window."

But, on the examination, he gave an excellent performance, and translated from sight beautifully. He was saved. Buck Benson commended his paper publicly with lazy astonishment, and gave him a fair grade. Thereafter, they slipped quickly into an easier relation: by Spring, he was reading Euripides with some confidence.

But that which remained most vividly, later, in the drowning years which cover away so much of beauty, was the vast sea-surge of Homer which beat in his brain, his blood, his pulses, as did the sea-sound in Gant's parlor shells, when first he heard it to the slowly pacing feet and the hexametrical drawl of Buck Benson, the lost last weary son of Hellas.

Dwaney de clangay genett, argereoyo beeoyo—above the whistle's shriek, the harsh scream of the wheel, the riveter's tattoo, the vast long music endures, and ever shall. What dissonance can quench it? What jangling violence can disturb or conquer it—entombed in our flesh when we were young, remembered like "the apple tree, the singing, and the gold"?

29

Before his first year was ended, the boy had changed his lodging four or five times. He finished the year living alone in a big bare carpetless room—an existence rare at Pulpit Hill, where the students, with very few exceptions, lived two or three to a room. In that room began a physical isolation, hard enough to bear at first, which later became indispensable to him, mind and body.

He had come to Pulpit Hill with Hugh Barton, who met him at Exeter and drove him over in the big roadster. After his registration, he had secured lodging quickly at the house of an Altamont widow whose son was a student. Hugh Barton looked relieved and departed, hoping to reach home and his bride by nightfall.

With fine enthusiasm, but poor judgment, Eugene paid the widow two months in advance. Her name was Bradley: she was a flabby petulant woman with a white face and heart-disease. But her food was excellent. Mrs. Bradley's student son answered to his initial letters— "G. T." G. T. Bradley, a member of the sophomore class, was a surly scowling youth of nineteen—a mixture, in equal parts, of servility and insolence. His chief, but thwarted, ambition was to be elected to membership in a fraternity. Having failed to win recognition by the exercise of his natural talents, he was driven by an extraordinary obsession that fame and glory would come to him if he were known as the slave-driver of a number of Freshmen.

But these tactics, tried on Eugene, produced at once defiance and resentment. Their hostility was bitter: G. T. set himself to thwart and ruin the beginnings of the boy's university life. He trapped him into public blunders, and solicited audiences to witness his humiliation; he wheedled his confidence and betrayed it. But there is a final mockery, an ultimate treachery that betrays us into shame; our capacity for villainy, like all our other capacities, is so small. The day came when Eugene was free from bondage. He was free to leave the widow's house of sorrow. G. T. approached him, scowling, diffidently.

"I hear you're leaving us, 'Gene," he said.

"Yes," said Eugene.

"Is it because of the way I've acted?"

"Yes," said Eugene.

"You take things too seriously, 'Gene," he said.

"Yes," said Eugene.

"I don't want you to go having hard feelings, 'Gene. Let's shake hands and be friends."

He thrust his hand out stiffly. Eugene looked at the hard weak face, the furtive, unhappy eyes casting about for something they might call their own. The thick black hair was plastered stiff with grease; he saw white points of dandruff at the roots. There was an odor of talcum powder. He had been borne and nourished in the body of his white-faced mother—for what? To lap the scornful stroking fingers of position; to fawn miserably before an emblem. Eugene had a moment of nausea.

"Let's shake hands, 'Gene," said the boy once more, waggling his out-thrust fingers.

"No," said Eugene.

"You don't hate me, do you?" whined G. T.

"No," said Eugene.

He had a moment of pity, of sickness. He forgave because it was necessary to forget.

Eugene lived in a small world, but its ruins for him were actual. His misfortunes were trifling, but their effect upon his spirit was deep and calamitous. He withdrew deeply and scornfully into his cell. He was friendless, whipped with scorn and pride. He set his face blindly against all the common united life around him.

It was during this bitter and desperate autumn that Eugene first met Jim Trivett.

Jim Trivett, the son of a rich tobacco farmer in the eastern part of the State, was a good tempered young tough of twenty years. He was a strong, rather foul-looking boy, with a coarse protruding mouth, full-meated and slightly ajar, constantly rayed with a faint loose smile and blotted at the corner with a brown smear of tobacco juice. He had bad teeth. His hair was light-brown, dry, and unruly: it stuck out in large untidy mats. He was dressed in the last cheap extreme of the dreadful fashion of the time: skin-tight trousers that ended an inch above his oxford shoes exposing an inch of clocked hose, a bobtailed coat belted in across his kidneys, large striped collars of silk. Under his coat he wore a big sweater with high-school numerals.

Jim Trivett lived with several other students from his community in a lodging-house near Mrs. Bradley's but closer to the west gate of the university. There were four young men banded together for security and companionship in two untidy rooms heated to a baking dryness by small cast-iron stoves. They made constant preparations for study, but they never studied: one would enter sternly, announcing that he had "a hell of a day tomorrow," and begin the most minute preparations for a long contest with his books: he would sharpen his pencils carefully and deliberately, adjust his lamp, replenish the red-hot stove, move his chair, put on an eyeshade, clean his pipe, stuff it carefully with tobacco, light, relight, and empty it, then, with an expression of profound relief, hear a rapping on his door.

"Come in the house, Goddamn it!" he would roar hospitably.

"Hello, 'Gene! Pull up a chair, son, and sit down," said Tom Grant. He was a thickly built boy, gaudily dressed; he had a low forehead, black hair, and a kind, stupid, indolent temper.

"Have you been working?"

"Hell, yes!" shouted Jim Trivett. "I've been working like a son-of-a-bitch."

"God!" said Tom Grant, turning slowly to look at him. "Boy, you're going to choke to death on one of those some day." He shook his head slowly and sadly, then continued with a rough laugh: "If old man Trivett knew what you were doing with his money, damn if he wouldn't bust a gut."

" 'Gene!" said Jim Trivett, "what the hell do you know about this damned English, anyway?"

"What he doesn't know about it," said Tom Grant, "you could write out on the back of a postage stamp. Old man Sanford thinks you're hell, 'Gene."

"I thought you had Torrington," said Jim Trivett.

"No," said Eugene, "I wasn't English enough. Young and crude. I changed, thank God! What is it you want, Jim?" he asked.

"I've got a long paper to write. I don't know what to write about," said Jim Trivett.

"What do you want me to do? Write it for you?"

"Yes," said Jim Trivett.

"Write your own damn paper," said Eugene with mimic toughness, "I won't do it for you. I'll help you if I can."

"When are you going to let Hard Boy take you to Exeter?" said Tom Grant, winking at Jim Trivett.

Eugene flushed, making a defensive answer.

"I'm ready to go any time he is," he said uneasily.

"Look here, Legs!" said Jim Trivett, grinning loosely. "Do you really want to go with me or are you just bluffing?"

"I'll go with you! I've told you I'd go with you!" Eugene said angrily. He trembled a little.

Tom Grant grinned slyly at Jim Trivett.

"It'll make a man of you, 'Gene," he said. "Boy, it'll sure put hair on your chest." He laughed, not loudly, but uncontrollably, shaking his head as at some secret thought.

Jim Trivett's loose smile widened. He spat into the woodbox.

"Gawd!" he said. "They'll think Spring is here when they see old Legs. They'll need a stepladder to git at him."

Tom Grant was shaken with hard fat laughter.

"They sure God will!" he said.

"Well, what about it, 'Gene?" Jim Trivett demanded suddenly. "Is it a go? Saturday?"

"Suits me!" said Eugene.

When he had gone, they grinned thirstily at each other for a moment, the pleased corrupters of chastity.

"Pshaw!" said Tom Grant. "You oughtn't to do that, Hard Boy. You're leading the boy astray."

"It's not going to hurt him," said Jim Trivett. "It'll be good for him."

He wiped his mouth with the back of his hand, grinning.

"Wait a minute!" whispered Jim Trivett. "I think this is the place."

They had turned away from the centre of the dreary tobacco town. For a quarter of an hour they had walked briskly through drab autumnal streets, descending finally a long rutted hill that led them, past a thinning squalor of cheap houses, almost to the outskirts. It was three weeks before Christmas: the foggy air was full of chill menace. There was a brooding quietness, broken by far small sounds. They turned into a sordid little road, unpaved, littered on both sides with negro shacks and the dwellings of poor whites. It was a world of rickets. The road was unlighted. Their feet stirred dryly through fallen leaves.

They paused before a two-storey frame house. A lamp burned dimly behind lowered yellow shades, casting a murky pollen out upon the smoky air.

"Wait a minute," said Jim Trivett, in a low voice, "I'll find out."

They heard scuffling steps through the leaves. In a moment a negro man prowled up.

"Hello, John," said Jim Trivett, almost inaudibly.

"Evenin', boss!" the negro answered wearily, but in the same tone.

"We're looking for Lily Jones' house," said Jim Trivett. "Is this it?"

"Yes, suh," said the negro, "dis is it."

Eugene leaned against a tree, listening to their quiet conspiratorial talk. The night, vast and listening, gathered about him its evil attentive consciousness. His lips were cold and trembled. He thrust a cigarette between them and, shivering, turned up the thick collar of his overcoat.

"Does Miss Lily know you're comin'?" the negro asked.

"No," said Jim Trivett. "Do you know her?"

"Yes, suh," said the negro. "I'll go up dar wid yo'."

Eugene waited in the shadow of the tree while the two men went up to the house. They avoided the front veranda, and went around to the side. The negro rapped gently at a latticed door. There were always latticed doors. Why?

He waited, saying farewell to himself. He stood over his life, he felt, with lifted assassin blade. He was mired to his neck, inextricably, in complication. There was no escape.

There had been a faint closed noise from the house: voices and laughter, and the cracked hoarse tone of an old phonograph. The sound stopped quickly as the negro rapped: the shabby house seemed to listen. In a moment, a hinge creaked stealthily: he caught the low startled blur of a woman's voice. Who is it? Who?

In another moment Jim Trivett returned to him, and said quietly:

"It's all right, 'Gene. Come on."

He slipped a coin into the negro's hand, thanking him. Eugene looked for a moment into the black broad friendliness of the man's face. He had a flash of warmth through his cold limbs. The black bawd had done his work eagerly and kindly: over their bought unlovely loves lay the warm shadow of his affection.

They ascended the path quietly and, mounting two or three steps, went in under the latticed door. A woman stood beside it, holding it open. When they had entered, she closed it securely. Then they crossed the little porch and entered the house.

They found themselves in a little hall which cleft the width of the house.

A smoky lamp, wicked low, cast its dim circle into the dark. An uncarpeted stair mounted to the second floor. There were two doors both to left and right, and an accordion hat-rack, on which hung a man's battered felt hat.

Jim Trivett embraced the woman immediately, grinning, and fumbling in her breast.

"Hello, Lily," he said.

"Gawd!" She smiled crudely, and continued to peer at Eugene, curious at what the maw of night had thrown in to her. Then, turning to Jim Trivett with a coarse laugh, she said:

"Lord a' mercy! Any woman that gits him will have to cut off some of them legs."

"I'd like to see him with Thelma," said Jim Trivett, grinning.

Lily Jones laughed hoarsely. The door to the right opened and Thelma, a small woman, slightly built, came out, followed by high empty yokel laughter. Jim Trivett embraced her affectionately.

"My Gawd!" said Thelma, in a tinny voice. "What've we got here?" She thrust out her sharp wrenny face, and studied Eugene insolently.

"I brought you a new beau, Thelma," said Jim Trivett.

"Ain't he the lankiest feller you ever seen?" said Lily Jones impersonally. "How tall are you, son?" she added, addressing him in a kind drawl.

He winced a little.

"I don't know," he said. "I think about six three."

"He's more than that!" said Thelma positively. "He's seven foot tall or I'm a liar."

"He hasn't measured since last week," said Jim Trivett. "He can't be sure about it."

"He's young, too," said Lily, staring at him intently. "How old are you, son?"

Eugene turned his pallid face away, indefinitely.

"Why," he croaked, "I'm about——"

"He's going on eighteen," said Jim Trivett loyally. "Don't you worry about him. Old Legs knows all the ropes, all right. He's a bearcat. I wouldn't kid you. He's been there."

"He don't look that old," said Lily doubtfully. "I wouldn't call him more'n fifteen, to look at his face. Ain't he got a little face, though?" she demanded in a slow puzzled voice.

"It's the only one I've got," said Eugene angrily. "Sorry I can't change it for a larger one."

"It looks so funny stickin' way up there above you," she went on patiently.

Thelma nudged her sharply.

"That's because he's got a big frame," she said. "Legs is all right. When he begins to fill out an' put some meat on them bones he's goin' to make a big man. You'll be a heartbreaker sure, Legs," she said harshly, taking his cold hand and squeezing it. In him the ghost, his stranger, turned grievously away. O God! I shall remember, he thought.

"Well," said Jim Trivett, "let's git goin'." He embraced Thelma again. They fumbled amorously.

"You go on upstairs, son," said Lily. "I'll be up in a minute. The door's open."

"See you later, 'Gene," said Jim Trivett. "Stay with them, son."

He hugged the boy roughly with one arm, and went into the room to the left with Thelma.

Eugene mounted the creaking stairs slowly and entered the room with the open door. A hot mass of coals glowed flamelessly in the hearth. He took off his hat and overcoat and threw them across a wooden bed. Then he sat down tensely in a rocker and leaned forward, holding his trembling fingers to the heat. There was no light save that of the coals; but, by their dim steady glow, he could make out the old and ugly wall-paper, stained with long streaks of water rust, and scaling, in dry tattered scrolls, here and there. He sat quietly, bent forward, but he shook violently, as with an ague, from time to time. Why am I here? This is not I, he thought.

Presently he heard the woman's slow heavy tread upon the stairs: she entered in a swimming tide of light, bearing a lamp before her. She put the lamp down on a table and turned the wick. He could see her now more plainly. Lily was a middle-aged country woman, with a broad heavy figure, unhealthily soft. Her smooth peasant face was mapped with fine little traceries of wrinkles at the corners of mouth and eyes, as if she had worked much in the sun. She had black hair, coarse and abundant. She was whitely plastered with talcum powder. She was dressed shapelessly in a fresh loose dress of gingham, unbelted. She was dressed like a housewife, but she conceded to her profession stockings of red silk, and slippers of red felt, trimmed with fur, in which she walked with a flat-footed tread.

The woman fastened the door, and returned to the hearth where the boy was now standing. He embraced her with feverish desire, fondling her with his long nervous hands. Indecisively, he sat in the rocker and drew her down clumsily on his knee. She yielded her kisses with the coy and frigid modesty of the provincial harlot, turning her mouth away. She shivered as his cold hands touched her.

"You're cold as ice, son," she said. "What's the matter?"

She chafed him with rough embarrassed professionalism. In a moment she rose impatiently.

"Let's git started," she said. "Where's my money?"

He thrust two crumpled bills into her hand.

Then he lay down beside her. He trembled, unnerved and impotent. Passion was extinct in him.

The massed coals caved in the hearth. The lost bright wonder died.

When he went down stairs, he found Jim Trivett waiting in the hall, holding Thelma by the hand. Lily led them out quietly, after peering through the lattice into the fog, and listening for a moment.

"Be quiet," she whispered, "there's a man across the street. They've been watching us lately."

"Come again, Slats," Thelma murmured, pressing his hand.

They went out softly, treading gently until they reached the road. The fog had thickened: the air was saturated with fine stinging moisture.

At the corner, in the glare of the street-lamp, Jim Trivett released his breath with loud relief, and stepped forward boldly.

"Damn!" he said. "I thought you were never coming. What were you trying to do with the woman, Legs?" Then, noting the boy's face, he added quickly, with warm concern: "What's the matter, 'Gene? Don't you feel good?"

"Wait a minute!" said Eugene thickly. "Be all right!"

He went to the curb, and vomited into the gutter. Then he straightened, mopping his mouth with a handkerchief.

"How do you feel?" asked Jim Trivett. "Better?"

"Yes," said Eugene, "I'm all right now."

"Why didn't you tell me you were sick?" said Jim Trivett chidingly.

"It came on all of a sudden," said Eugene. He added presently: "I think it was something I ate at that damn Greek's to-night."

"I felt all right," said Jim Trivett. "A cup of coffee will fix you up," he added with cheerful conviction.

They mounted the hill slowly. The light from winking cornerlamps fell with a livid stare across the fronts of the squalid houses.

"Jim," said Eugene, after a moment's pause.

"Yes. What is it?"

"Don't say anything about my getting sick," he said awkwardly.

Surprised, Jim Trivett stared at him.

"Why not? There's nothing in that," he said. "Pshaw, boy, any one's likely to get sick."

"Yes, I know. But I'd rather you wouldn't."

"Oh, all right. I won't. Why should I?" said Jim Trivett.

Eugene was haunted by his own lost ghost: he knew it to be irrecoverable. For three days he avoided every one: the brand of his sin, he felt, was on him. He was published by every gesture, by every word. His manner grew more defiant, his greeting to life more unfriendly. He clung more closely to Jim Trivett, drawing a sad pleasure from his coarse loyal praise. His unappeased desire began to burn anew: it conquered his bodily disgust and made new pictures. At the end of the week he went again, alone, to Exeter. No more of him, he felt, could be lost. This time he sought out Thelma.

When he went home for Christmas, his loins were black with vermin. The great body of the State lay like a barren giant below the leaden reek of the skies. The train roared on across the vast lift of the Piedmont: at night, as he lay in his berth, in a diseased coma, it crawled up into the great fortress of the hills. Dimly, he saw their wintry bulk, with its bleak foresting. Below a trestle, silent as a dream, a white rope of water coiled between its frozen banks. His sick heart lifted in the haunting eternity of the hills. He was hillborn. But at dawn, as he came from the cars with the band of returning students, his depression revived. The huddle of cheap buildings at the station seemed meaner and meaner than ever before. The hills, above the station flats, with their cheap propped houses, had the unnatural closeness of a vision. The silent Square seemed to have rushed together during his absence, and as he left the car and descended the street to Dixieland, it was as if he devoured toy-town distances with a giant's stride.

The Christmas was gray and chill. Helen was not there to give it warmth. Gant and Eliza felt the depression of her absence. Ben came and went like a ghost. Luke was not coming home. And he himself was sick with shame and loss.

He did not know where to turn. He paced his chill room at night, muttering, until Eliza's troubled face appeared above her wrapper. His father was gentler, older than he had ever seen him; his pain had returned on him. He was absent and sorrowful. He talked perfunctorily with his son about college. Speech choked in Eugene's throat. He stammered a few answers and fled from the house and the vacant fear in Gant's eyes. He walked prodigiously, day and night, in an effort to command his own fear. He believed himself to be rotting with a leprosy. And there was nothing to do but rot. There was no cure. For such had been the instruction of the moralists of his youth.

He walked with aimless desperation, unable to quiet for a moment his restless limbs. He went up on the eastern hills that rose behind Niggertown. A winter's sun labored through the mist. Low on the meadows, and high on the hills, the sunlight lay on the earth like milk.

He stood looking. A shaft of hope cut through the blackness of his spirit. I will go to my brother, he thought.

He found Ben still in bed at Woodson Street, smoking. He closed the door, then spun wildly about as if caged.

"In God's name!" Ben cried angrily. "Have you gone crazy? What's wrong with you?"

"I'm—I'm sick!" he gasped.

"What's the matter? Where've you been?" asked Ben sharply. He sat up in bed.

"I've been with a woman," said Eugene.

"Sit down, 'Gene," said Ben quietly, after a moment. "Don't be a little idiot. You're not going to die, you know. When did this happen?"

The boy blurted out his confession.

Ben got up and put on his clothes.

"Come on," said he, "we'll go to see McGuire."

As they walked townward, he tried to talk, explaining himself in babbling incoherent spurts.

"It was like this," he began, "if I had known, but at that time I didn't— of course I know it was my own fault for——"

"Oh, for God's sake!" said Ben impatiently. "Dry up! I don't want to hear about it. I'm not your damned Guardian Angel."

The news was comforting. So many people, after our fall from grace, are.

They mounted to the wide dark corridor of the Doctors' and Surgeons', with its sharp excitement of medical smells. McGuire's anteroom was empty. Ben rapped at the inner door. McGuire opened it: he pulled away the wet cigarette that was plastered on his heavy lip, to greet them.

"Hello, Ben. Hello, son!" he barked, seeing Eugene. "When'd you get back?"

"He thinks he's dying of galloping consumption, McGuire," said Ben, with a jerk of the head. "You may be able to do something to prolong his life."

"What's the matter, son?" said McGuire.

Eugene gulped dryly, craning his livid face.

"If you don't mind," he croaked. "See you alone." He turned desperately upon his brother. "You stay here. Don't want you with me."

"I don't want to go with you," said Ben surlily. "I've got troubles enough of my own."

Eugene followed McGuire's burly figure into the office; McGuire closed the door, and sat down heavily at his littered desk.

"Sit down, son," he commanded, "and tell me about it." He lit a cigarette and stuck it deftly on his sag wet lip. He glanced keenly at the boy, noting his contorted face.

"Take your time, son," he said kindly, "and control yourself. Whatever it is, it's probably not as bad as you think."

"It was this way," Eugene began in a low voice. "I've made a mistake. I know that. I'm willing to take my medicine. I'm not making any excuses for what has happened," his voice rose sharply; he got half-way out of his chair, and began to pound fiercely upon the untidy desk. "I'm putting the blame on no one. Do you understand that?"

McGuire turned a bloated bewildered face slowly upon his patient. His wet cigarette sagged comically from his half-opened mouth.

"Do I understand what?" he said. "See here, 'Gene: what the hell are you driving at? I'm no Sherlock Holmes, you know. I'm your doctor. Spit it out."

"What I've done," he said dramatically, "thousands have done. Oh, I know they may pretend not to. But they do! You're a doctor—you know that. People high-up in society, too. I'm one of the unlucky ones. I got caught. Why am I any worse than they are? Why—" he continued rhetorically.

"I think I catch your drift," said McGuire dryly. "Let's have a look, son."

Eugene obeyed feverishly, still declaiming.

"Why should I bear the stigma for what others get away with? Hypocrites —a crowd of damned, dirty, whining hypocrites, that's what they are. The Double-Standard! Hah! Where's the justice, where's the honor of that? Why should I be blamed for what people in High Society——"

McGuire lifted his big head from its critical stare, and barked comically.

"Who's blaming you? You don't think you're the first one who ever had this sort of trouble, do you? There's nothing wrong with you, anyway."

"Can—can you cure me?" Eugene asked.

"No. You're incurable, son!" said McGuire. He scrawled a few hieroglyphics on a prescription pad. "Give this to the druggist," he said, "and be a little more careful hereafter of the company you keep. People in High Society, eh?" he grinned. "So that's where you've been?"

The great weight of blood and tears had lifted completely out of the boy's heart, leaving him dizzily buoyant, wild, half-conscious only of his rushing words.

He opened the door and went into the outer room. Ben got up quickly and nervously.

"Well," he said, "how much longer has he got to live?" Seriously, in a low voice, he added: "There's nothing wrong with him, is there?"

"No," said McGuire, "I think he's a little off his nut. But, then, you all are."

When they came out on the street again, Ben said:
"Have you had anything to eat?"
"No," said Eugene.
"When did you eat last?"
"Some time yesterday," said Eugene. "I don't remember."
"You damned fool!" Ben muttered. "Come on—let's eat."

The idea became very attractive. The world was washed pleasantly in the milky winter sunshine. The town, under the stimulus of the holidays and the returning students, had wakened momentarily from its winter torpor: warm brisk currents of life seethed over the pavements. He walked along at Ben's side with a great bounding stride, unable to govern the expanding joy that rose yeastily in him. Finally, as he turned in on the busy avenue, he could restrain himself no longer: he leaped high in the air, with a yelp of ecstasy:

"Squee-ee!"

"You little idiot!" Ben cried sharply. "Are you crazy!"

He scowled fiercely, then turned to the roaring passersby, with a thin smile.

"Hang on to him, Ben!" yelled Jim Pollock. He was a deadly little man, waxen and smiling under a black mustache, the chief compositor, a Socialist.

"If you cut off his damned big feet," said Ben, "he'd go up like a balloon."

They went into the big new lunch-room and sat at one of the tables.

"What's yours?" said the waiter.

"A cup of coffee and a piece of mince pie," said Ben.

"I'll take the same," said Eugene.

"Eat!" said Ben fiercely. "Eat!"

Eugene studied the card thoughtfully.

"Bring me some veal cutlets breaded with tomato sauce," he said, "with a side-order of hash-brown potatoes, a dish of creamed carrots and peas, and a plate of hot biscuits. Also a cup of coffee."

Eugene got back his heart again. He got it back fiercely and carelessly, with an eldritch wildness. During the remainder of his holiday, he plunged recklessly through the lively crowds, looking boldly but without insolence at the women and young girls. They grew unexpectedly out of the waste drear winter like splendid flowers. He was eager and alone. Fear is a dragon that lives among crowds—and in armies. It lives hardly with men who are alone. He felt released—beyond the last hedge of desperation.

Freed and alone, he looked with a boding detachment at all the possessed and possessing world about him. Life hung for his picking fingers like a strange and bitter fruit. *They*—the great clan huddled there behind the stockade for warmth and safety—could hunt him down some day and put him to death: he thought they would.

But he was not now afraid—he was content, if only the struggle might be fruitful. He looked among the crowds printed with the mark of his danger, seeking that which he might desire and take.

He went back to the university sealed up against the taunts of the young men: in the hot green Pullman they pressed about him with thronging jibe, but they fell back sharply, as fiercely he met them, with constraint.

There came and sat beside him Tom French, his handsome face vested in the hard insolence of money. He was followed by his court jester, Roy Duncan, the slave with the high hard cackle.

"Hello, Gant," said Tom French harshly. "Been to Exeter lately?" Scowling, he winked at grinning Roy.

"Yes," said Eugene, "I've been there lately, and I'm on my way there now. What's it to you, French?"

Discomfited by this hard defiance, the rich man's son drew back.

"We hear you're stepping out among them, 'Gene," said Roy Duncan, cackling.

"Who's we?" said Eugene. "Who's them?"

"They say," said Tom French, "that you're as pure as the flowing sewer."

"If I need cleaning," said Eugene, "I can always use the Gold Dust

Twins, can't I? French and Duncan, the Gold Dust Twins—who never do any work."

The cluster of grinning students, the young impartial brutes who had gathered above them on the seats back and front, laughed loudly.

"That's right! That's right! Talk to them, 'Gene!" said Zeno Cochran, softly. He was a tall lad of twenty, slender and powerful, with the grace of a running horse. He had punted against the wind for eighty yards in the Yale Bowl. He was a handsome fellow, soft-spoken and kindly, with the fearless gentleness of the athlete.

Confused and angry, with sullen boastfulness, Tom French said:

"Nobody has anything on me. I've been too slick for them. Nobody knows anything about me."

"You mean," said Eugene, "that every one knows all about you, and nobody wants to know anything about you."

The crowd laughed.

"Wow!" said Jimmy Revell.

"What about that, Tom?" he asked challengingly. He was very small and plump, the son of a carpenter, offensively worthy, working his way through college by various schemes. He was a "kidder," an egger-on, finding excuse for his vulgarity and malice in a false and loud good-humor.

Eugene turned quietly on Tom French. "Stop it!" he said. "Don't go on because the others are listening. I don't think it's funny. I don't like it. I don't like you. I want you to leave me alone now. Do you hear?"

"Come on," said Roy Duncan, rising, "leave him alone, Tom. He can't take a joke. He takes things too seriously."

They left him. Unperturbed, relieved, he turned his face toward the vast bleak earth, gray and hoary in the iron grip of winter.

Winter ended. The sleety frozen earth began to soften under thaw and the rain. The town and campus paths were dreary trenches of mud and slime. The cold rain fell: the grass shot up in green wet patches. He hurtled down the campus lanes, bounding along like a kangaroo, leaping high at the lower boughs to clip a budding twig with his teeth. He cried loudly in his throat—a whinnying squeal—the centaur-cry of man or beast, trying to unburden its overladen heart in one blast of pain and joy and passion. At other times he slouched by, depressed by an unaccountable burden of weariness and dejection.

He lost count of the hours—he had no sense of time—no regular periods for sleep, work, or recreation, although he attended his classes faithfully, and ate with fair regularity by compulsion of dining-hall or boarding-house schedules. The food was abundant, coarse, greasily and badly cooked. It was very cheap: at the college commons, twelve dollars a month; at the boarding-houses, fifteen. He ate at the commons for a month: his interest in food was too profound and too intelligent to stand it longer. The commons was housed in a large bleak building of white brick. It was called officially Stiggins Hall, but in the more descriptive epithet of the students— The Sty.

He went to see Helen and Hugh Barton several times. They lived thirty-five miles away at Sydney, the State capital. It was a town of thirty thousand people, sleepy, with quiet leafy pavements, and a capitol Square in the centre, with radial streets. At the head of the main street, across from the capitol, a brown weathered building of lichened stone, was a cheap hotel— the largest and most notorious brothel in town. There were also three denominational colleges for young women.

The Bartons had rented quarters in an old house on the street above the Governor's Mansion. They lived in three or four rooms on the ground floor.

It was to Sydney that Gant had come, a young man, from Baltimore, on his slow drift to the South. It was in Sydney that he had first started business for himself and conceived, from the loss of his first investments, his hatred of property. It was in Sydney that he had met and wedded the sainted Cynthia, the tubercular spinstress who had died within two years of their marriage.

Their father's great ghost haunted them: it brooded over the town, above the scouring oblivion of the years that wipes all trace of us away.

Together, they hunted down into the mean streets, until they stood at length before a dreary shop on the skirts of the negro district.

"This must be it," she said. "His shop stood here. It's gone now."

She was silent a moment. "Poor old Papa." She turned her wet eyes away.

There was no mark of his great hand on this bleak world. No vines grew round the houses. That part of him which had lived here was buried— buried with a dead woman below the long gray tide of the years. They stood quietly, frightened, in that strange place, waiting to hear the summons of his voice, with expectant unbelief, as some one looking for the god in Brooklyn.

In April the nation declared war on Germany. Before the month was out, all the young men at Pulpit Hill who were eligible—those who were twenty-one—were going into service. At the gymnasium he watched the doctors examine them, envying them the careless innocence with which they stripped themselves naked. They threw off their clothes in indifferent heaps and stood, laughing and certain, before the doctors. They were clean-limbed, sound and white of tooth, graceful and fast in their movements. The fraternity men joined first—those merry and extravagant snobs of whom he had never known, but who now represented for him the highest reach of urbane and aristocratic life. He had seen them, happy and idle, on the wide verandas of their chapter houses—those temples where the last and awful rites of initiation were administered. He had seen them, always together, and from the herd of the uninitiated always apart, laughing over their mail at the post-office, or gambling for "black cows," at the drug store. And, with a stab of failure, with regret, with pain at his social deficiency, he had watched their hot campaigns for the favor of some desirable freshman—some one vastly more elegant than himself, some one with blood and with money. They were only the sons of the little rich men, the lords of the village and county, but as he saw them go so surely, with such laughing unconstraint, in well-cut clothes, well-groomed, well-brushed, among the crowd of humbler students, who stiffened awkwardly with peasant hostility and constraint,—they were the flower of chivalry, the sons of the mansion-house. They were Sydney, Raleigh, Nash. And now, like gentlemen, they were going to war.

The gymnasium was thick with the smell of steam and of sweating men coming in to the showers from the playing fields. Washed, with opened shirt, Eugene walked slowly away into the green budding shade of the campus, companioned by an acquaintance, Ralph Hendrix.

"Look!" said Ralph Hendrix, in a low angry tone. "Look at that, will you!" He nodded toward a group of students ahead. "That little Horse's Neck is booting the Dekes all over the campus."

Eugene looked, then turned to examine the bitter common face beside him. Every Saturday night, after the meeting of the literary society, Ralph Hendrix went to the drug-store and bought two cheap cigars. He had bent narrow shoulders, a white knobby face, and a low forehead. He spoke in a monotonous painful drawl. His father was foreman in a cotton mill.

"They're all Horse's Necks," he said. "They can go to hell before I'll boot to get in."

"Yes," said Eugene.

But he wanted to get in. He wanted to be urbane and careless. He wanted to wear well-cut clothes. He wanted to be a gentleman. He wanted to go to war.

On the central campus, several students who had been approved by the examining board, descended from the old dormitories, bearing packed valises. They turned down under the trees, walking toward the village street. From time to time they threw up an arm in farewell.

"So long, boys! See you in Berlin." The shining and dividing sea was closer and not so wide.

He read a great deal—but at random, for pleasure. He read Defoe, Smollet, Sterne, and Fielding—the fine salt of the English novel lost, during the reign of the Widow of Windsor, beneath an ocean of tea and molasses. He read the tales of Boccaccio, and all that remained of a tattered copy of the *Heptameron*. At Buck Benson's suggestion, he read Murray's *Euripides* (at the time he was reading the Greek text of the *Alcestis*—noblest and loveliest of all the myths of Love and Death). He saw the grandeur of the *Prometheus* fable—but the fable moved him more than the play of Æschylus. In fact, Æschylus he found sublime—and dull: he could not understand his great reputation. Rather—he could. He was Literature—a writer of masterpieces. He was almost as great a bore as Cicero—that windy old moralist who came out so boldly in favor of Old Age and Friendship. Sophocles was an imperial poet—he spoke like God among flashes of lightning: the *Œdipus Rex* is not only one of the greatest plays in the world, it is one of the greatest stories. This story—perfect, inevitable, and fabulous—wreaked upon him the nightmare coincidence of Destiny. It held him birdlike before its great snake-eye of wisdom and horror. And Euripides (whatever the disparagement of pedantry) he thought one of the greatest lyrical singers in all poetry.

He liked all weird fable and wild invention, in prose or verse, from the *Golden Ass* to Samuel Taylor Coleridge, the chief prince of the moon and magic. But he liked the fabulous wherever he found it, and for whatever purpose.

The best fabulists have often been the greatest satirists: satire (as with Aristophanes, Voltaire, and Swift) is a high and subtle art, quite beyond the barnyard snipings and wholesale geese-slaughterings of the present degenerate age. Great satire needs the sustenance of great fable. Swift's power of invention is incomparable: there's no better fabulist in the world.

He read Poe's stories, *Frankenstein,* and the plays of Lord Dunsany. He read *Sir Gawayne and the Greene Knight* and the *Book of Tobit*. He did not want his ghosts and marvels explained. Magic was magic. He wanted old ghosts—not Indian ghosts, but ghosts in armor, the spirit of old kings, and pillioned ladies with high coned hats. Then, for the first time, he thought of the lonely earth he dwelt on. Suddenly, it was strange to him that he should read Euripides there in the wilderness.

Around him lay the village; beyond, the ugly rolling land, sparse with cheap farmhouses; beyond all this, America—more land, more wooden houses, more towns, hard and raw and ugly. He was reading Euripides, and all around him a world of white and black was eating fried food. He was reading of ancient sorceries and old ghosts, but did an old ghost ever come to haunt this land? The ghost of Hamlet's Father, in Connecticut.

> ". . . . . . I am thy father's spirit,
> Doomed for a certain term to walk the night
> Between Bloomington and Portland, Maine."

He felt suddenly the devastating impermanence of the nation. Only the earth endured—the gigantic American earth, bearing upon its awful breast a world of flimsy rickets. Only the earth endured—this broad terrific earth that had no ghosts to haunt it. Stogged in the desert, half-broken and over-thrown, among the columns of lost temples strewn, there was no ruined image of Menkaura, there was no alabaster head of Akhnaton. Nothing had been done in stone. Only this earth endured, upon whose lonely breast he read Euripides. Within its hills he had been held a prisoner; upon its plain he walked, alone, a stranger.

O God! O God! We have been an exile in another land and a stranger in our own. The mountains were our masters: they went home to our eye and our heart before we came to five. Whatever we can do or say must be forever hillbound. Our senses have been fed by our terrific land; our blood has learned to run to the imperial pulse of America which, leaving, we can never lose and never forget. We walked along a road in Cumberland, and stooped, because the sky hung down so low; and when we ran away from London, we went by little rivers in a land just big enough. And nowhere that we went was far: the earth and the sky were close and near. And the old hunger returned—the terrible and obscure hunger that haunts and hurts Americans, and that makes us exiles at home and strangers wherever we go.

Eliza visited Helen in Sydney in the Spring. The girl was quieter, sadder, more thoughtful than she had ever been. She was subdued by the new life; chastened by her obscurity. She missed Gant more than she would confess. She missed the mountain town.

"What do you have to pay for this place?" said Eliza, looking around critically.

"Fifty dollars a month," said Helen.

"Furnished?"

"No, we had to buy furniture."

"I tell you what, that's pretty high," said Eliza, "just for down stairs. I believe rents are lower at home."

"Yes, I know it's high," said Helen. "But good heavens, mama! Do you realize that this is the best neighborhood in town? We're only two blocks from the Governor's Mansion, you know. Mrs. Mathews is no common boarding-house keeper, I can assure you! No sir!" she exclaimed, laughing. "She's a real swell—goes to all the big functions and gets in the papers all the time. You know Hugh and I have got to try to keep up appearances. He's a young man just starting out here."

"Yes. I know," Eliza agreed thoughtfully. "How's he been doing?"

"O'Toole says he's the best agent he's got," said Helen. "Hugh's all right. We could get along together anywhere, as long as there's no damned family about. It makes me furious at times to see him slaving to feather O'Toole's pockets. He works like a dog. You know, O'Toole gets a commission on every sale he makes. And Mrs. O'T. and those two girls ride around in a big car and never turn their hands over. They're Catholics, you know, but they get to go everywhere."

"I tell you what," said Eliza with a timid half-serious smile, "it might not be a bad idea if Hugh became his own boss. There's no use doing it all for the other fellow. Say, child!" she exclaimed, "why wouldn't it be a good idea if he tried to get the Altamont agency? I don't believe that fellow they've got is much account. He could get it without trying."

There was a pause.

"We've been thinking of that," the girl admitted slowly. "Hugh has written in to the main office. Anyway," she said a moment later, "he'd be his own boss. That's something."

"Well," said Eliza slowly, "I don't know but what it'd be a good idea. If he works hard there's no reason why he shouldn't build a good business up. Your papa's been complaining here lately about his trouble. He'd be glad to have you back." She shook her head slowly for a moment. "Child! they didn't do him a bit of good, up there. It's all come back."

They drove over to Pulpit Hill at Easter for a two days' visit. Eliza took him to Exeter and bought him a suit of clothes.

"I don't like those skimpy trousers," she told the salesman. "I want something that makes him look more of a man."

When he was newly dressed, she puckered her lips, smiling, and said: "Spruce up, boy! Throw your shoulders back! That's one thing about your father—he carries himself straight as an arrow. If you go all humped over like that, you'll have lung trouble before you're twenty-five."

"I want you to meet my mother," he said awkwardly to Mr. Joseph Ballantyne, a smooth pink young man who had been elected president of the Freshman class.

"You're a good smart-looking fellow," said Eliza smiling, "I'll make a trade with you. If you drum up some boarders for me among your friends here in this part of the State, I'll throw in your board free. Here are some of my cards," she added, opening her purse. "You might hand a few of them out, if you get a chance, and say a good word for Dixieland in the Land of the Sky."

"Yes, ma'am," said Mr. Ballantyne, in a slow surprised voice, "I certainly will."

Eugene turned a hot distressed face toward Helen. She laughed huskily, ironically, then turning to the boy, said:

"You're welcome at any time, Mr. Ballantyne, boarders or not. We'll always find a place for you."

When they were alone, in answer to his stammering and confused protests, she said with an annoyed grin:

"Yes, I know. It's pretty bad. But you're away from it most of the time. You're the lucky one. You see what I've had to listen to, the last week, don't you? You see, don't you?"

When he went home at the end of the year, late in May, he found that Helen and Hugh Barton had preceeded him. They were living with Gant, at Woodson Street. Hugh Barton had secured the Altamont agency.

The town and the nation boiled with patriotic frenzy—violent, in a chaotic sprawl, to little purpose. The spawn of Attila must be crushed ("exterminated," said the Reverend Mr. Smallwood) by the sons of freedom. There were loans, bond issues, speech-making, a talk of drafts, and a thin trickle of Yankees into France. Pershing arrived in Paris, and said, "Lafayette, we are here!", but the French were still looking. Ben went up before the enlistment board and was rejected. "Lungs— weak!" they said quite definitely. "No—not tubercular. A tendency. Underweight." He cursed. His face was a little more like a blade—thinner, grayer. The cleft of his scowl was deeper. He seemed more alone.

Eugene came up into the hills again and found them in their rich young summer glory. Dixieland was partly filled by paying guests. More arrived.

Eugene was sixteen years old. He was a College Man. He walked among the gay crowd of afternoon with a sense of elation, answering the hearty greetings with joy, warming to its thoughtless bombast.

"They tell me you're batting a thousand down there, son," yelled Mr. Wood, the plump young pharmacist, who had been told nothing at all. "That's right, boy! Go get 'em." The man passed forward cheerfully, up the prosperous glade of his store. Fans droned.

After all, Eugene thought, he had not done so badly. He had felt his first wounds. He had not been broken. He had seen love's bitter mystery. He had lived alone.

30

There was at Dixieland a girl named Laura James. She was twenty-one years old. She looked younger. She was there when he came back.

Laura was a slender girl, of medium height, but looking taller than she was. She was very firmly moulded: she seemed fresh and washed and clean. She had thick hair, very straight and blonde, combed in a flat bracelet around her small head. Her face was white, with small freckles. Her eyes were soft, candid, cat-green. Her nose was a little too large for her face: it was tilted. She was not pretty. She dressed very simply and elegantly in short plaid skirts and waists of knitted silk.

She was the only young person at Dixieland. Eugene spoke to her with timid hauteur. He thought her plain and dull. But he began to sit with her on the porch at night. Somehow, he began to love her.

He did not know that he loved her. He talked to her arrogantly and boastfully as they sat in the wooden porch-swing. But he breathed the clean perfume of her marvellous young body. He was trapped in the tender cruelty of her clear green eyes, caught in the subtle net of her smile.

Laura James lived in the eastern part of the State, far east even of

Pulpit Hill, in a little town built on a salt river of the great coastal plain. Her father was a wealthy merchant—a wholesale provisioner. The girl was an only child: she spent extravagantly.

Eugene sat on the porch rail one evening and talked to her. Before, he had only nodded, or spoken stiffly a word or two. They began haltingly, aware painfully of gaps in their conversation.

"You're from Little Richmond, aren't you?" he said.

"Yes," said Laura James, "do you know any one from there?"

"Yes," said he, "I know John Bynum and a boy named Ficklen. They're from Little Richmond, aren't they?"

"Oh, Dave Ficklen! Do you know him? Yes. They both go to Pulpit Hill. Do you go there?"

"Yes," he said, "that's where I knew them."

"Do you know the two Barlow boys? They're Sigma Nus," said Laura James.

He had seen them. They were great swells, football men.

"Yes, I know them," he said, "Roy Barlow and Jack Barlow."

"Do you know 'Snooks' Warren? He's a Kappa Sig."

"Yes. They call them Keg Squeezers," said Eugene.

"What fraternity are you?" said Laura James.

"I'm not any," he said painfully. "I was just a Freshman this year."

"Some of the best friends I have never joined fraternities," said Laura James.

They met more and more frequently, without arrangement, until by silent consent they met every night upon the porch. Sometimes they walked along the cool dark streets. Sometimes he squired her clumsily through the town, to the movies, and later, with the uneasy pugnacity of youth, past the loafing cluster at Wood's. Often he took her to Woodson Street, where Helen secured for him the cool privacy of the veranda. She was very fond of Laura James.

"She's a nice girl. A lovely girl. I like her. She's not going to take any beauty prizes, is she?" She laughed with a trace of good-natured ridicule.

He was displeased.

"She looks all right," he said. "She's not as ugly as you make out."

But she *was* ugly—with a clean lovely ugliness. Her face was freckled lightly, over her nose and mouth: her features were eager, unconscious, turned upward in irregular pertness. But she was exquisitely made and exquisitely kept: she had the firm young line of Spring, budding, slender, virginal. She was like something swift, with wings, which hovers in a wood—among the feathery trees suspected, but uncaught, unseen.

He tried to live before her in armor. He showed off before her. Perhaps, he thought, if he were splendid enough, she would not see the ugly disorder and meanness of the world he dwelt in.

Across the street, on the wide lawn of the Brunswick—the big brick gabled house that Eliza once had coveted—Mr. Pratt, who crawled in that mean world in which only a boarding-house husband can exist, was watering wide green spaces of lawn with a hose. The flashing water motes gleamed in the red glare of sunset. The red light fell across the shaven pinched face. It glittered on the buckles of his arm-bands. Across the walk, on the other lobe of grass, several men and women were playing croquet. There was laughter on the vine-hid porch. Next door, at the Belton, the boarders were assembled on the long porch in bright hash-house chatter. The comedian of the Dixie Ramblers arrived with two chorus girls. He was a little man, with the face of a weasel and no upper teeth. He wore a straw hat with a striped band, and a blue shirt and collar. The boarders gathered in around him. In a moment there was shrill laughter.

Julius Arthur sped swiftly down the hill, driving his father home. He grinned squintily and flung his arm up in careless greeting. The prosperous lawyer twisted a plump Van Dyked face on a wry neck curiously. Unsmiling, he passed.

A negress in the Brunswick struck on the several bells of a Japanese gong. There was a scramble of feet on the porch; the croquet players dropped their mallets and walked rapidly toward the house. Pratt wound his hose over a wooden reel.

A slow bell-clapper in the Belton sent the guests in a scrambling drive for the doors. In a moment there was a clatter of heavy plates and a loud foody noise. The guests on the porch at Dixieland rocked more rapidly, with low mutters of discontent.

Eugene talked to Laura in thickening dusk, sheeting his pain in pride and indifference. Eliza's face, a white blur in the dark, came up behind the screen.

"Come on out, Mrs. Gant, and get a breath of fresh air," said Laura James.

"Why no-o, child. I can't now. Who's that with you?" she cried, obviously flustered. She opened the door. "Huh? Heh? Have you seen 'Gene? Is it 'Gene?"

"Yes," he said. "What's the matter?"

"Come here a minute, boy," she said.

He went into the hall.

"What is it?" he asked.

"Why, son, what in the world! I don't know. You'll have to do something," she whispered, twisting her hands together.

"What is it, mama? What are you talking about?" he cried irritably.

"Why—Jannadeau's just called up. Your papa's on a rampage again and he's coming this way. Child! There's no telling what he'll do. I've all these people in the house. He'll ruin us." She wept. "Go and try to stop him. Head him off if you can. Take him to Woodson Street."

He got his hat quickly and ran through the door.

"Where are you going?" asked Laura James. "Are you going off without supper?"

"I've got to go to town," he said. "I won't be long. Will you wait for me?"

"Yes," she said.

He leaped down on the walk just as his father lurched in from the street by the high obscuring hedge that shut the house from the spacious yard of the attorney Hall. Gant reeled destructively, across a border of lilies, on to the lawn, and strode for the veranda. He stumbled, cursing, on the bottom step and plunged forward in a sprawl upon the porch. The boy jumped for him, and half dragged, half lifted his great drunken body erect. The boarders shrank into a huddle with a quick scattering of chairs: he greeted them with a laugh of howling contempt.

"Are you there? I say, are you there? The lowest of the low—boarding-house swine! Merciful God! What a travesty! A travesty on Nature! That it should come to this!"

He burst into a long peal of maniacal laughter.

"Papa! Come on!" said Eugene in a low voice. He took his father cautiously by the sleeve. Gant flung him half across the porch with a gesture of his hand. As he stepped in again swiftly, his father struck at him with a flailing arm. He evaded the great mowing fist without trouble, and caught the falling body, swung from its own pivot, in his arms. Then quickly, before Gant could recover, holding him from behind, he rushed him toward the door. The boarders scattered away like sparrows. But Laura James was at the screen before him: she flung it open.

"Get away! Get away!" he cried, full of shame and anger. "You stay out of this." For a moment he despised her for seeing his hurt.

"Oh, let me help you, my dear," Laura James whispered. Her eyes were wet, but she was not afraid.

Father and son plunged chaotically down the wide dark hall, Eliza, weeping and making gestures, just before them.

"Take him in here, boy. Take him in here," she whispered, motioning to a large bed-room on the upper side of the house. Eugene propelled his father through a blind passage of bath room, and pushed him over on the creaking width of an iron bed.

"You damned scoundrel!" Gant yelled, again trying to reap him down with the long arm, "let me up or I'll kill you!"

"For God's sake, papa," he implored angrily, "try to quiet down. Every one in town can hear you."

"To hell with them!" Gant roared. "Mountain Grills—all of them, fattening upon my heart's-blood. They have done me to death, as sure as there's a God in heaven."

Eliza appeared in the door, her face contorted by weeping.

"Son, can't you do something to stop him?" she said. "He'll ruin us all. He'll drive every one away."

Gant struggled to stand erect when he saw her. Her white face stirred him to insanity.

"There it is! There! There! Do you see! The fiend-face I know so well, gloating upon my misery. Look at it! Look! Do you see its smile of evil cunning? Greeley, Will, The Hog, The Old Major! The Tax Collector will get it all, and I shall die in the gutter!"

"If it hadn't been for me," Eliza began, stung to retaliation, "you'd have died there long ago."

"Mama, for God's sake!" the boy cried. "Don't stand there talking to him! Can't you see what it does to him! Do something, in heaven's name! Get Helen! Where is she?"

"I'll make an end to it all!" Gant yelled, staggering erect. "I'll do for us both now."

Eliza vanished.

"Yes, sir, papa. It's going to be all right," Eugene began soothingly, pushing him back on the bed again. He dropped quickly to his knees, and began to draw off one of Gant's soft tongueless shoes, muttering reassurances all the time: "Yes, sir. We'll get you some good hot soup and put you to bed in a jiffy. Everything's going to be all right," the shoe came off in his hand and, aided by the furious thrust of his father's foot, he went sprawling back.

Gant got to his feet again and, taking a farewell kick at his fallen son, lunged toward the door. Eugene scrambled up quickly, and leaped after him. The two men fell heavily into the roughly grained plaster of the wall. Gant cursed, flailing about clumsily at his tormentor. Helen came in.

"Baby!" Gant wept, "they're trying to kill me. O Jesus, do something to save me, or I perish."

"You get back in that bed," she commanded sharply, "or I'll knock your head off."

Very obediently he suffered himself to be led back to bed and undressed. In a few minutes she was sitting beside him with a bowl of smoking soup. He grinned sheepishly as she spooned it into his opened mouth. She laughed—almost happily—thinking of the lost and irrevocable years. Suddenly, before he slept, he lifted himself strongly from the pillows that propped him, and with staring eyes, called out in savage terror:

"Is it a cancer? I say, is it a cancer?"

"Hush!" she cried. "No. Of course not! Don't be foolish."

He fell back exhausted, with eyes closed. But they knew that it was. He had never been told. The terrible name of his malady was never uttered save by him. And in his heart he knew—what they all knew and never spoke of before him—that it was, it was a cancer. All day, with fear-stark eyes, Gant had sat, like a broken statue, among his marbles, drinking. It was a cancer.

The boy's right hand bled very badly across the wrist, where his father's weight had ground it into the wall.

"Go wash it off," said Helen. "I'll tie it up for you."

He went into the dark bathroom and held his hand under a jet of lukewarm water. A very quiet despair was in his heart, a weary peace that brooded too upon the house of death and tumult, that flowed, like a soft exploring wind, through its dark halls, bathing all things quietly with peace and weariness. The boarders had fled like silly sheep to the two houses across the street: they had eaten there, they were clustered there upon the porches, whispering. And their going brought him peace and freedom, as if his limbs had been freed from a shackling weight. Eliza, amid the slow smoke of the kitchen, wept more quietly over the waste of supper; he saw the black mournful calm of the negress's face. He walked slowly up the dark hall, with a handkerchief tied loosely round his wound. He felt suddenly the peace that comes with despair. The sword that pierces very deep had fared through the folds of his poor armor of pride. The steel had sheared his side, had bitten to his heart.

But under his armor he had found himself. No more than himself could be known. No more than himself could be given. What he was—he was: evasion and pretense could not add to his sum. With all his heart he was glad.

By the door, in the darkness, he found Laura James.

"I thought you had gone with the others," he said.

"No," said Laura James, "how is your father?"

"He's all right now. He's gone to sleep," he answered. "Have you had anything to eat?"

"No," she said, "I didn't want it."

"I'll bring you something from the kitchen," he said. "There's plenty there." In a moment he added: "I'm sorry, Laura."

"What are you sorry for?" she asked.

He leaned against the wall limply, drained of his strength at her touch.

"Eugene. My dear," she said. She pulled his drooping face down to her lips and kissed him. "My sweet, my darling, don't look like that."

All his resistance melted from him. He seized her small hands, crushing them in his hot fingers, and devouring them with kisses.

"My dear Laura! My dear Laura!" he said in a choking voice. "My sweet, my beautiful Laura! My lovely Laura. I love you, I love you." The words rushed from his heart, incoherent, unashamed, foaming through the broken levees of pride and silence. They clung together in the dark, with their wet faces pressed mouth to mouth. Her perfume went drunkenly to his brain; her touch upon him shot through his limbs a glow of magic; he felt the pressure of her narrow breasts, eager and lithe, against him with a sense of fear—as if he had dishonored her—with a sickening remembrance of his defilement.

He held between his hands her elegant small head, so gloriously wound with its thick bracelet of fine blonde hair, and spoke the words he had never spoken—the words of confession, filled with love and humility.

"Don't go! Don't go! Please don't go!" he begged. "Don't leave, dear. Please!"

"Hush!" she whispered. "I won't go! I love you, my dear."

She saw his hand, wrapped in its bloody bandage: she nursed it gently with soft little cries of tenderness. She fetched a bottle of iodine from her room and painted the stinging cut with a brush. She wrapped it with clean strips of fine white cloth, torn from an old waist, scented with a faint and subtle perfume.

Then they sat upon the wooden swing. The house seemed to sleep in darkness. Helen and Eliza came presently from its very quiet depth.

"How's your hand, 'Gene?" Helen asked.

"It's all right," he said.

"Let me see! O-ho, you've got a nurse now, haven't you?" she said, with a good laugh.

"What's that? What's that? Hurt his hand? How'd you do that? Why, here—say—I've got the very thing for it, son," said Eliza, trying to bustle off in all directions.

"Oh, it's all right now, mama. It's been fixed," he said wearily, reflecting that she had the very thing always too late. He looked at Helen grinning:

"God bless our Happy Home!" he said.

"Poor old Laura!" she laughed, and hugged the girl roughly with one hand. "It's too bad you have to be dragged into it."

"That's all right," said Laura. "I feel like one of the family now anyhow."

"He needn't think he can carry on like this," said Eliza resentfully. "I'm not going to put up with it any longer."

"Oh forget about it!" said Helen wearily. "Good heavens, mama. Papa's a sick man. Can't you realize that?"

"Pshaw!" said Eliza scornfully. "I don't believe there's a thing in the world wrong with him but that vile licker. All his trouble comes from that."

"Oh—how ridiculous! How ridiculous! You can't tell me!" Helen exclaimed angrily.

"Let's talk about the weather," said Eugene.

Then they all sat quietly, letting the darkness soak into them. Finally Helen and Eliza went back into the house: Eliza went unwillingly, at the girl's insistence, casting back the doubtful glimmer of her face upon the boy and girl.

The wasting helve of the moon rode into heaven over the bulk of the hills. There was a smell of wet grass and lilac, and the vast brooding symphony of the million-noted little night things, rising and falling in a constant ululation, and inhabiting the heart with steady unconscious certitude. The pallid light drowned out the stars, it lay like silence on the earth, it dripped through the leafy web of the young maples, printing the earth with swarming moths of elvish light.

Eugene and Laura sat with joined hands in the slowly creaking swing. Her touch shot through him like a train of fire: as he put his arm around her shoulders and drew her over to him, his fingers touched the live firm cup of her breast. He jerked his hand away, as if he had been stung, muttering an apology. Whenever she touched him, his flesh got numb and weak. She was a virgin, crisp like celery—his heart shrank away from the pollution of his touch upon her. It seemed to him that he was much the older, although he was sixteen, and she twenty-one. He felt the age of his loneliness and his dark perception. He felt the gray wisdom of sin—a waste desert, but seen and known. When he held her hand, he felt as if he had already seduced her. She lifted her lovely face to him, pert and ugly as a boy's; it was inhabited by a true and steadfast decency, and his eyes were wet. All the young beauty in the world dwelt for him in that face that had kept wonder, that had kept innocency, that had lived in such immortal blindness to the terror and foulness of the world. He came to her, like a creature who had travelled its life through dark space, for a moment of peace and conviction on some lonely planet, where now he stood, in the vast enchanted plain of moonlight, with moonlight falling on the moonflower of her face. For if a man should dream of heaven and, waking, find within his hand a flower as token that he had really been there—what then, what then?

"Eugene," she said presently, "how old are you?"

His vision thickened with his pulse. In a moment he answered with terrible difficulty.

"I'm—just sixteen."

"Oh, you child!" she cried. "I thought you were more than that!"

"I'm—old for my age," he muttered. "How old are you?"

"I'm twenty-one," she said. "Isn't it a pity?"

"There's not much difference," he said. "I can't see that it matters."

"Oh, my dear," she said. "It does! It matters so much!"

And he knew that it did—how much he did not know. But he had his moment. He was not afraid of pain, he was not afraid of loss. He cared nothing for the practical need of the world. He dared to say the strange and marvellous thing that had bloomed so darkly in him.

"Laura," he said, hearing his low voice sound over the great plain of the moon, "let's always love each other as we do now. Let's never get married. I want you to wait for me and to love me forever. I am going all over the world. I shall go away for years at a time; I shall become famous, but I shall always come back to you. You shall live in a house away in the mountains, you shall wait for me, and keep yourself for me. Will you?" he said, asking for her life as calmly as for an hour of her time.

"Yes, dear," said Laura in the moonlight, "I will wait for you forever."
She was buried in his flesh. She throbbed in the beat of his pulses.
She was wine in his blood, a music in his heart.

"He has no consideration for you or any one else," Hugh Barton
growled. He had returned late from work at his office, to take Helen
home. "If he can't do better than this, we'll find a house of our own.
I'm not going to have you get down sick on account of him."

"Forget about it," Helen said. "He's getting old."

They came out on the veranda.

"Come down to-morrow, honey," she said to Eugene. "I'll give you
a real feed. Laura, you come too. It's not always like this, you know."
She laughed, fondling the girl with a big hand.

They coasted away downhill.

"What a lovely girl your sister is," said Laura James. "Aren't you
simply crazy about her?"

Eugene made no answer for a moment.

"Yes," he said.

"She is about you. Any one can see that," said Laura.

In the darkness he caught at his throat.

"Yes," he said.

The moon quartered gently across heaven. Eliza came out again,
timidly, hesitantly.

"Who's there? Who's there?" she spoke into the darkness. "Where's
'Gene? Oh! I didn't know! Are you there, son?" She knew very well.

"Yes," he said.

"Why don't you sit down, Mrs. Gant?" asked Laura. "I don't see
how you stand that hot kitchen all day long. You must be worn out."

"I tell you what!" said Eliza, peering dimly at the sky. "It's a fine
night, isn't it? As the fellow says, a night for lovers." She laughed uncertainly, then stood for a moment in thought.

"Son," she said in a troubled voice, "why don't you go to bed and
get some sleep? It's not good for you staying up till all hours like this."

"That's where I should be," said Laura James, rising.

"Yes, child," said Eliza. "Go get your beauty sleep. As the saying
goes, early to bed and early to rise——"

"Let's all go, then. Let's all go!" said Eugene impatiently and angrily,
wondering if she must always be the last one awake in that house.

"Why law, no!" said Eliza. "I can't, boy. I've all those things to
iron."

Beside him, Laura gave his hand a quiet squeeze, and rose. Bitterly, he watched his loss.

"Good-night, all. Good-night, Mrs. Gant."

"Good-night, child."

When she had gone, Eliza sat down beside him, with a sigh of weariness.

"I tell you what," she said. "That feels good. I wish I had as much time as some folks, and could sit out here enjoying the air." In the darkness, he knew her puckering lips were trying to smile.

"Hm!" she said, and caught his hand in her rough palm. "Has my baby gone and got him a girl?"

"What of it? What if it were true?" he said angrily. "Haven't I a right as much as any one?"

"Pshaw!" said Eliza. "You're too young to think of them. I wouldn't pay any attention to them, if I were you. Most of them haven't an idea in the world except going out to parties and having a good time. I don't want my boy to waste his time on them."

He felt her earnestness beneath her awkward banter. He struggled in a chaos of confused fury, trying for silence. At last he spoke in a low voice, filled with his passion:

"We've got to have something, mama. We've got to have something, you know. We can't go on always alone—alone."

It was dark. No one could see. He let the gates swing open. He wept.

"I know!" Eliza agreed hastily. "I'm not saying——"

"My God, my God, where are we going? What's it all about? He's dying—can't you see it? Don't you know it? Look at his life. Look at yours. No light, no love, no comfort—nothing." His voice rose frantically: he beat on his ribs like a drum. "Mama, mama, in God's name, what is it? What do you want? Are you going to strangle and drown us all? Don't you own enough? Do you want more string? Do you want more bottles? By God, I'll go around collecting them if you say so." His voice had risen almost to a scream. "But tell me what you want. Don't you own enough? Do you want the town? What is it?"

"Why, I don't know what you're talking about, boy," said Eliza angrily. "If I hadn't tried to accumulate a little property none of you would have had a roof to call your own, for your papa, I can assure you, would have squandered everything."

"A roof to call our own!" he yelled, with a crazy laugh. "Good God, we haven't a bed to call our own. We haven't a room to call our own. We have not a quilt to call our own that might not be taken from us to warm the mob that rocks upon this porch and grumbles."

"Now, you may sneer at the boarders all you like—" Eliza began sternly.

"No," he said. "I can't. There's not breath or strength enough in me to sneer at them all I like."

Eliza began to weep.

"I've done the best I could!" she said. "I'd have given you a home if I could. I'd have put up with anything after Grover's death, but he never gave me a moment's peace. Nobody knows what I've been through. Nobody knows, child. Nobody knows."

He saw her face in the moonlight, contorted by an ugly grimace of sorrow. What she said, he knew, was fair and honest. He was touched deeply.

"It's all right, mama," he said painfully. "Forget about it! I know."

She seized his hand almost gratefully and laid her white face, still twisted with her grief, against his shoulder. It was the gesture of a child: a gesture that asked for love, pity, and tenderness. It tore up great roots in him, bloodily.

"Don't!" he said. "Don't, mama! Please!"

"Nobody knows," said Eliza. "Nobody knows. I need some one too. I've had a hard life, son, full of pain and trouble." Slowly, like a child again, she wiped her wet weak eyes with the back of her hand.

Ah, he thought, as his heart twisted in him full of wild pain and regret, she will be dead some day and I shall always remember this. Always this. This.

They were silent a moment. He held her rough hand tightly, and kissed her.

"Well," Eliza began, full of cheerful prophecy, "I tell you what: I'm not going to spend my life slaving away here for a lot of boarders. They needn't think it. I'm going to set back and take things as easy as any of them." She winked knowingly at him. "When you come home next time, you may find me living in a big house in Doak Park. I've got the lot—the best lot out there for view and location, far better than the one W. J. Bryan has. I made the trade with old Dr. Doak himself, the other day. Look here! What about!" She laughed. "He said, 'Mrs. Gant, I can't trust any of my agents with you. If I'm to make anything on this deal, I've got to look out. You're the sharpest trader in this town.' 'Why, pshaw! Doctor,' I said (I never let on I believed him or anything), 'all I want is a fair return on my investment. I believe in every one making his profit and giving the other fellow a chance. Keep the ball a-rolling!' I said, laughing as big as you please. 'Why, Mrs. Gant!' he said—" She was off on a lengthy divagation, recording with an absorbed gusto the interminable minutia of her transaction with the worthy Quinine King, with the attendant phenomena, during the time, of birds, bees, flowers, sun, clouds, dogs, cows, and people. She was pleased. She was happy.

Presently, returning to an abrupt reflective pause, she said: "Well, I may do it. I want a place where my children can come to see me and bring their friends, when they come home."

"Yes," he said, "yes. That would be nice. You mustn't work all your life."

He was pleased at her happy fable: for a moment he almost believed in a miracle of redemption, although the story was an old one to him.

"I hope you do," he said. "It would be nice. . . . Go on to bed now, why don't you, mama? It's getting late." He rose. "I'm going now."

"Yes, son," she said, getting up. "You ought to. Well, good-night." They kissed with a love, for the time, washed clean of bitterness. Eliza went before him into the dark house.

But before he went to bed, he descended to the kitchen for matches. She was still there, beyond the long littered table, at her ironing board, flanked by two big piles of laundry. At his accusing glance she said hastily:

"I'm a-going. Right away. I just wanted to finish up these towels."

He rounded the table, before he left, to kiss her again. She fished into a button-box on the sewing-machine and dug out the stub of a pencil. Gripping it firmly above an old envelope, she scrawled out on the ironing board a rough mapping. Her mind was still lulled in its project.

"Here, you see," she began, "is Sunset Avenue, coming up the hill. This is Doak Place, running off here at right angles. Now this corner-lot here belongs to Dick Webster; and right here above it, at the very top is——"

Is, he thought, staring with dull interest, the place where the Buried Treasure lies. Ten paces N.N.E. from the Big Rock, at the roots of the Old Oak Tree. He went off into his delightful fantasy while she talked. What if there *was* a buried treasure on one of Eliza's lots? If she kept on buying, there might very well be. Or why not an oil-well? Or a coal-mine? These famous mountains were full (they said) of minerals. 150 Bbl. a day right in the backyard. How much would that be? At $3.00 a Bbl., there would be over $50.00 a day for every one in the family. The world is ours!

"You see, don't you?" she smiled triumphantly. "And right there is where I shall build. That lot will bring twice its present value in five years."

"Yes," he said, kissing her. "Good-night, mama. For God's sake, go to bed and get some sleep."

"Good-night, son," said Eliza.

He went out and began to mount the dark stairs. Benjamin Gant, entering at this moment, stumbled across a mission-chair in the hall. He cursed fiercely, and struck at the chair with his hand. Damn it! Oh damn it! Mrs. Pert whispered a warning behind him, with a fuzzy laugh. Eugene paused, then mounted softly the carpeted stair, so that he would not be heard, entering the sleeping-porch at the top of the landing on which he slept.

He did not turn on the light, because he disliked seeing the raw blistered varnish of the dresser and the bent white iron of the bed. It sagged, and the light was dim—he hated dim lights, and the large moths, flapping blindly around on their dusty wings. He undressed in the moon. The moonlight fell upon the earth like a magic unearthly dawn. It wiped away all rawness, it hid all sores. It gave all common and familiar things—the sagging drift of the barn, the raw shed of the creamery, the rich curve of the lawyer's crab-apple trees—a uniform bloom of wonder. He lighted a cigarette, watching its red glowing suspiration in the mirror, and leaned upon the rail of his porch, looking out. Presently, he grew aware that Laura James, eight feet away, was watching him. The moonlight fell upon them, bathing their flesh in a green pallor, and steeping them in its silence. Their faces were blocked in miraculous darkness, out of which, seeing but unseen, their bright eyes lived. They gazed at each other in that elfin light, without speaking. In the room below them, the light crawled to his father's bed, swam up the cover, and opened across his face, thrust sharply upward. The air of the night, the air of the hills, fell on the boy's bare flesh like a sluice of clear water. His toes curled in to grip wet grasses.

On the landing, he heard Mrs. Pert go softly up to bed, fumbling with blind care at the walls. Doors creaked and clicked. The house grew solidly into quiet, like a stone beneath the moon. They looked, waiting for a spell and the conquest of time. Then she spoke to him— her whisper of his name was only a guess at sound. He threw his leg across the rail, and thrust his long body over space to the sill of her window, stretching out like a cat. She drew her breath in sharply, and cried out softly, "No! No!" but she caught his arms upon the sills and held him as he twisted in.

Then they held each other tightly in their cool young arms, and kissed many times with young lips and faces. All her hair fell down about her like thick corn-silk, in a sweet loose wantonness. Her straight dainty legs were clad in snug little green bloomers, gathered in by an elastic above the knee.

They were locked limb to limb: he kissed the smooth sheen of her arms and shoulders—the passion that numbed his limbs was governed by a religious ecstasy. He wanted to hold her, and go away by himself to think about her.

He stooped, thrusting his arm under her knees, and lifted her up exultantly. She looked at him frightened, holding him more tightly.

"What are you doing?" she whispered. "Don't hurt me."

"I won't hurt you, my dear," he said. "I'm going to put you to bed. Yes. I'm going to put you to bed. Do you hear?" He felt he must cry out in his throat for joy.

He carried her over and laid her on the bed. Then he knelt beside her, putting his arm beneath her and gathering her to him.

"Good-night, my dear. Kiss me good-night. Do you love me?"

"Yes." She kissed him. "Good-night, my darling. Don't go back by the window. You may fall."

But he went, as he came, reaching through the moonlight exultantly like a cat. For a long time he lay awake, in a quiet delirium, his heart thudding fiercely against his ribs. Sleep crept across his senses with goose-soft warmth: the young leaves of the maples rustled, a cock sounded his distant elfin minstrelsy, the ghost of a dog howled. He slept.

He awoke with a high hot sun beating in on his face through the porch awnings. He hated to awake in sunlight. Some day he would sleep in a great room that was always cool and dark. There would be trees and vines at his windows, or the scooped-out lift of the hill. His clothing was wet with night-damp as he dressed. When he went downstairs he found Gant rocking miserably upon the porch, his hand gripped over a walkingstick.

"Good-morning," he said, "how do you feel?"

His father cast his uneasy flickering eyes on him, and groaned.

"Merciful God! I'm being punished for my sins."

"You'll feel better in a little," said Eugene. "Did you eat anything?"

"It stuck in my throat," said Gant, who had eaten heartily. "I couldn't swallow a bite. How's your hand, son?" he asked very humbly.

"Oh, it's all right," said Eugene quickly. "Who told you about my hand?"

"She said I had hurt your hand," said Gant sorrowfully.

"Ah-h!" said the boy angrily. "No. I wasn't hurt."

Gant leaned to the side and, without looking, clumsily, patted his son's uninjured hand.

"I'm sorry for what I've done," he said. "I'm a sick man. Do you need money?"

"No," said Eugene, embarrassed. "I have all I need."

"Come to the office to-day, and I'll give you something," said Gant. "Poor child, I suppose you're hard up."

But instead, he waited until Laura James returned from her morning visit to the city's bathing-pool. She came with her bathing-suit in one hand, and several small packages in the other. More arrived by negro carriers. She paid and signed.

"You must have a lot of money, Laura?" he said. "You do this every day, don't you?"

"Daddy gets after me about it," she admitted, "but I love to buy clothes. I spend all my money on clothes."

"What are you going to do now?"

"Nothing—whatever you like. It's a lovely day to do something, isn't it?"

"It's a lovely day to do nothing. Would you like to go off somewhere, Laura?"

"I'd love to go off somewhere with you," said Laura James.

"That is the idea, my girl. That is the idea," he said exultantly, in throaty and exuberant burlesque. "We will go off somewhere alone—we will take along something to eat," he said lusciously.

Laura went to her room and put on a pair of sturdy little slippers. Eugene went into the kitchen.

"Have you a shoe-box?" he asked Eliza.

"What do you want that for?" she said suspiciously.

"I'm going to the bank," he said ironically. "I wanted something to carry my money in." But immediately he added roughly:

"I'm going on a picnic."

"Huh? Hah? What's that you say?" said Eliza. "A picnic? Who are you going with? That girl?"

"No," he said heavily, "with President Wilson, the King of England, and Dr. Doak. We're going to have lemonade—I've promised to bring the lemons."

"I'll vow, boy!" said Eliza fretfully. "I don't like it—your running off this way when I need you. I wanted you to make a deposit for me, and the telephone people will disconnect me if I don't send them the money to-day."

"O mama! For God's sake!" he cried annoyed. "You always need me when I want to go somewhere. Let them wait! They can wait a day."

"It's overdue," she said. "Well, here you are. I wish I had time to go off on picnics." She fished a shoe-box out of a pile of magazines and newspapers that littered the top of a low cupboard.

"Have you got anything to eat?"

"We'll get it," he said, and departed.

They went down the hill, and paused at the musty little grocery around the corner on Woodson Street, where they bought crackers, peanut butter, currant jelly, bottled pickles, and a big slice of rich yellow cheese. The grocer was an old Jew who muttered jargon into a rabbi's beard as if saying a spell against Dybbuks. The boy looked closely to see if his hands touched the food. They were not clean.

On their way up the hill, they stopped for a few minutes at Gant's. They found Helen and Ben in the dining-room. Ben was eating breakfast, bending, as usual, with scowling attention, over his coffee, turning from eggs and bacon almost with disgust. Helen insisted on contributing boiled eggs and sandwiches to their provision: the two women went back into the kitchen. Eugene sat at table with Ben, drinking coffee.

"O-oh my God!" Ben said at length, yawning wearily. He lighted a cigarette. "How's the Old Man this morning?"

"He's all right, I think. Said he couldn't eat breakfast."

"Did he say anything to the boarders?"

" 'You damned scoundrels! You dirty Mountain Grills! Whee—!' That was all."

Ben snickered quietly.

"Did he hurt your hand? Let's see."

"No. You can't see anything. It's not hurt," said Eugene, lifting his bandaged wrist.

"He didn't hit you, did he?" asked Ben sternly.

"Oh, no. Of course not. He was just drunk. He was sorry about it this morning."

"Yes," said Ben, "he's always sorry about it—after he's raised all the hell he can." He drank deeply at his cigarette, inhaling the smoke as if in the grip of a powerful drug.

"How'd you get along at college this year, 'Gene?" he asked presently.

"I passed my work. I made fair grades—if that's what you mean? I did better—this Spring," he added, with some difficulty. "It was hard getting started—at the beginning."

"You mean last Fall?"

Eugene nodded.

"What was the matter?" said Ben, scowling at him. "Did the other boys make fun of you?"

"Yes," said Eugene, in a low voice.

"Why did they? You mean they didn't think you were good enough for them? Did they look down on you? Was that it?" said Ben savagely.

"No," said Eugene, very red in the face. "No. That had nothing to do with it. I look funny, I suppose. I looked funny to them."

"What do you mean you look funny?" said Ben pugnaciously. "There's nothing wrong with you, you know, if you didn't go around looking like a bum. In God's name," he exclaimed angrily, "when did you get that hair cut last? What do you think you are: the Wild Man from Borneo?"

"I don't like barbers!" Eugene burst out furiously. "That's why! I don't want them to go sticking their damned dirty fingers in my mouth. Whose business is it, if I never get my hair cut?"

"A man is judged by his appearance to-day," said Ben sententiously. "I was reading an article by a big business man in *The Post* the other day. He says he always looks at a man's shoes before he gives him a job."

He spoke seriously, haltingly, in the same way that he read, without genuine conviction. Eugene writhed to hear his fierce condor prattle this stale hash of the canny millionaires, like any obedient parrot in a teller's cage. Ben's voice had a dull flat quality as he uttered these admirable opinions: he seemed to grope behind it all for some answer, with hurt puzzled eyes. As he faltered along, with scowling intensity, through a success-sermon, there was something poignantly moving in his effort: it was the effort of his strange and lonely spirit to find some entrance into life—to find success, position, companionship. And it was as if, spelling the words out with his mouth, a settler in the Bronx from the fat Lombard plain, should try to unriddle the new world by deciphering the World Almanac, or as if some woodsman, trapped by the winter, and wasted by an obscure and terrible disease, should hunt its symptoms and its cure in a book of Household Remedies.

"Did the Old Man send you enough money to get along on?" Ben asked. "Were you able to hold your own with the other boys? He can afford it, you know. Don't let him stint you. Make him give it to you, 'Gene."

"I had plenty," said Eugene, "all that I needed."

"This is the time you need it—not later," said Ben. "Make him put you through college. This is an age of specialization. They're looking for college-trained men."

"Yes," said Eugene. He spoke obediently, indifferently, the hard bright mail of his mind undinted by the jargon: within, the Other One, who had no speech, saw.

"So get your education," said Ben, scowling vaguely. "All the Big Men—Ford, Edison, Rockefeller—whether they had it or not, say it's a good thing."

"Why didn't you go yourself?" said Eugene curiously.

"I didn't have any one to tell me," said Ben. "Besides, you don't think the Old Man would give me anything, do you?" He laughed cynically. "It's too late now."

He was silent a moment; he smoked.

"You didn't know I was taking a course in advertising, did you?" he asked, grinning.

"No. Where?"

"Through the Correspondence School," said Ben. "I get my lessons every week. I don't know," he laughed diffidently, "I must be good at it. I make the highest grades they have—98 or 100 every time. I get a diploma, if I finish the course."

A blinding mist swam across the younger brother's eyes. He did not know why. A convulsive knot gathered in his throat. He bent his head quickly and fumbled for his cigarettes. In a moment he said:

"I'm glad you're doing it. I hope you finish, Ben."

"You know," Ben said seriously, "they've turned out some Big Men. I'll show you the testimonials some time. Men who started with nothing: now they're holding down big jobs."

"I hope you do," said Eugene.

"So, you see you're not the only College Man around here," said Ben with a grin. In a moment, he went on gravely: "You're the last hope, 'Gene. Go on and finish up, if you have to steal the money. The rest of us will never amount to a damn. Try to make something out of yourself. Hold your head up! You're as good as any of them—a damn sight better than these little pimps about town." He became very fierce; he was very excited. He got up suddenly from the table. "Don't let them laugh at you! By God, we're as good as they are. If any of them laughs at you again, pick up the first damn thing you get your hand on and knock him down. Do you hear?" In his fierce excitement he snatched up the heavy carving steel from the table and brandished it.

"Yes," said Eugene awkwardly. "I think it's going to be all right now. I didn't know how to do at first."

"I hope you have sense enough now to leave those old hookers alone?" said Ben very sternly. Eugene made no answer. "You can't do that and be anything, you know. And you're likely to catch everything. This looks like a nice girl," he said quietly, after a pause. "For heaven's sake, fix yourself up and try to keep fairly clean. Women notice that, you know. Look after your fingernails, and keep your clothes pressed. Have you any money?"

"All I need," said Eugene, looking nervously toward the kitchen. "Don't, for God's sake!"

"Put it in your pocket, you little fool," Ben said angrily, thrusting a bill into his hand. "You've got to have some money. Keep it until you need it."

Helen came out on the high front porch with them as they departed. As usual, she had added a double heaping measure to what they needed. There was another shoe-box stuffed with sandwiches, boiled eggs, and fudge.

She stood on the high step-edge, with a cloth wound over her head, her gaunt arms, pitted with old scars, akimbo. A warm sunny odor of nasturtiums, loamy earth, and honeysuckle washed round them its hot spermy waves.

"O-ho! A-ha!" she winked comically. "I know something! I'm not as blind as you think, you know—" She nodded with significant jocularity, her big smiling face drenched in the curious radiance and purity that occasionally dwelt so beautifully there. He thought always when he saw her thus, of a sky washed after rain, of wide crystalline distances, cool and clean.

With a rough snigger she prodded him in the ribs:

"Ain't love grand! Ha-ha-ha-ha! Look at his face, Laura." She drew the girl close to her in a generous hug, laughing, Oh, with laughing pity, and as they mounted the hill, she stood there, in the sunlight, her mouth slightly open, smiling, touched with radiance, beauty, and wonder.

They mounted slowly toward the eastern edge of town, by the long upward sweep of Academy Street, which bordered the negro settlement sprawled below it. At the end of Academy Street, the hill loomed abruptly; a sinuous road, well paved, curved up along the hillside to the right. They turned into this road, mounting now along the eastern edge of

Niggertown. The settlement fell sharply away below them, rushing down along a series of long clay streets. There were a few frame houses by the roadside: the dwellings of negroes and poor white people, but these became sparser as they mounted. They walked at a leisurely pace up the cool road speckled with little dancing patches of light that filtered through the arching trees and shaded on the left by the dense massed foliage of the hill. Out of this green loveliness loomed the huge raw turret of a cement reservoir: it was streaked and blotted coolly with water-marks. Eugene felt thirsty. Further along, the escape from a smaller reservoir roared from a pipe in a foaming hawser, as thick as a man's body.

They climbed sharply up, along a rocky trail, avoiding the last long corkscrew of the road, and stood in the gap, at the road's summit. They were only a few hundred feet above the town: it lay before them with the sharp nearness of a Sienese picture, at once close and far. On the highest ground, he saw the solid masonry of the Square, blocked cleanly out in light and shadow, and a crawling toy that was a car, and men no bigger than sparrows. And about the Square was the treeless brick jungle of business—cheap, ragged, and ugly, and beyond all this, in indefinite patches, the houses where all the people lived, with little bright raw ulcers of suburbia further off, and the healing and concealing grace of fair massed trees. And below him, weltering up from the hollow along the flanks and shoulders of the hill, was Niggertown. There seemed to be a kind of centre at the Square, where all the cars crawled in and waited, yet there was no purpose anywhere.

But the hills were lordly, with a plan. Westward, they widened into the sun, soaring up from buttressing shoulders. The town was thrown up on the plateau like an encampment: there was nothing below him that could resist time. There was no idea. Below him, in a cup, he felt that all life was held: he saw it as might one of the old schoolmen writing in monkish Latin a Theatre of Human Life; or like Peter Breughel, in one of his swarming pictures. It seemed to him suddenly that he had not come up on the hill from the town, but that he had come out of the wilderness like a beast, and was staring now with steady beast-eye at this little huddle of wood and mortar which the wilderness must one day repossess, devour, cover over.

The seventh from the top was Troy—but Helen had lived there; and so the German dug it up.

They turned from the railing, with recovered wind, and walked through the gap, under Philip Roseberry's great arched bridge. To the left, on the summit, the rich Jew had his cattle, his stables, his horses, his cows, and his daughters. As they went under the shadow of the bridge Eugene lifted his head and shouted. His voice bounded against the arch like a stone. They passed under and stood on the other side of the gap, looking from the road's edge down into the cove. But they could not yet see the cove, save for green glimmers. The hillside was thickly wooded, the road wound down its side in a white perpetual corkscrew. But they could look across at the fair wild hills on the other side of the cove, cleared half-way up their flanks with ample field and fenced meadow, and forested above with a billowing sea of greenery.

The day was like gold and sapphires: there was a swift flash and sparkle, intangible and multifarious, like sunlight on roughened water, all over the land. A rich warm wind was blowing, turning all the leaves back the same way, and making mellow music through all the lute-strings of flower and grass and fruit. The wind moaned, not with the mad fiend-voice of winter in harsh boughs, but like a fruitful woman, deep-breasted, great, full of love and wisdom; like Demeter unseen and hunting through the world. A dog bayed faintly in the cove, his howl spent and broken by the wind. A cowbell tinkled gustily. In the thick wood below them the rich notes of birds fell from their throats, straight down, like nuggets. A woodpecker drummed on the dry unbarked hole of a blasted chestnut-tree. The blue gulf of the sky was spread with light massy clouds: they cruised like swift galleons, tacking across the hills before the wind, and darkening the trees below with their floating shadows.

The boy grew blind with love and desire: the cup of his heart was glutted with all this wonder. It overcame and weakened him. He grasped the girl's cool fingers. They stood leg to leg, riven into each other's flesh. Then they left the road, cutting down across its loops along steep wooded paths. The wood was a vast green church; the bird-cries fell like plums. A great butterfly, with wings of blue velvet streaked with gold and scarlet markings, fluttered heavily before them in freckled sunlight, tottering to rest finally upon a spray of dogwood. There were light skimming noises in the dense undergrowth to either side, the swift bullet-shadows of birds. A garter snake, greener than wet moss, as long as a shoelace and no thicker than a woman's little finger, shot across the path, its tiny eyes bright with terror, its small forked tongue playing from its mouth like an electric spark. Laura cried out, drawing back in sharp terror; at her cry he snatched up a stone in a wild lust to kill the tiny creature that shot at them, through its coils, the old snake-fear, touching

them with beauty, with horror, with something supernatural. But the
snake glided away into the undergrowth and, with a feeling of strong
shame, he threw the stone away. "They won't hurt you," he said.

At length, they came out above the cove, at a forking of the road.
They turned left, to the north, toward the upper and smaller end. To
the south, the cove widened out in a rich little Eden of farm and pasture.
Small houses dotted the land, there were green meadows and a glint of
water. Fields of young green wheat bent rhythmically under the wind;
the young corn stood waist-high, with light clashing blades. The chimneys
of Rheinhart's house showed above its obscuring grove of maples; the
fat dairy cows grazed slowly across the wide pastures. And further
below, half tree-and-shrub-hidden, lay the rich acres of Judge Webster
Tayloe. The road was thickly coated with white dust; it dipped down
and ran through a little brook. They crossed over on white rocks, strewn
across its bed. Several ducks, scarcely disturbed by their crossing, waddled
up out of the clear water and regarded them gravely, like little children
in white choir aprons. A young country fellow clattered by them in a
buggy filled with empty milk-cans. He grinned with a cordial red face,
saluting them with a slow gesture, and leaving behind an odor of milk
and sweat and butter. A woman, in a field above them, stared curiously
with shaded eyes. In another field, a man was mowing with a scythe,
moving into the grass like a god upon his enemies, with a reaping hook
of light.

They left the road near the head of the cove, advancing over the fields
on rising ground to the wooded cup of the hills. There was a powerful
masculine strench of broad dock-leaves, a hot weedy odor. They moved
over a pathless field, knee-high in a dry stubbly waste, gathering on their
clothes clusters of brown cockle-burrs. All the field was sown with hot
odorous daisies. Then they entered the wood again, mounting until they
came to an island of tender grass, by a little brook that fell down from
the green hill along a rocky ferny bed in bright cascades.

"Let's stop here," said Eugene. The grass was thick with dandelions:
their poignant and wordless odor studded the earth with yellow magic.
They were like gnomes and elves, and tiny witchcraft in flower and acorn.

Laura and Eugene lay upon their backs, looking up through the high
green shimmer of leaves at the Caribbean sky, with all its fleet of cloudy
ships. The water of the brook made a noise like silence. The town behind
the hill lay in another unthinkable world. They forgot its pain and
conflict.

"What time is it?" Eugene asked. For, they had come to a place where no time was. Laura held up her exquisite wrist, and looked at her watch.

"Why!" she exclaimed, surprised. "It's only half-past twelve!"

But he scarcely heard her.

"What do I care what time it is!" he said huskily, and he seized the lovely hand, bound with its silken watch-cord, and kissed it. Her long cool fingers closed around his own; she drew his face down to her mouth.

They lay there, locked together, upon that magic carpet, in that paradise. Her gray eyes were deeper and clearer than a pool of clear water; he kissed the little freckles on her rare skin; he gazed reverently at the snub tilt of her nose; he watched the mirrored dance of the sparkling water over her face. All of that magic world—flower and field and sky and hill, and all the sweet woodland cries, sound and sight and odor—grew into him, one voice in his heart, one tongue in his brain, harmonious, radiant, and whole—a single passionate lyrical noise.

"My dear! Darling! Do you remember last night?" he asked fondly, as if recalling some event of her childhood.

"Yes," she gathered her arms tightly about his neck, "why do you think I could forget it?"

"Do you remember what I said—what I asked you to do?" he insisted eagerly.

"Oh, what are we going to do? What are we going to do?" she moaned, turning her head to the side and flinging an arm across her eyes.

"What is it? What's the matter? Dear?"

"Eugene—my dear, you're only a child. I'm so old—a grown woman."

"You're only twenty-one," he said. "There's only five years' difference. That's nothing."

"Oh!" she said. "You don't know what you're saying. It's all the difference in the world."

"When I'm twenty, you'll be twenty-five. When I'm twenty-six, you'll be thirty-one. When I'm forty-eight, you'll be fifty-three. What's that?" he said contemptuously. "Nothing."

"Everything," she said, "everything. If I were sixteen, and you twenty-one it would be nothing. But you're a boy and I'm a woman. When you're a young man I'll be an old maid; when you grow old I shall be dying. How do you know where you'll be, what you'll be doing five years from now?" she continued in a moment. "You're only a boy—you've just started college. You have no plans yet. You don't know what you're going to do."

"Yes, I do!" he yelled furiously. "I'm going to be a lawyer. That's what they're sending me for. I'm going to be a lawyer, and I'm going into politics. Perhaps," he added with gloomy pleasure, "you'll be sorry then, after I make a name for myself." With bitter joy he foresaw his lonely celebrity. The Governor's Mansion. Forty rooms. Alone. Alone

"You're going to be a lawyer," said Laura, "and you're going everywhere in the world, and I'm to wait for you, and never get married. You poor kid!" She laughed softly. "You don't know what you're going to do."

He turned a face of misery on her; brightness dropped from the sun.

"You don't care?" he choked. "You don't care?" He bent his head to hide his wet eyes.

"Oh, my dear," she said, "I do care. But people don't live like that. It's like a story. Don't you know that I'm a grown woman? At my age, dear, most girls have begun to think of getting married. What—what if I had begun to think of it, too?"

"Married!" The word came from him in a huge gasp of horror as if she had mentioned the abominable, proposed the unspeakable. Then, having heard the monstrous suggestion, he immediately accepted it as a fact. He was like that.

"So! That's it!" he said furiously. "You're going to get married, eh? You have fellows, have you? You go out with them, do you? You've known it all the time, and you've tried to fool me."

Nakedly, with breast bare to horror, he scourged himself, knowing in the moment that the nightmare cruelty of life is not in the remote and fantastic, but in the probable—the horror of love, loss, marriage, the ninety seconds treason in the dark.

"You have fellows—you let them feel you. They feel your legs, they play with your breasts, they—" His voice became inaudible through strangulation.

"No. No, my dear. I haven't said so," she rose swiftly to a sitting position, taking his hands. "But there's nothing unusual about getting married, you know. Most people do. Oh, my dear! Don't look like that! Nothing has happened. Nothing! Nothing!"

He seized her fiercely, unable to speak. Then he buried his face in her neck.

"Laura! My dear! My sweet! Don't leave me alone! I've been alone! I've always been alone!"

"It's what you want, dear. It's what you'll always want. You couldn't stand anything else. You'd get so tired of me. You'll forget this ever happened. You'll forget me. You'll forget—forget."

"Forget! I'll never forget! I won't live long enough."

"And I'll never love any one else! I'll never leave you! I'll wait for you forever! Oh, my child, my child!"

They clung together in that bright moment of wonder, there on the magic island, where the world was quiet, believing all they said. And who shall say—whatever disenchantment follows—that we ever forget magic, or that we can ever betray, on this leaden earth, the apple-tree, the singing, and the gold? Far out beyond that timeless valley, a train, on the rails for the East, wailed back its ghostly cry: life, like a fume of painted smoke, a broken wrack of cloud, drifted away. Their world was a singing voice again: they were young and they could never die. This would endure.

He kissed her on her splendid eyes; he grew into her young Mænad's body, his heart numbed deliciously against the pressure of her narrow breasts. She was as lithe and yielding to his sustaining hand as a willow rod—she was bird-swift, more elusive in repose than the dancing water-motes upon her face. He held her tightly lest she grow into the tree again, or be gone amid the wood like smoke.

Come up into the hills, O my young love. Return! O lost, and by the wind grieved, ghost, come back again, as first I knew you in the timeless valley, where we shall feel ourselves anew, bedded on magic in the month of June. There was a place where all the sun went glistering in your hair, and from the hill we could have put a finger on a star. Where is the day that melted into one rich noise? Where the music of your flesh, the rhyme of your teeth, the dainty languor of your legs, your small firm arms, your slender fingers, to be bitten like an apple, and the little cherry-teats of your white breasts? And where are all the tiny wires of finespun maidenhair? Quick are the mouths of earth, and quick the teeth that fed upon this loveliness. You who were made for music, will hear music no more: in your dark house the winds are silent. Ghost, ghost, come back from that marriage that we did not foresee, return not into life, but into magic, where we have never died, into the enchanted wood, where we still lie, strewn on the grass. Come up into the hills, O my young love: return. O lost, and by the wind grieved, ghost, come back again.

31

One day, when June was coming to its end, Laura James said to him: "I shall have to go home next week." Then, seeing his stricken face, she added, "but only for a few days—not more than a week."

"But why? The summer's only started. You will burn up down there."

"Yes. It's silly, I know. But my people expect me for the Fourth of July. You know, we have an enormous family—hundred of aunts, cousins, and in-laws. We have a family re-union every year—a great barbecue and picnic. I hate it. But they'd never forgive me if I didn't come."

Frightened, he looked at her for a moment.

"Laura! You're coming back, aren't you?" he said quietly.

"Yes, of course," she said. "Be quiet."

He was trembling violently; he was afraid to question her more closely.

"Be quiet," she whispered, "quiet!" She put her arms around him.

He went with her to the station on a hot mid-afternoon. There was a smell of melted tar in the streets. She held his hand beside her in the rattling trolley, squeezing his fingers to give him comfort, and whispering from time to time:

"In a week! Only a week, dear."

"I don't see the need," he muttered. "It's over 400 miles. Just for a few days."

He passed the old one-legged gateman on the station platform very easily, carrying her baggage. Then he sat beside her in the close green heat of the pullman until the train should go. A little electric fan droned uselessly above the aisle; a prim young lady whom he knew, arranged herself amid the bright new leather of her bags. She returned his greeting elegantly, with a shade of refined hauteur, then looked out the window again, grimacing eloquently at her parents who gazed at her raptly from the platform. Several prosperous merchants went down the aisle in expensive tan shoes that creaked under the fan's drone.

"Not going to leave us, are you, Mr. Morris?"

"Hello, Jim. No, I'm running up to Richmond for a few days." But even the gray weather of their lives could not deaden the excitement of that hot chariot to the East.

" 'Board!"

He got up trembling.

"In a few days, dear." She looked up, taking his hand in her small gloved palms.

"You will write as soon as you get there? Please!"

"Yes. To-morrow—at once."

He bent down suddenly and whispered, "Laura—you will come back. You will come back!"

She turned her face away and wept bitterly. He sat beside her once more; she clasped him tightly as if he had been a child.

"My dear, my dear! Don't forget me ever!"

"Never. Come back. Come back."

The salt print of her kiss was on his mouth, his face, his eyes. It was, he knew, the guttering candle-end of time. The train was in motion. He leaped blindly up the passage with a cry in his throat.

"Come back again!"

But he knew. Her cry followed him, as if he had torn something from her grasp.

Within three days he had his letter. On four sheets of paper, bordered with victorious little American flags, this:

"My dear: I got home at half-past one, just too tired to move. I couldn't sleep on the train at all last night, it seemed to get hotter all the way down. I was so blue when I got here, I almost cried. Little Richmond is too ghastly for words—everything burned up and every one gone away to the mountains or the sea. How can I ever stand it even for a week!" (Good! he thought. If the weather holds, she will come back all the sooner.) "It would be heaven now to get one breath of mountain air. Could you find your way back to our place in the valley again?" (Yes, even if I were blind, he thought.) "Will you promise to look after your hand until it gets well? I worried so after you had gone, because I forgot to change the bandage yesterday. Daddy was glad to see me: he said he was not going to let me go again but, don't worry, I'll have my own way in the end. I always do. I don't know any one at home any more—all of the boys have enlisted or

gone to work in the shipyards at Norfolk. Most of the girls I know are getting married, or married already. That leaves only the kids." (He winced.
As old as I am, maybe older.) "Give my love to Mrs. Barton, and tell your
mother I said she must not work so hard in that hot kitchen. And all the
little cross-marks at the bottom are for you. Try to guess what they are.

LAURA."

He read her prosy letter with rigid face, devouring the words more
hungrily than if they had been lyrical song. She would come back! She
would come back! Soon.

There was another page. Weakened and relaxed from his excitement, he
looked at it. There he found, almost illegibly written, but at last in her own
speech, as if leaping out from the careful aimlessness of her letter, this note:

"July 4.

"Richard came yesterday. He is twenty-five, works in Norfolk. I've been
engaged to him almost a year. We're going off quietly to Norfolk to-
morrow and get married. My dear! My dear! I couldn't tell you! I tried to,
but couldn't. I didn't want to lie. Everything else was true. I meant all I
said. If you hadn't been so young, but what's the use of saying that? Try
to forgive me, but please don't forget me. Good-by and God bless you. Oh,
my darling, it was heaven! I shall never forget you."

When he had finished the letter, he re-read it, slowly and carefully. Then
he folded it, put it in his inner breast-pocket, and leaving Dixieland, walked
for forty minutes, until he came up in the gap over the town again. It was
sunset. The sun's vast rim, blood-red, rested upon the western earth, in a
great field of murky pollen. It sank beyond the western ranges. The clear
sweet air was washed with gold and pearl. The vast hills melted into
purple solitudes: they were like Canaan and rich grapes. The motors of
cove people toiled up around the horse-shoe of the road. Dusk came. The
bright winking lights in the town went up. Darkness melted over the
town like dew: it washed out all the day's distress, the harsh confusions.
Low wailing sounds came faintly up from Niggertown.

And above him the proud stars flashed into heaven: there was one, so
rich and low, that he could have picked it, if he had climbed the hill beyond
the Jew's great house. One, like a lamp, hung low above the heads of men
returning home. (O Hesperus, you bring us all good things.) One had
flashed out the light that winked on him the night that Ruth lay at the feet

of Boaz; and one on Queen Isolt; and one on Corinth and on Troy. It was night, vast brooding night, the mother of loneliness, that washes our stains away. He was washed in the great river of night, in the Ganges tides of redemption. His bitter wound was for the moment healed in him: he turned his face upward to the proud and tender stars, which made him a god and a grain of dust, the brother of eternal beauty and the son of death——alone, alone.

"Ha-ha-ha-ha!" Helen laughed huskily, prodding him in the ribs. "Your girl went and got married, didn't she? She fooled you. You got left."

"Wh-a-a-a-t!" said Eliza banteringly, "has my boy been—as the fellow says" (she sniggered behind her hand) "has my boy been a-courtin'?" She puckered her lips in playful reproach.

"Oh, for God's sake," he muttered angrily, "What fellow says!"

His scowl broke into an angry grin as he caught his sister's eye. They laughed.

"Well, 'Gene," said the girl seriously, "forget about it. You're only a kid yet. Laura is a grown woman."

"Why, son," said Eliza with a touch of malice, "that girl was fooling you all the time. She was just leading you on."

"Oh, stop it, please."

"Cheer up!" said Helen heartily. "Your time's coming. You'll forget her in a week. There are plenty more, you know. This is puppy love. Show her that you're a good sport. You ought to write her a letter of congratulation."

"Why, yes," said Eliza, "I'd make a big joke of it all. I wouldn't let on to her that it affected me. I'd write her just as big as you please and laugh about the whole thing. I'd show them! That's what I'd——"

"Oh, for God's sake!" he groaned, starting up. "Leave me alone, won't you?"

He left the house.

But he wrote the letter. And the moment after the lid of the mailbox clanged over it, he was writhen by shame. For it was a proud and boastful letter, salted with scatterings of Greek, Latin, and English verse, quotable scraps, wrenched into the text without propriety, without accuracy, without anything but his pitiful and obvious desire to show her his weight in the point of his wit, the depth of his learning. She would be sorry when she knew her loss! But, for a moment at the end, his fiercely beating heart stormed through:

". . . and I hope he's worth having you—he can't deserve you, Laura; no one can. But if he knows what he has, that's something. How lucky he is! You're right about me—I'm too young. I'd cut off my hand now for eight or ten years more. God bless and keep you, my dear, dear Laura.

"Something in me wants to burst. It keeps trying to, but it won't, it never has. O God! If it only would! I shall never forget you. I'm lost now and I'll never find the way again. In God's name write me a line when you get this. Tell me what your name is now—you never have. Tell me where you're going to live. Don't let me go entirely, I beg of you, don't leave me alone."

He sent the letter to the address she had given him—to her father's house. Week melted into week: his life mounted day by day in a terrible tension to the delivery of the mail, morning and afternoon, fell then into a miasmic swamp when no word came. July ended. The summer waned. She did not write.

Upon the darkening porch, awaiting food, the boarders rocked, oh rocked with laughter.

The boarders said: "Eugene's lost his girl. He doesn't know what to do, he's lost his girl."

"Well, well! Did the Old Boy lose his girl?"

The little fat girl, the daughter of one of the two fat sisters whose husbands were hotel clerks in Charleston, skipped to and from him, in slow May dance, with fat calves twinkling brownly above her socks.

"Lost his girl! Lost his girl! Eugene, Eugene, has lost his girl."

The fat little girl skipped back to her fat mother for approbation: they regarded each other with complacent smiles loosely netted in their full-meated mouths.

"Don't let them kid you, big boy. What's the matter: did some one get your girl?" asked Mr. Hake, the flour salesman. He was a dapper young man of twenty-six years, who smoked large cigars; he had a tapering face, and a high domey head, bald on top, fringed sparsely with fine blond hair. His mother, a large grass-widow near fifty, with the powerful craggy face of an Indian, a large mass of dyed yellow hair, and a coarse smile, full of gold and heartiness, rocked mightily, laughing with hoarse compassion:

"Git another girl, 'Gene. Why, law! I'd not let it bother me two minutes."

He always expected her to spit, emphatically, with gusto, after speaking.

"You should worry, boy. You should *worry!*" said Mr. Farrel, of Miami, the dancing instructor. "Women are like street-cars: if you miss one, there's another along in fifteen minutes. Ain't that right, lady?" he said pertly, turning to Miss Clark, of Valdosta, Georgia, for whom it had been uttered. She answered with a throaty confused twiddle-giggle of laughter. "Oh, aren't men the awfullest——"

Leaning upon the porch rail in the thickening dusk, Mr. Jake Clapp, a well-to-do widower from Old Hominy, pursued his stealthy courtship of Miss Florry Mangle, the trained nurse. Her limp face made a white blot in the darkness; she spoke in a tired whine:

"I thought she was too old for him when I saw her. 'Gene's only a kid. He's taken it hard, you can tell by looking at him how miserable he is. He's going to get sick if he keeps on at this rate. He's thin as a bone. He hardly eats a bite. People get run down like that and catch the first disease that comes along——"

Her melancholy whine continued as Jake's stealthy thigh fumbled against her. She kept her arms carefully folded across her sagging breasts.

In the gray darkness, the boy turned his starved face on them. His dirty clothes lapped round his scarecrow body: his eyes burned like a cat's in the dark, his hair fell over his forehead in a matted net.

"He'll git over it," said Jake Clapp, in a precise country drawl, streaked with a note of bawdry. "Every boy has got to go through the Calf-Love stage. When I was about 'Gene's age——" He pressed his hard thigh gently against Florry, grinning widely and thinly with a few gold teeth. He was a tall solid man, with a hard precise face, lewdly decorous, and slanting Mongol eyes. His head was bald and knobby.

"He'd better watch out," whined Florry sadly. "I know what I'm talking about. That boy's not strong—he has no business to go prowling around to all hours the way he does. He's on the verge of——"

Eugene rocked gently on his feet, staring at the boarders with a steady hate. Suddenly he snarled like a wild beast, and started down the porch, unable to speak, reeling, but snarling again and again his choking and insane fury.

"Miss Brown" meanwhile sat primly at the end of the porch, a little apart from the others. From the dark sun-parlor at the side came swiftly the tall elegant figure of Miss Irene Mallard, twenty-eight, of Tampa, Florida. She caught him at the step edge, and pulled him round sharply, gripping his arms lightly with her cool long fingers.

"Where are you going, 'Gene?" she said quietly. Her eyes of light violet were a little tired. There was a faint exquisite perfume of rosewater.

"Leave me alone!" he muttered.

"You can't go on like this," she said in a low tone. "She's not worth it—none of them are. Pull yourself together."

"Leave me alone!" he said furiously. "I know what I'm doing!" He wrenched away violently, and leaped down into the yard, plunging around the house in a staggering run.

"Ben!" said Irene Mallard sharply.

Ben rose from the dark porch-swing where he had been sitting with Mrs. Pert.

"See if you can't do something to stop him," said Irene Mallard.

"He's crazy," Ben muttered. "Which way did he go?"

"By there—around the house. Go quick!"

Ben went swiftly down the shallow steps and loped back over the lawn. The yard sloped sharply down: the gaunt back of Dixieland was propped upon a dozen rotting columns of whitewashed brick, fourteen feet high. In the dim light, by one of these slender piers, already mined with crumbling ruins of wet brick, the scarecrow crouched, toiling with the thin grapevine of his arms against the temple.

"I will kill you, House," he gasped. "Vile and accursed House, I will tear you down. I will bring you down upon the whores and boarders. I will wreck you, House."

Another convulsion of his shoulders brought down a sprinkling rain of dust and rubble.

"I will make you fall down on all the people in you, House," he said.

"Fool!" cried Ben, leaping upon him, "what are you trying to do?" He caught the boy's arms from behind and dragged him back. "Do you think you can bring her back to you by wrecking the house? Are there no other women in the world, that you should let one get the best of you like this?"

"Let me go! Let me go!" said Eugene. "What does it matter to you?"

"Don't think, fool, that I care," said Ben fiercely. "You're hurting no one but yourself. Do you think you'll hurt the boarders by pulling the house down on your own head? Do you think, idiot, that any one cares if you kill yourself?" He shook the boy. "No. No. I don't care what you do, you know. I simply want to save the family the trouble and expense of burying you."

With a great cry of rage and bafflement Eugene tried to free himself. But the older brother held on as desperately as the Old Man of the Sea. Then, with a great effort of his hands and shoulders, the boy lifted his captor off the ground, and dashed him back against the white brick wall of the cellar. Ben collapsed, releasing him, with a fit of dry coughing, holding his hand against his thin breast.

"Don't be a fool," he gasped.

"Did I hurt you?" said Eugene dully.

"No. Go into the house and wash yourself. You ought to comb your hair once or twice a week, you know. You can't go around like a wild man. Get something to eat. Have you any money?"

"Yes—I have enough."

"Are you all right now?"

"Yes—don't talk about it, please."

"I don't want to talk about it, fool. I want you to learn a little sense," said Ben. He straightened, brushing his whitened coat. In a moment, he went on quietly: "To hell with them, 'Gene. To hell with them all. Don't let them worry you. Get all that you can. Don't give a damn for anything. Nothing gives a damn for you. To hell with it all! To hell with it! There are a lot of bad days. There are a lot of good ones. You'll forget. There are a lot of days. Let it go."

"Yes," said Eugene wearily, "let it go. It's all right now. I'm too tired. When you get tired you don't care, do you? I'm too tired to care. I'll never care any more. I'm too tired. The men in France get tired and don't care. If a man came and pointed a gun at me now, I wouldn't be scared. I'm too tired." He began to laugh, loosely, with a sense of delicious relief. "I don't care for any one or anything. I've always been afraid of everything, but when I got tired I didn't care. That's how I shall get over everything. I shall get tired."

Ben lighted a cigarette.

"That's better," he said. "Let's get something to eat." He smiled thinly. "Come along, Samson."

They walked out slowly around the house.

He washed himself, and ate a hearty meal. The boarders finished, and wandered off into the darkness variously—some to the band-concert on the Square, some to the moving-pictures, some for walks through the town. When he had fed he went out on the porch. It was dark and almost empty save where, at the side, Mrs. Selborne sat in the swing with a wealthy lumber man from Tennessee. Her low rich laughter bubbled up softly from the vat of the dark. "Miss Brown" rocked quietly and decorously by herself. She was a heavily built and quietly dressed woman of thirty-nine years, touched with that slightly comic primness—that careful gentility—that marks the conduct of the prostitute incognito. She was being very refined. She was a perfect lady and would, if aroused, assert the fact.

"Miss Brown" lived, she said, in Indianapolis. She was not ugly: her face was simply permeated with the implacable dullness of the Mid-Westerner. In spite of the lewdness of her wide thin mouth, her look was smug. She had a fair mass of indifferent brown hair, rather small brown eyes, and a smooth russet skin.

"Pshaw!" said Eliza. "I don't believe her name's 'Miss Brown' any more than mine is."

There had been rain. The night was cool and black; the flower-bed before the house was wet, with a smell of geraniums and drenched pansies. He lighted a cigarette, sitting upon the rail. "Miss Brown" rocked.

"It's turned off cool," she said. "That little bit of rain has done a lot of good, hasn't it?"

"Yes, it was hot," he said. "I hate hot weather."

"I can't stand it either," she said. "That's why I go away every summer. Out my way we catch it. You folks here don't know what hot weather is."

"You're from Milwaukee, aren't you?"

"Indianapolis."

"I knew it was somewhere out there. Is it a big place?" he asked curiously.

"Yes. You could put Altamont in one corner of it and never miss it."

"How big is it?" he said eagerly. "How many people have you there?"

"I don't know exactly—over three hundred thousand with the suburbs."

He reflected with greedy satisfaction.

"Is it pretty? Are there a lot of pretty houses and fine buildings?"

"Yes—I think so," she said reflectively. "It's a nice homelike place."

"What are the people like? What do they do? Are they rich?"

"Why—yes. It's a business and manufacturing place. There are a lot of rich people."

"I suppose they live in big houses and ride around in big cars, eh?" he demanded. Then, without waiting for a reply, he went on: "Do they have good things to eat? What?"

She laughed awkwardly, puzzled and confused.

"Why, yes. There's a great deal of German cooking. Do you like German cooking?"

"Beer!" he muttered lusciously. "Beer—eh? You make it out there?"

"Yes." She laughed, with a voluptuous note in her voice. "I believe you're a bad boy, Eugene."

"And what about the theatres and libraries? You have lots of shows, don't you?"

"Yes. A lot of good shows come to Indianapolis. All the big hits in New York and Chicago."

"And a library—you have a big one, eh?"

"Yes. We have a nice library."

"How many books has it?"

"Oh, I can't say as to that. But it's a good big library."

"Over 100,000 books, do you suppose? They wouldn't have half a million, would they?" He did not wait for an answer, he was talking to himself. "No, of course not. How many books can you take out at a time? What?"

The great shadow of his hunger bent over her; he rushed out of himself, devouring her with his questions.

"What are the girls like? Are they blonde or brunette? What?"

"Why, we have both kinds—more dark than fair, I should say." She looked through the darkness at him, grinning.

"Are they pretty?"

"Well! I can't say. You'll have to draw your own conclusions, Eugene. I'm one of them, you know." She looked at him with demure lewdness, offering herself for inspection. Then, with a laugh of teasing reproof, she said: "I believe you're a bad boy, Eugene. I believe you're a bad boy."

He lighted another cigarette feverishly.

"I'd give anything for a smoke," muttered "Miss Brown." "I don't suppose I could here?" She looked round her.

"Why not?" he said impatiently. "There's no one to see you. It's dark. What does it matter anyway?"

Little electric currents of excitement played up his spine.

"I believe I will," she whispered. "Have you got a cigarette?"

He gave her his package; she stood up to receive the flame he nursed in his cupped hands. She leaned her heavy body against him as, with puckered face and closed eyes, she held her cigarette to the fire. She grasped his shaking hands to steady the light, holding them for a moment after.

"What," said "Miss Brown," with a cunning smile, "what if your mother should see us? You'd catch it!"

"She'll not see us," he said. "Besides," he added generously, "why shouldn't women smoke the same as men? There's no harm in it."

"Yes," said "Miss Brown," "I believe in being broad-minded about these things, too."

But he grinned in the dark, because the woman had revealed herself with a cigarette. It was a sign—the sign of the province, the sign unmistakable of debauchery.

Then, when he laid his hands upon her, she came very passively into his embrace as he sat before her on the rail.

"Eugene! Eugene!" she said in mocking reproof.

"Where is your room?" he said.

She told him.

Later, Eliza came suddenly and silently out upon them, on one of her swift raids from the kitchen.

"Who's there? Who's there?" she said, peering into the gloom suspiciously. "Huh? Hah? Where's Eugene? Has any one seen Eugene?" She knew very well he was there.

"Yes, here I am," he said. "What do you want?"

"Oh! Who's that with you? Hah?"

" 'Miss Brown' is with me."

"Won't you come out and sit down, Mrs. Gant?" said "Miss Brown." "You must be tired and hot."

"Oh!" said Eliza awkwardly, "is that you, 'Miss Brown'? I couldn't see who it was." She switched on the dim porch light. "It's mighty dark out here. Some one coming up those steps might fall and break a leg. I tell you what," she continued conversationally, "this air feels good. I wish I could let everything go and just enjoy myself."

She continued in amiable monologue for another half hour, her eyes probing about swiftly all the time at the two dark figures before her. Then hesitantly, by awkward talkative stages, she went into the house again.

"Son," she said before she went, troubled, "it's getting late. You'd better go to bed. That's where we all ought to be."

"Miss Brown" assented gracefully and moved toward the door.

"I'm going now. I feel tired. Good-night, all."

He sat quietly on the rail, smoking, listening to the noises in the house. It went to sleep. He went back and found Eliza preparing to retire to her little cell.

"Son!" she said, in a low voice, after shaking her puckered face reproachfully for a moment, "I tell you what—I don't like it. It doesn't look right—your sitting out alone with that woman. She's old enough to be your mother."

"She's *your* boarder, isn't she?" he said roughly, "not mine. I didn't bring her here."

"There's one thing sure," said Eliza, wounded. "You don't catch me associating with them. I hold up my head as high as any one." She smiled at him bitterly.

"Well, good-night, mama," he said, ashamed and hurt. "Let's forget about them for a while. What does it matter?"

"Be a good boy," said Eliza timidly. "I want you to be a good boy, son."

There was a sense of guilt in her manner, a note of regret and contrition.

"Don't worry!" he said, turning away suddenly, wrenched bitterly, as he always was, by a sense of the child-like innocence and steadfastness that lay at the bottom of her life. "It's not your fault if I'm not. I shan't blame you. Good-night."

The kitchen-light went out; he heard his mother's door click gently. Through the dark house a shaft of air blew coolly. Slowly, with thudding heart, he began to mount the stairs.

But on that dark stair, his foot-falls numbed in the heavy carpet, he came squarely upon a woman's body that, by its fragrance, like magnolia, he knew was that of Mrs. Selborne. They held each other sharply by the arms, discovered, with caught breath. She bent toward him: a few strands of her blonde hair brushed his face, leaving it aflame.

"Hush-h!" she whispered.

So they paused there, holding each other, breast to breast, the only time that they had ever touched. Then, with their dark wisdom of each other confirmed, they parted, each a sharer in the other's life, to meet thereafter before the world with calm untelling eyes.

He groped softly back along the dark corridor until he came to the door of "Miss Brown's" room. It was slightly ajar. He went in.

She took all his medals, all that he had won at Leonard's school—the one for debating, the one for declaiming, the one in bronze for William Shakespeare. W. S. 1616-1916—Done for a Ducat!

He had no money to give her: she did not want much—a coin or two at a time. It was, she said, not the money: it was the principle of the thing. He saw the justice of her argument.

"For," said she, "if I wanted money, I wouldn't fool with you. Somebody tries to get me to go out every day. One of the richest men in this town (old man Tyson) has been after me ever since I came. He's offered me ten dollars if I'll go out in his car with him. I don't need your money. But you've got to give me something. I don't care how little it is. I wouldn't feel decent unless you did. I'm not one of your little Society Chippies that you see every day uptown. I've too much self-respect for that."

So, in lieu of money, he gave her his medals as pledges.

"If you don't redeem them," said "Miss Brown," "I'll give them to my own son when I go home."

"Have you a son?"

"Yes. He's eighteen years old. He's almost as tall as you are and twice as broad. All the girls are mad about him."

He turned his head away sharply, whitening with a sense of nausea and horror, feeling in him an incestuous pollution.

"That's enough, now," said "Miss Brown" with authority. "Go to your room and get some sleep."

But, unlike the first one in the tobacco town, she never called him "son."

"Poor Butterfly, for her heart was break-king,
Poor Butterfly, for she loved him so-o——"

Miss Irene Mallard changed the needle of the little phonograph in the sun-parlor, and reversed the well-worn record. Then as with stately emphasis, the opening measure of "Katinka" paced out, she waited for him, erect, smiling, slender, beautiful, with long lovely hands held up like wings to his embrace. She was teaching him to dance. Laura James had danced beautifully: it had maddened him to see her poised in the arms of a young man dancing. Now, clumsily, he moved off on a conscientious left foot, counting to himself. One, two, three, four! Irene Mallard slipped and veered to his awkward pressure, as bodiless as a fume of smoke. Her left hand rested on his bony shoulder lightly as a bird: her cool fingers were threaded into his hot sawing palm.

She had thick hair of an oaken color, evenly parted in the middle; her skin was pearl-pale, and transparently delicate; her jaw was long, full, and sensuous—her face was like that of one of the pre-Raphaelite women. She carried her tall graceful body with beautiful erectness, but with the slightly worn sensuousness of fragility and weariness: her lovely eyes were violet, always a little tired, but full of slow surprise and tenderness. She was like a Luini madonna, mixed of holiness and seduction, the world and heaven. He held her with reverent care, as one who would not come too near, who would not break a sacred image. Her exquisite and subtle perfume stole through him like a strange whisper, pagan and divine. He was afraid to touch her—and his hot palm sweated to her fingers.

Sometimes she coughed gently, smiling, holding a small crumpled hand-kerchief, edged with blue, before her mouth.

She had come to the hills not because of her own health, but because of her mother's, a woman of sixty-five, rustily dressed, with the petulant hang-dog face of age and sickness. The old woman suffered from asthma and heart-disease. They had come from Florida. Irene Mallard was a very capable business woman; she was the chief bookkeeper of one of the Altamont banks. Every evening Randolph Gudger, the bank president, telephoned her.

Irene Mallard pressed her palm across the mouthpiece of the telephone, smiling at Eugene ironically, and rolling her eyes entreatingly aloft.

Sometimes Randolph Gudger drove by and asked her to go with him. The boy went sulkily away until the rich man should leave: the banker looked bitterly after him.

"He wants me to marry him, 'Gene," said Irene Mallard. "What am I going to do?"

"He's old enough to be your grandfather," said Eugene. "He has no hair on the top of his head; his teeth are false, and I don't know what-all!" he said resentfully.

"He's a rich man, 'Gene," said Irene, smiling. "Don't forget that."

"Go on, then! Go on!" he cried furiously. "Yes—go ahead. Marry him. It's the right thing for you. Sell yourself. He's an old man!" he said melodramatically. Randolph Gudger was almost forty-five.

But they danced there slowly in a gray light of dusk that was like pain and beauty; like the lost light undersea, in which his life, a lost merman, swam, remembering exile. And as they danced she, whom he dared not touch, yielded her body unto him, whispering softly to his ear, pressing with slender fingers his hot hand. And she, whom he would not touch, lay there, like a sheaf of grain, in the crook of his arm, token of the world's remedy—the refuge from the one lost face out of all the faces, the anodyne against the wound named Laura—a thousand flitting shapes of beauty to bring him comfort and delight. The great pageantry of pain and pride and death hung through the dusk its awful vision, touching his sorrow with a lonely joy. He had lost; but all pilgrimage across the world was loss: a moment of cleaving, a moment of taking away, the thousand phantom shapes that beaconed, and the high impassionate grief of stars.

It was dark. Irene Mallard took him by the hand and led him out on the porch.

"Sit down here a moment, 'Gene. I want to talk to you." Her voice was serious, low-pitched. He sat beside her in the swing, obediently, with the sense of an impending lecture.

"I've been watching you these last few days," said Irene Mallard. "I know what's been going on."

"What do you mean?" he said thickly, with thudding pulses.

"You know what I mean," said Irene Mallard sternly. "Now you're too fine a boy, 'Gene, to waste yourself on that Woman. Any one can see what she is. Mother and I have both talked about it. A woman like that can ruin a young boy like you. You've got to stop it."

"How did you know about it?" he muttered. He was frightened and ashamed. She took his trembling hand and held it between her cool palms until he grew quieter. But he drew no closer to her: he halted, afraid, before her loveliness. As with Laura James, she seemed too high for his passion. Hs was afraid of her flesh; he was not afraid of "Miss Brown's." But now he was tired of the woman and didn't know how he could pay her. She had all his medals.

All through the waning summer he walked with Irene Mallard. They walked at night through the cool streets filled with the rustle of tired leaves. They went together to the hotel roof and danced; later "Pap" Rheinhart, kind and awkward and shy, and smelling of his horse, came to their little table, sitting and drinking with them. He had spent the years since Leonard's at a military school, trying to straighten the wry twist of his neck. But he remained the same as ever—quizzical, dry, and humorous. Eugene looked at that good shy face, remembering the lost years, the lost faces. And there was sorrow in his heart for what would come no more. August ended.

September came, full of departing wings. The world was full of departures. It had heard the drums. The young men were going to the war. Ben had been rejected again in the draft. Now he was preparing to drift off in search of employment in other towns. Luke had given up his employment in a war-munitions factory at Dayton, Ohio, and had enlisted in the Navy. He had come home on a short leave before his departure for the training-school at Newport, Rhode Island. The street roared as he came down at his vulgar wide-legged stride, in flapping blues, his face all on the grin, thick curls of his unruly hair coiling below the band of his hat. He was the cartoon of a gob.

"Luke!" shouted Mr. Fawcett, the land-auctioneer, pulling him in from the street to Wood's pharmacy, "by God, son, you've done your bit. I'm going to set you up. What are you going to have?"

"Make it a dope," said Luke. "Colonel, yours truly!" He lifted the frosty glass in a violently palsied hand, and stood posed before the grinning counter. "F-f-f-forty years ago," he began, in a hoarse voice, "I might have refused, but now I can't, G-G-G-God help me! I c-c-c-c-can't!"

Gant's sickness had returned on him with increased virulence. His face was haggard and yellow: a tottering weakness crept into his limbs. It was decided that he must go again to Baltimore. Helen would go with him.

"Mr. Gant," said Eliza persuasively, "why don't you just give up everything and settle down to take things easy the rest of your days? You don't feel good enough to tend to business any more; if I were you, I'd retire. We could get $20,000 for your shop without any trouble—If I had that much money to work with, I'd show them a thing or two." She nodded pertly with a smart wink. "I could turn it over two or three times within two years' time. You've got to trade quick to keep the ball a-rolling. That's the way it's done."

"Merciful God!" he groaned. "That's my last refuge on earth. Woman, have you no mercy? I beg of you, leave me to die in peace: it won't be long now. You can do what you please with it after I'm gone, but give me a little peace now. In the name of Jesus, I ask it!" He sniffled affectedly.

"Pshaw!" said Eliza, thinking no doubt to encourage him. "There's nothing wrong with you. Half of it's only imagination."

He groaned, turning his head away.

Summer died upon the hills. There was a hue, barely guessed, upon the foliage, of red rust. The streets at night were filled with sad lispings: all through the night, upon his porch, as in a coma, he heard the strange noise of autumn. And all the people who had given the town its light thronging gaiety were vanished strangely overnight. They had gone back into the vast South again. The solemn tension of the war gathered about the nation. A twilight of grim effort hovered around him, above him. He felt the death of joy; but the groping within him of wonder, of glory. Out of the huge sprawl of its first delirium, the nation was beginning to articulate the engines of war—engines to mill and print out hatred and falsehood, engines to pump up glory, engines to manacle and crush opposition, engines to drill and regiment men.

But something of true wonder had come upon the land—the flares and rockets of the battle-fields cast their light across the plains as well. Young men from Kansas were going to die in Picardy. In some foreign earth lay the iron, as yet unmoulded, that was to slay them. The strangeness of death and destiny was legible upon lives and faces which held no strangeness of their own. For, it is the union of the ordinary and the miraculous that makes wonder.

Luke had gone away to the training-school at Newport. Ben went to Baltimore with Helen and Gant, who, before entering the hospital again for radium treatment, had gone on a violent and unruly spree which had compelled their rapid transference from one hotel to another and had finally brought Gant moaning to his bed, hurling against God the anathemas that should have been saved for huge riotings in raw oysters washed down chaotically with beer and whisky. They all drank a great deal: Gant's excesses, however, reduced the girl to a state of angry frenzy, and Ben to one of scowling and cursing disgust.

"You damned old man!" cried Helen, seizing and shaking his passive shoulders as he lay reeking and sodden on an untidy bed. "I could wear you out! You're not sick; I've wasted my life nursing you, and you're not as sick as I am! You'll be here long after I'm gone, you selfish old man! It makes me furious!"

"Why, baby!" he roared, with a vast gesture of his arms, "God bless you, I couldn't do without you."

"Don't 'baby' me!" she cried.

But she held his hand next day as they rode out to the hospital, held it as, quaking, he turned for an instant and looked sadly at the city stretched behind and below him.

"I was a boy here," he muttered.

"Don't worry," she said, "we're going to make you well again. Why! You'll be a boy again!"

Hand in hand they entered the lobby where, flanked with death and terror and the busy matter-of-factness of the nurses and the hundred flitting shapes of the quiet men with the gray faces and gimlet eyes who walk so surely in among the broken lives—with arms proposed in an attitude of enormous mercy—many times bigger than Gant's largest angel—is an image of gentle Jesus.

Eugene went to see the Leonards several times. Margaret looked thin and ill, but the great light in her seemed on this account to burn more brightly. Never before had he been so aware of her enormous tranquil patience, the great health of her spirit. All of his sin, all of his pain, all the vexed weariness of his soul were washed away in that deep radiance: the tumult and evil of life dropped from him its foul and ragged cloak. He seemed to be clothed anew in garments of seamless light.

But he could confess little that lay on his heart: he talked freely of his work at the university, he talked of little else. His heart was packed with its burden for confessional, but he knew he could not speak, that she would not understand. She was too wise for anything but faith. Once, desperately, he tried to tell her of Laura: he blurted out a confession awkwardly in a few words. Before he had finished she began to laugh.

"Mr. Leonard!" she called. "Imagine this rascal with a girl! Pshaw, boy! You don't know what love is. Get along with you. There'll be time enough to think of that ten years from now." She laughed tenderly to herself, with absent misty gaze.

"Old 'Gene with a girl! Pity the poor girl! Ah, Lord, Boy! That's a long way off for you. Thank your stars!"

He bent his head sharply, and closed his eyes. O My lovely Saint! he thought. How close you have been to me, if any one. How I have cut my brain open for you to see, and would my heart, if I had dared, and how alone I am, and always have been.

He walked through the streets at night with Irene Mallard; the town was thinned and saddened by departures. A few people hurried past, as if driven along by the brief pouncing gusts of wind. He was held in the lure of her subtle weariness: she gave him comfort and he never touched her. But he unpacked the burden of his heart, trembling and passionate. She sat beside him and stroked his hand. It seemed to him that he never knew her until he remembered her years later.

The house was almost empty. At night Eliza packed his trunk carefully, counting the ironed shirts and mended socks with satisfaction.

"Now, you have plenty of good warm clothes, son. Try to take care of them." She put Gant's check in his inner pocket and fastened it with a safety-pin.

"Keep a sharp eye on your money, boy. You never know who you'll run up with on a train."

He dawdled nervously toward the door, wishing to melt away, not end in leave-taking.

"It does seem you might spend one night at home with your mother," she said querulously. Her eyes grew misty at once, her lips began to work tremulously in a bitter self-pitying smile. "I tell you what! It looks mighty funny, doesn't it? You can't stay with me five minutes any more without wanting to be up and off with the first woman that comes along. It's all right! It's all right. I'm not complaining. It seems as if all I was fit for is to cook and sew and get you ready to go off." She burst volubly into tears. "It seems that that's the only use you have for me. I've hardly laid eyes on you all summer."

"No," he said bitterly, "you've been too busy looking after the boarders. Don't think, mama, that you can work on my feelings here at the last minute," he cried, already deeply worked-on. "It's easy to cry. But I was here all the time if you had had time for me. Oh, for God's sake! Let's make an end to this! Aren't things bad enough without it? Why must you act this way whenever I go off? Do you want to make me as miserable as you can?"

"Well, I tell you," said Eliza hopefully, becoming dry-eyed at once, "if I make a couple of deals and everything goes well, you may find me waiting for you in a big fine house when you come back next Spring. I've got the lot picked out. I was thinking about it the other day," she went on, giving him a bright and knowing nod.

"Ah-h!" he made a strangling noise in his throat and tore at his collar. "In God's name! Please!" There was a silence.

"Well," said Eliza gravely, plucking at her chin, "I want you to be a good boy and study hard, son. Take care of your money—I want you to have plenty of good food and warm clothes—but you mustn't be extravagant, boy. This sickness of your papa's has cost a lot of money. Everything is going out and nothing's coming in. Nobody knows where the next dollar's coming from. So you've got to watch out."

Again silence fell. She had said her say; she had come as close as she could, but suddenly she felt speechless, shut out, barred from the bitter and lonely secrecy of his life.

"I hate to see you go, son," she said quietly, with a deep and indefinable sadness.

He cast his arms up suddenly in a tortured incomplete gesture.

"What does it matter! Oh God, what does it matter!"

Eliza's eyes filled with tears of real pain. She grasped his hand and held it.

"Try to be happy, son," she wept, "try to be a little more happy. Poor child! Poor child! Nobody ever knew you. Before you were born," she shook her head slowly, speaking in a voice that was drowned and husky with her tears. Then, huskily, clearing her throat, she repeated, "Before you were born——"

32

When he returned to the university for his second year, he found the place adjusted soberly to war. It seemed quieter, sadder—the number of students was smaller and they were younger. The older ones had gone to war. The others were in a state of wild, but subdued, restlessness. They were careless of colleges, careers, successes—the war had thrilled them with its triumphing *Now*. Of what use To-morrow! Of what use all labor for To-morrow! The big guns had blown all spun schemes to fragments: they hailed the end of all planned work with a fierce, a secret joy. The business of education went on half-heartedly, with an abstracted look: in the classroom, their eyes were vague upon the book, but their ears cocked attentively for alarums and excursions without.

Eugene began the year earnestly as room-mate of a young man who had been the best student in the Altamont High School. His name was Bob Sterling. Bob Sterling was nineteen years old, the son of a widow. He was of middling height, always very neatly and soberly dressed; there was nothing conspicuous about him. For this reason, he could laugh good-naturedly, a little smugly, at whatever was conspicuous. He had a good mind—bright, attentive, studious, unmarked by originality or inventiveness. He had a time for everything: he apportioned a certain time for the preparation of each lesson, and went over it three times, mumbling rapidly to himself. He sent his laundry out every Monday. When in merry company he laughed heartily and enjoyed himself, but he always kept track of the time. Presently, he would look at his watch, saying: "Well, this is all very nice, but it's getting no work done," and he would go.

Every one said he had a bright future. He remonstrated with Eugene, with good-natured seriousness, about his habits. He ought not to throw his clothes around. He ought not to let his shirts and drawers accumulate in a dirty pile. He ought to have a regular time for doing each lesson; he ought to live by regular hours.

They lived in a private dwelling on the edge of the campus, in a large bright room decorated with a great number of college pennants, all of which belonged to Bob Sterling.

Bob Sterling had heart-disease. He stood on the landing, gasping, when he had climbed the stairs. Eugene opened the door for him. Bob Sterling's pleasant face was dead white, spotted by pale freckles. His lips chattered and turned blue.

"What is it, Bob? How do you feel?" said Eugene.

"Come here," said Bob Sterling with a grin. "Put your head down here." He took Eugene's head and placed it against his heart. The great pump beat slowly and irregularly, with a hissing respiration.

"Good God!" cried Eugene.

"Do you hear it?" said Bob Sterling, beginning to laugh. Then he went into the room, chafing his dry hands briskly.

But he fell sick and could not attend classes. He was taken to the College Infirmary, where he lay for several weeks, apparently not very ill, but with lips constantly blue, a slow pulse, and a sub-normal temperature. Nothing could be done about it.

His mother came and took him home. Eugene wrote him regularly twice a week, getting in return short but cheerful messages. Then one day he died.

Two weeks later the widow returned to gather together the boy's belongings. Silently she collected the clothing that no one would ever wear. She was a stout woman in her forties. Eugene took all the pennants from the wall and folded them. She packed them in a valise and turned to go.

"Here's another," said Eugene.

She burst suddenly into tears and seized his hand.

"He was so brave," she said, "so brave. Those last days—I had not meant to— Your letters made him so happy."

She's alone now, Eugene thought.

I cannot stay here, he thought, where he has been. We were here together. Always I should see him on the landing, with the hissing valve and the blue lips, or hear him mumbling his lessons. Then, at night, the other cot would be empty. I think I shall room alone hereafter.

But he roomed the remainder of the term in one of the dormitories.

He had two room-mates—one, an Altamont young man who answered to the name of L. K. Duncan (the "L" stood for Lawrence, but every one called him "Elk") and the other, the son of an Episcopal minister, Harold Gay. Both were several years older than Eugene: Elk Duncan was twenty-four, and Harold Gay, twenty-two. But it is doubtful whether a more precious congress of freaks had ever before gathered in two small rooms, one of which they used as a "study."

Elk Duncan was the son of an Altamont attorney, a small Democratic politician, mighty in county affairs. Elk Duncan was tall—an inch or two over six feet—and incredibly thin, or rather narrow. He was already a little bald, he had a high prominent forehead, and large pale bulging eyes: from that point his long pale face sloped backward to his chin. His shoulders were a trifle bowed and very narrow; the rest of his body had the symmetry of a lead pencil. He always dressed very foppishly, in tight suits of blue flannel, with high stiff collars, fat silken cravats, and colored silk handkerchiefs. He was a student in the Law School, but he spent a large part of his time, industriously, in avoiding study.

The younger students—particularly the Freshmen—gathered around him after meals with mouths slightly ajar, feeding upon his words like manna, and hungrily demanding more, the wilder his fable became. His posture toward life was very much that of the barker of a carnival side-show: loquacious, patronizing, and cynical.

The other room-mate, Harold Gay, was a good soul, no older than a child. He wore spectacles, which gave the only glister to the dull grayness of his face; he was plain and ugly without any distinction: he had been puzzled so long by at least four-fifths of the phenomena of existence that he no longer made any effort to comprehend them. Instead, he concealed his shyness and bewilderment under a braying laugh that echoed at all the wrong places, and a silly grin full of an absurd and devilish knowingness. His association with Elk Duncan was one of the proud summits of his life: he weltered in the purple calcium which bathed that worthy, he smoked cigarettes with a debauched leer, and cursed loudly and uneasily with the accent of a depraved clergyman.

"Harold! Harold!" said Elk Duncan reprovingly. "Damn, son! You're getting hard! If you go on like this, you'll begin to chew gum, and fritter away your Sunday-school money at the movies. Think of the rest of us, please. 'Gene here's only a young boy, as pure as a barnyard privy, and, as for me, I've always moved in the best circles, and associated with only the highest class of bartenders and ladylike streetwalkers. What would

your father say if he could hear you? Don't you know he'd be shocked?
He'd cut off your cigarette money, son."

"I don't give a damn what he'd do, Elk, nor you either!" said Harold
toughly, grinning. "So, what the hell!" he roared as loudly as he could.
There was an answering howl from the windows of the whole dormitory
—cries of "Go to hell!" "Cut it out!" and ironical cheers, at which
he was pleased.

The scattered family drew together again at Christmas. A sense of
impending dissolution, of loss and death, brought them back. The surgeon
at Baltimore had given no hope. He had, rather, confirmed Gant's death-
warrant.

"Then how long can he live?" asked Helen.

He shrugged his shoulders. "My dear girl!" he said. "I have no idea.
The man's a miracle. Do you know that he's Exhibit A here? Every
surgeon in the place has had a look. How long can he last? I'll swear to
nothing—I no longer have any idea. When your father left here, the
first time, after his operation, I never expected to see him again. I doubted
if he would last the winter through. But he's back again. He may be
back many times."

"Can you help him at all? Do you think the radium does any good?"

"I can give him relief for a time. I can even check the growth of the
disease for a time. Beyond that, I can do nothing. But his vitality is
enormous. He is a creaking gate which hangs by one hinge—but which
hangs, nevertheless."

Thus, she had brought him home, the shadow of his death suspended
over them like a Damocles sword. Fear prowled softly through their
brains on leopard feet. The girl lived in a condition of repressed hysteria:
it had its outburst daily at Eliza's or in her own home. Hugh Barton
had purchased a house to which he had taken her.

"You'll get no peace," he said, "as long as you're near them. That's
what's wrong with you now."

She had frequent periods of sickness. She went constantly to the doctors
for treatment and advice. Sometimes she went to the hospital for several
days. Her illness manifested itself in various ways—sometimes in a terrible
mastoid pain, sometimes in nervous exhaustion, sometimes in an hysterical
collapse in which she laughed and wept by turns, and which was governed

partly by Gant's illness and a morbid despair over her failure to bear a child. She drank stealthily at all times—she drank in nibbling draughts for stimulants, never enough for drunkenness. She drank vile liquids—seeking only the effect of alcohol and getting at it in strange ways through a dozen abominations called "tonics" and "extracts." Almost deliberately she ruined her taste for the better sort of potable liquors, concealing from herself, under the convenient labellings of physic, the ugly crawling hunger in her blood. This self-deception was characteristic of her. Her life expressed itself through a series of deceptions—of symbols: her dislikes, affections, grievances, brandishing every cause but the real one.

But, unless actually bedridden, she was never absent from her father for many hours. The shadow of his death lay over their lives. They shuddered below its horror; its protracted menace, its unsearchable enigma, deprived them of dignity and courage. They were dominated by the weary and degrading egotism of life, which is blandly philosophical over the death of the alien, but sees in its own the corruption of natural law. It was as hard for them to think of Gant's death as of God's death: it was a great deal harder, because he was more real to them than God, he was more immortal than God, he was God.

This hideous twilight into which their lives had passed froze Eugene with its terror, and choked him with fury. He would grow enraged after reading a letter from home and pound the grained plaster of the dormitory wall until his knuckles were bloody. They have taken his courage away! he thought. They have made a whining coward out of him! No, and if I die, no damned family about. Blowing their messy breaths in your face! Snuffling down their messy noses at you! Gathering around you till you can't breathe. Telling you how well you're looking with hearty smiles, and boo-hooing behind your back. O messy, messy, messy death! Shall we never be alone? Shall we never live alone, think alone, live in a house by ourselves alone? Ah! but I shall! I shall! Alone, alone, and far away, with falling rain. Then, bursting suddenly into the study, he found Elk Duncan, with unaccustomed eye bent dully upon a page of Torts, a bright bird held by the stare of that hypnotic snake, the law.

"Are we to die like rats?" he said. "Are we to smother in a hole?"

"Damn!" said Elk Duncan, folding the big calfskin and cowering defensively behind it.

"Yes, that's right, that's right! Calm yourself. You are Napoleon Bonaparte and I'm your old friend, Oliver Cromwell. Harold!" he called. "Help! He killed the keeper and got out."

" 'Gene!" yelled Harold Gay, hurling a thick volume from him under the spell of Elk's great names. "What do you know about history? Who signed Magna Charta, eh?"

"It wasn't signed," said Eugene. "The King didn't know how to write, so they mimeographed it."

"Correct!" roared Harold Gay. "Who was Æthelred the Unready?"

"He was the son of Cynewulf the Silly and Undine the Unwashed," said Eugene.

"On his Uncle Jasper's side," said Elk Duncan, "he was related to Paul the Poxy and Genevieve the Ungenerous."

"He was excommunicated by the Pope in a Bull of the year 903, but he refused to be cowed," said Eugene.

"Instead, he called together all the local clergy, including the Archbishop of Canterbury, Dr. Gay, who was elected Pope," said Elk Duncan. "This caused a great schism in the Church."

"But as usual, God was on the side of the greatest number of canons," said Eugene. "Later on, the family migrated to California, and made its fortune in the Gold Rush of '49."

"You boys are too good for me!" yelled Harold Gay, getting up abruptly. "Come on! Who's going to the Pic?"

The Pic was the only purchasable entertainment that the village afforded steadily. It was a moving-picture theatre, inhabited nightly by a howling tribe of students who rushed down aisles, paved with peanut-shells, through a shrapnel fire of flying goobers, devoting themselves studiously for the remainder of the evening to the unhappy heads and necks of Freshmen, and less attentively, but with roars of applause, indignation, or advice, to the poor flicker-dance of puppets that wavered its way illegibly across the worn and pleated screen. A weary but industrious young woman with a scrawny neck thumped almost constantly at a battered piano. If she was idle for five minutes, the whole pack howled ironically, demanding: "Music, Myrtle! Music!"

It was necessary to speak to every one. If one spoke to every one, one was "democratic"; if one did not, one was a snob, and got few votes. The appraisal of personality, like all other appraisal with them, was coarse and blunt. They were suspicious of all eminence. They had a hard peasant hostility to the unusual. A man was brilliant? Was there a bright sparkle to him? Bad, bad! He was not safe; he was not sound. The place was a democratic microcosmos—seething with political interests: national, regional, collegiate.

The campus had its candidates, its managers, its bosses, its machines, as had the State. A youngster developed in college the political craft he was later to exert in Party affairs. The son of a politician was schooled by his crafty sire before the down was off his cheeks: at sixteen, his life had been plotted ahead to the governorship, or to the proud dignities of a Congressman. The boy came deliberately to the university to bait and set his first traps: deliberately he made those friendships that were most likely to benefit him later. By his junior year, if he was successful, he had a political manager, who engineered his campus ambitions; he moved with circumspection, and spoke with a trace of pomp nicely weighed with cordiality:

"Ah, there, gentlemen." "Gentlemen, how are you?" "A nice day, gentlemen."

The vast champaign of the world stretched out its limitless wonder, but few were seduced away from the fortress of the State, few ever heard the distant reverberation of an idea. They could get no greater glory for themselves than a seat in the Senate, and the way to glory—the way to all power, highness, and distinction whatsoever—was through the law, a string tie, and a hat. Hence politics, law schools, debating societies, and speechmaking. The applause of listening senates to command.

The yokels, of course, were in the saddle—they composed nine-tenths of the student body: the proud titles were in their gift, and they took good care that their world should be kept safe for yokelry and the home-spun virtues. Usually, these dignities—the presidencies of student bodies, classes, Y. M. C. A.'s, and the managerships of athletic teams—were given to some honest serf who had established his greatness behind a plough before working in the college commons, or to some industrious hack who had shown a satisfactory mediocrity in all directions. Such an industrious hack was called an "all-round man." He was safe, sound, and reliable. He would never get notions. He was the fine flower of university training. He was a football scrub, and a respectable scholar in all subjects. He was a universal Two Man. He always got Two on everything, except Moral Character, where he shone with a superlative Oneness. If he did not go into the law or the ministry, he was appointed a Rhodes Scholar.

In this strange place Eugene flourished amazingly. He was outside the pale of popular jealousies: it was quite obvious that he was not safe, that he was not sound, that decidedly he was an irregular person. He could never be an all-round man. Obviously, he would never be governor.

Obviously, he would never be a politician, because he said funny things. He was not the man to lead a class or say a prayer; he was a man for curious enterprise. Well, thought they benevolently, we need some such. We are not all made for weighty business.

He was happier that he had ever been in his life, and more careless. His physical loneliness was more complete and more delightful. His escape from the bleak horror of disease and hysteria and death impending, that hung above his crouched family, left him with a sense of aerial buoyance, drunken freedom. He had come to the place alone, without companions. He had no connections. He had, even now, not one close friend. And this isolation was in his favor. Every one knew him at sight: every one called him by name, and spoke to him kindly. He was not disliked. He was happy, full of expansive joy, he greeted every one with enthusiastic gusto. He had a vast tenderness, an affection for the whole marvellous and unvisited earth, that blinded his eyes. He was closer to a feeling of brotherhood than he had ever been, and more alone. He was filled with a divine indifference for all appearance. Joy ran like a great wine through his young expanding limbs; he bounded down the paths with wild cries in his throat, leaping for life like an apple, trying to focus the blind desire that swept him apart, to melt down to a bullet all of his formless passion, and so, slay death, slay love.

He began to join. He joined everything. He had never "belonged" to any group before, but now all groups were beckoning him. He had without much trouble won a place for himself on the staff of the college paper and the magazine. The small beginning trickle of distinctions widened into a gushet. It began to sprinkle, then it rained. He was initiated into literary fraternities, dramatic fraternities, theatrical fraternities, speaking fraternities, journalistic fraternities, and in the Spring into a social fraternity. He joined enthusiastically, submitted with fanatical glee to the hard mauling of the initiations, and went about lame and sore, more pleased than a child or a savage, with colored ribbons in his coat lapel, and a waistcoat plastered with pins, badges, symbols, and Greek letterings.

But not without labor had his titles come. The early autumn was lustreless and slack: he could not come from the shadow of Laura. She haunted him. When he went home at Christmas, he found the hills bleak and close, and the town mean and cramped in the grim stinginess of winter. There was a ludicrous, a desperate gaiety in the family.

"Well!" said Eliza sorrowfully, as she peered above the stove, "let's all try to be happy this time and enjoy a quiet Christmas. You never know! You never know!" She shook her head, unable to continue. Her eyes were wet. "It may be the last time we're all together. The old trouble! The old trouble!" she said hoarsely, turning to him.

"What old trouble?" he said angrily. "Good God, why are you so mysterious?"

"My heart!" she whispered, with a brave smile. "I've said nothing to any one. But last week—I thought I was gone." This was delivered in a boding whisper.

"Oh, my God!" he groaned. "You'll be here when the rest of us are rotten."

Helen burst into a raucous angry laugh, looking at his sullen face, and prodding him roughly with her big fingers.

"K-K-K-K-K-K! Did you ever know it to fail? Did you? If you come to her with one of your kidneys gone, she's always got something worse the matter with her. No, sir! I've never known it to fail!"

"You may laugh! You may laugh!" said Eliza with a smile of watery bitterness. "But I may not be here to laugh at much longer."

"Good heavens, mama!" the girl cried irritably. "There's nothing wrong with you. You're not the sick one! Papa's the sick one. He's the one that needs attention. Can't you realize that—he's dying. He may not last the winter out. I'm the sick one! You'll be here long after we're both gone."

"You never know," said Eliza mysteriously. "You never know who'll be the first one to go. Only last week, there was Mr. Cosgrave, as fine a looking man as——"

"They're off!" Eugene screamed with a crazy laugh, stamping up and down the kitchen in a frenzy. "By God! They're off!"

At this moment, one of the aged harpies, of whom the house always sheltered two or three during the grim winter, lurched from the hall back into the door-space. She was a large raw-boned hag, a confirmed drug-eater, who moved by a violent and dissonant jerking of her gaunt limbs, pawing abruptly at the air with a gnarled hand.

"Mrs. Gant," said she, writhing her loose gray lips horribly before she could speak. "Did I get a letter? Have you seen him?"

"Seen who? Go on!" said Eliza fretfully. "I don't know what you're talking about, and I don't believe you do, either."

Smiling hideously at them all, and pawing the air, the monster got under way again, disappearing like an old wagon with loose wheels.

Helen began to laugh, hoarsely, as Eugene's face hung forward with mouth half-open in an expression of sullen stupefaction. Eliza laughed, too, slily, rubbing her nosewing with a finger.

"I'll vow!" she said. "I believe she's crazy. She takes dope of some sort—that's certain. It makes my flesh crawl when she comes around."

"Then why do you keep her in the house?" said Helen resentfully. "Good heavens, mama! You could get rid of her if you wanted to. Poor old 'Gene!" she said, beginning to laugh again. "You always catch it, don't you?"

"The time draws near the birth of Christ," said he, piously.

She laughed; then, with abstracted eyes, plucked vaguely at her large chin.

His father spent most of the day staring vacantly into the parlor fire. Miss Florry Mangle, the nurse, gave him the morbid comfort of her silence: she rocked incessantly before the fire, thirty heel-taps to the minute, with arms tight-folded on her limp breasts. Occasionally she talked of death and disease. Gant had aged and wasted shockingly. His heavy clothes wound round his feeble shanks: his face was waxen and transparent—it was like a great beak. He looked clean and fragile. The cancer, Eugene thought, flowered in him like some terrible but beautiful plant. His mind was very clear, not doting, but sad and old. He spoke little, with almost comical gentleness, but he ceased to listen almost as soon as one answered.

"How have you been, son?" he asked. "Are you getting along all right?"

"Yes. I am a reporter on the paper now; I may be managing editor next year. I have been elected to several organizations," he went on eagerly, glad of the rare chance to speak to one of them about his life. But when he looked up again, his father's stare was fixed sadly in the fire. The boy stopped in confusion, pierced with a bitter pain.

"That's good," said Gant, hearing him speak no more. "Be a good boy, son. We're proud of you."

Ben came home two days before Christmas: he prowled through the house like a familiar ghost. He had left the town early in the autumn, after his return from Baltimore. For three months he had wandered alone through the South, selling to the merchants in small towns space for advertisements upon laundry cards. How well this curious business succeeded he did not say: he was scrupulously neat, but threadbare and haggard, and more fiercely secretive than ever. He had found employment at length upon a newspaper in a rich tobacco town of the Piedmont. He was going there after Christmas.

He had come to them, as always, bearing gifts.

Luke came in from the naval school at Newport, on Christmas eve. They heard his sonorous tenor shouting greetings to people in the street; he entered the house upon a blast of air. Everyone began to grin.

"Well, here we are! The Admiral's back! Papa, how's the boy! Well, for God's sake!" he cried, embracing Gant, and slapping his back. "I thought I was coming to see a sick man! You're looking like the flowers that bloom in the Spring."

"Pretty well, my boy. How are you?" said Gant, with a pleased grin.

"Couldn't be better, Colonel. 'Gene, how are you, Old Scout? Good!" he said, without waiting for an answer. "Well, well, if it isn't Old Baldy," he cried, pumping Ben's hand. "I didn't know whether you'd be here or not. Mama, old girl," he said, as he embraced her, "how're they going? Still hitting on all six. Fine!" he yelled, before any one could reply to anything.

"Why, son,—what on earth!" cried Eliza, stepping back to look at him. "What have you done to yourself? You walk as if you are lame."

He laughed idiotically at sight of her troubled face and prodded her.

"Whah—whah! I got torpedoed by a submarine," he said. "Oh, it's nothing," he added modestly. "I gave a little skin to help out a fellow in the electrical school."

"What!" Eliza screamed. "How much did you give?"

"Oh, only a little six-inch strip," he said carelessly. "The boy was badly burned: a bunch of us got together and chipped in with a little hide."

"Mercy!" said Eliza. "You'll be lame for life. It's a wonder you can walk."

"He always thinks of others—that boy!" said Gant proudly. "He'd give you his heart's-blood."

The sailor had secured an extra valise, and stocked it on the way home with a great variety of beverages for his father. There were several bottles of Scotch and rye whiskies, two of gin, one of rum, and one each of port and sherry wine.

Every one grew mildly convivial before the evening meal.

Let's give the poor kid a drink," said Helen. "It won't hurt him."

"What! My ba-a-by! Why, son, you wouldn't drink, would you?" Eliza said playfully.

"Wouldn't he!" said Helen, prodding him. "Ho! ho! ho!"

She poured him out a stiff draught of Scotch whiskey.

"There!" she said cheerfully. "That's not going to hurt him."

"Son," said Eliza gravely, balancing her wine-glass, "I don't want you ever to acquire a taste for it." She was still loyal to the doctrine of the good Major.

"No," said Gant. "It'll ruin you quicker than anything in the world, if you do."

"You're a goner, boy, if that stuff ever gets you," said Luke. "Take a fool's advice."

They lavished fair warnings on him as he lifted his glass. He choked as the fiery stuff caught in his young throat, stopping his breath for a moment and making him tearful. He had drunk a few times before—minute quantities that his sister had given him at Woodson Street. Once, with Jim Trivett, he had fancied himself tipsy.

When they had eaten, they drank again. He was allowed a small one. Then they all departed for town to complete their belated shopping. He was left alone in the house.

What he had drunk beat pleasantly through his veins in warm pulses, bathing the tips of ragged nerves, giving to him a feeling of power and tranquillity he had never known. Presently, he went to the pantry where the liquor was stored. He took a water tumbler and filled it experimentally with equal portions of whiskey, gin, and rum. Then, seating himself at the kitchen table, he began to drink the mixture slowly.

The terrible draught smote him with the speed and power of a man's fist. He was made instantly drunken, and he knew instantly why men drank. It was, he knew, one of the great moments in his life—he lay, greedily watching the mastery of the grape over his virgin flesh, like a girl for the first time in the embrace of her lover. And suddenly, he knew how completely he was his father's son—how completely, and with what added power and exquisite refinement of sensation, was he Gantian. He exulted in the great length of his limbs and his body, through which the mighty liquor could better work its wizardry. In all the earth there was no other like him, no other fitted to be so sublimely and magnificently drunken. It was greater than all the music he had ever heard; it was as great as the highest poetry. Why had he never been told? Why had no one ever written adequately about it? Why, when it was possible to buy a god in a bottle, and drink him off, and become a god oneself, were men not forever drunken?

He had a moment of great wonder—the magnificent wonder with which we discover the simple and unspeakable things that lie buried and known, but unconfessed, in us. So might a man feel if he wakened after death and found himself in Heaven.

Then a divine paralysis crept through his flesh. His limbs were numb; his tongue thickened until he could not bend it to the cunning sounds of words. He spoke aloud, repeating difficult phrases over and over, filled with wild laughter and delight at his effort. Behind his drunken body his brain hung poised like a falcon, looking on him with scorn, with tenderness, looking on all laughter with grief and pity. There lay in him something that could not be seen and could not be touched, which was above and beyond him—an eye within an eye, a brain above a brain, the Stranger that dwelt in him and regarded him and was him, and that he did not know. But, thought he, I am alone now in this house; if I can come to know him, I will.

He got up, and reeled out of the alien presences of light and warmth in the kitchen; he went out into the hall where a dim light burned and the high walls gave back their grave-damp chill. This, he thought, is the house.

He sat down upon the hard mission settle, and listened to the cold drip of silence. This is the house in which I have been an exile. There is a stranger in the house, and there's a stranger in me.

O house of Admetus, in whom (although I was a god) I have endured so many things. Now, house, I am not afraid. No ghost need fear come by me. If there's a door in silence, let it open. My silence can be greater than your own. And you who are in me, and who I am, come forth beyond this quiet shell of flesh that makes no posture to deny you. There is none to look at us: O come, my brother and my lord, with unbent face. If I had 40,000 years, I should give all but the ninety last to silence. I should grow to the earth like a hill or a rock. Unweave the fabric of nights and days; unwind my life back to my birth; subtract me into nakedness again, and build me back with all the sums I have not counted. Or let me look upon the living face of darkness; let me hear the terrible sentence of your voice.

There was nothing but the living silence of the house: no doors were opened.

Presently, he got up and left the house. He wore no hat or coat; he could not find them. The night was blanketed in a thick steam of mist:

sounds came faintly and cheerfully. Already the earth was full of Christmas. He remembered that he had bought no gifts. He had a few dollars in his pocket; before the shops closed he must get presents for the family. Bareheaded he set off for the town. He knew that he was drunk and that he staggered; but he believed that with care and control he could hide his state from any one who saw him. He straddled the line that ran down the middle of the concrete sidewalk, keeping his eyes fixed on it and coming back to it quickly when he lurched away from it. When he got into the town the streets were thronged with late shoppers. An air of completion was on everything. The people were streaming home to Christmas. He plunged down from the Square into the narrow avenue, going in among the staring passersby. He kept his eye hotly on the line before him. He did not know where to go. He did not know what to buy.

As he reached the entrance to Wood's pharmacy, a shout of laughter went up from the lounging beaux. The next instant he was staring into the friendly grinning faces of Julius Arthur and Van Yeats.

"Where the hell do you think you're going?" said Julius Arthur.

He tried to explain; a thick jargon broke from his lips.

"He's cock-eyed drunk," said Van Yeats.

"You look out for him, Van," said Julius. "Get him in a doorway, so none of his folks will see him. I'll get the car."

Van Yeats propped him carefully against the wall; Julius Arthur ran swiftly into Church Street, and drew up in a moment at the curb. Eugene had a vast inclination to slump carelessly upon the nearest support. He placed his arms around their shoulders and collapsed. They wedged him between them on the front seat; somewhere bells were ringing.

"Ding-dong!" he said, very cheerfully. "Cris-muss!"

They answered with a wild yell of laughter.

The house was still empty when they came to it. They got him out of the car, and staggered up the steps with him. He was sorry enough that their fellowship was broken.

"Where's your room, 'Gene?" said Julius Arthur, panting, as they entered the hall.

"This one's as good as any," said Van Yeats.

The door of the front bed-room, opposite the parlor, was open. They took him in and put him on the bed.

"Let's take off his shoes," said Julius Arthur. They unlaced them and pulled them off.

"Is there anything else you want, son?" said Julius.

He tried to tell them to undress him, put him below the covers, and close the door, in order to conceal his defection from his family, but he had lost the power of speech. After looking and grinning at him for a moment, they went out without closing the door.

When they had gone he lay upon the bed, unable to move. He had no sense of time, but his mind worked very clearly. He knew that he should rise, fasten the door, and undress. But he was paralyzed.

Presently the Gants came home. Eliza alone was still in town, pondering over gifts. It was after eleven o'clock. Gant, his daughter, and his two sons came into the room and stared at him. When they spoke to him, he burned helplessly.

"Speak! Speak!" yelled Luke, rushing at him and choking him vigorously. "Are you dumb, idiot?"

I shall remember that, he thought.

"Have you no pride? Have you no honor? Has it come to this?" the sailor roared dramatically, striding around the room.

Doesn't he think he's hell, though? Eugene thought. He could not fashion words, but he could make sounds, ironically, in the rhythm of his brother's moralizing. "Tuh-tuh-tuh-tuh! Tuh-tuh-tuh-tuh! Tuh-tuh-tuh-tuh!" he said, with accurate mimicry. Helen, loosening his collar, bent over him laughing. Ben grinned swiftly under a cleft scowl.

Have you no this? Have you no that? Have you no this? Have you no that?—he was cradled in their rhythm. No, ma'am. We've run out of honor to-day, but we have a nice fresh lot of self-respect.

"Ah, be quiet," Ben muttered. "No one's dead, you know."

"Go heat some water," said Gant professionally, "he's got to get it off his stomach." He no longer seemed old. His life in a marvellous instant came from its wasting shadow; it took on a hale sinew of health and action.

"Save the fireworks," said Helen to Luke, as she left the room. "Close the door. For heaven's sake, try to keep it from mama, if you can."

This is a great moral issue, thought Eugene. He began to feel sick.

Helen returned in a very few minutes with a kettle of hot water, a glass, and a box of soda. Gant fed him the solution mercilessly until he began to vomit. At the summit of his convulsion Eliza appeared. He lifted his sick head dumbly from the bowl, and saw her white face at the door, and her weak brown eyes, that could take on so much sharpness and sparkle when her suspicion was awakened.

"Hah? Huh? What is it?" said Eliza.

But she knew, of course, instantly, what it was.

"What say?" she asked sharply. No one had said anything. He grinned feebly at her, tickled, above his nausea and grief, at the palpable assumption of blind innocence which always heralded her discoveries. Seeing her thus, they all laughed.

"Oh, my Lord!" said Helen. "Here she is. We were hoping you wouldn't get here till it was over. Come and look at your Baby," she said, with a good-humored snicker, keeping his head comfortably supported on the palm of her hand.

"How do you feel now, son?" Gant asked kindly.

"Better," he mumbled, discovering, with some elation, that his vocal paralysis was not permanent.

"Well, you see!" Helen began, kindly enough, but with a brooding satisfaction. "It only goes to show we're all alike. We all like it. It's in our blood."

"That awful curse!" Eliza said. "I had hoped that I might have one son who might escape it. It seems," she said, bursting into tears, "as if a Judgment were on us. The sins of the fathers——"

"Oh! for heaven's sake!" Helen cried angrily. "Stop it! It's not going to kill him: he'll learn a lesson from it."

Gant gnawed his thin lip, and wetted his great thumb in the old manner.

"You might know," he said, "that I'd get the blame for it. Yes— if one of them broke a leg it would be the same."

"There's one thing sure!" said Eliza. "None of them ever got it from my side of the house. Say what you will, his grandfather, Major Pentland, never in his life allowed a drop in his house."

"Major Pentland be damned!" said Gant. "If you'd depended on him for anything you'd have gone hungry."

Certainly, thought Eugene, you'd have gone thirsty.

"Forget it!" said Helen. "It's Christmas. Let's try to have a little peace and quiet once a year."

When they had left him, the boy tried to picture them lulled in the dulcet tranquillity they so often invoked. Its effects, he thought, would be more disastrous than any amount of warfare.

In the darkness, everything around and within him swam hideously. But presently he slid down into a pit of distressed sleep.

Every one had agreed on a studious forgiveness. They stepped with obtrusive care around his fault, filled pleasantly with Christmas and mercy. Ben scowled at him quite naturally, Helen grinned and prodded him, Eliza and Luke surrendered themselves to sweetness, sorrow, and silence. Their forgiveness made a loud noise in his ears.

During the morning his father asked him to come for a walk. Gant was embarrassed and hang-dog; a duty of gentle admonishment devolved upon him—he had been counselled to it by Helen and Eliza. Now, no man in his time could carry on in the big, Bow-wow style better than Gant, but none was less fitted to scatter the blossoms of sweetness and light. His wrath was sudden, his invective sprang from the moment, but he had for this occasion no thunder-bolts in his quiver, and no relish for the business before him. He had a feeling of personal guilt; he felt like a magistrate fining for intoxication a culprit with whom he has been on a spree the night before. Besides—what if the Bacchic strain in him had been passed on to his son?

They walked on in silence across the Square, by the rimmed fountain. Gant cleared his throat nervously several times.

"Son," said he presently, "I hope you'll take last night as a warning. It would be a terrible thing if you let whiskey get the best of you. I'm not going to speak harshly to you about it: I hope you'll learn a lesson by it. You had better be dead than become a drunkard."

There! He was glad it was over.

"I will!" Eugene said. He was filled with gratitude and relief. How good every one was. He wanted to make passionate avowals, great promises. He tried to speak. But he couldn't. There was too much to be said.

But they had their Christmas, beginning thus with parental advice and continuing through all the acts of contrition, love, and decorum. They put on, over their savage lives, the raiment of society, going diligently through the forms and conventions, and thinking, "now, we are like all other families"; but they were timid and shy and stiff, like rustics dressed in evening-clothes.

But they could not keep silence. They were not ungenerous or mean: they were simply not bred to any restraint. Helen veered in the wind of hysteria, the strong uncertain tides of her temperament. At times when, before her own fire, her vitality sank, and she heard the long howl of the wind outside, she almost hated Eugene.

"It's ridiculous!" she said to Luke. "His behaving like this. He's only a kid—he's had everything, we've had nothing! You see what it's come to, don't you?"

"His college education has ruined him," said the sailor, not unhappy that his candle might burn more brightly in a naughty world.

"Why don't you speak to her?" she said irritably. "She may listen to you—she won't to me! Tell her so! You've seen how she's rubbed it in to poor old papa, haven't you? Do you think that old man—sick as he is—is to blame? 'Gene's not a Gant, anyway. He takes after her side of the house. He's queer—like all of them! *We're* Gants!" she said with a bitter emphasis.

"There was always some excuse for papa," said the sailor. "He's had a lot to put up with." All his convictions in family affairs had been previously signed with her approval.

"I wish you'd tell her that. With all his moping into books, he's no better than we are. If he thinks he's going to lord it over me, he's mistaken."

"I'd like to see him try it when I'm around," said Luke grimly.

The boy was doing a multiple penance—he had committed his first great wrong in being at once so remote from them and so near to them. His present trouble was aggravated by the cross-complication of Eliza's thrusts at his father, and the latent but constantly awakening antagonism of mother and daughter. In addition, he bore directly Eliza's nagging and carping attack. All this he was prepared for—it was the weather of his mother's nature (she was as fond of him as of any of them, he thought), and the hostility of Helen and Luke was something implacable, unconscious, fundamental, that grew out of the structure of their lives. He was of them, he was recognizably marked, but he was not with them, nor like them. He had been baffled for years by the passionate enigma of their dislike—their tenders of warmth and affection, when they came, were strange to him: he accepted them gratefully and with a surprise he did not wholly conceal. Otherwise, he had grown into a shell of sullenness and quiet: he spoke little in the house.

He was wearing ragged from the affair and its consequences. He felt that he was being unfairly dealt with, but as the hammering went on he drew his head bullishly down and held his tongue, counting the hours until his holiday should end. He turned silently to Ben—he should have turned nowhere. But the trusted brother, frayed and bitter on his own accord, scowled bitterly, and gave him the harsh weight of his tongue. This finally was unendurable. He felt betrayed—utterly turned against and set upon.

The outbreak came three nights before his departure as he stood, tense and stolid, in the parlor. For almost an hour, in a savage monotone, Ben had tried deliberately, it seemed, to goad him to an attack. He had listened without a word, smothering in pain and fury, and enraging by his silence the older brother who was finding a vent for his own alien frustration.

"—and don't stand there scowling at me, you little thug. I'm telling you for your own good. I'm only trying to keep you from being a jailbird, you know."

"The trouble with you," said Luke, "is that you have no appreciation for what's been done for you. Everything's been done for you, and you haven't sense enough to appreciate it. Your college education has ruined you."

The boy turned slowly on Ben.

"All right, Ben," he muttered. "That's enough, now. I don't care what he says, but I've had enough of it from you."

This was the admission the older one had wanted. They were all in very chafed and ugly temper.

"Don't talk back to me, you little fool, or I'll bat your brains out."

The boy sprang at his brother like a cat, with a snarling cry. He bore him backward to the floor as if he were a child, laying him down gently and kneeling above him, because he had been instantly shocked by the fragility of his opponent and the ease of his advantage. He struggled with such mixed rage and shame as those who try quietly to endure the tantrum of a trying brat. As he knelt above Ben, holding his arms pinned, Luke fell heavily on his back, uttering excited cries, strangling him with one arm and cuffing awkwardly with the other.

"All right, B-B-Ben," he chattered, "you grab his legs."

A free scrimmage upon the floor followed, with such a clatter of upset scuttles, fire-irons, and chairs, that Eliza was brought at a fast gallop from the kitchen.

"Mercy!" she shrieked, as she reached the door. "They'll kill him!"

But, although being subdued—in the proud language of an older South "defeated, sir, but never beaten"—Eugene was doing very well for his age, and continued to chill the spines of his enemies with strange noises in his larynx, even after they had all clambered panting to their feet.

"I f-f-f-fink he's gone crazy," said Luke. "He j-j-jumped on us without a word of warning."

The hero replied to this with a drunken roll of the head, a furious dilation of the nostrils, and another horrible noise in his throat.

"What's to become of us!" wept Eliza. "When brother strikes brother, it seems that the smash-up has come." She lifted the padded arm-chair, and placed it on its legs again.

When he could speak, Eugene said quietly, to control the trembling of his voice:

"I'm sorry I jumped on you, Ben. You," he said to the excited sailor, "jumped on my back like a coward. But I'm sorry for what's happened. I'm sorry for what I did the other night and now. I said so, and you wouldn't leave me alone. You've tried to drive me crazy with your talk. And I didn't," he choked, "I didn't think you'd turn against me as you have. I know what the others are like—they hate me!"

"Hate you!" cried Luke excitedly. "For G-g-god's sake! You talk like a fool. We're only trying to help you, for your own good. Why should we hate you!"

"Yes, you hate me," Eugene said, "and you're ashamed to admit it. I don't know why you should, but you do. You wouldn't ever admit anything like that, but it's the truth. You're afraid of the right words. But it's been different with you," he said, turning to Ben. "We've been like brothers—and now, you've gone over against me."

"Ah!" Ben muttered, turning away nervously. "You're crazy. I don't know what you're talking about!" He lighted a cigarette, holding the match in a hand that trembled.

But although the boy had used a child's speech of woe and resentment, they knew there was a core of truth in what he had said.

"Children, children!" said Eliza sadly. "We must try to love one another. Let's try to get along together this Christmas—what time's left. It may be the last one we'll ever have together." She began to weep: "I've had such a hard life," she said, "it's been strife and turmoil all the way. It does seem I deserve a little peace and happiness now."

They were touched with the old bitter shame: they dared not look at one another. But they were awed and made quiet by the vast riddle of pain and confusion that scarred their lives.

"No one, 'Gene," Luke began quietly, "has turned against you. We want to help you—to see you amount to something. You're the last chance—if booze gets you the way it has the rest of us, you're done for."

The boy felt very tired; his voice was flat and low. He began to speak with the bluntness of despair: what he said had undebatable finality.

"And how are you going to keep booze from getting me, Luke?" he said. "By jumping on my back and trying to strangle me? That's on a level with every other effort you're ever made to know me."

"Oh," said Luke ironically, "you don't think we understand you?"

"No," Eugene said quietly. "I don't think you do. You know nothing whatever about me. I know nothing about you—or any of you. I have lived here with you for seventeen years and I'm a stranger. In all that time have you ever talked to me like a brother? Have you ever told me anything of yourself? Have you ever tried to be a friend or a companion to me?"

"I don't know what you want," Luke answered, "but I thought I was acting for the best. As to telling you about myself, what do you want to know?"

"Well," said Eugene slowly, "you're six years older than I am: you've been away to school, you've worked in big cities, and you are now enlisted in the United States Navy. Why do you always act like God Almighty," he continued with rankling bitterness. "I know what sailors do! You're no better than I am! What about liquor? What about women?"

"That's no way to talk before your mother," said Luke sternly.

"No, son," said Eliza in a troubled voice. "I don't like that way of talking."

"Then I won't talk like that," Eugene said. "But I had expected you to say that. We do not want to be told what we know. We do not want to call things by their names, although we're willing to call one another bad ones. We call meanness nobility and hatred honor. The way to make yourself a hero is to make me out a scoundrel. You won't admit that either, but it's true. Well, then, Luke, we won't talk of the ladies, black or white, you may or may not know, because it would make you uncomfortable. Instead, you can keep on being God and I'll listen to your advice, like a little boy in Sunday School. But I'd rather read the Ten Commandments where it's written down shorter and better."

"Son," said Eliza again with her ancient look of trouble and frustration, "we must try to get on together."

"No," he said. "Alone. I have done an apprenticeship here with you for seventeen years, but it is coming to an end. I know now that I shall escape; I know that I have been guilty of no great crime against you, and I am no longer afraid of you."

"Why, boy!" said Eliza. "We've done all we could for you. What crime have we accused you of?"

"Of breathing your air, of eating your food, of living under your roof, of having your life and your blood in my veins, of accepting your sacrifice and privation, and of being ungrateful for it all."

"We should all be thankful for what we have," said Luke sententiously. "Many a fellow would give his right eye for the chance you've been given."

"I've been given nothing!" said Eugene, his voice mounting with a husky flame of passion. "I'll go bent over no longer in this house. What chance I have I've made for myself in spite of you all, and over your opposition. You sent me away to the university when you could do nothing else, when it would have been a crying disgrace to you among the people in this town if you hadn't. You sent me off after the Leonards had cried me up for three years, and then you sent me a year too soon— before I was sixteen—with a box of sandwiches, two suits of clothes, and instructions to be a good boy."

"They sent you some money, too," said Luke. "Don't forget that."

"I'd be the only one who would, if I did," the boy answered. "For that is really what is behind everything, isn't it? My crime the other night was not in getting drunk, but in getting drunk without any money of my own. If I did badly at the university with money of my own, you'd dare say nothing, but if I do well on money you gave me, I must still be reminded of your goodness and my unworthiness."

"Why, son!" said Eliza diplomatically, "no one has a word to say against the way you've done your work. We're very proud of you."

"You needn't be," he said sullenly. "I've wasted a great deal of time and some money. But I've had something out of it—more than most—I've done as much work for my wages as you deserve. I've given you a fair value for your money; I thank you for nothing."

"What's that! What's that!" said Eliza sharply.

"I said I thank you for nothing, but I take that back."

"That's better!" said Luke.

"Yes, I have a great deal to give thanks for," said Eugene. "I give thanks for every dirty lust and hunger that crawled through the polluted blood of my noble ancestors. I give thanks for every scrofulous token that may ever come upon me. I give thanks for the love and mercy that kneaded me over the washtub the day before my birth. I give thanks for the country slut who nursed me and let my dirty bandage fester across my navel. I give thanks for every blow and curse I had from any of you during my childhood, for every dirty cell you ever gave me to sleep in, for the ten million hours of cruelty or indifference, and the thirty minutes of cheap advice."

"Unnatural!" Eliza whispered. "Unnatural son! You will be punished if there's a just God in heaven."

"Oh, there is! I'm sure there is!" cried Eugene. "Because I have been punished. By God, I shall spend the rest of my life getting my heart back, healing and forgetting every scar you put upon me when I was a child. The first move I ever made, after the cradle, was to crawl for the door, and every move I have made since has been an effort to escape. And now at last I am free from you all, although you may hold me for a few years more. If I am not free, I am at least locked up in my own prison, but I shall get me some beauty, I shall get me some order out of this jungle of my life: I shall find my way out of it yet, though it take me twenty years more—alone."

"Alone?" said Eliza, with the old suspicion. "Where are you going?"

"Ah," he said, "you were not looking, were you? I've gone."

33

During the few remaining days of his holiday, he stayed almost entirely away from the house, coming for a brief and mumbled meal, and late at night, for bed. He waited for departure as a prisoner for release. The dolorous prelude to a journey—the wet platform eyes, the sudden radiation of hectic warmth, the declarations of love at sound of the whistle—left him this time unmoved. The tear-ducts, he was beginning to discover, had, like sweat-glands, dermic foundations, and were easily brought to a salty sparkle at mere sight of a locomotive. He had, therefore, the somewhat detached composure of a gentleman on his way to a comfortable week-end, who stands in a noisy crowd, waiting for the ferry.

He gave benediction to the words in which he had so happily defined his position as wage-earner. They stated and confirmed an attitude, and in some measure protected him against the constant betrayals of sentiment. During the Spring he worked stupendously at joining activities, knowing that here was coin whose ring they could hear. He wrote conscientiously each item of his distinctions; his name found its way back more than once to the indulgent Altamont papers. Gant kept the clippings proudly, and gave public readings when he could.

The boy had two short awkward letters from Ben, who was now stationed one hundred miles away, in the tobacco town. At Easter, Eugene visited him, staying at his lodgings, where again his unerring destiny had thrown him into the welcoming arms of a gray-haired widow. She was under fifty—a handsome silly woman, who prodded and teased him as she would an adored child. She addressed him—with a loose giggle—as "Old Curly-Head," at which he fetched out his usual disgusted plea to his Maker. "O my God! Listen to this!" She had reverted to an astonishing romping girlhood, and would exercise her playfulness by leaping suddenly upon Old Curly-Head, dealing him a stiff dig in the ribs, and skipping away with a triumphant "Hah! Got you that time!"

There was forever in that town a smell of raw tobacco, biting the nostrils with its acrid pungency: it smote the stranger coming from the train, but all the people in the town denied it, saying: "No; there is no smell at all." And within a day the stranger too could smell it no more.

On Easter morning he arose in the blue light and went with the other pilgrims to the Moravian cemetery.

"You ought to see it," Ben said. "It's a famous custom: people come from everywhere." But the older brother did not go. Behind massed bands of horns, the trumpeting blare of trombones, the big crowds moved into the strange burial ground where all the stones lay flat upon the graves—symbol, it was said, of all-levelling Death. But as the horns blared, the old ghoul-fantasy of death returned, the grave slabs made him think of table-cloths: he felt as if he were taking part in some obscene feast.

Spring was coming on again across the earth like a light sparkle of water-spray: all of the men who had died were making their strange and lovely return in blossom and flower. Ben walked along the streets of the tobacco town looking like asphodel. It was strange to find a ghost there in that place: his ancient soul prowled wearily by the cheap familiar brick and all the young facades.

There was a Square on high ground; in the centre a courthouse. Cars were parked in close lines. Young men loitered in the drug-store.

How real it is, Eugene thought. It is like something we have always known about and do not need to see. The town would not have seemed strange to Thomas Aquinas,—but he to the town.

Ben prowled along, greeting the merchants with a grave scowl, leaning his skull against their round skulls of practicality, across their counters— a phantom soliciting advertisement in a quiet monotone.

"This is my kid brother, Mr. Fulton."

"Hello, son! Dogged if they don't grow tall 'uns up there, Ben. Well, if you're like Old Ben, young fellow, we won't kick. We think a lot of him here."

That's like thinking well of Balder, in Connecticut, Eugene thought.

"I have only been here three months," said Ben, resting in bed on his elbow and smoking a cigarette. "But I know all the leading business men already. I'm well thought of here." He glanced at his brother quickly and grinned, with a shy charm of rare confession. But his fierce eyes were desperate and lonely. Hill-haunted? For—home? He smoked.

"You see, they think well of you, once you get away from your people. You'll never have a chance at home, 'Gene. They'll ruin everything for you. For heaven's sake, get away when you can.—What's the matter with you? Why are you looking at me like that?" he said sharply, alarmed at the set stare of the boy's face. In a moment he said: "They'll spoil your life. Can't you forget about her?"

"No," said Eugene. In a moment he added: "She's kept coming back all Spring."

He twisted his throat with a wild cry.

The Spring advanced with a mounting hum of war. The older students fell out quietly and drifted away to enlistments. The younger strained tensely, waiting. The war brought them no sorrow: it was a pageant which might, they felt, pluck them instantly into glory. The country flowed with milk and honey. There were strange rumors of a land of Eldorado to the north, amid the war industry of the Virginia coast. Some of the students had been there, the year before: they brought back stories of princely wages. One could earn twelve dollars a day, with no experience. One could assume the duties of a carpenter, with only a hammer, a saw, and a square. No questions were asked.

War is not death to young men; war is life. The earth had never worn raiment of such color as it did that year. The war seemed to unearth pockets of ore that had never been known in the nation: there was a vast unfolding and exposure of wealth and power. And somehow—this imperial wealth, this display of power in men and money, was blended into a lyrical music. In Eugene's mind, wealth and love and glory melted into a symphonic noise: the age of myth and miracle had come upon the world again. All things were possible.

He went home stretched like a bowstring and announced his intention of going away into Virginia. There was protest, but not loud enough to impede him. Eliza's mind was fastened on real-estate and the summer trade. Gant stared into the darkness at his life. Helen laughed at him and scolded him; then fell to plucking at her chin, absently.

"Can't do without her? You can't fool me! No, sir. I know why you want to go," she said jocularly. "She's a married woman now: she may have a baby, for all you know. You've no right to go after her."

Then abruptly, she said:

"Well, let him go if he wants to. It looks silly to me, but he's got to decide for himself."

He got twenty-five dollars from his father—enough to pay his railway fare to Norfolk and leave him a few dollars.

"Mark my words," said Gant. "You'll be back in a week's time. It's a wild-goose chase you're going on."

He went.

All through the night he drew toward her across Virginia, propped on his elbow in the berth and staring bewitched upon the great romantic country clumped with dreaming woodlands and white as a weird dawn beneath the blazing moonlight.

Early in the morning he came to Richmond. He had to change trains; there was a wait. He went out from the station and walked up the hill toward the fine old State House drenched cleanly in the young morning light. He ate breakfast at a lunchroom on Broad Street, filled already with men going to their work. This casual and brief contact with their lives, achieved after his lonely and magnificent approach through the night, thrilled him by its very casualness. All the little ticking sounds of a city beginning its day, the strange familiarity of voices in an alien place, heard curiously after the thunder of the wheels, seemed magical and unreal. The city had no existence save that which he conferred on it: he wondered how it had lived before he came, how it would live after he left. He looked at all the men, feeding with eyes that held yet the vast moon-meadows of the night and the cool green width of the earth. They were like men in a zoo; he gazed at them, looking for all the little particular markings of the town, the fine mapping upon their limbs and faces of their own little cosmos. And the great hunger for voyages rose up in him—to come always, as now at dawn, into strange cities, striding in among them, and sitting with them unknown, like a god in exile, stored with the enormous vision of the earth.

The counterman yawned and turned the crackling pages of a morning paper. That was strange.

Cars clanked by, beginning to work through the town. Merchants lowered their awnings; he left them as their day began.

An hour later he was riding for the sea. Eighty miles away lay the sea and Laura. She slept unwitting of the devouring wheels that brought him to her. He looked at the aqueous blue sky whitened with little clouds, and at the land wooded with pines and indefinable tokens of the marshes and bright salt.

The train drew under the boat-shed at Newport News. The terrific locomotive, as beautiful as any ship, breathed with unlaborious fatigue at the rail-head. There, by lapping water, she came to rest, like a completed destiny.

The little boat lay waiting at the dock. Within a few minutes he had left the hot murky smell of the shed and was cruising out into the blue water of the Roads. A great light wind swept over the water, making a singing noise through the tackle of the little boat, making a music and a glory in his heart. He drove along the little decks at a bounding stride, lunging past the staring people, with wild noises in his throat. The lean destroyers, the bright mad camouflage of the freighters and the transports, the lazy red whirl of a propeller, half-submerged, and the light winey sparkle of the waves fused to a single radiance and filled him with glory. He cried back into the throat of the enormous wind, and his eyes were wet.

Upon the decks of the boats, clean little figures in white moved about; under the bulging counter of a huge Frenchman young naked men were swimming. They come from France, he thought, and it is strange that they should be here.

O, the wonder, the magic and the loss! His life was like a great wave breaking in the lonely sea; his hungry shoulder found no barriers— he smote his strength at nothing, and was lost and scattered like a wrack of mist. But he believed that this supreme ecstasy which mastered him and made him drunken might some day fuse its enormous light into a single articulation. He was Phaeton with the terrible horses of the sun: he believed that his life might pulse constantly at its longest stroke, achieve an eternal summit.

The hot Virginias broiled under the fierce blue oven of the sky, but in the Roads the ships rocked in the freshening breeze of war and glory.

Eugene remained in the furnace of Norfolk for four days, until his money was gone. He watched it go without fear, with a sharp quickening of his pulses, tasting the keen pleasure of his loneliness and the unknown turnings of his life. He sensed the throbbing antennae of the world: life purred like a hidden dynamo, with the vast excitement of ten thousand glorious threats. He might do all, dare all, become all. The far and the mighty was near him, around him, above him. There was no great bridge to span, no hard summit to win. From obscurity, hunger, loneliness, he might be lifted in a moment into power, glory, love. The transport loading at the docks might bear him war-ward, love-ward, fame-ward Wednesday night.

He walked by lapping water through the dark. He heard its green wet slap against the crusted pier-piles: he drank its strong cod scent, and watched the loading of great boats drenched in blazing light as they weltered slowly down into the water. And the night was loud with the rumble of huge cranes, the sudden loose rattle of the donkey-engines, the cries of the overseers, and the incessant rumbling trucks of stevedores within the pier.

His imperial country, for the first time, was gathering the huge thrust of her might. The air was charged with murderous exuberance, rioting and corrupt extravagance.

Through the hot streets of that town seethed the toughs, the crooks, the vagabonds of a nation—Chicago gunmen, bad niggers from Texas, Bowery bums, pale Jews with soft palms, from the shops of the city, Swedes from the Middle-West, Irish from New England, mountaineers from Tennessee and North Carolina, whores, in shoals and droves, from everywhere. For these the war was a fat enormous goose raining its golden eggs upon them. There was no thought or belief in any future. There was only the triumphant *Now*. There was no life beyond the moment. There was only an insane flux and re-flux of getting and spending.

Young men from Georgia farms came, in the evenings, from their work on piers, in camps, in shipyards, to dress up in their peacock plumage. And at night, hard and brown and lean of hand and face, they stood along the curbing in $18.00 tan leathers, $80.00 suits, and $8.00 silk shirts striped with broad alternating bands of red and blue. They were carpenters, masons, gang overseers, or said they were: they were paid ten, twelve, fourteen, eighteen dollars a day.

They shifted, veered from camp to camp, worked for a month, loafed opulently for a week, enjoying the brief bought loves of girls they met upon the ocean-beach or in a brothel.

Strapping black buck-niggers, with gorilla arms and the black paws of panthers, earned $60 a week as stevedores, and spent it on a mulatto girl in a single evening of red riot.

And more quietly, soberly, in this crowd, moved the older thriftier workmen: the true carpenters, the true masons, the true mechanics—the canny Scotch-Irish of North Carolina, the fishermen of the Virginia coast, the careful peasantry of the Middle-West, who had come to earn, to save, to profit from the war.

Everywhere amid this swarming crowd gleamed the bright raimant of blood and glory: the sailors thronged the streets in flapping blues and spotless whites—brown, tough, and clean. The marines strode by in arrogant twos, stiff as rods in the loud pomp of chevrons and striped trousers. Commanders gray and grim, hard-handed C. P. O.'s, and elegant young ensigns out of college, with something blonde and fluffy at their side, went by among the red cap-buttons of French matelots, or the swagger sea-wise port of the Englishmen.

Through this crowd, with matted uncut hair that fell into his eyes, that shot its spirals through the rents of his old green hat, that curled a thick scroll up his dirty neck, Eugene plunged with hot devouring eyes—soaked in his sweat by day, sharp and stale by night.

In this great camp of vagrant floaters he lost himself: he came home into this world from loneliness. The hunger for voyages, the hunger that haunts Americans, who are a nomad race, was half-assuaged here in this maelstrom of the war.

He lost himself in the crowd. He lost count of the days. His little store of money melted. He moved from a cheap hotel, loud at night with the noise of harlotry, to a little attic room in a lodging-house, an oven of hot pine and tarred roof; he moved from the lodging-house to a fifty-cent cot in the Y. M. C. A., where, returning night by night, he paid his fee, and slept in a room with forty snoring sailors.

Finally, his money gone, he slept, until driven out, in all-night lunch-rooms; upon the Portsmouth ferry; and over lapping water on a rotting pier.

By night he prowled about among the negroes; he listened to their rich proposed seductions; he went where the sailors went, down Church Street, where the women were. He prowled the night with young beast-lust, his thin boy-body stale with sweat, his hot eyes burning through the dark.

He grew hungry for food. His money was gone. But there was a hunger and thirst in him that could not be fed. Over the chaos of his brain hung the shadow of Laura James. Her shadow hung above the town, above all life. It had brought him here; his heart was swollen with pain and pride; he would not go to find her.

He was obsessed with the notion that he would find her in the crowd, upon the street, around the corner. He would not speak to her if he met her. He would go proudly and indifferently by. He would not see her. She would see him. She would see him at some heroic moment, just as he was receiving the love and respect of beautiful women. She would speak to him; he would not speak to her. She would be stricken; she would be beaten down; she would cry to him for love and mercy.

Thus, unclean, unkempt, clothed in rags and hunger and madness, he saw himself victorious, heroic and beautiful. He was mad with his obsession. He thought he saw Laura on the streets a dozen times a day: his heart turned rotten; he did not know what he should do or say, whether to run or remain. He brooded for hours over her address in the telephone directory; sitting by the phone, he trembled with excitement because its awful magic could be sounded at a gesture, because within a minute he could be with her, voice to voice.

He hunted out her home. She was living in an old frame house far out from the centre of the town. He stalked carefully about the neighborhood, keeping a block away from the house at all times, observing it obliquely, laterally, from front and back, with stealthy eye and a smothering thud of the heart, but never passing before it, never coming directly to it.

He was foul and dirty. The soles of his shoes wore through: his calloused feet beat against hot pavements. He stank.

At length, he tried to get work. Work there was in great abundance—but the princely wages of which he had been told were hard to find. He could not swear he was a carpenter, a mason. He was a dirty boy, and looked it. He was afraid. He went to the Navy Yard at Portsmouth, the Naval Base at Norfolk, the Bush Terminal—everywhere there was work, abundant work—hard labor that paid four dollars a day. This he would gladly have taken; but he found that he could not have his wages until after the second week, and that one week's pay would be withheld to tide him over in illness, trouble, or departure.

And he had no money left.

He went to a Jew and pawned the watch Eliza had given him upon his birthday. He got five dollars on it. Then he went by boat once more to Newport News, and by trolley up the coast to Hampton. He had heard, in the thronging rumor of Norfolk, that there was work upon the flying field, and that the worker was fed and housed upon the field, at company expense.

In the little employment shack at the end of the long bridge that led across into the field, he was signed on as a laborer and searched by the sentry, who made him open his valise. Then he labored across the bridge, kneeing his heavy bag, which bulged with his soiled and disorderly belongings, before him.

He staggered at length into the rude company office and sought out the superintendent, a man in the thirties, shaven, pale, weary, who wore a blue eyeshade, armbands, and talked with a limp cigarette plastered on his lip.

Eugene thrust out his employment slip in shaking fingers. The man looked briefly at it.

"College boy, aren't you, son?" he said, glancing at Eugene.

"Yes, sir," said Eugene.

"Did you ever do day labor before?" said the man.

"No, sir," said Eugene.

"How old are you, son?" the man asked.

Eugene was silent for a moment. "I'm—nineteen," he said at length, wondering, since he had lied, why he had not had courage to say twenty.

The superintendent grinned wearily.

"It's hard work, son," the man said. "You'll be among the wops and the Swedes and the hunkies. You'll live in the same bunkhouse, you'll eat with them. They don't smell nice, son."

"I have no money," said Eugene. "I'll work hard. I won't get sick. Give me the job. Please!"

"No," said the man. "No, I won't do that."

Eugene turned blindly away.

"I tell you what I'll do," said the superintendent. "I'll give you a job as a checker. You'll be with the office force. That's where you belong. You'll live with them in their own bunkhouse. They're nice fellows," he said elegantly, "college fellows, like yourself."

"Thank you," said Eugene, clenching his fingers, with husky emotion. "Thank you."

"The checker we've got is quitting," said the superintendent. "You'll go to the stables with him in the morning to get your horse."

"H-h-h-horse?" said Eugene.

"You'll have a horse," said the superintendent, "to ride around on."

With strong bowel-excitement Eugene began to think of the horse, with joy, with fear. He turned to go. He could not bear to talk of money.

"H-h-how much—?" he finally croaked, feeling that he must. Business.

"I'll give you $80 a month to begin with," said the manager with a touch of magnificence. "If you make good, I'll give you a hundred."

"And my keep?" whispered Eugene.

"Sure!" said the manager. "That's thrown in."

Eugene reeled away with his valise, and with a head full of exploding rockets.

These months, although filled with terror and hunger, must be passed in rapid summary with bare mention of the men and actions that a lost boy knew. They belong to a story of escape and wandering—valuable here to indicate the initiation to the voyage this life will make. They are a prelude to exile, and into their nightmare chaos no other purpose may be read than the blind groping of a soul toward freedom and isolation.

Eugene worked upon the Flying Field for a month. Three times a day he rode around the field to check the numbers of two dozen gangs who were engaged in the work of grading, levelling, blasting from the spongy earth the ragged stumps of trees and filling interminably, ceaselessly, like the weary and fruitless labor of a nightmare, the marshy earth-craters, which drank their shovelled toil without end. The gangs were of all races and conditions: Portugee niggers, ebony-black, faithful and childlike, who welcomed him with great toothy grins, each pointing to his big white pin, on which was printed his number, crying out in strange outlandish voices, "feefety-nine, nine-net-ty seex," and so on; Bowery bums, in greasy serge and battered derbies, toying distastefully with pick-handles that shredded their dirty uncalloused palms—their hard evil faces, with their smudge of beard, were like things corrupt, green-yellow, that grow under barrels. And there were also drawling fishermen from the Virginia coast, huge gorilla niggers from Georgia and the lower South, Italians, Swedes, Irishmen—part of the huge compost of America.

He came to know them and their overseers—tough reckless men, gray-haired and lustful, full of swift action and coarse humor.

Stuck like a jigging doll upon the horse, whom he feared, he rode, staring into heaven, sometimes almost unconscious of the great engine expanding and contracting below him with a brown sensual rhythm. The bird-men filled the blue Virginia weather with the great drone of the Liberties.

At length, hungry again for the ships and faces, he left his work and spent his earnings in a week of gaudy riot in Norfolk and on the Virginia beaches. Almost penniless again, with only the savage kaleidoscope of a thousand streets, a million lights, the blazing confusion and the strident noise of carnival, he returned to Newport News in search of employment, accompanied by another youth from Altamont, likewise a thriftless adventurer in war-work, whom he had found upon the beach. This worthy, whose name was Sinker Jordan, was three years older than Eugene. He was a handsome reckless boy, small in stature, and limping from an injury he had received in a football game. His character was weak and volatile—he hated effort, and was obstinate only in cursing ill-fortune.

The two young men had a few dollars between them. They pooled their resources, and, with wild optimism, purchased from a pawnbroker in Newport News the rudiments of carpenter's equipment—hammers, saws, and T-squares. They went inland fifteen or twenty miles to a dreary government camp sweltering in the Virginia pines. They were refused employment here and in black dejection returned in the afternoon to the town they had left so hopefully in the morning. Before sundown they had secured employment in the Shipbuilding Yards, but they had been discharged five minutes after they reported for work, when they confessed to a grinning foreman in a room full of woodshavings and quietly slatting belts, that they had no knowledge of the intensely special carpentry of ship's carving. Nor (they might have added) of any other.

They were quite moneyless now, and once on the street again, Sinker Jordan had hurled upon the pavement the fatal tools, cursing savagely the folly that threatened now to keep them hungry. Eugene picked the tools up, and took them back to the imperturbable Uncle, who repurchased them for only a few dollars less than the sum they had paid him in the morning.

Thus the day. They found a lodging in a dingy house where, as an appropriate climax to his folly, Sinker Jordan surrendered their remaining capital into the greedy palm of the landlady—and a real lady too, she admitted. But, having previously eaten, they had all the hope of a full belly and their youth—they slept, Sinker without care and without effort.

Eugene was early up at dawn, and after futile efforts to waken the luxuriously somnolent Sinker, he was off to the dingy yellow piers along the waterfront, which were stored with munitions for the war. After a morning tramping up and down the dusty road outside the guarded enclosure, he had obtained employment for himself and Sinker from the chief checker, a nervous ugly man, swollen with petty tyranny. He had gimlet eyes, glittering below spectacles, and hard muscular jaws that writhed constantly.

Eugene went to work at seven the next morning—Sinker, a day or two later, only when his last small coin had vanished. Eugene screwed up his pride and borrowed a few dollars from one of the other checkers. On this he and Sinker lived meagerly until pay-day—which was only a few days off. This money slipped quickly through their careless fingers. Down to a few coins again, with the next pay-day almost two weeks off, Sinker gambled at dice with the checkers, behind the great fortress of sacked oats upon the pier—lost, won, lost, rose penniless and cursing God. Eugene knelt beside the checkers, with his last half-dollar in his palm, heedless of Sinker's bitter taunt. He had never thrown dice before: naturally, he won—$8.50. He rose exultantly from their profane surprise, and took Sinker to dinner at the best hotel.

A day or two later, he went behind the oats again, gambled with his last dollar—and lost.

He began to starve. Day crawled into weary day. The fierce eye of July beat down upon the pier with a straight insufferable glare. The boats and trains slid in and out, crammed to the teeth with munitions—with food for the soldiers. The hot grainy air on the pier swam before his eyes speckled with dancing patches, and he made weary tallies on a sheet as the big black stevedores swarmed past him with their trunks. Sinker Jordan cadged small sums from the other checkers, and lived miserably on bottled pop and cheese at a little grocery across the road from the pier. Eugene was unable to beg or borrow. Partly from pride, but more from the powerful brooding inertia of his temper, which more and more was governing his will to act, he found himself unable to speak. Each day he said: "I shall speak to one of them to-day. I shall say that I must eat, and that I have no money." But when he tried to speak he could not.

As they grew more efficient in their work they were called back, after the day's end, for work at night. This extra work, with its time-and-a-half pay, he would otherwise have been glad to get, but stumbling from exhaustion, the command to return was horrible. For several days now he had not been home to the dingy little room which he shared with Sinker Jordan. At the end of his day's work, he would climb to a little oasis in the enormous wall of sacked oats and sink into exhausted sleep, with the rattling of cranes and winches, the steady rumble of the trucks, and the remote baying of boats anchored in the stream—mixing in a strange faint symphony in his ears.

And he lay there, with the fading glimmer of the world about him, as the war mounted to its climax of blood and passion during that terrible month. He lay there, like his own ghost, thinking with pain, with grief, of all the million towns and faces he had not known. He was the atom for which all life had been aplot—Caesar had died and a nameless wife of Babylon, and somewhere here, upon this marvellous dying flesh, this myriad brain, their mark, their spirit, rested.

And he thought of the strange lost faces he had known, the lonely figures of his family, damned in chaos, each chained to a destiny of ruin and loss—Gant, a fallen Titan, staring down enormous vistas of the Past, indifferent to the world about him; Eliza, beetle-wise, involved in blind accretions; Helen, childless, pathless, furious—a great wave breaking on the barren waste; and finally, Ben—the ghost, the stranger, prowling at this moment in another town, going up and down the thousand streets of life, and finding no doors.

But the next day, on the pier, Eugene was weaker than ever. He sat sprawled upon a throne of plump oat sacks, with blurred eyes watching the loading of the bags at the spout, marking raggedly his tally upon the sheet as the stevedores plunged in and out. The terrible heat steamed through the grainy pollen of the air: he moved each limb with forethought, picking it up and placing it as if were a detached object.

At the end of the day he was asked to return for night-work. He listened, swaying on his feet, to the far-sounding voice of the chief checker.

The supper hour came, upon the heated pier, with the sudden noise of silence. There were small completed noises up and down the enormous shed: a faint drumming of footfalls of workers walking toward the entrance, a slap of water at the ship's hull, a noise from the bridge.

Eugene went behind the oat pile and climbed blindly up until he reached his little fortress at the top. The world ebbed from his fading sense: all sound grew fainter, more far. Presently, he thought, when I have rested here, I shall get up and go down to work. It has been a hot day. I am tired. But when he tried to move he could not. His will struggled against the imponderable lead of his flesh, stirring helplessly like a man in a cage. He thought quietly, with relief, with tranquil joy. They will not find me here. I cannot move. It is over. If I had thought

of this long ago, I would have been afraid. But I'm not, now. Here—
upon the oat pile—doing my bit—for Democracy. I'll begin to stink.
They'll find me then.

Life glimmered away out of his weary eyes. He lay, half-conscious,
sprawled upon the oats. He thought of the horse.

In this way the young checker, who had loaned him money, found
him. The checker knelt above him, supporting Eugene's head with one
hand, and putting a bottle of raw hard liquor to his mouth with the
other. When the boy had revived somewhat, the checker helped him
to descend the pile and walked slowly with him up the long wooden
platform of the pier.

They went across the road to a little grocery-store. The checker
ordered a bottle of milk, a box of crackers, and a big block of cheese.
As Eugene ate, the tears began to flow down his grimy face, dredging
dirty gullies on his skin. They were tears of hunger and weakness: he
could not restrain them.

The checker stood over him watchfully, with a kindly troubled stare.
He was a young man with a lantern jaw, and a thin dish face: he wore
scholarly spectacles, and smoked a pipe reflectively.

"Why didn't you tell me, boy? I'd have let you have the money,"
he said.

"I—don't—know," said Eugene, between bites of cheese. "Couldn't."

With the checker's loan of five dollars he and Sinker Jordan lived
until pay-day. Then, after dining together on four pounds of steak,
Sinker Jordan departed for Altamont and the enjoyment of an inherit-
ance which had fallen due a few days before, on his twenty-first birthday.
Eugene stayed on.

He was like a man who had died, and had been re-born. All that
had gone before lived in a ghostly world. He thought of his family, of
Ben, of Laura James, as if they were ghosts. The world itself turned
ghost. All through that month of August, while the war marched to
its ending, he looked upon its dying carnival. Nothing seemed any
longer hard and hot and raw and new. Everything was old. Everything
was dying. A vast aerial music, forever far-faint, like the language of
his forgotten world, sounded in his ears. He had known birth. He had
known pain and love. He had known hunger. Almost he had known
death.

At night, when he was not called back for work he rode out by trolley to one of the Virginia beaches. But the only sound that was real, that was near and present, was the sound in his heart, in his brain, of the everlasting sea. He turned his face toward it: behind him, the cheap million lights of the concessionaires, the clatter, the racket, the confetti, the shrill blare of the saxophones, all the harsh joyless noise of his country, was softened, was made sad, far, and phantom. The wheeling merry-go-round, the blaring dance-orchestra, played *K-K-K-Katy Beautiful Katy, Poor Little Buttercup,* and *Just a Baby's Prayer at Twilight.*

And that cheap music turned elfin and lovely; it was mixed into magic—it became a part of the romantic and lovely Virginias, of the surge of the sea, as it rolled in from the eternal dark, across the beach, and of his own magnificent sorrow—his triumphant loneliness after pain and love and hunger.

His face was thin and bright as a blade, below the great curling shock of his hair; his body as lean as a starved cat's; his eyes bright and fierce.

O sea! (he thought) I am the hill-born, the prison-pent, the ghost, the stranger, and I walk here at your side. O sea, I am lonely like you, I am strange and far like you, I am sorrowful like you; my brain, my heart, my life, like yours, have touched strange shores. You are like a woman lying below yourself on the coral floor. You are an immense and fruitful woman with vast thighs and a great thick mop of curling woman's hair floating like green moss above your belly. And you will bring me to the happy land, you will wash me to glory in bright ships.

There by the sea of the dark Virginias, he thought of the forgotten faces, of all the million patterns of himself, the ghost of his lost flesh. The child that heard Swain's cow, the lost boy in the Ozarks, the carrier of news among the blacks, and the boy who went in by the lattice with Jim Trivett. And the waitress, and Ben, and Laura? Dead, too? Where? How? Why? Why has the web been woven? Why do we die so many deaths? How came I here beside the sea? O lost, O far and lonely, where?

Sometimes, as he walked back among the dancers, a scarecrow in flapping rags, he looked and saw himself among them. He seemed to be two people: he constantly saw himself with dark bent face sitting upon the top rail of a fence, watching himself go by with a bright herd of young people. He saw himself among the crowds, several inches shorter than he was, fitting comfortably into a world where everything was big enough for him.

And while he stared and saw himself beloved and admitted, he heard them laugh: he felt suddenly the hard white ring of their faces about him, and he plunged away, with cursing mouth.

O my sweet bitches! My fine cheap sluts! You little crawling itch of twiddlers: you will snigger at me! At me! At me! (He beat his hands against his ribs.) You will mock at me, with your drug-store pimps, your Jazz-bo apes, your gorilla gobs, you cute little side-porch chippies! What do you understand? The lust of a goat, the stink of your kind—that does for you, my girls. And yet you laugh at me! Ah, but I'll tell you why you laugh: you are afraid of me because I am not like the others. You hate me because I do not belong. You see I am finer and greater than any one you know: you cannot reach me and you hate me. That's it! The ethereal (yet manly) beauty of my features, my boyish charm (for I am Just a Boy) blended with the tragic wisdom of my eyes (as old as life and filled with the brooding tragedy of the ages), the sensitive and delicate flicker of my mouth, and my marvellous dark face blooming inward on strange loveliness like a flower—all this you want to kill because you cannot touch it. Ah me! (Thinking of his strange beauty, his eyes grew moist with love and glory, and he was forced to blow his nose.) Ah, but She will know. The love of a lady. Proudly, with misty eyes, he saw her standing beside him against the rabble: her elegant small head, wound with a bracelet of bright hair, against his shoulder, and with two splendid pearls in her ears. Dearest! Dearest! We stand here on a star. We are beyond them now. Behold! They shrink, they fade, they pass—victorious, enduring, marvellous love, my dearest, we remain.

Brooding thus on the vision of his own beauty, stirred by his own heroic music, with misty eyes, he would pass over into the forbidden settlement, with its vigilant patrols of naval and military police on the watch for their own, and prowl softly down a dark little street to a dingy frame house with drawn blinds, where dwelt a love that for three dollars could be bought and clothed with his own fable. Her name was Stella Blake. She was never in a hurry.

With her lived a young corn-haired girl of twenty years whose family lived in Pulpit Hill. Sometimes he went to see her.

Twice a week the troops went through. They stood densely in brown and weary thousands on the pier while a council of officers, tabled at the gangways, went through their clearance papers. Then, each below the sweating torture of his pack, they were filed from the hot furnace of the pier into the hotter prison of the ship. The great ships, with their motley jagged patches of deception, waited in the stream: they slid in and out in unending squadrons.

Sometimes the troops were black—labor regiments from Georgia and Alabama; big gorilla bucks from Texas. They gleamed with sweat and huge rich laughter: they were obedient as children and called their cursing officers "boss."

"And don't you call me 'boss' again, you bastards!" screamed a young Tennessee lieutenant, who had gone slowly insane during the moving, as he nursed his charges through hell. They grinned at him cheerfully, with affection, like good obedient children, as he stamped, raving, up and down the pier. From time to time they goaded him into a new frenzy with complaints about lost hats, bayonets, small arms, and papers. Somehow he found things for them; somehow he cursed his way through, keeping them in order. They grinned affectionately, therefore, and called him boss.

"And what in Jesus' name have you done now?" he yelled, as a huge black sergeant with several enlisted men, who had gathered at the examiner's table, burst suddenly into loud roars of grief.

The fiery lieutenant rushed at the table, cursing.

The sergeant and several enlisted men, all Texas darkies, had come away from camp without a clean bill of health: they were venereals and had not been cured.

"Boss," blubbered the big black sergeant, "we wants to go to France. We don't want to git lef' in dis Gawd-dam hole."

(Nor do I blame them, thought Eugene.)

"I'll kill you! So help me God, I'll kill you!" screamed the officer, hurling his trim cap upon the ground and stamping upon it. But, a moment later, with a medical officer he was leading them away for examination behind the great wall of sacked oats. Five minutes later they emerged. The negroes were cavorting with joy: they pressed around their fierce commander, seizing and kissing his hand, fawning upon him, adoring him.

"You see," said the dish-faced checker, while he and Eugene watched, "that's what it takes to hold a crowd of niggers. You can't be nice to 'em. They'd do anything for that guy."

"He would for them," said Eugene.

These negroes, he thought, who came from Africa, were sold at the block in Louisiana, and live in Texas, are now on their way to France.

Mr. Finch, the chief checker with the ugly slit eyes, approached Eugene with a smile of false warmth. His gray jaws worked.

"I've got a job for you, Gant," he said. "Double-time pay. I want you to get in on some of the easy money."

"What is it?" said Eugene.

"They're loading this ship with big stuff," said Mr. Finch. "They're taking her out into the stream to get it on. I want you to go out with her. They'll take you off in a tug to-night."

The dish-faced checker, when jubilantly he told him of his appointment, said:

"They asked me to go, but I wouldn't."

"Why not?" said Eugene.

"I don't want the money bad enough. They're loading her with T. N. T. and nitro-glycerin. The niggers play baseball with those cases. If they ever drop one, they'll bring you home in a bucket."

"It's all in the day's work," said Eugene dramatically.

This was danger, war. He was definitely in on it, risking his hide for Democracy. He was thrilled.

When the big freighter slid away from the pier, he stood in the bow with spread legs, darting his eyes about with fierce eagle glances. The iron decks blistered his feet through the thin soles of his shoes. He did not mind. He was the captain.

She anchored seaward down the Roads, and the great barges were nosed in by the tugs. All through the day, under a broiling sun, they loaded her from the rocking barges: her huge yellow booms swung up and down; by nightfall she rode deeply in the water, packed to her throat with shells and powder, and bearing on the hot plates of her deck 1200 grisly tons of field artillery.

Eugene stood with fierce appraising eyes, walking about the guns with a sense of authority, jotting down numbers, items, pieces. From time to time he thrust a handful of moist scrap-tobacco into his mouth, and chewed with an air of relish. He spat hot sizzling gobs upon the iron deck. God! thought he. This is man's work. Heave-ho, ye black devils! There's a war on! He spat.

The tug came at nightfall and took him off. He sat apart from the stevedores, trying to fancy the boat had come for him alone. The lights went twinkling up the far Virginia shores. He spat into the swirling waters.

When the trains slid in and out, the stevedores raised the wooden bridges that spanned the tracks. Foot by foot, with rhythmic pull and halt, the gangs tugged at the ropes, singing, under the direction of their leader their song of love and labor:

"Jelly Roll! (Heh!) Je-e-elly Roll."

They were great black men, each with his kept woman. They earned fifty or sixty dollars a week.

Once or twice again, in the dying summer, Eugene went to Norfolk. He saw the sailor, but he no longer tried to see Laura. She seemed far and lost.

He had not written home all summer. He found a letter from Gant, written in his father's Gothic sprawl—a sick and feeble letter, written sorrowfully and far away. O lost! Eliza, in the rush and business of the summer trade, had added a few practical lines. Save his money. Get plenty of good food. Keep well. Be a good boy.

The boy was a lean column of brown skin and bone. He had lost over thirty pounds during the summer: he was over six foot four and weighed little more than one hundred and thirty pounds.

The sailor was shocked at his emaciation, and bullied him with blustering reproof:

"Why didn't you t-t-tell me where you were, idiot? I'd have sent you money. For G-g-god's sake! Come on and eat!" They ate.

The summer waned. When September came, Eugene quit his work and, after a luxurious day or two in Norfolk, started homeward. But, at Richmond, where there was a wait of three hours between trains, he changed his plans suddenly and went to a good hotel.

He was touched with pride and victory. In his pockets he had $130 that he had won hardily by his own toil. He had lived alone, he had known pain and hunger, he had survived. The old hunger for voyages fed at his heart. He thrilled to the glory of the secret life. The fear of the crowd, a distrust and hatred of group life, a horror of all bonds that tied him to the terrible family of the earth, called up again the vast Utopia of his loneliness. To go alone, as he had gone, into strange cities; to meet strange people and to pass again before they could know him; to wander, like his own legend, across the earth—it seemed to him there could be no better thing than that.

He thought of his own family with fear, almost with hatred. My God! Am I never to be free? he thought. What have I done to deserve this slavery? Suppose—suppose I were in China, or in Africa, or at the South Pole. I should always be afraid of his dying while I was away.

(He twisted his neck as he thought of it.) And how they would rub it in to me if I were not there! Enjoying yourself in China (they would say) while your father was dying. Unnatural son! Yes, but curse them! Why should I be there? Can they not die alone? Alone! O God, is there no freedom on this earth?

With quick horror, he saw that such freedom lay a weary world away, and could be bought by such enduring courage as few men have.

He stayed in Richmond several days, living sumptuously in the splendid hotel, eating from silver dishes in the grill, and roaming pleasantly through the wide streets of the romantic old town, to which he had come once as a Freshman at Thanksgiving, when the university's team had played Virginia there. He spent three days trying to seduce a waitress in an ice-cream and candy-store: he lured her finally to a curtained booth in a chop-suey restaurant, only to have his efforts fail when the elaborate meal he had arranged for with the Chinaman aroused her distaste because it had onions in it.

Before he went home he wrote an enormous letter to Laura James at Norfolk, a pitiable and boasting letter which rose at its end to an insane crow: "I was there all summer and I never looked you up. You were not decent enough to answer my letters; I saw no reason why I should bother with you any more. Besides, the world is full of women; I got my share and more this summer."

He mailed the letter, with a sense of malevolent triumph. But the moment the iron lid of the box clanged over it, his face was contorted by shame and remorse: he lay awake, writhing as he recalled the schoolboy folly of it. She had beaten him again.

34

Eugene returned to Altamont two weeks before the term began at Pulpit Hill. The town and the nation seethed in the yeasty ferment of war. The country was turning into one huge camp. The colleges and universities were being converted into training-camps for officers. Every one was "doing his bit."

It had been a poor season for tourists. Eugene found Dixieland almost deserted, save for a glum handful of regular or semi-regular guests. Mrs. Pert was there, sweet, gentle, a trifle more fuzzy than usual. Miss Newton, a wrenny and neurotic old maid, with asthma, who had gradually become Eliza's unofficial assistant in the management of the house, was there. Miss Malone, the gaunt drug-eater with the loose gray lips, was there. Fowler, a civil engineer with blond hair and a red face, who came and departed quietly, leaving a sodden stench of corn-whiskey in his wake, was there. Gant, who had now moved definitely from the house on Woodson Street, which he had rented, to a big back room at Eliza's, was there—a little more waxen, a little more petulant, a little feebler than he had been before. And Ben was there.

He had been home for a week or two when Eugene arrived. He had been rejected again by both army and navy examining-boards, he had been rejected as unfit in the draft; he had left his work suddenly in the tobacco town and come quietly and sullenly home. He was thinner and more like old ivory than ever. He prowled softly about the house, smoking innumerable cigarettes, cursing in brief snarling fury, touched with despair and futility. His old surly scowl was gone, his old angry mutter; his soft contemptuous laugh, touched with so much hidden tenderness, had given way to a contained but savage madness.

During the brief two weeks that Eugene remained at home before departing again for Pulpit Hill, he shared with Ben a little room and sleeping-porch upstairs. And the quiet one talked—talked himself from a low fierce mutter into a howling anathema of bitterness and hate that carried his voice, high and passionate, across all the sleeping world of night and rustling autumn.

"What have you been doing to yourself, you little fool?" he began, looking at the boy's starved ribs. "You look like a scarecrow."

"I'm all right," said Eugene. "I wasn't eating for a while. But I didn't write them," he added proudly. "They thought I couldn't hold out by myself. But I did. I didn't ask for help. And I came home with my own money. See?" He thrust his hand into his pocket and pulled out his soiled roll of banknotes, boastfully displaying it.

"Who wants to see your lousy little money?" Ben yelled furiously. "Fool. You come back, looking like a dead man, as if you'd done something to be proud of. What've you done? What've you done except make a monkey of yourself?"

"I've paid my own way," Eugene cried resentfully, stung and wounded. "That's what I've done."

"Ah-h," said Ben, with an ugly sneer, "you little fool! That's what they've been after! Do you think you've put anything over on them? Do you? Do you think they give a damn whether you die or not, as long as you save them expense? What are you bragging about? Don't brag until you've got something out of them."

Propped on his arm, he smoked deeply, in bitter silence, for a moment. Then more quietly, he continued.

"No, 'Gene. Get it out of them any way you can. Make them give it to you. Beg it, take it, steal it—only get it somehow. If you don't, they'll let it rot. Get it, and get away from them. Go away and don't come back. To hell with them!" he yelled.

Eliza, who had come softly upstairs to put out the lights, and had been standing for a moment outside the door, rapped gently and entered. Clothed in a tattered old sweater and indefinable under-lappings, she stood for a moment with folded hands, peering in on them with a white troubled face.

"Children," she said, pursing her lips reproachfully, and shaking her head, "it's time every one was in bed. You're keeping the whole house awake with your talk."

"Ah-h," said Ben with an ugly laugh, "to hell with them."

"I'll vow, child!" she said fretfully. "You'll break us up. Have you got that porch light, on, too?" Her eyes probed about suspiciously. "What on earth do you mean by burning up all that electricity!"

"Oh, listen to this, won't you?" said Ben, jerking his head upward with a jeering laugh.

"I can't afford to pay all these bills," said Eliza angrily, with a smart shake of her head. "And you needn't think I can. I'm not going to put up with it. It's up to us all to economize."

"Oh, for God's sake!" Ben jeered. "Economize! What for? So you can give it all away to Old Man Doak for one of his lots?"

"Now, you needn't get on your high-horse," said Eliza. "You're not the one who has to pay the bills. If you did, you'd laugh out of the other side of your mouth. I don't like any such talk. You've squandered every penny you've earned because you've never known the value of a dollar."

"Ah-h!" he said. "The value of a dollar! By God, I know the value of a dollar better than you do. I've had a little something out of mine, at any rate. What have you had out of yours? I'd like to know that. What the hell's good has it ever been to any one? Will you tell me that?" he yelled.

"You may sneer all you like," said Eliza sternly, "but if it hadn't been for your papa and me accumulating a little property, you'd never have had a roof to call your own. And this is the thanks I get for all my drudgery in my old age," she said, bursting into tears. "Ingratitude! Ingratitude!"

"Ingratitude!" he sneered. "What's there to be grateful for? You don't think I'm grateful to you or the old man for anything, do you? What have you ever given me? You let me go to hell from the time I was twelve years old. No one has ever given me a damned nickel since then. Look at your kid here. You've let him run around the country like a crazy man. Did you think enough of him this summer to send him a post-card? Did you know where he was? Did you give a damn, as long as there was fifty cents to be made out of your lousy boarders?"

"Ingratitude!" she whispered huskily, with a boding shake of the head. "A day of reckoning cometh."

"Oh, for God's sake!" he said, with a contemptuous laugh. He smoked for a moment. Then he went on quietly:

"No, mama. You've done very little to make us grateful to you. The rest of us ran around wild and the kid grew up here among the dope-fiends and street-walkers. You've pinched every penny and put all you've had into real estate which has done no one any good. So don't wonder if your kids aren't grateful to you."

"Any son who will talk that way to his mother," said Eliza with rankling bitterness, "is bound to come to a bad end. Wait and see!"

"The hell you say!" he sneered. They stared at each other with hard bitter eyes. He turned away in a moment, scowling with savage annoyance, but stabbed already with fierce regret.

"All right! Go on, for heaven's sake! Leave us alone! I don't want you around!" He lit a cigarette to show his indifference. The lean white fingers trembled, and the flame went out.

"Let's stop it!" said Eugene wearily. "Let's stop it! None of us is going to change! Nothing's going to get any better. We're all going to be the same. We've said all this before. So, for God's sake, let's stop it! Mama, go to bed, please. Let's all go to bed and forget about it." He went to her, and with a strong sense of shame, kissed her.

"Well, good-night, son," said Eliza slowly, with gravity. "If I were you I'd put the light out now and turn in. Get a good night's sleep, boy. You mustn't neglect your health."

She kissed him, and went away without another glance at the older boy. He did not look at her. They were parted by hard and bitter strife.

After a moment, when she had gone, Ben said without anger:

"I've had nothing out of life. I've been a failure. I've stayed here with them until I'm done for. My lungs are going: they won't even take a chance on me for the army. They won't even give the Germans a chance to shoot at me. I've never made good at anything. By God!" he said, in a mounting blaze of passion. "What's it all about? Can you figure it out, 'Gene? Is it really so, or is somebody playing a joke on us? Maybe we're dreaming all this. Do you think so?"

"Yes," said Eugene, "I do. But I wish they'd wake us up." He was silent, brooding over his thin bare body, bent forward on the bed for a moment. "Maybe," he said slowly, "maybe—there's nothing, nobody to wake."

"To hell with it all!" said Ben. "I wish it were over."

Eugene returned to Pulpit Hill in a fever of war excitement. The university had been turned into an armed camp. Young men who were eighteen years old were being admitted into the officers' training corps. But he was not yet eighteen. His birthday was two weeks off. In vain he implored the tolerance of the examining board. What did two weeks matter? Could he get in as soon as his birthday arrived? They told him he could not. What, then, could he do? They told him that he must wait until there was another draft. How long would that be? Only two or three months, they assured him. His wilted hope revived. He chafed impatiently. All was not lost.

By Christmas, with fair luck, he might be eligible for service in khaki: by Spring, if God was good, all the proud privileges of trench-lice, mustard gas, spattered brains, punctured lungs, ripped guts, asphyxiation, mud and gangrene, might be his. Over the rim of the earth he heard the glorious stamp of the feet, the fierce sweet song of the horns. With a tender smile of love for his dear self, he saw himself wearing the eagles of a colonel on his gallant young shoulders. He saw himself as Ace Gant, the falcon of the skies, with 63 Huns to his credit by his nineteenth year. He saw himself walking up the Champs-Elysées, with a handsome powdering of gray hair above his temples, a left forearm of the finest cork, and the luscious young widow of a French marshal at his side. For the first time he saw the romantic charm of mutilation. The perfect and unblemished heroes of his childhood now seemed cheap to him—fit only to illustrate advertisements for collars and toothpaste. He longed for that subtle distinction, that air of having lived and suffered that could only be attained by a wooden leg, a rebuilt nose, or the seared scar of a bullet across his temple.

Meanwhile, he fed voraciously, and drank gallons of water in an effort to increase his poundage. He weighed himself a half-dozen times a day. He even made some effort at systematic exercise: swinging his arms, bending from his hips, and so on.

And he talked about his problem with the professors. Gravely, earnestly, he wrestled with his soul, mouthing with gusto the inspiring jargon of the crusade. For the present, said the professors, was his Place not Here? Did his Conscience tell him that he Had to go? If it did, they said gravely, they would say nothing more. But had he considered the Larger Issues?

"Is not," said the Acting Dean persuasively, "is not this your Sector? Is your own Front Line not here on the campus? Is it not here that you must Go Over The Top? Oh, I know," he went on with a smile of quiet pain, "I know it would be easier to go. I have had to fight that battle myself. But we are all part of the Army now; we are all enlisted in the Service of Liberty. We are all Mobilized for Truth. And each must Do His Bit where it will count for most."

"Yes," said Eugene, with a pale tortured face, "I know. I know it's wrong. But oh, sir,—when I think of those murderous beasts, when I think of how they have menaced All that we Hold Dear, when I think of Little Belgium, and then of My Own Mother, My Own Sister—" He turned away, clenching his hands, madly in love with himself.

"Yes, yes," said the Acting Dean gently, "for boys with a spirit like yours it's not easy."

"Oh, sir, it's hard!" cried Eugene passionately. "I tell you it's hard."

"We must endure," said the Dean quietly. "We must be tempered in the fire. The Future of Mankind hangs in the balance."

Deeply stirred they stood together for a moment, drenched in the radiant beauty of their heroic souls.

Eugene was managing editor of the college paper. But, since the editor was enlisted in the corps, the entire work of publication fell to the boy. Every one was in the army. With the exception of a few dozen ratty Freshmen, a few cripples, and himself, every one, it seemed, was in the army. All of his fraternity brothers, all of his college mates, who had not previously enlisted, and many young men who had never before thought of college, were in the army. "Pap" Rheinhart, George Graves, Julius Arthur —who had experienced brief and somewhat unfortunate careers at other universities, and a host of young Altamonters who had never known a campus before, were all enlisted now in the Student's Army.

During the first days, in the confusion of the new order, Eugene saw a great deal of them. Then, as the cogs of the machine began to grind more smoothly, and the university was converted into a big army post, with its punctual monotony of drilling, eating, studying, inspection, sleeping, he found himself detached, alone, occupying a position of unique and isolated authority.

He Carried On. He Held High the Torch. He Did His Bit. He was editor, reporter, censor, factotum of the paper. He wrote the news. He wrote the editorials. He seared them with flaming words. He extolled the crusade. He was possessed of the inspiration for murder.

He came and he went as he chose. When the barracks went dark at night, he prowled the campus, contemptuous of the electric flash and the muttered apologies of the officious shavetails. He roomed in the village with a tall cadaver, a gaunt medical student with hollow cheeks and a pigeon-breast, named Heston. Three or four times a week he was driven over the rutted highway to Exeter where, in a little print shop, he drank the good warm smell of ink and steel.

Later, he prowled up the dreary main street of the town as the lights went up, ate at the Greek's, flirted with a few stray furtive women until the place went dead at ten o'clock, and came back through the dark country-side in a public-service car beside a drunken old walrus who drove like a demon, and whose name was "Soak" Young.

October began, and a season of small cold rain. The earth was a sodden reek of mud and rotten leaves. The trees dripped wearily and incessantly. His eighteenth birthday came, and he turned again, with a quivering tension, toward the war.

He got a brief sick letter from his father; a few pages, practical, concrete with her blunt pungent expression, from Eliza:

"Daisy has been here with all her tribe. She went home two days ago, leaving Caroline and Richard. They have all been down sick with the flu. We've had a siege of it here. Every one has had it, and you never know who's going to be next. It seems to get the big strong ones first. Mr. Hanby, the Methodist minister, died last week. Pneumonia set in. He was a fine healthy man in the prime of life. The doctors said he was gone from the start. Helen has been laid up for several days. Says it's her old kidney trouble. They had McGuire in Thursday night. But they can't fool me, no matter what they say. Son, I hope you will never surrender to that awful craving. It has been the curse of my life. Your papa seems to go along about the same as usual. He eats well, and gets lots of sleep. I can't notice any change in him from a year ago. He may be here long after some of the rest of us are under the sod. Ben is still here. He mopes around the house all day and complains of having no appetite. I think he needs to get to work again doing something that will take his mind off himself. There are only a few people left in the house. Mrs. Pert and Miss Newton hang on as usual. The Crosbys have gone back to Miami. If it gets much colder here I'll just pack up and go too. I guess I must be getting old. I can't stand the cold the way I could when I was young. I want you to buy yourself a good warm overcoat before the winter sets in. You must also eat plenty of good substantial food. Don't squander your money but . . ."

He heard nothing more for several weeks. Then, one drizzling evening at six o'clock, when he returned to the room that he occupied with Heston, he found a telegram. It read: "Come home at once. Ben has pneumonia. Mother."

35

There was no train until the next day. Heston quieted him during the evening with a stiff drink of gin manufactured from alcohol taken from the medical laboratory. Eugene was silent and babbled incoherently by starts: he asked the medical student a hundred questions about the progress and action of the disease.

"If it were double pneumonia she would have said so. Doesn't it seem that way to you? Hey?" he demanded feverishly.

"I should think so," said Heston. He was a kind and quiet boy.

Eugene went to Exeter the next morning to catch the train. All through a dreary gray afternoon it pounded across the sodden State. Then, there was a change and a terrible wait of several hours at a junction. Finally, as dark came, he was being borne again toward the hills.

Within his berth he lay with hot sleepless eyes, staring out at the black mass of the earth, the bulk of the hills. Finally, in the hours after midnight, he dropped into a nervous doze. He was wakened by the clatter of the trucks as they began to enter the Altamont yards. Dazed, half-dressed, he was roused by the grinding halt, and a moment later was looking out through the curtains into the grave faces of Luke and Hugh Barton.

"Ben's very sick," said Hugh Barton.

Eugene pulled on his shoes and dropped to the floor, stuffing his collar and tie into a coat pocket.

"Let's go," he said. "I'm ready."

They went softly down the aisle, amid the long dark snores of the sleepers. As they walked through the empty station toward Hugh Barton's car, Eugene said to the sailor:

"When did you get home, Luke?"

"I came in last night," he said. "I've been here only a few hours."

It was half-past three in the morning. The ugly station settlement lay fixed and horrible, like something in a dream. His strange and sudden return to it heightened his feeling of unreality. In one of the cars lined at the station curbing, the driver lay huddled below his blanket. In the Greek's lunch-room a man sat sprawled faced downward on the counter. The lights were dull and weary: a few burned with slow lust in the cheap station-hotels.

Hugh Barton, who had always been a cautious driver, shot away with a savage grinding of gears. They roared townward through the rickety slums at fifty miles an hour.

"I'm afraid B-B-B-Ben is one sick boy," Luke began.

"How did it happen?" Eugene asked. "Tell me."

He had taken influenza, they told Eugene, from one of Daisy's children. He had moped about, ill and feverish, for a day or two, without going to bed.

"In that G-g-g-god dam cold barn," Luke burst out. "If that boy dies it's because he c-c-c-couldn't keep warm."

"Never mind about that now," Eugene cried irritably, "go on."

Finally he had gone to bed, and Mrs. Pert had nursed him for a day or two.

"She was the only one who d-d-d-did a damn thing for him," said the sailor. Eliza, at length, had called in Cardiac.

"The d-d-damned old quack," Luke stuttered.

"Never mind! Never mind!" Eugene yelled. "Why dig it up now? Get on with it!"

After a day or two, he had grown apparently convalescent, and Cardiac told him he might get up if he liked. He got up and moped about the house for a day, in a cursing rage, but the next day he lay a-bed, with a high fever. Coker at length had been called in, two days before——

"That's what they should have done at the start," growled Hugh Barton over his wheel.

"Never mind!" screamed Eugene. "Get on with it."

And Ben had been desperately ill, with pneumonia in both lungs, for over a day. The sad prophetic story, a brief and terrible summary of the waste, the tardiness, and the ruin of their lives, silenced them for a moment with its inexorable sense of tragedy. They had nothing to say.

The powerful car roared up into the chill dead Square. The feeling of unreality grew upon the boy. He sought for his life, for the bright lost years,
in this mean cramped huddle of brick and stone. Ben and I, here by the
City Hall, the Bank, the grocery-store (he thought). Why here? In Gath
or Ispahan. In Corinth or Byzantium. Not here. It is not real.

A moment later, the big car sloped to a halt at the curb, in front of Dixieland. A light burned dimly in the hall, evoking for him chill memories of
damp and gloom. A warmer light burned in the parlor, painting the
lowered shade of the tall window a warm and mellow orange.

"Ben's in that room upstairs," Luke whispered, "where the light is."

Eugene looked up with cold dry lips to the bleak front room upstairs,
with its ugly Victorian bay-window. It was next to the sleeping-porch where,
but three weeks before, Ben had hurled into the darkness his savage curse
at life. The light in the sickroom burned grayly, bringing to him its grim
vision of struggle and naked terror.

The three men went softly up the walk and entered the house. There was
a faint clatter from the kitchen, and voices.

"Papa's in here," said Luke.

Eugene entered the parlor and found Gant seated alone before a bright
coal-fire. He looked up dully and vaguely as his son entered.

"Hello, papa," said Eugene, going to him.

"Hello, son," said Gant. He kissed the boy with his bristling cropped
mustache. His thin lip began to tremble petulantly.

"Have you heard about your brother?" he snuffled. "To think that this
should be put upon me, old and sick as I am. O Jesus, it's fearful—"

Helen came in from the kitchen.

"Hello, Slats," she said, heartily embracing him. "How are you, honey?
He's grown four inches more since he went away," she jeered, sniggering.
"Well, 'Gene, cheer up! Don't look so blue. While there's life there's hope.
He's not gone yet, you know." She burst into tears, hoarse, unstrung,
hysterical.

"To think that this must come upon me," Gant sniffled, responding
mechanically to her grief, as he rocked back and forth on his cane and
stared into the fire. "O boo-hoo-hoo! What have I done that God
should——"

"You shut up!" she cried, turning upon him in a blaze of fury. "Shut
your mouth this minute. I don't want to hear any more from you! I've given
my life to you! Everything's been done for you, and you'll be here when
we're all gone. You're not the one who's sick." Her feeling toward him had,
for the moment, gone rancorous and bitter.

"Where's mama?" Eugene asked.

"She's back in the kitchen," Helen said. "I'd go back and say hello before you see Ben if I were you." In a low brooding tone, she continued: "Well, forget about it. It can't be helped now."

He found Eliza busy over several bright bubbling pots of water on the gas-stove. She bustled awkwardly about, and looked surprised and confused when she saw him.

"Why, what on earth, boy! When'd you get in?"

He embraced her. But beneath her matter-of-factness, he saw the terror in her heart: her dull black eyes glinted with bright knives of fear.

"How's Ben, mama?" he asked quietly.

"Why-y," she pursed her lips reflectively, "I was just saying to Doctor Coker before you came in. 'Look here,' I said. 'I tell you what, I don't believe he's half as bad off as he looks. Now, if only we can hold on till morning. I believe there's going to be a change for the better.' "

"Mama, in heaven's name!" Helen burst out furiously. "How can you bear to talk like that? Don't you know that Ben's condition is critical? Are you never going to wake up?"

Her voice had its old cracked note of hysteria.

"Now, I tell you, son," said Eliza, with a white tremulous smile, "when you go in there to see him, don't make out as if you knew he was sick. If I were you, I'd make a big joke of it all. I'd laugh just as big as you please and say, 'See here, I thought I was coming to see a sick man. Why, pshaw!' (I'd say) 'there's nothing wrong with you. Half of it's only imagination!' "

"O mama! for Christ's sake!" said Eugene frantically. "For Christ's sake!"

He turned away, sick at heart, and caught at his throat with his fingers.

Then he went softly upstairs with Luke and Helen, approaching the sick-room with a shrivelled heart and limbs which had gone cold and bloodless. They paused for a moment, whispering, before he entered. The wretched conspiracy in the face of death filled him with horror.

"N-n-n-now, I wouldn't stay but a m-m-m-minute," whispered Luke. "It m-m-might make him nervous."

Eugene, bracing himself, followed Helen blindly into the room.

"Look who's come to see you," her voice came heartily. "It's High-pockets."

For a moment Eugene could see nothing, for dizziness and fear. Then, in the gray shaded light of the room, he descried Bessie Gant, the nurse, and the long yellow skull's-head of Coker, smiling wearily at him, with big stained teeth, over a long chewed cigar. Then, under the terrible light which fell directly and brutally upon the bed alone, he saw Ben. And in that moment of searing recognition he saw, what they had all seen, that Ben was dying.

Ben's long thin body lay three-quarters covered by the bedding; its gaunt outline was bitterly twisted below the covers, in an attitude of struggle and torture. It seemed not to belong to him, it was somehow distorted and detached as if it belonged to a beheaded criminal. And the sallow yellow of his face had turned gray; out of this granite tint of death, lit by two red flags of fever, the stiff black furze of a three-day beard was growing. The beard was somehow horrible; it recalled the corrupt vitality of hair, which can grow from a rotting corpse. And Ben's thin lips were lifted, in a constant grimace of torture and strangulation, above his white somehow dead-looking teeth, as inch by inch he gasped a thread of air into his lungs.

And the sound of this gasping—loud, hoarse, rapid, unbelievable, filling the room, and orchestrating every moment in it—gave to the scene its final note of horror.

Ben lay upon the bed below them, drenched in light, like some enormous insect on a naturalist's table, fighting, while they looked at him, to save with his poor wasted body the life that no one could save for him. It was monstrous, brutal.

As Eugene approached, Ben's fear-bright eyes rested upon the younger brother for the first time and bodilessly, without support, he lifted his tortured lungs from the pillow, seizing the boy's wrists fiercely in the hot white circle of his hands, and gasping in strong terror like a child: "Why have you come? Why have you come home, 'Gene?"

The boy stood white and dumb for a moment, while swarming pity and horror rose in him.

"They gave us a vacation, Ben," he said presently. "They had to close down on account of the flu."

Then he turned away suddenly into the black murk, sick with his poor lie, and unable to face the fear in Ben's gray eyes.

"All right, 'Gene," said Bessie Gant, with an air of authority. "Get out of here—you and Helen both. I've got one crazy Gant to look after already. I don't want two more in here." She spoke harshly, with an unpleasant laugh.

She was a thin woman of thirty-eight years, the wife of Gant's nephew, Gilbert. She was of mountain stock: she was coarse, hard, and vulgar, with little pity in her, and a cold lust for the miseries of sickness and death. These inhumanities she cloaked with her professionalism, saying:

"If I gave way to my feelings, where would the patient be?"

When they got out into the hall again, Eugene said angrily to Helen:

"Why have you got that death's-head here? How can he get well with her around? I don't like her!"

"Say what you like—she's a good nurse." Then, in a low voice, she said: "What do you think?"

He turned away, with a convulsive gesture. She burst into tears, and seized his hand.

Luke was teetering about restlessly, breathing stentorously and smoking a cigarette, and Eliza, working her lips, stood with an attentive ear cocked to the door of the sick-room. She was holding a useless kettle of hot water.

"Huh? Hah? What say?" asked Eliza, before any one had said anything. "How is he?" Her eyes darted about at them.

"Get away! Get away! Get away!" Eugene muttered savagely. His voice rose. "Can't you get away?"

He was infuriated by the sailor's loud nervous breathing, his large awkward feet. He was angered still more by Eliza's useless kettle, her futile hovering, her "huh?" and "hah?"

"Can't you see he's fighting for his breath? Do you want to strangle him? It's messy! Messy! Do you hear?" His voice rose again.

The ugliness and discomfort of the death choked him; and the swarming family, whispering outside the door, pottering uselessly around, feeding with its terrible hunger for death on Ben's strangulation, made him mad with alternate fits of rage and pity.

Indecisively, after a moment, they went downstairs, still listening for sounds in the sick-room.

"Well, I tell you," Eliza began hopefully. "I have a feeling, I don't know what you'd call it—" She looked about awkwardly and found herself deserted. Then she went back to her boiling pots and pans.

Helen, with contorted face, drew him aside, and spoke to him in whispered hysteria, in the front hall.

"Did you see that sweater she's wearing? Did you see it? It's filthy!" Her voice sank to a brooding whisper. "Did you know that he can't bear to look at her? She came into the room yesterday, and he grew perfectly sick. He turned his head away and said 'O Helen, for God's sake, take her out of here.' You hear that, don't you. Do you hear? He can't stand to have her come near him. He doesn't want her in the room."

"Stop! Stop! For God's sake, stop!" Eugene said, clawing at his throat. The girl was for the moment insane with hatred and hysteria.

"It may be a terrible thing to say, but if he dies I shall hate her. Do you think I can forget the way she's acted? Do you?" Her voice rose almost to a scream. "She's let him die here before her very eyes. Why, only day before yesterday, when his temperature was 104, she was talking to Old Doctor Doak about a lot. Did you know that?"

"Forget about it!" he said frantically. "She'll always be like that! It's not her fault. Can't you see that? O God, how horrible! How horrible!"

"Poor old mama!" said Helen, beginning to weep. "She'll never get over this. She's scared to death! Did you see her eyes? She knows, of course she knows!"

Then suddenly, with mad brooding face, she said: "Sometimes I think I hate her! I really think I hate her." She plucked at her large chin, absently. "Well, we mustn't talk like this," she said. "It's not right. Cheer up. We're all tired and nervous. I believe he's going to get all right yet."

Day came gray and chill, with a drear reek of murk and fog. Eliza bustled about eagerly, pathetically busy, preparing breakfast. Once she hurried awkwardly upstairs with a kettle of water, and stood for a second at the door as Bessie Gant opened it, peering in at the terrible bed, with her white puckered face. Bessie Gant blocked her further entrance, and closed the door rudely. Eliza went away making flustered apologies.

For, what the girl had said was true, and Eliza knew it. She was not wanted in the sick-room; the dying boy did not want to see her. She had seen him turn his head wearily away when she had gone in. Behind her white face dwelt this horror, but she made no confession, no complaint. She bustled around doing useless things with an eager matter-of-factness. And Eugene, choked with exasperation at one moment, because of her heavy optimism, was blind with pity the next when he saw the terrible fear and pain in her dull black eyes. He rushed toward her suddenly, as she stood above the hot stove, and seized her rough worn hand, kissing it and babbling helplessly.

"O mama! Mama! It's all right! It's all right! It's all right."

And Eliza, stripped suddenly of her pretenses, clung to him, burying her white face in his coat sleeve, weeping bitterly, helplessly, grievously, for the sad waste of the irrevocable years—the immortal hours of love that might never be relived, the great evil of forgetfulness and indifference that could never be righted now. Like a child she was grateful for his caress, and his heart twisted in him like a wild and broken thing, and he kept mumbling:

"It's all right! It's all right! It's all right!"—knowing that it was not, could never be, all right.

"If I had known. Child, if I had known," she wept, as she had wept long before at Grover's death.

"Brace up!" he said. "He'll pull through yet. The worst is over."

"Well, I tell you," said Eliza, drying her eyes at once, "I believe it is. I believe he passed the turning-point last night. I was saying to Bessie——"

The light grew. Day came, bringing hope. They sat down to breakfast in the kitchen, drawing encouragement from every scrap of cheer doctor or nurse would give them. Coker departed, non-committally optimistic. Bessie Gant came down to breakfast and was professionally encouraging.

"If I can keep his damn family out of the room, he may have some chance of getting well."

They laughed hysterically, gratefully, pleased with the woman's abuse.

"How is he this morning?" said Eliza. "Do you notice any improvement?"

"His temperature is lower, if that's what you mean."

They knew that a lower temperature in the morning was a fact of no great significance, but they took nourishment from it: their diseased emotion fed upon it—they had soared in a moment to a peak of hopefulness.

"And he's got a good heart," said Bessie Gant. "If that holds out, and he keeps fighting, he'll pull through."

"D-d-don't worry about his f-f-fighting," said Luke, in a rush of eulogy. "That b-b-boy'll fight as long as he's g-g-got a breath left in him."

"Why, yes," Eliza began, "I remember when he was a child of seven—I know I was standing on the porch one day—the reason I remember is Old Mr. Buckner had just come by with some butter and eggs your papa had——"

"O my God!" groaned Helen, with a loose grin. "Now we'll get it."

"Whah—whah!" Luke chortled crazily, prodding Eliza in the ribs.

"I'll vow, boy!" said Eliza angrily. "You act like an idiot. I'd be ashamed!"

"Whah—whah—whah!"

Helen sniggered, nudging Eugene.

"Isn't he crazy, though? Tuh-tuh-tuh-tuh-tuh." Then, with wet eyes, she drew Eugene roughly into her big bony embrace.

"Poor old 'Gene. You always got on together, didn't you? You'll feel it more than any of us."

"He's not b-b-buried yet," Luke cried heartily. "That boy may be here when the rest of us are pushing d-d-daisies."

"Where's Mrs. Pert?" said Eugene. "Is she in the house?"

A strained and bitter silence fell upon them.

"I ordered her out," said Eliza grimly, after a moment. "I told her exactly what she was—a whore." She spoke with the old stern judiciousness, but in a moment her face began to work and she burst into tears. "If it hadn't been for that woman I believe he'd be well and strong to-day. I'll vow I do!"

"Mama, in heaven's name!" Helen burst out furiously. "How dare you say a thing like that? She was the only friend he had: when he was taken sick she nursed him hand and foot. Why, the idea! The idea!" she panted in her indignation. "If it hadn't been for Mrs. Pert he'd have been dead by now. Nobody else did anything for him. You were willing enough, I notice, to keep her here and take her money until he got sick. No, sir!" she declared with emphasis. "Personally, I like her. I'm not going to cut her now."

"It's a d-d-d-damn shame!" said Luke, staunch to his goddess. "If it hadn't been for Mrs. P-P-P-Pert and you, Ben would be S. O. L. Nobody else around here gave a damn. If he d-d-d-dies, it's because he didn't get the proper care when it would have done him some good. There's always been too d-d-damn much thought of saving a nickel, and too d-d-damn little about flesh and blood!"

"Well, forget about it!" said Helen wearily. "There's one thing sure: I've done everything I could. I haven't been to bed for two days. Whatever happens, I'll have no regrets on that score." Her voice was filled with a brooding ugly satisfaction.

"I know you haven't! I know that!" The sailor turned to Eugene in his excitement, gesticulating. "That g-g-girl's worked her fingers to the bone. If it hadn't been for her—" His eyes got wet; he turned his head away and blew his nose.

"Oh, for Christ's sake!" Eugene yelled, springing up from the table. "Stop it, won't you! Let's wait till later."

In this way, the terrible hours of the morning lengthened out, while they spent themselves trying to escape from the tragic net of frustration and loss in which they were caught. Their spirits soared to brief moments of insane joy and exultancy, and plunged into black pits of despair and hysteria. Eliza alone seemed consistently hopeful. Trembling with exacerbated nerves, the sailor and Eugene paced the lower hall, smoking incessant cigarettes, bristling as they approached each other, ironically polite when their bodies touched. Gant dozed in the parlor or in his own room, waking and sleeping by starts, moaning petulantly, detached, vaguely aware only of the meaning of events, and resentful because of the sudden indifference to him. Helen went in and out of the sick-room constantly, dominating the dying boy by the power of her vitality, infusing him with moments of hope and confidence. But when she came out, her hearty cheerfulness was supplanted by the strained blur of hysteria; she wept, laughed, brooded, loved, and hated by turns.

Eliza went only once into the room. She intruded with a hotwater bag, timidly, awkwardly, like a child, devouring Ben's face with her dull black eyes. But when above the loud labor of his breath his bright eyes rested on her, his clawed white fingers tightened their grip in the sheets, and he gasped strongly, as if in terror:

"Get out! Out! Don't want you."

Eliza left the room. As she walked she stumbled a little, as if her feet were numb and dead. Her white face had an ashen tinge, and her dull eyes had grown bright and staring. As the door closed behind her, she leaned against the wall and put one hand across her face. Then, in a moment, she went down to her pots again.

Frantically, angrily, with twitching limbs they demanded calm and steady nerves from one another; they insisted that they keep away from the sick-room—but, as if drawn by some terrible magnet, they found themselves again and again outside the door, listening, on tiptoe, with caught breath, with an insatiate thirst for horror, to the hoarse noise of his gasping as he strove to force air down into his strangled and cemented lungs. And eagerly, jealously, they sought entrance to the room, waiting their turn for carrying water, towels, supplies.

Mrs. Pert, from her refuge in the boarding-house across the street, called Helen on the phone each half-hour, and the girl talked to her while Eliza came from the kitchen into the hall, and stood, hands folded, lips pursed, with eyes that sparkled with her hate.

The girl cried and laughed as she talked.

"Well . . . that's all right, Fatty. . . . You know how I feel about it. . . . I've always said that if he had one true friend in the world, it's you . . . and don't think we're *all* ungrateful for what you've done. . . ."

During the pauses, Eugene could hear the voice of the other woman across the wires, sobbing.

And Eliza said, grimly: "If she calls up again you let me talk to her. I'll fix her!"

"Good heavens, mama!" Helen cried angrily. "You've done enough already. You drove her out of the house when she'd done more for him than all his family put together." Her big strained features worked convulsively. "Why, it's ridiculous!"

Within Eugene, as he paced restlessly up and down the hall or prowled through the house a-search for some entrance he had never found, a bright and stricken thing kept twisting about like a trapped bird. This bright thing, the core of him, his Stranger, kept twisting its head about, unable to look at horror, until at length it gazed steadfastly, as if under a dreadful hypnosis, into the eyes of death and darkness. And his soul plunged downward, drowning in that deep pit: he felt that he could never again escape from this smothering flood of pain and ugliness, from the eclipsing horror and pity of it all. And as he walked, he twisted his own neck about, and beat the air with his arm like a wing, as if he had received a blow in his kidneys. He felt that he might be clean and free if he could only escape into a single burning passion—hard, and hot, and glittering—of love, hatred, terror, or disgust. But he was caught, he was strangling, in the web of futility—there was no moment of hate that was not touched by a dozen shafts of pity: impotently, he wanted to seize them, cuff them, shake them, as one might a trying brat, and at the same time to caress them, love them, comfort them.

As he thought of the dying boy upstairs, the messy ugliness of it—as they stood whimpering by while he strangled—choked him with fury and horror. The old fantasy of his childhood came back to him: he remembered his hatred of the semi-private bathroom, his messy discomfort while he sat at stool and stared at the tub filled with dirty wash, sloppily puffed and ballooned by cold gray soapy water. He thought of this as Ben lay dying.

Their hopes revived strongly in the forenoon when word came to them that the patient's temperature was lower, his pulse stronger, the congestion of the lungs slightly relieved. But at one o'clock, after a fit of coughing, he grew delirious, his temperature mounted, he had increasing difficulty in getting his breath. Eugene and Luke raced to Wood's pharmacy in Hugh Barton's car, for an oxygen tank. When they returned, Ben had almost choked to death.

Quickly they carried the tank into the room, and placed it near his head. Bessie Gant seized the cone, and started to put it over Ben's mouth, commanding him to breathe it in. He fought it away tigerishly: curtly the nurse commanded Eugene to seize his hands.

Eugene gripped Ben's hot wrists: his heart turned rotten. Ben rose wildly from his pillows, wrenching like a child to get his hands free, gasping horribly, his eyes wild with terror:

"No! No! 'Gene! 'Gene! No! No!"

Eugene caved in, releasing him and turning away, white-faced, from the accusing fear of the bright dying eyes. Others held him: he was given temporary relief. Then he became delirious again.

By four o'clock it was apparent that death was near. Ben had brief periods of consciousness, unconsciousness, and delirium—but most of the time he was delirious. His breathing was easier, he hummed snatches of popular songs, some old and forgotten, called up now from the lost and secret adyts of his childhood; but always he returned, in his quiet humming voice, to a popular song of war-time—cheap, sentimental, but now tragically moving: "Just a Baby's Prayer at Twilight,"

> ". . . when lights are low.
> Poor baby's years"

Helen entered the darkening room.

> "Are filled with tears."

The fear had gone out of his eyes: above his gasping he looked gravely at her, scowling, with the old puzzled child's stare. Then, in a moment of fluttering consciousness, he recognized her. He grinned beautifully, with the thin swift flicker of his mouth.

"Hello, Helen! It's Helen!" he cried eagerly.

She came from the room with a writhen and contorted face, holding the sobs that shook her until she was half-way down the stairs.

As darkness came upon the gray wet day, the family gathered in the parlor, in the last terrible congress before death, silent, waiting. Gant rocked petulantly, spitting into the fire, making a weak whining moan from time to time. One by one, at intervals, they left the room, mounting the stairs softly, and listening outside the door of the sick-room. And they heard Ben, as, with incessant humming repetition, like a child, he sang his song,

> "There's a mother there at twilight
> Who's glad to know——"

Eliza sat stolidly, hands folded, before the parlor fire. Her dead white face had a curious carven look; the inflexible solidity of madness.

"Well," she said at length, slowly, "you never know. Perhaps this is the crisis. Perhaps——" her face hardened into granite again. She said no more.

Coker came in and went at once, without speaking, to the sick-room. Shortly before nine o'clock Bessie Gant came down.

"All right," she said quietly. "You had all better come up now. This is the end."

Eliza got up and marched out of the room with a stolid face. Helen followed her: she was panting with hysteria, and had begun to wring her big hands.

"Now, get hold of yourself, Helen," said Bessie Gant warningly. "This is no time to let yourself go."

Eliza went steadily upstairs, making no noise. But, as she neared the room, she paused, as if listening for sounds within. Faintly, in the silence, they heard Ben's song. And suddenly, casting away all pretense, Eliza staggered, and fell against the wall, turning her face into her hand, with a terrible wrenched cry:

"O God! If I had known! If I had known!"

Then, weeping with bitter unrestraint, with the contorted and ugly grimace of sorrow, mother and daughter embraced each other. In a moment they composed themselves, and quietly entered the room.

Eugene and Luke pulled Gant to his feet and supported him up the stairs. He sprawled upon them, moaning in long quivering exhalations.

"Mer-ci-ful God! That I should have to bear this in my old age. That I should——"

"Papa! For God's sake!" Eugene cried sharply. "Pull yourself together! It's Ben who's dying—not us! Let's try to behave decently to him for once."

This served to quiet Gant for a moment. But as he entered the room, and saw Ben lying in the semi-conscious coma that precedes death, the fear of his own death overcame him, and he began to moan again. They seated him in a chair, at the foot of the bed, and he rocked back and forth, weeping:

"O Jesus! I can't bear it! Why must you put this upon me? I'm old and sick, and I don't know where the money's to come from. How are we ever going to face this fearful and croo-el winter? It'll cost a thousand dollars before we're through burying him, and I don't know where the money's to come from." He wept affectedly with sniffling sobs.

"Hush! hush!" cried Helen, rushing at him. In her furious anger, she seized him and shook him. "You damned old man you, I could kill you! How dare you talk like that when your son's dying? I've wasted six years of my life nursing you, and you'll be the last one to go!" In her blazing anger, she turned accusingly on Eliza:

"You've done this to him. You're the one that's responsible. If you hadn't pinched every penny he'd never have been like this. Yes, and Ben would be here, too!" She panted for breath for a moment. Eliza made no answer. She did not hear her.

"After this, I'm through! I've been looking for you to die—and Ben's the one who has to go." Her voice rose to a scream of exasperation. She shook Gant again. "Never again! Do you hear that, you selfish old man? You've had everything—Ben's had nothing. And now he's the one to go. I hate you!"

"Helen! Helen!" said Bessie Gant quietly. "Remember where you are."

"Yes, that means a lot to us," Eugene muttered bitterly.

Then, over the ugly clamor of their dissension, over the rasp and snarl of their nerves, they heard the low mutter of Ben's expiring breath. The light had been re-shaded: he lay, like his own shadow, in all his fierce gray lonely beauty. And as they looked and saw his bright eyes already blurred with death, and saw the feeble beating flutter of his poor thin breast, the strange wonder, the dark rich miracle of his life surged over them its enormous loveliness. They grew quiet and calm, they plunged below all the splintered wreckage of their lives, they drew together in a superb communion of love and valiance, beyond horror and confusion, beyond death.

And Eugene's eyes grew blind with love and wonder: an enormous organ-music sounded in his heart, he possessed them for a moment, he was a part of their loveliness, his life soared magnificently out of the slough and pain and ugliness. He thought:

"That was not all! That really was not all!"

Helen turned quietly to Coker, who was standing in shadow by the window, chewing upon his long unlighted cigar.

"Is there nothing more you can do? Have you tried everything? I mean—*everything?*"

Her voice was prayerful and low. Coker turned toward her slowly, taking the cigar between his big stained fingers. Then, gently, with his weary yellow smile, he answered: "Everything. Not all the king's horses, not all the doctors and nurses in the world, can help him now."

"How long have you known this?" she said.

"For two days," he answered. "From the beginning." He was silent for a moment. "For ten years!" he went on with growing energy. "Since I first saw him, at three in the morning, in the Greasy Spoon, with a doughnut in one hand and a cigarette in the other. My dear, dear girl," he said gently as she tried to speak, "we can't turn back the days that have gone. We can't turn life back to the hours when our lungs were sound, our blood hot, our bodies young. We are a flash of fire—a brain, a heart, a spirit. And we are three-cents-worth of lime and iron—which we cannot get back."

He picked up his greasy black slouch hat, and jammed it carelessly upon his head. Then he fumbled for a match and lit the chewed cigar.

"Has everything been done?" she said again. "I want to know! Is there anything left worth trying?"

He made a weary gesture of his arms.

"My dear girl!" he said. "He's drowning! Drowning!"

She stood frozen with the horror of his pronouncement.

Coker looked for a moment at the gray twisted shadow on the bed. Then, quietly, sadly, with tenderness and tired wonder, he said: "Old Ben. When shall we see *his* like again?"

Then he went quietly out, the long cigar clamped firmly in his mouth.

In a moment, Bessie Gant, breaking harshly in upon their silence with ugly and triumphant matter-of-factness, said: "Well, it will be a relief to get this over. I'd rather be called into forty outside cases than one in which any of these damn relations are concerned. I'm dead for sleep."

Helen turned quietly upon her.

"Leave the room!" she said. "This is our affair now. We have the right to be left alone."

Surprised, Bessie Gant stared at her for a moment with an angry, resentful face. Then she left the room.

The only sound in the room now was the low rattling mutter of Ben's breath. He no longer gasped; he no longer gave signs of consciousness or struggle. His eyes were almost closed; their gray flicker was dulled, coated with the sheen of insensibility and death. He lay quietly upon his back, very straight, without sign of pain, and with a curious upturned thrust of his sharp thin face. His mouth was firmly shut. Already, save for the feeble mutter of his breath, he seemed to be dead—he seemed detached, no part of the ugly mechanism of that sound which came to remind them of the terrible chemistry of flesh, to mock at illusion, at all belief in the strange passage and continuance of life.

He was dead, save for the slow running down of the worn-out machine, save for that dreadful mutter within him of which he was no part. He was dead.

But in their enormous silence wonder grew. They remembered the strange flitting loneliness of his life, they thought of a thousand forgotten acts and moments—and always there was something that now seemed unearthly and strange: he walked through their lives like a shadow— they looked now upon his gray deserted shell with a thrill of awful recognition, as one who remembers a forgotten and enchanted word, or as men who look upon a corpse and see for the first time a departed god.

Luke, who had been standing at the foot of the bed, now turned to Eugene nervously, stammering in an unreal whisper of wonder and disbelief:

"I g-g-g-guess Ben's gone."

Gant had grown very quiet: he sat in the darkness at the foot of the bed, leaning forward upon his cane, escaped from the revery of his own approaching death, into the waste land of the past, blazing back sadly and poignantly the trail across the lost years that led to the birth of his strange son.

Helen sat facing the bed, in the darkness near the windows. Her eyes rested not on Ben but on her mother's face. All by unspoken consent stood back in the shadows and let Eliza repossess the flesh to which she had given life.

And Eliza, now that he could deny her no longer, now that his fierce bright eyes could no longer turn from her in pain and aversion, sat near his head beside him, clutching his cold hand between her rough worn palms.

She did not seem conscious of the life around her. She seemed under a powerful hypnosis: she sat very stiff and erect in her chair, her white face set stonily, her dull black eyes fixed upon the gray cold face.

They sat waiting. Midnight came. A cock crew. Eugene went quietly to a window and stood looking out. The great beast of night prowled softly about the house. The walls, the windows seemed to bend inward from the thrusting pressure of the dark. The low noise in the wasted body seemed almost to have stopped. It came infrequently, almost inaudibly, with a faint fluttering respiration.

Helen made a sign to Gant and Luke. They rose and went quietly out. At the door she paused, and beckoned to Eugene. He went to her.

"You stay here with her," she said. "You're her youngest. When it's over come and tell us."

He nodded, and closed the door behind her. When they had gone, he waited, listening for a moment. Then he went to where Eliza was sitting. He bent over her.

"Mama!" he whispered. "Mama!"

She gave no sign that she had heard him. Her face did not move; she did not turn her eyes from their fixed stare.

"Mama!" he said more loudly. "Mama!"

He touched her. She made no response.

"Mama! Mama!"

She sat there stiffly and primly like a little child.

Swarming pity rose in him. Gently, desperately, he tried to detach her fingers from Ben's hand. Her rough clasp on the cold hand tightened. Then, slowly, stonily, from right to left, without expression, she shook her head.

He fell back, beaten, weeping, before that implacable gesture. Suddenly, with horror, he saw that she was watching her own death, that the unloosening grip of her hand on Ben's hand was an act of union with her own flesh, that, for her, Ben was not dying—but that a part of *her,* of *her* life, *her* blood, *her* body, was dying. Part of her, the younger, the lovelier, the better part, coined in her flesh, borne and nourished and begun with so much pain there twenty-six years before, and forgotten since, was dying.

Eugene stumbled to the other side of the bed and fell upon his knees. He began to pray. He did not believe in God, nor in Heaven or Hell, but he was afraid they might be true. He did not believe in angels with soft faces and bright wings, but he believed in the dark spirits that hovered above the heads of lonely men. He did not believe in devils or angels, but he believed in Ben's bright demon to whom he had seen him speak so many times.

Eugene did not believe in these things, but he was afraid they might be true. He was afraid that Ben would get lost again. He felt that no one but he could pray for Ben now: that the dark union of their spirits made only *his* prayers valid. All that he had read in books, all the tranquil wisdom he had professed so glibly in his philosophy course, and the great names of Plato and Plotinus, of Spinoza and Immanuel Kant, of Hegel and Descartes, left him now, under the mastering surge of his wild Celtic superstition. He felt that he must pray frantically as long as the little ebbing flicker of breath remained in his brother's body.

So, with insane sing-song repetition, he began to mutter over and over again: "Whoever You Are, be good to Ben to-night. Show him the way . . . Whoever You Are, be good to Ben to-night. Show him the way . . ." He lost count of the minutes, the hours: he heard only the feeble rattle of dying breath, and his wild synchronic prayer.

Light faded from his brain, and consciousness. Fatigue and powerful nervous depletion conquered him. He sprawled out on the floor, with his arms pillowed on the bed, muttering drowsily. Eliza, unmoving, sat across the bed, holding Ben's hand. Eugene, mumbling, sank into an uneasy sleep.

He awoke suddenly, conscious that he had slept, with a sharp quickening of horror. He was afraid that the little fluttering breath had now ceased entirely, that the effect of his prayer was lost. The body on the bed was almost rigid: there was no sound. Then, unevenly, without rhythm, there was a faint mutter of breath. He knew it was the end. He rose quickly and ran to the door. Across the hall, in a cold bedroom, on two wide beds, Gant, Luke, and Helen lay exhausted.

"Come," cried Eugene. "He's going now."

They came quickly into the room. Eliza sat unmoving, oblivious of them. As they entered the room, they heard, like a faint expiring sigh, the final movement of breath.

The rattling in the wasted body, which seemed for hours to have given over to death all of life that is worth saving, had now ceased. The body appeared to grow rigid before them. Slowly, after a moment, Eliza withdrew her hands. But suddenly, marvellously, as if his resurrection and rebirth had come upon him, Ben drew upon the air in a long and powerful respiration; his gray eyes opened. Filled with a terrible vision of all death to the dark spirit who had brooded upon each footstep of his pillows without support—a flame, a light, a glory—joined at length in death to the dark spirit who had brooded upon each footstep of his lonely adventure on earth; and, casting the fierce sword of his glance with utter and final comprehension upon the room haunted with its gray pageantry of cheap loves and dull consciences and on all those uncertain mummers of waste and confusion fading now from the bright window of his eyes, he passed instantly, scornful and unafraid, as he had lived, into the shades of death.

We can believe in the nothingness of life, we can believe in the nothingness of death and of life after death—but who can believe in the nothingness of Ben? Like Apollo, who did his penance to the high god in the sad house of King Admetus, he came, a god with broken feet, into the gray hovel of this world. And he lived here a stranger, trying to recapture the music of the lost world, trying to recall the great forgotten language, the lost faces, the stone, the leaf, the door.

O Artemidorus, farewell!

36

In that enormous silence, where pain and darkness met, some birds were waking. It was October. It was almost four o'clock in the morning. Eliza straightened out Ben's limbs, and folded his hands across his body. She smoothed out the rumpled covers of the bed, and patted out the pillows, making a smooth hollow for his head to rest in. His flashing hair, cropped close to his well-shaped head, was crisp and crinkly as a boy's, and shone with bright points of light. With a pair of scissors, she snipped off a little lock where it would not show.

"Grover's was black as a raven's without a kink in it. You'd never have known they were twins," she said.

They went downstairs to the kitchen.

"Well, Eliza," said Gant, calling her by name for the first time in thirty years, "you've had a hard life. If I'd acted different, we might have got along together. Let's try to make the most of what time's left. Nobody is blaming you. Taking it all in all, you've done pretty well."

"There are a great many things I'd like to do over again," said Eliza gravely. She shook her head. "We never know."

"We'll talk about it some other time," said Helen. "I guess every one is worn out. I know I am. I'm going to get some sleep. Papa, go on to bed, in heaven's name! There's nothing you can do now. Mama, I think you'd better go, too——"

"No," said Eliza, shaking her head. "You children go on. I couldn't sleep now anyway. There are too many things to do. I'm going to call up John Hines now."

"Tell him," said Gant, "to spare no expense. I'll foot the bills."

"Well," said Helen, "whatever it costs, let's give Ben a good funeral. It's the last thing we can ever do for him. I want to have no regrets on that score."

"Yes," said Eliza, nodding slowly. "I want the best one that money will buy. I'll make arrangements with John Hines when I talk to him. You children go on to bed now."

"Poor old 'Gene," said Helen, laughing. "He looks like the last rose of summer. He's worn out. You pile in and get some sleep, honey."

"No," he said, "I'm hungry. I haven't had anything to eat since I left the university."

"Well, for G-G-G-God's sake!" Luke stuttered. "Why didn't you speak, idiot? I'd have got you something. Come on," he said, grinning. "I wouldn't mind a bite myself. Let's go uptown and eat."

"Yes," said Eugene. "I'd like to get out for a while from the bosom of the family circle."

They laughed crazily. He poked around the stove for a moment, peering into the oven.

"Huh? Hah? What are you after, boy?" said Eliza suspiciously.

"What you got good to eat, Miss Eliza?" he said, leering crazily at her. He looked at the sailor: they burst into loud idiot laughter, pronging each other in the ribs. Eugene picked up a coffee-pot half-filled with a cold weak wash, and sniffed at it.

"By God!" he said. "That's one thing Ben's out of. He won't have to drink mama's coffee any more."

"Whah-whah-whah!" said the sailor.

Gant grinned, wetting a thumb.

"You ought to be ashamed of yourself," said Helen, with a hoarse snigger. "Poor old Ben!"

"Why, what's wrong with that coffee?" said Eliza, vexed. "It's *good* coffee."

They howled. Eliza pursed her lips for a moment.

"I don't like that way of talking, boy," she said. Her eyes blurred suddenly. Eugene seized her rough hand and kissed it.

"It's all right, mama!" he said. "It's all right. I didn't mean it!" He put his arms around her. She wept, suddenly and bitterly.

"Nobody ever knew him. He never told us about himself. He was the quiet one. I've lost them both now." Then, drying her eyes, she added: "You boys go get something to eat. A little walk will do you good. And, say," she added, "why don't you go by *The Citizen* office? They ought to be told. They've been calling up every day to find out about him."

"They thought a lot of that boy," said Gant.

They were tired, but they all felt an enormous relief. For over a day, each had known that death was inevitable, and after the horror of the incessant strangling gasp, this peace, this end of pain touched them all with a profound, a weary joy.

"Well, Ben's gone," said Helen slowly. Her eyes were wet, but she wept quietly now, with gentle grief, with love. "I'm glad it's over. Poor old Ben! I never got to know him until these last few days. He was the best of the lot. Thank God, he's out of it now."

Eugene thought of death now, with love, with joy. Death was like a lovely and tender woman, Ben's friend and lover, who had come to free him, to heal him, to save him from the torture of life.

They stood there together, without speaking, in Eliza's littered kitchen, and their eyes were blind with tears, because they thought of lovely and delicate death, and because they loved one another.

Eugene and Luke went softly up the hall, and out into the dark. Gently, they closed the big front door behind them, and descended the veranda steps. In that enormous silence, birds were waking. It was a little after four o'clock in the morning. Wind pressed the boughs. It was still dark. But above them the thick clouds that had covered the earth for days with a dreary gray blanket had been torn open. Eugene looked up through the deep ragged vault of the sky and saw the proud and splendid stars, bright and unwinking. The withered leaves were shaking.

A cock crew his shrill morning cry of life beginning and awaking. The cock that crew at midnight (thought Eugene) had an elfin ghostly cry. His crow was drugged with sleep and death: it was like a far horn sounding under sea; and it was a warning to all the men who are about to die, and to the ghosts that must go home.

But the cock that crows at morning (he thought), has a voice as shrill as any fife. It says, we are done with sleep. We are done with death. O waken, waken into life, says his voice as shrill as any fife. In that enormous silence, birds were waking.

He heard the cock's bright minstrelsy again, and by the river in the dark, the great thunder of flanged wheels, and the long retreating wail of the whistle. And slowly, up the chill deserted street, he heard the heavy ringing clangor of shod hoofs. In that enormous silence, life was waking.

Joy awoke in him, and exultation. They had escaped from the prison of death; they were joined to the bright engine of life again. Life, ruddered life, that would not fail, began its myriad embarkations.

A paper-boy came briskly, with the stiff hobbled limp that Eugene knew so well, down the centre of the street, hurling a blocked paper accurately upon the porch of the Brunswick. As he came opposite Dixieland, he moved in to the curb, tossing his fresh paper with a careful plop. He knew there was sickness in the house.

The withered leaves were shaking.

Eugene jumped to the sidewalk from the sodded yard. He stopped the carrier.

"What's your name, boy?" he said.

"Tyson Smathers," said the boy, turning upon him a steady Scotch-Irish face that was full of life and business.

"My name is 'Gene Gant. Did you ever hear of me?"

"Yes," said Tyson Smathers, "I've heard of you. You had number 7."

"That was a long time ago," said Eugene, pompously, grinning. "I was just a boy."

In that enormous silence, birds were waking.

He thrust his hand into a pocket and found a dollar-bill.

"Here," he said. "I carried the damn things once. Next to my brother Ben, I was the best boy they ever had. Merry Christmas, Tyson."

"It ain't Christmas yet," said Tyson Smathers.

"You're right, Tyson," said Eugene, "but it will be."

Tyson Smathers took the money, with a puzzled, freckled grin. Then he went on down the street, throwing papers.

The maples were thin and sere. Their rotting leaves covered the ground. But the trees were not leafless yet. The leaves were quaking. Some birds began to chatter in the trees. Wind pressed the boughs, the withered leaves were shaking. It was October.

As Luke and Eugene turned up the street toward town, a woman came out of the big brick house across the street, and over the yard toward them. When she got near, they saw she was Mrs. Pert. It was October, but some birds were waking.

"Luke," she said fuzzily. "Luke? Is it Old Luke?"

"Yes," said Luke.

"And 'Gene? Is it old 'Gene?" She laughed gently, patting his hand, peering comically at him with her bleared oaken eyes, and swaying back and forth gravely, with alcoholic dignity. The leaves, the withered leaves, were shaking, quaking. It was October, and the leaves were shaking.

"They ran old Fatty away, 'Gene," she said. "They won't let her come in the house any more. They ran her away because she liked Old Ben. Ben. Old Ben." She swayed gently, vaguely collecting her thought. "Old Ben. How's Old Ben, 'Gene?" she coaxed. "Fatty wants to know."

"I'm m-m-m-mighty sorry, Mrs. P-P-P-Pert . . ." Luke began.

Wind pressed the boughs, the withered leaves were quaking.

"Ben's dead," said Eugene.

She stared at him for a moment, swaying on her feet.

"Fatty liked Ben," she said gently, in a moment. "Fatty and Old Ben were friends."

She turned and started unsteadily across the street, holding one hand out gravely, for balance.

In that enormous silence, birds were waking. It was October, but some birds were waking.

Then Luke and Eugene walked swiftly townward, filled with great joy because they heard the sounds of life and daybreak. And as they walked, they spoke often of Ben, with laughter, with old pleasant memory, speaking of him not as of one who had died, but as of a brother who had been gone for years, and was returning home. They spoke of him with triumph and tenderness, as of one who had defeated pain, and had joyously escaped. Eugene's mind groped awkwardly about. It fumbled like a child, with little things.

They were filled with a deep and tranquil affection for each other: they talked without constraint, without affectation, with quiet confidence and knowledge.

"Do you remember," Luke began, "the t-t-t-time he cut the hair of Aunt Pett's orphan boy—Marcus?"

"He—used—a chamber-pot—to trim the edges," Eugene screamed, waking the street with wild laughter.

They walked along hilariously, greeting a few early pedestrians with ironical obsequiousness, jeering pleasantly at the world in brotherly alliance. Then they entered the relaxed and weary offices of the paper which Ben had served so many years, and gave their stick of news to the tired man there.

There was regret, a sense of wonder, in that office where the swift record of so many days had died—a memory that would not die, of something strange and passing.

"Damn! I'm sorry! He was a great boy!" said the men.

As light broke grayly in the empty streets, and the first car rattled up to town, they entered the little beanery where he had spent, in smoke and coffee, so many hours of daybreak.

Eugene looked in and saw them there, assembled as they had been many years before, like the nightmare ratification of a prophecy: McGuire, Coker, the weary counter-man, and, at the lower end, the press-man, Harry Tugman.

Luke and Eugene entered, and sat down at the counter.

"Gentlemen, gentlemen," said Luke sonorously.

"Hello, Luke," barked McGuire. "Do you think you'll ever have any sense? How are you, son? How's school?" he said to Eugene. He stared at them for a moment, his wet cigarette plastered comically on his full sag lip, his bleared eyes kindly and drunken.

"General, how's the boy? What're you drinking these days—turpentine or varnish?" said the sailor, tweaking him roughly in his larded ribs. McGuire grunted.

"Is it over, son?" said Coker quietly.

"Yes," said Eugene.

Coker took the long cigar from his mouth and grinned malarially at the boy.

"Feel better, don't you, son?" he said.

"Yes," said Eugene. "A hell of a lot."

"Well, Eugenics," said the sailor briskly, "what are you eating?"

"What's the man got?" said Eugene, staring at the greasy card. "Have you got any young roast whale left?"

"No," said the counter-man. "We did have some, but we run out."

"How about the fricasseed bull?" said Luke. "Have you got any of that?"

"You don't need any one to fricassee your bull, son," said McGuire. "You've got plenty as it is."

Their bull-laughter bellowed in the beanery.

With puckered forehead, Luke stuttered over the menu.

"F-f-f-fried chicken à la Maryland," he muttered. "A la Maryland?" he repeated as if puzzled. "Now, ain't that nice?" he said, looking around with mincing daintiness.

"Bring me one of your this week's steaks," said Eugene, "well done, with a meat-axe and the sausage-grinder."

"What do you want the sausage-grinder for, son?" said Coker.

"That's for the mince pie," said Eugene.

"Make it two," said Luke, "with a coupla cups of Mock-a, just like mother still makes."

He looked crazily around at Eugene, and burst into loud whah-whahs, prodding him in the ribs.

"Where they got you stationed now, Luke?" said Harry Tugman, peering up snoutily from a mug of coffee.

"At the p-p-p-present time in Norfolk at the Navy Base," Luke answered, "m-m-making the world safe for hypocrisy."

"Do you ever get out to sea, son?" said Coker.

"Sure!" said Luke. "A f-f-five-cent ride on the street-car brings me right out to the beach."

"That boy has had the makings of a sailor in him ever since he wet the bed," said McGuire. "I predicted it long ago."

Horse Hines came in briskly, but checked himself when he saw the two young men.

"Look out!" whispered the sailor to Eugene, with a crazy grin. "You're next! He's got his fishy eye glued on you. He's already getting you measured up for one."

Eugene looked angrily around at Horse Hines, muttering. The sailor chortled madly.

"Good-morning, gentlemen," said Horse Hines, in an accent of refined sadness. "Boys," he said, coming up to them sorrowfully, "I was mighty sorry to hear of your trouble. I couldn't have thought more of that boy if he'd been my own brother."

"Don't go on, Horse," said McGuire, holding up four fat fingers of protest. "We can see you're heart-broken. If you go on, you may get hysterical with your grief, and break right out laughing. We couldn't bear that, Horse. We're big strong men, but we've had hard lives. I beg of you to spare us, Horse."

Horse Hines did not notice him.

"I've got him over at the place now," he said softly. "I want you boys to come in later in the day to see him. You won't know he's the same person when I'm through."

"God! An improvement over nature," said Coker. "His mother will appreciate it."

"Is this an undertaking shop you're running, Horse," said McGuire, "or a beauty parlor?"

"We know you'll d-d-do your best, Mr. Hines," said the sailor with ready earnest insincerity. "That's the reason the family got you."

"Ain't you goin' to eat the rest of your steak?" said the counter-man to Eugene.

"Steak! Steak! It's not steak!" muttered Eugene. "I know what it is now." He got off the stool and walked over to Coker. "Can you save me? Am I going to die? Do I look sick, Coker?" he said in a hoarse mutter.

"No, son," said Coker. "Not sick—crazy."

Horse Hines took his seat at the other end of the counter. Eugene, leaning upon the greasy marble counter, began to sing:

> "Hey, ho, the carrion crow,
>   Derry, derry, derry, derr—oh!"

"Shut up, you damn fool!" said the sailor in a hoarse whisper, grinning.

> "A carrion crow sat on a rock,
>   Derry, derry, derry, derr—oh!"

Outside, in the young gray light, there was a brisk wakening of life. A street-car curved slowly into the avenue, the motorman leaning from his window and shifting the switch carefully with a long rod, blowing the warm fog of his breath into the chill air. Patrolman Leslie Roberts, sallow and liverish, slouched by anæmically, swinging his club. The negro man-of-all-work for Wood's Pharmacy walked briskly into the post-office to collect the morning mail. J. T. Stearns, the railway passenger-agent, waited on the curb across the street for the depot car. He had a red face, and he was reading the morning paper.

"There they go!" Eugene cried suddenly. "As if they didn't know about it!"

"Luke," said Harry Tugman, looking up from his paper, "I was certainly sorry to hear about Ben. He was one fine boy." Then he went back to his sheet.

"By God!" said Eugene. "This is news!"

He burst into a fit of laughter, gasping and uncontrollable, which came from him with savage violence. Horse Hines glanced craftily up at him. Then he went back to his paper.

The two young men left the lunch-room and walked homeward through the brisk morning. Eugene's mind kept fumbling with little things. There was a frosty snap and clatter of life upon the streets, the lean rattle of wheels, the creak of blinds, a cold rose-tint of pearled sky. In the Square, the motormen stood about among their cars, in loud foggy gossip. At Dixieland, there was an air of exhaustion, of nervous depletion. The house slept; Eliza alone was stirring, but she had a smart fire crackling in the range, and was full of business.

"You children go and sleep now. We've all got work to do later in the day."

Luke and Eugene went into the big dining-room which Eliza had converted into a bed-room.

"D-d-d-damn if I'm going to sleep upstairs," said the sailor angrily. "Not after this!"

"Pshaw!" said Eliza. "That's only superstition. It wouldn't bother me a bit."

The brothers slept heavily until past noon. Then they went out again to see Horse Hines. They found him with his legs comfortably disposed on the desk of his dark little office, with its odor of weeping ferns, and incense, and old carnations.

He got up quickly as they entered, with a starchy crackle of his hard boiled shirt, and a solemn rustle of his black garments. Then he began to speak to them in a hushed voice, bending forward slightly.

How like Death this man is (thought Eugene). He thought of the awful mysteries of burial—the dark ghoul-ritual, the obscene com-

munion with the dead, touched with some black and foul witch-magic.
Where is the can in which they throw the parts? There is a restaurant
near here. Then he took the cold phthisic hand, freckled on its back,
that the man extended, with a sense of having touched something embalmed. The undertaker's manner had changed since the morning: it
had become official, professional. He was the alert marshal of their
grief, the efficient master-of-ceremonies. Subtly he made them feel there
was an order and decorum in death: a ritual of mourning that must be
observed. They were impressed.

"We thought we'd like to s-s-s-see you f-f-f-first, Mr. Hines, about
the c-c-c-c-casket," Luke whispered nervously. "We're going to ask your
advice. We want you to help us find something appropriate."

Horse Hines nodded with grave approval. Then he led them softly
back, into a large dark room with polished waxen floors where, amid a
rich dead smell of wood and velvet, upon wheeled trestles, the splendid
coffins lay in their proud menace.

"Now," said Horse Hines quietly, "I know the family doesn't want
anything cheap."

"No, sir!" said the sailor positively. "We want the b-b-b-best you have."

"I take a personal interest in this funeral," said Horse Hines with
gentle emotion. "I have known the Gant and Pentland families for
thirty years or more. I have had business dealings with your father for
nigh on to twenty years."

"And I w-w-want you to know, Mr. Hines, that the f-f-f-family ap-
preciates the interest you're taking in this," said the sailor very earnestly.

He likes this, Eugene thought. The affection of the world. He must
have it.

"Your father," continued Horse Hines, "is one of the oldest and
most respected business men in the community. And the Pentland family
is one of the wealthiest and most prominent."

Eugene was touched with a moment's glow of pride.

"You don't want anything shoddy," said Horse Hines. "I know that.
What you get ought to be in good taste and have dignity. Am I right?"

Luke nodded emphatically.

"That's the way we feel about it, Mr. Hines. We want the best you
have. We're not pinching p-p-p-pennies where Ben's concerned," he said
proudly.

"Well, then," said Horse Hines, "I'll give you my honest opinion.
I could give you this one cheap," he placed his hand upon one of the
caskets, "but I don't think it's what you want. Of course," he said, "it's

good at the price. It's worth the money. It'll give you service, don't worry. You'll get value out of it——"

Now there's an idea, thought Eugene.

"They're all good, Luke. I haven't got a bad piece of stock in the place. But——"

"We want something b-b-b-better," said Luke earnestly. He turned to Eugene. "Don't you think so, 'Gene?"

"Yes," said Eugene.

"Well," said Horse Hines, "I could sell you this one," he indicated the most sumptuous casket in the room. "They don't come better than that, Luke. That's the top. She's worth every dollar I ask for her."

"All right," said Luke. "You're the judge. If that's the best you've g-g-g-got, we'll take it."

No, no! thought Eugene. You mustn't interrupt. Let him go on.

"But," said Horse Hines relentlessly, "there's no need for you to take that one, either. What you're after, Luke, is dignity and simplicity. Is that right?"

"Yes," said the sailor meekly, "I guess you're right at that, Mr. Hines."

Now we'll have it, thought Eugene. This man takes joy in his work.

"Well, then," said Horse Hines decisively, "I was going to suggest to you boys that you take this one." He put his hand affectionately upon a handsome casket at his side.

"This is neither too plain nor too fancy. It's simple and in good taste. Silver handles, you see—silver plate here for the name. You can't go wrong on this one. It's a good buy. She'll give you value for every dollar you put into it."

They walked around the coffin, staring at it critically.

After a moment, Luke said nervously:

"How—wh—wh—wh-what's the price of this one?"

"That sells for $450," said Horse Hines. "But," he added, after a moment's dark reflection, "I'll tell you what I'll do. Your father and I are old friends. Out of respect for the family, I'll let you have it at cost—$375."

"What do you say, 'Gene?" the sailor asked. "Does it look all right to you?"

Do your Christmas shopping early.

"Yes," said Eugene, "let's take it. I wish there were another color. I don't like black," he added. "Haven't you got any other color?"

Horse Hines stared at him a moment.

"Black *is* the color," he said.

Then, after a moment's silence, he went on:

"Would you boys care to see the body?"

"Yes," they said.

He led them on tiptoe down the aisle of the coffins, and opened a door to a room behind. It was dark. They entered and stood with caught breath. Horse Hines switched on a light and closed the door.

Ben, clad in his best suit of clothes, a neat one of dark gray-black, lay in rigid tranquillity upon a table. His hands, cold and white, with clean dry nails, withered a little like an old apple, were crossed loosely on his stomach. He had been closely shaved: he was immaculately groomed. The rigid head was thrust sharply upward, with a ghastly counterfeit of a smile: there was a little gum of wax at the nostrils, and a waxen lacing between the cold firm lips. The mouth was tight, somewhat bulging. It looked fuller than it ever had looked before.

There was a faint indefinably cloying odor.

The sailor looked with superstition, nervously, with puckered forehead. Then he whispered to Eugene:

"I g-g-guess that's Ben, all right."

Because, Eugene thought, it is not Ben, and we are lost. He looked at the cold bright carrion, that bungling semblance which had not even the power of a good wax-work to suggest its image. Nothing of Ben could be buried here. In this poor stuffed crow, with its pathetic barbering, and its neat buttons, nothing of the owner had been left. All that was there was the tailoring of Horse Hines, who now stood by, watchfully, hungry for their praise.

No, this is not Ben (Eugene thought). No trace of him is left in this deserted shell. It bears no mark of him. Where has he gone? Is this his bright particular flesh, made in his image, given life by his unique gesture, by his one soul? No, he is gone from that bright flesh. This thing is one with all carrion; it will be mixed with the earth again. Ben? Where? O lost!

The sailor, looking, said:

"That b-b-b-boy sure suffered." Suddenly, turning his face away into his hand, he sobbed briefly and painfully, his confused stammering life drawn out of its sprawl into a moment of hard grief.

Eugene wept, not because he saw Ben there, but because Ben had gone, and because he remembered all the tumult and the pain.

"It is over now," said Horse Hines gently. "He is at peace."

"By God, Mr. Hines," said the sailor earnestly, as he wiped his eyes on his jacket, "that was one g-g-great boy."

Horse Hines looked raptly at the cold strange face.

"A fine boy," he murmured as his fish-eye fell tenderly on his work. "And I have tried to do him justice."

They were silent for a moment, looking.

"You've d-d-done a fine job," said the sailor. "I've got to hand it to you. What do you say, 'Gene?"

"Yes," said Eugene, in a small choking voice. "Yes."

"He's a b-b-b-bit p-p-p-pale, don't you think?" the sailor stammered, barely conscious of what he was saying.

"Just a moment!" said Horse Hines quickly, lifting a finger. Briskly he took a stick of rouge from his pocket, stepped forward, and deftly, swiftly, sketched upon the dead gray cheeks a ghastly rose-hued mockery of life and health.

"There!" he said, with deep satisfaction; and, rouge-stick in hand, head critically cocked, like a painter before his canvas, he stepped back into the terrible staring prison of their horror.

"There are artists, boys, in every profession," Horse Hines continued in a moment, with quiet pride, "and though I do say it myself, Luke, I'm proud of my work on this job. Look at him!" he exclaimed with sudden energy, and a bit of color in his gray face. "Did you ever see anything more natural in your life?"

Eugene turned upon the man a grim and purple stare, noting with pity, with a sort of tenderness, as the dogs of laughter tugged at his straining throat the earnestness and pride in the long horse-face.

"Look at it!" said Horse Hines again in slow wonder. "I'll never beat that again! Not if I live to be a million! That's art, boys!"

A slow strangling gurgle escaped from Eugene's screwed lips. The sailor looked quickly at him, with a crazy suppressed smile.

"What's the matter?" he said warningly. "Don't, fool!" His grin broke loose.

Eugene staggered across the floor and collapsed upon a chair, roaring with laughter while his long arms flapped helplessly at his sides.

"'Scuse!" he gasped. "Don't mean to—A-r-rt! Yes! Yes! That's it!" he screamed, and he beat his knuckles in a crazy tattoo upon the polished floor. He slid gently off the chair, slowly unbuttoning his vest, and with a languid hand loosening his necktie. A faint gurgle came from his weary throat, his head lolled around on the floor languidly, tears coursed down his swollen features.

"What's wrong with you? Are you c-c-c-crazy?" said the sailor, all a-grin.

Horse Hines bent sympathetically and assisted the boy to his feet. "It's the strain," he said knowingly to the sailor. "The pore fellow has become hysterical."

37

So, to Ben dead was given more care, more time, more money than had ever been given to Ben living. His burial was a final gesture of irony and futility: an effort to compensate carrion death for the unpaid wage of life—love and mercy. He had a grand funeral. All the Pentlands sent wreaths, and came with their separate clans, bringing along with their hastily assumed funeral manners a smell of recent business. Will Pentland talked with the men about politics, the war, and trade conditions, paring his nails thoughtfully, pursing his lips and nodding in his curiously reflective way, and occasionally punning with a birdy wink. His pleased self-laughter was mixed with Henry's loud guffaw. Pett, older, kinder, gentler than Eugene had ever seen her, moved about with a rustling of gray silk, and a relaxed bitterness. And Jim was there, with his wife, whose name Eugene forgot, and his four bright hefty daughters, whose names he confused, but who had all been to college and done well, and his son, who had been to a Presbyterian college, and had been expelled for advocating free love and socialism while editor of the college paper. Now he played the violin, and loved music, and helped his father with the business: he was an effeminate and mincing young man, but of the breed. And there was Thaddeus Pentland, Will's bookkeeper, the youngest and poorest of the three. He was a man past fifty, with a pleasant red face, brown mustaches, and a gentle placid manner. He was full of puns and pleased good-nature, save when he quoted from Karl Marx and Eugene Debs. He was a Socialist, and had once received eight votes for Congress. He was there with his garrulous wife (whom Helen called Jibber-Jibber) and his two daughters, languid good-looking blondes of twenty and twenty-four.

There they were, in all their glory—that strange rich clan, with its fantastic mixture of success and impracticality, its hard monied sense, its visionary fanaticism. There they were, in their astonishing contradictions: the business man who had no business method, and yet had made his million dollars; the frantic antagonist of Capital who had given the loyal service of a lifetime to the thing he denounced; the wastrel son, with the bull vitality of the athlete, a great laugh, animal charm—no more; the musician son, a college rebel, intelligent, fanatic, with a good head for figures; insane miserliness for oneself, lavish expenditure for one's children.

There they were, each with the familiar marking of the clan—broad nose, full lips, deep flat cheeks, deliberate pursed mouths, flat drawling voices, flat complacent laughter. There they were, with their enormous vitality, their tainted blood, their meaty health, their sanity, their insanity, their humor, their superstition, their meanness, their generosity, their fanatic idealism, their unyielding materialism. There they were, smelling of the earth and Parnassus—that strange clan which met only at weddings or funerals, but which was forever true to itself, indissoluble and forever apart, with its melancholia, its madness, its mirth: more enduring than life, more strong than death.

And as Eugene looked, he felt again the nightmare horror of destiny: he was of them—there was no escape. Their lust, their weakness, their sensuality, their fanaticism, their strength, their rich taint, were rooted in the marrow of his bones.

But Ben, with the thin gray face (he thought) was not a part of them. Their mark was nowhere on him.

And among them, sick and old, leaning upon his cane, moved Gant, the alien, the stranger. He was lost and sorrowful, but sometimes, with a flash of his old rhetoric, he spoke of his grief and the death of his son.

The women filled the house with their moaning. Eliza wept almost constantly; Helen by fits, in loose hysterical collapse. And all the other women wept with gusto, comforting Eliza and her daughter, falling into one another's arms, wailing with keen hunger. And the men stood sadly about, dressed in their good clothes, wondering when it would be over. Ben lay in the parlor, bedded in his expensive coffin. The room was heavy with the incense of the funeral flowers.

Presently the Scotch minister arrived: his decent soul lay above all the loud posturings of grief like a bolt of hard clean wool. He began the service for the dead in a dry nasal voice, remote, monotonous, cold, and passionate.

Then, marshalled by Horse Hines, the pallbearers, young men from the paper and the town, who had known the dead man best, moved slowly out, gripping the coffin-handles with their nicotined fingers. In proper sequence, the mourners followed, lengthening out in closed victorias that exhaled their funeral scent of stale air and old leather.

To Eugene came again the old ghoul fantasy of a corpse and cold pork, the smell of the dead and hamburger steak—the glozed corruption of Christian burial, the obscene pomps, the perfumed carrion. Slightly nauseated, he took his seat with Eliza in the carriage, and tried to think of supper.

The procession moved off briskly to the smooth trotting pull of the velvet rumps. The mourning women peered out of the closed carriages at the gaping town. They wept behind their heavy veils, and looked to see if the town was watching. Behind the world's great mask of grief, the eyes of the mourners shone through with a terrible and indecent hunger, an unnameable lust.

It was raw October weather—gray and wet. The service had been short, as a precaution against the pestilence which was everywhere. The funeral entered the cemetery. It was a pleasant place, on a hill. There was a good view of the town. As the hearse drove up, two men who had been digging the grave, moved off. The women moaned loudly when they saw the raw open ditch.

Slowly the coffin was lowered onto the bands that crossed the grave. Again Eugene heard the nasal drone of the Presbyterian minister. The boy's mind fumbled at little things. Horse Hines bent ceremoniously, with a starched crackle of shirt, to throw his handful of dirt into the grave. "Ashes to ashes—" He reeled and would have fallen in if Gilbert Gant had not held him. He had been drinking. "I am the resurrection and the life—" Helen wept constantly, harshly and bitterly. "He that believeth in me—" The sobs of the women rose to sharp screams as the coffin slid down upon the bands into the earth.

Then the mourners got back into their carriages and were driven briskly away. There was a fast indecent hurry about their escape. The long barbarism of burial was at an end. As they drove away, Eugene peered back through the little glass in the carriage. The two grave-diggers were already returning to their work. He watched until the first shovel of dirt had been thrown into the grave. He saw the raw new graves, the sere long grasses, noted how quickly the mourning wreaths had wilted. Then he looked at the wet gray sky. He hoped it would not rain that night.

It was over. The carriages split away from the procession. The men dropped off in the town at the newspaper office, the pharmacy, the cigar-store. The women went home. No more. No more.

Night came, the bare swept streets, the gaunt winds. Helen lay before a fire in Hugh Barton's house. She had a bottle of chloroform liniment in her hand. She brooded morbidly into the fire, reliving the death a hundred times, weeping bitterly and becoming calm again.

"When I think of it, I hate her. I shall never forget. And did you hear her? Did you? Already she's begun to pretend how much he loved her. But you can't fool me! I know! He wouldn't have her around. You saw that, didn't you? He kept calling for me. I was the only one he'd let come near him. You know that, don't you?"

"You're the one who always has to be the goat," said Hugh Barton sourly. "I'm getting tired of it. That's what has worn you out. If they don't leave you alone, I'm going to take you away from here."

Then he went back to his charts and pamphlets, frowning impor-tantly over a cigar, and scrawling figures on an old envelope with a stub of pencil gripped between his fingers.

She has him trained, too, Eugene thought.

Then, hearing the sharp whine of the wind, she wept again.

"Poor old Ben," she said. "I can't bear to think of him out there to-night."

She was silent for a moment, staring at the fire.

"After this, I'm through," she said. "They can get along for them-selves. Hugh and I have a right to our own lives. Don't you think so?"

"Yes," said Eugene. I'm merely the chorus, he thought.

"Papa's not going to die," she went on. "I've nursed him like a slave for six years, and he'll be here when I'm gone. Every one was expecting papa to die, but it was Ben who went. You never can tell. After this, I'm through."

Her voice had a note of exasperation in it. They all felt the grim trickery of Death, which had come in by the cellar while they waited at the window.

"Papa has no right to expect it of me!" she burst out resentfully. "He's had his life. He's an old man. We have a right to ours as well as any one. Good heavens! Can't they realize that! I'm married to Hugh Barton! I'm *his* wife!"

Are you? thought Eugene. Are you?

But Eliza sat before the fire at Dixieland with hands folded, reliving a past of tenderness and love that never had been. And as the wind howled in the bleak street, and Eliza wove a thousand fables of that lost and bitter spirit, the bright and stricken thing in the boy twisted about in horror, looking for escape from the house of death. No more! No more! (it said). You are alone now. You are lost. Go find yourself, lost boy, beyond the hills.

This little bright and stricken thing stood up on Eugene's heart and talked into his mouth.

O but I can't go now, said Eugene to it. (Why not? it whispered.) Because her face is so white, and her forehead is so broad and high, with the black hair drawn back from it, and when she sat there at the bed she looked like a little child. I can't go now and leave her here alone. (She is alone, it said, and so are you.) And when she purses up her mouth and stares, so grave and thoughtful, she is like a little child. (You are alone now, it said. You must escape, or you will die.) It is all like death: she fed me at her breast, I slept in the same bed with her, she took me on her trips. All of that is over now, and each time it was like a death. (And like a life, it said to him. Each time that you die, you will be born again. And you will die a hundred times before you become a man.) I can't! I can't! Not now—later, more slowly. (No. Now, it said.) I am afraid. I have nowhere to go. (You must find the place, it said.) I am lost. (You must hunt for yourself, it said.) I am alone. Where are you? (You must find me, it said.)

Then, as the bright thing twisted about in him, Eugene heard the whine of the bleak wind about the house that he must leave, and the voice of Eliza calling up from the past the beautiful lost things that never happened.

"—and I said, 'Why, what on earth, boy, you want to dress up warm around your neck or you'll catch your death of cold.'"

Eugene caught at his throat and plunged for the door.

"Here, boy! Where are you going?" said Eliza, looking up quickly.

"I've got to go," he said in a choking voice. "I've got to get away from here."

Then he saw the fear in her eyes, and the grave troubled child's stare. He rushed to where she sat and grasped her hand. She held him tightly and laid her face against his arm.

"Don't go yet," she said. "You've all your life ahead of you. Stay with me just a day or two."

"Yes, mama," he said, falling to his knees. "Yes, mama." He hugged her to him frantically. "Yes, mama. God bless you, mama. It's all right, mama. It's all right."

Eliza wept bitterly.

"I'm an old woman," she said, "and one by one I've lost you all. He's dead now, and I never got to know him. O son, don't leave me yet. You're the only one that's left: you were my baby. Don't go! Don't go." She laid her white face against his sleeve.

It is not hard to go (he thought). But when can we forget?

It was October and the leaves were quaking. Dusk was beginning. The sun had gone, the western ranges faded in chill purple mist, but the western sky still burned with ragged bands of orange. It was October.

Eugene walked swiftly along the sinuous paved curves of Rutledge Road. There was a smell of fog and supper in the air: a warm moist blur at window-panes, and the pungent sizzle of cookery. There were mist-far voices, and a smell of burning leaves, and a warm yellow blur of lights.

He turned into an unpaved road by the big wooden sanitarium. He heard the rich kitchen laughter of the negroes, the larded sizzle of food, the dry veranda coughing of the lungers.

He walked briskly along the lumpy road, with a dry scuffling of leaves. The air was a chill dusky pearl: above him a few pale stars were out. The town and the house were behind him. There was a singing in the great hill-pines.

Two women came down the road and passed him. He saw that they were country women. They were dressed rustily in black, and one of them was weeping. He thought of the men who had been laid in the earth that day, and of all the women who wept. Will they come again? he wondered.

When he came to the gate of the cemetery he found it open. He went in quickly and walked swiftly up the winding road that curved around the crest of the hill. The grasses were dry and sere; a wilted wreath of laurel lay upon a grave. As he approached the family plot, his pulse quickened a little. Some one was moving slowly, deliberately, in among the grave-stones. But as he came up he saw that it was Mrs. Pert.

"Good-evening, Mrs. Pert," said Eugene.

"Who is it?" she asked, peering murkily. She came to him with her grave unsteady step.

"It's 'Gene," he said.

"Oh, is it Old 'Gene?" she said. "How are you, 'Gene?"

"Pretty well," he said. He stood awkwardly, chilled, not knowing how to continue. It was getting dark. There were long lonely preludes to winter in the splendid pines, and a whistling of wind in the long grasses. Below them, in the gulch, night had come. There was a negro settlement there—Stumptown, it was called. The rich voices of Africa wailed up to them their jungle dirge.

But in the distance, away on their level and above, on other hills, they saw the town. Slowly, in twinkling nests, the lights of the town went up, and there were frost-far voices, and music, and the laughter of a girl.

"This is a nice place," said Eugene. "You get a nice view of the town from here."

"Yes," said Mrs. Pert. "And Old Ben's got the nicest place of all. You get a better view right here than anywhere else. I've been here before in the daytime." In a moment she went on. "Old Ben will turn into lovely flowers. Roses, I think."

"No," said Eugene, "dandelions—and big flowers with a lot of thorns on them."

She stood looking about fuzzily for a moment, with the blurred gentle smile on her lips.

"It is getting dark, Mrs. Pert," said Eugene hesitantly. "Are you out here alone?"

"Alone? I've got Old 'Gene and Old Ben here, haven't I?" she said.

"Maybe we'd better go back, Mrs. Pert?" he said. "It's going to turn cold to-night. I'll go with you."

"Fatty can go by herself," she said with dignity. "Don't worry, 'Gene. I'll leave you alone."

"That's all right," said Eugene, confused. "We both came for the same reason, I suppose."

"Yes," said Mrs. Pert. "Who'll be coming here this time next year, I wonder? Will Old 'Gene come back then?"

"No," said Eugene. "No, Mrs. Pert. I shall never come here again."

"Nor I, 'Gene," she said. "When do you go back to school?"

"To-morrow," he said.

"Then Fatty will have to say good-bye," she said reproachfully. "I'm going away too."

"Where are you going?" he asked, surprised.

"I'm going to live with my daughter in Tennessee. You didn't know

Fatty was a grandmother, did you?" she said, with her soft blurred smile. "I've a little grandson two years old."

"I'm sorry to see you go," Eugene said.

Mrs. Pert was silent a moment, rocking vaguely upon her feet.

"What did they say was wrong with Ben?" she asked.

"He had pneumonia, Mrs. Pert," said Eugene.

"Oh, pneumonia! That's it!" She nodded her head wisely as if satisfied. "My husband's a drug salesman, you know, but I never can remember all the things that people have. Pneumonia."

She was silent again, reflecting.

"And when they shut you up in a box and put you in the ground, the way they did Old Ben, what do they call that?" she asked with a soft inquiring smile.

He did not laugh.

"They call that death, Mrs. Pert."

"Death! Yes, that's it," said Mrs. Pert brightly, nodding her head in agreement. "That's one kind, 'Gene. There are some other kinds, too. Did you know that?" She smiled at him.

"Yes," said Eugene. "I know that, Mrs. Pert."

She stretched out her hands suddenly to him, and clasped his cold fingers. She did not smile any more.

"Good-bye, my dear," she said. "We both knew Ben, didn't we? God bless you."

Then she turned and walked away down the road, at her portly uncertain gait, and was lost in the gathering dark.

The great stars rode proudly up into heaven. And just over him, just over the town, it seemed, there was one so rich and low he could have touched it. Ben's grave had been that day freshly sodded: there was a sharp cold smell of earth there. Eugene thought of Spring, and the poignant and wordless odor of the elvish dandelions that would be there. In the frosty dark, far-faint, there was the departing wail of a whistle.

And suddenly, as he watched the lights wink cheerfully up in the town, their warm message of the hived life of men brought to him a numb hunger for all the words and the faces. He heard the far voices and laughter. And on the distant road a powerful car, bending around the curve, cast over him for a second, over that lonely hill of the dead, its great shaft of light and life. In his numbed mind, which for days now had fumbled curiously with little things, with little things alone, as a child fumbles with blocks or with little things, a light was growing.

His mind gathered itself out of the wreckage of little things: out of all that the world had shown or taught him he could remember now only the great star above the town, and the light that had swung over the hill, and the fresh sod upon Ben's grave, and the wind, and far sounds and music, and Mrs. Pert.

Wind pressed the boughs, the withered leaves were shaking. It was October, but the leaves were shaking. A star was shaking. A light was waking. Wind was quaking. The star was far. The night, the light. The light was bright. A chant, a song, the slow dance of the little things within him. The star over the town, the light over the hill, the sod over Ben, night over all. His mind fumbled with little things. Over us all is something. Star, night, earth, light . . . light . . . O lost! . . . a stone . . . a leaf . . . a door . . . O ghost! . . . a light . . . a song . . . a light . . . a light swings over the hill . . . over us all . . . a star shines over the town . . . over us all . . . a light.

We shall not come again. We never shall come back again. But over us all, over us all, over us all is—something.

Wind pressed the boughs; the withered leaves were shaking. It was October, but some leaves were shaking.

A light swings over the hill. (We shall not come again.) And over the town a star. (Over us all, over us all that shall not come again.) And over the day the dark. But over the darkness—what?

We shall not come again. We never shall come back again.

Over the dawn a lark. (That shall not come again.) And wind and music far. O lost! (It shall not come again.) And over your mouth the earth. O ghost! But, over the darkness—what?

Wind pressed the boughs; the withered leaves were quaking.

We shall not come again. We never shall come back again. It was October, but we never shall come back again.

When will they come again? When will they come again?

The laurel, the lizard, and the stone will come no more. The women weeping at the gate have gone and will not come again. And pain and pride and death will pass, and will not come again. And light and dawn will pass, and the star and the cry of a lark will pass, and will not come again. And we shall pass, and shall not come again.

What things will come again? O Spring, the cruellest and fairest of the seasons, will come again. And the strange and buried men will come again, in flower and leaf the strange and buried men will come again, and death and the dust will never come again, for death and the dust will die. And Ben will come again, he will not die again, in flower and leaf, in wind and music far, he will come back again.

O lost, and by the wind grieved, ghost, come back again!

It had grown dark. The frosty night blazed with great brilliant stars. The lights in the town shone with sharp radiance. Presently, when he had lain upon the cold earth for some time, Eugene got up and went away toward the town.

Wind pressed the boughs; the withered leaves were shaking.

38

Three weeks after Eugene's return to the university the war ended. The students cursed and took off their uniforms. But they rang the great bronze bell, and built a bonfire on the campus, leaping around it like dervishes.

Life fell back into civilian patterns. The gray back of winter was broken: the Spring came through.

Eugene was a great man on the campus of the little university. He plunged exultantly into the life of the place. He cried out in his throat with his joy: all over the country, life was returning, reviving, awaking. The young men were coming back to the campus. The leaves were out in a tender green blur: the quilled jonquil spouted from the rich black earth, and peach-bloom fell upon the shrill young isles of grass. Everywhere life was returning, awaking, reviving. With victorious joy, Eugene thought of the flowers above Ben's grave.

He was wild with ecstasy because the Spring had beaten death. The grief of Ben sank to a forgotten depth in him. He was charged with the juice of life and motion. He did not walk: he bounded along. He joined everything he had not joined. He made funny speeches in chapel, at smokers, at meetings of all sorts. He edited the paper, he wrote poems and stories—he flung outward without pause or thought.

Sometimes at night he would rush across the country, beside a drunken driver, to Exeter and Sydney, and there seek out the women behind the chained lattices, calling to them in the fresh dawn-dusk of Spring his young goat-cry of desire and hunger.

Lily! Louise! Ruth! Ellen! O mother of love, you cradle of birth and living, whatever your billion names may be, I come, your son, your lover. Stand, Maya, by your opened door, denned in the jungle web of Niggertown.

Sometimes, when he walked softly by, he heard the young men talking in their rooms of Eugene Gant. Eugene Gant was crazy. Eugene Gant was mad. Oh, I (he thought) am Eugene Gant!

Then a voice said: "He didn't change his underwear for six weeks. One of his fraternity brothers told me so." And another: "He takes a bath once a month, whether he needs it or not." They laughed; one said then that he was "brilliant"; they all agreed.

He caught the claw of his hand into his lean throat. They are talking of me, of me! I am Eugene Gant—the conqueror of nations, lord of the earth, the Siva of a thousand beautiful forms.

In nakedness and loneliness of soul he paced along the streets. Nobody said, I know you. Nobody said, I am here. The vast wheel of life, of which he was the hub, spun round.

Most of us think we're hell, thought Eugene. I do. I think I'm hell. Then, in the dark campus path, he heard the young men talking in their rooms, and he gouged at his face bloodily, with a snarl of hate against himself.

I think I am hell, and they say I stink because I have not had a bath. But I could not stink, even if I never had a bath. Only the others stink. My dirtiness is better than their cleanliness. The web of my flesh is finer; my blood is a subtle elixir: the hair of my head, the marrow of my spine, the cunning jointure of my bones, and all the combining jellies, fats, meats, oils, and sinews of my flesh, the spittle of my mouth, the sweat of my skin, is mixed with rarer elements, and is fairer and finer than their gross peasant beef.

There had appeared that year upon the nape of his neck a small tetter of itch, a sign of his kinship with the Pentlands—a token of his kinship with the great malady of life. He tore at the spot with frantic nails; he burned his neck to a peeled blister with carbolic acid—but the spot, as if fed by some ineradicable leprosy in his blood, remained. Sometimes, during cool weather, it almost disappeared; but in warm weather it returned angrily, and he scraped his neck red in an itching torture.

He was afraid to let people walk behind him. He sat, whenever possible, with his back to the wall; he was in agony when he descended a crowded stair, holding his shoulders high so that the collar of his coat might hide the terrible patch. He let his hair grow in a great thick mat, partly to hide his sore, and partly because exposing it to the view of the barber touched him with shame and horror.

He would become at times insanely conscious of spotless youth: he was terrified before the loud good health of America, which is really a sickness, because no man will admit his sores. He shrank back at the memory of his lost heroic fantasies: he thought of Bruce-Eugene, of all his thousand romantic impersonations, and never could he endure himself with an itching tetter upon his flesh. He became morbidly conscious of all his blemishes, real and fancied: for days he would see nothing but people's teeth—he would stare into their mouths when he talked to them, noting the fillings, the extractions, the plates and bridges. He would gaze with envy and fear at the sound ivory grinders of the young men, baring his own, which were regular but somewhat yellowed with smoking, a hundred times a day. He scrubbed at them savagely with a stiff brush until the gums bled; he brooded for hours upon a decaying molar which must one day be extracted, and, wild with despair, he would figure out on paper the age at which he might become toothless.

But if, he thought, I lose only one every two years after I am twenty, I shall still have over fifteen left when I am fifty, since we have thirty-two, including wisdom-teeth. And it will not look so bad, if only I can save the front ones. Then, with his hope in futures, he thought: But by that time perhaps the dentists can give me real ones. He read several dental magazines to see if there was any hope for the transplanting of sound teeth for old ones. Then, with brooding satisfaction, he studied his sensual deeply scalloped mouth with the pouting underlip, noting that even when he smiled he barely revealed his teeth.

He asked the medical students innumerable questions about the treatment or cure of inherited blood maladies, venereal diseases, intestinal and inguinal cancers, and the transference of animal glands to men. He went to the movies only to examine the teeth and muscles of the hero; he pored over the toothpaste and collar advertisements in the magazines; he went to the shower-rooms at the gymnasium and stared at the straight toes of the young men, thinking with desperate sick pain of his own bunched and crooked ones. He stood naked before a mirror, looking at his long gaunt body, smooth and white save for the crooked toes and the terrible spot on his neck—lean, but moulded with delicate and powerful symmetry.

Then, slowly, he began to take a terrible joy in his taint. The thing on his neck that could not be gouged or burnt away he identified with a tragic humor of his blood that plunged him downward at times into melancholia and madness. But there was, he saw, a great health in him as well, that could bring him back victoriously from desolation. In his reading of fiction, in the movies, in the collar advertisements, in all his thousand fantasies of Bruce-Eugene, he had never known a hero with crooked toes, a decaying tooth, and a patch of tetter on his neck. Nor had he ever known a heroine, whether among the society women of Chambers and Phillips, or among the great elegants of Meredith and Ouida, who had borne such a blemish. But, in all his fantasies now, he loved a woman with hair of carrot silk and eyes of a faintly weary violet, webbed delicately at the corners. Her teeth were small, white and irregular, and she had one molar edged with gold which was visible when she smiled. She was subtle, and a little weary: a child and a mother, as old and as deep as Asia, and as young as germinal April who returns forever like a girl, a mistress, a parent, and a nurse.

Thus, through the death of his brother, and the sickness that was rooted in his own flesh, Eugene came to know a deeper and darker wisdom than he had ever known before. He began to see that what was subtle and beautiful in human life was touched with a divine pearl-sickness. Health was to be found in the steady stare of the cats and dogs, or in the smooth vacant chops of the peasant. But he looked on the faces of the lords of the earth— and he saw them wasted and devoured by the beautiful disease of thought and passion. In the pages of a thousand books he saw their portraits: Coleridge at twenty-five, with the loose sensual mouth, gaping idiotically, the vast staring eyes, holding in their opium depths the vision of seas haunted by the albatross, the great white forehead—head mixed of Zeus and the village degenerate; the lean worn head of Caesar, a little thirsty in the flanks; and the dreaming mummy face of Kublai Khan, lit with eyes that flickered with green fires. And he saw the faces of the great Thothmes, and Aspalta and Mycerinus, and all the heads of subtle Egypt—those smooth unwrinkled faces that held the wisdom of 1,200 gods. And the strange wild faces of the Goth, the Frank, the Vandal, that came storming up below the old tired eyes of Rome. And the weary craftiness on the face of the great Jew, Disraeli; the terrible skull-grin of Voltaire; the mad ranting savagery of Ben Jonson's; the dour wild agony of Carlyle's; and the faces of Heine, and Rousseau, and Dante, and Tiglath-Pileser, and Cervantes— these were all faces on which life had fed. They were faces wasted by the vulture, Thought; they were faces seared and hollowed by the flame of Beauty.

And thus, touched with the terrible destiny of his blood, caught in the trap of himself and the Pentlands, with the little flower of sin and darkness on his neck, Eugene escaped forever from the good and the pretty, into a dark land that is forbidden to the sterilized. The creatures of romantic fiction, the vicious doll-faces of the movie women, the brutal idiot regularity of the faces in the advertisements, and the faces of most of the young college-men and women, were stamped in a mould of enamelled vacancy, and became unclean to him.

The national demand for white shiny plumbing, toothpaste, tiled lunch-rooms, hair-cuts, manicured dentistry, horn spectacles, baths, and the insane fear of disease that sent the voters whispering to the druggist after their brutal fumbling lecheries—all of this seemed nasty. Their outer cleanliness became the token of an inner corruption: it was something that glittered and was dry, foul, and rotten at the core. He felt that, no matter what leper's taint he might carry upon his flesh, there was in him a health that was greater than they could ever know—something fierce and cruelly wounded, but alive, that did not shrink away from the terrible sunken river of life; something desperate and merciless that looked steadily on the hidden and unspeakable passions that unify the tragic family of this earth.

Yet, Eugene was no rebel. He had no greater need for rebellion than have most Americans, which is none at all. He was quite content with any system which might give him comfort, security, enough money to do as he liked, and freedom to think, eat, drink, love, read, and write what he chose. And he did not care under what form of government he lived—Republican, Democrat, Tory, Socialist, or Bolshevist—if it could assure him these things. He did not want to reform the world, or to make it a better place to live in: his whole conviction was that the world was full of pleasant places, enchanted places, if he could only go and find them. The life around him was beginning to fetter and annoy him: he wanted to escape from it. He felt sure things would be better elsewhere. He always felt sure things would be better elsewhere.

It was not his quality as a romantic to escape out of life, but into it. He wanted no land of Make-believe: his fantasies found extension in reality, and he saw no reason to doubt that there really were 1,200 gods in Egypt, and that the centaur, the hippogriff, and the winged bull might all be found in their proper places. He believed that there was magic in Byzantium, and genii stoppered up in wizards' bottles. Moreover, since Ben's death, the conviction had grown on him that men do not escape from life because life is dull, but that life escapes from men because men are little. He felt that the passions of the play were greater than the actors. It seemed to him that he had never had a great moment of living in which he had measured up to its fulness. His pain at Ben's death had been greater than he, the love and loss of Laura had left him stricken and bewildered, and when he embraced young girls and women he felt a desperate frustration: he wanted to eat them like cake and to have them, too; to roll them up into a ball; to entomb them in his flesh; to possess them more fully than they may ever be possessed.

Further, it annoyed and wounded him to be considered "queer." He exulted in his popularity among the students, his heart pounded with pride under all the pins and emblems, but he resented being considered an eccentric, and he envied those of his fellows who were elected to office for their solid golden mediocrity. He wanted to obey the laws and to be respected: he believed himself to be a sincerely conventional person—but, some one would see him after midnight, bounding along a campus path, with goat-cries beneath the moon. His suits went baggy, his shirts and drawers got dirty, his shoes wore through—he stuffed them with cardboard strips—his hats grew shapeless and wore through at the creases. But he did not mean to go unkempt—the thought of going for repairs filled him with weary horror. He hated to act—he wanted to brood upon his entrails for fourteen hours a day. At length, goaded, he would lash his great bulk, lulled in the powerful inertia of its visions, into a cursing and violent movement.

He was desperately afraid of people in crowds: at class meetings, or smokers, or at any public gathering, he was nervous and constrained until he began to talk to them, and got them under him. He was always afraid that some one would make a joke about him, and that he would be laughed at. But he was not afraid of any man alone: he felt that he could handle any one if he got him away from his crowd. Remembering his savage fear and hatred of the crowd, with a man alone he would play cruelly, like a cat, snarling gently at him, prowling in on him softly, keeping cocked and silent the terrible tiger's paw of his spirit. All of their starch oozed out of them; they seemed to squeak and twitter, and look round for the door. He would get some loud pompous yokel—the student president of the Y. M. C. A., or the class president—and bear down on him with evil gentle matter-of-factness.

"Don't you think," he would begin with earnest piety, "don't you think that a man should kiss his wife on her belly?"

And he would fasten all the eager innocence of his face into a stare.

"For, after all, the belly is sometimes more beautiful than the mouth, and far cleaner. Or do you believe in the belly-less marriage? I, for one," he went on with proud passion, "do not! I stand for more and better Belly-Kissing. Our wives, our mothers, and our sisters expect it of us. It is an act of reverence to the seat of life. Nay! it is even an act of religious worship. If we could get our prominent business men and all the other right-thinking people interested in it, it would bring about the mightiest revolution ever known in a nation's life. In five years it would do away with divorce and re-establish the prestige of the home. In twenty years it would make our nation the proud centre of civilization and the arts. Don't you think so? Or do you?"

Eugene thought so. It was one of his few Utopias.

Sometimes, when he was in a chafed and bitter temper, he would hear a burst of laughter from a student's room, and he would turn snarling, and curse them, believing they laughed at him. He inherited his father's conviction at times that the world was gathered in an immense conspiracy against him: the air about him was full of mockery and menace, the leaves whispered with treason, in a thousand secret places people were assembled to humiliate, degrade, and betray him. He would spend hours under the terrible imminence of some unknown danger: although he was guilty of nothing but his own nightmare fantasies, he would enter a class, a meeting, a gathering of students, with cold constricted heart, awaiting exposure, sentence, and ruin, for he knew not what crime. Again, he would be wild, extravagant, and careless, squealing triumphantly in their faces and bounding along possessed with goaty joy, as he saw life dangling like a plum for his taking.

And thus, going along a campus path at night, fulfilled with his dreams of glory, he heard young men talking of him kindly and coarsely, laughing at his antics, and saying he needed a bath and clean underwear. He clawed at his throat as he listened.

I think I'm hell, thought Eugene, and they say I stink because I have not had a bath. Me! Me! Bruce-Eugene, the Scourge of the Greasers, and the greatest fullback Yale ever had! Marshal Gant, the saviour of his country! Ace Gant, the hawk of the sky, the man who brought Richthofen down! Senator Gant, Governor Gant, President Gant, the restorer and uniter of a broken nation, retiring quietly to private life in spite of the weeping protest of one hundred million people, until, like Arthur or Barbarossa, he shall hear again the drums of need and peril.

Jesus-of-Nazareth Gant, mocked, reviled, spat upon, and imprisoned for the sins of others, but nobly silent, preferring death rather than cause pain to the woman he loves. Gant, the Unknown Soldier, the Martyred President, the slain God of Harvest, the Bringer of Good Crops. Duke Gant of Westmoreland, Viscount Pondicherry, twelfth Lord Runnymede, who hunts for true love, incognito, in Devon and ripe grain, and finds the calico white legs embedded in sweet hay. Yes, George-Gordon-Noel-Byron Gant, carrying the pageant of his bleeding heart through Europe, and Thomas-Chatterton Gant (that bright boy!), and François-Villon Gant, and Ahasuerus Gant, and Mithridates Gant, and Artaxerxes Gant, and Edward-the-Black-Prince Gant; Stilicho Gant, and Jugurtha Gant, and Vercinge-torix Gant, and Czar-Ivan-the-Terrible Gant. And Gant, the Olympian Bull; and Heracles Gant; and Gant, the Seductive Swan; and Ashtaroth and Azrael Gant, Proteus Gant, Anubis and Osiris and Mumbo-Jumbo Gant.

But what, said Eugene very slowly into the darkness, if I'm not a Genius? He did not ask himself the question often. He was alone: he spoke aloud, but in a low voice, in order to feel the unreality of this blasphemy. It was a moonless night, full of stars. There was no thunder and no lightning.

Yes, but what, he thought with a livid snarl, but what if anybody else thinks I'm not? Ah, but they'd like to, the swine. They hate me, and are jealous of me because they can't be like me, so they'll belittle me if they can. They'd like to say it, if they dared, just to hurt me. For a moment his face was convulsed with pain and bitterness: he craned his neck, holding his throat with his hand.

Then, as was his custom, when he had burnt his heart out, he began to look nakedly and critically at the question.

Well, he went on very calmly, what if I'm not? Am I going to cut my throat, or eat worms, or swallow arsenic? He shook his head slowly but emphatically. No, he said, I am not. Besides, there are enough geniuses. They have at least one in every high school, and one in the orchestra of every small-town movie. Sometimes Mrs. Von Zeck, the wealthy patroness of the arts, sends a genius or two off to New York to study. So that, he estimated, this broad land of ours has by the census not less than 26,400 geniuses and 83,752 artists, not counting those in business and advertising. For his personal satisfaction, Eugene then muttered over the names of 21 geniuses who wrote poetry, and 37 more who devoted themselves to the drama and the novel. After this, he felt quite relieved.

What, he thought, can I be, besides a genius? I've been one long enough. There must be better things to do.

Over that final hedge, he thought, not death, as I once believed—but new life—and new lands.

Erect, with arm akimbo on his hip, he stood, his domed head turned out toward the light: sixty, subtle and straight of body, deep-browed, with an old glint of hawk-eyes, lean apple-cheeks, a mustache bristle-cropped. That face on which the condor Thought has fed, arched with high subtle malice, sophist glee.

Below, benched in rapt servility, they waited for his first husky word. Eugene looked at the dull earnest faces, lured from the solid pews of Calvinism to the shadowland of metaphysics. And now his mockery will play like lightning around their heads, but they will never see it, nor feel it strike. They will rush forward to wrestle with his shadow, to hear his demon's laughter, to struggle solemnly with their unborn souls.

The clean cuffed hand holds up an abraded stick. Their stare follows obediently along its lustre.

"Mr. Willis?"

White, bewildered, servile, the patient slave's face.

"Yes, sir."

"What have I here?"

"A stick, sir."

"What is a stick?"

"It's a piece of wood, sir."

A pause. Ironic eyebrows ask their laughter. They snicker smugly for the wolf that will devour them.

"Mr. Willis says a stick is a piece of wood."

Their laughter rattles against the walls. Absurd.

"But a stick *is* a piece of wood," says Mr. Willis.

"So is a tree or a telephone-pole. No, I'm afraid that will not do. Does the class agree with Mr. Willis?"

"A stick is a piece of wood cut off at a certain length."

"Then we agree, Mr. Ransom, that a stick is not simply wood with unlimited extension?"

The stunned peasant's face with its blink of effort.

"I see that Mr. Gant is leaning forward in his seat. There is a light in his face that I have seen there before. Mr. Gant will not sleep of nights, for thinking."

"A stick," said Eugene, "is not only wood but the negation of wood. It is the meeting in Space of Wood and No-Wood. A stick is finite and unextended wood, a fact determined by its own denial."

The old head listens gravely above the ironic intake of their breath. He will bear me out and praise me, for I am measured against this peasant earth. He sees me with the titles of proud office; and he loves victory.

"We have a new name for him, Professor Weldon," said Nick Mabley. "We call him Hegel Gant."

He listened to their shout of laughter; he saw their pleased faces turn back on him. That was meant well. I shall smile—their Great Original, the beloved eccentric, the poet of substantial yokels.

"That's a name he may be worthy of," said Vergil Weldon seriously.

Old Fox, I too can juggle with your phrases so they will never catch me. Over the jungle of their wits our unfoiled minds strike irony and passion. Truth? Reality? The Absolute? The Universal? Wisdom? Experience? Knowledge? The Fact? The Concept? Death—the great negation? Parry and thrust, Volpone! Have we not words? We shall prove anything. But Ben, and the demon-flicker of his smile? Where now?

The Spring comes back. I see the sheep upon the hill. The belled cows come along the road in wreaths of dust, and the wagons creak home below the pale ghost of the moon. But what stirs within the buried heart? Where are the lost words? And who has seen his shadow in the Square?

"And if they asked you, Mr. Rountree?"

"I'd have told the truth," said Mr. Rountree, removing his glasses.

"But they had built a good big fire, Mr. Rountree."

"That doesn't matter," said Mr. Rountree, putting his glasses on again. How nobly we can die for truth—in conversation.

"It was a very hot fire, Mr. Rountree. They'd have burned you if you hadn't recanted."

"Ah. I'd have let them burn," said the martyred Rountree through moistening spectacles.

"I think it might be painful," Vergil Weldon suggested. "Even a little blister hurts."

"Who wants to be burned for anything?" said Eugene. "I'd have done what Galileo did—backed out of it."

"So should I," said Vergil Weldon, and their faces arched with gleeful malice over the heavy laughter of the class.

Nevertheless, it moves.

"On one side of the table stood the combined powers of Europe; on the other stood Martin Luther, the son of a blacksmith."

The voice of husky passion, soul-shaken. This they can remember, and put down.

"There, if ever, was a situation to try the strongest soul. But the answer came like a flash. *Ich kann nicht anders*—I can't do otherwise. It was one of the great utterances of history."

That phrase, used now for thirty years, relic of Yale and Harvard: Royce and Munsterberg. In all this jugglery, the Teutons were Weldon's masters, yet mark how thirstily the class lap it up. He will not let them read, lest some one find the rag-quilt of his takings from Zeno to Immanuel Kant. The crazy patchwork of three thousand years, the forced marriage of irreconcilables, the summation of all thought, in his old head. Socrates begat Plato. Plato begat Plotinus. Plotinus begat St. Augustine. . . . Kant begat Hegel. Hegel begat Vergil Weldon. Here we pause. There's no more to beget. An Answer to All Things in Thirty Easy Lessons. How sure they are they've found it!

And to-night they will carry their dull souls into his study, will make unfleshly confessions, will writhe in concocted tortures of the spirit, revealing struggles that they never had.

"It took character to do a thing like that. It took a man who refused to crack under pressure. And that is what I want my boys to do! I want them to succeed! I want them to absorb their negations. I want them to keep as clean as a hound's tooth!"

Eugene winced, and looked around on all the faces set in a resolve to fight desperately for monogamy, party politics, and the will of the greatest number.

And yet the Baptists fear this man! Why? He has taken the whiskers off their God, but for the rest, he has only taught them to vote the ticket.

So here is Hegel in the Cotton Belt!

During these years Eugene would go away from Pulpit Hill, by night and by day, when April was a young green blur, or when the Spring was deep and ripe. But he liked best to go away by night, rushing across a cool Spring countryside full of dew and starlight, under a great beach of the moon ribbed with clouds.

He would go to Exeter or Sydney; sometimes he would go to little towns he had never before visited. He would register at hotels as "Robert Herrick," "John Donne," "George Peele," "William Blake," and "John Milton." No one ever said anything to him about it. The people in those small towns had such names. Once he registered at a hotel, in a small Piedmont town, as "Ben Jonson."

The clerk spun the book critically.

"Isn't there an *h* in that name?" he said.

"No," said Eugene. "That's another branch of the family. I have an uncle, Samuel, who spells his name that way."

Sometimes, at hotels of ill-repute, he would register, with dark buried glee, as "Robert Browning," "Alfred Tennyson," and "William Wordsworth."

Once he registered as "Henry W. Longfellow."

"You can't fool me," said the clerk, with a hard grin of disbelief. "That's the name of a writer."

He was devoured by a vast strange hunger for life. At night, he listened to the million-noted ululation of little night things, the great brooding symphony of dark, the ringing of remote churchbells across the country. And his vision widened out in circles over moon-drenched meadows, dreaming woods, mighty rivers going along in darkness, and ten thousand sleeping towns. He believed in the infinite rich variety of all the towns and faces: behind any of a million shabby houses he believed there was strange buried life, subtle and shattered romance, something dark and unknown. At the moment of passing any house, he thought, some one therein might be at the gate of death, lovers might lie twisted in hot embrace, murder might be doing.

He felt a desperate frustration, as if he were being shut out from the rich banquet of life. And against all caution, he determined to break the pattern of custom, and look within. Driven on by this hunger, he would suddenly rush away from Pulpit Hill and, as dusk came on, prowl up and down the quiet streets of towns. Finally, lifted beyond all restraint, he would mount swiftly to a door and ring the bell. Then, to whoever came, reeling against the wall and clutching at his throat, he would say:

"Water! In God's name, water! I am ill!"

Sometimes there were women, seductive and smiling, aware of his trick, but loath to let him go; sometimes women touched with compassion and tenderness. Then, having drunk, he would smile with brave apology into startled and sympathetic faces, murmuring:

"Pardon me. It came on suddenly—one of my attacks. I had no time to go for help. I saw your light."

Then they would ask him where his friends were.

"Friends!" he glanced about wildly and darkly. Then, with a bitter laugh, he said, "Friends! I have none! I am a stranger here."

Then they would ask him what he did.

"I am a Carpenter," he would answer, smiling strangely.

Then they would ask him where he came from.

"Far away. Very far," he would say deeply. "You would not know if I told you."

Then he would rise, looking about him with grandeur and compassion.

"And now I must go!" he would say mysteriously. "I have a long way to go before my journey is done. God bless you all! I was a stranger and you gave me shelter. The Son of Man was treated not so well."

Sometimes, he would ring bells with an air of timid inquiry, saying: "Is this number 26? My name is Thomas Chatterton. I am looking for a gentleman by the name of Coleridge—Mr. Samuel T. Coleridge. Does he live here? . . . No? I'm sorry. . . . Yes, 26 is the number I have, I'm sure. . . . Thank you . . . I've made a mistake . . . I'll look it up in the telephone directory."

But what, thought Eugene, if one day, in the million streets of life, I should really find him?

These were the golden years.

39

Gant and Eliza came to his graduation. He found them lodgings in the town: it was early June—hot, green, fiercely and voluptuously Southern. The campus was a green oven; the old grads went about in greasy pairs; the cool pretty girls, who never sweated, came in to see their young men graduate, and to dance; the mamas and papas were shown about dumbly and shyly.

The college was charming, half-deserted. Most of the students, except the graduating class, had departed. The air was charged with the fresh sensual heat, the deep green shimmer of heavy leafage, a thousand spermy earth and flower-scents. The young men were touched with sadness, with groping excitement, with glory.

On this rich stage, Gant, who had left his charnel-house of death for three days, saw his son Eugene. He came, gathered to life again, out of his grave. He saw his son enthroned in all the florid sentiment of commencement, and the whole of his heart was lifted out of the dust. Upon the lordly sward, shaded by great trees, and ringed by his solemn classmen and their families, Eugene read the Class Poem ("O Mother Of Our Myriad Hopes"). Then Vergil Weldon spoke, high-husky, deep, and solemn-sad; and Living Truth welled in their hearts. It was a Great Utterance. Be true! Be clean! Be good! Be men! Absorb the Negation! The world has need of. Life was never so worth. Never in history had there been. No other class had shown so great a promise as. Among other achievements, the editor of the paper had lifted the moral and intellectual level of the State two inches. The university spirit! Character! Service! Leadership!

Eugene's face grew dark with pride and joy there in the lovely wilderness. He could not speak. There was a glory in the world: life was panting for his embrace.

Eliza and Gant listened attentively to all the songs and speeches. Their son was a great man on the campus. They saw and heard him before his class, on the campus, and at graduation, when his prizes and honors were announced. And his teachers and companions spoke to them about him, and said he would have "a brilliant career." And Eliza and Gant were touched a little by the false golden glow of youth. They believed for a moment that all things were possible.

"Well, son," said Gant, "the rest is up to you now. I believe you're going to make a name for yourself." He laid a great dry hand clumsily upon his son's shoulder, and for a moment Eugene saw in the dead eyes the old dark of umber and unfound desire.

"Hm!" Eliza began, with a tremulous bantering smile, "your head will get turned by all the things they're saying about you." She took his hand in her rough warm grasp. Her eyes grew suddenly wet.

"Well, son," she said gravely. "I want you to go ahead now and try to be Somebody. None of the others ever had your opportunity, and I hope you do something with it. Your papa and I have done the best we could. The rest is up to you."

He took her hand in a moment of wild devotion and kissed it.

"I'll do something," he said. "I will."

They looked shyly at his strange dark face, with all its passionate and naïve ardor, and they felt tenderness and love for his youth and all that was unknown to it. And a great love and pity welled up in him because of their strange and awkward loneliness, and because he felt, through some terrible intuition, that he was already indifferent to the titles and honors they desired for him, and because those which he had come to desire for himself were already beyond the scale of their value. And, before the vision of pity and loss and loneliness, he turned away, clutching his lean hand into his throat.

It was over. Gant, who under the stimulus of his son's graduation had almost regained the vitality of his middle years, relapsed now into whining dotage. The terrible heat came down and smote him. He faced with terror and weariness the long hot trip into the hills again.

"Merciful God!" he whined. "Why did I ever come! O Jesus, how will I ever face that trip again! I can't bear it. I'll die before I get there! It's fearful, it's awful, it's cruel." And he wept weak snuffling sobs.

Eugene took them to Exeter and got them comfortably disposed in a Pullman. He was remaining for a few days to gather his belongings— the clutter of four years, letters, books, old manuscript, worthless rubbish of every description, for he seemed to inherit Eliza's mania for blind accumulation. Extravagant with money, and unable to husband it, he saved everything else even when his spirit grew sick at the stale and dusty weariness of the past.

"Well, son," said Eliza, in the quiet moment before departure. "Have you thought yet of what you're going to do?"

"Yes," said Gant, wetting his thumb, "for you've got to shift for yourself from now on. You've had the best education money can buy. The rest is up to you."

"I'll talk to you in a few days when I see you at home," said Eugene. "I'll tell you about it then."

Mercifully the train began to move: he kissed them quickly and ran down the aisle.

He had nothing to tell them. He was nineteen; he had completed his college course; but he did not know what he was going to do. His father's plan that he should study law and "enter politics" had been forgotten since his sophomore year, when it became apparent that the impulse of his life was not toward law. His family felt obscurely that he was an eccentric—"queer," they called it—and of an impractical or "literary" turn.

Without asking sharply why, they felt the absurdity of clothing this bounding figure, with the wild dark face, in a frock-coat and string tie: he did not exist in business, trade, or law. More vaguely, they classified him as bookish and a dreamer—Eliza referred to him as "a good scholar," which, in fact, he had never been. He had simply performed brilliantly in all things that touched his hunger, and dully, carelessly, and indifferently in all things that did not. No one saw very clearly what he was going to do—he, surely, least of all—but his family, following the tack of his comrades, spoke vaguely and glibly of "a career in journalism." This meant newspaper work. And, however unsatisfactory this may have been, their inevitable question was drugged for the moment by the glitter of success that had surrounded his life at the university.

But Eugene was untroubled by thought of a goal. He was mad with such ecstasy as he had never known. He was a centaur, moon-eyed and wild of mane, torn apart with hunger for the golden world. He became at times almost incapable of coherent speech. While talking with people, he would whinny suddenly into their startled faces, and leap away, his face contorted with an idiot joy. He would hurl himself squealing through the streets and along the paths, touched with the ecstasy of a thousand unspoken desires. The world lay before him for his picking—full of opulent cities, golden vintages, glorious triumphs, lovely women, full of a thousand unmet and magnificent possibilities. Nothing was dull or tarnished. The strange enchanted coasts were unvisited. He was young and he could never die.

He went back to Pulpit Hill for two or three days of delightful loneliness in the deserted college. He prowled through the empty campus at midnight under the great moons of the late rich Spring; he breathed the thousand rich odors of tree and grass and flower, of the opulent and seductive South; and he felt a delicious sadness when he thought of his departure, and saw there in the moon the thousand phantom shapes of the boys he had known who would come no more.

And in the day he went to talk with Vergil Weldon. The old man was charming, confidential, full of wise intimacy, gentle humor. They sat beneath the great trees of his yard and drank iced tea. Eugene was thinking of California, Peru, Asia, Alaska, Europe, Africa, China. But he mentioned Harvard. For him, it was not the name of a university—it was rich magic, wealth, elegance, joy, proud loneliness, rich books and golden browsing; it was an enchanted name like Cairo and Damascus. And he felt somehow that it gave a reason, a goal of profit, to his wild ecstasy.

"Yes," said Vergil Weldon approvingly. "It's the place for you, Mr. Gant. It doesn't matter about the others. They're ready now. But a mind like yours must not be pulled green. You must give it a chance to ripen. There you will find yourself."

And he talked enchantingly about the good free life of the mind, cloistered study, the rich culture of the city, and about the food. "They give you food there that a man can eat, Mr. Gant," he said. "Your mind can do its work on it." Then he spoke of his own student days there, and of the great names of Royce and Everett, and William James.

Eugene looked with passionate devotion at the grand old head, calm, wise and comforting. In a moment of vision, he saw that, for him, here was the last of the heroes, the last of those giants to whom we give the faith of our youth, believing like children that the riddle of our lives may be solved by their quiet judgment. He believed, and no experience, he knew, would ever make him disbelieve, that one of the great lives of his time had unfolded itself quietly in the little college town.

Oh, my old Sophist, he thought. What were all the old philosophies that you borrowed and pranked up to your fancy, to you, who were greater than all? What was the Science of Thinking, to you, who were Thought? What if all your ancient game of metaphysics never touched the dark jungle of my soul? Do you think you have replaced my childhood's God with your Absolute? No, you have only replaced his beard with a mustache, and a glint of demon hawk-eyes. To me, you were above good, above truth, above righteousness. To me, you were the sufficient negation to all your teachings. Whatever you did was, by its doing, right. And now I leave you throned in memory. You will see my dark face burning on your bench no more; the memory of me will grow mixed and broken; new boys will come to win your favor and your praise. But you? Forever fixed, unfading, bright, my lord.

Then, while the old man talked, Eugene leaped suddenly to his feet, and grasped the lean hand tightly in his own.

"Mr. Weldon!" he said. "Mr. Weldon! You are a great man! I shall never forget you!"

Then, turning, he plunged off blindly down the path.

He still loitered, although his baggage had been packed for days. With a desperate pain, he faced departure from that Arcadian wilderness where he had known so much joy. At night he roamed the deserted campus, talking quietly until morning with a handful of students who lingered strangely, as he did, among the ghostly buildings, among the phantoms of lost boys. He could not face a final departure. He said he would return early in autumn for a few days, and at least once a year thereafter.

Then one hot morning, on sudden impulse, he left. As the car that was taking him to Exeter roared down the winding street, under the hot green leafiness of June, he heard, as from the sea-depth of a dream, far-faint, the mellow booming of the campus bell. And suddenly it seemed to him that all the beaten walks were thudding with the footfalls of lost boys, himself among them, running for their class. Then, as he listened, the far bell died away, and the phantom runners thudded into oblivion. Soon the car roared up by Vergil Weldon's house, and as he passed, he saw the old man sitting below his tree.

Eugene stood up in the car and waved his long arm in a gesture of farewell.

"Good-bye," he cried. "Good-bye."

The old man stood up with a quiet salute of parting, slow, calm, eloquently tender.

Then, even while Eugene stood looking back upon the street, the car roared up across the lip of the hill, and drove steeply down into the hot parched countryside below. But as the lost world faded from his sight, Eugene gave a great cry of pain and sadness, for he knew that the elfin door had closed behind him, and that he would never come back again.

He saw the vast rich body of the hills, lush with billowing greenery, ripe-bosomed, dappled by far-floating cloud-shadows. But it was, he knew, the end.

Far-forested, the horn-note wound. He was wild with the hunger for release: the vast champaign of earth stretched out for him its limitless seduction.

It was the end, the end. It was the beginning of the voyage, the quest of new lands.

Gant was dead. Gant was living, death-in-life. In his big back room at Eliza's he waited death, lost and broken in a semi-life of petulant memory. He hung to life by a decayed filament, a corpse lit by infrequent flares of consciousness. The sudden death whose menace they had faced so long that it had lost its meaning, had never come to him. It had come where they had least expected it—to Ben. And the conviction which Eugene had had at Ben's death, more than a year and a half before, was now a materialized certainty. The great wild pattern of the family had been broken forever. The partial discipline that had held them together had been destroyed by the death of their brother: the nightmare of waste and loss had destroyed their hope. With an insane fatalism they had surrendered to the savage chaos of life.

Except for Eliza. She was sixty, sound of body and mind, triumphantly healthy. She still ran Dixieland, but she had given up the boarders for roomers, and most of the duties of management she intrusted to an old maid who lived in the house. Eliza devoted most of her time to real estate.

She had, during the past year, got final control of Gant's property. She had begun to sell it immediately and ruthlessly, over his indifferent mutter of protest. She had sold the old house on Woodson Street for $7,000—a good enough price, she had said, considering the neighborhood. But, stark, bare, and raw, stripped of its girdling vines, annex now to a quack's sanitarium for "nervous diseases," the rich labor of their life was gone. In this, more than in anything else, Eugene saw the final disintegration of his family.

Eliza had also sold a wild tract of mountain farmland for $6,000, fifty acres on the Reynoldsville road for $15,000, and several smaller pieces. Finally she had sold Gant's shop upon the Square for $25,000 to a syndicate of real estate people who were going to erect on the site the town's first "skyscraper." With this money as capital, she began to "trade," buying, selling, laying down options, in an intricate and bewildering web.

"Dixieland" itself had become enormously valuable. The street which she had foreseen years before had been cut through behind her boundaries: she lacked thirty feet of meeting the golden highway, but she had bought the intervening strip, paying without complaint a stiff price. Since then she had refused, with a puckered smile, an offer of $100,000 for her property.

She was obsessed. She talked real estate unendingly. She spent half her time talking to real estate men; they hovered about the house like flesh-flies. She drove off with them several times a day to look at property. As her land investments grew in amount and number, she became insanely niggardly in personal expenditure. She would fret loudly if a light was kept burning in the house, saying that ruin and poverty faced her. She seldom ate unless the food was given to her; she went about the house holding a cup of weak coffee and a crust of bread. A stingy careless breakfast was the only meal to which Luke and Eugene could look forward with any certainty: with angry guffaw and chortle, they ate, wedged in the little pantry—the dining-room had been turned over to the roomers.

Gant was fed and cared for by Helen. She moved back and forth in ceaseless fret between Eliza's house and Hugh Barton's, in constant rhythms of wild energy and depletion, anger, hysteria, weariness and indifference. She had had no children and, it seemed, would have none. For this reason, she had long periods of brooding morbidity, during which she drugged herself with nibbling potations of patent tonics, medicines with a high alcoholic content, home-made wines, and corn whiskey. Her large eyes grew lustreless and dull, her big mouth had a strain of hysteria about it, she would pluck at her long chin and burst suddenly into tears. She talked restlessly, fretfully, incessantly, wasting and losing herself in a net of snarled nerves, in endless gossip, incoherent garrulity about the townsfolk, the neighbors, disease, doctors, hospitals, death.

The deliberate calm of Hugh Barton sometimes goaded her to a frenzy. He would sit at night, oblivious of her tirade, gravely chewing his long cigar, absorbed in his charts, or in a late issue of *System* or of *The*

American Magazine. This power of losing himself in solitary absorption would madden her. She did not know what she wanted, but his silence before her exasperated indictment of life drove her to frenzy. She would rush at him with a sob of rage, knock the magazine from his hands, and seize his thinning hair in the grip of her long fingers.

"You answer when I speak!" she cried, panting with hysteria. "I'm not going to sit here, night after night, while you sit buried in a story. The idea! The idea!" She burst into tears. "I might as well have married a dummy."

"Well, I'm willing to talk to you," he protested sourly, "but nothing I say to you seems to suit you. What do you want me to say?"

It seemed, indeed, when she was in this temper, that she could not be pleased. She was annoyed and irritable if people agreed carefully with all her utterances; she was annoyed equally by their disagreement and by their silence. A remark about the weather, the most studiously uncontroversial opinion, aroused her annoyance.

Sometimes at night she would weep hysterically upon her pillow, and turn fiercely upon her mate.

"Leave me! Go away! Get out! I hate you!"

He would rise obediently and go downstairs, but before he reached the living-room she would call fearfully after him, asking him to return.

She lavished kisses and abuse on him by turns: the mothering tenderness, in which she was drowning for want of a child, she poured out on a dirty little mongrel dog which had trotted in from the streets one night, half-dead from starvation. He was a snarling little brute with a rough black-and-white pelt, and an ugly lift of teeth for every one but his master and mistress, but he had grown waddling-fat upon choice meats and livers; he slept warmly on a velvet cushion and rode out with them, snarling at passers-by. She smothered the little cur with slaps and kisses, devoured him with baby-talk, and hated any one who disliked his mongrel viciousness. But most of her time, her love, her blazing energy, she gave to the care of her father. Her feeling toward Eliza was more bitter than ever: it was one of constant chaffering irritability, mounting at times to hatred. She would rail against her mother for hours:

"I believe she's gone crazy. Don't you think so? Sometimes I think we ought to get guardians appointed and keep her under custody. Do you know that I buy almost every bite of food that goes into that house? Do you? If it weren't for me, she'd let him die right under her eyes. Don't you know she would? She's got so stingy she won't even buy food for herself. Why, good heavens!" she burst out in strong exasperation. "It's not my place to do those things. He's her husband, not mine! Do you think it's right? Do you?" And she would almost weep with rage.

And she would burst out on Eliza, thus: "Mama, in God's name! Are you going to let that poor old man in there die for lack of proper care? Can't you ever get it into your head that papa's a sick man? He's got to have good food and decent treatment."

And Eliza, confused and disturbed, would answer: "Why, child! What on earth do you mean? I took him in a big bowl of vegetable soup myself, for his lunch: he ate it all up without stopping. 'Why, pshaw! Mr. Gant,' I said (just to cheer him up), 'I don't believe there can be much wrong with any one with an appetite like that. Why, say,' I said . . ."

"Oh, for heaven's sake!" cried Helen furiously. "Papa's a sick man. Aren't you ever going to understand that? Surely Ben's death should have taught us something," her voice ended in a scream of exasperation.

Gant was a spectre in waxen yellow. His disease, which had thrust out its branches to all parts of his body, gave him an appearance of almost transparent delicacy. His mind was sunken out of life in a dim shadowland: he listened wearily and indifferently to all the brawling clamor around him, crying out and weeping when he felt pain, cold, or hunger, smiling when he was comfortable and at ease. He was taken back to Baltimore two or three times a year now for radium treatments: he had a brief flare of vitality and ease after each visit, but every one knew his relief would be only temporary. His body was a rotten fabric which had thus far miraculously held together.

Meanwhile, Eliza talked incessantly about real estate, bought, sold and traded. About her own ventures she was insanely secretive; she would smile craftily when questioned about them, wink in a knowing fashion, and make a bantering noise in her throat.

"I'm not telling all I know," she said.

This goaded her daughter's bitter curiosity almost past endurance, for, despite her angry mockery, the mania for property had bitten into her and Hugh Barton as well: secretly they respected Eliza's shrewdness and got her advice on property into which he was putting all his surplus earnings. But when Eliza refused to reveal her own investments, the girl would cry out in a baffled hysteria:

"She has no right to do that! Don't you know she hasn't? It's papa's property just as much as hers, you know. If she should die now, that estate would be in a terrible mess. No one knows what she's done: how much she's bought and sold. I don't think she knows herself. She keeps her notes and papers hidden away in little drawers and boxes."

Her distrust and fear had been so great that, much to Eliza's annoyance, she had persuaded Gant, a year or two before, to make a will: he had left $5,000 to each of his five children, and the remainder of his property and money to his wife. And, as the summer advanced, she again persuaded him to appoint as executors the two people in whose honesty she had the greatest trust: Hugh Barton and Luke Gant.

To Luke, who, since his discharge from the navy, had been salesman, in the mountain district, for electrical farm-lighting plants, she said:

"We're the ones who've always had the interests of the family at heart, and we've had nothing for it. We've been the generous ones, but Eugene and Steve will get it all in the end. 'Gene's had everything: we've had nothing. Now he's talking of going to Harvard. Had you heard about that?"

"His m-m-m-majesty!" said Luke ironically. "Who's going to p-p-p-pay the bills?"

Thus, as the summer waned, over the slow horror of Gant's death was waged this ugly warfare of greed and hatred. Steve came in from Indiana; within four days he was insane from whiskey and veronal. He began to follow Eugene around the house, backing him ominously into corners, seizing him belligerently by the arm, as he breathed upon him his foul yellow stench, and spoke to him with maudlin challenge.

"I've never had your chance. Every one was down on Stevie. If he'd had the chance some folks have, he'd be right up there with the Big Boys now. And at that, he's got more brains than a lot of people I know who've been to college. You get that, don't you?"

He thrust his pustulate face, foul and snarling, close to Eugene's.

"Get away, Steve! Get away!" the boy muttered. He tried to move, but his brother blocked him. "I tell you to get away, you swine!" he screamed suddenly, and he struck the evil face away from him.

Then, as Steve sprawled dazed and witless on the floor, Luke sprang upon him with stammering curse, and, past reason, began to drag him up and down. And Eugene sprang upon Luke to stop him, and all three stammered and cursed and begged and accused, while the roomers huddled at the door, and Eliza wept, calling for help, and Daisy, who was up from the South with her children, wrung her plump hands, moaning "Oh, they'll kill him! They'll kill him. Have mercy on me and my poor little children, I beg of you."

Then the shame, the disgust, the maudlin grievance, the weeping women, the excited men.

"You m-m-m-miserable degenerate!" cried Luke. "You c-c-came home because you thought p-p-p-papa would die and leave you a little money. You d-d-don't deserve a penny!"

"I know what you're trying to do," Steve screamed in an agony of suspicion. "You're all against me! You've framed up on me and you're trying to beat me out of my share."

He was weeping with genuine rage and fear, with the angry suspicion of a beaten child. Eugene looked at him with pity and nausea: he was so foul, whipped, and frightened. Then, with a sense of unreal horror and disbelief, he listened while they bawled out their accusations. This disease of money and greed tainted other people, the people in books, not one's own. They were snarling like curs over one bone—their little shares in the money of an unburied dead man who lay, with low moanings of disease, not thirty feet away.

The family drew off in two camps of hostile watchfulness: Helen and Luke on one side and Daisy and Steve, subdued but stubborn, on the other. Eugene, who had no talent for parties, cruised through sidereal space with momentary anchorings to earth. He loafed along the avenue, and lounged in Wood's; he gossiped with the pharmacy rakes; he courted the summer girls on boarding-house porches; he visited Roy Brock in a high mountain village, and lay with a handsome girl in the forest; he went to South Carolina; he was seduced by a dentist's wife at Dixieland. She was a prim ugly woman of forty-three, who wore glasses and had sparse hair. She was a Daughter of the Confederacy and wore the badge constantly on her starched waists.

He thought of her only as a very chill and respectable woman. He played Casino—the only game he knew—with her and the other boarders, and called her "ma'am." Then one night she took his hand, saying she would show him how to make love to a girl. She tickled the palm, put it around her waist, lifted it to her breast, and plumped over on his shoulder, breathing stertorously through her pinched nostrils and saying, "God, boy!" over and over. He plunged around the dark cool streets until three in the morning, wondering what he would do about it. Then he came back to the sleeping house, and crept on shoeless feet into her room. Fear and disgust were immediate. He climbed the hills to ease his tortured spirit and stayed away from the house for hours. But she would follow him down the halls or open her door suddenly on him, clad in a red kimono. She became very ugly and bitter, and accused him of betraying, dishonoring, and deserting her. She said that where she came from—the good old State of South Carolina—a man who treated a woman in such fashion would get a bullet in him. Eugene thought of new lands. He was in an agony of repentance and guilty abasement: he framed a long plea for pardon and included it in his prayers at night, for he still prayed, not from devout belief, but from the superstition of habit and number, muttering a set formula over sixteen times, while he held his breath. Since childhood he had believed in the magical efficacy of certain numbers—on Sunday he would do only the second thing that came into his head and not the first—and this intricate ritual of number and prayer he was a slave to, not to propitiate God, but to fulfil a mysterious harmonic relation with the universe, or to pay worship to the demonic force that brooded over him. He could not sleep of nights until he did this.

Eliza finally grew suspicious of the woman, picked a quarrel with her, and ejected her.

No one said very much to him about going to Harvard. He himself had no very clear reason for going, and only in September, a few days before the beginning of the term, decided to go. He talked about it at intervals during the summer, but, like all his family, he needed the pressure of immediacy to force a decision. He was offered employment on several newspapers in the State, and on the teaching staff of the run-down military academy that topped a pleasant hill two miles from town.

But in his heart he knew he was going to leave. And no one opposed him very much. Helen railed against him at times to Luke, but made only a few indifferent and unfriendly comments to himself about it. Gant moaned wearily, saying: "Let him do as he likes. I can't pay out any more money on his education. If he wants to go, his mother must send him." Eliza pursed her lips thoughtfully, made a bantering noise, and said:

"Hm! Harvard! That's mighty big talk, boy. Where are you going to get the money?"

"I can get it," he said darkly. "People will lend it to me."

"No, son," she said with instant grave caution. "I don't want you to do anything like that. You mustn't start life by accumulating debts."

He was silent, trying to force the terrible sentence through his parched lips.

"Then," he said finally, "why can't I pay my way from my share in papa's estate?"

"Why, child!" said Eliza angrily. "You talk as if we were millionaires. I don't even know that there's going to be any share for anybody. Your papa was persuaded into that against his better judgment," she added fretfully.

Eugene began to beat suddenly against his ribs.

"I want to go!" he said. "I've got to have it now! Now!"

He was mad with a sense of frustration.

"I don't want it when I'm rotten! I want it now! To hell with the real estate! I want none of your dirt! I hate it! Let me go!" he screamed; and in his fury he began to beat his head against the wall.

Eliza pursed her lips for a moment.

"Well," she said, at length. "I'll send you for a year. Then we'll see."

But, two or three days before his departure, Luke, who was taking Gant to Baltimore the next day, thrust a sheet of typed paper into his hand.

"What is it?" he asked, looking at it with sullen suspicion.

"Oh, just a little form Hugh wants you to sign, in case anything should happen. It's a release."

"A release from what?" said Eugene, staring at it.

Then, as his mind picked its way slowly through the glib jargon of the law, he saw that the paper was an acknowledgment that he had already received the sum of five thousand dollars in consideration of college fees and expenses. He lifted his scowling face to his brother. Luke looked at him for a moment, then burst into a crazy whah-whah, digging him in the ribs. Eugene grinned sullenly, and said:

"Give me your pen."

He signed the paper and gave it back to his brother with a feeling of sad triumph.

"Whah-whah! Now you've done it!" said Luke, with witless guffaw.

"Yes," said Eugene, "and you think me a fool for it. But I'd rather be done now than later. That's my release, not yours."

He thought of Hugh Barton's grave foxy face. There was no victory for him there and he knew it. After all, he thought, I have my ticket and the money for my escape in my pocket. Now, I am done with it cleanly. It's a good ending, after all.

When Eliza heard of this occurrence, she protested sharply:

"Why here!" she said. "They've no right to do that. The child's still a minor. Your papa always said he intended to give him his education."

Then, after a thoughtful pause, she said doubtfully: "Well, we'll see, then. I've promised to send him for a year."

In the darkness by the house, Eugene clutched at his throat. He wept for all the lovely people who would not come again.

Eliza stood upon the porch, her hands clasped loosely across her stomach. Eugene was leaving the house and going toward the town. It was the day before his departure; dusk was coming on, the hills were blooming in strange purple dusk. Eliza watched him go.

"Spruce up there, boy!" she called. "Spruce up! Throw your shoulders back!"

In the dusk he knew that she was smiling tremulously at him, pursing her lips. She caught his low mutter of annoyance:

"Why, yes," she said, nodding briskly. "I'd show them! I'd act as if I thought I was Somebody. Son," she said more gravely, with a sudden change from her tremulous banter, "it worries me to see you walk like that. You'll get lung-trouble as sure as you're born if you go all humped over. That's one thing about your papa: he always carried himself as straight as a rod. Of course, he's not as straight now as he used to be— as the fellow says" (she smiled tremulously)—"I reckon we all have a tendency to shrink up a little as we get older. But in his young days there wasn't a straighter man in town."

And then the terrible silence came between them again. He had turned sullenly upon her while she talked. Indecisively she stopped, peered down at him with white pursed face, and in that silence, behind the trivial arras of her talk, he heard the bitter song of all her life.

The marvellous hills were blooming in the dusk. Eliza pursed her lips reflectively a moment, then continued:

"Well, when you get way up there—as the fellow says—in Yankeedom, you want to look up your Uncle Emerson and all your Boston kin. Your Aunt Lucy took a great liking to you when they were down here— they always said they'd be glad to see any of us if we ever came up— when you're a stranger in a strange land it's mighty good sometimes to have some one you know. And say—when you see your Uncle Emerson, you might just tell him not to be surprised to see me at any time now" (She nodded pertly at him)—"I reckon I can pick right up and light out the same as the next fellow when I get ready—I may just pack up and come—without saying a word to any one—I'm not going to spend all my days slaving away in the kitchen—it don't pay—if I can turn a couple of trades here this Fall, I may start out to see the world like I always intended to—I was talking to Cash Rankin about it the other day— 'Why, Mrs. Gant,' he said, 'if I had your head I'd be a rich man in five years—you're the best trader in this town,' he said. 'Don't you talk to me about any more trades,' I said—'when I get rid of what I've got now I'm going to get out of it, and not even listen to any one who says

real-estate to me—we can't take any of it with us, Cash,' I said—'there
are no pockets in shrouds and we only need six feet of earth to bury us
in the end—so I'm going to pull out and begin to enjoy life—or as the
feller says—before it's too late'—'Well, I don't know that I blame you,
Mrs. Gant,' he said—'I reckon you're right—we can't take any of it with
us,' he said—'and besides, even if we could, what good would it do us
where we're goin'?'—Now here" (she addressed Eugene with sudden
change, with the old loose masculine gesture of her hand)—"here's the
thing I'm going to do—you know that lot I told you I owned on Sunset
Crescent——"

And now the terrible silence came between them once again.

The marvellous hills were blooming in the dusk. We shall not come
again. We never shall come back again.

Without speech now they faced each other, without speech they knew
each other. In a moment Eliza turned quickly from him and with the
queer unsteady steps with which she had gone out from the room where
Ben lay dying, she moved toward the door.

He rushed back across the walk and with a single bound took the steps
that mounted to the porch. He caught the rough hands that she held
clasped across her body, and drew them swiftly, fiercely, to his breast.

"Good-bye," he muttered harshly. "Good-bye! Good-bye, mama!" A
wild, strange cry, like that of a beast in pain, was torn from his throat.
His eyes were blind with tears; he tried to speak, to get into a word, a
phrase, all the pain, the beauty, and the wonder of their lives—every
step of that terrible voyage which his incredible memory and intuition
took back to the dwelling of her womb. But no word came, no word
could come; he kept crying hoarsely again and again, "Good-bye,
good-bye."

She understood, she knew all he felt and wanted to say, her small weak
eyes were wet as his with tears, her face was twisted in the painful
grimace of sorrow, and she kept saying:

"Poor child! Poor child! Poor child!" Then she whispered huskily,
faintly: "We must try to love one another."

The terrible and beautiful sentence, the last, the final wisdom that the
earth can give, is remembered at the end, is spoken too late, wearily. It
stands there, awful and untraduced, above the dusty racket of our lives.
No forgetting, no forgiving, no denying, no explaining, no hating.

O mortal and perishing love, born with this flesh and dying with this
brain, your memory will haunt the earth forever.

And now the voyage out. Where?

40

The Square lay under blazing moonlight. The fountain pulsed with a steady breezeless jet: the water fell upon the pool with a punctual slap. No one came into the Square.

The chimes of the bank's clock struck the quarter after three as Eugene entered from the northern edge, by Academy Street.

He came slowly over past the fire department and the City Hall. On Gant's corner, the Square dipped sharply down toward Niggertown, as if it had been bent at the edge.

Eugene saw his father's name, faded, on the old brick in moonlight. On the stone porch of the shop, the angels held their marble posture. They seemed to have frozen, in the moonlight.

Leaning against the iron railing of the porch, above the sidewalk, a man stood smoking. Troubled and a little afraid, Eugene came over. Slowly, he mounted the long wooden steps, looking carefully at the man's face. It was half-obscured in shadow.

"Is there anybody there?" said Eugene.

No one answered.

But, as Eugene reached the top, he saw that the man was Ben.

Ben stared at him a moment without speaking. Although Eugene could not see his face very well under the obscuring shadow of his gray felt hat, he knew that he was scowling.

"Ben?" said Eugene doubtfully, faltering a little on the top step. "Is it you, Ben?"

"Yes," said Ben. In a moment, he added in a surly voice: "Who did you think it was, you little idiot?"

"I wasn't sure," said Eugene somewhat timidly. "I couldn't see your face."

They were silent a moment. Then Eugene, clearing his throat in his embarrassment, said: "I thought you were dead, Ben."

"Ah-h!" said Ben contemptuously, jerking his head sharply upward. "Listen to this, won't you?"

514

He drew deeply on his cigarette: the spiral fumes coiled out and melted in the moon-bright silence.

"No," he said in a moment, quietly. "No, I am not dead."

Eugene came up on the porch and sat down on a limestone base, up-ended. Ben turned, in a moment, and climbed up on the rail, bending forward comfortably upon his knees.

Eugene fumbled in his pockets for a cigarette, with fingers that were stiff and trembling. He was not frightened: he was speechless with wonder and strong eagerness, and afraid to betray his thoughts to ridicule. He lighted a cigarette. Presently he said, painfully, hesitantly, in apology:

"Ben, are you a ghost?"

Ben did not mock.

"No," he said. "I am not a ghost."

There was silence again, while Eugene sought timorously for words.

"I hope," he began presently, with a small cracked laugh, "I hope, then, this doesn't mean that I'm crazy?"

"Why not?" said Ben, with a swift flickering grin. "Of course you're crazy."

"Then," said Eugene slowly, "I'm imagining all this?"

"In heaven's name!" Ben cried irritably. "How should I know? Imagining all what?"

"What I mean," said Eugene, "is, are we here talking together, or not?"

"Don't ask me," said Ben. "How should I know?"

With a strong rustle of marble and a cold sigh of weariness, the angel nearest Eugene moved her stone foot and lifted her arm to a higher balance. The slender lily stipe shook stiffly in her elegant cold fingers.

"Did you see that?" Eugene cried excitedly.

"Did I see what?" said Ben, annoyed.

"Th-th-that angel there!" Eugene chattered, pointing with a trembling finger. "Did you see it move? It lifted its arm."

"What of it?" Ben asked irritably. "It has a right to, hasn't it? You know," he added with biting sarcasm, "there's no law against an angel lifting its arm if it wants to."

"No, I suppose not," Eugene admitted slowly, after a moment. "Only, I've always heard——"

"Ah! Do you believe all you hear, fool?" Ben cried fiercely. "Because," he added more calmly, in a moment, drawing on his cigarette, "you're in a bad way if you do."

There was again silence while they smoked. Then Ben said:

"When are you leaving, 'Gene?"

"To-morrow," Eugene answered.

"Do you know why you are going, or are you just taking a ride on the train?"

"I know! Of course—I know why I'm going!" Eugene said angrily, confused. He stopped abruptly, bewildered, chastened. Ben continued to scowl at him. Then, quietly, with humility, Eugene said:

"No, Ben. I don't know why I'm going. Perhaps you're right. Perhaps I just want a ride on the train."

"When are you coming back, 'Gene?" said Ben.

"Why—at the end of the year, I think," Eugene answered.

"No," said Ben, "you're not."

"What do you mean, Ben?" Eugene said, troubled.

"You're not coming back, 'Gene," said Ben softly. "Do you know that?"

There was a pause.

"Yes," said Eugene, "I know it."

"Why aren't you coming back?" said Ben.

Eugene caught fiercely at the neckband of his shirt with a clawed hand. "I want to go! Do you hear!" he cried.

"Yes," said Ben. "So did I. Why do you want to go?"

"There's nothing here for me," Eugene muttered.

"How long have you felt like this?" said Ben.

"Always," said Eugene. "As long as I can remember. But I didn't know about it until you—" He stopped.

"Until I what?" said Ben.

There was a pause.

"You are dead, Ben," Eugene muttered. "You must be dead. I saw you die, Ben." His voice rose sharply. "I tell you, I saw you die. Don't you remember? The front room upstairs that the dentist's wife has now? Don't you remember, Ben? Coker, Helen, Bessie Gant who nursed you, Mrs. Pert? The oxygen tank? I tried to hold your hands together when they gave it to you." His voice rose to a scream. "Don't you remember? I tell you, you are dead, Ben."

"Fool," said Ben fiercely. "I am not dead."

There was a silence.

"Then," said Eugene very slowly, "which of us is the ghost, I wonder?"

Ben did not answer.

"Is this the Square, Ben? Is it you I'm talking to? Am I really here or not? And is this moonlight in the Square? Has all this happened?"

"How should I know?" said Ben again.

Within Gant's shop there was the ponderous tread of marble feet. Eugene leaped up and peered through the broad sheet of Jannadeau's dirty window. Upon his desk the strewn vitals of a watch winked with a thousand tiny points of bluish light. And beyond the jeweller's fenced space, where moonlight streamed into the ware-room through the tall side-window, the angels were walking to and fro like huge wound dolls of stone. The long cold pleats of their raiment rang with brittle clangor; their full decent breasts wagged in stony rhythms, and through the moonlight, with clashing wings the marble cherubim flew round and round. With cold ewe-bleatings the carved lambs grazed stiffly across the moon-drenched aisle.

"Do you see it?" cried Eugene. "Do you see it, Ben?"

"Yes," said Ben. "What about it? They have a right to, haven't they?"

"Not here! Not here!" said Eugene passionately. "It's not right, here! My God, this is the Square! There's the fountain! There's the City Hall! There's the Greek's lunch-room."

The bank-chimes struck the half hour.

"And there's the bank" he cried.

"That makes no difference," said Ben.

"Yes," said Eugene, "it does!"

I am thy father's spirit, doomed for a certain term to walk the night——

"But not here! Not here, Ben!" said Eugene.

"Where?" said Ben wearily.

"In Babylon! In Thebes! In all the other places. But not here!" Eugene answered with growing passion. "There is a place where all things happen! But not here, Ben!"

My gods, with bird-cries in the sun, hang in the sky.

"Not here, Ben! It is not right!" Eugene said again.

The manifold gods of Babylon. Then, for a moment, Eugene stared at the dark figure on the rail, muttering in protest and disbelief: "Ghost! Ghost!"

"Fool," said Ben again, "I tell you I am not a ghost."

"Then, what are you?" said Eugene with strong excitement. "You are dead, Ben."

In a moment, more quietly, he added: "Or do men die?"

"How should I know," said Ben.

"They say papa is dying. Did you know that, Ben?" Eugene asked.

"Yes," said Ben.

"They have bought his shop. They are going to tear it down and put up a skyscraper here."

"Yes," said Ben, "I know it."

We shall not come again. We never shall come back again.

"Everything is going. Everything changes and passes away. To-morrow I shall be gone and this——" he stopped.

"This—what?" said Ben.

"This will be gone or— O God! Did all this happen?" cried Eugene.

"How should I know, fool?" cried Ben angrily.

"What happens, Ben? What really happens?" said Eugene. "Can you remember some of the same things that I do? I have forgotten the old faces. Where are they, Ben? What were their names? I forget the names of people I knew for years. I get their faces mixed. I get their heads stuck on other people's bodies. I think one man has said what another said. And I forget—forget. There is something I have lost and have forgotten. I can't remember, Ben."

"What do you want to remember?" said Ben.

A stone, a leaf, an unfound door. And the forgotten faces.

"I have forgotten names. I have forgotten faces. And I remember little things," said Eugene. "I remember the fly I swallowed on the peach, and the little boys on tricycles at Saint Louis, and the mole on Grover's neck, and the Lackawanna freight-car, number 16356, on a siding near Gulfport. Once, in Norfolk, an Australian soldier on his way to France asked me the way to a ship; I remember that man's face."

He stared for an answer into the shadow of Ben's face, and then he turned his moon-bright eyes upon the Square.

And for a moment all the silver space was printed with the thousand forms of himself and Ben. There, by the corner in from Academy Street, Eugene watched his own approach; there, by the City Hall, he strode with lifted knees; there, by the curb upon the step, he stood, peopling the night with the great lost legion of himself—the thousand forms that came, that passed, that wove and shifted in unending change, and that remained unchanging Him.

And through the Square, unwoven from lost time, the fierce bright horde of Ben spun in and out its deathless loom. Ben, in a thousand moments, walked the Square: Ben of the lost years, the forgotten days, the unremembered hours; prowled by the moonlit façades; vanished, returned, left and rejoined himself, was one and many—deathless Ben in search of the lost dead lusts, the finished enterprise, the unfound door—unchanging Ben multiplying himself in form, by all the brick façades entering and coming out.

And as Eugene watched the army of himself and Ben, which were not ghosts, and which were lost, he saw himself—his son, his boy, his lost and virgin flesh—come over past the fountain, leaning against the

loaded canvas bag, and walking down with rapid crippled stride past
Gant's toward Niggertown in young pre-natal dawn. And as he passed
the porch where he sat watching, he saw the lost child-face below the
lumpy ragged cap, drugged in the magic of unheard music, listening for
the far-forested horn-note, the speechless almost captured pass-word. The
fast boy-hands folded the fresh sheets, but the fabulous lost face went
by, steeped in its incantations.

Eugene leaped to the railing.

"You! You! My son! My child! Come back! Come back!"

His voice strangled in his throat: the boy had gone, leaving the memory
of his bewitched and listening face turned to the hidden world. O lost!

And now the Square was thronging with their lost bright shapes, and
all the minutes of lost time collected and stood still. Then, shot from
them with projectile speed, the Square shrank down the rails of destiny,
and was vanished with all things done, with all forgotten shapes of
himself and Ben.

And in his vision he saw the fabulous lost cities, buried in the drifted
silt of the earth—Thebes, the seven-gated, and all the temples of the
Daulian and Phocian lands, and all Oenotria to the Tyrrhene gulf. Sunk
in the burial-urn of earth he saw the vanished cultures: the strange
sourceless glory of the Incas, the fragments of lost epics upon a broken
shard of Gnossic pottery, the buried tombs of the Memphian kings,
and imperial dust, wound all about with gold and rotting linen, dead
with their thousand bestial gods, their mute unwakened *ushabtii,* in their
finished eternities.

He saw the billion living of the earth, the thousand billion dead: seas
were withered, deserts flooded, mountains drowned; and gods and demons
came out of the South, and ruled above the little rocket-flare of centuries,
and sank—came to their Northern Lights of death, the muttering death-
flared dusk of the completed gods.

But, amid the fumbling march of races to extinction, the giant rhythms
of the earth remained. The seasons passed in their majestic processionals,
and germinal Spring returned forever on the land—new crops, new men,
new harvests, and new gods.

And then the voyages, the search for the happy land. In his moment
of terrible vision he saw, in the tortuous ways of a thousand alien places,
his foiled quest of himself. And his haunted face was possessed of that
obscure and passionate hunger that had woven its shuttle across the seas,

that had hung its weft among the Dutch in Pennsylvania, that had darkened his father's eyes to impalpable desire for wrought stone and the head of an angel. Hill-haunted, whose vision of the earth was mountain-walled, he saw the golden cities sicken in his eye, the opulent dark splendors turn to dingy gray. His brain was sick with the million books, his eyes with the million pictures, his body sickened on a hundred princely wines.

And rising from his vision, he cried: "I am not there among the cities. I have sought down a million streets, until the goat-cry died within my throat, and I have found no city where I was, no door where I had entered, no place where I had stood."

Then, from the edges of moon-bright silence, Ben replied: "Fool, why do you look in the streets?"

Then Eugene said: "I have eaten and drunk the earth, I have been lost and beaten, and I will go no more."

"Fool," said Ben, "what do you want to find?"

"Myself, and an end to hunger, and the happy land," he answered. "For I believe in harbors at the end. O Ben, brother, and ghost, and stranger, you who could never speak, give me an answer now!"

Then, as he thought, Ben said: "There is no happy land. There is no end to hunger."

"And a stone, a leaf, a door? Ben?" Spoke, continued without speaking, to speak. "Who are, who never were, Ben, the seeming of my brain, as I of yours, my ghost, my stranger, who died, who never lived, as I? But if, lost seeming of my dreaming brain, you have what I have not—an answer?"

Silence spoke. ("I cannot speak of voyages. I belong here. I never got away," said Ben.)

"Then I of yours the seeming, Ben? Your flesh is dead and buried in these hills: my unimprisoned soul haunts through the million streets of life, living its spectral nightmare of hunger and desire. Where, Ben? Where is the world?"

"Nowhere," Ben said. "*You* are your world."

Inevitable catharsis by the threads of chaos. Unswerving punctuality of chance. Apexical summation, from the billion deaths of possibility, of things done.

"I shall save one land unvisited," said Eugene. *Et ego in Arcadia.*

And as he spoke, he saw that he had left the million bones of cities, the skein of streets. He was alone with Ben, and their feet were planted on darkness, their faces were lit with the cold high terror of the stars.

On the brink of the dark he stood, with only the dream of the cities, the million books, the spectral images of the people he had loved, who had loved him, whom he had known and lost. They will not come again. They never will come back again.

With his feet upon the cliff of darkness, he looked and saw the lights of no cities. It was, he thought, the strong good medicine of death.

"Is this the end?" he said. "Have I eaten life and have not found him? Then I will voyage no more."

"Fool," said Ben, "*this* is life. You have been nowhere."

"But in the cities?"

"There are none. There is one voyage, the first, the last, the only one."

"On coasts more strange than Cipango, in a place more far than Fez, I shall hunt him, the ghost and haunter of myself. I have lost the blood that fed me; I have died the hundred deaths that lead to life. By the slow thunder of the drums, the flare of dying cities, I have come to this dark place. And this is the true voyage, the good one, the best. And now prepare, my soul, for the beginning hunt. I will plumb seas stranger than those haunted by the Albatross."

He stood naked and alone in darkness, far from the lost world of the streets and faces; he stood upon the ramparts of his soul, before the lost land of himself; heard inland murmurs of lost seas, the far interior music of the horns. The last voyage, the longest, the best.

"O sudden and impalpable faun, lost in the thickets of myself, I will hunt you down until you cease to haunt my eyes with hunger. I heard your foot-falls in the desert, I saw your shadow in old buried cities, I heard your laughter running down a million streets, but I did not find you there. And no leaf hangs for me in the forest; I shall lift no stone upon the hills; I shall find no door in any city. But in the city of myself, upon the continent of my soul, I shall find the forgotten language, the lost world, a door where I may enter, and music strange as any ever sounded; I shall haunt you, ghost, along the labyrinthine ways until—— until? O Ben, my ghost, an answer?"

But as he spoke, the phantom years scrolled up their vision, and only the eyes of Ben burned terribly in darkness, without an answer.

And day came, and the song of waking birds, and the Square, bathed in the young pearl light of morning. And a wind stirred lightly in the Square, and, as he looked, Ben, like a fume of smoke, was melted into dawn.

And the angels on Gant's porch were frozen in hard marble silence, and at a distance life awoke, and there was a rattle of lean wheels, a slow clangor of shod hoofs. And he heard the whistle wail along the river.

Yet, as he stood for the last time by the angels of his father's porch, it seemed as if the Square already were far and lost; or, I should say, he was like a man who stands upon a hill above the town he has left, yet does not say "The town is near," but turns his eyes upon the distant soaring ranges.

The End.